The **Rough Guide** to

Jamaica

written and researched by

Polly Thomas, Adam Vaitilingam and Robert Coates

with additional contributions from
Laura Henzell

ROUGH GUIDES

www.roughguides.com

Contents

Jamaican food and drink colour section following p.112

Jamaican nightlife colour section following p.208

◄◄ Bob Marley Museum, Kingston ◄ Doctor's Cave Beach, Montego Bay

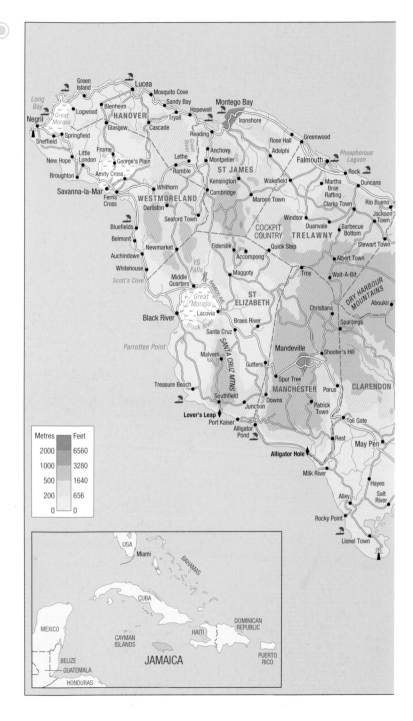

CARIBBEAN SEA

Parish boundary

0   10 miles

Discovery Bay
Runaway Bay
Browns Town
Priory
Sevilla Nueva
St Ann's Bay
Philadelphia
Alexandria
ST ANN
Nine Mile
Claremont
Albion
Golden Grove
Pedro
Ocho Rios
Dunn's River Falls
Prospect Plantation
Galina Point
Fern Gully
Oracabessa
Moneague
Firefly
Cabarita Island
Port Maria
White River
Kellits
ST MARY
Robins Bay
Whitehall
Troja
Richmond
Annotto Bay
Linstead
Castleton
Chovey
Glengoffe
Buff Bay
Bog Walk
Orange Bay
Colbeck
Balcarres
ST CATHERINE
ST ANDREW
PORTLAND
Hope Bay
Old Harbour
Spanish Town
Somerset Falls
St. Margaret's Bay
Freetown
Stony Hill
Wakefield
Old Harbour Bay
Fruitful Vale
Port Antonio
Port Esquivel
Portmore
KINGSTON
Newcastle
BLUE MTNS
Winnifred
Little Goat Island
Port Henderson
August Town
Site of Nanny Town
Great Goat Island
HELLSHIRE HILLS
Port Royal
JOHN CROW MTNS
Boston Bay
Lime Cay
Bull Bay
Ramble
Comfort Castle
Long Bay
Eleven Miles
Millbank
Manchioneal
ST THOMAS
Reach Falls
Hector's River
Yallahs
Wilmington
Bath
Salt Ponds
Rozelle
Golden Grove
Morant Bay
Lyssons
Retreat
Port Morant
Rio Grande

Introduction to

Jamaica

**Rightly famous for its beaches and music, beautiful, brash
Jamaica is much more besides. There's certainly plenty
of white sand, gin-clear sea and swaying palm trees, but
there's also a huge amount to see away from the coast:
spectacular mountains and rivers, tumbling waterfalls
and cactus-strewn savannah plains. The towns and cities
also affirm that Jamaica is far more than a mere tourist
attraction – in particular, the dynamic, sprawling metropolis
of Kingston remains the island's cultural hub and the best
place to experience the explosive reggae scene.**

Despite its natural allure, it's not just the physical
aspect that makes the country so absorbing and, to
many visitors, so utterly addictive. Jamaica retains
an attitude – a personality – that's more resonant and
distinctive than you'll find in any other Caribbean
nation, and the island's rich musical heritage has
helped to create a prominent and vibrant culture that's
imitated the world-over – quite a feat, and one that's out of all proportion
to the island's relatively tiny size. It's a country with a swagger in its step
– proud of its history, sporting success and musical genius – but also with
a weight upon its shoulders. Jamaica has not avoided the familiar problems
of a developing country, such as dramatic inequality of wealth and social
tensions that spill over into localized violence or worldwide headlines. The
mixture is potent, and has produced a people as renowned for being as sharp,
sassy and straight-talking as they are laid-back and hip. People don't tend to
beat around the bush here; Jamaicans get on with life, and their directness
can sometimes make them appear rude or uncompromising. Particularly
around the big resorts, this is taken to extremes at times, though the

Fact file

• Ninety miles south of Cuba and six hundred miles south of Miami, Jamaica sits 18 degrees north of the equator. The largest English-speaking island in the Caribbean, Jamaica is 146 miles long, with widths varying between 22 and 51 miles, and boasts 633 miles of coastline.

• Almost half of Jamaica lies 327 feet above sea level; the highest point, Blue Mountain Peak, stands at 7402 feet.

• Jamaica has more than 120 rivers; the Plantain Garden River in St Thomas is the only one that flows to the west.

• Around 3800 varieties of flowering plants and ferns, some 720 of which are endemic, grow on the island.

• Measuring just 2.5 inches (6cm) from head to tailfeather, Jamaica's bee hummingbird is one of the world's smallest birds, while the endemic Giant Swallowtail butterfly, with a wingspan of up to six inches (15cm), is the largest in the western hemisphere and the second largest in the world.

• Sugar cane, bananas, plantains, mangoes, breadfruit, ackees, bamboo and coconut palms are not native to Jamaica, having been imported by the Taino, Spanish, Africans and British.

• Jamaica's population is almost three million. Just over half of the island's residents live in urban areas, 22 percent in greater Kingston.

• Some 76 percent of Jamaicans are of African origin, 15 percent are of mixed African/European heritage, 3.5 percent are East Indian/African East Indian, 1.2 percent are Chinese/African Chinese and 0.8 are European.

harassment of tourists that once bedevilled the resorts is a lot less noticeable these days.

But there's absolutely no reason to be put off. The Jamaican authorities have spent millions making sure the island treats its tourists right, and as a foreign visitor, your chances of encountering any trouble are minuscule. As the birthplace of the **"all-inclusive"** hotel, Jamaica has become well-suited for those who (like many people) want to head straight from plane to beach, never leaving their hotel compound. But to get any sense of the country at all, you'll need to do some exploring. It's undoubtedly worth it, as this is a place packed with first-class attractions and natural attributes, oozing with character, and with a rich musical scene: if you're a reggae fan, you're in heaven.

Where to go

Most of Jamaica's tourist business is concentrated in the "big three" **resorts** of Montego Bay, Negril and Ocho Rios. A busy commercial city, **Montego Bay** has a string of hotels, bars and restaurants along its beach-lined tourist strip, and manicured golf courses and high-end all-inclusives hogging the coast to the east. West of here, its low-rise hotels slung along seven miles of fantastic white sand and two miles of dramatic cliffs, **Negril** is younger, more laid-back and with a long-standing reputation for hedonism. East of MoBay, and the least individualistic of the big three, **Ocho Rios** embodies high-impact tourism – purpose-built in the 1960s to provide the ultimate package of sun, sand and sea. The beaches aren't wonderful, but the tourist infrastructure is undeniably strong and you're right by several excellent attractions, including the famous **Dunn's River** waterfall.

Away from these resorts, you'll have to look a bit harder to find your entertainment – Jamaica's quieter east and south coasts offer a less packaged product. In the island's **east**, lush, rain-fed, sleepy **Port Antonio** and its increasingly popular neighbour, **Long Bay**, provide gateways to some of Jamaica's greatest natural attractions, like the cascading **waterfalls** at Reach and Somerset and outdoor activities such as **rafting** on the majestic Rio Grande. The **south coast** offers different pleasures, from gentle beach action at the terminally easy-going **Treasure Beach** – the perfect base for exploring local delights like the YS waterfalls or boat safaris in search of crocodiles on the **Black River**. Set in the upper reaches of the Santa Cruz Mountains, the south's

◄ Dunn's River Falls

inland towns, such as **Mandeville** and **Christiana**, offer respite from the heat of the coast and an interesting insight into Jamaica away from the resorts.

Kingston is the true heart of Jamaica. A thrilling place pulsating with energy and spirit, it's not just the nation's political capital but the focus of its art, theatre and music scenes, with top-class hotels, restaurants and shopping, electric nightlife and legendary fried fish on offer at the fabulous **Hellshire beach**. A stunning backdrop to the city, the cool **Blue Mountains** are a captivating antidote, with plenty of marvellous hiking, while the nearby fishing village of **Port Royal**, once a great pirate city, provides some historic diversion.

Going off the beaten track

Though beaches and buzzing resort areas are Jamaica's most obvious draws, one of the island's greatest assets is its spectacular **interior**. With everything from mist-swathed mountains to steamy rainforest, lush wetland and cane-covered agricultural plains, the Jamaican countryside is one of the most diverse in the Caribbean and is a joy to explore, as much for its scenic delights as for its profusion of one-horse towns, where you can sink a few glasses of overproof in the obligatory rum shop and get a flavour of Jamaican life that couldn't be more different to that in the resorts. And whether your goal is a swim in a waterfall or river, or a hike into the hills, the journey can be as much of a joy as the destination itself, especially if you stop off en route to sample pepper shrimp, roast yam and saltfish or jerk chicken from one of the country's innumerable roadside stalls.

When to go

Jamaica's **climate** means hot sun year-round, but the weather is at its most appealing during the peak tourist season (mid-Dec to mid-April), when rainfall is lowest and the heat is tempered by cooling trade winds known as the "Doctor Breeze".

▼ Blue Mountains

Jake's hotel, Treasure Beach

Nights can get chilly during this period, and you'll probably want to bring a sweater. Things get noticeably hotter during the summer and, particularly in September and October, the humidity can become oppressive. September is also the most threatening month of the annual hurricane season, which runs officially from June 1 to October 31.

Prices and crowds are at their highest during peak season, when the main attractions and beaches get pretty busy. Outside this period everywhere is quieter and, though the main resorts throb with life pretty much year-round and the summer school holidays see an upsurge in visitor arrivals, less popular tourist areas like Port Antonio and Treasure Beach can feel a little lifeless. The good news is that hotel prices everywhere fall by up to 25 percent, there are more bargains to be had in every field of activity and a number of **festivals** – including the massive annual Reggae Sumfest – inject some summertime zip.

Average daily temperatures and monthly rainfall

	Jan	Feb	March	April	May	June	July	Aug	Sept	Oct	Nov	Dec
Temperature												
Max/min (°F)	86/67	86/67	86/68	87/70	87/72	89/74	90/73	90/73	89/73	88/73	87/71	87/69
Max/min (°C)	30/19	30/19	30/20	31/21	31/22	32/23	32/23	32/23	32/23	31/23	31/22	31/21
Rainfall												
inch/mm	0.9/23	0.6/15	0.9/23	1.2/30	4.0/100	3.4/86	3.4/86	3.5/89	3.8/96	7.0/178	3.0/76	1.4/36

These figures are for Kingston, but are virtually identical islandwide with the exception of Port Antonio and the Blue Mountains, where rainfall is considerably higher.

15

things not to miss

It's not possible to see everything that Jamaica has to offer in one trip — and we don't suggest you try. What follows, in no particular order, is a selective and subjective taste of the country's highlights: outstanding natural features, marvellous beaches, festivals and clubs and delicious food and drink. They're arranged in five colour-coded categories to help you find the very best things to see, do and experience. All entries have a page reference to take you straight into the guide, where you can find out more.

01 Negril sunsets Page **218** • Right at Jamaica's western tip, Negril is in pole position for the best sunset-watching in Jamaica.

02 **Hiking in the Blue Mountains** Page **98** • Cool, misty and fragrant with coffee and wild ginger flowers, the Blue Mountains are perfect hiking territory, the ultimate challenge being the highest point in Jamaica, Blue Mountain Peak.

04 **Mineral springs** Page **121** • Jamaica's interior abounds with these deliciously cool, deep turquoise swimming holes, offering a perfect antidote to the heat of the day.

03 **National Gallery** Page **62** • This Kingston institution offers the country's premier collection of work by Jamaican artists – look out for pieces by John Dunkley, Mallica "Kapo" Reynolds, Barrington Watson and Edna Manley.

05 Port Royal Page **84** • This former pirate haunt and British military command centre bristles with character, from Fort Charles to bars and seafood restaurants, and is also the jumping-off point for the white sand and clear waters of nearby Lime Cay.

06 Kingston Page **51** • The cultural heart of the nation, Jamaica's atmospheric capital holds museums to Marley, galleries galore, blissful public parks and some simply brilliant bars, restaurants and clubs.

07 Beaches Page **177** • From the north coast's strips of fine white sand to the wind-whipped breakers and black volcanic sand in the south, Jamaica's shoreline is immensely varied – but the Caribbean sea is always warm and inviting.

09 Take a boat cruise Pages **139**, **176** & **216** • The catamarans, sail-swathed pirate boats and souped-up pirogues that cruise Jamaica's coastline offer a wonderful perspective of the island as well as access to some of Jamaica's best snorkelling spots.

08 River rafting Page **127** • A gentle glide through the cool waters of one of Jamaica's innumerable rivers is a gentle and beguiling way to see the countryside.

10 Ackee and saltfish Page **27** • Sample Jamaica's national dish, a delectable and addictive combination of salt cod and the little-known ackee fruit.

11 **Pelican Bar** Page **249** • Perched on stilts atop a sandbar 1km from the shore, this marvellously ramshackle bar is a unique place to catch the sunset.

12 **Waterfalls** Pages **140**, **255** & **126**, respectively • Whether it's joining the cruise-shippers to clamber up the multiple tiers of Dunn's River, swinging Tarzan-style over the water at YS or getting a natural jacuzzi at Reach, Jamaica's waterfalls are a delight.

13 Nightlife See *Jamaican nightlife* **colour section** • From huge stageshows such as Rebel Salute or Reggae Sumfest to the island's legendary street dances, Jamaica's music and nightlife scene is unforgettable.

14 Treasure Beach
Page **244** • With its supremely laid-back atmosphere and community-based tourism ethos, Treasure Beach offers a restorative antidote to the high-octane north coast resorts.

15 Firefly Page **151** • Left just as it was when he died, Noël Coward's former home offers a poignant insight into his life, and with a spectacular location above the St Mary coastline, Firefly has the ultimate "room with a view".

Basics

Basics

Getting there

As one of the Caribbean's most visited islands as well as a regional transport hub, Jamaica is well served with direct flights from North America, the UK and other parts of Europe. Most visitors buy packages that include flight, accommodation and airport transfers, but there are plenty of good flight-only deals available. The majority of airlines fly into Montego Bay, and some also land at Kingston – more convenient if you're heading for Port Antonio or the Blue Mountains.

Airfares always depend on the **season**, with the highest prices around December to mid-January, when the weather is best, and around the summer school holidays (July to early Sept). Fares drop during the "shoulder" seasons – November and mid-January to April (excluding Easter) – and you'll get the best prices during the low season, May to November.

Flights from the US and Canada

The popularity of all-inclusive **package** holidays means that the majority of visitors fly to Jamaica with a charter airline. However, there are also plenty of daily **direct flights** from many parts of the US, though Canada is not as well served.

Flying time **from the US** varies enormously. The flight from Miami to Montego Bay only takes 1 hour 25 minutes, making the city the main US departure point to Jamaica, while from New York, flying time is 3 hours 20 minutes, and from LA 5 hours 30 minutes. **Air Jamaica** has an extensive timetable of direct flights, with services to Montego Bay and Kingston from Philadelphia (3hr 15min), Chicago (3hr), Fort Lauderdale (1hr 30min), Orlando (2hr), Baltimore (3hr) and New York (3hr 20min). Their high-and-low-season **fares** to Montego Bay average US$680/440, and special deals are often incredibly good value – recent offers have included a $183 round-trip (plus taxes of an average $115) from Orlando to Montego Bay. Other excellent deals are available with budget carriers. Spirit offers no-frills round-trip services from Fort Lauderdale to Montego Bay and Kingston for as little as $92 plus taxes. Jet

Blue fly from New York (JFK and La Guardia) to Montego Bay and Kingston from $179 plus taxes, and also have connections to numerous US cities including LA, Phoenix and Chicago. A number of other US airlines also fly direct to Jamaica: American Airlines from Miami to Kingston; Continental from Houston and New York to Montego Bay and Kingston; Delta from Atlanta and New York to Kingston and Atlanta, New York and LA to Montego Bay; Northwest from Memphis, Detroit, Washington and Minneapolis to Montego Bay; and US Airways from Boston, Charlotte and Philadelphia to Montego Bay.

From **Canada**, Air Jamaica and Air Canada have direct flights from Toronto to Kingston and Montego Bay. Flying time from Toronto is around 4 hours, and high/low season **fares** average Can$1150/770. Passengers from other parts of Canada have to either fly first to Toronto or to a regional hub in the US, and then take a connecting flight to Jamaica.

Flights from the UK and Ireland

From the UK, Air Jamaica, British Airways and Virgin have direct flights to Montego Bay and Kingston from Gatwick. Flying time from the UK is around 9 hours, and average high/low season scheduled fares are £850/600, though special deals can bring fares down to the £400 mark. Your best bet for deals with these airlines are Caribbean specialist agents such as Newmont Travel (see p.21), who often have cheaper fares than those offered by the airlines themselves.

Booking a **charter flight** can cut costs, with an average fare of around £450 and

Six steps to a better kind of travel

At Rough Guides we are passionately committed to travel. We feel strongly that only through travelling do we truly come to understand the world we live in and the people we share it with – plus tourism has brought a great deal of **benefit** to developing economies around the world over the last few decades. But the extraordinary growth in tourism has also damaged some places irreparably, and of course **climate change** is exacerbated by most forms of transport, especially flying. This means that now more than ever it's important to **travel thoughtfully** and **responsibly**, with respect for the cultures you're visiting – not only to derive the most benefit from your trip but also to preserve the best bits of the planet for everyone to enjoy. At Rough Guides we feel there are six main areas in which you can make a difference:

- Consider what you're contributing to the **local economy**, and how much the services you use do the same, whether it's through employing local workers and guides or sourcing locally grown produce and local services.
- Consider the **environment** on holiday as well as at home. Water is scarce in many developing destinations, and the biodiversity of local flora and fauna can be adversely affected by tourism. Try to patronize businesses that take account of this.
- Travel with a purpose, not just to tick off experiences. Consider **spending longer** in a place, and getting to know it and its people.
- Give thought to how often you **fly**. Try to avoid short hops by air and more harmful night flights.
- Consider **alternatives to flying**, travelling instead by bus, train, boat and even by bike or on foot where possible.
- Make your trips **"climate neutral"** via a reputable carbon offset scheme. All Rough Guide flights are offset, and every year we donate money to a variety of charities devoted to combating the effects of climate change.

the occasional deal of as low as £300; charter airlines' flight and accommodation packages also represent great savings. Charter operators currently offering flights to Montego Bay are First Choice, from Gatwick, Birmingham and Manchester; Thomas Cook from Gatwick and Manchester; and Thomson from Gatwick. Charters are best booked by doing Internet searches, or visiting the individual company websites.

As there are no direct flights to Jamaica **from Ireland**, the easiest way to get to Jamaica is to travel to the UK and take a direct flight from there.

Flights from Australia and New Zealand

There are **no direct flights** from Australia or New Zealand to Jamaica; the best option is to fly to the US, the UK or Europe (Italy or the Netherlands) and pick up an onward connection. The least expensive and most

straightforward **route** is via Los Angeles. To LA, Quantas flies regularly from Sydney, Brisbane, Melbourne and Auckland. Average round-trip **fares** to LA are NZ$2320 from Auckland or A$1760 from Sydney.

Airlines, agents and operators

Airlines

Air Canada ⓦ www.aircanada.com.
Air Jamaica ⓦ www.airjamaica.com.
Air New Zealand ⓦ www.airnz.co.nz.
American Airlines ⓦ www.aa.com.
British Airways ⓦ www.ba.com.
Continental Airlines ⓦ www.continental.com.
Delta ⓦ www.delta.com.
Jet Blue ⓦ www.jetblue.com.
Northwest ⓦ www.nwa.com.
Qantas Airways ⓦ www.qantas.com.
Spirit ⓦ www.spiritair.com.
Virgin Atlantic ⓦ www.virgin-atlantic.com.

Agents and operators

Air Jamaica Vacations US ☎1-800/LOVEBIRD, Ⓦwww.airjamaicavacations.com. All-inclusive or flight-and-room trips. Offers occasional good specials.

Caribbean Destinations Australia ☎03/9813 5258 or 1800/354 104, Ⓦwww.caribbeanislands .com.au. Themed holidays to Jamaica and the Caribbean, based around everything from cricket to festivals.

Caribbean Journey US ☎1-888/343-2101, Ⓦwww.caribbeanjourney.com. Caribbean specialists offering all-in packages, weddings and holidays.

Caribtours UK ☎020/7751 0660, Ⓦwww.carib tours.co.uk. Long-established, fairly upmarket company offering all types of trips and plenty of personalized advice.

Dragonfly Expeditions US ☎1-888/9-WANDER, Ⓦwww.dragonflyexpeditions.com/jamaica. A well-run, energetic company featuring interesting holidays in western Jamaica with an eco-tourism slant.

First Choice UK ☎0870-850-3999, Ⓦflights.first choice.co.uk. Cheap charter flights and package holidays.

MyTravel UK ☎0870-241-5333, Ireland ☎0818/300 012; Ⓦwww.mytravel.com. Cheap flights to Montego Bay and package deals to all the main resorts.

Newmont Travel UK ☎020/8920 1155, Ⓦwww .newmont.co.uk. Caribbean flight specialist that's been around for years and offers some excellent deals; worth trying before any others.

North South Travel UK ☎01245/608 291, Ⓦwww.northsouthtravel.co.uk. Friendly, competitive travel agency, offering discounted fares worldwide. Profits are used to support projects in the developing world, especially the promotion of sustainable tourism.

Sackville Travel UK ☎020/7274 2242, Ⓦwww .sackvilletravel.com. Caribbean specialists offering cheap charter and scheduled fares.

Simply Jamaica ☎876/802 2023, Ⓦwww .seejamaicacheaply.com. Jamaica-based agent representing an excellent selection of hotels and guesthouses islandwide.

Spring Break Travel US ☎1-800/678-6386, Ⓦwww.springbreaktravel.com. Large tour company specializing exclusively in Spring Break packages.

Sunbird Tours UK ☎01767/262522, Ⓦwww .sunbirdtours.co.uk. Birdwatching specialists offering eight-day trips to Jamaica covering all the top spots.

Thomas Cook UK ☎0870/750 0316, Ⓦwww .thomascook.com. Inexpensive flight and accommodation packages, with hotels in all the big resorts, and flight-only deals too.

Thomsonfly UK ☎0870-1900-737, Ireland ☎01247-77723; Ⓦwww.thomsonfly.com. No-frills budget flights and package deals.

TourScan Inc US ☎1-800/962-2080 or 203/655-8091, Ⓦwww.tourscan.com. Caribbean specialist with a searchable database that scans offerings from a large number of Jamaica's hotels, as well as tour operators and airlines.

Trips Worldwide, UK ☎0117/311 4400, Ⓦwww .tripsworldwide.co.uk. Classy outfit featuring excellent Jamaica packages with an alternative twist.

Wings Birding Tours US ☎1-888/293-6443, Ⓦwww.wingsbirds.com. Specialists in birding holidays, offering eight-day trips to Jamaica.

Getting around

Many visitors to Jamaica spend their entire holiday tanning on the beach, but the less sedentary will find a variety of ways to get around. Privately run minibuses provide a comprehensive and cheap – if very chaotic – public transport system, while shared route taxis are great for short hops. Renting a car is the most convenient way of seeing the island, however, but it's expensive in comparison to the US or UK; if you just want to make the odd excursion, it can work out more cost-effective to hire a driver.

Minibuses and buses

Comprising anything from pockmarked minivans to air-conditioned, window-tinted coaches, Jamaica's fleet of privately owned buses and **minibuses** (the names are used interchangeably) is nothing if not eclectic. Though minibus transport is pretty anarchic, with no timetables and regulation stopping at the red "PPV" plates that denote a vehicle is licensed for public carriage, the system does work, and is a viable option for short hops and cross-island trips. One exception to the rule is the **Knutsford Express** (☎971 9822, ⓦwww.knutsfordexpress.com), whose smart, air-conditioned buses connect Kingston, Ocho Rios, Montego Bay and Negril according to scheduled services. Kingston, meanwhile, is served by a fairly comprehensive network of government-owned buses (see p.57).

Regular minibuses do have some definite downsides: drivers can show little interest in the rules of the road, and passengers are squeezed in with scant regard for comfort – and if you're one of the first to board, you'll have to wait until the vehicle is full before it'll leave. On the other hand, they are a great way to get a window into Jamaican life away from the resorts. Bear in mind that you may not be able to get a direct service to your destination, especially if you're travelling a fair distance – the journey from Montego Bay to Port Antonio, for example, might involve changing buses in Ochi, Port Maria and Annotto Bay. Non-stop long-distance buses do exist, though, so if you're not up for an interrupted journey, ask the locals if and when direct buses leave. In general, services start at around 6am and continue until 7 or 8pm, and services are severely reduced on Sundays.

All towns have a **bus terminal** of sorts, either a proper bus station or a designated area along the main road, often near the market, and buses have their routes written on the front, back and sides of the vehicle. Conductors shout out the destination repeatedly before departure, scouting the area for potential passengers and cramming in as many as possible. Once on the road, buses and minibuses will stop anywhere to pick up or drop off passengers (except in Kingston, where they're restricted to bus stops and terminals). If you want to get off before the terminus, tell the conductor and fellow passengers where you're going when you get on, or yell "one stop", or something similar, when you get there. To get on a bus mid-route, just stand by the side of the road and flag it down, but bear in mind that the earlier in the day you travel, the better – being stuck in a bursting Jamaican bus on a boiling afternoon is no picnic.

Fares are paid to a conductor after boarding, and having the right change, or at least small bills, will make your life easier.

Cars

Renting a car is by far the best way of getting around and seeing the island. Though some of the roads beggar belief, Jamaica is a relatively easy country to drive in. Distances are small, and while some locals have a kamikaze approach to driving, most are extremely courteous. However, rental **prices** are high, averaging around US$50 per day – though rates can go as low as US$30, and you'll usually get a discount if you rent for more than a few days. Third-party insurance is normally included in the rental rate; you'll have to pay another US$12–25 per day to cover potential damage to the car. If you choose not to take this out, you're liable for every scratch on the car, whether caused by your own error or not.

There are **rental companies** all over the island, from international outfits to small-scale local offices, with the best selection in Kingston, Montego Bay and Ocho Rios – we've listed the main players below, and local operators within the Guide. You'll often get a better deal by going with a local company, especially as the better ones offer guaranteed roadside assistance and allow you to pick up and drop off in different major towns for no extra fee. To rent a car, you'll need a current licence from your home country or an international licence and, in theory, you'll need to have held it for at least a year. Most companies stipulate that drivers must be at least 21 years old (though some will rent only to drivers over 25). Before you set off, check the car to ensure that every dent, scratch or missing part is inventoried, and that the petrol tank is full (bear in mind

that you'll have to return the vehicle with the same amount of petrol).

Car rental agencies

International operators

Avis Ⓦ www.avis.com.
Budget Ⓦ www.budget.com.
Hertz Ⓦ www.hertz.com.

Jamaican operators

Eden Ⓦ www.edencarrental.com.
Fiesta Ⓦ www.fiestacarrentals.com.
Island Ⓦ www.islandcarrentals.com.

Rules of the road

Driving in Jamaica is on the **left**, and **speed limits** are 30mph/50kph in towns and on minor roads, 50mph/80kph on main roads and highways (though some stretches of the new highways have 70mph/110kph limits). Note that although Jamaica generally follows the Imperial measurement system, speed limit signs are in kph, and road-sign distances in kilometres. The Jamaican police often set up **roadblocks**, and **speed checks** by way of radar gun – the safest bet is to stick to 30mph/50kph unless you see a sign indicating otherwise. Jamaican drivers have an informal system of flashing their lights to other drivers to indicate police presence ahead. If you're stopped, be polite and cooperate fully. Note that wearing front **seat-belts** is mandatory.

Unless there's been recent heavy weather, most main A-roads are in pretty good condition, while the new highways along the north and south coasts are pristine and a pleasure to drive (bear in mind that the south's Highway 2000, and the new causeway from Kingston to Portmore have a minimal **toll fee**). Minor roads, however, are often badly potholed – take it slowly.

Jamaicans can be pretty cavalier behind the wheel, with many drivers (particularly those in charge of taxis or air-braked, diesel-spitting juggernauts) often dangerously macho and impatient. Always **drive defensively**; watch out for overtaking traffic coming towards you, as passing a long line of cars (even if it's impossible to see what's coming) is common practice; untethered animals also stray onto roads

Many Jamaicans **hitch** rides – and will flag you down for a lift if you're driving through a rural area in a half-empty car. But very few tourists hitchhike, and it's not something we recommend for safety reasons – if you're short of cash, you're better off sticking to buses or shared taxis.

in country areas, so be on the lookout at all times. At night, many locals drive with undipped headlights; keeping your eyes on the left verge helps to avoid being dazzled. You should use your horn as freely as most Jamaicans do; a toot is just as likely to mean "thank you" as it is an indication of some kind of hazard or an intention to overtake (and in the case of the latter, it's always safest to slow down and let the overtaker pass you). Daredevil stunts notwithstanding, Jamaican drivers tend to be pretty courteous toward visitors, often giving way at junctions and offering loud vocal suggestions as to how best to handle situations.

Taxis

Jamaican taxis vary from the gleaming white vans and fancy cars of the **Jamaican Union of Travellers Association** (JUTA; MoBay ☎952 0813, Negril ☎957 9197, Ocho Rios ☎974 2292, Kingston ☎927 4534; ⓦwww .jutatours.com), the official carriers, to the Japanese estate cars that are the vehicle of choice for most taxi men. Licensed taxis carry red number plates with "PP" or "PPV" on them, but there are a number of rogues. We've given numbers of taxi firms throughout the Guide, but during the day, it's usually just as easy to flag a car down in the street.

Fares are pretty reasonable in Kingston and the less touristed areas, even for long journeys; on the north coast, prices are rather more hefty – around US$25 for ten miles, and you'll always pay a little more if you take a taxi affiliated with a hotel. As taxis are unmetered, always establish a price before you get in (or over the phone if you're calling for a taxi). If you hail a vehicle on the street, the first figure may be just an opener; don't be afraid of negotiating.

Shared taxis, or "route taxis", operate on short, busy set routes picking up and dropping off passengers anywhere along the way. Some are marked by the PPV

number plate, but many more are not, making them difficult to identify, except by the squash of passengers and the wad of small bills in the drivers' hands. They're used more by Jamaicans than visitors, so it's not uncommon for a driver to assume that you want to charter the whole taxi if you flag one down, in which case he'll throw the other passengers out – make it clear that this is not what you want. Prices are much closer to bus fares than to charter taxi rates.

If you don't drive – or don't want to – but still want to travel independently around the island, hiring a **local taxi driver** for a day or more is an excellent option, and generally costs about US$100 a day. Local drivers often make good tour guides, too. We've recommended reliable drivers throughout the Guide.

Bikes and scooters

Jamaica should be much better for **cycling** than it is. Places like the Blue Mountains, perfect for biking, are not well geared towards independent cyclists, though several tour companies offer an easy, and pricey, way of seeing them on a bike (see p.96). Throughout the island, rental outlets are thin on the ground; we've listed them where they're available – Treasure Beach is particularly popular.

Renting a **scooter** or small motorbike is easier, and can be an exhilarating way of touring the island, though not all resorts have outlets – most are in Negril. Rates are US$35 per day, and though in theory you'll need to show a driving licence, these are rarely asked for. Under Jamaican law, all motorcycle or scooter riders must wear helmets – you'd be a fool not to in any case. Zooming about on two wheels, though hugely enjoyable, does of course bring the usual dangers; be on your guard for potholes and daft goats and dogs straying onto the tarmac.

Organized tours

There's plenty on offer if you're after an **organized tour**; most hotels have a tour desk which organize trips to well-known attractions like Rose Hall or Dunn's River Falls, or "highlight" tours of the local area, usually run by one of the "conventional" operators below. At best, they're a hassle-free and comfortable means of getting around; at worst, they barely skim the surface of the country and its culture from the shelter of an air-conditioned bus. **Prices** are comparable, starting from around US$50 for a simple half-day excursion to US$100 for full day-trips. Tours of specific sights are listed in the relevant chapters throughout the Guide. The trips offered by the **alternative** companies listed below tend to be more rewarding and, consequently, more expensive – booking in a group spreads always ensures cheaper rates.

The Jamaica Tourist Board's **Meet the People** programme introduces holiday-makers to local Jamaicans with shared interests – religion, nature, art and culture – for no charge. You can register online (ⓦ www.visitjamaica.com) or contact your local JTB branch.

Conventional tour operators

Caribic Vacations ☎ 953 2600, ⓦ www.caribic vacations.com.
Glamour Tours ☎ 940 3277, ⓦ www.glamour toursdmc.com.

Tourwise ☎ 974 2323, ⓦ tourwise.org.
Tropical Tours ☎ 953 9100, ⓦ www.tropical tours-ja.com.

Alternative tour operators

Barrett Adventures Rose Hall, Montego Bay ☎ 382 6384, ⓦ www.barrettadventures.com. Customized packages to waterfalls, plantations and beaches islandwide.
Cockpit Country Adventure Tours Albert Town PO, Trelawny ☎ 610 0818 or 869 3243, ⓦ www.stea.net. Excellent offshoot of an environmental NGO offering hiking, caving and river-swimming trips in and around Cockpit Country, all led by charming local guides. Profits are channelled directly back into the community.
Our Story Tours ☎ 377 5693, ⓔ ourstorytours @gmail.com. Offbeat and fascinating historical islandwide tours. Emphasis is on Kingston, Spanish Town and Port Royal, but custom-designed tours are available to any part of the island. It's the only company to offer trips to see the racing at Caymanas Park – unmissable.
Sun Venture 30 Balmoral Ave, Kingston 10 ☎ 960 6685, ⓦ www.sunventuretours.com. Reliable, innovative and eco-friendly scheduled and custom-designed tours – the best on the island for offbeat excursions. Mainstays include Blue Mountain hikes, Cockpit Country hikes, bicycle tours, south coast safaris, caving and city tours.
Treasure Tours Calabash Bay, Treasure Beach ☎ 965 0126, ⓦ treasuretoursjamaica.com. Small, personal tour company with eight different day tours to south coast attractions, and a popular day-long "non-tourist tour" that visits inland St Elizabeth and some of the local deserted and hidden beaches.

Accommodation

Jamaica has a huge amount of choice when it comes to accommodation, including some of the world's finest luxury hotels, but it's extremely rare to find anywhere to stay for less than US$40 per night in the resorts (Treasure Beach and Port Antonio being notable exceptions), and you'll usually pay twice that for anything approaching luxury. If you haven't booked a flight package that includes accommodation, it's worth reserving a room for your first night or two to save hassle on arrival, and to satisfy immigration requirements.

If you're in the mood, it is always worth **haggling** over the price of a room. Even in high season, a lot of hotels have surplus capacity and are sometimes desperate for customers – and doing so over the phone will save you having to traipse around.

Finally note that hotels often add a **service charge** (up to 15 percent) as well as a 15 percent **government tax** (GCT) to your bill; before you agree on anything, check whether taxes are included in quoted rates.

Hotels and guesthouses

Jamaica has no youth hostels, and the cheapest places to stay are usually small, family-run **guesthouses** with pretty basic facilities. Rooms in our ❶ or ❷ price code will be basic but clean and functional – though sometimes cramped and box-like – with spartan furniture, shared bathrooms and a fan rather than a/c. Places in the ❸ or ❹ brackets may have a little more ambience, and possibly a/c, while accommodation in the ❺ and ❻ categories, usually **hotels** rather than guesthouses, will offer cable TV, phone, a/c and on-site facilities such as pool, bar and restaurant. In the ❼ and ❽ categories, options vary wildly from slick, modern chain-style behemoths to chic, creatively decorated boutique hotels, while the ❾ bracket covers Jamaica's top-end places – expect notable architectural design, lavish artwork in the rooms and lobby, impeccably dressed staff, excellent facilities and fabulous cuisine.

All-inclusives

Jamaica was the birthplace of the **all-inclusive** hotel, where a single price covers your room, all meals, drinks and watersports too. **Sandals** (🌐 www.sandals.com) and **Superclubs** (🌐 www.superclubs.com) are the best known of the all-inclusive chains, with around twenty hotels between them, while concrete jungles of Spanish chain Riu (🌐 www.riujamaica.com) are colonizing huge chunks of the north coast. Prices vary

Accommodation price codes

All accommodation listed in this guide has been graded according to the following **price categories**, based on the cheapest available **double** or **twin room** during the high season – normally mid-November to mid-April. During the low season, rates are liable to decrease by up to forty percent (though this is rare at the cheaper hotels), and proprietors may be more amenable to bargaining. Many of the all-inclusive hotels have a minimum-stay requirement – where this is the case, we have mentioned it in the text – and rates are quoted per person per night based on double occupancy. Although the law requires prices to be quoted in Jamaican dollars, most hotels give their rates in US dollars; payment can be made in either currency.

❶ $30 and under
❷ $31–$50
❸ $51–70
❹ $71–$100
❺ $101–$150
❻ $151–$200
❼ $201–$250
❽ $251–$300
❾ $301 and over

enormously, and it's possible to get bargain deals during low season. However, as all-inclusives tend to make a very negligible contribution to the local economy, as well as eating up precious natural resources and often ruining the pristine coastal environments, we don't recommend staying in one, and haven't reviewed these properties in this guide. For more on the negative impact of the all-inclusive boom, check out Polly Pattulo's excellent book *Last Resorts* (see Contexts, p.310).

Villas

Throughout Jamaica, there are hundreds of **villas** available for visitors to rent, normally by the week. Ranging from small beachside chalets to grand mansions, these are typically self-catering places, often with maid service (occasionally with a cook and a security guard), and can make a reasonably priced alternative to hotels if you are travelling as a family or in a group, as well as offering a wonderful level of privacy. We've listed individual properties throughout the Guide, but the Jamaica Association of Villas and Apartments (JAVA), PO Box 298, Ocho Rios (☎974 2508, ⓦwww.villasinjamaica .com) represents three hundred or so places, and a quick net search will turn up a host of other options.

Food and drink

From fiery jerk pork and chicken to inventive seafood and ubiquitous rice and peas, Jamaican cuisine is delicious and varied, and even vegetarians are fairly well catered for with the meatless offerings of Rastafarian Ital dishes. Snacking is good, too, with spicy meat, vegetable or seafood patties the staple fare, along with a vast selection of fresh fruits and vegetables.

Eating out

All the resorts, as well as cosmopolitan Kingston, have a wide variety of eating options, from posh seafood places to Italian, Indian, Japanese and Mediterranean cuisine. Elsewhere on the island, Jamaica's **restaurants** tend to be of two types: no-frills filling stations patronized mostly by locals and with a standard menu of Jamaican staples, or tourist-oriented places with more in the way of decor and a menu geared towards American and European palates. If you're after fast food, you'll find chains such as *Burger King*, *Wendy's*, *KFC* and *Pizza Hut* in all the larger settlements. Jamaica has the honour of being one of the few countries in which lack of demand prompted *McDonald's* to close its few local franchises, and the island is now golden arch-free.

Breakfast

The classic – and totally addictive – Jamaican breakfast is **ackee** and **saltfish**. The soft yellow flesh of the ackee fruit is sautéed with onions, sweet and hot peppers, fresh tomatoes and flaked salted cod, producing a dish similar to scrambled eggs in looks and consistency but wildly superior in taste. You'll often find it served with the leafy, spinach-like **callaloo**, boiled green bananas, fried breadfruit, a hunk of hard-dough bread (a dense, slightly sweet white loaf), and fried or boiled dumplings, the former also called Johnny cakes. Other popular morning options include delicious and filling cornmeal, plantain, hominy corn or peanut porridge; or smoked mackerel "rundown", cooked with coconut milk, onions and seasoning. All hotels and restaurants in resorts serve more international breakfasts, from continental (rolls, jam, juice and coffee) to omelettes and American-style bacon, pancakes and scrambled eggs), as well as fresh fruit plates.

Lunch and dinner

Chicken and **fish** are the mainstays of lunch and dinner. Chicken is stewed, fried, jerked or curried, while fish can be grilled, steamed with okra and pimento, brown-stewed in a tasty tomato-based sauce or "**escovitched**" – seasoned, fried, and then doused in a spicy sauce of onions, hot peppers and vinegar. Red snapper and parrot are the most common (and the tastiest) varieties of fish, but you'll also be offered juicy steaks of kingfish, jackfish, tuna and dolphin (mahi-mahi, rather than the mammal). Other staples include stewed beef, curried goat, oxtail with butterbeans, and **pepperpot soup**, made from callaloo, okra and beef or pork. More adventurous palates might fancy "**mannish water**" (goat soup that includes the testicles, considered an aphrodisiac), **cowfoot** (a gelatinous and arguably delicious stew of bovine hooves) or **fish tea**, a delicious broth of fish and veg, sold by the cup at roadside stalls. Pumpkin soup, often made with chicken stock, is also a delicious lunch filler. Another great option for a quick meal is a hunk of **jerk chicken** or **pork** (jerk fish or seafood are also widely available): spicy, marinated meat cooked slowly over an open fire and served with **festival** (a deliciously light sweet fried dumpling), roast yam or breadfruit or slices of hard-dough bread. Specialist jerk centres are scattered all over Jamaica, while **pan chicken**, seasoned in the same way as jerk but barbecued in a modified ex-oil barrel over coal rather than the traditional pimento wood, is cooked up by vendors who set up on street corners in the evenings, typically on Friday and Saturday nights. For more on jerk cooking, see the *Jamaican food and drink* colour section.

Seafood is another Jamaican joy, with fresh **lobster** – curried or grilled with garlic butter – and **shrimp** widely available, and surprisingly inexpensive, too. Fresh-water **crayfish** (known as janga) are pulled from rivers across Jamaica, and in Middle Quarters, vendors sell bags of them, hotly peppered and ready to eat; an equally tasty alternative is janga soup. Though it's not the most visually appealing fruit of the sea, **conch** (the inhabitant of the huge pink shells sold in the resorts) is dense and delicious, cooked up into a fortifying soup or curried in silver-foil parcels at roadside stalls and served with **bammy** (a substantial bread made from cassava flour which is soaked in milk or water and then fried or steamed). **Seapuss**, also occasionally on menus, is octopus or squid.

Rice and peas (white rice cooked with coconut, spices and red kidney beans) is the accompaniment to most meals, though you'll sometimes get bammy, festival, sweet or regular **potatoes** (the latter often referred to as Irish potatoes), yam, dasheen, Johnny cakes or fried or boiled **dumplings**.

Though the island produces a fabulous array of fresh produce, **vegetarians** are only really catered for at Rastafarian **Ital** restaurants, where meals are exclusively meat-free and, in theory, cooked without salt. Mainstays include ackee and vegetable stews served with rice and peas; tofu, gluten and soya are cooked up in various forms as alternative sources of protein. You should usually be able to get patties filled with pulses, soya chunks and ackee. The majority of Ital restaurants are in Kingston, though there are places in Ocho Rios, Montego Bay, Negril and Port Antonio.

Snacks

Along with jerk meat, **patties** are Jamaica's best-known snack, a flaky pastry case usually filled with highly spiced minced beef, though also available in veg, chicken, shrimp, ackee and saltfish, soya or lobster varieties, and sold at bakeries, cafés and snack bars. Brands to look out for are Tastee and Juici Beef. Other popular snacks are **bun and cheese** – a sweet currant bun sold with a hunk of processed cheese – or **meatloaf** and **callaloo loaf**, both made with bread rather than pastry. Bakeries also offer buttery folds of **coco bread** (eaten wrapped around a patty for the classic working-man's lunch), **bullas** (flat, heavy ginger cakes, improved upon in the Portland area by the creation of lighter "holey bullas"), rock cakes, rich cakes and **gizzadas** (tarts filled with shredded coconut and spiced with nutmeg and

In a bid to boost decimated fish stocks, the Jamaican government has enforced **closed seasons** on lobster and conch during their reproductive cycles – April 1 to June 30 and July 1 to October 31, respectively. It is **illegal** for restaurants to serve lobster or conch caught during these times, and while many will tell you that the stock is frozen and predates the deadline, this is obviously not always true, and you should avoid restaurants that don't comply with the law.

ginger). If you're lucky, you'll find **duckanoo** (also known as "blue drawers"), made from cornflour, sugar and nutmeg, wrapped in a banana leaf and steamed.

Jamaicans are enthusiastic **roadside** eaters, and you shouldn't miss out on breaking long journeys with a cup of fish tea, conch or pepperpot soup, which are all sold from steaming mobile cauldrons, or a chunk of buttered roast yam and saltfish. Peanuts and cashews are also hawked at major road junctions, sold salted or "Ital"; if he's not holding a pile of them aloft, you'll recognize a "nuts man" by the high-pitched, steam-driven whine that emanates from the pushcart roasting equipment.

Fruit and vegetables

One of the delights of touring Jamaica is stopping off at roadside stalls to try the local fruits. Bananas, oranges, guavas, pineapples and paw-paws (papaya) are the most common, while **mangoes** come in all shapes and sizes (though the juicy, non-stringy Julie variety is a universal favourite). Of more unusual offerings, the suitably named **ugli fruit** looks like a disfigured grapefruit but is more tasty, while the origins and flavour of the Jamaican-bred **ortanique** are described by its hybrid name – orange, tangerine, unique. Something like a green-skinned lychee, with delicate flesh around a large pip, **guineps** (in season from July to October) have a refreshingly tart sweetness; the brown, orange-sized **naseberries** are sweeter and slightly gritty; **sweetsops**, or custard apples, look like pine cones and, as they ripen, the sections separate for eating.

Other options include **soursops** (a bigger, sharper and indescribably better version of the sweetsop, often made into a juice); green or deep purple, milky-fleshed **star apples**; and the perfumed, rose-tinted flesh of **otaheite** (or "Ethiopian") **apples**, crimson-red, pear-shaped and with white, delicately perfumed and very refreshing flesh.

Ubiquitous **vegetables** include the whitish-blue **dasheen**, a slightly chewy and very delicious tuber. Of a variety of squashes, the watery **cho-cho** is the most common, and you'll also find **callaloo**, **okra**, **yams**, **cassava**, **breadfruit** and **plantains**, the latter ripened and served as a fried accompaniment to main meals.

Drinking

Jamaica's water is safe to drink, but locally bottled **spring water** is widely available and much nicer. For a tasty non-alcoholic **drink**, look no further than the roadside piles of coconuts in every town and village, often advertised with a sign saying "**ice-cold jelly**". The vendor will open one up with a few strokes from a machete, and you drink straight from the nut (with a straw if you're lucky), after which the vendor will split the shell so you can scoop out the soft flesh using a piece of the shell. **Sky juice** – shaved ice flavoured with syrup or fresh cane juice – is also popular, usually served in a plastic bag with a straw.

Elsewhere, you'll find the usual imported **sodas**, plus Jamaica's own D&G brands: Ting (a refreshing sparkling grapefruit drink), Malta (a fortifying malt drink), and throat-tingling ginger beer. Most places also sell "**box drinks**" – from additive-filled, over-sweetened peanut punch or eggnog to sweetened fruit juices. The unsweetened Tru-Juice brand comes in some interesting varieties, including West Indian cherry or June plum with ginger. **Fresh natural fruit juices** – tamarind, June plum, guava, soursop, strawberry and cucumber – are always delicious, and are available at local restaurants, while blended fruit juices are a meal in themselves; if you haven't got a sweet tooth, ask for yours to be made without syrup.

Jamaican **coffee** (see p.106) is usually excellent. Blue Mountain beans are among the best and most expensive in the world,

Stamina potions

Ever careful to safeguard his powerful libido, the average Jamaican man couldn't live without gallons of potions concocted to supplement the diet and ensure health and sexual stamina. With self-explanatory names such as **tan-pon-it-long** or **front-end lifter**, these vitamin and mineral-rich drinks often include peanuts, oats and **Irish moss**, a seaweed boiled and strained into a glutinous milky-white potion and which serves as the main component of the ubiquitous **magnum** (Irish moss and linseed), **strong back** (Irish moss, oats, peanuts, paw-paw, Dragon stout and a decoction of the strong-back herb) and **pep-up** (Irish moss, Dragon stout, Red Label wine and liquefied green corn). Most people have their own favourite blend with a suitably libidinous name to match.

Another popular tonic is **roots wine**, now commercially produced and sold in shops and bars islandwide – look out for Zion's Bedroom Bully, Ital Jockey and Mandingo varieties, as well as the Baba Roots brand. Roots wine is classically made by Rastafarian herbalists, however, who mix various quantities of roots and herbs such as arrowroot, chainy root, bridal wisp, strong back and occasionally ganja, boiling them with molasses or honey to make an evil-smelling brew. Most people have their own recipes, but as preparation is time-consuming, many prefer to visit their favourite "juice man", who sells old rum bottles full of the stuff in most markets.

though the other local brews, such as High Mountain, Low Mountain or Mountain Blend, are also good. Made from balls of locally grown cocoa spiced up with cinnamon and nutmeg and then boiled with water and condensed milk, **hot chocolate**, known as cocoa tea, is a traditional but rather labour-intensive breakfast drink. **Tea**, in Jamaica, can mean any hot drink, from regular, insipid Lipton's to fish tea, herbal tea or even ganja tea.

Alcohol and bars

Jamaica's national **beer** is the excellent Red Stripe, available in distinctive squat bottles and occasionally on draught; Red Stripe Light is a lower-alcohol version. Heineken is also widely available, as is locally brewed Guinness (stronger than British varieties), which competes with the sweeter Dragon as the island's stout of choice.

Wine is also widely available in restaurants and bars by the glass or bottle, though it's more expensive than locally produced drinks; supermarkets sell wine at more reasonable prices. A rum-shop staple, the local Red Label wine is a pretty grim fortified tipple.

Rum is the liquor of choice, with a huge variety at a range of prices – for more on rum, see p.256 & the *Jamaican food and drink* colour section. Rum-based **liqueurs** are the other local speciality; Sangster's make award-winning rum creams and liqueurs flavoured with orange, coffee, pimento and more, while the coffee-infused Tia Maria is quite delicious. **Alcopops** are becoming increasingly popular, with imported, vodka-based Smirnoff Ice leading the charge.

Jamaica's traditional rum shops are hole-in-the-wall places patronized by groups of men drinking rum, playing dominoes and gazing at the scantily clad ladies on the Red Stripe posters, but within the cities and resorts, there are hordes of drinking holes, from sports bars to English-style pubs.

The media

Newspapers

Of Jamaica's three daily **newspapers**, the broadsheet **Daily Gleaner** (🌐www.jamaica-gleaner.com) is the market leader, with solid coverage of local news and sports, the pick of the island's feature writers and good entertainment listings. It's rivalled by the **Observer** (🌐www.jamaicaobserver.com), with a similar mix of news and features. The **Star** (🌐www.jamaica-star.com) is the island's tabloid, full of salacious tittle-tattle and the "Dear Pastor" problem page is also worth a glance. Sunday brings fat weekend issues of the *Gleaner* and *Observer*, and the weighty **Sunday Herald** (🌐www.sunday heraldjamaica.com), which has the odd good feature.

International newspapers – the main US dailies and the UK's broadsheets – are sold in major pharmacies and the gift shops of the bigger hotels, usually a couple of days out of date.

Radio

Jamaica's **radio stations** are predictably awash with local music, from hyped-up dancehall to roots reggae, R&B and hip-hop. Music faces tough competition from daytime phone-in talk shows, which offer a pertinent insight into the local psyche, as well as sports coverage.

Irie FM (🌐www.iriefm.net) is easily the most listened-to music station, with a non-stop reggae playlist and some of the island's best-known DJs. **Zip FM** (🌐www.zipfm.net) has a slightly more eclectic mix of musical styles, from soca and Latin to techno and rock, as well as local tunes, and **Fame FM** (🌐www.fame95fm.com), with plenty of upfront dancehall, R&B and hip-hop. **Kool 97** (🌐www.kool97fm.com) is another worthy choice, offering a laid-back mix of music, with some excellent 1980s soul as well as reggae, soft rock and oldies. For many Jamaicans, talk shows are essential listening, with main

players including **RJR** (🌐www.rjr94fm.com) and **Power 106** (🌐www.go-jamaica.com /power). Note that most of the radio station websites allow you to listen in live online.

The excellent **BBC Caribbean** (🌐www .bbc.co.uk/caribbean), broadcasting from Jamaica, is a solid source of local and international news.

Radio stations and frequencies

KLAS 89FM
RJR 90.5/91.1/92.9/94.5/103.3FM
Fame 95FM
Roots 96.1FM (in Kingston area only)
Love 101.1FM
Hot 102 102FM
Zip FM 103 FM
Irie FM 105.5/107.7FM
Power 106 106.5FM
BBC Caribbean 104FM

Television

You'll find a **television** set in most hotel rooms, usually hooked up to the cable network with countless American-based channels as well as the two domestic channels, **TVJ** (🌐www.televisionjamaica.com) and **CVM** (🌐www.cvmtv.com), competent if rarely thrilling; look out, though, for the excellent music-based programme *Entertainment Report* on TVJ. Output is dominated by news, local sport and US re-runs. Those desperate for international sports coverage will find that most towns have one or two bars with big-screen TVs broadcasting major US sporting events – NFL and NBA games and occasionally baseball – though you won't find much from Europe other than the odd football game.

Local cable channels have mushroomed in recent years, with Hype and RETV broadcasting from dances and parties islandwide and showing local music videos on a loop. Look out also for Tempo, MTV's Caribbean music channel.

Festivals

From regional food festivals to massive music concerts, Jamaica plays host to a huge variety of annual events, with as many geared toward tourists as they are to locals. We've detailed the main and most interesting events here, but for comprehensive listings, visit the website of the JTB (ⓦ www.visitjamaica.com) for details of each year's programme.

Throughout the year, the **Jamaican Cultural Development Commission** stages various events centred around traditional Jamaica song, dance and the arts, with the Festival Song Competition Finals at the Ranny Williams Entertainment Centre in Kingston being one of the highlights; see ⓦ www.jcdc .org.jm for full details.

Calendar of events

January

Accompong Maroon Festival Accompong, St Elizabeth. All-day celebration of the 1739 Maroon peace treaty, held on January 6. Food and craft stalls, drumming, traditional dancing, speeches and a sound-system dance till dawn.

Air Jamaica Jazz and Blues Festival Wyndham Rose Hall, Montego Bay ⓦ www.jamaicajazzandblues .com. This increasingly popular event has a fabulous setting and a big enough purse to attract some excellent international performers, from John Legend to Al Green.

Annual National Exhibition National Gallery, Kingston ⓦ about.galleryjamaica.org. Annual showpiece exhibition of new artists and established names.

Rebel Salute Kaiser Sports Club, St Elizabeth ⓦ www.rebelsaluteproduction.com. Large-scale annual concert with a festival atmosphere, featuring a huge line-up of cultural artists and attracting a large rootsy crowd. Meat and alcohol are banned from the grounds (but ganja certainly isn't).

February

A Fi Wi Sinting Port Antonio ⓦ www.fiwisinting .com. Daytime event highlighting Jamaica's African heritage, with dub poetry, drumming, fashion and traditional food and craft stalls.

Bob Marley Birthday Week Nine Mile; Bob Marley Museum, Kingston; James Bond Beach, Oracabessa; and Negril ⓦ www.bobmarley-foundation.com. Celebrations for the king of reggae are held on

and around the anniversary of Marley's birthday on February 6, from seminars to live shows or sound-system jams.

Jamaica Carnival Kingston, Ocho Rios and Montego Bay ⓦ www.jamaicacarnival.com or www.bacchanaljamaica.com. Trinidad-style carnival parties (with performances from top soca artists) in the capital and elsewhere, of which the best is Beach Jouvert in Oracabessa. Carnival culminates in a costumed parade through the streets of Kingston in April.

Misty Bliss Holywell National Park, Blue Mountains ⓦ www.jcdt.org. Annual Sunday fair designed to showcase the mountain region and environmental matters, with market stalls selling herbs and spices grown in the area, nature tours, live mento and kumina music.

Jamaica Fat Tyre Festival Ocho Rios ⓦ www .Smorba.com. Mountain biking festival, with organized rides and plenty of parties.

March

Spring Break In early March, American college students descend on the main resorts (particularly Negril) for a two-week JTB-sponsored orgy of beer drinking and slapstick antics. Student ID gets discounts on hotels and events.

April

Trelawny Yam Festival Albert Town, Trelawny ⓦ www.stea.net. This tiny town, with a stunning setting on the outskirts of Cockpit Country, plays host to an incongruously large open-air party. As well as the prize tubers, competition categories include cooking and best-dressed goat.

Western Consciousness Savannah-la-Mar. Excellent rootsy stage show featuring the best of Jamaica's cultural artists.

May

Calabash International Literary Festival Treasure Beach, St Elizabeth ⓦ www.calabash festival.org. Fabulous free literary festival in the laid-back surrounds off Treasure Beach, with book and poetry readings, seminars, discussions and some excellent parties too.

June

Ocho Rios Jazz Festival Ocho Rios Ⓦ www .jamaicaculture.org/jazz. Jamaica's original jazz festival, attracting top performers from all over the world. Concerts take place in hotels and open spaces in Ocho Rios, with a few events in Montego Bay and Kingston.

July

International Dancehall Queen Contest Pier One, Montego Bay Ⓣ 940 7661. Excellent annual event in which Jamaica's most accomplished movers (as well as contestants from overseas) don sequins, fishnet and plenty of bling to vie for the coveted title of Dancehall Queen. Expect a brilliant display of all the latest dances and dancehall fashions, as well as some seriously sexy gyrating.

Kingston on the Edge Kingston Ⓦ www .myspace.com/kingstonedge. This brilliant urban arts festival sees a series of events, from gallery shows to poetry readings, dance performances and concerts, staged across the capital and showcasing the work of the country's most interesting young artists and performers.

Little Ochi Seafood Carnival Manchester. Great seafood and music at this renowned beachside seafood joint.

Portland Jerk Festival Boston Bay, Portland Ⓦ www.portlandjerkfestival.com. Celebration of Jamaica's most famous dish, with jerk everything and all the trimmings cooked up by Portland's finest amid music, kids' attractions and games.

Reggae Sumfest Catherine Hall Entertainment Centre, Montego Bay Ⓦ www.reggaesumfest.com. This massive four-night festival is the main event in

the musical calendar, with sets from all the big players in the local music scene as well as international artists from Beyonce to Ne-Yo. See p.183.

August

Red Stripe Dream Weekend Negril. The "Jamaican Spring Break", held over Independence weekend, which sees thousands of well-heeled young Jamaicans descend on Negril for four nights of all-inclusive parties and stageshows.

Denbigh Agricultural Show Denbigh Showground, May Pen Ⓦ www.jas.org.jm. Creative displays of farm produce and livestock by farmers from across the country.

October

Peter Tosh Birthday Celebration Savannah-la-Mar, Westmoreland. Annual roots and culture tribute concert in memory of the reggae great, held on or around the anniversary of his October 19 birthday.

November

Restaurant Week Ⓦ www.go-jamaica.com/rw. A great chance to delve into the dining scene, with some of the best restaurants in Kingston, Ocho Rios and Montego Bay offering three-course set menus at significantly discounted prices.

December

LTM National Pantomime Little Theatre, Kingston and theatres around the island. Annual theatrical institution, with ribald jokes, great costumes, political commentary and traditional Jamaican song and dance.

Sting Portmore, Kingston Ⓦ www.stingjamaica .com.jm. Annual New Year's Eve concert featuring current top DJs and singers. The atmosphere can get a bit hairy.

Sports and outdoor activities

As you'll quickly discover, sport is a Jamaican obsession – hardly surprising in a country that continues to produce so many world-class athletes – and you'll find newspapers and TV news awash with sports reports. Jamaica is also a great place to indulge your own sporting passion, with excellent watersports and top-class golfing in particular.

Spectator sports

Virtually every Jamaican has an opinion on **cricket**, the national game, and bringing it up in conversation is a sure-fire way to break the ice – though if you want to win friends, gloating over the recent failings of the West Indies cricket team may not be a brilliant idea. If you get the chance to catch a match, particularly a Test fixture or 20/20 game at Sabina Park, you'll find the atmosphere very Jamaican – thumping reggae between overs, vendors hawking jerk chicken and Red Stripe and a full-scale party at the Mound stand. As well as Sabina and the new Greenfield

---

The rules of cricket

The rules of cricket are so complex that the official rulebook runs to some twenty pages. The basics, however, are by no means as Byzantine as the game's detractors make out.

There are two teams of eleven players. A team wins by scoring more runs than the other team and dismissing all the opposition – in other words, a team could score many more runs than the opposition, but still not win if the last enemy batsman doggedly stays "in" (hence ensuring a draw). The match is divided into **innings**, when one team bats and the other fields. The number of innings varies depending on the type of competition: one-day matches have one per team; test matches have two.

The aim of the fielding side is to limit the runs scored and get the batsmen "out". Two players from the batting side are on the pitch at any one time. The bowling side has a bowler, a wicket keeper and nine fielders. Two umpires, one standing behind the stumps at the bowler's end and one square on to the play, are responsible for adjudicating if a batsman is out. Each innings is divided into **overs**, consisting of six deliveries, after which the wicket keeper changes ends, the bowler is changed and the fielders move positions.

The batsmen **score runs** either by running up and down from wicket to wicket (one length equals one run), or by hitting the ball over the boundary rope, scoring four runs if it crosses the boundary having touched the ground, and six runs if it flies straight over. The main ways a batsman can be dismissed are: by being "clean bowled", where the bowler dislodges the bails of the wicket (the horizontal pieces of wood resting on top of the stumps); by being "run out", which is when one of the fielding side dislodges the bails with the ball while the batsman is running between the wickets; by being caught, which is when any of the fielding side catches the ball after the batsman has hit it and before it touches the ground; or "LBW" (leg before wicket), where the batsman blocks with his leg a delivery that would otherwise have hit his stumps.

These are the bare rudiments of a game whose beauty lies in the subtlety of its skills and tactics. The captain, for example, chooses which bowler to play and where to position his fielders to counter the strengths of the batsman, the condition of the pitch and a dozen other variables. Cricket also has a beauty in its esoteric language, used to describe such things as fielding positions ("silly mid-off", "cover point", etc) and the various types of bowling delivery ("googly", "yorker", and so on).

Stadium in Trelawny, built for the Cricket World Cup in 2007, there are smaller venues throughout the island: Melbourne Oval in Kingston; Chedwin Park near Spanish Town; Alpart Sports Club in Nain, St Elizabeth; Jarrett Park in Montego Bay; and Kaiser sports ground in Discovery Bay, St Ann. For more on West Indies cricket, visit ⓦwww .windiescricket.com.

Since Jamaica's national team, the **Reggae Boyz** (ⓦwww.thereggaeboyz.com), qualified for the 1998 World Cup, **football** (soccer) has become another national obsession, more popular amongst young people than cricket. Although international matches, held at the National Stadium in Kingston, are relatively rare, league games (the main one being the Wray and Nephew Premier League) attract large and passionate crowds at grounds across the island. These are well worth attending, as much for the atmosphere as for the action on the pitch – visit ⓦwww.golocaljamaica.com/premier league for details of fixtures.

Watersports

Scuba diving and **snorkelling** are concentrated on the north coast, between Negril and Ocho Rios, where visibility is best. The state of the reefs is variable – pollution and aggressive fishing techniques have affected many areas, but there are still some gorgeous sites very close to the shore. The fish are nonetheless impressive, with multitudes of parrot, angel and trigger fish, as well as moray eels, turtles and the evil-looking barracuda. There are a handful of wreck dives – including several plane wrecks off the coast of Negril – and good trenches, overhangs and wall dives.

The main resorts are packed with operators offering dive trips and snorkelling excursions; the most reputable are listed throughout the Guide. For beginners, the most popular options are the one-day introductory **resort courses**, for around US$70, which offer basic instruction and a short supervised shallow dive close to shore. The longer **PADI** (Professional Association of Diving Instructors) **open-water certification course** costs around US$350 and takes a few days, with practical and theoretical tests, safety training and several dives. Once you're certified, you can dive without an instructor, though you'll still need to go with a licensed operator – expect to pay US$95 for a three-tank dive, and remember to take your certification with you.

Parasailing, jet-skiing, water-skiing, kayaking, glass-bottom boat rides and **sailing** are available at all of the major resorts. You can **surf** at Boston Bay and Long Bay in Portland and Bull Bay just east of Kingston, though board rentals are scarce. **Deep-sea fishing** is best around Portland, particularly during October's Blue Marlin tournament. Fully equipped boats are available for rent in all the major resorts; at about US$700 per day, the pursuit of big fish doesn't come cheap, though.

Away from the coast, **river rafting** was first popularized in the 1950s by movie idol **Errol Flynn**, who saw that the bamboo rafts used to transport bananas along Portland's Rio Grande could be used for pleasure punting. The Rio Grande remains the most spectacular spot for an idle glide, but operators have also set up in Ocho Rios, Falmouth and Montego Bay. Costs start at around $50 for a two-person raft, more if you need transport to and from your hotel.

River swimming is idyllic in Jamaica, particularly in the Rio Grande in Portland, the Great River in Montego Bay and the White River in Ocho Rios. Dunn's River in Ocho Rios offers the island's ultimate **waterfall climb**, but there are plenty more cascades, many untouristed. For more relaxing options, **mineral springs** and **natural spas** are Jamaica's hidden gems – locals flock to Bath in St Thomas (p.111), Rockfort in Kingston (p.82) and Milk River in Clarendon (p.254) for the restorative powers of the radioactive water. **River rising pools**, such as Roaring River in Westmoreland (p.232), Cranbrook in St Ann (see p.157) or the Blue Lagoon in Portland (see p.121), are also a delight.

Golf

Jamaica boasts no fewer than twelve **golf courses**, from the magnificent championship Tryall course near Montego Bay and the world-class course at the Ritz Carlton Hotel in Rose Hall, just east of Montego Bay, to less testing nine-hole links in Mandeville and Port Antonio. All are open to the public, except during tournaments. **Green fees** vary wildly from course to course, and there are additional charges for caddies, club and cart rental. For more on golf, visit ⓦwww.visit jamaica.com or www.jamaicagolf.com.

Hiking

Though the heat doesn't encourage strenuous exercise, **hiking** is by far the best way to get a flavour of the Jamaican country-side. The best opportunities are in the dense wildernesses of the **Blue and John Crow mountains**, where the ultimate trek is to the top of Jamaica's highest point, Blue Mountain Peak; and in **Cockpit Country**, where trails originally blazed by Maroon warriors lead deep into the Jamaican interior, though there are enjoyable minor walks elsewhere; all are fully covered in the text.

It is strongly recommended that you use a **guide** for all but the shortest of hikes, as it's perilously easy to get lost (see p.25 for major operators). Always stick to paths and trails; veering off into uncharted foliage not only encourages disorientation, but can destroy plants and lead to soil erosion. Never throw rubbish when hiking; even cigarette butts should be pocketed – a carelessly discarded cigarette can easily start a massive bush fire.

Other activities

A labyrinth of **caves** networks Jamaica's limestone interior, and many have been opened up as attractions with lights and stairs, so you don't have to be an experienced spelunker to enjoy them. Best of the bunch are Nonsuch Cave in Portland (p.126), Roaring River in Westmoreland (p.232) and Dromilly Cave in Trelawny (p.199). Serious cavers should head for Cockpit Country, where the limestone is at its thickest and

many of the caves are unexplored; Windsor (p.202) is the only easily accessible cavern. Contact Sun Venture Tours or Cockpit Country Adventure Tours (see p.199) for caving trips. For more information on caving in Jamaica, see p.199.

Horseback trail riding is a lovely way of exploring the island, though some stables and their mounts are rather run-down; stick to those listed in the chapters or check with the JTB. The best stables are Hooves in St Ann (see p.157), Chukka Cove in St Ann and Chukka Caribbean in Hanover (see p.157 & p.230), the Good Hope stables in Trelawny (see p.196) and the Half Moon Equestrian Centre in Montego Bay (see p.185); the latter also offers **polo**, **dressage** and **show-jumping** lessons. If you're inter-ested in watching a polo match, contact the Jamaica Polo Association (☎952 4370); fixtures are held throughout the year.

Cycling is surprisingly underpromoted in Jamaica. An alternative to demure proces-sions aboard colour coordinated resort cycles is a guided **mountain-bike tour**, available in the Blue Mountains (see p.96); more serious mountain bikers should contact the St Mary Off-Road Biking Association (ⓦwww.smorba.com).

If you're after some well-regimented thrills, Chukka Adventures (ⓦwww.chukka caribbean.com) have the island's **soft adventure** market completely sewn up, with bases in or around the three main resorts offering everything from zip-lining "canopy tours" to river kayaking and tubing, ATV rides and dogsled tours, with sleds pulled by rehabilitated pot-hounds.

Finally, many hotels offer **tennis courts**, and for those who can't survive without their workout, plenty of resorts also provide **gyms** and **aerobics classes**.

Trouble, harassment and drugs

Jamaica has a bad reputation for violent crime, but while the island certainly does have its problems, you're very unlikely to get mixed up in them.

The resorts are well policed, and the JTB are keen to stress that you are more likely to be robbed in New York than Montego Bay. Most tourists still steer clear of the capital – even rural Jamaicans are wary of going into "Town", and you'll be warned against going at all of the resorts – but such trepidation is largely misplaced. You'll be surprised at how safe and friendly Kingston feels. Drug-related organized crime is a frightening reality, but it is a reality that affects poor Jamaicans rather than tourists. It's almost always restricted to ghetto areas – pockets of west Kingston and Spanish Town that you're never going to go to; elsewhere, the vast majority of visitors experience no crime or violence during their stay.

At the same time, robberies, assaults and other crimes against tourists do occur, and it's wise to apply the **precautions** you'd take in any foreign city. Don't flaunt fat rolls of bank notes, avoid walking alone late at night, don't go mad smoking ganja in the street, lock your hotel room door at night – in short, use your common sense and you'll prevent potential problems before they happen. You might also want to read the travel advice of your own government; contacts are listed below.

Government travel advice

Australian Department of Foreign Affairs Ⓦ www.dfat.gov.au, Ⓦ www.smartraveller.gov.au.
British Foreign & Commonwealth Office Ⓦ www.fco.gov.uk.

Police

The **emergency number** for the Jamaican **police** is ☎ 119. Individual police stations are detailed throughout the text.

Canadian Department of Foreign Affairs Ⓦ www.dfait-maeci.gc.ca.
Irish Department of Foreign Affairs Ⓦ www.foreignaffairs.gov.ie.
New Zealand Ministry of Foreign Affairs Ⓦ www.mft.govt.nz.
US State Department Ⓦ www.travel.state.gov.

Hustling

Hustling – the hard-nosed, hard-sell pitches you'll be endlessly subjected to on the north coast – can be the chief irritation of time spent in Jamaica. The tourist trade has long been adversely affected by the stream of young hopefuls aggressively (or humorously) accosting foreigners in the street with offers of transport, ganja, aloe massages, hair braiding and crafts. It's wearisome, but much of what is perceived as harassment is simply an attempt to make a living in an economically deprived country, and while some locals see tourists as easy prey for exploitation, many street touts are genuine. Hustling is a game played in the true entrepreneurial Jamaican spirit; the sales pitch is finely honed and modified to match the perceived nature of the potential client, and the national aptitude for "lyrics" (artful banter designed to break down even the most hardened sensibility) can make encounters with street vendors an entertaining and educative experience rather than a trial. This often depends on your attitude to the approaches, so try to respond with humour and charm rather than irritation and frustration (which, admittedly, can be difficult when the fiftieth taxi driver of the day offers his services). For more on ways to deal with approaches, see p.178.

Homophobia

Jamaica is not a gay-friendly country. Sodomy (and so-called lewd acts, taken to mean any homosexual activity) is illegal here, condemned as a sin by the church and the moral majority, and fuel for much hysterical press coverage. And while there's a sizeable gay community here, it's very much an undercover scene, with parties and events publicized by word of mouth.

Attempting to argue with freely expressed prejudices is almost always a lesson in futility – it'll be you against the Bible. But this doesn't mean that gay and lesbian travellers should avoid Jamaica – many hotels are managed by gay men, and a lot of the smarter ones won't turn a hair if you ask for a double room – but don't expect to be able to display affection in public without attracting catcalls, sniggers, downright aggression and maybe even physical violence. For more information contact J-Flag, the Jamaican gay and lesbian support group (☎978 1954, ⓦwww.jflag.org).

Marijuana

Tourism officials are loathe to acknowledge it, but many people do come to Jamaica in search of what aficionados agree is some of the finest marijuana in the world, and certainly **ganja** is part-and-parcel of the culture here to a greater degree than in other Caribbean islands, smoked more openly and available more freely. Be warned that quite apart from being **illegal**, Jamaican ganja, or "herb", packs a mightier punch than anything you've experienced before. Yellow-eyed

Jamaicans who've been smoking since their teens can cope with a spliff before breakfast – fresh-off-the-plane visitors probably can't.

Bear in mind, also, that despite the stereotypical view of an island populated by ganja fiends, those Jamaicans who smoke are in a minority; most locals neither smoke nor approve of those who do. And despite its links with the Rastafarian religion and frequent use as a medicinal draught, possession, use and export of any quantity of ganja is **against the law** and carries stiff penalties. Tourists are just as eligible for prosecution as Jamaicans; at any one time there are hundreds of foreigners serving sentences in Jamaican jails, in horrifyingly harsh conditions.

If you choose to smoke ganja, trust your instincts. You will be approached with offers; buy only from someone you feel you can trust. You should be equally wary of carrying ganja around the island; if you pass a car at the roadside flanked by a worried-looking white person and a swarm of cops, you can bet that the police are conducting one of their routine searches.

Finally, do not attempt to smuggle ganja out of the country under any circumstances; however devious you think your method, customs officials have seen it before, while sophisticated scanning machines can pick up the tiniest amounts. Even carrying rolling papers can prompt protracted questioning.

Culture and etiquette

Take a look at a roomful of Jamaicans enjoying a night out and you might easily think this is one of the most free, open societies on the planet, what with the downright sexiness of the dancing and the frankness of the chat-up lines. But the party scene is just one aspect of Jamaican culture, and the society as a whole is actually pretty conservative. The vast majority of Jamaicans are practising Christians, far more likely to spend Sunday mornings in church than recovering from the night before.

Jamaica can be quite a paradoxical place; it's fine to turn up at a sound-system party wearing little more than a few strips of fabric, but wear your bikini anywhere away from the beach and you're likely to cause offence. Similarly, as most locals take a great deal of pride in their appearance, grubbing around in a crumpled T-shirt speckled with last night's jerk sauce is a guaranteed way to not be taken seriously. In terms of general **dress codes**, though, you'll want something smart if you plan on clubbing, and men will need long trousers if planning to dine at the better restaurants (jackets are required only at the most expensive places).

Jamaicans are refreshingly direct; your big nose or bald head will be seen as fair game for comment, and while an open invitation to bed within the first five minutes of meeting someone can be disconcerting, you at least know where you stand. At the same time, old-fashioned **manners** are maintained here; passing someone on a rural street without acknowledging them will be seen as rude, as will failing to greet a shop assistant with a "good morning/ afternoon" before launching into your request. The elderly are revered in Jamaican culture, and it's usual to preface someone's name with Mr or Miss when addressing someone much older than you; kids are taught to respect their elders at all times and never answer back. Bear in mind, too, that many locals are a bit weary of serving as the "Jamaican Rasta" or "market lady" in the holiday snaps of a thousand visitors – it's polite to ask before taking someone's picture (and don't be surprised if they ask for a little money should they say yes).

Women travellers

For women **travelling solo**, Jamaica can be hard work until you get used to the constant male attention. In the resorts particularly, unaccompanied women can expect to receive a barrage of attention from Jamaican men, from hopeful innuendo – "gal, me a cry for you"– to frankly pornographic propositions, and a walk down the street will have you sized up by a thousand eyes. All of this is somewhat abated after the first couple of days, particularly if your holiday plans don't include "climbing aboard the big bamboo". Cope with your new status as a sex goddess with humility and humour; it probably has more to do with your foreign allure – or perceived economic clout – than your personal charms, and a lot of the come-ons can be extremely amusing.

As lots of women do come to Jamaica in search of "exotic" romance, many locals will inevitably assume that single female travellers have come here to find a man – or several. The news that you're not will often be greeted with incredulity, and the semi-professional **gigolos** (and full-blown male prostitutes) who work the resorts will do their best to get you to change your mind. If you're not interested, saying "no" and meaning it, dressing fairly conservatively and avoiding idle chat with men you don't know are good lines of defence. Learn to listen to your instincts; the slightest hint of flirting means that you are probably about to be propositioned, so assume that even the most innocent reaction may be interpreted as a sign of acquiescence.

Shopping

The Jamaican souvenir industry is precisely that – many of the carvings and knick-knacks are mass-produced, with little variation from maker to maker. However, the most common products tend to be the best, and though your "lignum vitae" Lion of Judah may be a pitch-pine copy of a thousand others, quality is generally good. Haggling is a natural part of the trade at craft markets and stalls, but not in hotel boutiques and the more expensive, air-conditioned shops.

Where to shop

Virtually every town in Jamaica has at least one **market**, most selling fruit, vegetables and other produce, and often a limited selection of crafts, too. The resorts have dedicated craft markets selling T-shirts, wooden carvings, jewellery, straw goods, hats and assorted knick-knacks, and these, along with the ubiquitous roadside **craft stalls**, are the most enjoyable places to browse and buy.

Specialist **souvenir stores** also have a good stock of crafts and indigenous art as well as rum and cigars, while local galleries often have paintings, sculptures and woodcarvings for sale. Both souvenir stores and galleries tend to be pricier than the markets and stalls, but the standard of merchandise is higher.

In-bond – or duty-free – shops are usually clustered together in glitzy plazas and malls, stocked with perfume, spirits, designer clothes, brand-name watches, crystal, porcelain, diamonds and gold. Savings range from twenty to forty percent; all goods must be paid for in foreign (ie US) currency, and major credit cards are usually accepted. You'll need your passport and proof of onward travel.

What to buy

There are many alternatives to "Rasta" tams with attached fake locks or bamboo shakers: a custom-designed pair of leather sandals, the ubiquitous red-gold-and-green string vests, and bandanas and tassels for car mirrors are all available in market areas of most towns. T-shirts have improved immeasurably in recent years; there are still plenty of dreadful ones emblazoned with caricature Rastas yowling "Yeh Mon it Irie", but you can also get some fantastically stylish alternatives; look for the Stoosh or Cooyah brands, among others.

Not surprisingly, **reggae music** is big business in Jamaica, and fans will have a field day. The best music stores are in downtown Kingston (see p.80), but there are adequate outlets in most other towns. Compilation CDs are available from roadside vendors throughout Jamaica (though note these are usually illegal copies); they also sell recordings of the most recent sound-system dances.

Other good Jamaican gifts include the prettily packaged range of essential oils, soaps, candles and bodycare accessories from Blue Mountain Aromatics and Starfish Oils, all made from natural local ingredients; both are available from more upmarket gift shops.

Food and drink

For a taste of Jamaica back home, you can pick up fiery **jerk sauce** or delicious **guava jelly** at any supermarket – the main locally made brands, such as Walkers Wood and Busha Brown, are substantially cheaper when purchased in non-tourist shops.

> Especially on the north coast, you'll see **coral** (particularly black coral) and "**tortoiseshell**" products (made from the endangered hawksbill turtle) on sale, but the trade in these protected species is **illegal**. Don't buy; you're liable to serious fines if you're caught with them. Though not illegal, conch shells, too, should be avoided, as demand has eclipsed supply and conch are slowly disappearing from Jamaican waters.

Cocoa tea balls, used to make the local version of hot chocolate, fresh **nutmeg**, and the delectable **honey**, sold in old rum bottles at any market, will all bring your memories flooding back. At both international airports, you can buy boxes of frozen Juici Beef and Tastee patties.

Rum (see *Jamaican food and drink* colour section) is an obligatory memento – gift shops sell cardboard "Jamaica Farewell" packages holding two or three bottles for easy transit, though these are usually cheaper in the airport departure lounge; you can also save if you buy from a wholesale liquor shop or supermarket. The Sangster's company produces excellent **liqueurs**, on sale everywhere, and the ubiquitous Tia Maria coffee liqueur is another must-have. Finally, a packet of **Blue Mountain coffee**, sold all over the island but most reasonably *in situ*, is an essential souvenir; by far the best brand is Old Tavern, available in more upmarket outlets, but the JABLUM brands, sold in fetching hessian pouches, are good too.

Travel essentials

Costs

Jamaica's reputation as a "luxury" destination combined with the high cost of living compared to most developing countries means that this isn't a cheap destination by any means, though there are ways to make savings if you're on a budget. Some things, like car rental and petrol (and hence taxis, too), cost more than in Europe and a lot more than in the US, while you'll pay a fair bit extra for a drink or a meal in a tourist-oriented restaurant or bar than you will in a locals' joint. Eating at local restaurants, and taking shared taxis and public transport are the main ways to keep costs down, and there are inexpensive (if rather basic) accommodation options across the island. Equally, don't be scared to negotiate on prices – particularly in taxis and at markets and roadside stalls, the first price quoted is often an opening gambit, and even hotels and guesthouses are generally fair game for a bit of bargaining, especially during low season.

In terms of daily budgets, **accommodation** is likely to be the major expense. If you're prepared to put up with extremely basic options, you can find rooms in most of the main resort areas for around US$30 (£18/€20) per night, though don't expect to be close to the beach or to have a room where you'll want to spend much time (there are some notable exceptions to this in less developed areas such as Port Antonio and Treasure Beach, however). The most inexpensive options in the resorts will set you back around US$50 (£30/€33) per night for a room with a fan or a/c and a private bathroom, while US$60–120 (£36/€39–£72/€79) will get you nicer decor and public facilities such as a pool, tennis courts, restaurant and bar. Above this, the sky is the limit. Note also that government tax (GCT; 15 percent) and a service charge (up to 15 percent) are not always included in room rates – ask before you check in, as these can add significantly to the final price. With regards to **eating** and **drinking**, a breakfast or lunch in a locals' restaurant will cost J$500–800 (US$6/£3.60/€4–$9.50/£5.70/€6.30), a fish dinner around $1000 (US$11.80/£7/€7.80). In tourist restaurants and bars, breakfasts might start at $800 ($9.50/£5.70/€6.30), while a standard lunch or dinner will be around J$1500 (US$17.75/£10.75/€11.80), a mixed drink J$400 (US$4.70/£2.90/€3.15) and a beer about J$250 (US$2.95/£1.80/€2). Note that 15 percent service charge is often added to restaurant bills in touristy places. In terms of **getting around**, renting a car will cost roughly US$50 (£30/€33) per day, a car and driver US$100 (£60/€66) per day, and

Tipping

No tip is necessary at any **restaurant** that imposes an automatic service charge (although obviously you can leave one if service is good); ten to fifteen percent is the norm anywhere else. Tip **taxi drivers** at your discretion; route taxi drivers do not expect a tip. A small consideration for services rendered, from minding your car to carrying your bag to your room, is the norm for most Jamaicans, and will always be appreciated, as will leaving something for your hotel **chambermaid** at the end of your stay.

shared taxi rides around town will be about J$120 (US$1.40/£0.85/€0.95) per trip. For more on bus/minibus prices, see p.22.

Electricity IIO V

The island standard is 110 volts, with two-pin sockets, though some older hotels still use 220 volts. Take adapters for essential items – some of the upmarket hotels and guesthouses have them, but you shouldn't rely on it. Current is poor in some areas, and foreign appliances can run slowly.

Entry requirements

Visitors from North America, the UK and Australasia do not need a visa and are allowed stays of up to six months without one. On arrival, your passport will be stamped by an immigration officer who may ask you for proof of adequate funds, where you're staying during your holiday (if you don't know yet, pick any hotel in our listings, as you may be delayed if you can't name a place) and evidence of a return or onward flight.

If you want to stay longer than six months, it's possible to apply for an **extension** for up to twelve further months. You'll need to contact the Ministry of National Security, located at the Mutual Life Building, North Tower, 2 Oxford Rd, Kingston 10 (☎876/906 4908 to 4933, ⍉www.mnsj.gov.jm) or, in Montego Bay, the Immigration Office at Overton Plaza, Union St (☎952 5381).

Jamaican embassies and consulates abroad

Canada Jamaica High Commission, 75 Slater Street, Suite 800, Ottawa, Ontario K1P 5H9 ☎613/233-9311, ⍉www.jhcottawa.ca.
UK and Ireland Jamaica High Commission, 1–2 Prince Consort Rd, London SW7 2BQ ☎020/7823 9911, ⍉jhcuk.org.

US Embassy of Jamaica, 1520 New Hampshire Ave NW, Washington DC 20036 ☎202/452-0660, ⍉www.jamaicaembassy.org.

There are no Jamaican embassies or consulates in Australia, New Zealand or South Africa.

Health

Health-wise, travelling in Jamaica poses few problems. Food tends to be well and hygienically prepared and the filtered and the heavily chlorinated tap water is safe to drink. Unless you've travelled to Asia, Africa, Central or South America, the Dominican Republic, Haiti or Trinidad and Tobago within six weeks of landing in Jamaica, **no vaccinations** are required to enter the island. Jamaica is not generally malarial, and though there was a brief outbreak in 2006, malaria prophylaxis are not considered necessary for visitors. There are occasional outbreaks of **dengue fever**, carried by the *Aedes aegypti* mosquito, found throughout the island, which can be serious for the infirm, very young or very old. Symptoms include extreme aches and pains in the bones and joints, rashes around the torso, dizziness, headaches, fever and vomiting. There's no effective vaccination.

To avoid being bitten by **sandflies** and **mosquitoes**, cover arms and legs at dusk and dawn, and apply lots of DEET-rich repellent. Mosquito coils are sold everywhere and can be effective, if a bit smelly, and many hotels provide plug-in anti-mossi devices, too. Of more natural alternatives, the locally-produced Starfish Oil of No Mosquito is a nice citronella-based repellent. Once you've been bitten (and you will be), gently apply some antihistamine, after which you shouldn't touch the area at all. Though hellishly tempting, scratching (or even a light investigative rub) will always lead to more irritation, bigger red marks and possibly infection.

If you're unused to it, Jamaica's **humid climate** can bring on a host of minor complaints. Open wounds take longer to heal and easily become septic: clean cuts straight away, and dress with iodine, dry antiseptic spray or powder rather than creams. Blocked sweat ducts can cause uncomfortable and unsightly **prickly heat** rashes; to treat or avoid these, wear loose cotton clothes, take frequent cool showers without soap, dust with medicated talcum powder and don't use sunscreen or moisturizer on affected areas. It's also important to remember to drink plenty of water, and always apply high factor sunscreen when outside (and, if possible, keep out of the sun between 11am and 3pm).

Jamaica has no poisonous snakes, but there are a few underwater hazards to be aware of. **Spiny black sea urchins** are easily missed in a bed of sea grass – if you tread on one, remove the spines immediately, soak the skin in vinegar (or urine) and see a doctor; water heated as hot as you can stand is useful for getting out the spines. Never touch **coral**; apart from the fact that contact kills the organism, coral can cut and you'll come away with a painful, slow-to-heal rash. If you do have a brush with the reefs, don't touch the affected area directly, but wash it with a diluted vinegar or ammonia solution.

Jamaica has the third-highest incidence of **AIDS** in the Caribbean, with the disease being the leading cause of death for Jamaicans in their 20s. Unofficial sex tourism has long been a part of the scenery in the resorts; if you do have sex while away, always use a condom. Brand-names such as Durex are available in pharmacies and larger gas stations.

There are two good, sizeable public **hospitals** in Kingston, while Cornwall Regional in Montego Bay is the best equipped on the north coast. There are also private hospitals in the main towns, with MoBay Hope in Montego Bay being one of the best. The easiest way to find a **doctor** in a hurry is to ask at your hotel; some have a resident nurse, and all will be able to recommend a doctor or private clinic locally. Most of these are reliable, but you'll have to fork out for the treatment and claim on your insurance once back home, so make sure you get receipts.

Every town has at least one **pharmacy**, with those in resort towns well stocked with expensive brand-name products; they will only issue antibiotics with a doctor's prescription.

Hospitals, private doctors, clinics and pharmacies are found throughout the island and are listed in each chapter.

Insurance

It's always sensible to take out **travel insurance** before visiting Jamaica to cover against theft, loss and illness or injury. A typical policy will provide cover for loss of baggage, tickets and – up to a certain limit – cash or cheques, as well as cancellation or curtailment of your journey. Most exclude so-called dangerous sports unless an extra premium is paid: in Jamaica, this can mean scuba diving, windsurfing or white-water rafting, though probably not kayaking or jeep safaris. When securing baggage cover, make sure that the per-article limit will cover your camera or any other valuables. If you need to make a claim, you should keep receipts for medicines and medical treatment, and in

Rough Guides travel insurance

Rough Guides has teamed up with WorldNomads.com to offer great **travel insurance** deals. Policies are available to residents of over 150 countries, with cover for a wide range of **adventure sports**, 24hr emergency assistance, high levels of medical and evacuation cover and a stream of **travel safety information**. Roughguides.com users can take advantage of their policies online 24/7, from anywhere in the world – even if you're already travelling. And since plans often change when you're on the road, you can extend your policy and even claim online. Roughguides.com users who buy travel insurance with WorldNomads.com can also leave a positive footprint and donate to a community development project. For more information go to ⓦ**www .roughguides.com/shop**.

the event of having anything stolen, you must obtain an official statement from the police.

Internet

Internet access is available in all towns and resorts, with both dedicated cybercafés and wi-fi in many bars and restaurants. Almost all hotels have a connection, too, with terminals for guests' use and/or wi-fi, while libraries and larger post offices sometimes have free access.

Laundry

Most hotels have a **laundry service**, but check prices before handing over a huge load as charges can be per-item and not at all cheap. Many large towns have at least one public laundry (listed in the relevant chapters), which is a less expensive option.

Mail

Considering how small Jamaica is, it's amazing how long it can take for inland mail to get across the country. Don't expect a letter from Kingston to the north coast (or vice versa) to arrive in less than a week. **International mail** is also slow – reckon on around ten days to a fortnight for airmail to reach Europe or North America. If you're really in a hurry to send something overseas, try DHL (toll-free ☎1-888/225 5345, ⓦwww .dhl.com.jm) or FedEx (toll-free ☎1-888/463 3339, ⓦfedex.com/jm); within Jamaica, Tara Couriers (toll-free ☎1-888/827 2226, ⓦwww .taracan.com) will get packages from one side of the island to another within a day.

Most towns and villages have a **post office**, normally open Monday to Friday from 9am to 5pm; smaller postal agencies in rural areas keep shorter hours. Those in large towns have **poste restante** facilities – mail is held for about a month, and you'll need your passport or other identification to collect it. **Stamps** are sold at post offices and in many hotels. It costs J$50 to mail a postcard to anywhere in the world; rates for international letters are J$60–90. Rates for parcels are available online at ⓦwww.jamaicapost.gov.jm.

Maps

For touring or driving around the island, the best map to get a hold of is the **Shell** **Jamaica Road Map** (1:250,000), which is contoured and includes excellent street maps of Kingston, Montego Bay and Ocho Rios as well as Spanish Town, Mandeville and Port Antonio. It's sold at good book shops in Jamaica and in selected Shell petrol stations islandwide. Also useful, and a more manageable size, is the JTB road map, *Discover Jamaica*, which includes a 1:350,000 map of the entire island, a 1:34,000 map of Kingston and small maps of the other main towns. It's available from JTB offices abroad, and, in Jamaica, from the offices in Kingston and Montego Bay – you may have to pay a small fee.

Note that some of these maps don't show the new coastal highways.

Money

Jamaica's unit of currency is the **Jamaican dollar** (J$), divided into 100 cents. It comes in bills of J$1000, J$500, J$100 and J$50 and coins of J$20, J$10, J$5 and J$1, plus seldom-used copper coins (in locals' stores, it's common to be given boiled sweets in lieu of small change). Note that the J$100 and $1000 bills look very similar – it's surprisingly easy to mix them up. At the time of writing, exchange rates were US$1=J$87, £1=J$143 and €1=J$130. Given the constant fluctuation of the Jamaican dollar, the **US dollar** has long served as an unofficial parallel currency, particularly at the north coast resorts, and prices for tourist services – hotels, car rental, sightseeing tours, etc – are usually quoted in US$. Restaurants and bars vary, with some quoting US, others Jamaican; for minor items like bus fares, short taxi rides or roadside snacks, drivers and vendors will always quote Jamaican dollars. In the resorts, US dollars are as widely accepted as Jamaican, but when paying a bill, check in advance that your change will be given in the same currency or, if in Jamaican dollars, at a decent exchange rate. It's a good idea to always carry some Jamaican dollars to pay for small things like snacks, drinks, tips and taxi fares.

Credit/debit cards and travellers' cheques

The easiest way to access funds in Jamaica is by using your ATM card; machines are widespread, at some shopping malls and petrol stations as well as banks. Before you leave home, check with your bank that your card is cleared to use abroad, and find out what the fees for overseas withdrawals are. Some can be quite high, so you may want to make one large withdrawal rather than several small ones. ATMs dispense local cash and, in large resorts, US dollars. Major **credit cards** – American Express, Visa, MasterCard – are widely accepted in the larger tourist hotels, but smaller hotels and restaurants may not take them.

Banks and exchange M-Th 9-2pm

Banking hours in Jamaica are generally Monday to Thursday 9am to 2pm and Friday 9am to 3pm or 4pm, and will often have a separate queue for foreign exchange. Given their limited hours, though, you'll probably find you make more use of **cambios**, ubiquitous in the resorts and also within many supermarkets. They usually offer a better exchange rate than the banks, particularly when the currency is fluctuating wildly, as well as opening longer hours. A firm favourite, with consistently good rates, are the islandwide branches of FX Trader, often conveniently situated within supermarkets and shopping malls; you can find out the location of the nearest office by calling toll-free on ☎1-888/398 7233. Exchange bureaux at the main airports offer rates slightly lower than the banks, and at **hotels**, the rate is invariably significantly lower – it's only worth changing money at hotels if you have no other choice.

Opening hours and public holidays

Jamaican offices are normally open for business between 8.30am and 4.30 or 5pm Monday to Friday, often closing for an hour at lunch, while **shops** are typically open from 8am to 5pm Monday to Saturday, although **supermarkets** tend to open until 8 or 9pm, as well as on Sundays. **Museums** normally close for one day a week, either Sunday or Monday, while most other places you'll want to visit – private beaches, waterfalls, gardens, churches and so on – are generally open daily.

Public holidays

The main **national holidays**, when virtually all shops and offices close, are as follows:

New Year's Day (January 1)
Ash Wednesday
Good Friday
Easter Monday
Labour Day (May 23)
Emancipation Day (August 1)
Independence Day (first Mon in August)
National Heroes Day (third Mon in October)
Christmas Day (December 25)
Boxing Day (December 26)

Phones

The national telecommunications network in Jamaica, run as a monopoly for many years by Cable & Wireless, has undergone a massive revolution since the entrance of Irish-based company Digicel (🔘www .digicel.com) made mobile phones available to all at a relatively low cost. Several other cell phone companies have since muscled in on the act, and Jamaicans are now said to have more mobiles per household than anywhere else in the world – locals have all but abandoned the public phone system. Payphones do exist – you'll need to purchase a phonecard from a supermarket or pharmacy to use one.

If you have a tri-band **mobile phone**, you can use it in Jamaica by way of roaming. You'll pay a lot less for local and international calls if you buy a local SIM card from any of the innumerable outlets islandwide (around US$15). You're given a local number, and you can top up your credit at shops, bars, petrol stations and restaurants islandwide. *cell phone*

Another cheap way to make international calls from hotel phones or private land-lines is to use pre-paid WorldTalk **phonecards**, widely available from hotels, post offices, gift shops and supermarkets.

The **area code** for Jamaica is 876.

Calling home from Jamaica

Note that the initial zero is omitted from the area code when dialling the UK, Ireland, Australia and New Zealand from abroad.

US and Canada international access code + 1 + area code.

Australia international access code + 61 + city code.

New Zealand international access code + 64 + city code.

UK international access code + 44 + city code.

Ireland international access code + 353 + city code.

South Africa international access code + 27 + city code.

Photography

Jamaica is made for pretty pictures, though overexposure can also be a problem: watch out for the glare from sea and sand, and try to take pictures early or late in the day when the sun is less bright. When photographing people (or their homes and property), always ask permission – some like it, others don't – and anticipate a request for a donation.

Time

Jamaica is on Eastern Standard Time and does not adjust for Daylight Saving Time. Accordingly, it's on the same time as New York (one hour behind from spring to autumn) and five hours behind London (six hours from spring to autumn).

Tourist information

Though Jamaica spends a great deal on lavish advertising campaigns, the **Jamaica Tourist Board** (JTB) isn't a user-friendly source of information on the island. Offices in Jamaica – in Montego Bay, Kingston and Port Antonio (see p.172, p.57 & p.115 respectively) – aren't really geared up to deal with enquiries from visitors, though they can answer basic questions. The **Internet** is a far better source of information; start off at the JTB's website, ⓦwww.visitjamaica.com, which has a regularly updated calendar of events, plus accommodation, resort and attraction listings and hoards of local information. Other good

general sites include ⓦwww.jamaicans.com, a huge site with everything from language and culture to cookery and tourist info, plus busy message boards; and ⓦwww.top5jamaica.com, which has links to the most popular Jamaican sites on the Web.

Jamaica has no entertainment listings magazine, so to find out what's going on, you have to rely on the **radio** (particularly Irie FM; see p.31), **newspapers** (see p.31), and – the usual way of announcing forthcoming events – **flyers** and **banners** posted up all around the towns. There are also a host of websites dedicated to entertainment listings; try ⓦwww.whatsonjamaica.com, www.yardflex.com, www.whata-gwan.com, www.yardyvibes.com or www.partyinc.com. We've given more specific advice on finding out what's on in the individual chapters.

Travellers with disabilities

Large- to medium-sized hotels, and most of the big all-inclusive chains, have ramps or lifts on their properties, though Jamaica isn't particularly geared toward people with disabilities – expect accessibility to be a recurrent problem. However, though facilities are poor, you'll find that most people are quick to help out should you have mobility issues. The Combined Disabilities Association of Jamaica, 18 Ripon Rd, Kingston (☎929 1177) may be able to help with further advice; you could also visit the US-based website ⓦwww.access-able.com.

Travelling with children

Pellucid seas, gently shelving beaches, no serious health risks and an indulgent attitude toward kids make Jamaica an ideal destination if you're travelling with children. Though some larger hotels (the *Sandals* chain in particular) operate under a couples-only policy, most welcome families, and some all-inclusive properties are specially geared for families, with extensive facilities, daily events and personal nannies: best are the *Pebbles* resorts, in Falmouth and Runaway Bay (ⓦwww.fdrholidays.com); and the *Beaches* resorts in Negril, Boscobel and Sandy Bay (ⓦwww.beaches.com). There are also many hotels with kids' clubs that offer vacationing parents an afternoon off. Equally, it's usually easy to arrange babysitting through your hotel.

Guide

Guide

Kingston and around

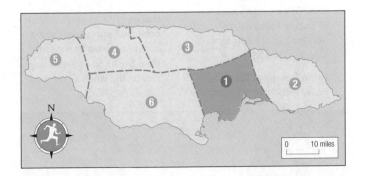

CHAPTER 1 # Highlights

* **National Gallery** A wealth of works from Jamaica's most important artists, from Edna Manley to Kapo. See p.62

* **Bob Marley pilgrimage** Tour the Trench Town Culture Yard, where Marley grew up; the museum in his former home; and, the family's Tuff Gong recording studio. See p.63 & p.73

* **Sports events** Music, flowing Red Stripe and plenty of crowd participation are fine accompaniments to seeing a football match at "The Office", some cricket at Sabina Park or the horseracing at Caymanas. See p.71 & p.88

* **Hope Botanical Gardens** A lovely respite from the urban din, with palms to sit under and a fantastic vegetarian restaurant. See p.74

* **Nightlife** From high-octane clubbing and outdoor parties to roots and rock sessions to classic Kingston street jams, the capital's nightlife scene is legendary. See p.77

* **Port Royal and Lime Cay** Peppered with eighteenth-century military buildings, this former pirate stronghold is an atmospheric place for a plate of fresh seafood or a dance under the stars. See p.84

* **Hellshire** White sand, brightly coloured fishing boats and a cool sea breeze provide the ideal backdrop for what may well be the world's best fried fish. See p.88

▲ Craft shop, Trench Town Culture Yard

Kingston and around

Overwhelming and fascinating in equal measure, **Kingston** is quite unlike anywhere else in the Caribbean. Overhung by the magnificent Blue Mountains to the north and lapped by a huge natural harbour to the south, the city holds as many pockets of opulence as it does zinc-fenced ghettos, and its wide boulevards see top-of-the-range SUVs fighting for space with pushcarts and the odd goat or cow. Nonetheless, in the 1950s, Ian Fleming called Kingston a "tough city", and that still holds true today. Jamaica's capital is rough and ready, a little uncompromising, but always exciting – and though its troubled reputation means that few tourists visit (it's not, perhaps, a place for the faint-hearted), Kingston is infinitely more absorbing than any of the resorts.

With some 700,000 residents (22 percent of the island's total population), Kingston seethes with life, noise and activity, the glitzy malls of uptown and the faded, rough charm of downtown revealing a side of Jamaica that couldn't be more different to the north coast. As well as being the seat of government and the island's administrative centre, Kingston is Jamaica's cultural and historical heart, the city that spawned Bob Marley, Buju Banton, Beenie Man and countless other reggae stars, and the place where Marcus Garvey first preached his tenets of black empowerment. And, with a plethora of theatres and galleries, it's one of the best places on the island to fully appreciate the country's home-grown art, theatre and dance scenes.

If you do decide to visit – and it's well worth the effort for anyone with even a passing interest in Jamaican culture – you'll find that not only is it easy to steer clear of trouble, but that there's none of the persistent **harassment** that bedevils parts of the north coast. In comparison to Ochi or Negril, the capital feels refreshingly real, with most Kingstonians far more interested in going about their business than trifling with a tourist. That's not to say that city dwellers are unfriendly; in fact, it's far easier to strike up a decent conversation here than in more conventional tourist honeypots, where every interaction can seem like a precursor to a sales pitch. The pulsating, live-for-today vitality of the place, combined with the urbane outlook of its citizens, injects a shot of adrenaline that often proves addictive, and the exuberant atmosphere is tempered by a cool elegance and a strong sense of national history. If you follow the herd and avoid the capital, you'll have missed one of Jamaica's undoubted highlights.

For many, the sights and sounds of the capital's street life are entertainment in themselves, but the city is packed with more substantial draws besides. A handful of interesting **museums**, galleries and churches can easily fill a couple of days of sightseeing, while the island's best clubs, theatres and some great restaurants will take care of the evenings.

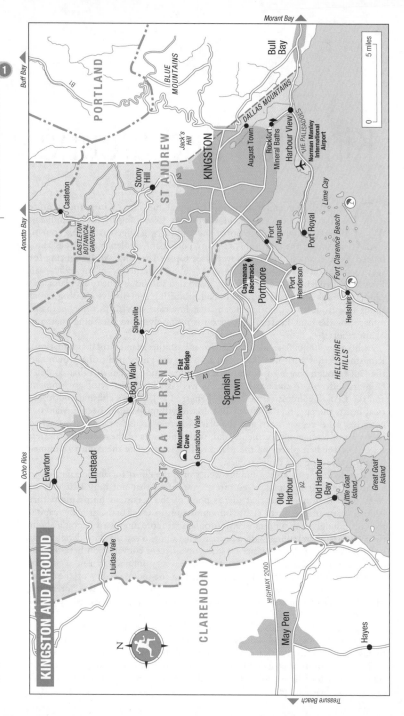

KINGSTON AND AROUND

Morant Bay

Bull Bay

PORTLAND

BLUE MOUNTAINS

DALLAS MOUNTAINS

Buff Bay

Jack's Hill

ST ANDREW

August Town

KINGSTON

Rockfort Mineral Baths

Harbour View

THE PALISADOES

Norman Manley International Airport

Annotto Bay

Castleton

CASTLETON BOTANICAL GARDENS

Stony Hill

Lime Cay

Fort Augusta

Port Royal

Fort Clarence Beach

Caymanas Racetrack

Portmore

Port Henderson

Hellshire

Sligoville

HELLSHIRE HILLS

Ocho Rios

Bog Walk

Flat Bridge

Spanish Town

Linstead

Mountain River Cave

Guanaboa Vale

Ewarton

Old Harbour

Old Harbour Bay

Little Goat Island

Great Goat Island

Lluidas Vale

HIGHWAY 2000

CLARENDON

N

May Pen

Hayes

Treasure Beach

5 miles

0

Kingston

Founded at the tail end of the seventeenth century, **KINGSTON** fast became the greatest city in the West Indies. The main impetus to growth was its fabulous location, built on an expansive **natural harbour** – the seventh largest in the world – which was to prove the cornerstone of future trading success. Since those early days, the city streets have gradually found their way north and now reach as far as the foothills of the **Blue Mountains**, a truly glorious backdrop and a useful means of orientating yourself.

Kingston's main sights are divided between the area known as "downtown", which stretches north from the waterfront to the busy traffic junction of Cross Roads, and "uptown", spreading up into the ritzy suburbs of Jack's Hill and Cherry Gardens at the base of the mountains. **Downtown** is the city's industrial centre, its factories and all-important port providing most of the city's blue-collar employment; the law firms, stock exchange and the Bank of Jamaica are also prominent features.

Uptown is different, and you may be surprised at how attractive and easy-going it feels, as suited businessmen and office workers go about their daily routines. Most of Kingston's hotels, restaurants, clubs and shopping centres are here, and it's where you'll spend most of your time. In terms of **highlights**, many visitors make straight for the **Bob Marley Museum**, former home of the island's greatest reggae star and musical ambassador. But there are also some grand old **colonial houses**, recently restored as museums, and an excellent **national art gallery**. There are plenty of good hotels and restaurants, and the city is the heartbeat of the country's music industry, with top-quality clubs and a busy live-music scene. The annual **Carnival** is well worth catching if you're on the island between February and April.

Some history

Though the Spanish first settled in Jamaica in 1510, replaced by British colonists in 1655, there was little development in present-day Kingston until 1692. The area held just a small pig-rearing village, glamorously known as Colonel Beeston's Hog Crawle, and a handful of fishing shacks. All of the action was across the harbour on the island of Port Royal, then Jamaica's second city (after Spanish Town) and home to most of the country's leading lights. In 1692, however, a violent **earthquake** devastated Port Royal; several thousand people died instantly and the rest went scurrying for a more hospitable place to live. The Hog Crawle was the obvious choice – on the mainland but beside the harbour – and the former citizens of Port Royal promptly snapped up two hundred acres of land there.

Within a few months, the plans for the new town had been drawn up. Newborn Kingston was named in honour of William of Orange, king of England from 1689 to 1702, and the town was laid out beside the water to take advantage of the existing **sea trade**. The road plan mostly followed a grid system (which remains largely intact today) with the big central square of the **Parade** left open in the heart of town.

By the early eighteenth century, Kingston had become a **major port** for the transhipment of English goods and African slaves to the Spanish colonies of South America. Merchants, traders and brokers made rapid fortunes and began to build themselves ostentatious homes, while fresh waves of **immigrants** piled into the booming city – some from Europe, some from other Caribbean islands, some from other parts of Jamaica, all in search of opportunity.

With its swelling population and rising wealth, the city soon began to challenge for the role of the **nation's capital**, though the authorities in Spanish Town – comfortably ensconced in their grand Georgian buildings – proved stubborn in handing over the title to their upstart neighbour. By 1872, when Kingston finally became Jamaica's capital city, many wealthy families were already moving beyond the original town boundaries to the more genteel areas that today comprise **uptown** Kingston. Meanwhile, the less affluent huddled downtown and in the **shanty towns** that began to spring up on the outskirts of old Kingston, particularly west of the city, their ranks swollen by a tide of former slaves hoping to find prosperity beyond the sugar estates.

Jamaica's turn-of-the-century boom, engineered by tourism and agriculture, largely bypassed Kingston's poor and helped to reinforce the divide between uptown and downtown. While the rich got richer and sequestered themselves in the new suburbs uptown, the **downtown** area continued to deteriorate. Those who could afford to do so continued to move out, leaving behind an increasingly destitute population that proved fertile recruitment ground for the **Rastafari** movement during the 1920s and 1930s.

There were major **riots** during the 1930s, with the city feeling the knock-on effects of an islandwide economic crisis sparked by the plunging price of key crops like bananas and sugar on world markets. The riots led to the development of local trade unions and political parties during the 1940s; these organizations spoke for the workers and the dispossessed, but improvements in working conditions and the physical infrastructure were slow in coming. Finally, in the 1960s, the city authorities began to show some interest in reversing the decay. Efforts were made to give the old downtown area a face-lift; redevelopment of the waterfront resulted in a much-needed expansion of the city's **port facility** (still a vital part of the city's commerce today) and a smartening-up of the harbour area with the introduction of shops, offices and even the island's major art gallery.

A mini-**tourist boom** was sparked by the new-look Kingston (and by the growing popularity of Jamaican music abroad), with cruise ships arriving to inject a fresh air of hope into the city. Sadly, the optimism proved short-lived. For the people of downtown Kingston, the redevelopment of downtown was only cosmetic. Crime – an inevitable feature in the crowded ghettos – was getting out of control, sponsored by politicians who distributed weapons and patronage to their supporters. At election time (particularly in 1976 and 1980), hundreds of people were killed in bloody campaigns, many of them innocent bystanders. Tourists ran for cover, heading for the new beach resorts on the island's north coast, and the city sank into a quagmire of unemployment, poverty and crime. (For more on Kingston's ghettos, see p.65.)

Today, Kingston remains a divided city. The wealthy have moved further and further into the suburbs, coming in to work in the downtown business district or the smart uptown area of New Kingston but rarely venturing downtown after dark while the ghettos remain firmly under the control of gangs, led by infamous characters euphemistically referred to as "area leaders". You have to look hard to find rays of hope, but there are hints that the city's fortunes may be turning.

Arrival and information

All international and some domestic **flights** land at **Norman Manley International Airport** (T 924 8456 or 1-888/247 7678, W www.nmia.aero) on the Palisadoes – a strip of land that juts out into the Caribbean Sea southeast of the city. There's a currency exchange desk just past immigration, and a number of **car rental** firms have desks alongside the arrivals area (see p.81); others will meet you there on request. City

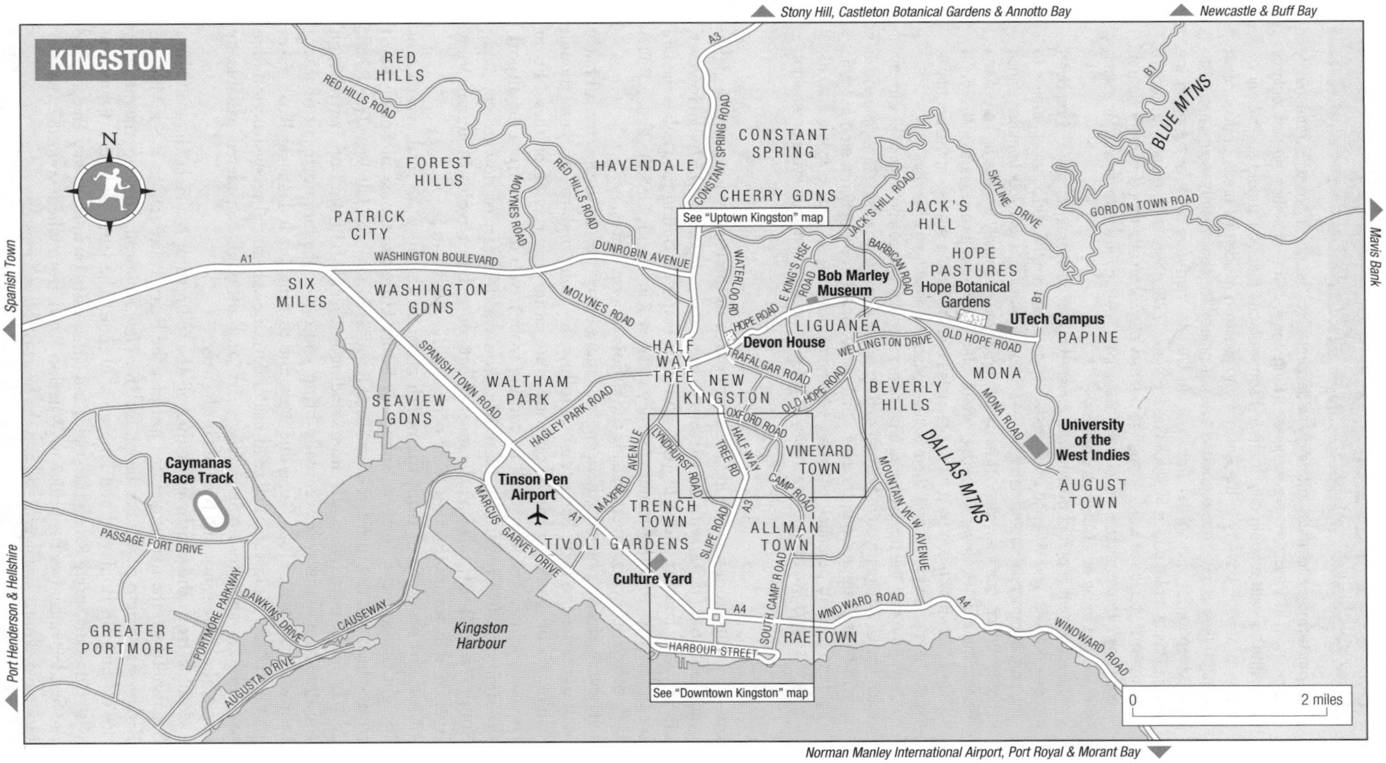
KINGSTON
Stony Hill, Castleton Botanical Gardens & Annotto Bay
Newcastle & Buff Bay
Mavis Bank
Spanish Town
Port Henderson & Hellshire
Norman Manley International Airport, Port Royal & Morant Bay
N
RED HILLS
RED HILLS ROAD
FOREST HILLS
PATRICK CITY
HAVENDALE
CONSTANT SPRING
CONSTANT SPRING ROAD
CHERRY GDNS
JACK'S HILL
JACK'S HILL ROAD
SKYLINE DRIVE
BLUE MTNS
B1
GORDON TOWN ROAD
HOPE PASTURES
Hope Botanical Gardens
UTech Campus
PAPINE
See "Uptown Kingston" map
A3
A1
WASHINGTON BOULEVARD
DUNROBIN AVENUE
MOLYNES ROAD
SIX MILES
WASHINGTON GDNS
WATERLOO RD
E KING'S HSE ROAD
Bob Marley Museum
BARBICAN ROAD
HOPE ROAD
Devon House
LIGUANEA
WELLINGTON DRIVE
OLD HOPE ROAD
MONA
MONA ROAD
University of the West Indies
AUGUST TOWN
HALF WAY TREE
NEW KINGSTON
TRAFALGAR ROAD
BEVERLY HILLS
DALLAS MTNS
SPANISH TOWN ROAD
WALTHAM PARK
HAGLEY PARK ROAD
SEAVIEW GDNS
OXFORD ROAD
HALF WAY TREE RD
VINEYARD TOWN
CAMP ROAD
MOUNTAIN VIEW AVENUE
LYNDHURST ROAD
MAXFIELD AVENUE
Caymanas Race Track
Tinson Pen Airport
MARCUS GARVEY DRIVE
TRENCH TOWN
TIVOLI GARDENS
SLIPE ROAD
ALLMAN TOWN
PASSAGE FORT DRIVE
Culture Yard
SOUTH CAMP ROAD
WINDWARD ROAD
A4
PORTMORE PARKWAY
DAWKINS DRIVE
CAUSEWAY
Kingston Harbour
GREATER PORTMORE
AUGUSTA DRIVE
HARBOUR STREET
RAE TOWN
See "Downtown Kingston" map
0
2 miles

Safety and harassment

The **pestering** of tourists, irritatingly widespread on the north coast, is refreshingly uncommon in Kingston. Nevertheless, Kingston's crime statistics are undeniably ugly, and as with any big city, there are some places that you should steer clear of. There is serious poverty in the eastern and western residential areas of downtown Kingston (see p.65) – these ghettos are not places for casual sightseeing and, with the exception of visiting the Trench Town Culture Yard (see p.64) or taking in the Passa Passa street dance in Tivoli Gardens (see p.78), there is no reason to venture into them. If you are unlucky enough to be the victim of an attempted robbery, do not, under any circumstances, resist your assailant – hand over whatever they're asking for, and get away as quickly as possible.

The more central part of **downtown**, covered in this guide, has its share of impoverished enclaves, and violence occasionally spills over from the surrounding ghettos to the core commercial streets described in this book, but if you use your common sense and don't flash cash, jewellery or fancy cameras, you're unlikely to have any problems during the day. However, once the area's office workers have departed at around 5.30pm, downtown can be a bit risky – unless you're seeing a show at the brightly lit Ward Theatre on the Parade, there is little reason to head here after dark.

During the day, the **uptown** area feels fine, particularly once you're familiar with the main roads. At night, you're best off getting a taxi if you're travelling any distance. If you're driving late at night, be aware that some local drivers may not stop at traffic lights to prevent potential robberies; whether or not you choose to follow suit, it's wise to slow down and look each way at junctions even when you have a green light.

bus #98 runs from just outside the arrivals area to the Parade downtown roughly every half-hour (J$50), with the last service leaving the airport at 10.57pm. However, unless you're familiar with Kingston, you're far better off opting for a **cab** – the fare for the twenty- to thirty-minute journey to New Kingston is US$20–25 in a JUTA taxi; there are always drivers outside the airport to meet flights.

If you're arriving by **car**, there are four main **entry points** to the city, all fairly well signposted to New Kingston on "follow the hummingbird" markers, though you're best off getting a handle on your route rather than relying on these. **From the east**, which is where you'll be coming from if you drive in from the airport, the signposts direct you into New Kingston via the heart of downtown, along South Camp Road; this isn't the most direct route, but it avoids Mountain View Avenue, which runs through some occasionally volatile areas.

Most visitors come in **from the north coast** on the busy A3 road, which runs straight through the northern suburb of Stony Hill onto Constant Spring Road from which you can turn left onto Hope Road or head onto Half Way Tree Road. Also from the north coast, the more winding but scenic B3 from Buff Bay through the Blue Mountains will eventually bring you out at Papine, northeast of town; following the main Hope Road due west, and turning left at Trafalgar Road, takes you into New Kingston. The road has undergone substantial reconstruction (due to landslides and erosion in recent years) and although considered passable by some, the drive is not one for the fainthearted.

Coming **from the southwest**, either off the toll road or Mandela Highway from Spanish Town, the road is elevated just past the Ferry Police station at Six Miles on Kingston's western edge; take the left fork for New Kingston, carrying straight along on Washington Boulevard and Dunrobin Avenue. The latter ends at a T-junction with Constant Spring Road; turn right, and either carry on to Half Way Tree, or take the first left once over the bridge to Waterloo Road, from where you can cross over Hope Road onto Trafalgar Road and the heart of New Kingston.

Most of the **buses** into Kingston pull in at the swarming **terminal** at the junction of Beckford and Pechon streets, just west of the crowded Parade, though some terminate at the safer and more convenient Half Way Tree. If you have a lot of luggage, you're best off hopping straight into a **taxi** from the busy rank on Parade, but if you want to use public transport, local bus #76 runs from nearby Duke Street to New Kingston and Liguanea; from Half Way Tree buses #70 and #75 run to Liguanea and Papine. For more on city buses, see below.

Information

The main office of the **Jamaica Tourist Board** (Mon–Fri 9am–4.30pm; ℡ 929 9200) is right in the heart of New Kingston at 64 Knutsford Blvd. Staff can provide basic information, but the office is not really geared up to assist visitors. There's a smaller, more tourist-oriented booth at Norman Manley airport. The most useful **map** of the Kingston area is on the back of the JTB's Esso island map, which is sold at the tourist office and the airport booth (J$150).

For entertainment **listings**, the Friday editions of the *Daily Gleaner* and *Observer* newspapers are particularly good; most of the theatres, cinemas and clubs also advertise their activities on radio stations such as Irie, Zip and Roots.

Getting around

Finding your way around Kingston is pretty straightforward. Downtown uses a grid system, while uptown is defined by a handful of major roads. You'll quickly get used to the main landmarks, and as a reliable fallback, the mountains to the northeast and the high-rises of New Kingston serve as good compass references should you lose your way, while locals are invariably helpful with directions. The heat and the distances between places mean you're not going to want to do a lot of **walking**, though the downtown sights, in particular, are fairly easy to navigate on foot. It's not advisable to walk the streets at night in any part of the city; most Kingstonians don't.

Taxis are the best way of getting around the city and are reasonably cheap; a ride from New Kingston to downtown costs around J$400. Bear in mind that cabs don't carry meters and you'll need to fix a price before you get in. Although it's standard practice to phone for a taxi (see p.82 for a list of companies), particularly at night, they can almost always be flagged down on the main streets (look out for red "PP" or "PPV" plates). There's also a bustling rank downtown at Parade, and taxis can always be found on and around Knutsford Boulevard in New Kingston.

Operated by the government-run Jamaica Urban Transit Company (JUTC), Kingston's **buses** are a viable option for visitors. Smart and clean "bendy" buses cover all the main routes; all have numbers displayed, along with their destination, on the dot-matrix boards at the front. The best way to ensure you get to your destination is to ask – most bus users seem to have an exhaustive knowledge of schedules and services. Alternatively for **routes**, fares and general information, call ℡ 1-888/588 2287 (toll-free) or 749 3192; there's also a full list of routes online at ⓦ www.jutc.com. **Fares** are very cheap, at J$50 for any journey in and around the city. You can use cash to pay fares, but if you plan on using buses a lot, get hold of a pre-paid Smart Card; these cover multiple rides and are widely available at specialist outlets. Main bus terminals are at Parade and Half Way Tree.

Though traffic jams are a real problem, particularly around the morning and evening rush hours (roughly 7.30–9.30am and 4–6.30pm), when traffic slows to a crawl along all the main roads, **renting a car** is the best way to explore Kingston. Signage on the roads has improved immeasurably in recent years, and if you plan on spending more than a couple of days in the capital, it'll work out cheaper to drive yourself than to keep forking out for taxis. A car of your own also makes it a lot easier to check out Kingston's nightlife (it's not advisable to walk from venue to venue). Rental is usually cheaper in Kingston than at the resorts; for a list of reliable operators, see p.81. See the box on p.56 for a couple of tips on safety while driving.

Finally, **city tours** can be an excellent way to negotiate the main sights efficiently and check out the capital's nightlife, and not all of the available roster are of the twenty-people-in-a-bus variety. For a list of operators, see p.81.

Accommodation

Most of Kingston's **hotels** and **guesthouses** are in and around the small uptown district of **New Kingston**, convenient for sightseeing and close to most of the restaurants, theatres, cinemas and clubs (see the map on p.70 for accommodation locations). Only a few of the city's accommodation options cater specifically to the tourist trade, relying instead on a steady stream of Jamaican and international business visitors; as a result, rates show no seasonal variation, and the price codes given in this chapter are valid year-round. Although it's normally wise to reserve in advance, finding a room in Kingston is rarely a problem.

If you don't fancy the hustle of the big city or the noise of Kingston's traffic and very vocal dog population, you might want to stay in Port Royal (see p.84). There are also a couple of small hotels and guesthouses in the foothills of the Blue Mountains just north of Kingston (see p.99). If you want to explore the city, though, it can be expensive and time-consuming getting back and forth from a hotel in one of the outlying areas – and certainly, without a car, you're better off staying in New Kingston. Unless otherwise stated all rooms have air conditioning, cable TV and phone.

Alhambra Inn 1 Tucker Ave ℡978 9072–3, ℮alhambra@cwjamaica.com. Pretty complex set back from the road near the National Stadium, with a pool, outdoor restaurant and Internet access. The appealing rooms have parquet floors, king/queen beds (or two doubles) and are great value. Rates include breakfast. ❺

Altamont Court 1 Altamont Terrace ℡929 4498, ⓦwww.altamontcourt.com. Kingston's best mid-range option by far, Altamont is ranged around a flower-filled courtyard. The comfortable, modern rooms boast pleasant decor, all the usual amenities, plus there's wireless Internet throughout, a swimming pool, sun deck, jacuzzi and a good restaurant and bar. Rates include breakfast, and the staff speak several languages. ❺–❻

Christar Villas 99 Hope Rd, near Bob Marley Museum ℡978 3933. Appealing studios, suites and apartments – all with kitchens. The more luxurious ones have private jacuzzis and exercise equipment. Wireless Internet and a business centre, gym, pool, sun deck, a/c restaurant, popular sports bar and free airport transfers (Mon–Sat 8am–5pm). Rooms ❺, apartments ❽

Courtleigh 85 Knutsford Blvd ℡929 9000, ⓦwww.courtleigh.com. Featuring a tasteful lobby decked out in Chinese style, a business centre, good restaurant, bar/nightclub, pool, gym and a coin-op laundry for guests. Each of the luxurious rooms has a balcony and lots of welcome extras, and there's wireless Internet access. ❼–❾

The Gardens 23 Liguanea Ave ℡927 5957. This delightful and secure complex of expansive two-bedroom townhouses is one of Kingston's best choices. You can choose a double en-suite room, a double with shared kitchen, living room and patio, or rent the whole two-bedroom townhouse. The grounds feature gorgeous flowered gardens and a pool. ❹–❺

Hilton Kingston 77 Knutsford Blvd ℡926 5430, ⓦwww.kingston.hilton.com. Lively, landmark New Kingston hotel popular with visiting execs. All the trappings, from Olympic-size pool, tennis courts and health club to nightclub, business centre and three restaurants, including an excellent Japanese diner above the glitzy lobby. Rooms have good views and all mod cons, and there's a huge range of suites, too. ❼–❾

Indies 5 Holborn Rd ☎926 2952, ⓦwww
.indieshotel.com. Compact, clean and appealing
little hotel next to *Holborn Manor*, set on two levels
around a garden courtyard and small restaurant.
The cheapest rooms are on the small side, with fan
only, but there are more spacious a/c options with
cable TV. ➍

Jamaica Pegasus 81 Knutsford Blvd ☎926 3690,
ⓦwww.jamaicapegasus.com. Seventeen-storey
business-oriented behemoth with a slightly 1970s
air. The three hundred luxurious rooms and suites,
in American-chic decor, all have balconies. The
hotel also offers a business centre, wireless
Internet in public areas, a gym, two pools, floodlit
tennis courts, a jogging trail, four restaurants, two
bars, a gaming room and acres of conference
space. Rate includes full buffet breakfast. ➎

Knutsford Court 16 Chelsea Ave ☎929 1000,
ⓦwww.knutsfordcourt.com. Formerly the *Sutton
Place* hotel. Refurbished, with lots of greenery
outside and redecorated rooms with all mod
cons including irons and boards. Business centre,
coin-op laundry, pool and restaurant are on site.
Rates include continental breakfast. ➎–➏

Mayfair 4 West King's House Close ☎926 1610,
ⓔmayfair-hotel@cwjamaica.com. Unremarkable
but sound choice in a quiet residential area, with a
pool, restaurant and bar. Standard rooms have fan
only, while superior ones have a/c, cable TV and a
balcony; there are also studios and suites with a
dining/living room and kitchenette. ➍, studios ➎

Medallion Hall 53 Hope Rd ☎927 5721,
ⓔmedallionhall@cwjamaica.com. Roomy 21-room
property in a central location, popular for confer-
ences. A range of comfy units (some sleep four);
ask for one of the breezier rooms upstairs, or the

good-value, spacious bridal suite. There's a good
Jamaican restaurant, too. ➍

Mikuzi 5 Upper Montrose Rd ☎876/978 4859
or 813 0098, ⓦwww.mikuzijamaica.com.
Wonderful and unique guesthouse set in and
around a lovely colonial-era house in residential
New Kingston. The eclectic en-suite rooms have
stylish, funky decor, fans and kitchenettes; some
have a/c and cable TV, and there are also a couple
of budget cottages in the pretty flower-filled
gardens. Very friendly. ➌–➍

Shirley Retreat House 7 Maeven Ave
☎946 2679, ⓔjeshirl@cwjamaica.com. Tucked
down a quiet cul-de-sac off Hope Rd, this is a
pleasant and friendly getaway operated by the
United Church. The rooms are spacious, light and
appealing; superior ones have two double beds
rather than the two twin beds of standard units.
Meals are available, and rates include continental
breakfast. ➍–➎

Spanish Court Hotel 1 St Lucia Ave
☎926 0000, ⓦwww.spanishcourthotel
.com. With its modern reception area and overall
chic look – flat screen TVs, premium linens, free
wireless access and rooftop pool – it seems that
Kingston's first central business-boutique hotel
has finally arrived. A range of suites; rates include
continental breakfast. ➎–➏

Terra Nova 17 Waterloo Rd ☎926 2211,
ⓦwww.terranovajamaica.com. Smart hideaway set
in landscaped gardens, with a small pool, charming
terrace restaurant and a formal dining room hung
with chandeliers. The elegant rooms are suitably
upscale, with Internet access and fluffy bathrobes,
and there are some extremely opulent suites, too.
Rates include a buffet breakfast. ➏–➒

The City

Kingston is divided into downtown and uptown, with the division lying roughly
at Half Way Tree. It'll take you a couple of days to check out the main sights
downtown, and about the same amount of time to catch those uptown.

Downtown

Flattened by an earthquake in 1907, **downtown Kingston** has lost most of its
grand eighteenth-century architecture, and much of what remains is slowly
crumbling into dereliction. Nevertheless, numerous historic buildings can still be
found along Rum Lane, Water Lane and King Street, and if you peer into the most
unlikely yards you can often find evidence of the intricate structures that used to
proliferate here, with their fancy ironwork, red-brick facades and wraparound
verandahs. It's an intensely atmospheric place, one that's suffused with a sense of
history and of Kingston as the great, proud port city it once was. And though
many locals wouldn't dream of pounding the downtown streets, you'll find that

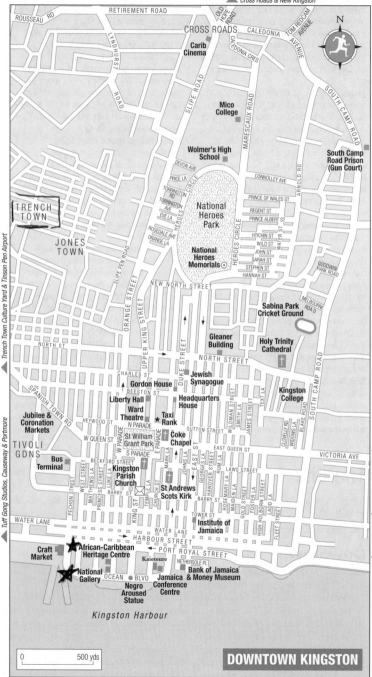

Cross Roads & New Kingston

RETIREMENT ROAD

ROUSSEAU RD

LYNDHURST ROAD

OLD HOPE ROAD

CROSS ROADS

CALEDONIA

TOM REDCAM AVENUE

CALEDONIA CRES

N

Carib Cinema

SLIPE ROAD

Mico College

MARESCAUX ROAD

SOUTH CAMP ROAD

Wolmer's High School

CONNOLLEY AVE

ARNOLD RD

South Camp Road Prison (Gun Court)

DEVON AVE

PRICE LA

CIRCLE

PRINCE OF WALES ST

TORRINGTON RD

TORRINGTON AVE

EVE LA

REGENT ST

PRINCE ALBERT ST

HTICHIN ST

WATER ST

National Heroes Park

WILD ST

JOHN ST

GOODWIN PARK ROAD

ROSEDALE AVE

ORANGE LA

HEROES CIRCLE

National Heroes Memorials ⊙

SARAH ST

STEPHEN ST

HANNAH ST

TRENCH TOWN

JONES TOWN

SLIPE PEN ROAD

Trench Town Culture Yard & Tinson Pen Airport

NEW NORTH STREET

MELBOURNE ROAD

Sabina Park Cricket Ground

ORANGE STREET

UPPER KING STREET

DUKE STREET

Gleaner Building

Holy Trinity Cathedral

NORTH STREET

NORTH ST

CHARLES LA

Kingston College

SOUTH CAMP ROAD

SPANISH TOWN RD

BEESTON ST

Gordon House

Jewish Synagogue

TEXT LA

Liberty Hall

Headquarters House

Ward Theatre

★ Taxi Rank

N PARADE

CLOKELY RD

WIDONS LA

BLAKE ROAD

Jubilee & Coronation Markets

HEYWOOD ST

W QUEEN ST

W PARADE

St William Grant Park

E PARADE

Coke Chapel

SUTTON STREET

WOMAN STREET

SMITH LA

JAMES STREET

TIVOLI GDNS

Bus Terminal

BECKFORD STREET

PRINCESS STREET

LUKE LA

MARK LA

EAST QUEEN ST

EAST ST

JOHNS LA

GEORGES LA

HANOVER LA

RUM LA

VICTORIA AVE

Airport, Rae Town, Port Royal & Morant Bay

WEST STREET

MATTHEWS LA

Kingston Parish Church

LAWS STREET

MAIDEN LA

ROSEMARY LA

Tuff Gong Studios, Causeway & Portmore

PECHON STREET

BARRY ST

St Andrews Scots Kirk

BARRY ST

GOLD STREET

FOSTER LA

HIGH HOLBORN STREET

LADD LA

FLEET STREET

WATER LANE

KING ST

TEMPLE LA

TOWER ST

WATER LANE

Institute of Jamaica

HARBOUR STREET

Craft Market

★ African-Caribbean Heritage Centre

PORT ROYAL STREET

NETHERSOLE PL

★ National Gallery

OCEAN BLVD

Kaieteure

Negro Aroused Statue

Jamaica Conference Centre

Bank of Jamaica & Money Museum

Kingston Harbour

0   500 yds

DOWNTOWN KINGSTON

exploring on foot is not only the best way to get the full flavour of the area but it also feels surprisingly **safe**. The usual common-sense rules apply, of course (for more on which, see p.56), but unless the violence that habitually breaks out in the surrounding ghettos spills over into downtown's central commercial streets, there's no reason to expect any problems.

Much of Kingston's economic strength still derives from its impressively huge natural **harbour**. It's one of the world's best, but grimly polluted these days, despite concerted government efforts to clean it up. Once buzzing with trading ships, the **waterfront** is a good spot to start a tour of the downtown area. It's close to the **National Gallery** and a short walk from the main **Parade**, above which you'll find **Headquarters House** and, just outside the old city boundaries to the north, **National Heroes Park**.

The waterfront

Despite the fuel silos, loading cranes and the container ships moored just offshore, the wind-whipped **waterfront** is a surprisingly pleasant place: people and pelicans fish off the concrete piers, couples and the odd vagrant sit on the harbour wall or walk the wide grassy boulevard between the road and the sea, and planes swoop overhead en route to Norman Manley Airport across the water. The chief beneficiary of the city council's 1960s' bid to beautify elements of downtown, the waterfront saw its historic buildings swept away and replaced by spanking new high-rises – the icons of the era.

▲ *Negro Aroused* sculpture, Kingston waterfront

Today, these modern monuments define the eastern end of the waterfront's main strip, Ocean Boulevard. They include the high-rise headquarters of the Bank of Jamaica on Nethersole Place, whose small **Money Museum** (Mon–Fri 9am–4pm; free; Ⓦ www.boj.org.jm) is a surprisingly absorbing, if compact, exhibition on the country's currency. The well-labelled collection takes you through a history of money, from barley grains, cowrie shells and Taino beads to notes and coins, including the "anchors" and "Christian quatties" first issued by the British in Jamaica. It's worth calling ahead to arrange a (free) guided tour with one of the very informative curators. A short stroll away, at 14 Duke St, you should also be able to get a free tour (ask at reception) of the enormous **Jamaica Conference Centre** (Mon–Fri 9am–4pm), built in 1981 to host meetings of the United Nations' International Seabed Authority. This in itself probably won't have you queuing at dawn, but the building's lofty design and abundant use of glass and local crafts is impressive and provides a poignant glimpse of a time when downtown Kingston looked forward to a heady future at the centre of a vibrant Caribbean economic community. Upstairs, the breezy upstairs cafeteria (see p.76) is a great spot for lunch; just beyond the dining area, look out for a huge rendition of the Jamaican coat of arms, wrought out of metal and forming the end to one of the building's corridors, with a lovely view stretching down to the sea visible between the figures.

Further along the boulevard, at the bottom of King Street, is a striking reproduction of the sculpture **Negro Aroused** by the late Edna Manley, one of Jamaica's leading artists and wife and mother, respectively, of former Prime Ministers Norman Manley and Michael Manley. One of the icons of twentieth-century Jamaican art, the bronze sculpture captures the incipient labour movement and the spirit of unrest of the 1930s, and is dedicated to the workers of Jamaica (though you wouldn't know it, as the title plaque is long gone).

The National Gallery and around

The pleasantly air-conditioned **National Gallery**, at 12 Ocean Blvd, but entered around the corner on Orange Street (Tues–Thurs 10am–4.30pm, Fri 10am–4pm, Sat 10am–3pm; J$200, university students with ID and children free; ☎922 1561, Ⓦ www.galleryjamaica.org), is one of the highlights of a visit to Kingston. The permanent collection here is superb, ranging from delicate woodcarvings to flamboyant religious paintings, while the temporary exhibitions, such as the Biennial (alternate years, Dec–Feb) or the excellent regular Curator's Eye series (the latter put together by guest curators), showcase the best of contemporary Jamaican art from the new vanguard of Jamaican painters, sculptors and mixed-media artists. **Guided tours** of the gallery (J$1500; call in advance to arrange) are well worth taking. They provide essential background to, and interpretation of, the works on show, and if you have any special interest – Jamaican intuitive art, say – your tour can be tailored accordingly. The permanent collection consists of ten chronological galleries housed on the first floor, representing the Jamaican School, 1922 to the present. Dominating the earlier rooms are works by artists deemed to have been the forerunners of the art movement in Jamaica, including Edna Manley, John Dunkley, Albert Huie and David Pottinger. Later galleries feature the prolific work of Carl Abrahams and show a move towards abstraction which was capped by Colin Garland and David Boxer (a longtime curator of the gallery). Realism returned later with Barrington Watson, Kay Brown and Dawn Scott, whose *A Cultural Object* is a particularly unique and powerful re-creation of a Kingston ghetto and not to be missed. Look out for colourful, spiritual works by Everald Brown, Karl Parboosingh, Gloria Escoffery and Ralph Campbell. There is also an entire room that houses the Larry Wirth Collection of African-style

Jamaican art

Although the Tainos left paintings on cave walls and visiting British artists captured the colonial era on canvas, **Jamaican art** really only came into its own in the twentieth century. The island's modern art movement was led by **Edna Manley** (1900–87), an English sculptor who had married prime-minister-to-be Norman Manley and moved to Jamaica in 1921, and whose arresting work has come to be seen as a turning point in Jamaican art. In 1939, she led a group of artists who stormed the annual meeting at the Institute of Jamaica to demand an end to the domination of Anglophile attitudes to art, and the replacement of the colonial portraits that hung in the galleries with works by local artists. Though more symbolic than revolutionary, their gesture did galvanize Jamaican painters and sculptors, and Manley's classes at the **Jamaica School of Art** (now the Edna Manley College of the Visual and Performing arts), which she co-founded, helped give direction to a new wave of local artists.

There were two distinct artistic styles in the work of this new crop of Jamaican artists. Most studied in England at one time or another and followed a classical European approach. **Albert Huie** (1920–2010) and **Barrington Watson** (born 1931) used natural forms and landscapes as reference points, incorporating the lives of black Jamaicans into their work for the first time, while **Gloria Escoffery** (1923–2002) played with abstract themes, depicting a range of subjects, from quiet pastoral scenes to the traditional Saturday market.

The paintings of the self-taught artists, known as **"intuitives"**, were perhaps more distinctive. The prodigious **John Dunkley** (1891–1947), made his name by covering every inch of his Kingston barber shop with pictures of trees, vines and flowers; his later paintings (now much sought-after) continued his obsession with dark, brooding scenes from nature. Many intuitive artists focused their work around religious imagery. **Mallica "Kapo" Reynolds** (1911–89), the shepherd (head) of a Revivalist group in Kingston, became the first self-taught Jamaican painter to be fully accepted by local and foreign audiences, and is still seen as the island's foremost intuitive sculptor and painter. Other artists such as **Albert Artwell** (born 1942) and **Everald Brown** (1917–2002) – a priest in the Ethiopian Coptic Church – concentrate on Rasta beliefs.

In the 1960s and 1970s, Jamaican art became more experimental, most noticeably in the surrealism represented by the work of **David Boxer** (born 1946) and Australian-born **Colin Garland** (1935–2007). Today, Jamaica's art scene continues its diversity. At the bottom end, it's dominated by the huge carving and painting industry that has grown up around mass tourism, and although much of it is relentlessly mediocre, there is some decent art at the craft markets in Kingston and across the north coast, and in Kingston's clutch of galleries. The establishment of the **National Gallery** in 1974 gave the art scene an important institutional infrastructure, and the regular exhibits of Jamaican art continue to encourage the development of young painters and sculptors, as witnessed by the proliferation of studios and galleries islandwide. You can also see the best of contemporary Jamaican art during the annual **Kingston on the Edge** arts festival (see p.33).

sculpture and paintings by Revivalist Shepherd Mallica "Kapo" Reynolds, as well as a slew of beautiful wood sculptures.

Before leaving the gallery, check out the small gift shop selling postcards, prints and books on Jamaican art.

Tuff Gong and Culture Yard

If you're a Bob Marley devotee, you might want to jump in a taxi at the waterfront and head west along Port Royal Street and its western continuation Marcus Garvey Drive, the latter a battered but wide thoroughfare lined with warehouses and factories. At 220 Marcus Garvey Drive you'll find the state-of-the-art

Tuff Gong Recording Studios (Mon–Fri 8.30am–5pm; ☎923 9383, Ⓦwww .bobmarley-foundation.com), established by Bob Marley and now one of Kingston's premier recording studios, as well as one of its biggest CD pressing plants. It's a commercial venture rather than a tourist sight, but you can **tour** the facility (J$600; 35–40 min) to see the self-same mixing board used on Wailers' classics such as *Stir It Up*, *Concrete Jungle* and *No Woman, No Cry*. If the studios are in use, you may not get access to all areas – it's up to whoever's recording. While not wildly exciting, it's a nice stop for Marley disciples, with a gift shop for that essential CD.

North of Marcus Garvey Drive are the government social housing communities of West Kingston: Tivoli Gardens, Denham Town, Jones Town and **Trench Town**. Eulogized in Marley and the Wailer's *Trench Town Rock*, *No Woman No Cry* and *Natty Dread*, Trench Town has earned the title of the birthplace of popular Jamaican urban culture. Trench Town was the first Kingston home of Bob Marley, who earned his nickname – the "Tuff Gong" – on the community's football fields after his mother relocated to the capital when he was a small boy and moved into a government-built house at 19 Second Street. In Trench Town Bob Marley found a community rich in music, religion, nationalism and sports. Though the area's "**government yards**", built in the colonial 1940s, were conceived as a part of a planned community and were seen as desirable places to live when Mother Booker moved there in 1956, the political violence of Jamaica in the 1970s soon took its toll. Trench Town today is as infamous for garrison politics and gang feuds as it is for having spawned some of the biggest names in the rock steady and reggae pantheon, including The Wailers, Joe Higgs, Delroy Wilson, Alton Ellis, Ernie Ranglin, Dean Fraser and the Abbyssinians. Also from here are numerous Jamaican notables, from Labour leader and Garveyite St William Grant to the late Rastafarian elder Mortimer Planno, and famous sports personalities such as cricketer Collie Smith and footballer Carl Brown. Trench Town is also home to two top Premier Club League football teams, Boys Town and Arnette Gardens. It remains a tough place to live; many of its inhabitants still reside in the 1940s buildings and have enclosed zinc-fenced yards. Nonetheless, it is a vibrant, proud and creative community that holds an edgy allure for anyone with a serious interest in the roots of Jamaican culture.

And though Trench Town remains one of Kingston's poorest areas, the picture isn't entirely bleak. In the last few years, enterprising members of this tight-knit community have clubbed together to find ways in which to regenerate their area using their heritage and cultural status for economic development. The first initiative was the establishment, in 1993, of the **Trench Town Reading Centre** on First Street (Ⓦwww.trenchtownreadingcentre.com), a library and resource centre with a mission to arm local people with information rather than weapons. By 1996, the aim had widened, and the **Trench Town Development Association** (TTDA; ☎757 6739 or 922 8462) was formed to address the pressing issues of sanitation, security, housing, health and employment. On February 6, 2000 (the anniversary of Marley's birthday) the **Trench Town Culture Yard** was officially opened (TTCY; daily 6am–6pm; US$10), set in the government yard at 6 & 8 Lower First Street where Marley sought refuge after returning from living in the US, and where he was taught to play the guitar by his mentor, community elder Vincent "Tarta" Ford, who himself wrote *No Woman, No Cry* here. Shaded from the street by a lush canopy of mango-tree leaves, it's also where Peter Tosh, Bunny Wailer and Bob formed the Wailers and wrote the *Catch a Fire* LP and, according to his widow Rita, where son Ziggy was conceived. The museum is a work in progress; its galleries have greatly improved, but it's still awaiting funding grants to complete the museum installations and minor infrastructure. Even so, the overall restoration of the buildings has been successful, and the experience and presentation commendable, and the Trench Town Culture Yard was declared a National Heritage Site by the Government of Jamaica in 2007.

A tour guide is always on the property, or you can call ahead to arrange a guided tour with the manager Clifford "Ferdie" Bent (℡572.4085), local architect Christopher Whyms-Stone (℡546.1559, ⓔstonec@kasnet.com), one of the project's curators, or TTDA Chairman Wayne Gray (℡532.0352).

The museum's **collection** is contained in six rooms in one of the property's restored residential buildings. These well-designed buildings are oriented around the yard's central open-air courtyard, where residents would have washed clothes, gardened and socialized; the rusting remains of Marley's powder-blue VW van sit in a corner, while around the back is Jah Bobby's original, colourful and rather odd statue of Marley with his preferred guitar and football, which formerly graced the front yard of the Hope Road museum (see p.73). Sensitively refurbished and retaining many original features and fittings, from "Tarta" Ford's graffitied bedroom walls to the single bed on which Bob and Rita slept, the rooms also hold one of Tarta's and Marley's first acoustic guitars and a selection of Adrian Boot's

Kingston's ghettos

Taking up huge swathes of downtown, Kingston's **ghetto communities** are the country's urban nightmare. Bob Marley sang fondly of growing up in the "government yards in Trench Town", but the contemporary reality is a huge underclass confined to crowded, makeshift homes enclosed by rusting, graffiti-daubed zinc, their communities bearing suitably apocalyptic names, from Dunkirk and Jungle to Tel Aviv and Zimbabwe.

In the city's early years, downtown was a popular residential zone – well laid out and central. Trench Town's government yards were planned communities that proudly boasted all the modern conveniences and for a time (despite their cramped nature) provided a desirable place to live for Jamaica's working class. Before long, however, the combination of a high influx of rural job seekers, a soaring rate of unemployment and a lack of housing made downtown a grim place to live. Criminal elements were quick to take advantage of these conditions, recruiting and arming gang members from the ranks of the poor. The crime problem was exacerbated in the **1970s** as politicians provided guns and favours for their supporters, asking them to intimidate – at the very least – opponents or drive them out of their "**garrisons**" or constituencies. The "PNP zone" or "JLP enter at your own risk" graffiti that you'll still see plastered over downtown walls stands testament to the strong political allegiances of the communities, many of which remain divided along political lines.

While political violence still flares up at election times and army-enforced night-time curfews are In effect sometimes months on end, the people of the ghettos have largely washed their hands of a political stance that seems to have done them no long-term favours despite the years of promises. Instead, many now give their allegiance to high-profile "**area leaders**" or "**dons**", who earn the favour of their communities as much as by staging free "fun days" for local people and doling out school books and cash to the needy as they do by "keeping the peace" through sheer fire-power and their publicly declared truces with rival areas. Although the country's anti-crime initiative, Operation Kingfish, has made some headway with several high-profile arrests in recent years, profits from drug trafficking and protection rackets (said to be worth millions) makes it seem unlikely that the government will have much success in curtailing the dons and their gangs simply by regenerating the ghettos – these days it's money, not party politics, that rules.

For more on the capital's ghettos, Laurie Gunst's book *Born Fi Dead,* David Howard's *Kingston* and Orlando Patterson's powerful novel *Children of Sisyphus* provide an interesting insiders' view of life here. For a cinematic perspective, check out *Third World Cop*, while Perry Henzell's seminal *The Harder They Come*, though released in the early 1970s, still has much relevance today. (All these books and films are reviewed in Contexts.)

beautiful photographs of the man himself taken during his time in the yard. There is also a gallery featuring the famous Trench Town personalities, and the inevitable gift shop, where resident artist Starliner sells her "Made in Trench Town" Rasta belts, tams and the like. Tours end at the *Casbah Bar* at the front of the property which, together with the shady verandah outside, provides a lovely space to kick back and reflect on the life and work of a man whose music and message has achieved such long-standing and universal appeal.

After exploring the museum, it's well worth paying another US$5 for an accompanied **tour to Second Street**, taking in the Reading Centre and Victory Basic School, Marley's childhood home on Second Street and the former home of Delroy Wilson. A further US$10 buys an extended tour of the area and surrounding enclaves, and if you're keen to spend more time in Trench Town and soak up the atmosphere, you can arrange to **stay** in the basic one-room cottage at the back of the yard (rates negotiable).

While your safety is assured in and around the Culture Yard and Government Yards District (there's a community-based vested interest in ensuring the success of the project, after all), wider Trench Town itself remains a volatile place. Getting to Trench Town is possible by arranged tour (Tourwise Ltd, Mandy Sprague ℡ 974 2323; around US$70/person), local taxi or private car. Though a taxi is the best plan, bear in mind that you may have a hard job persuading some drivers to venture this far into the "ghetto" – you'll probably have to call a few firms. It's also worth keeping an ear out for reports of trouble in the area. Don't carry too much money with you, and it's also a good idea to start early, as you may not want to be touring here after dark. But you'll be fine if you come for the night-time **concert** that's staged here around the time of the Marley birthday and other celebrations – and there's something very special about, in the words of Bob Marley himself, "grooving in Kingston 12".

The Institute of Jamaica

Back in central downtown Kingston, head two blocks north of the National Gallery, turn right into Harbour Street, then left into East Street and you'll reach the **Institute of Jamaica** (Mon–Thurs 9am–4.30pm, Fri 9am–3.30pm; free; ℡ 922 0621, ⓦ www.ioj.org.jm). Here you'll find the **National Library** (℡ 967 1526 or 967 2494, ⓦ www.nlj.org.jm,), home to the best collection of books and old newspapers in the country, and the **Natural History Museum** (entrance round the corner at 10 Tower St; J$200). Focusing on Jamaica's natural history, the museum's main exhibition consists of a collection of musty cabinets filled with dust-gathering stuffed birds, and displays explaining the origins of the country's most important "economic plants" – sugar cane, bananas, coconuts and pineapples – almost all imported from areas of Asia during the early years of Spanish and British colonialism, and now widely grown for export. The museum was being refurbished at the time of writing, but if the excellence of the Institute's new temporary exhibitions is anything to go by, the main collection may well improve. These **temporary exhibitions**, staged in the entrance hall of the National Museum on Tower Street and curated by a dynamic IoJ team, offer some illuminating insights into Jamaican culture; past displays include "Of Things Sacred", an exploration of faith in Jamaica, which featured everything from a re-creation of a Revival altar to the basis of Rastafari, as well as the Centenary of the Great Kingston Earthquake.

The Parade and around

From the Institute, turn left onto Tower Street and right onto King Street, which runs north to the **Parade**, a large square left open by the original city planners and used as a parade ground by British troops during the eighteenth century. Today, as downtown's transport hub, Parade is one of the busiest spots in town.

In the middle of the Parade is **St William Grant Park**, originally Victoria Park but renamed in 1977 for the often overlooked 1930s leader of the infant Jamaican trade union movement. Cynically upstaged by the more charismatic Alexander Bustamante, Grant ended his life as a security guard for the Ministry of Social Security. Rather fierce statues of political rivals Norman Manley and Bustamante guard the park's north and south entrances, while Queen Victoria – the one-time "Supreme Lady of Jamaica" – stands to the east, looking a little lost among all the mayhem.

Up from the park on North Parade, looking like an elaborately iced birthday cake, the elegant **Ward Theatre** occupies a site with a long theatrical tradition. It is reckoned that public performances have been staged here since at least the mid-eighteenth century and probably earlier. The present building, bestowed on the city by one-time Custos and rum baron Colonel Charles Ward, dates from 1911, but sadly, it's showing its age these days. Also looming over the northeast corner of the Parade, is the large red-brick **Coke Chapel**, a Methodist church that dates from 1840. It was erected over the remains of a smaller eighteenth-century chapel built by Thomas Coke, one of the first Methodist missionaries to the island.

On South Parade, just below the park, the **Kingston Parish Church** was first built in 1699, although little of the present structure predates the 1907 earthquake. Airy and spacious, the church is used for important state funerals and such, although the regular congregation has dwindled to almost nothing due to migration out of the downtown area.

Queen Street runs west and east of the park. To the west, **Jubilee Market** (Mon–Sat) spills over into **Coronation Market** (same days), the island's biggest, busiest and loudest – an experience even if you're not here to buy. Backing onto the fringes of the volatile Tivoli Gardens area, Coronation is not a traditional tourist spot, and is best visited in the company of someone who knows where he or she is going.

King Street and Liberty Hall

Striking north and south from the centre of the Parade, **King Street** was once downtown's grandest thoroughfare and the heart of the island's financial district. Some illustrious structures still remain – look out for the courthouse and the GPO buildings south of the Parade near the junction with Tower Street – and though the usual melee of fast-food restaurants, haberdasheries and general stores vastly outnumber the banks and government buildings these days, King Street remains an absorbing place for a wander. At no. 76, set back from the street in a tree-shaded yard, stands **Liberty Hall** (Mon–Thurs 10am–4pm, Fri 10am–3.30pm; guided tour J$200; ☎948 8639, ⓦwww.garveylibertyhall.com, ⓔlibertyhall @cwjamaica.com), site of the Kingston headquarters of **Marcus Garvey**'s United Negro Improvement Association, or **UNIA**. Over a thousand Liberty Halls were established by the UNIA worldwide, and this one, first opened in 1923, was a hotbed of activity in Garvey's heyday, serving both as a community resource – with a laundry, canteen, job centre and cooperative bank – and as social club-cum-meeting place for UNIA members and associated organizations; it was from here in 1927, following his deportation from the US, that Garvey addressed a huge crowd of supporters. After Garvey's departure for England in 1935, however, the building was used variously as an entertainment and sports centre before falling into disrepair. It was acquired by the Jamaica National Heritage Trust in 1987, and restored and reopened in 2003; today, as in Garvey's time, it serves as a community resource, with a reference library and a multimedia centre offering low-cost computing courses. It runs educational outreach programmes for local children, including a summer arts course, as evidenced by the lovely mosaic on the exterior walls and the murals around the top-floor Great Hall. Also on site is an engaging **museum** (Mon–Fri 10am–4pm; J$100), with interactive touch-screens, a collection of UNIA-related memorabilia, a small theatre screening films on Garvey and pan-Africanism and, of course, a shop. The building is also used for regular concerts, poetry performances and lectures.

Duke Street and around

From Liberty Hall, it's a couple of blocks east via Beeston Street to the fretworked Georgian edifice of **Headquarters House** on Duke Street (Mon–Fri 8.30am–4.30pm; free), which affords a brief glimpse of Jamaican history. Built in 1755 by Thomas Hibbert, a wealthy local merchant, it served as its military headquarters (hence the name) until Jamaica's legislative assembly moved in full time and operated there between 1872 and 1960.

Next to Headquarters House is the rather less imposing **Gordon House**, a contemporary slab of concrete that's been home to the Jamaican parliament since 1960. Named after National Hero George William Gordon, today the House of Representatives meets here most Tuesdays at 2pm (and at the same time on Wednesdays and Thursdays if there is sufficient business), while the Senate sits in the chamber on Fridays at 11am. At these times, surrounding streets are sometimes cordoned off. Entrance to the public gallery is free, and when the chamber is empty you can ask the marshal to show you round.

The striking white building on the opposite side of Duke Street above Gordon House is the **Jewish synagogue**. In 1882, the synagogues of the two Jewish congregations in Kingston, the Ashkenhazi and the Sephardic, were both destroyed by fire and an amalgamated synagogue was built on this site; the present building dates from after the 1907 earthquake. The building, with its mahogany staircase and gallery, is still worth a visit if you're passing; it's kept locked, but you can normally find the caretaker on the premises during the week. If you want to learn more about the history of Jamaica's Jews, call ahead to arrange to see the small **exhibition** (Mon–Fri 9am–4pm, closes a little earlier on Friday; donation US$5; ☏ 922 5931, ⓦ www.ucija.org) in the adjacent hall, which includes a short and engaging film.

National Heroes Park and around

A ten-minute walk north of the Gleaner Building, **National Heroes Park** is a large stretch of scrubby, dusty, sun-bleached grass enclosed by iron railings. If you're on foot it offers a chance to escape the traffic that hammers around it, but it's not a place for a promenade these days; its proximity to the volatile Vineyard Town community means that it's favoured more by grazing goats than casual strollers. The park held the city's racecourse for more than a century before it got shifted to the safer New Kingston, and from there to its present location west of the city at Caymanas Park (see p.88). After independence, the government converted the southern portion of what was then the George IV Memorial Park into a monument to Jamaica's **National Heroes** (see box opposite), patrolled by gun-toting soldiers and guarded by two JDF sentries sweltering in full ceremonial uniform (there's a foot-stomping changing of the guard each hour).

Adjacent to the main Heroes' plots is a bust of Antonio Maceo and a statue of Simon Bolivar, independence leaders in Cuba and Venezuela respectively, and inspirational to Jamaica's early nationalists. Bolivar was exiled to Jamaica for a year in 1815 following his unsuccessful revolt against Spanish rule in Venezuela. Whilst living in a boarding house on the corner of Princess and Tower streets, he survived an assassination attempt by the Spanish and penned his "Letter from Jamaica", in which he laid out the reasoning behind his struggle for South American liberation.

At the north end of the park, on Marescaux Road, are the colourful wooden buildings of **Wolmer's High School** and **Mico College**. Wolmer's, founded in 1729, has proved a formidable centre of academic achievement, counting prime

Jamaica's National Heroes

Since independence, the Jamaican parliament has elevated seven of the island's greatest people to the status of **National Hero**, all of whom carry the title "The Right Excellent". As yet, none of the Heroes hail from the worlds of sport or music, but it is widely anticipated that Bob Marley will be next to join the pantheon. Michael Manley, who died in 1997, is another popular candidate. The present National Heroes are:

Paul Bogle (unknown–1865). Baptist preacher who led the 1865 Morant Bay Rebellion and was executed for his participation.

Alexander Bustamante (1884–1977). Labour leader, founder of the Jamaica Labour Party and first prime minister of the independent country from 1962 to 1967.

Marcus Garvey (1887–1940). Founder of the Universal Negro Improvement Association and widely viewed as the father of the black power movement.

George William Gordon (1820–65). "Free coloured" leader of Jamaica's nationalist movement after slavery, executed by the British for his part in the Morant Bay Rebellion.

Norman Manley (1893–1969). Lawyer, founder of the People's National Party and leader of Jamaica's movement for independence.

Nanny (birth and death years unknown). Legendary eighteenth-century female leader of the Windward Maroons in their battles with the English.

Sam Sharpe (1801–32). Baptist preacher executed after leading the 1831 slave rebellion in Jamaica's western parishes.

ministers and governor generals among its alumni. Nearby Mico, the largest teacher-training school in the West Indies, owes its foundation in 1834 to the eleventh-hour refusal of Englishman Samuel Mico to marry one of the six nieces of his aunt, Lady Mico, back in 1670. The intended dowry was invested for a number of charitable purposes and eventually used to found teacher-training colleges in various parts of the Caribbean. Dedicated to "liberating minds from the bondage of ignorance", Mico was founded to fund education for newly emancipated Africans and was one of the only colleges in Jamaica that operated on non-racial grounds.

Uptown

The phrase "uptown Kingston" is used as a catch-all for areas of the city north of Cross Roads, including the business and commercial centres of **Half Way Tree** and **New Kingston** as well as residential areas like **Hope Pastures Mona** and **Beverly Hills**.

New Kingston

The heart of uptown is the high-rise district of **New Kingston**, contained in an eccentric triangle bounded by Trafalgar Road, Old Hope Road and Half Way Tree Road.

The chances are that you'll **stay** and do much of your **eating** and **drinking** in or around this area; some of the interesting sights are within walking distance, the rest are a short bus or taxi ride away. There are few places of note in New Kingston itself, although the **Liguanea Club**, opposite the *Jamaica Pegasus* hotel on Knutsford Boulevard, still retains its old colonial buildings as well as lots of lovely tennis courts (available for hire). In theory the club is open to members only, but it's easily accessible if you're passing. The building served as the fictional Queens Club, where James Bond took cocktails on the verandah with Professor Dent in the classic movie *Dr No*. It's sometimes used for outdoor parties these days.

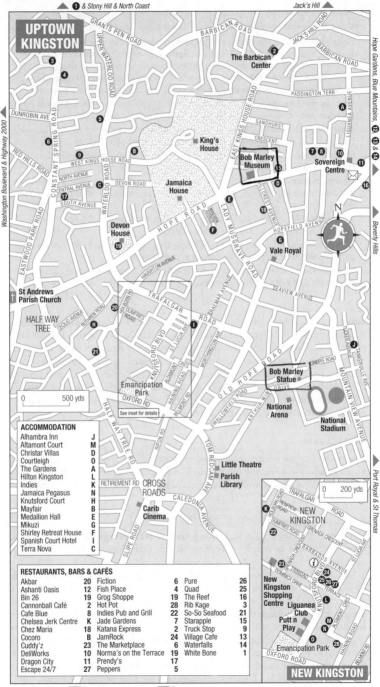

UPTOWN KINGSTON

Washington Boulevard & Highway 2000

Hope Gardens, Blue Mountains, 12, 13 & 14

Beverly Hills

Port Royal & St Thomas

ACCOMMODATION

Alhambra Inn	J
Altamont Court	M
Christar Villas	D
Courtleigh	O
The Gardens	A
Hilton Kingston	L
Indies	K
Jamaica Pegasus	N
Knutsford Court	H
Mayfair	B
Medallion Hall	E
Mikuzi	G
Shirley Retreat House	F
Spanish Court Hotel	I
Terra Nova	C

RESTAURANTS, BARS & CAFÉS

Akbar	20	Fiction	6	Pure	26
Ashanti Oasis	12	Fish Place	4	Quad	25
Bin 26	19	Grog Shoppe	19	The Reef	16
Cannonball Café	2	Hot Pot	28	Rib Kage	3
Cafe Blue	8	Indies Pub and Grill	22	So-So Seafood	21
Chelsea Jerk Centre	K	Jade Gardens	7	Starapple	15
Chez Maria	18	Katana Express	2	Truck Stop	9
Cocoro	B	JamRock	24	Village Cafe	13
Cuddy'z	23	The Marketplace	6	Waterfalls	14
DeliWorks	10	Norma's on the Terrace	19	White Bone	1
Dragon City	11	Prendy's	17		
Escape 24/7	27	Peppers	5		

NEW KINGSTON

0   200 yds

0   500 yds

Downtown   Downtown

A little further down Knutsford, the buildings give way to the wide-open space of **Emancipation Park** (Mon–Fri 5am–11pm, Sat & Sun 5am–midnight; free), opened in 2002 as a memorial to the 1838 cessation of slavery in Jamaica. It's a manicured and well-maintained space, with more concrete than grass, ever-watchful security, piped jazz from boulder-shaped speakers, a well-used jogging track and a stage which hosts frequent free concerts. Make a beeline for the stunning **Redemption Song** by local sculptor Laura Facey-Cooper, a majestic study of a Jamaican couple facing each other and looking skywards; their ample breasts and genitals inevitably caused outrage when the sculpture was first installed in 2003. Though the park is a nice spot to take a breather in the daytime, it comes into its own at night, when couples canoodle and families turn out to promenade and gaze at the central "sky cascade" fountain, its ever-changing jets of water lit by coloured lights to delightful effect. If you're here in the evening or at the weekend, you might want to head across the boundary road to **Putt 'n' Play** (Mon–Thurs 5–11pm, Fri 5pm–midnight, Sat & Sun 11am–midnight). It's a prettily landscaped 18-hole mini-golf course, with a few kids' rides to boot, that attracts a healthy clique of Kingston teenagers after dark, and families at the weekends.

The National Stadium and around

Just east of New Kingston on Arthur Wint Drive, the 40,000-capacity **National Stadium**, known to sports fans as "The Office", hosts most of Jamaica's premier sporting events. The stadium was built to coincide with Jamaica's independence celebrations in 1962; the first event here was the raising of the new nation's black, green and gold flag, followed soon after by the 1962 Commonwealth Games. The facilities for athletics and cycling are first-rate, but the centrepiece is the refurbished football pitch, surrounded by towering aisles of bleachers and overlooked by arc lights. The home of Jamaica's **Reggae Boyz**, the stadium comes alive when

Jamaica's sporting success

Although historically famous for its contribution to West Indies cricket, Jamaica's recent outstanding achievements in the area of track and field have propelled the island nation into the limelight of the sporting world. Spearheading this international success is Trelawny native **Usain "Lightning" Bolt** who, along with other members of the now famous **Team Jamaica** (which included Asafa Powell, Michael Frater, Nestor Carter, Shelly Ann Fraser, Melaine Walker, Veronica Campbell-Brown and Kerron Stewart) dominated the track events at the Beijing Olympics in 2008.

In an astonishing performance Bolt swept both the world and Olympic records in the 100- and 200-metre races, with times of 9.69 seconds and 10.30 seconds, respectively. He is the first man in history to break both world records at one Olympic Game and the first man to win both the 100- and 200-metre events at the same Olympics since Carl Lewis in 1984.

This record of achievement, remarkable for such a small country with limited resources, began in 1948 when the island, still a British colony, entered its first Olympics and has included the successes of medalists such as Arthur Wint, Herb McKenley, Don Quarrie and Merlene Ottey.

Despite their base in Jamaica, it is rare to see Bolt and others in action on their home turf. Failing that, other exciting sporting events worth taking in are the one-day and four-day international **cricket matches** held in Jamaica at the refurbished **Sabina Park**. While grandstand seats are available for purchase (for serious spectators), most locals tend to grab their portable lawn chairs or throw down towels on the newly rebranded Appleton Rum Mound where for a premium price patrons can enjoy an all-inclusive bar and party-like atmosphere.

there's a game on. If the national team are playing, it's usually packed to capacity – Air Jamaica planes fly low overhead, and the shouts of "GOAAALLLL" can be heard across town. For information on tickets, call ☎929 4970. Just inside the railings by the car park is a statue of Jamaican athlete Herb McKinley coming off the starting blocks; at the 1952 Helsinki Olympics, McKinley became the first man in the world to run in the 200-, 400- and 800-metre races (see box, p.71). A smaller stadium, for minor events, is adjacent, while the **National Arena** next door also houses smaller-scale sporting events and other shows.

Further south from the National Arena, on Tom Redcam Avenue, the squat, wooden **Little Theatre** was built in 1961 to house the Little Theatre Movement (LTM), which from its inception in 1942 pioneered organized theatre in Kingston. Alongside regular productions of Jamaican roots plays, the theatre hosts the LTM's annual pantomime as well as seasons by the globally recognized National Dance Theatre Company and other local dance groups, and its more secure uptown location has seen it overtake the Ward (see p.67) as Jamaica's premier performing arts venue. The wooden memorial outside is to Greta Fowler, energetic founder of the LTM, while the small building next door is the site of the innovative **Little Little Theatre**, where the works of modern Jamaican playwrights are given an airing. For more on performances, see p.80.

Half Way Tree

On the other side of New Kingston, a mile or so away, is the congested area known as **Half Way Tree**. Before it got swallowed up by the expanding city, Half Way Tree was a tiny village and the capital of the parish of St Andrew. Its central plaza – today a busy shopping area and one of Kingston's key road intersections – once provided a resting place for farmers travelling into the city's markets. The eponymous cotton tree under which they sheltered is long gone, and a clock tower now stands in its place, a 1913 memorial to British King Edward VII. With back-to-back traffic sweltering under the sun, vendors hawking iced-water and newspapers at the traffic lights, and queues of hungry workers standing in line at the pretty-pink *Tastee Patties* outlet, Half Way Tree today is about as far away from a resting place as it's possible to imagine.

A handful of restored colonial buildings stand near the square, the most notable of which is the red-brick **St Andrew's Parish Church** (always open; free), which stands oddly marooned between the streams of traffic and city life. Though largely submerged by the modern buildings that have arisen around it, this is still a tranquil and gently alluring edifice. Built in 1666, it's one of the oldest religious sites on the island, though the present model is the fourth incarnation. Striking north from Half Way Tree, **Constant Spring Road** boasts Kingston's largest conglomeration of shopping malls; it's also the route to the cool greens of the Constant Spring Golf Course.

Devon House and around

Fifteen minutes' walk east from Half Way Tree, tall iron railings overhung by towering trees mark the grassy complex ranged around **Devon House**, 26 Hope Rd (vehicular entrance on Waterloo Road; call for information about tours on ☎929 6602), built in 1881 by Jamaica's first black millionaire and still one of the city's grandest buildings. Rumour has it that nearby Lady Musgrave Road, which circuitously bypasses Devon House, was built at the request of the wife of Anthony Musgrave, Jamaica's governor from 1874 to 1883, so that she could get to King's House (see opposite) without having to pass such a fine house owned by a black Jamaican.

Born in Kingston in 1820, building contractor **George Stiebel** made his fortune mining gold in Venezuela, returning home in 1873 to snap up 99 properties throughout Jamaica (ownership of a hundred was prohibited by law). Among these was Devon Pen, where he built the house that was his Kingston home until he died in 1896. Bought by the Jamaican government in 1967, and first used to house the National Gallery before it moved to its present downtown location, the house has gradually been furnished with West Indian and European antiques as well as more modern Jamaican reproductions.

The landscaped grounds of Devon House make a fine place for a leisurely stroll, with plenty of breezy benches and shady spots to while away the midday heat. You've a good chance of running into one of the numerous wedding parties who come here for their photos. Most visitors, though, make straight for the former stables, which now house a handful of gift shops stocking a good range of rather expensive ephemera, as well as a smattering of cafés and restaurants (for full reviews of which, see p.76). Chief attractions include the shop selling heavenly home-made "**I Scream**" (soursop and Guinness flavours are sublime), and the *Brick Oven* bakery, which features excellent gooey cakes and some of Kingston's best patties. You can also get a decent sit-down lunch at the *Grog Shoppe*, which is not as painfully quaint as its name would suggest, or even afternoon tea or a gourmet meal at the elegant *Norma's on the Terrace*.

Further up Hope Road from Devon House mark the entrances to **Jamaica House** (closed to visitors), used as the prime minister's office, and **King's House** (Mon–Fri by appointment; free; ☎ 927 6424), which is the official residence of the governor general, who is the Queen of England's representative in Jamaica, and has the notional powers of a head of state.

The Bob Marley Museum

For reggae fans, the **Bob Marley Museum** at 56 Hope Rd (Mon–Sat 9.30am–4pm, last tour at 4pm; U$20; ☎ 927 9152, ⓦ www.bobmarley-foundation.com) is the whole point of a visit to Kingston, and even if you're not a serious devotee, it's well worth an hour of your time – though don't expect a Disney-type theme-park ambience. Hidden from the street by a red-, gold- and green-painted wall and marked by fluttering Rasta banners, this beautiful colonial-era wooden building was Marley's Kingston home from 1975 until his death from cancer in 1981, and was designated a National Heritage site in 2006. It's been kept much as it looked when he lived here, and is a gentle monument to Jamaica's greatest musical legend. The hour-long **tour** starts as soon as you pass through the gates (no photography, filming or taping is allowed inside the house), with the guide pointing out photographs of the singer and his family mounted on the walls, a battered jeep formerly owned by Marley and Pierre Rouzier's fine sculpture of the man himself. You're then led around the back of the house to the room where Marley was almost assassinated during the 1976 election campaign. Blown-up newspaper reports from the time cover the walls, with space left for the bullet holes which riddle the brickwork. After the shooting, Marley left Jamaica for a two-year exile in Britain.

Inside, the house is decorated with gold and platinum discs depicting sales of the albums *Exodus* (1977), *Uprising* (1980) and *Legend* (1984), as well as the covers of all the LPs, a commemoration of Marley's induction into the Rock and Roll Hall of Fame in 2003, his Grammy Lifetime Achievement Award, posthumously presented in 2001 and his Order of Merit from the Jamaican government. Upstairs, there is a re-creation of Wail 'n' Soul, Marley's tiny, shack-like Trench Town record shop, where he once hung out with band members Peter Tosh and Bunny Wailer, while the walls of another room are entirely covered with yellowing newspaper articles from home and abroad, which make fascinating reading. There's also a chart of all the cities the Wailers played in worldwide – prominence is given to shows in Africa, particularly the independence celebrations in Zimbabwe in 1980, but the band clearly worked hard, notching up performances in places as far-flung as the Mediterranean party island of Ibiza. You can peek into Marley's bedroom and kitchen, the latter complete with the blender in which he made his natural juices.

The tour ends behind the house in the air-conditioned movie theatre that once housed Marley's Tuff Gong recording studio. There's moving footage of the "One Love" concert held during the bloody election year of 1980, at which Marley brought together rival party leaders Michael Manley and Edward Seaga, and interviews with the great man cut together with appropriate music videos – the return to Africa and *Exodus*, celebration of "herb" and *Easy Skanking*.

Afterwards, you can escape from the clutches of the guide to look at the excellent photo gallery. There are pictures of Marley in New York during his final tour, with the police after the assassination attempt, and playing a lot of football. In the yard opposite the cinema, a shop sells daughter Cedella's wonderful Catch a Fire clothing alongside hordes of Marley paraphernalia.

Hope Botanical Gardens and around

A quarter of a mile east of the Marley museum, just past the Sovereign shopping centre, Hope Road becomes Old Hope Road and heads east towards Papine and the Blue Mountains. On the way it passes the ample grounds of **Jamaica College**, one of the island's premier schools, which count both Norman and Michael Manley among its ex-pupils. In the early days of English settlement in Jamaica, Major Richard Hope, an officer with the invading British forces of Penn and Venables, set up a thriving sugar estate here, with a stone aqueduct (parts of which can still be seen today) bringing water down from the Hope River. In 1881 the government acquired two hundred acres of land from the Hope Estate and laid out the **Hope Botanical Gardens** (daily 6am–7pm; free) in much the same form as you see them today.

Entered on your left as you head up Old Hope Road, the **gardens** took a heavy knock from hurricanes Gilbert in 1988 and Ivan in 2004, but remain a lovely escape from the clamour of the city and a popular venue for weekend strolls, picnics and get-togethers. There are huge lawns, bougainvillea walks, a lily-smothered pond

▲ Hope Botanical Gardens

and a dizzying variety of unusual trees, including a great collection of palms. After exploring, you can grab a bite at the wonderful *Ashanti Oasis* vegetarian restaurant (see p.76) in the middle of the gardens. Adjacent to the gardens is a small and sadly underfunded **zoo** (Mon–Fri 10am–4pm, Sat & Sun 10am–4pm; J$150 adults, J$100 kids under 12, kids under 3 are free), with crocodiles, monkeys, mongooses, tapirs, peccaries, snakes and tropical birds. A wooden tower overlooks the lot and provides a handsome view of the city. If you're driving from downtown or New Kingston, turn off the Old Hope Road about four hundred yards past the signposted main entrance to the garden and follow it around to the left to a small parking area.

University of the West Indies
A few hundred yards west of Hope Gardens along Old Hope Road, and just before the Sovereign Centre mall, Mona Road swings southeast towards the extensive campus of the **University of the West Indies** (Ⓦ www.uwimona .edu.jm), usually just called UWI. It was first established here in 1948, as a College of the University of London, and achieved full university status in 1962. With sister campuses in Trinidad and Barbados, UWI accepts students from all over the Caribbean. Look out for sections of the 1758 **Paine-Mona Aqueduct**, which once sluiced water from the Hope River in the Blue Mountain foothills to a sugar-processing works that was part of the old Mona, Hope and Papine estates. The university's Jamaican-Georgian **chapel**, located elsewhere on campus, has an interesting history. Built in 1799, the building was originally a warehouse on a Trelawney sugar estate, but was brought here and rebuilt brick by brick in 1955 at the suggestion of a former UWI chancellor. You can see the name of its former owner, one Edward Morant Gale, esquire, inscribed along the northern outer wall. If you're in Kingston around the February 6 anniversary of Bob Marley's birthday, try to attend the annual Marley lecture presented here by the university's Reggae Studies unit; past speakers have included Finance Minister Omar Davies discoursing on Peter Tosh, and there's usually a reggae performance afterwards. Otherwise, finish off your campus visit with a browse around the excellent bookshop.

Eating

After the sun goes down and the heat lifts, the Kingston area is hard to beat for **eating**. Particularly uptown – which is where you'll want to be in the evenings – you'll find a wider choice of **restaurants** than anywhere else in Jamaica and an excellent standard of food. Most places offer variations on traditional Jamaican fare, from tiny jerk bars to exquisite local seafood establishments, but there's also good Chinese, Japanese, Indian, Italian and Middle Eastern cuisine, as well as a good spread of vegetarian restaurants.

For **patties**, *Tastee's* most convenient branches are at 11 Knutsford Blvd, at Half Way Tree and at Papine Square, or try *Juici Beef* at 7 Hope Rd, just up from the Sovereign Centre, and at 7 Trinidad Terrace, off Knutsford Boulevard; *Juici* also does a great breakfast – try the cornmeal porridge.

Lastly, if you're after truly authentic **jerk chicken**, try any of the smoking oil-drum barbecues that set up on street corners. An excellent choice is the vendor just outside Northside Plaza in the Liguanea section of Hope Road, who sells from Thursday to Saturday.

Note that we've given a phone number only for those places where you might need to reserve a table. Unless otherwise stated, all the places below are marked on the Uptown Kingston map, p.70.

Inexpensive

Ashanti Oasis Hope Gardens. Right in the centre of the gardens, and with a waterfall running through the open-sided dining area, this wonderful vegetarian restaurant is a must. The daily-changing lunch/early dinner menu always includes a delicious thick soup (split peas, red peas or pumpkin) and main dishes such as soya and veg balls served with rice, salad and ratatouille. Also available are veggie burgers with chutney, natural juices, aloe wine and soya ice cream. Unmissable.

Chelsea Jerk Centre 7 Chelsea Ave. Businesslike a/c diner popular with New Kingston workers, and offering, obviously, great jerk chicken alongside large plates of no-nonsense Jamaican daily specials, usually including a fish dish amongst the meaty treats.

Cocoro Mayfair Hotel. Tasty sushi restaurant with rolls, teriyaki and tempura in a no-frills setting at the Mayfair hotel – sit on the verandah if possible.

Deli Works Sovereign Centre, Hope Rd. Reliable a/c canteen-style diner that's a great lunch spot, with local fare alongside veggie or meat lasagne, macaroni cheese and lots of salads. Good breakfasts, too, and a reasonably priced Sunday brunch (9am–3pm, starting at J$800).

Hot Pot 2 Altamont Terrace. Popular spot for typical, inexpensive Jamaican meals in the heart of New Kingston. Excellent breakfasts, from cornmeal or banana porridge to various ackee and saltfish combinations, and lunches of fish and bammy, curry goat, stewed beef and other Jamaican staples.

Kaieteure Foods Jamaica Conference Centre, 14 Duke St. (see Downtown Kingston map, p.60). This first-floor dining area, popular with local business folk, is the best place in downtown Kingston for lunch, with sea breezes fanning over the tables which are arranged around the open-sided dining area. The excellent food is served canteen-style, and there's a wide choice of quality salads and daily specials, from fish and chicken to Jamaican favourites such as oxtail.

Mother Earth 13 Oxford Terrace. Central, businesslike vegetarian restaurant doing a cracking trade. The menu changes daily; expect good Jamaican staples for breakfast and imaginative lunches with lots of pulses, soya and tofu. Patties – chickpea, lentils, veg mince, ackee – are excellent, as are the natural juices and soya ice cream.

The Reef 124 Old Hope Rd. Cafeteria-style seafood restaurant in Liguanea serving tasty food from a mid-sized menu – try the pumpkin-steamed fish.

Moderate

Café Blue Sovereign Center, Hope Rd. Clean, bright café serving delicious Blue Mountain coffee and great light snacks. Open early (7am Mon–Fri, Sat 8 am and Sun 9am), so it's perfect for breakfast as well as a light lunch, with a nice selection of omelettes, bagels and pastries and coffee beverages. Try their extra-ordinarily calorific Mochaccino and definitely visit their other location on the way to Newcastle (just past Irish Town on the right before the entrance to Strawberry Hill). Wireless.

Cannonball Cafe Loshusan Shopping Centre. One of three great locations (Manor Park and New Kingston being the others), Cannonball has garnered a well-deserved reputation of light tasty sandwiches, salads and meals with comfortable seating conducive to family outings, small meetings and get-togethers with girlfriends. Serves wine, and also has wireless and a great bulletin board to find out what's happening locally.

Chez Maria 7 Hillcrest Ave. A lovely outdoor setting, with tables scattered around a garden, and tasty Italian and Lebanese food, from mezes and kebabs to bruschetta and pizza and the full range of pasta dishes – try the lobster spaghetti with garlic, olives and chili.

Cuddy'z 25 Dominica Drive Owned and operated by ex-Windies cricket superstar Courtney Walsh, this slick, modern a/c restaurant offers a wide-ranging, mid-priced international-style menu of build-your-own salads, steaks, ribs, pasta and local favourites.

Dragon City 17 Northside Plaza, Liguanea ☎ 927 0939. The best of the multitude of Chinese restaurants that line this mini Chinatown opposite the Liguanea Shopping Centre on Hope Rd, with a huge variety of tasty dishes at medium prices. Take-away available.

Indies Pub and Grill 8 Holborn Rd, opposite Indies Hotel. Easy-going café-cum-bar with seating in a semi-outdoor terrace and an eclectic, reasonably priced menu featuring Jamaican staples alongside fish and chips, pizza and Lebanese dishes.

JamRock 69 Knutsford Blvd. Busy combination of sports bar and restaurant, this a/c indoor diner offers the sumptuous "Jerk Nyamwich" alongside salads, local staples, pasta dishes, a good fish soup and cakes and pastries from the patisserie.

Katana Express Loshusan Supermarket. 29 East Kings House Rd. Tasty sushi from a small, simple menu, in a convenient but not so glamorous (supermarket) setting – reasonably priced and quick.

Our Place 102 Hope Rd. This laid-back place features excellent Jamaican cooking and attracts a regular crew of locals who play dominoes on the verandah or wolf down the local cooking at tables indoors. All the staples, from conch soup to curry

The Marketplace – 67 Constant Spring Road

This lovely piazza-style courtyard offers seating under the stars. Diners can choose from five premium **restaurants** (prices range from moderate to expensive), including *East*, a sushi bar with lunch specials and sushi/sashimi combos; *Habibi Latino*, which is particularly favoured for its delicious Middle Eastern food; *Café Aubergine*, with French-Italian style fare in a romantic café-like setting; *Jewel of India*, a high-end Indian restaurant serving delicious small plates; and the no-frills *China Express*, which serves tasty Jamaican-Chinese food. It's busy throughout the week and even more so on the weekend; come for dinner, and afterwards head to the nearby *Fiction* for after-hours drinks and dancing.

goat, and a seafood night on Fridays. The bar is nice for a quiet drink, and there's outdoor seating at the back.

Rib Kage 149 Constant Spring Rd ⓣ905 1858. Popular amongst meat-loving locals, with rustic wooden tables under the stars and a US-style menu of melt-in-the-mouth pork or beef ribs smothered in barbecue sauce and served with a baked potato. Steaks, pizzas, fish and chicken dishes are also available, as is delivery.

So-So Seafood 4 Chelsea Ave. Busy place with an appealing outdoor setting featuring a mini waterfall and strings of fairy lights, and a decently priced seafood-based menu, from garlic, curry, coconut, stir-fried or pepper shrimp and lobster to fish priced by the pound, as well as Jamaican daily blackboard specials and an excellent conch soup on Thursdays and Fridays.

Starapple 94 Hope Rd. Set in a lovely old house, all creaky polished floors and fretworked "gingerbread" woodwork, and offering a solid, mid-priced Jamaican menu, from yam and saltfish and oxtail and beans to steamed fish and all the usual variations. Interesting veggie options include callaloo quiche, vegetable rundown and aloo and channa curry.

White Bones 1 Mannings Hill Rd ⓣ925 2813. Charming outdoor seafood restaurant serving an extensive menu of great seafood.

Expensive

Akbar 11 Holborn Rd ⓣ926 3480. The best Indian food in town, in a tastefully decorated a/c dining room. All the regular dishes, roti and plenty of vegetarian choices.

Jade Garden Sovereign Centre ⓣ978 3476. Smart business-set restaurant with some of the best Chinese dishes in town.

Norma's on the Terrace Devon House ⓣ968 5488. Kingston's most upscale eatery, situated on the terrace of the old Devon House stables and serving gourmet Jamaican food with an international twist. Menu highlights include smoked marlin with onions and capers, jerk smoked pork chop marinated in ginger and Red Stripe and glazed with guava preserve, and a delicious seafood lasagne. Vegetarian dishes run from home-made ravioli to jerk tofu, and service is excellent. Closed Sun.

Red Bones Blues Café 21 Braemar Ave ⓣ978 6091, ⓦwww.redbonesbluescafe.com. Stylish, upmarket restaurant-cum-music venue with a distinguished but laid-back atmosphere, and tables in a pretty dining room or on an outdoor terrace overlooking the gardens. The imaginative and delicious food has a contemporary flavour, from herb-crusted snapper or lamb chops stuffed with feta and a peppercorn sauce to a callaloo strudel, and the kitchen takes last orders at a satisfyingly late 11pm. Closed Sun.

Drinking and nightlife

Kingston has legions of great places for a **drink**, from sophisticated hangouts with live jazz and a long wine list to buzzy bars crowded with the capital's bright young things. For an overall idea of what's going on, it's a good idea to check the entertainment sections of the *Gleaner* and *Observer* on a Friday, and keep an eye and an ear out for press and radio ads throughout the week.

When choosing a bar, bear in mind that you'll rarely want to walk between places at night, and taxis are the best way of getting around. In line with the growing popularity of **gaming lounges** throughout Jamaica, Kingston features several places where you can hit the slots or roulette machine. Even if you don't want to gamble, some spots such as *Treasure Hunt* on Trinidad Terrace off Knutsford Boulevard, are open round-the-clock, and are sound places to get a drink in the wee hours. In-hotel lounges with shorter hours include those at the *Terra Nova* (Mon–Thurs & Sun 11am–4am, Fri & Sat 11am–6am) and the *Hilton* (daily 11.30am–3am).

Kingston's active **club** scene ranges from jam-packed, air-conditioned indoor venues with big-name DJs, state-of-the-art equipment and the latest tunes to small, dark, oldies' clubs for the more mature dancers. Anticipate a cover of less than US$5 – more if there's a live performance or a big-name sound system; the *Gleaner* advertises regular ladies' nights, when women get in free. As you'll find island-wide, nothing much happens before midnight except on Friday, when after-work jams pull an early evening crowd. **Security** at most of the clubs is tight, and you'll often be searched on your way in.

Live music in the capital is less predictable, but almost always more interesting than the anaesthetized reggae dished up for tourists on the north coast. In terms of regular events, look out for the excellent Heineken Startime concerts, featuring the best of Jamaica's vintage artists; Startime also put on brilliant "back in times" parties. Bars such as the *Red Bones*, *Village Café*, and venues such as *Backyaad* (126 Constant Spring Rd) and *Weekenz* (80 Constant Spring Rd) feature regular live

---

Kingston's street dances

The clubs and bars serve as an excellent sampler of the capital's nightlife, but there's nothing like partying under the stars, and you shouldn't leave Kingston without taking in one of the various outdoor parties staged in and around the city. The last few years have seen an explosion in popularity of free **street parties**, huge dancehall sessions that are now among the biggest events in Kingston's nightlife scene. Held outdoors in the capital's less salubrious areas and with a raw, earthy atmosphere, weekly parties such as Passa Passa and Hot Mondays have become legendary, attracting huge crowds of dancehall aficionados who dress to impress and come to hear the cream of the island's sound systems and selectors, as well as rub shoulders with the big names in the dancehall fraternity – from dancers who come to "bring out" their latest move to Jamaica's best-known DJs, who might take to the mic for an impromptu perform-ance. And surprisingly, given their ghetto locations, the parties have a healthy following amongst uptown dancehall devotees, and you'll see the odd tourist there, too.

Though you'll need to be a fan of the music and reasonably well informed about dancehall culture to get the best out of a street dance, your **security** is pretty much guaranteed – anyone foolish enough to ruin everyone's fun by starting trouble or attempting a robbery will inevitably be swiftly dealt with by irate locals, backed up by the area leaders who provide the security. Nonetheless, it's obviously sensible to keep your wits about you, leave your valuables at home and, if possible, go with a local escort. Similarly, avoid street dances if there's been recent trouble in any of the areas – just ask around.

Parties come and go, but at the time of writing, the main jams were Early Monday at Savannah Plaza (Constant Spring Road); Boasty Tuesday at Lyndhurst Road Plaza; Bembe on Thursdays at Weekenz (Constant Spring Road); Cadillac Saturday at Limelight (Half Way Tree); and Prendy's on Sundays at Hellshire. **Weddy Wednesdays**, staged at Stone Love's headquarters on Burlington Avenue, is the only regular uptown street dance, and is a great warm-up for the daddy of them all, **Passa Passa**, 47 Spanish Town Rd, the pride of Tivoli Gardens and by far the busiest party of the week. The action doesn't start until the small hours of Wednesday morning, though, and there's not much point turning up before 1am.

shows as well as, occasionally, *Mas Camp*, although most of the live music parties happen here during Carnival.

If you're in Kingston between January and April, you can take in Jamaica's **Carnival**. Adopted from the Trinidadian event, Carnival is on a smaller scale here and focused more on all-inclusive parties and outdoor street jams, though it does culminate with an early-hours Jouvert (a body-paint-spattered street parade) and a traditional-style costume parade through new Kingston. Though there's plenty of soca, dancehall is inevitably a big part of Carnival here, and you'll see lots of DJs and bands (including local stalwarts Byron Lee and the Dragonaires) as well as big stars from Trinidad and the Eastern Caribbean – Alison Hinds, Machel Montano, TC, Bunji Garlin and the like. Events are widely publicized on the radio and in the press, and you can also contact the JTB (☎ 929 9200) or visit ⓦ www.jamaicacarnival.com or www.bacchanaljamaica.com.

Bin 26 Devon House. Kingston's first wine bar fills its tiny floor space with a wide selection of wines, liqueurs and champagnes, as well as cigars. Patrons can sip by the glass or buy bottles; tapas-like snacks are also available.

Carlos Café 22 Belmont Rd. Intimate and friendly place to sink a few drinks or shoot some pool, with various theme nights throughout the week.

Cuddy'z 25 Dominica Drive. Operated by cricketing legend Courtney Walsh, who often passes through to the delight of patrons, this well-equipped, high-tech sports bar is a lively place for a drink or to catch a baseball, cricket or football game shown on numerous TVs.

The Deck 14 Trafalgar Rd. Spacious, easy-going and central open-air bar under a cavernous thatched roof, popular with a friendly, older set. Good bar snacks, and the DJ's oldies selection keeps things moving on the dancefloor.

Escape 24-7 24 Knutsford Blvd. Semi-outdoor bar in a great central location, popular with a youngish crowd and offering good – if sometimes ear-shattering – music, inexpensive drinks (a rarity in the vicinity) and basic light meals such as fish and chips. Particularly good for after hours.

Fiction Marketplace, 67 Constant Spring Rd. Large indoor club with two bars, private booths and great music, this newcomer to the Kingston club scene has become the premier spot for nightlife with a swinging party every night of the week.

Grog Shoppe Devon House. Under new management and swinging again on Fridays, this bar/restaurant benefits from its beautiful location right beside the lit-up Devon House, where crowds circle around the bar below a giant cotton tree.

Indies 8 Holborn Rd, opposite the *Indies* hotel. Long-standing place with a central location, a mellow, friendly atmosphere and a big screen for sports events. There's a popular karaoke night on Thursday, an after-work jam on Fridays and

dancing on Saturday nights, with DJs playing hip-hop, soca, soul and reggae.

Jonkanoo Lounge *Hilton Kingston*, 77 Knutsford Blvd ☎ 926 5430. Relatively smart and sedate, as you'd expect from a hotel-based venue. Rarely crowded, it attracts a mature and upmarket clientele who come to dance or take in occasional live bands. Call ahead for details of special events.

Mingles *Courtleigh Hotel*, 85 Knutsford Blvd ☎ 929 9000. Indoor and outdoor sections of this in-hotel nightclub provide pleasant settings for a drink during the week.

Peppers 31 Upper Waterloo Rd. Late-opening and permanently popular outdoor bar that pulls in post-work drinkers and then younger clubbers, who pack out the outdoor dancefloor. There's a huge line of pool tables, and inexpensive Jamaican food is available. Especially good every other Saturday night when the bar hosts Kingston's best Latin party.

Pure Trinidad Terrace, in the heart of New Kingston. Modern, sophisticated and uber-trendy, Pure is the first lounge to open in Kingston and is a perfect spot for early evening cocktails. Patrons can take advantage of valet service, reserve a private VIP booth, enjoy bottle service, listen to great house music and feel like you're a million miles away from the island city outside the door. Above *Pure* is the nightclub *Plush*, with a lively dancefloor.

Quad 20–22 Trinidad Terrace, off Knutsford Blvd. Kingston's flashiest club, this upmarket indoor venue has Christopher's Jazz Café on the ground floor, a comfortable a/c lounge with a weekday happy hour (5–8pm). Above, Oxygen is a swish North American-style nightclub, playing commercial dance music for a youngish crowd; the Wednesday retro night is a good bet. The top-floor Voodoo Lounge is aimed at the slightly more mature punter, with music from the 1960s to 1990s and a small outdoor deck.

Red Bones Blues Café 21 Braemar Ave ☎ 978 8262. Sophisticated place for a quiet drink amongst a mixed crowd of expats and well-heeled locals. Look out for live music sessions, with everything from classical to blues and jazz, and a good wine list.

Truckstop 16 West Kings House Rd. New after-work spot with a great, lively vibe, breezy outdoor seating and a tasty jerk-based menu.

Village Café Orchid Village Plaza, Barbican Rd. One of Kingston's busiest bars, this open-air,

split-level venue at the top of a small plaza stages a range of popular and ever-changing events, including live music from up-and-coming acts to fashion shows from local designers. It's also a great place for a dance at the weekend.

Waterfalls 9 Mona Plaza, Liguanea ☎977 0652. Great Thursday nights with Merritone playing on the turntables. Much older crowd but nice vibes.

Theatre and dance

Next to nightlife, **theatre** is Kingston's strongest cultural suit. The performance scene is limited but buoyant, with a small core of first-rate writers, directors and actors – including Trevor Rhone, Oliver Samuels and David Heron – producing work of a high standard. Most of the plays are sprinkled with Jamaican patois, but you'll still get the gist. Comedies (particularly sexual romps and political satire) are popular, and the normally excellent annual **pantomime** – a musical with a message, totally different from the English variety – is a major event, running from December to April at both the **Ward Theatre** (☎922 0453; see p.67) and, later, the **Little Theatre** (☎926 6129; see p.72). Other theatres include the Barn, 5 Oxford Rd (☎926 6469), Center Stage Theatre, 18 Dominica Drive (☎968 7529), the Pantry Playhouse, 2 Dumfries Rd (☎960 9845), and the New Green Gables Playhouse, 6 Cargill Ave (☎920 0858). For details of performances, check the *Gleaner* or *Observer* newspapers, particularly the Friday entertainment sections. Many of these venues also stage dance performances featuring the acclaimed National Dance Theatre Company or L'Acadco; check the press to see what's on.

Shopping

As you'd expect, reggae fans are in shopping heaven in Kingston. Downtown's Orange Street is the place to go – you'll find loads of **record stores**, many of them attached to studios and pressing plants. For vinyl as well as CDs, GG's Records, on the corner of Orange Street and Parade, is particularly well stocked, and as vibrant and loud as its location. Prince Busta's, further down Orange Street, is known for its collection of rare oldies. Augustus Pablo's Rockers International, 135 Orange St, carries an extensive stock of old rock steady and reggae classics, and Techniques, at no. 99, has a good selection of old and new stock. Elsewhere, a good place to check is Rock and Groove Muzic, 8 Northside Plaza in Liguanea. Mobile Music, at Lane Plaza in Liguanea, has helpful staff and a good selection of reggae and R&B; Derrick Harriot's One Stop in Twin Gates Plaza, Constant Spring Road, is good for old and new reggae.

Kingston also has a vibrant art scene, and there are excellent **galleries** across the city, which host exhibitions by contemporary Jamaican artists (call to see what's on) as well as offering works for sale. The main players are the Frame Centre, 10 Tangerine Place (☎926 4644); Grosvenor Galleries, 1 Grosvenor Terrace (☎924 6684); the Bolivar Gallery, 1d Grove Rd (☎926 8799); Hi Q, Shop 19, Island Life Mall, 1 St Lucia Ave (☎926 4183); and the Mutual Gallery, 2 Oxford Rd (☎929 4302).

Listings

Airlines Air Canada, Norman Manley Airport ☎924 8211; Air Jamaica, 4 St Lucia Ave ☎1-888/359 2475; Air Link ☎940 6660; American Airlines, 26 Trafalgar Rd ☎924 8248-9 or 1-800/744 0006; British Airways, 25 Dominica Drive ☎929 9020–5, Norman Manley Airport ☎924 8187; Caribbean Airlines ☎1-800/744 2225; Cayman Airways, 23 Dominica Drive ☎926 1762 (reservations), ☎924 8092 (flight info); Continental, 81 Knutsford Blvd ☎1-800/231 0856; Delta ☎968 2623, 924 8180; Northwest/KLM ☎1-800/225 2525; Spirit Airlines ☎932 7137, 924 8636; Virgin Atlantic ☎924 8592.

Ambulances For a public ambulance, call ☎110 or St John's Ambulance on ☎926 7656; for a private ambulance, call Ambucare on ☎978 2327.

Banks and exchange The main banks have branches citywide; uptown branches with ATMs include: Citibank, 63 Knutsford Blvd; National Commercial Bank, 1–7 Knutsford Blvd and Northside Plaza, Hope Rd; RBTT, Sovereign Centre, 106 Hope Rd, 17 Dominica Drive, 6 St Lucia Ave; ScotiaBank, 125 Old Hope Rd, 2 Knutsford Blvd and 6 Oxford Rd. However, you'll get better rates at FX Trader (2–6 Trafford Place).

Car rental Reliable firms include: Alamo ☎908 2397; Avis, Norman Manley Airport ☎924 8542 or 1 Merrick Ave ☎926 8021; Budget, 53 South Camp Rd ☎759 1793, Norman Manley Airport ☎942 8762; Caribbean, 31 Old Hope Rd ☎926 6339; Econocars, 11 Lady Musgrave Rd ☎927 6761 or 9989; Island, 17 Antigua Ave ☎926 8012, Norman Manley Airport ☎924 8075.

Doctors and dentists Your hotel should be able to make recommendations. Otherwise, for doctors call Dr Trevor McCartney ☎927 766 or Dr Richard Gomes ☎563 0132. Reliable dentists include the Oxford Dental Centre, 22g Old Hope Rd ☎926 7311. For a pediatrician, try Dr Leslie Gabay ☎978 0907.

Embassies Almost all of the embassies and consulates are based in New Kingston. They include the British High Commission, 28 Trafalgar Rd ☎510 0700; the American Embassy, 142 Old Hope Rd, ☎970 2268; and the Canadian High Commission, 3 West Kings House Rd ☎926 1500.

Hospitals Kingston's best public hospital is the University Hospital at Mona (☎927 1620); otherwise there's the Kingston Public Hospital downtown on North St (☎922 0210), and the

Tours from Kingston

All of the places around Kingston can be explored on an **organized tour** from the city. You shouldn't need a tour to see Port Royal, which is small, safe and relaxed enough to wander around alone, as well as being a straightforward bus or taxi ride from the city. But a tour is not a bad option for Spanish Town, which is a bit awkward to get to and, with its ongoing violent outbursts, better navigated with someone who knows where they're going. Generally, you'll get a fuller perspective on all the sights by engaging the services of a tour company, many of which offer individualized, small-scale jaunts. **Our Story Tours** (☎377 5693, ⓔourstorytours @gmail.com) is brilliant for historical perspectives, offering custom-designed tours of Kingston, Spanish Town and Port Royal, Caymanas Park for horseracing, and other destinations across the island. Tours start at US$120 per day, with reductions for groups, and transport is extra. Another good option is Kingston-based **Sun Venture** (30 Balmoral Ave ☎960 6685, ⓦwww.sunventuretours.com), which offers interesting, professional day-long city tours of the more conventional sights – the National Gallery, Bob Marley Museum, Devon House, as well as Tuff Gong recording studios and out to Port Royal – for US$100 per person for two, less for larger groups. Sun Venture is also your best choice if heading into the Blue Mountains.

For the lowdown on the Kingston music scene, or just to see the capital from a locals' perspective, look no further than **Beat'n'Track Music Tours** (☎395 8959), where operator Andrea Lewis conducts excellent trips. A typical itinerary might have you checking out the record stores of Orange Street, visiting recording studios or even jamming with local musicians or hanging out with reggae stars. Other options include the Trench Town Culture Yard, Port Royal (including the Friday-night street jam), Hellshire, Caymanas mineral spring, Cane River and surfing at Bull Bay. Tours cost US$100 per person per day for transportation and guide (meals and entry fees are extra).

Bustamante Hospital for Children, Arthur Wint Drive (☎926 5721). There are a number of well-equipped private hospitals in New Kingston, including Medical Associates, 18 Tangerine Place ☎926 1400; Nuttall Memorial, 6 Caledonia Ave ☎926 2139; and Andrews Memorial, 27 Hope Rd ☎926 7401.

Internet Although there aren't many Internet cafés in Kingston, two reliable, a/c options are Sangsters bookstore in the Sovereign Center and the Liguanea Cyber Center at the Half Way Tree Post Office.

Pharmacies There are pharmacies at most of the shopping malls. Late-opening options are Monarch, at the Sovereign Centre (Mon–Fri 8am–10pm, Sat 9am–10pm, Sun 9am–8pm), York Pharmacy at the Half Way Tree junction (daily 8am–11pm), and Discount Pharmacy, Liguanea and Manor Park (8–11pm).

Police The main station is at 79 Duke St (☎922 9321). Stations uptown include Matilda's Corner, Old Hope Rd (☎926 6517). In an emergency, call ☎119.

Post offices The GPO is at 13 King St downtown, and there are post offices in the Liguanea Post Mall, 115 Hope Rd, in and at the airport. Stamps can also be bought at most hotels.

Sports International and major domestic soccer and cricket matches are played at the National Stadium call the Football Federation at ☎929 8036 and Sabina Park ☎967 0322 or 922 3338 respectively. Horseracing can be seen at Caymanas Park (☎922 3338 or 988 2523).

Taxis For JUTA taxis, call ☎924 8511. Reputable 24hr taxi companies include: El Shaddai ☎969 7633; Mortec ☎924 4833 or 925 5227; and On Time ☎926 3866.

Around Kingston

There are some excellent options around Kingston if you want to escape from the city for a day or two. The one-time pirate haunt of **Port Royal** in particular is well worth a day-trip, with nearby **Lime Cay** providing a good spot for a swim, too. **Spanish Town**, the nation's capital from 1534 to 1872, offers the third limb of Jamaica's "Historic Triangle" (with Kingston and Port Royal); half a day is more than ample to see the remains of the city's superb Georgian architecture and to tour the oldest Anglican cathedral in the "New World", while the Blue Mountains (see Chapter 2) and **Castleton Botanical Gardens** offer hiking and undisturbed nature. Just south of the city, **Hellshire**'s lovely white-sand bays are immensely popular at the weekends, both as a place to swim and to eat some of the best fried fish in Jamaica, and you can wash off the salt at the **Nature's Paradise mineral spring** behind Caymanas Polo Club.

East of Kingston

The main route east out of the city, Windward Road follows the coastline out of Kingston, scything through an industrial zone of oil tanks and a cement works that towers over the ruined defensive bastion of Fort Rock, now the **Rockfort Mineral Baths**. If the scenery looks familiar, you may be recalling the classic scene in the **James Bond** movie *Dr No*, in which Bond leaves Norman Manley Airport in a nifty red Sunbeam Alpine. A mile or so further on, turning right at the roundabout takes you on to the **Palisadoes**, a narrow ten-mile spit of land that leads out past the international airport to the ancient city of **Port Royal**, from where it's a short hop to the tiny island of **Lime Cay**.

Rockfort Mineral Baths

Huddled below the immense Carib Cement works and suffering somewhat from a surfeit of dust, **Rockfort Mineral Baths** (Tues–Fri 8am–4pm, Sat–Sun 7am–6pm;

Jamaica on film

From *Dr No* to the *Blue Lagoon*, with *Club Paradise* and *The Mighty Quinn* in between, Hollywood has long used Jamaica as a tropical backdrop against which tales of international adventure and romance are set. Dig a bit deeper, though, and you'll find a solid tradition of Jamaican film-making. The island's best-known and best-loved movie is Perry Henzell's **The Harder They Come**, which tells the story of Ivan (played by Jimmy Cliff) as he strives to make a better life for himself in Kingston. Pulling no punches in its gritty depiction of life in 1970s Jamaica, it offers a unique window into the life of the "sufferer", and has rightly become a cult classic. Equally realistic but with a dollop of humour, **Smile Orange** (1974) features Ringo, a head waiter in a resort hotel, played by Carl Bradshaw, who uses all his guile and wit on tourists to overcome the harsh economic realities of contemporary Jamaica. Unsurprisingly, it still has plenty of relevance today, and is well worth seeking out despite the often poor audio quality.

The man who brought Bob Marley to the attention of the world, Jamaican impresario Chris Blackwell has also had a hand in classic Jamaican films. As well as acting as location scout on *Dr No* in 1962 and releasing *The Harder They Come* soundtrack on his Island label, he established Island Pictures in 1982 with the production of **Countryman**, a gorgeous tale woven around a scheme operated by corrupt government officials to discredit their opposition through the framing of two innocent American tourists as CIA gunrunners, and with a killer soundtrack to boot. Island were also behind **The Lunatic**, adapted by Jamaican author Anthony Winkler from his novel. An engaging, achingly funny mixture of burlesque humour, folklore and satirical comment on the sexual tourism prevalent in Jamaica, it stars Paul Campbell as the insane Aloysius. Campbell also starred in both **Dancehall Queen** (1997) and **Third World Cop** (1999), which together defined modern Jamaican cinema. The former tracks the fortunes of Marcia (played by Audrey Reid) as she struggles to support her family by way of being crowned dancehall queen; its underlying themes of incest and the exploitation of women generated plenty of controversy in Jamaica, and it still makes for a gripping watch. *Third World Cop*, meanwhile, takes the stock characters, action sequences and narrative cliché associated with the modern Hollywood action thriller and fleshes them out with distinctively Jamaican motivations and language, with Campbell playing the truly sinister baddie, Capone. A Jamaican take on the classic gangster movie, **Shottas** (2002) mines the same vein of violence, albeit much more graphically, with Kymani Marley and DJ Spragga Benz playing two Kingston boys who take their life of crime from Jamaica to the US. Released in 2005, the sweet and delightful **One Love** represents a departure from the action genre; producer Sheelagh Farrell deliberately avoided focusing on the drugs-and-guns Jamaica, instead choosing to concentrate on the social tensions created when a pastor's daughter falls controversially in love with a Rasta musician.

J$250 to use the pool) offers one of the few public swimming pools in the Kingston area, as well as private spa pools seating two to twelve people. This was the site of the British Fort Rock, first strengthened against a threatened French invasion in 1694 and remanned in 1865 amid fears that the Morant Bay Rebellion further east might spread to Kingston. Today, the baths sit in a neat modern facility and offer a chance to enjoy some laid-back pampering. Fed by a spring high in the hills that appeared following the 1907 earthquake, the mineral spas are all fitted with jacuzzis, and you're allowed to wallow in them for up to 45 minutes. Piped from a local spring, the mineral water is moderately radioactive; it's claimed that the radioactivity helps to infuse the therapeutic minerals into the body. Therapeutic massage is available using natural essential oils, and there's a canteen serving Jamaican food.

The hills above Rockfort rise up to the **Dallas Mountains**, named after Robert Dallas, a local eighteenth-century plantation owner whose grandson, George

Miflin Dallas, became vice president of the United States in 1845 and founded the eponymous city in Texas.

Port Royal

PORT ROYAL, a short drive from downtown Kingston, once captured the spirit of early colonial adventure. For several decades in the late seventeenth century, Port Royal was a riotous town – the notorious haunt of cut-throats and buccaneers, and condemned by the church as the "the wickedest city in the world". Little of that past remains, and it's now a pleasant and hospitable little town, home to the base of the Jamaica Defence Force Coastguard and a small fishing industry. Port Royal depends largely on visitors for its income, and you'll find a number of popular eating places around town, including a few excellent seafood joints. Port Royal is also the place to take off for an outing to Lime Cay, a small sandy cay that offers lovely swimming and snorkelling.

Some history

In 1655, when the English sailed into what is now Kingston harbour they passed a cay known as "cayo de carena", as it was where the Spanish careened their vessels to clean and caulk them. Having captured Spanish Town, the invaders set about fortifying this point, eventually building five separate **forts** to defend the inner harbour (the world's seventh largest) and the town, soon to be called Port Royal, that grew up within. Over the next fifteen years, Port Royal grew through trade and was enriched by the booty of the **buccaneers** armed with royal commissions. It was recognized that its location at the entrance to the harbour of what became Jamaica's capital city, Kingston, needed to be strengthened and several fortifications were built in the tumultuous period between 1655 and 1692, the year of the catastrophic **earthquake**, which swallowed two-thirds of the landmass. Port Royal never recovered its mercantile prominence, although it remained the western Caribbean headquarters of the Royal Navy for two centuries.

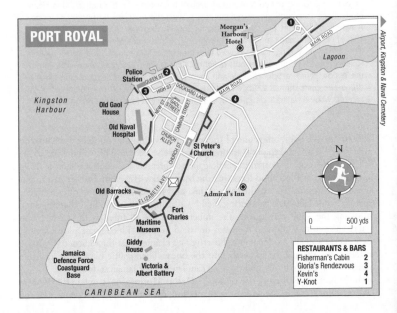

Pirates and buccaneers

To assist with the defence of their new Caribbean colonies, English, French and Dutch governors turned to the **buccaneers**, who were more than willing to plunder Spain's towns in the Caribbean and Gulf of Mexico. The earliest buccaneers were a ragged assortment of deserters, fugitives and even runaway slaves who banded together on the island of Tortuga on the Atlantic coast of present-day Haiti. They lived by hunting wild pigs and cattle (brought to the island by European settlers), smoking their meat on a wooden frame over a pit known as a *boucan* (hence the name *boucaniers*). When the game became scarce they took to the open sea to prey on shipping, especially Spanish.

As their numbers and their skills increased, the buccaneers became a serious fighting force under resourceful leaders like **Henry Morgan**, who had arrived with the English army. Morgan's successful sack of the city of Panama with three thousand men in 1671 coincided with the conclusion of a peace treaty between England and Spain. After a brief incarceration in the Tower of London to appease the Spanish, Morgan returned to Jamaica as Lieutenant Governor with a mandate to eradicate what was now deemed piracy.

Reminders of the era of piracy at Port Royal include Gallows Point at the end of the promontory and, offshore, Rackham's Cay where "**Calico Jack**" Rackham, after being executed, was squeezed into a cage and hung in the air as a warning to others. His two accomplices, Anne Bonney and Mary Read, escaped punishment by declaring themselves pregnant.

Getting there

Since the ferry service from Kingston's waterfront was scrapped in 2004, the only way to get to Port Royal is to **drive** – follow the signs southeast from Kingston to the airport and bear left at the roundabout halfway along the Palisadoes – or to take **bus** #98, which leaves from the Parade in downtown Kingston. A **taxi** will set you back around US$25 in each direction, though you may well be able to negotiate.

The Town

Port Royal is easily navigable on foot. Head straight on along the main road into town, here called Church Street, and you'll reach **St Peter's Church**, built in 1725 on the site of a church lost in the earthquake. It contains several examples of fine commemorative art and a beautiful eighteenth-century organ loft. You will need to call Rhona Wade ("Molly") at ☏899-1315 to arrange entry. Ask to see the exquisite communion plate said to be a gift of Sir Henry Morgan. More interesting though, are the ancient tombs in the small and rambling graveyard, particularly that of the Frenchman **Lewis Galdy**. Swallowed by the earthquake in 1692, an eruption seconds later spat him out into the sea from where, amazingly, he scrambled to safety and lived until 1739.

A left turn out of the church leads down to fascinating **Fort Charles** (daily 9am–5pm; J$200). Originally known as Fort Cromwell (but renamed after King Charles II was restored to the British throne in 1660). The present fort looks much as it did in 1692, except that then it was immediately bordered by the sea on three sides. Clearly identified is Nelson's Quarterdeck, where the hero of the Battle of Trafalgar, Horatio Nelson, served as a young lieutenant in the English navy. There are two small museums containing artefacts recovered from the sunken city. The two structures that now stand between the fort and the water both date from the 1880s. The squat, rectangular **Giddy House**, an ammunition store, partially sank in 1907, while the circular bunker beside it was the **Victoria and Albert Battery**, an emplacement for a nineteenth-century supergun that was fired only once. The 1907 earthquake dropped the gun turret several yards into the earth, while the storeroom somehow remained intact but tilted making walking across it without slipping over a challenge.

Other points of interest in Port Royal lead you to head back along Church Street the way you've come, turning left after St Peter's Church, then right and third left onto Gaol Street. On Gaol Street stands the **Old Gaol**, a sturdy example of shipwrights' work which has survived fourteen hurricanes, six earthquakes and two disastrous fires in the area. Turn left at the end of Gaol Street onto New Street and, behind the old garrison wall, you'll find the decaying red bricks of the **Old Naval Hospital**. Built by the Bowling Ironworks in Bradford, England, the two-storey iron prefab, shipped over and erected here in 1819, remains the oldest prefabricated structure in the New World. Unfortunately it has been closed since it was damaged in Hurricane Gilbert.

Slightly out of town on the road back to Kingston, the **Naval Cemetery** – its entrance marked by an anchor-shaped memorial to the crew of HMS *Goshawk*, who drowned when their vessel sank in Port Royal harbour – marks the final resting place of many of Port Royal's long-forgotten sailors. Buccaneer-turned-enforcer Henry Morgan (see box, p.85) was buried here too, but the earthquake tipped his body into the sea, along with a large part of the old graveyard.

Finally, there are a couple of **beaches** around Port Royal, but both sea and sand are pretty dirty; if you want to **swim**, you're better off taking a boat out to Lime Cay. The hotel can arrange deep-sea **fishing**, and evening drop-line fishing (check the front desk for current rates), while the owners of *Admiral's Inn* (see opposite; rates negotiable) offer **boat rides** into the mangrove swamps.

Lime Cay and other islands

Just fifteen minutes from Port Royal, **Lime Cay** is a tiny uninhabited island with white sand, blue water and easy snorkelling. It was here that Ivanhoe ("Rhygin") Martin – the cop-killing gangster and folk-hero immortalized in the classic Jamaican movie *The Harder They Come* – met his demise in 1948. Boats run regularly from Port Royal, from *Y-Knot* and *Morgan's Harbour* (see opposite); both

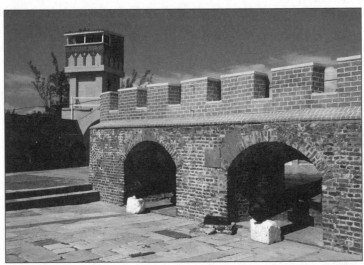

▲ Fort Charles, Port Royal

establishments' boats are well maintained and carry life jackets. The per-person fare is J$700 return or J$350 for kids; tell the boatman what time you want to be picked up. Alternatively, you can ask one of the fishermen around the ferry pier to take you – their going rates may be a little cheaper. Though you'll often find the beach deserted on weekdays (bring your own refreshments), it's a very different story at the weekends, when hordes of Kingstonians descend to display their latest designer swimwear and relax with friends, and music blares from the stalls selling cooked meals and cold beers.

If you desperately want your own private island, ask to be dropped at **Maiden Cay**, a tiny, shadeless sandspit, or **Twin Cays**, shadier but with poorer swimming than at Lime Cay. En route to any of these, you'll pass the once heavily armed **Gun Cay**, still bearing evidence of its eighteenth-century fortification by the British, and the fast-disappearing **Rackham's Cay**, a visible victim of beach erosion.

Practicalities

The glitziest place to **stay** in Port Royal is the elegant and atmospheric *Morgan's Harbour Hotel* (℡967 8075 or 8280; ❺–❽). Recently refurbished, the hotel is all dark wood and seafaring charm, with a pool, a gaming lounge, two restaurants and a salt-licked open-air bar. Rooms boast all mod cons, and most have a balcony overlooking the harbour; no. 105 was the setting for the *Dr No* scene in which James Bond is woken by the attentions of a large spider. Bond also tumbles amongst crates of Red Stripe at the bar, transformed for the movie into "*Puss Fellers*" nightclub. The only other option in town is the excellent *Admiral's Inn* (℡353 4202 or 365 6839, 750 0391; ❷), a friendly, family-run place in the housing scheme to the left by *Kevin's* restaurant as you enter Port Royal. The spic-and-span en-suite rooms have king, double or twin beds and a/c, fridge and microwave; there's a pretty garden out back, with a gazebo and a bar and grill where delicious fish and lobster are cooked up. The owners offer Lime Cay trips, boat tours and airport pick-ups and drop-offs with advance notice.

In terms of **eating**, *Morgan's Harbour Hotel* has two restaurants: the relatively informal *Red Jack*, with tables overlooking the harbour and a menu of sandwiches, salads, seafood and Jamaican dishes, and the more upscale *Quartermain*, serving up lovely plates of seafood. There are several cheaper eating options near the police station serving Port Royal's best fish and seafood, the stuff that Jamaicans will drive miles to get. The most popular is *Gloria's Rendezvous* at 5 Queen St, with shaded tables right on the road and inside, where you can enjoy a tasty and inexpensive plate of fish and bammy, or lobster and shrimp (the garlic shrimp is particularly good) and watch the pelicans and frigate birds fishing just offshore. Just down the road, *Fisherman's Cabin*, much less smart but with tables right by the water and on a short pier. You can also buy fried fish from stalls in the main square, and on Friday evening, make a beeline for the curried crab and conch soup sold at the *Martin's Sweetness* cart – it's delicious and usually runs out around 7pm.

The *Angler's Club*, at the corner of the square on Dockyard Lane, opens up for some hard **drinking**, and on Fridays, speakers are stacked up in the main square for an outdoor **party**. A friendly crowd piles down from Kingston, and it's a great opportunity to enjoy a very easy-going Jamaican street dance. Set around a large wooden deck over the water adjacent to *Morgan's Harbour*, *Y-Knot* (℡967 8448-9) is another excellent spot for a drink, a dance and something to eat. Most Kingstonians take their Lime Cay boats from here, and it's a busy scene at the weekends, with sand-dusted Cay visitors piling off the boats and heading straight to the bar, dancers staking out their portion of the deck and swift business at the charcoal grill. The fish, lobster, chicken and shrimp are cooked to perfection here, and the conch soup is excellent.

West of Kingston

Southwest of Kingston, off Marcus Garvey Drive, a **causeway** connects the city to the bland but booming dormitory town of **PORTMORE**. Home to an estimated 200,000 people (and built to accommodate far fewer, as the recent strain on the sewage system illustrates), Portmore itself has nothing much of interest save its **racecourse** and a few shopping malls. But **Port Henderson**, a brief detour away, has a handful of colonial-era relics and fine views across Kingston harbour. Below Portmore, the road cuts across the eastern fringe of the **Hellshire Hills** – a vast and scrubby limestone expanse – and down to Hellshire's white-sand **beaches**. Further northwest, the former capital city of **Spanish Town**, a run-down shadow of its former self, still retains some graceful architecture.

Caymanas Park racetrack

Once you've crossed the causeway, taking the right turn (Dawkins Drive) rather than the left onto Augusta Drive brings you into Portmore proper, an immense maze of identikit residential streets. You'll soon come to a roundabout adjacent to the Portmore Mall. Turn right at the PetCom petrol station onto Portmore Parkway, left at the sewage tank onto Passage Fort Drive and you'll see signs for **Caymanas Park** (℡ 988 2523). It's one of the best racetracks in the Caribbean, with a gorgeous backdrop of the Blue Mountains and Kingston shimmering across the harbour. Meets are held most Wednesdays and Saturdays (call ahead to check) and make a great day out, with much commentary and cursing from racegoers adding to the colourful scene. You can sit either in the air-conditioned North Stand (J$275) or, for a lot less, in the Grand Stand or outdoor bleachers, a more raucous affair with plenty of catcalls and shrieks of encouragement from the punters. You can visit Caymanas on your own, but you'll undoubtedly have a better time if you go with Our Story Tours (see p.81), with whom you'll get an explanation of the labyrinthine betting system as well as lunch and a seat in the North Stand; trips cost US$150 for 1–2 people, and include transportation and entry fee. Our Story Tours can also take you to nearby stud farms to see the horses up close.

Hellshire and around

Covered in low, dense scrub and towering cacti, the arid **Hellshire Hills** extend for around a hundred square miles west of Kingston. From Port Henderson, the signposted road to the Hellshire beaches runs under the flanks of the Hellshire Hills, passing a huge scar in the mountainside gouged out to provide marl for construction of Portmore's homes. Just before the quarry stands an abandoned high-rise building, formerly the *Forum Hotel*, built by the government in an unsuccessful attempt to entice tourists to the area. Past here, the road hits the coast again beside the **Great Salt Pond**. An old Taino fishing spot, the pond is a site of ecological significance that continues to be polluted by excesses from Portmore's woefully inadequate sewerage system. From there the road carries on to **Fort Clarence beach** (Mon–Fri 10am–5pm, Sat & Sun 8am–7pm; J$200), a pretty stretch of white sand and choppy waves (there's no outlying reef to protect the beach). Owned by the Urban Development Company (UDC), Fort Clarence is often used as a venue for dancehall stageshows, but it's a lovely place for a swim, with decent changing rooms and toilets and a snack shop/bar, and gets busy with families at the weekends. Lifeguards are on duty during opening hours.

If you're after atmosphere, though, it's far better to press on to **Hellshire beach** (no set hours; free), separated from Fort Clarence by a barrier reef that makes the water here a lot calmer. Hellshire is buzzing at the weekends, with sound systems (particularly on a Sunday) and a party atmosphere. Also present at the weekends are **watersports operators** touting jet skis and snorkelling equipment, while horses (wearing fetching eye-gear to protect against flying sand grains) parade up and down giving children rides. The powdery dunes are peppered with family groups that haven't been able to nab one of the wooden loungers set up under the shady eaves of the area's multiple **fish joints**, delightfully ramshackle and wholeheartedly Jamaican affairs which compete to sell the freshest fish, lobster and festival. Most Jamaicans come here for the food as much as the sea and sand, and Hellshire fried fish, best eaten with festival and vinegary home-made pepper sauce, is utterly delicious. The best cook shop is ℱ *Prendy's on the Beach*, directly in front of you as you follow the sandy main road in. You select your fish or lobster, have it weighed in front of you and receive a ticket showing the price, and you then choose how you want it cooked, and whether you want side orders of festival or bammy. As well as fried fish, *Prendy's* does a divine version of steamed fish, cooked in a thick pumpkin soup with potatoes, vegetables and bammy. If *Prendy's* is overrun, *Flo's* next door is also a good bet.

The only place to **stay** in the area is the friendly *Hellshire Beach Club* (☏ 989 8306; ⬤), a cavernous white building with a pool and restaurant. The clean, tiled rooms have air conditioning, fan and TV; the ceiling mirrors are a hint as to why most people rent by the hour.

Bus #1A from Parade and Half Way Tree in Kingston runs roughly every hour to the Hellshire beaches.

Practicalities

Buses and **minibuses** run to Port Henderson from Parade and to Portmore from Parade and Half Way Tree. There is nowhere to **stay** in Port Henderson itself, but Augusta Drive is lined with accommodation options, most of them short-time "motel no-tells" for couples seeking a discreet rendezvous. Despite being right on the sea, these aren't places with a holiday vibe, and there's little reason to stay here. *Rodney's Arms*, justifiably the most popular local **eatery**, serves excellent seafood in an atmospheric colonial-era setting. In terms of **entertainment**, *La Roose* on Augusta Drive is a lively venue for dancehall shows and sound-system parties (go with a Jamaican friend).

Spanish Town

Spanish Town, which was called St Jago de la Vega when it was found by the Spanish in 1534, remained the island's capital under the English until 1872. It sits 12 miles west of Kingston and these days contains only vestigial traces of its former glory. Although it attracts few tourists, it's still worth a half-day visit. Away from its vibrant buzzing streets is **Parade Square**, which holds possibly the finest collection of Georgian architecture in the Americas. A classical memorial to Admiral Rodney, who defeated the French in 1782 in the Battle of Les Saintes, dominates the northern side. An adjoining structure houses the National Archives (Mon–Thurs 9.30am–3.30pm, Fri 9am–3.30pm; free) containing a unique collection of records dating back to the seventeenth century.

Directly opposite the memorial on Parade Square is the Georgian-style parish **courthouse**, which replaced the original nineteenth-century structure destroyed by fire in 1986. On the westsssss of the square is the porticoed, red-brick facade of the **King's House**, built in 1762, the residence of Jamaica's governors until the capital was moved to Kingston in 1872. A plaque can be seen commemorating a proclamation declaring full emancipation from slavery in 1838. A catastrophic fire destroyed all but the facade of the King's House nearly a century ago. Also on the west side of the square sits the former House of Assembly, once the house of the island's governing body and now the parish offices.

From Parade Square, walk south down White Church Street to reach the **Cathedral of St Jago de la Vega** (daily 9am–5pm; free). It stands on the foundations of the sixteenth-century Church of the Red Cross and black-and-white tiles in the aisle are thought to date from the Spanish building. Important monuments crowd the cathedral, many of them carved in England by leading sculptors of the time such as John Bacon and John Wilton, reflecting the status and wealth of the colony during the eighteenth century. Inside, two chapels, the Blessed Sacrament Chapel and the Lady Chapel, contain memorials to former governors. Outside, you can spend an hour exploring and deciphering the ancient gravestones under the mango trees.

North of parade Square, at French and Williams streets, the ramshackle **Philippo's Church** is associated with James Philippo, a Baptist who campaigned for the abolition of slavery and the establishment of "free villages" for emancipated slaves, one of which is the nearby Sligoville.

When leaving Spanish Town, it's possible to pass the old **Iron Bridge** spanning the Rio Cobre. No longer in use for vehicular traffic, it was erected in 1801 after being cast in England and was the first of its kind in the Americas.

Practicalities

Spanish Town lies to the west of the Rio Cobre, with Bourkes Road, the main highway from Kingston, running across its southern end, fifteen minutes' walk from the central square. If you're **driving** from Kingston, you can go on the new highway, but it's easier to follow the old Mandela Highway: take Washington Boulevard (from uptown) or Marcus Garvey Drive (from downtown) out of the city, a half-hour journey. The Spanish Town turn-off is signposted at the huge roundabout at the end of the first section of Mandela. **Bus** #21A runs regularly from New Kingston to the terminus on Bourkes Road, while a **taxi** from New Kingston costs about US$20. Once here, the main sights can easily be explored on foot, as the city is still laid out on its original neat grid system.

North of Kingston

The main A3 artery shoots north from Kingston, shearing first through the affluent Stony Hill suburbs, all electric gates, expansive driveways and barking guard dogs. First stop, fourteen miles along, is **Castleton Botanical Gardens** (daily 9am–5pm; free), which occupy fifteen acres adjacent to the Wag Water River. Established in 1862, with support from London's Kew Gardens, Castleton quickly became the best-stocked garden in the Caribbean, and many of the plants that now dominate the island – the ubiquitous **poinciana** for example – were first introduced here. Despite the damage caused by recent hurricanes (and by official neglect), the gardens are still an important research station and well worth a stop if you're passing.

Beyond Castleton, the A3 winds a beautiful – but demanding if you're driving – route to Annotto Bay on the north coast (see Chapter 2, p.130). The road runs parallel to the Wag Water River and offers occasional marvellous views of the rocky river bed below. About halfway to the coast, the tiny community of **Friendship Gully** – better known to all as Junction – offers a couple of places to break your journey with a snack at a fried chicken/Chinese food joint or a small Jamaican eatery.

The Blue Mountains and the east

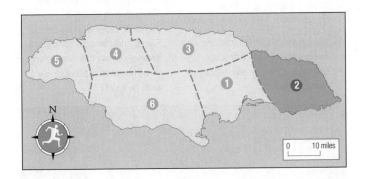

CHAPTER 2 # Highlights

✳ **Hiking in the Blue Mountains** From the arduous ascent for sunrise at Blue Mountain Peak to the nearly-as-spectacular climb to Cinchona Botanical Gardens, hiking in the region is the perfect antidote to beach inertia. See p.98

✳ **Sunday Brunch at Strawberry Hill Hotel** If you can't afford to stay in the finest hotel around Kingston, its Sunday brunch buffet is the next best thing. Take in a panoramic view of the capital while enjoying Caribbean gourmet food at its best. See p.102

✳ **Port Antonio** Small, historic town with lots of character set around two pretty bays. See p.113

✳ **The Blue Lagoon** To many water-lovers, the single most impressive site in Jamaica, made famous in the film of the same name. The "bottomless" lagoon features a curious mix of warm sea and cool fresh water. See p.121

✳ **Winnifred Beach** One of the last public beaches in Portland and the most atmospheric, with horse rides along the sand and little shacks serving fresh fried fish. See p.122

✳ **Rafting on the Rio Grande** The best rafting trip in Jamaica, pioneered by Errol Flynn. The bamboo rafts glide serenely down the river, taking three hours to reach journey's end. See p.127

▲ Pool at *Strawberry Hill Hotel*

2

The Blue Mountains and the east

owering behind Kingston and enticingly visible from anywhere in the island's eastern third, the **Blue Mountains** conform with few people's mental image of Jamaica, land of sand, sea and reggae. Forming one of the longest continuous ranges in the Caribbean, their cool, fragrant woodlands are shrouded in mist, and offer some of the best hiking on the island, including **Blue Mountain Peak**, the remarkable **botanical gardens** at Cinchona and estates producing some of the most expensive **coffee** on earth.

South of the range, **St Thomas** is one of the country's poorest and least developed regions, despite a rich history. Tourist development remains negligible and there are only a handful of hotels, but these are good bases nonetheless to visit the delightful mineral springs at **Bath**, or the deserted beaches around **Morant Point Lighthouse**.

Contrasting in scenery and atmosphere, on the other side of the mountains is the northeastern parish of **Portland**, justifiably touted as one of the most beautiful parts of Jamaica, with jungle-smothered hillsides cascading down to postcard-perfect Caribbean shoreline. Tourism is less conspicuous here than the other resorts, but it's all the more reason to come – the wetter climate supports some stupendous natural scenery, including beautiful waterfalls and the magical **Blue Lagoon**. The parish capital, **Port Antonio**, has plenty of historical charm, while inland you can hike in pristine **rainforest** or take a gentler rafting trip on the **Rio Grande**. Some of the island's best **beaches** are also found here, and they're far less crowded than those further west, with lovely places to stay to boot: the idyllic, surf-pounded stretch at Long Bay has become a haven for backpackers, who come for the waves and chilled-out atmosphere.

The main **A4 highway** runs all the way around the coastline of Portland and St Thomas, with most points reachable by bus and route taxi, though you'll need a car to explore much of the interior. Bear in mind unpredictable schedules for public transport (particularly in the mountains); ask around for probable departure times and try to travel during the morning.

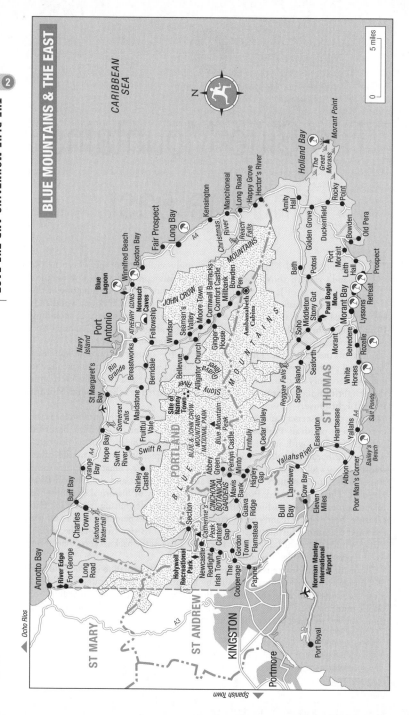

BLUE MOUNTAINS & THE EAST

CARIBBEAN SEA

N

0   5 miles

The Blue Mountains

The **Blue Mountains** begin where Kingston ends, and a starker contrast would be hard to imagine, with the chaotic concrete maelstrom fast replaced by lush tranquillity and staggering natural beauty. The mountains are named for the mists that colour them from a distance, and their craggy slopes form an unbroken, undulating spine across Jamaica's easternmost parishes, a fabulously fertile wilderness with a surprisingly cool, wet climate. The dense forest provided perfect cover for the Windward Maroons during the seventeenth and eighteenth centuries, though as a whole the mountains have proved largely inhospitable, with today's sparse population concentrated in settlements like **Gordon Town** and **Newcastle.**

The northern slopes of the mountains are covered by a huge quilt of dense, primary forest, but deforestation has badly affected the southern side, where great chunks have been cleared by coffee planters, farmers, and (catastrophically) hurricanes Gilbert

The mountain environment

The Blue Mountain range is Jamaica's oldest geographical feature, formed in the Cretaceous period (between 144 and 65 million years ago). Though the peaks are named for their cerulean tint when seen from afar, some of the rock actually is coloured blue by crossite minerals.

Categorized as montane (high-altitude woodland), the **forests** are mostly native cedar, soapwood, sweetwood and dogwood evergreens, with a few blue mahoe, mahogany and teak trees, but the eucalyptus and Caribbean pines introduced in the 1950s are also having an impact. The primeval-looking cyathea (**tree fern**), with its diamond-patterned trunk and top-heavy fronds is particularly distinctive; the tallest are more than 150 years old. Below the dense canopy are **shrubs**, of which the red tubular flowers of the cigar bush are the most identifiable. Every tree trunk or exposed rock is festooned with brightly coloured epiphytes, including inexhaustible swathes of dirty lime-coloured old man's beard. Wild strawberries, raspberries, blackberries and rose apples provide a free feast, and you'll doubtless encounter prickly climbing bamboo, the only variety native to Jamaica; each one blossoms simultaneously with tiny white flowers once every 33 years, – your next chance to see them is 2017. Alongside are over five hundred species of **flowering plant**, including 65 varieties of orchid. Begonias, blue iris, agapanthus, lobelias, busy lizzies and fuschias proliferate, while wild ginger lilies lend a delicate perfume.

Other than mongooses, coneys and the wild pigs that roam the northern slopes, there are few **mammals**. You may hear the scuffles of feral cats, mice and rats in the undergrowth, and a few Jamaican yellow boas inhabit the lower slopes. The presence of bats is poorly documented; you're most likely to see them around the limestone slopes of the John Crow Mountains to the east. By contrast, **bird life** flourishes; the forests ring out with the evocative whistle of the rufous-throated solitaire, and mockingbirds, crested quail doves (known as mountain witches), white-eyed thrushes, blackbirds and Jamaican todys add to the cacophony, backed by the squeaking mating calls of tree frogs.

The mountains are the sole habitat of one of the rarest and largest **butterflies** in the world, the six-inch **giant swallowtail**, but its distinctively patterned dark brown and gold wings rarely flutter into view – again, the warmer John Crow range yields the most sightings. Insects, on the other hand, are multitudinous – in summer it's common to see thousands of **fireflies** (known as peenie-wallies) clustering on a single bush and lighting it up like a Christmas tree.

and Ivan in 1988 and 2004. Though cattle is farmed on some of the denuded lower slopes, to try to protect the wilderness from further devastation, 200,000 acres were designated as a **national park** in 1993, with the stated aims of managing natural resources for long-term sustainable use and generating income opportunities through eco-tourism. To help in the latter, great **hiking trails** have been carved into the interior of the forest, often following ancient mule trails over the mountains.

Tourism here is small-scale with just a few hotels and budget options – though most have spectacular locations. **Coffee** is the mainstay of the local economy, and excellent **tours** for those keen to see how the stuff is produced are found at the coffee factory at **Mavis Bank** and smaller plantations at **Old Tavern** and **Craighton**. Dark and earthy, Blue Mountain coffee is considered one of the world's best by experts, and prices reflect that assessment, though you can usually find it cheaper here – at hotels, coffee factories or direct from the farmers – than anywhere else. Visitors also come here to hike up **Blue Mountain Peak** or to follow the well-maintained trails at **Holywell** – superb trekking for which you'll nonetheless need to be well prepared. Elsewhere, the botanical gardens at **Cinchona** are a delightful spot, a magical splash of colour 5000ft up.

Many visitors find mountain residents more gentle and welcoming than Jamaicans elsewhere – despite the evident poverty and grinding workload many of them face.

Getting around

You'll need a **car** to get the most out of the mountains. The principal access road, the **B1** (Gordon Town Road), leads straight from Papine in northeast Kingston though the southern edge of the Mona Valley before winding upward into the riverine hills. Continuing straight ahead at tiny hamlet **The Cooperage** leads to Gordon Town and then Mavis Bank, the main access point for Blue Mountain Peak, whereas a left turn here climbs precipitously up to Irish Town, the army barracks at Newcastle and onwards to Section. The road from here down to **Buff Bay** on the north coast has been impassable since landslides in 2004, though there's a good chance of its repair in the next year or so – ask around. Roads throughout the mountains come in for heavy assault during the wet season so expect some bone-rattling, though you won't need a 4WD unless you plan to head off the main routes, such as to Cinchona or Abbey Green. Though roads appear wide enough only for a single vehicle, snorting delivery trucks loaded with precariously balanced crates of Red Stripe frequently barrel up the slopes, sounding their presence with mighty blasts on the horn. It's wise to turn off the radio here and listen out, while also announcing your own presence with regular toots on the horn.

Minibuses and **route taxis** (roughly J$150) also ply the major routes from Papine to Redlight (via Irish Town), Gordon Town and Mavis Bank, though schedules are nonexistent and frequency poor – it's always best to travel first thing in the morning, or to arrange transport through your hotel. Avoid starting out on a Sunday.

Cycling is an attractive option with several hotels offering daylong biking expeditions, calling in at small coffee farms and private homes, among them *Mount Edge Guesthouse* (see p.99) and *Forres Park* (see p.103). Blue Mountain Tours (T 974 7075, W www.bmtoursja.com; US$93 including transfer, brunch, lunch and refreshments) is an excellent option for a day-trip; they'll drive you up into the mountains and let you freewheel eighteen miles or so down to Fishdone waterfall near Buff Bay.

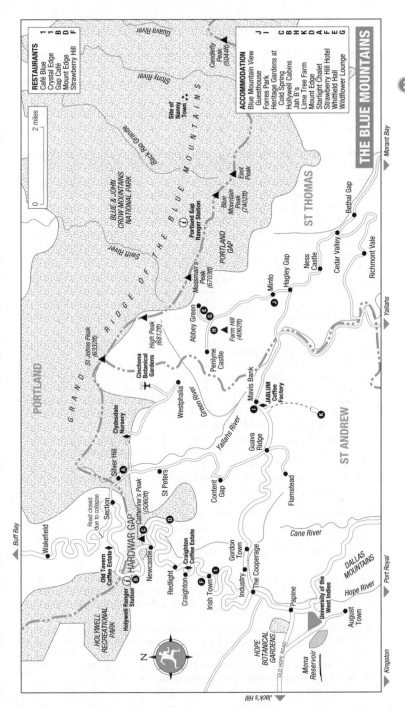

RESTAURANTS

Café Blue	1
Crystal Edge	B
Gap Café	1
Mount Edge	D
Strawberry Hill	F

ACCOMMODATION

Blue Mountain View Guesthouse	J
Forres Park	I
Heritage Gardens at Cold Spring	C
Hollywell Cabins	B
Jah B's	K
Lime Tree Farm	H
Mount Edge	D
Starlight Chalet	A
Strawberry Hill Hotel	F
Whitfield Hall	E
Wildflower Lounge	G

THE BLUE MOUNTAINS

Irish Town, Newcastle and Section

Taking the B1 from Papine, you follow the Hope River, which carries floodwater into the Mona Dam, its banks reinforced with high concrete walls. At around a mile and a half, the small village **THE COOPERAGE** is wrapped around a road junction. It's named for the Irish coopers who worked here in the early nineteenth century, making the wooden barrels in which Blue Mountain coffee was shipped abroad. A left turn here leads up a precipitous winding road which continues for three miles to **Irish Town**, dominated by the best hotel in the Kingston area,

Hiking in the Blue Mountains

Extreme weather conditions, ecological protection projects and lack of funding mean that of the thirty recognized **trails** in the national park, only twenty or so are open at any given time; information on weather conditions and trail access is available at the main **ranger station**, located at Holywell, and at smaller stations at Portland Gap and Millbank (not always manned). Ordnance survey maps are also on display. Phone contact is available through the Jamaica Conservation and Development Trust in Kingston, which runs the park. Bear in mind that hiking in the rainy season (May–June & Sept–Oct) pretty much guarantees getting drenched.

All usual common-sense guidelines apply to mountain hiking. Bring decent boots or shoes, plentiful **drinking water** (pine bromeliads hold much water between their leaves, but as they're home to insect nymphs and tree frogs, you'll only be tempted to sup in an emergency), snacks, insect repellent, and a flashlight in the event of unforeseen circumstances.

Guides and organized groups

It's almost always advisable to use a **guide** in the Blue Mountains; given changeable weather conditions and poor maps (alongside few obvious landmarks), it's very easy to get lost. Security can also be a problem for unaccompanied hikers, particularly on the Kingston side of the mountains. A guide will ensure your safety, clear overgrown paths and provide an informed commentary. Most hotels in the mountains are a good starting point for information and guided tours.

Forres Park Mavis Bank ☏927 8275 or 977 8141, ⊛www.forrespark.com. This recently expanded hotel and coffee farm organizes hiking and cycling tours, birding trips and transport across the national park (US$150/day per small group).

Jamaica Conservation and Development Trust 29 Dumbarton Ave, Kingston ☏960 2848/9, ⊛www.greenjamaica.org.jm. Conservation organization that manages trails at the Holywell park and organizes hikes across the old Maroon Cunha Cunha Pass trail between the Blue and John Crow mountain ranges; US$10–$50.

Mount Edge Just south of Newcastle ☏944 8151 or 351 5083, ⊛www.mountedge .com. Eccentric but friendly guesthouse with a limitless range of customized tours, standard trips to the Blue Mountain Peak (US$60/person) and cycling tours (US$40, 4hr).

Strawberry Hill Irish Town ☏944 8400 ⊛www.islandoutpost.com. The hotel offers a variety of hikes and nature tours for guests and non-guests, from US$40/person (2–3 hr). Options include the Gordon Town Trail, and the steep Copper Gully Trail to the beautiful hamlet of Greenwich.

Sun Venture 30 Balmoral Ave, Kingston 10 ☏960 6685 or 469 4444, ⊛www.sun venturetours.com. By far the most experienced option for Blue Mountain hikes; includes various daylong mountain walks (US$100, discount for four people) as well as treks to the peak with a night in Penlyne Castle (US$120). These prices are based on groups of two to four people, and transport is included.

THE BLUE MOUNTAINS AND THE EAST | Irish Town, Newcastle and Section

2

Strawberry Hill, before climbing further to the community of **Redlight** and the army training ground at **Newcastle**. This section of the mountains has a larger population than the Mavis Bank area to the east, and also offers a greater choice of accommodation and eating. Views are staggering throughout, the winding lanes cutting through mist-covered **coffee plantations** and dense woodland; at the northern end of the road the cool trails of Holywell are an excellent way to explore it further, while at **Section** beyond, the road loops back around to Clydesdale and Guava Ridge (see p.102).

Accommodation: Irish Town to Section

Accommodation on this side of the mountains caters to most budgets, with all options offering airport pick-ups or transport from Kingston. If you're exploring the Holywell Park, an alternative is to rent one of the on-site **cabins** (❷) from the Jamaica Conservation and Development Trust (see opposite). Each sleeps four to six people and are basic yet attractive, with fireplace, kitchenette, complete seclusion and a marvellous view. You can also **camp** here at one of two picturesque campsites (US$5/person).

Heritage Gardens at Cold Spring Newcastle ☏960 8627 or 978 4438, ⓦ www.heritagegardens jamaica.com. This delightful two-bedroom house is set in landscaped gardens, on the grounds of a former coffee plantation established by Irish naval officer Matthew Wallen while posted to Newcastle. Features a long, shady verandah and large bathroom with tub, and the hosts are friendly and welcoming. Rates include breakfast. ❸

Mount Edge Redlight/Newcastle ☏944 8151 or 351 5083, ⓦ www .mountedge.com. Clinging to the side of the valley, this laid-back guesthouse-cum-restaurant has phenomenal views and is run by wily local personality Michael Fox. Simple rooms inside the main house are perfect for backpackers, while separate units just outside are of a higher standard. Excellent meals (call ahead) are available, while the friendly bar ranges from chilled out to rowdy depending on who's there. ❶–❷

Starlight Chalet & Health Spa Silver Hill Gap ☏969 3070 or 924 3075, ⓦ www.starlightchalet .com. One of the most appealing and isolated

choices in the mountains, located in flower- and bird-filled gardens with a short trail down to a swimmable river. Carpeted rooms have balconies and private bathrooms, and there's a shared TV lounge, sauna and small gym, with yoga classes on offer. Kitchen for guest use, but fresh and inexpensive Jamaican meals are served at the on-site restaurant and bar. Bicycle rental available, and tours on offer. ❸–❹

Strawberry Hill ☏944 8400, ⓦ www .islandoutpost.com. Easily the classiest hotel in the wider Kingston area, yet it also maintains an unpretentious Jamaican feel. The fourteen cottages are perched right on the hillside, made from local materials and imaginatively designed to blend into their environment. The studios and two-bedroom villas boast hand-carved fretwork and muslin-draped mahogany four-poster beds with heated mattresses (it gets cold at night). Gardens are beautifully landscaped (look out for the unusual jade vine), and there's a glorious pool and deck affording breathtaking views, and a state-of-the-art spa. ❽–❾

Irish Town and Redlight

Named after the Irish coopers who settled here while working in the valley below, **IRISH TOWN** is a small farming community located at just over 3000ft above sea level, and now dominated by one magnificent **hotel**, *Strawberry Hill* (see above). The brainchild of Island Records magnate Chris Blackwell, this former coffee plantation opened as the first *Island Outpost* property in 1994, and offers a fabulous panorama from Kingston harbour to Spanish Town on one side, and of a lush Blue Mountain valley on the other. Bob Marley was brought here to convalesce after being shot in 1976, and many other artists have stayed here over the years – among them the Rolling Stones, U2, Stevie Wonder and Sting; the hotel's conference room contains numerous photos of the stars and Island's collection of gold and platinum discs from sales of Bob Marley's albums (open by appointment). Even if you can't afford to stay here, **eating** at *Strawberry Hill* is a must (see p.102).

Also in Irish Town is a new contemporary **art gallery**, The Observation Deck, where local fine-artist Tiffany Recas exhibits a range of paintings and sculpture, and also runs occasional art-themed retreats and workshops (Thurs–Sun; call ℡944 8592 for directions).

Beyond Irish Town, the B1 passes the near-vertical driveway for **Craighton Coffee Estate**, a private plantation owned by Japanese company UCC, who offer low-key tours of the 200-year-old plantation house (with its assortment of Japanese mementos and coffee oddments), a walk through the coffee farm and coffee tastings (weekends only by appointment; ℡929 8490, ⓦwww.craightonestate.com; 1hr 15min; US$15).

From Craighton, the road passes a ridiculously high boundary wall known locally as the Great Wall of China, built by the owner to protect against landslides, and continues through the tiny village of **REDLIGHT**, named for the former brothels that kept the Irish coopers entertained. It's a charming, laid-back place with a couple of basic rum/provision shops – look out for an attractive double-storey building boldly painted in red, green and gold, owned by a couple of friendly Rastafarians who are happy to help visitors find accommodation in private homes. The **Gordon Town Trail** loops downhill from Redlight, passing through small coffee plantations and precipitous fields of broccoli and scallion. The trail offers opportunities for swimming, with plenty of mini-waterfalls and deep pools; it's easy to follow once you get on to it – ask anyone in Redlight to direct you to the start, from where it takes about two and a half hours to get to Gordon Town.

Newcastle

Four thousand feet up from Redlight is **NEWCASTLE**, an old British military base established by Major William Gomm in 1841 to escape the yellow fever raging on the hot, swampy plains below. The main road cuts across the **parade ground** of the Jamaica Defence Force, which still features old cannons and the insignia of the various regiments stationed here during the past century or so. The nearby military graveyard remembers the dead of that period with its neat, white crosses. The views from the base across the mountains and down to Kingston are dazzling and almost vertiginous, while behind you, immediately above Newcastle, **Catherine's Peak** (5060ft) – named after Lady Catherine Long, the first woman to climb it (officially, at least) in 1760 – marks the highest point in the parish of St Andrew. You can make the steep, misty hike to the pylon-topped summit of Catherine's Peak via a concrete road that branches off the B1 just north of Newcastle and winds its way up, affording excellent views of Kingston when the mist clears.

A couple of miles past Newcastle, the mountain pass 4000ft up at **Hardwar Gap** is named for a British army captain who supervised the construction of the road from here to Buff Bay. The atmospheric **Gap Café** (see p.102) was constructed in the 1930s and originally designed as a way station for those traversing the mountains by horse and carriage, now serving lunch and afternoon drinks.

Holywell Recreational Park

Just beyond the *Gap Café* is the entrance to the **Holywell Recreational Park** (℡960 2848, ⓦwww.greenjamaica.org.jm; US$5 entry fee, US$10 including guided walks). At over 4000ft above sea level, the mountain air here is deliciously fresh, fragrant and cool – aided by a thick mist that clears to provide a spectacular unbroken view over the shimmering streets of Kingston, Port Royal and Portmore. The three hundred acres of parkland are latticed with enjoyable, well-maintained hiking trails, best of which is the gentle **Oatley Mountain Trail** (2 miles; 40min), an easy, varied circular hike through tunnel-like jungle. There are a couple of lookout towers and viewing platforms from which to enjoy the views, and several information boards explain the flora and fauna found in the area. You can continue on to the **Waterfall Trail** (1.5 miles; 1hr 30min), a mildly testing scramble along a river bed to the Cascade Waterfall; however, landslides have reduced the icy waters and swimming hole to a trickle. Oatley Mountain was extensively replanted with Caribbean pines after Hurricane Gilbert, and though it unfortunately suffered further damage during Ivan, it remains a sanctuary for a wide variety of birds. To the east lies Mount Horeb and the ecologically sensitive (and so off-limits) Fairy Glades Trail, where pines are outnumbered by the twisted trunks of soapwood and dogwood trees laden with clusters of orchids and wild pines.

Check in at the **ranger station** near the entrance before you set off, as rain can sometimes wreak havoc overnight and leave a few trails impassable. You'll also need to be accompanied by a ranger for some of the more difficult routes (sturdy boots advised). Near the entrance you'll find a picnic spot with tables, covered gazebos, water faucets and a toilet.

Look out for the annual "Misty Bliss" festival held on the last Sunday in February (10am–5pm; J$500), celebrating Jamaica's mountain environment and culture with foods, crafts, Maroon drumming and dancing, storytelling and nature tours (phone for additional information).

Old Tavern Coffee Estate ✗

A mile or so beyond Holywell at **Green Hills**, and stretching right up to Section, is the 120-acre **Old Tavern Coffee Estate** (☎924 2785 or 399 1222, ⓦwww.old taverncoffee.com; book in advance). It's run by Dorothy Twyman from her unmarked cottage, which hangs vertiginously just below the mountain road (look out for the late Alex Twyman's battered Land Rover outside), together with her Kingston-based son, David. The Twymans fought long and hard for the right to process their own crop due to archaic laws insisting that all coffee beans grown in the Blue Mountains be handled by licensed processors. In 1997, they became the only growers in the country to be awarded a licence to self-process, which set a precedent for the (near) free market that exists now. The Twymans are masters of coffee, and the resulting three roasts and subtler peaberry bean make for what is unquestionably the best Blue Mountain coffee in Jamaica. A visit to the farm includes a lesson on progression from plant to bean to pot, and the enjoyable trails also offer an appealing waterfall for swimming. You can buy Old Tavern coffee at a far lower price here than in the resorts; if you'd like to purchase while in Kingston, call David on ☎865 2978.

Section and around

Two miles past Old Tavern, **SECTION**, a friendly if slightly dishevelled little settlement straggled around a fork in the road, is home to several small-scale coffee farmers and is a good place to enquire about hiking guides or to buy some coffee (a pound of beans should cost about J$1200). Turning right and to the east here takes you around switchback turns towards **Silver Hill** and Clydesdale (see p.103), while turning left carries you towards the Maroon settlement of Charles Town and the coast at Buff Bay, though collapses in three separate locations have left upper reaches of the road impassable – ask around if it's been repaired before you travel. The views from here over the mountain gaps, planted with neat rows of coffee, are fantastic nonetheless. Nine miles before Buff Bay a dip at **Fishdone Waterfall** offers a natural power shower and wide, clear pool of cool water; turn left just before the white Silver Hill bridge at a sign for the Avocat Primary School.

Eating and drinking

The best option for **eating** in this part of the mountains is undoubtedly ⅍ *Strawberry Hill* (see p.99) at Irish Town. Set on the Great House terrace, the restaurant is the ultimate spot for a romantic dinner, with the sublime fare an eminently successful combination of fresh local ingredients and sophisticated international cooking, including baked crab backs with tropical remoulade and more conventional jerk chicken roti or plantain-crusted snapper. The restaurant's Sunday brunch buffet is an unmissable institution and worth every cent of the US$65 per person.

If you're looking for a less formal meal in Irish Town, friendly *Crystal Edge* has an outside terrace with great views and serves up a lovely *janga* (crayfish) or red-peas soup and delicious jerk chicken and pork cooked in the open air. Just next door is *Café Blue*, an air-conditioned Italian-style **coffee shop** with a great range of Blue Mountain lattes and cappuccinos, cheesecakes, and an assortment of Blue Mountain-themed gifts. The coffee here is sourced from the Clifton Mount Estate, and tours can be arranged from the shop.

Other options include *Mount Edge* guesthouse above Redlight (see p.99), offering a scrumptious range of dishes from crab in coconut milk to crayfish and chicken (order in advance). Higher up beyond Newcastle is the atmospheric **Gap Café** (℡ 997 3032; 10am–5pm Thurs–Sun), which serves Jamaican lunches as well as sandwiches, smoked marlin, escovitched fish, steaks or pasta (J$700–1500); the charming garden terrace is also a perfect place to sink a cocktail or a beer.

Gordon Town, Mavis Bank and Blue Mountain Peak

Back at the Kingston foothills of the Blue Mountains, continuing straight ahead at The Cooperage takes you past tiny riverside village **Industry**, where the Gordon Town River provides lots of swimming spots, and onwards to undistinguished **Gordon Town**. The only sizeable settlement in the Blue Mountains, it's built around a neat central square with a couple of snack bars and the usual giggling gaggles of smartly turned-out schoolchildren, and is only really worth stopping at to stock up on final supplies if you're heading to a remote area. Confusingly, the main road continues by taking an un-signposted right turn across a water-covered bridge; it rapidly deteriorates as it twists around hairpin bends all the way to Mavis Bank and beyond, but a little care and plenty of toots on the horn still make this a very enjoyable drive.

Three miles east of Gordon Town, the road splits at the hilltop junction **Guava Ridge**. Left up a steep slope takes you towards **Cinchona Botanical Gardens** and onwards to Section, while two consecutive right turns brings you past **Nyumbani** – the late Michael Manley's 1950s mountain home and coffee estate – to **Flamstead**, worth a visit for jaw-dropping vistas over Port Royal and the Caribbean. Once the site of a great house and plantation that was home to Governor Edward Eyre and British Admiral Horatio Nelson, the house was ruined by a series of hurricanes, though you can meander freely around the grounds and tip a gardener to let you into the tiny on-site **exhibition** on the property's history.

Coffee aside, the main motivation for visiting Mavis Bank is undoubtedly hiking; with the peak temptingly close and legions of fabulous walks nearby, you'd be crazy not to test out some of the trails.

Accommodation: Mavis Bank and Abbey Green

A more isolated part of the mountains, Mavis Bank is the gateway to Blue Mountain Peak, but also ideally placed to explore the surrounding ridges and Cinchona Botanical Gardens. **Staying** at Cinchona itself is also a possibility; US$8 buys you floor space in the main house, and camping is also permitted, though for both options you'll need to bring food and bedding with you.

A number of other options cater solely to the needs of hikers climbing the peak. The most common choices are detailed below, though if in a group you might wish to rent the whole of *Wildflower Lodge* at Abbey Green (T929 5395 or 364 0722; ●) a modern two-storey house containing double rooms, bunks, kitchen and dining room, set in gorgeous flowered gardens. Whichever lodge you choose, it's a good idea to arrange to have a hot meal prepared ready for your return; you'll need it.

Blue Mountain View Guesthouse Hagley Gap T842 5241. With four simple bedrooms, a communal kitchen and stupendous views, this option is located at the base of the steep road up to Abbey Green. Its genial Rastafarian owner, Staf, prepares vegetarian meals and organizes pick-ups from Mavis Bank (US$25 round-trip), and also arranges guides to the peak. ●
Forres Park Mavis Bank T927 8275 or 977 8141, Wwww.forrespark.com. A charming, friendly property with luxurious – though small – rooms with king-size beds and a shared verandah in the renovated main house, and slightly more basic timber cabins close by. Good food available by pre-order (non-residents welcome) and spa treatments offered. With 28 endemic and migrant bird species in the area, the property appeals to specialist birders, though hiking and mountain-biking tours are also available. "Gold Cup" (Wwww.100percentbluemountain.com) coffee is grown here, and tours of their Kingston factory are also available. ●–●
Jah B's Abbey Green T377 5206, Ebobotamo @yahoo.com. A simple, friendly dormitory-cum-guesthouse run by a local Rasta and his family, with good Ital food available. ●

Lime Tree Farm T881 8788, Wwww.lime treefarm.com. The most impressive setting of any hotel in Jamaica, this coffee estate owned by the grandson of former governor Hugh Foot appeals as much to hikers as to lovers of seclusion, astonishing views and equally fine food. The three spacious cottages are supremely comfortable, and large meals by Jamaican chef Suzy are served either on your verandah or at a communal terrace. Fruit trees of all varieties lie between the surrounding coffee terraces, which lead to excellent birding and tours to all neighbouring peaks are reasonably-priced. All-inclusive, with pick-up from Mavis Bank and wine with dinner. ●
Whitfield Hall Abbey Green T926 6612 or 927 0986. The most atmospheric, though also the most basic of Abbey Green's hostels, is set in an old coffee-planters' great house, with a huge communal sitting room with yellowing books lining the walls and a large blackened fireplace. Low ceilings and old-fashioned kitchen add to the archaic feel, as do oil lamps casting shadows throughout. The bunks are not especially comfortable, but you'll almost certainly meet other hikers preparing for the climb. Camping also allowed (US$5/person). ●

Clydesdale and Cinchona Botanical Gardens

The northern fork of Guava Ridge takes you five miles into the heart of coffee country, through the tiny hamlet of **Content Gap**, and onward to **Clydesdale**, tucked into a remote pocket of the mountains and accessible only by foot or 4WD. An old coffee plantation, it was converted into a nursery in 1937 by the Forestry Department with row upon row of Caribbean pines, networked by several paths that make for a pleasantly shady walk. Sadly, the plantation is no longer functioning as a financial enterprise – its buildings have long been abandoned and are in a state of advanced disrepair – but it's still a lovely, tranquil spot, and usually completely deserted so you'll need to bring a guide. Sun Venture Tours (see p.98) run day-trips up to Clydesdale and on to Cinchona, including along a hiking trail to a small, icy-cold waterfall and river pool on the Clydesdale River, known locally as the **Fountain of Life** for its supposedly healing properties. This was once a picnic and swimming spot, popular among locals and Kingstonians, a fact attested to by the now-derelict changing rooms; some people still make the tough journey up from Kingston.

Most people hike to **Cinchona Botanical Gardens** (no set hours; free) from Clydesdale, though it is possible to drive all the way from Westphalia or Mavis Bank in a 4WD (guide needed; see p.98) up the abysmal road that snakes through the precipitous coffee groves covering Top Mountain. The gardens are at the summit, and their orderliness is a surprise after the rugged and wild hillsides below. Clinging to the ridge opposite Blue Mountain Peak and overlooking the Yallahs River valley, the ten-acre maintained gardens were initially a commercial venture, planted with Assam tea and cinchona trees – which produce quinine, used as an anti-malarial before the advent of modern drugs – in 1886. However, the inaccessibility of the site and competition from Indian plantations led to the project's decline, and it became a government-run public garden in 1968. It's still an important centre for botanical research.

Today, the gardens have a magical feel, with eucalyptus whistling in the breeze, and Norfolk Island pine, Japanese cedar, weeping cypress, rubber and camphor trees flourishing in the mist. The vivid flower-beds are bursting with blooms, and wild coffee smothers the slopes. You can see it all on the **Panorama Walk** (preferably accompanied by one of the gardeners – leave a tip), which takes you through a tunnel-like thicket of Holland bamboo and eventually back to the main house, an ancient oblong of stone that still contains most of its original fittings. Other guided trails are also available, among the most rewarding the sweaty six-mile hike down to Mavis Bank, the four-mile hike to Catherine's Peak, and the historic, ten-mile **Vinegar Hill Trail** to Buff Bay, an old Maroon trading route that the British used to transport supplies from Kingston to the north coast. Though now largely impenetrable, it is still possible to navigate with a good guide.

Mavis Bank

Heading east from Guava Ridge, the next settlement along is **MAVIS BANK**, picturesquely nestled in the Yallahs River valley. Accessible by bus from Papine, neatly arranged Mavis Bank is the last full-scale village on the route to Blue Mountain Peak. If you're driving, this is the place to park – in the lay-by opposite the police station – because although it is possible to drive on to Hagley Gap with a normal car, parking can be a problem, and only the sturdiest 4WD can tackle the terrain beyond. There's little to Mavis Bank itself: the town's single street consists of a police station, several no-frills rum shops that also sell basic foods, a couple of churches and a smattering of homes. The main organized attraction is the **Mavis Bank Coffee Factory** (Mon–Fri 10am–2pm; US$10; phone in advance, ☎977 8015), owned by the National Investment Bank of Jamaica and the Munn family, and located on the west side of the village. In business for around a hundred years and handling some 70,000 bushels of coffee per year from 6000 farmers, the factory is Jamaica's main Blue Mountain coffee processing plant, and it is here that the precious beans are graded, roasted and packaged under the **JABLUM** consortium name. Beginning with an obligatory infusion of steaming caffeine at the on-site coffee bar, the tour takes you on an engaging journey "from the berry to the cup" through every part of the working factory, and at the end you can buy bags of beans far cheaper than in the shops.

▲ Sorting beans at the Mavis Bank Coffee Factory

Abbey Green

You can start the hike up to Blue Mountain Peak from Mavis Bank, along the steep and strenuous Farm Hill Trail from the church, but it's much more sensible to begin from **ABBEY GREEN** just over five miles northeast. At some 4500ft above sea level, it's a completely different world, where wind shrieks through eucalyptus trees and seemingly impenetrable mists billow over the mountainside only to evaporate after a few rays of sun. It's an intensely beautiful place, and you're unlikely to meet anyone save the odd coffee grower or scallion farmer. Three rustic **hostels** here act as bases for peak hikers (see p.103) and offer Land Rover pick-up from Mavis Bank for US$50 per carload (maximum six people). All also provide guides for the peak hike for around US$40.

On the way up, you'll turn left through **Hagley Gap** – a steeply inclining one-street village where you can buy last-ditch provisions and get a hot meal from a couple of small-scale cookshops – after which you'll traverse one of the least road-like roads in Jamaica, with huge gullies carved through the clay by coursing water. Shortly after embarking on this tortuous route, you pass through pretty **MINTO**, a drawn-out roadside community where proud locals have planted their gardens with brightly coloured flowers and shrubs.

Blue Mountain Peak

Undeniably the most rewarding hike in Jamaica, **Blue Mountain Peak** (7402ft), the highest point on the island, seems daunting but isn't the fearful climb you might imagine – though it's hardly a casual stroll, either. It is magnificent by day, when you can marvel at the opulence of the canopy, the thousands of orchids, mosses, bromeliads and lichens, the mighty shadows cast by the peak and the coils of smoke from invisible dwellings below. It's also thrilling by night, when after a magical moon-lit ascent, Kingston's lights occasionally twinkling in the distance, you find yourself at Jamaica's zenith as a new day dawns.

From Abbey Green, the climb to the peak is around eight miles, and can take anything from three to six hours depending on your fitness level. If you're staying at one of the hostels, you can start at around 1am and catch sunrise at around 5.15 to 6.15am, depending on the time of year. A full moon also means you'll get natural floodlighting – otherwise, take a flashlight. Signposts make much of the route easy to follow without a guide, but in this remote area it's sensible to go with someone who knows the way. Don't stray onto tempting "short cuts" – it's illegal, you'll damage the sensitive environment and you'll almost certainly get hopelessly lost. Rescue patrols can take days to mobilize effectively, by which time you'll be in serious trouble.

The first stretch of the trail, a steep series of switchback turns through thick forest aptly named **Jacob's Ladder**, is said to be the most arduous, and you'll appreciate arriving at the halfway point at **Portland Gap Ranger Station** (4.5 miles), where you can rest at the gazebo, top up water and let the rangers know that you're walking the trail (leave a note if you arrive in the early hours). Pit toilets and two very basic cabins can also be found here (camping costs J$150/person; book in advance via the Jamaica Conservation and Development Trust, see p.98).

Once past Portland Gap, it's another three and a half miles to the peak through twisted montane and then low-lying elfin forest, in which the gnarled soapwood

Blue Mountain coffee

Coffee trees from Ethiopia were introduced to Jamaica in 1728 by Governor Sir Nicholas Lawes, and they flourished on the cool slopes of the Blue Mountains. Cultivation reached new heights of excellence during the first half of the nineteenth century, when expert coffee growers arrived from revolution-torn Haiti, soon meeting an increased demand from European coffeehouses. Jamaica became one of the world's main coffee exporters, producing up to fifteen thousand tons of beans per year.

The industry suffered its first crushing blow with emancipation in 1838, as streams of former slaves left the plantations to set up their own small farms. Soon afterwards, Britain abolished preferential trade terms on coffee, and direct competition with the coffees of South America crippled small Jamaican farmers. The decline continued into the twentieth century, and it was only after World War II that the Jamaican government took belated steps to save the Blue Mountain plantations. It established **quality guidelines** for both cultivation and processing, stipulating that only coffee grown at a certain altitude could claim the Blue Mountain name (you'll see other coffee around the island called High Mountain or Low Mountain). This exclusivity heightened the coffee's cachet and helped to underpin its reputation as one of the world's finest. A further boost came during the 1980s as Japanese companies, with a big domestic market for Blue Mountain coffee, invested huge amounts in the best of the plantations. More than eighty percent of the crop is now sold to Japan, which contributes to the massive prices you'll pay for Blue Mountain coffee in Europe and North America.

Blue Mountain coffee has always been vulnerable to **hurricane damage**, and deforestation on the hillsides has only heightened this. Periodic hurricanes have wiped out entire plantations: during Hurricane Ivan in 2004, the entire usual rainfall for September fell in two days, resulting in the loss of valuable top soil and mature plants in landslides, and a subsequent shortage of beans for three years, all told costing Jamaica US$30 million. The burden was felt most heavily by small-scale mountain farmers, many of whom had effectively no income through 2005, a human cost which has heightened the need for tourism revenue in this rarely publicized but most picturesque of locations.

and dogwood evergreens are so stunted by low temperatures, exposure and lack of nutrients that they grow no higher than 8ft. You're still only about 6000ft up, but you might already be a little dizzy from the rising altitude; if so, go slowly and eat a high-energy snack. At 7000ft, the plateau at **Lazy Man's Peak** is where some call it a day, but it's certainly worth struggling on for another twenty minutes.

If you've arrived before dawn, you'll be completely bowled over. The inky black slowly melts into ever-intensifying pinks, oranges and purples until finally a hint of wispy blue heralds the sun and reveals the surrounding ranges. It's quite possible you'll be here alone, the highest person in Jamaica and feeling – literally – on top of the world. As the sun burns off the mist, the spectacular panorama becomes recognizable; you can make out Cinchona and, on a good day, Buff Bay and Port Antonio's Navy Island to the north and Kingston, Portmore and coastal St Thomas to the south.

Blue Mountain Peak is the furthest you can go into the Blue Mountains, as thick forest and treacherous terrain means that even the burly pig hunters seldom venture further east, preferring to enter the John Crow range from Millbank in Portland (see p.129).

St Thomas

St Thomas, nestling below the Blue Mountains, is the most neglected of Jamaica's parishes, and as a result, its villages are somewhat impoverished with meagre facilities for tourists. For some, however, the region offers a slice of the "real" Jamaica, untouched by the demands of tourism. The main attractions are the rambling old spa town of **Bath** in the foothills of the mountains, and also remote **Morant Point**, where a candy-striped lighthouse overlooks a stunning beach. A couple of waterfalls in other areas are interesting diversions, though there's little to the parish capital, **Morant Bay**, except to reflect on one of the bloodiest periods in Jamaica's volatile history. The parish's friendly people remain probably the biggest draw; large-scale sound-system parties and stageshows (such as the excellent roots-reggae East Fest, held in late December/early January) are to be found on public holidays, and, largely due to the presence of the descendants of free Africans, St Thomas is the cradle of Jamaica's African-based religions (see Contexts, p.289), with roadside Kumina sessions found frequently.

The main road to Morant Bay is served by regular **buses**, with route taxis continuing from there to Port Antonio, but it's difficult to reach more remote locations without a car.

Bull Bay to Morant Bay

The A4 hugs the coastline east of Kingston, past the tiny settlements of **BULL BAY** and **COW BAY**, named for the manatees that were caught and slaughtered here in the seventeenth and eighteenth centuries. These days Bull Bay is more well known as a **surfing** destination, with young groups of Kingstonians catching the few decent waves that roll in off the Atlantic. Contact Billy Mystic at *Jamnesia* if you'd like to know more or want to stay in one of the basic surfers' huts here (☎750 0103, ⓦwww.jamnesia.20megsfree.com; ❶; airport pick-up, meals, surfboard rental and instruction available). A roadside marker at the village of **ELEVEN MILES** recalls Jack Mansong (known as Three Finger Jack), a formidable nineteenth-century runaway slave who, after the bungled attempted murder of the slave trader who'd transported his parents from Africa – one Captain Henry Harrop – escaped from his execution and carrying Harrop to a cave where, with delicious irony, he forced his master to become his slave. Fuelled by the promise of a rich reward, Quashie, the Maroon who had relieved Mansong of his fingers, shot him in the stomach and cut off his head, preserving it in a bucket of rum all the way to Spanish Town.

Back on the coast, the road traverses the boulder-strewn mouth of the **Yallahs River**, which appears unfeasibly large in the dry season when the river slows to a trickle. **YALLAHS** itself is best known for its **salt ponds**, said to have been created by the tears of an English estate owner, distraught when his brother married the woman he loved. Bacteria occasionally go on the rampage here, turning the ponds a reddish colour, and scientists reckon that present archeo-bacteria are among the earliest of Earth life forms. UWI research teams study the pond's ecosystem – particularly artemia, shrimp-like creatures that are one of the few animals able to survive. For seafood of a more appetizing variety, however, try good local **restaurant** *Thelma's* on the western edge of town. East of the salt ponds, **Rozelle Beach** offers swimming opportunities on its popular brown-sand strip.

Two miles east of Rozelle, Bustamante Bridge takes you into dusty **MORANT BAY**, parish capital of St Thomas and best known for having witnessed some of the ugliest moments in Jamaica's post-emancipation history. Edna Manley's grim-faced statue of National Hero **Paul Bogle** stands in front of the courthouse here, where he was hanged after leading the 1865 **Morant Bay Rebellion** (see box opposite); a plaque honours the "patriots" who died alongside him. The courthouse you see today replaced the original building razed in the rebellion. Bogle is buried behind it with those tipped into a mass grave here after the uprising, and only afforded a proper burial when they were dug up by chance in 1965. Today, a memorial erected "in gratitude from the generation who now realize that they did not die in vain" marks the spot, poignantly dedicated to those "who fell because they loved freedom". Paul Bogle Day is celebrated yearly in Morant Bay on October 11. There's not much else to the town: the attractive 1865 red-brick **Anglican church** is of passing interest, as is the crowded **market** (Mon–Sat), and the **library** (Mon–Fri 9am–6pm, Sat 10am–4pm), which holds interesting material on Paul Bogle and offers **Internet** access (J$60/30min). A series of unassuming villages lie just east of town – the first, **LYSSONS**, notable chiefly for its palm-fringed **beach**.

Buses and **taxis** to all destinations pull up next to the petrol station on the coast road. For **accommodation**, best value is the supremely friendly *Brown's Guesthouse* (☎982 6205; ❶–❷) at Retreat east of town with immaculate, home-style rooms with TV, air conditioning and meals on request. Right on the beach at Winward Drive, Lyssons, *Golden Shore Beach Resort* (☎982 9657, ⓦwww.goldenshorehotel .com; ❸) has cool, airy, tiled rooms with air conditioning, TV, restaurant and bar. The best **food** is at the *Fish Cove* restaurant in **Leith Hall**, where you can choose your fish from a coolbox; conch soup is also on offer. In Morant Bay itself, the *Village Green* cafeteria by the Shell petrol station as you head in from Kingston has a large menu with fish stew, red-peas soup and vegetable chop suey.

Turn inland from the roundabout at the western outskirts of Morant Bay, followed by a right fork into the hills from the hamlet of Morant, to reach Paul Bogle's birthplace, **Stony Gut** (see box opposite). Central to Jamaica's history, it

The Morant Bay Rebellion

In August 1865, Baptist Deacon **Paul Bogle** – supported by **George William Gordon**, a wealthy mulatto member of the National Assembly – led a 54-mile march from St Thomas to Spanish Town to protest to the island's governor, Edward Eyre, against the inequity of the legal system, which invariably supported white landholders over small farmers, who struggled to find decent land to cultivate. A generation after emancipation, living conditions for Jamaica's black population remained abysmal, with food shortages, lack of access to property, and high taxation, and it was only a matter of time before people registered their grievances. After being turned away, the marchers returned to St Thomas with plans to create a "state within a state" at **Stony Gut**, Bogle's home village. Worried by the force of the uprising, the police had two of Bogle's supporters arrested on trumped-up charges of assault and trespass. On October 7, Bogle and his men marched military-style to the Morant Bay courthouse to disrupt proceedings by surrounding the building. Despite the protest's peaceful nature, the authorities issued a warrant for Bogle's arrest, yet police were thwarted by the sheer power of numbers and forced to swear oaths that they would no longer serve public officials.

Undeterred, on October 10, eight more policemen set out for Stony Gut, but again they underestimated his support and were quickly overpowered and forced to swear allegiance to Bogle. Back in Morant Bay, they impressed the seriousness of the situation on then-Custos Baron Von Ketelhadt, who promptly arranged for one hundred soldiers to set sail aboard the HMS *Wolverine*. On October 11, Bogle and his men again marched into Morant Bay, raided the police station for arms and attacked the courthouse where the council was meeting. Eighteen soldiers and council members were killed as frustrations erupted; the courthouse was burned to the ground, and arms, gunpowder and foodstuffs were taken from the town's shops. Unrest quickly spread, and the government troops aboard the *Wolverine* arrived too late to quell the disturbance when they put ashore on October 12. Fearing that the whole country would soon be engulfed, the authorities gave free rein to the army, and the protesters were crushed with brute ferocity. A staggering 437 people were **executed**, another six hundred men and women flogged, and over a thousand homes razed to the ground. Bogle evaded capture and fled to the hills, where he remained undetected for several days. In Kingston, Governor Eyre declared martial law in St Thomas and wrote a warrant for the arrest of George William Gordon, who was hung outside the Morant Bay courthouse on October 20. There was nowhere for Bogle to hide; he was captured at Stony Gut on October 23 and went to the gallows two days later.

The rebellion marked a key political and social watershed for Jamaica. Governor Eyre was immediately recalled to England and stripped of his position, and the island came under **direct rule** from the home country until reforms in education and the legal system could be put into place – policies that never would have got past the local elite. Though progress for the poor was still painfully slow, Bogle's defiant legacy ensured that Jamaica remained relatively peaceful until well into the next century. The Jamaican government eventually recognized Paul Bogle (and George Willam Gordon) as National Heroes, and monuments to them stand in Heroes Circle in Kingston (see p.68).

was from here that Deacon Bogle built the rockbed of support that enabled him to lead his rebellion. Opposite the Methodist church, a heavily hurricane-damaged lane leads down to Bogle's simple memorial, the **Stony Gut Monument**, atmospherically shaded by Otaheite apple trees and bearing a plaque that outlines his deeds. Bogle's great-grandson was caretaker of the site for many years and was interred behind the monument in 1995.

Continuing straight ahead on the main road out of Morant Bay, excellent **cookshop** *Lorna Searchwells Fastfood* is worth a stop, while straight ahead through residential Seaforth and a right turn (in effect going straight ahead) before the Morant River bridge, is the road to **Reggae Falls at Hillside Dam**, where shallow but fast-flowing waters meander along an improbably wide, boulder-strewn riverbed. Walk along the riverbank and you'll reach the dam after a few minutes. Once a hydroelectric plant, these days water cascades over to create a deep swimming pool. It's a fabulously secluded place and you're unlikely to meet another soul, though go in a pair or group to be sure of safety.

The Southeastern corner

Five miles east of Morant Bay, diminutive village **PORT MORANT** was a key banana-shipping point during the eighteenth century, but is now solely known for commercial **oyster-farming** at its **Bowden Wharf**. The shellfish are eaten locally with a sauce of fiery peppers, scallion, thyme, pimento, sugar and vinegar. At the centre of the village by the gas station, a road cuts inland for six exceptionally pretty miles to the little-visited village of **BATH** at the edge of the John Crow Mountains (route taxis run daily from Morant Bay, Port Antonio and Manchioneal; no fixed timetable). Born when a runaway Spanish slave stumbled across hot mineral springs in the late 1690s, it was discovered that the waters could cure wounds. Ironically, the same slave's master sold the spring and some 1130 acres of land surrounding it to the British in 1699 for £400, who swiftly carved a road through the hills and erected a spa building here in 1747.

The breadfruit and the *Bounty*

Up until the late eighteenth century, Jamaica was not self-sufficient in food, relying on imports to feed the ever-increasing slave population. As a result, the American War of Independence (1775–81), which severely disrupted food supplies, brought tragedy, with thousands dying of malnutrition and related disease. To eliminate this catastrophic dependence, planters lobbied the British government for a source of cheap food that could be grown locally. The starchy, nourishing **breadfruit** – about which Captain Cook had rhapsodized, "If a man plants ten of them...he will completely fulfil his duty to his own and future generations" – was at the top of their wish list.

Setting sail from England in 1787, the HMS *Bounty* commanded by **Captain William Bligh**, was assigned the task of procuring breadfruit plants from their native Tahiti. After a dangerous journey around Cape Horn, captain and crew were garlanded with flowers before loading up the breadfruit plants and moving on. Three weeks later, on another arduous crossing with a captain who seemed to care more for his plants than for his men, the ship's crew mutinied. Bligh was cast adrift in the Pacific with a handful of loyal followers, while the rest made for Ascension Island and their place in history. Incredibly, Bligh survived. He found his way back to England, where he was cleared of any blame and entrusted with another ship, HMS *Providence*, to complete his mission. The Jamaican House of Assembly voted him a substantial gift of 500 guineas to encourage his endeavours, and the *Providence* left England in 1791, finally delivering the breadfruit to the island in February 1793. The plants were propagated at Bath Botanical Gardens and eventually spread throughout the island, an important step towards Jamaican self-sufficiency.

In the 1700s Bath glittered in the colonial spotlight, but just a century later it fell from grace through a combination of political disputes and hurricane damage. A reminder of its heyday is to be found at the **Bath Botanical Gardens** (daily dawn to dusk; free) established in 1779, adjacent to the dilapidated Anglican Church. This was where many plants – including cinnamon, jacaranda, bougainvillea and mango – were first introduced to the island, but the ravages of time and Hurricane Gilbert (which levelled the village yet again in 1988) have ensured that little remains of the carefully ordered labels. You'll still see descendants of the **breadfruit trees** brought from Tahiti by Captain Bligh of HMS *Bounty* fame (see opposite) in 1793, alongside guava trees, royal palms, bamboo and crotons. The annual **breadfruit** festival in September commemorates the seminal event in Jamaican history.

Most visitors, though, come to take the waters at the rambling old 🏛 *Bath Fountain Hotel and Spa* (☎ 703 4345, ✉ bathmineralspahotelja@yahoo.com; ❷–❸), reached along a signposted one-mile road from the town centre. The **spa** (daily 8am–9.30pm; J$300 for a single-person bath, J$500 for a two-person bath, including towel and robe) has ten small cubicles, each with a sunken tiled bath. The water is high in sulphur and lime and, like most mineral baths, slightly (though not dangerously) radioactive – no more than thirty minutes is recommended due to the risk of dehydration. **Rooms** at the hotel are old-fashioned but comfortable and supremely quiet; rates include free access to the baths. Tasty Jamaican **meals** and fruit juices are also available. Bear in mind that outside the hotel you may well be accosted by a group of aggressive hustlers offering to take you to the open-air spring at the hotel's rear; while this hot and cold "Sulphur River" is a pleasant spot (water from the two springs is diverted to the spa inside and mixed to provide a bath of a more even temperature), the unofficial "guides" most certainly are not, and their amateur massages are inevitably exorbitantly priced.

Hiking trails lead from the hotel for miles across the Blue Mountains; the best is a recently reopened Maroon trading route through the John Crow range to Bowden Pen (see p.129) – for a guide contact the Jamaica Conservation and Development Trust or Sun Venture Tours (see p.98).

The far southeastern corner of the island, beyond Bath and Port Morant, is a seamless feast of banana, sugar and coconut plantations, the least developed yet one of the most picturesque corners of Jamaica. The slightly dishevelled communities of **Golden Grove** and **Duckenfield** hold neat but dilapidated rows of homes on stilts, accommodating cane cutters working at the Duckenfield sugar plantation, while **Rocky Point Bay** has a delightfully secluded beach and a fleet of small fishing boats. Though *Miss Nora's Cookhouse* in Duckenfield is a great spot for lunch, the highlight of the area is undoubtedly the rough drive to the right of the Duckenfield sugar factory, which leads five miles through cane fields and the mangroves of the Great Morass to the serenely isolated hundred-foot **Morant Point lighthouse** (ask locals for directions; often impassable in rainy season except by 4WD). The lighthouse itself was cast in London in 1841 and put up here by Kru men from Sierra Leone, among the first free Africans to be brought to the island after the abolition of slavery. Tip the lighthouse keeper to climb to the top; deserted and windswept, with Atlantic surf crashing onto the rocks, there's a magnificent panorama of the Blue Mountains, vast mangrove swamp, and of gorgeous **Holland Bay**, a deserted swath of fine white sand and pellucid water overlooked by a few ragged palms – the perfect place to live out your Robinson Crusoe fantasies. If you can't face the drive, come here by boat; *Zion Country Cottages* (see p.126) organizes tours.

Portland

Portland, north of the Blue Mountains, is generally considered the most beautiful of Jamaica's parishes – a rain-drenched land of luscious foliage, sparkling rivers and pounding waterfalls. Eastern Jamaica's largest town, **Port Antonio**, is an attractive destination in itself, but most visitors prefer to base themselves along the exquisite coastline heading east, with fabulous beaches and the **Blue Lagoon** nearby. The idyllic, surf-pounded stretch of beach at **Long Bay** is well established as a laid-back haven for backpackers, who come for the waves and chilled-out atmosphere – while roadside vendors in **Boston Bay** continue to offer the most authentic jerk pork and chicken in the country. The gorgeous waterfalls at **Somerset Falls** and **Reach Falls** are within striking distance wherever you stay, while heading into the **John Crow Mountains** in the interior you can be poled down the **Rio Grande** on a bamboo raft or hike through the rainforest along the centuries-old trails of the Windward Maroons.

Portland's **history** is distinctly one of boom and bust. The parish was officially formed in 1723, one of the last to be settled, despite Port Antonio being blessed with two natural harbours. Reports of the difficult terrain and the constant threat of Maroon warfare had deterred would-be settlers, though eventually the Crown was obliged to offer major incentives, including land grants, tax exemptions and free food supplies. The early economy was dependent on sugar until a surprise replacement crop – **bananas** – proved perfect for Portland's fertile soil towards the end of the nineteenth century (see box below). Port Antonio boomed, ushering in a golden era of prosperity with businessmen pouring in, and in 1905 the town's first **hotel** was built on the Titchfield peninsula. Cabin space on banana boats was sold

Bananas

Brought to Jamaica from the Canary Islands in 1520, the **banana** remarkably only became popular in 1871, when captain **Lorenzo Dow Baker** took a shipload of the foodstuff formerly deemed unpalatable from Port Antonio to Boston. His gamble paid off handsomely – the entire stock was sold for a healthy profit and mass demand ensued, earning him and others colossal fortunes. By the second half of the nineteenth century, sugar was already declining, and farmers rushed to plant the new "green gold". With high rainfall and fertile soil Portland was perfectly placed, and armies of planters and pickers arrived to earn pitiful wages, living in wretched conditions while production output hit thirty million stems per year.

The arrival of **banana ships** at the wharves was signalled by blasts on a conch shell, followed by frenetic activity as the labourers cut stems and carried the fresh fruit off the estates and onto waiting trucks. At the dock the banana stems were taken to the checkers, who ensured that each had the nine hands required to count as a bunch – hence, in the banana-boat song, *Day O*, "six hands, seven hands, eight hands, bunch!". Once aboard the ship, the tallyman gave the carrier a tally to redeem for payment, and workers made their weary way back to the plantation or to the bar.

Sadly for Portland, the boom didn't last – by the 1920s, Panama disease and hurricane damage had decimated the crop, and World War II compounded problems. Today, the end of long-standing preferential trade terms with Europe has caused many farmers to abandon bananas (being unable to compete with huge US operations) and the days of the banana as an important export crop certainly look numbered.

Jamaican food and drink

From a plate of grilled lobster served up by the sea to conch soup or jerk chicken from a roadside stall, Jamaica's cuisine is one of the island's main draws. Food is a serious business here, and any self-respecting Jamaican is a master of the myriad ways to season and cook the sumptuous array of local fish, seafood, meat, vegetables and fruits. To wash it all down, there's everything from fresh natural juices or coconut water straight from the nut to a frosty rum drink or a chilled Red Stripe.

Ackee ▲

Jamaican jerk

Ackee and saltfish may be the national dish, but **jerk cooking** is Jamaica's best-known culinary delight. The tradition of jerking dates back to the seventeenth century, when Maroon warriors used it to preserve the meat of wild pigs – it's now Jamaica's most ubiquitous cooking style, and the aromatic smoke that wafts from innumerable **jerk stands** is one of the island's more memorable and tantalizing aromas. Marinated in island-grown spices that include pimento, hot peppers, cinnamon and nutmeg, the meat – usually chicken or pork, but occasionally fish, lobster or sausage – is grilled slowly, often for hours, over a fire of pimento wood and under a cover of wooden slats or corrugated zinc sheets, with deliciously tender and flavoursome results. Common accompaniments are hard-dough bread or some roast breadfruit, yam or sweet potato, as well as an icy-cold Red Stripe. If you don't like things too hot, ask the server to hold off on the final dash of pepper sauce.

Jerk stand, Mammee Bay ▲

Streetside barbecue, Negril ▼

You'll find jerk sold from smoking **streetside barbecues** islandwide (usually from Thursday to Sunday only; head for the vendor with the longest line), but the best places to sample it are the legion of dedicated jerk centres, usually casual open-air affairs where you can watch the chefs at work. If you're after the real McCoy, head for Portland, the home of jerk cooking – the stalls at Boston Bay (see p.122) are renowned as the best in the island, though the Blueberry Hill jerk stop in St Mary (see p.130) is another local favourite. And don't leave the stall without purchasing a bottle of home-made jerk marinade, which gives a distinctive kick to any meat or fish dish.

Relaxing with a drink

It would be criminal to visit Jamaica without partaking of the island's award-winning rums, some of the finest in the Caribbean and whipped up into a huge array of fruity tropical cocktails. The classic brand is Wray and Nephew's overproof, an inexpensive and potent white rum notching up 63 percent alcohol that's best knocked back with a mixer of Ting grapefruit soda. There are plenty of less caustic brands of white rum, too, which are deployed in many a daiquiri; while piña coladas depend on the sweetened coconut-flavour varieties. If you're after taste rather than effect, though, go for the smooth gold rums and older, aged varieties produced by Appleton, left to mature in oak barrels for anything up to 21 years, and best savoured neat or over ice. Appleton Special or the tastier VX are delicious with coke and a slice of lime, or blended with fresh fruit juice into a classic rum punch. Of other locally produced specialities, Tia Maria is a sweet liqueur made with Blue Mountain coffee, while a variety of "roots wines", both with and without alcohol, utilize roots and herbs that the labels promise will invigorate the body and provide some extra stamina in the bedroom department.

No less celebrated is Jamaica's national beer, Red Stripe. While it has become an international brand, it never tastes as good as when sipped ice-cold straight from the bottle while gazing at a flaming Caribbean sunset.

If you're after something non-alcoholic, the water from fresh coconuts sold at roadside stands is the ultimate refresher, and supremely good for you too. Jamaican bartenders are aces with a blender, too, with tropical fruits whizzed up with ice to delicious effect.

▲ Jamaican rums

▼ Tropical cocktail, Negril

▼ Red Stripe beer at *Pelican Bar*, Parottee

Grilled lobster at *Rockhouse*, Negril ▲

Jack Sprat, Treasure Beach ▼

Best restaurants

Jamaica's restaurant scene runs the gamut from simple beachside seafood shacks to top-notch gourmet palaces offering a local take on international cuisine. The list below comprises some of the best spots to eat out.

▶▶ **Best barefoot dining: Jack Sprat, Treasure Beach**. This understated beachside restaurant offers fresh fish and pizza, served up to a backdrop of lilting reggae and the slap of dominoes on tabletops. See p.251

▶▶ **Most mouthwatering seaside dining: Prendy's, Hellshire**. The string of shacks on Kingston's closest beach are legendary for their seafood, but *Prendy's* is a cut above the rest: as well as the classic fried fish, they do a delicious steamed fish in a pumpkin and vegetable broth. See p.89

▶▶ **Best vegetarian food: Ashanti Oasis, Kingston**. A beautiful and peaceful setting amidst Hope Botanical Gardens, and some of the tastiest Ital cooking on the island. See p.76

▶▶ **Most succulent seafood: Little Ochi, Alligator Pond**. Right on the sand, with tables in reconditioned fishing boats, the seafood here is spectacular. See p.252

▶▶ **Most unusual setting: Houseboat Grill, Montego Bay**. This converted houseboat moored in Bogue Lagoon offers some seriously good food, including lobster fresh from a tank under the hull. See p.188

▶▶ **Most romantic venue: Toscanini, Ocho Rios**. Set in a beautiful former great house smothered in gingerbread fretwork, this is Jamaica's premier Italian restaurant. See p.145

▶▶ **Best sunset spot: Rockhouse, Negril**. With lovely fusion cooking, this classy restaurant atop the West End cliffs is perfect for a romantic dinner with the waves crashing below and the sun sinking into the horizon. See p.214

to curious tourists, who rubbed shoulders with the rich and famous – publishing magnate William Randolph Hearst, banker J.P. Morgan, actress Bette Davis – swanning in on their private yachts.

The boom proved to be short-lived, though the high-end tourism it had helped to engender remained. With the enthusiastic patronage of movie stars like Errol Flynn (see p.123), Port Antonio's place in the glitterati's global playground was assured, and Jamaica's first luxury hotel was built at *Frenchman's Cove* – to this day a testament to faded glamour. More recently, the movie business has injected much-needed capital, too – films shot here include *Cocktail*, *The Mighty Quinn*, *Club Paradise* and *Lord of the Flies*. Celebrities still sequester themselves in Portland, but the area can't compete with Montego Bay, Negril and Ocho Rios for mass tourism. Although Portland is a long way from the prosperity of its heyday, its natural water features and beauty spots are open to anyone who cares to find them – a lower-key Jamaica that's a welcome change for many visitors travelling the island.

Port Antonio

The days of movie stars coming to stay in **PORT ANTONIO** are long gone, and these days the town feels a little isolated. That said, sandwiched between the mountains and the sea, this somewhat sleepy place has a charm all its own – there are many remaining timber buildings and with a smart new marina and plans to develop Navy Island and the Titchfield peninsula, things seem to be stirring once again. There's not a huge amount to see here and there's little in the way of water sports or shopping, but "Portie" is a friendly and beguiling place with a bustling central market and a couple of lively nightspots.

Most people find Port Antonio something of a relief after the harassment of the north coast, and any hassle you do encounter tends to be fairly half-hearted. Even so, don't wander off the main streets after dark, and also be wary of police roadblocks east of town.

Arrival, information and getting around

Buses and **minibuses** from Kingston (2hr 30min) and Ocho Rios (2hr) pull in by the seafront on Gideon Avenue, which is also the place to get **public transport** onwards to the beaches and other places of interest – shared taxis run along the main road as far as Long Bay; you'll pay around J\$120 to Dragon Bay/Frenchman's Cove, J\$150 to Boston Bay and J\$200 to Long Bay. If you're **driving**, the A4 highway runs straight through the town, whether coming from east or west; **renting a car** is a tempting option with most sights scattered around the parish, but you'll get a better deal with a Kingston- or Ocho Rios-based company, with rental rates here slightly higher than elsewhere. If you're just planning a single day-trip – say to Reach Falls or the Rio Grande – it usually works out cheaper to use a **taxi**. The main taxi **stand** is at the town's central square on West Street; alternatively, call cheerful driver Mr Palmer on ☎993 3468, or the Port Antonio taxi cooperative/JUTA at 7 Harbour St (☎993 2684). If you want an easy life, you can enjoy all of the main draws with Attractions Link, a tour company based at Travel Express in the City Centre Plaza on Harbour Street (☎993 2102 or 4828, ✉attractionslink@cwjamaica.com).

The town is easily navigable, with two main streets, and you can **walk** the handful of sights in a couple of hours. **West Palm Avenue** runs into **West Street** (from the western entrance of Port Antonio to the central clock tower), while **Harbour Street** cuts through the middle. To get your bearings, take the steep climb up to the *Bonnie View Hotel* from the town centre; its terrace bar overlooks the entire town

PORT ANTONIO

▲ Blue Lagoon & Boston Bay

▼ Nonsuch, Berridale & Moore Town

◀ Somerset Falls & Buff Bay

N

0   500 yds

Woods Island
Folly
Folly Oval
Folly Point Lighthouse
CARIBBEAN SEA
Navy Island
Titchfield High School (Fort George)
Titchfield Peninsula
East Harbour
West Harbour
Folly Beach
Boundbrook Wharf
Port Antonio Marina
Musgrave Market
TPDCo
Carder Park
Bonnie View Hotel
Hospital
Annotto River

ALLAN AVENUE
A4
EVELEIGH PK RD
EAST PALM AVENUE
MANNINGS AVE
RED HASSELL ROAD
SUMMERS TOWN ROAD
BRIDGES LANE
BONNIE VIEW ROAD
LOVE LANE
W. BAPTIST AVE
EAST BAPTIST AVE
HALL'S AVE
FUN ALL RD
GIDEON AVENUE
FORT GEORGE ST
QUEEN ST
TITCHFIELD ST
FORT ST
GEORGE ST
HARBOUR ST
WILLIAM ST
WEST ST
WEST PALM AVENUE
RICE PIECE ROAD
BOUNDBROOK ROAD
See inset for detail

Inset:
Royal Mall
Courthouse
Clocktower
Scotia Bank
Bus Terminal
Pharmacy
Police Station
Christ Church
Musgrave Market
Port Antonio Marina

GROSSETT RD
LOVE LANE
WEST ST
BONNIE VIEW
HARBOUR ST
WILLIAM ST
GIDEON AVE
ALLAN AVE
BRIDGE ST
SPRINGBANK ROAD
BOUNDBROOK ROAD

RESTAURANTS & BARS/NIGHTLIFE

A&K Deluxe Restaurant	6
Anna Bananas	4
Dickie's Best Kept Secret	1
Dixon's Food Shop	11
Golden Happiness	13
The Hub	7
KS Kozy Knook	16
La Best Nite Club	14
Miss Shine-Eye	5
The New Debonaire	10
Norma's on the Marina	2
Oliver's Survival Beach	3
Pier View Jerk Centre	9
The Roof	15
Shadows	8
Yosch Cafe	12

ACCOMMODATION

Barcelona	F
Boundbrook Hilltop Guesthouse	D
De Montevin Lodge	C
Ivanhoes	B
Ocean Crest Guesthouse	A
Hotel Timbamboo	E

and provides great views. The landscaped **Errol Flynn Marina** (entrance opposite Royal Mall) has in its main complex a **TPDCO** information point (Mon–Fri 8.30am–4pm; ☎715 5324), but much more useful for **information** is the **website** ⓦwww.portantoniotravel.com, put together by a consortium of local businesses. Also close to the marina entrance, the **library** (Mon–Fri 9am–6pm, Sat 9am–1pm; ☎993 2793) has the cheapest and most reliable **Internet** connection; other Internet services can be found in Royal Mall or on West Palm Avenue. The marina also offers **boat mooring** and excellent maintenance facilities.

Independent guide Joanna Hart (☎831 8434 or 859 3758), described by the London *Daily Telegraph* as Port Antonio's most knowledgeable guide, offers a complete highlight tour of Port Antonio with emphasis on the history and culture of the area. Call for more details and prices. If you're interested in **deep-sea fishing** or a sunset **cruise**, Captain Paul Bohnenkamper (☎909 9552, ⓔCaribbeCapt@aol .com), based at Port Antonio Marina, rents out his fully equipped boat, and arranges trips to catch blue marlin and other big fish.

Accommodation

Port Antonio has a decent amount of budget **accommodation** close to the middle of town; if you're looking for more variety or glamour, stay east of town (see p.119) or at St Margaret's Bay (p.129). The Port Antonio Guesthouse Association (☎993 7118, ⓦwww.go-jam.com) is run by supremely friendly Maria Gullotta from *Drapers San* (see p.120), who can book rooms in some of the parish's most appealing properties, and also offers accompanied forays to nightspots and traditional African drumming sessions. If you want to **rent a house** in Port Antonio, *Barcelona* (☎368 1036, ⓔolivermagnusja@hotmail.com; ❸) is an attractive, well-equipped property off Summerstown Road, with three bedrooms, mosquito nets and fans, rustic outdoor shower, TV lounge, garden and porch area.

Boundbrook Hilltop Guesthouse 15 Boundbrook Crescent ☎715 1644, ⓦwww.bbhilltop.com. Great cheap option just west of the centre. Small doubles with fan, TV and bathroom, and also larger rooms with a/c and up to three beds. There's wireless throughout, good communal areas and a sea view. ❶

De Montevin Lodge 21 Fort George St ☎993 2604, ⓔdemontevin@cwjamaica.com. Good value in a lovely old gingerbread house, a relic from colonial days. Clean, cool and simple rooms, each with a balcony and shared or private bathroom, and a restaurant/bar downstairs with live music at weekends. ❷–❹

Ivanhoes 9 Queen St ☎993 3043, ⓦwww .go-jam.com. Scrupulously clean and tidy no-frills guesthouse in a flower-filled garden opposite

the ruins of the old *Titchfield Hotel*. Each of the appealing, reasonably priced rooms has fan and private hot-water bathroom. Meals available. ❷

Ocean Crest Guesthouse 7 Queen St ☎993 4024, ⓦwww.go-jam.com. Small, simple yet smart guesthouse with six rooms with private hot-water bathroom, some with a/c. Guests can use the large kitchen and dining area, though meals are available and there's a sunny terrace with a view over the harbour. ❷

Timbamboo Hotel 5 Everleigh Park Rd ☎993 2049, ⓦwww.hoteltimbamboo.com. A large a/c concrete block featuring clean, comfortable rooms with tiled floors, cable TV and private bathrooms. There's wi-fi in the lobby, and a fabulous roof terrace with views across the city. ❸–❹

The Town

The obvious starting point for a stroll is the town's **central square**, with a landmark **clock tower** opposite the red-brick, two-storey Georgian **courthouse** (now housing NCB bank), built in 1895 and fronted by an elegant fretworked verandah supported by cast-iron columns courtesy of William MacFarlane in Glasgow, Scotland. The area is always milling with people on court business or visiting the post office below. Looking to the other side of the road, your eyes can't help but be drawn to the **Royal Mall** (formerly the **Village of St George**), a mishmash of architectural styles from medieval to Tudor and Renaissance built over the old Delmar Theatre. Somehow its striking, opulent exterior, richly embellished with murals and sculptures, manages to complement its surrounding. The brainchild of locally infamous Zigi Fami, owner of the equally exuberant *Jamaican Palace* hotel and the woman behind Trident Castle (see p.121), the mall boasts a handful of ordinary stores, salons and a small café/bar.

Due north from here, the **Titchfield peninsula** juts out into the sea, dividing Port Antonio's **twin harbours**. The tip of the peninsula once held the British **Fort George**, whose ancient cannons and crumbling walls today form part of Titchfield High School, alive with noisy open-air lessons and frenetic games of football and netball. The short wander up from town takes you past the **De Montevin Lodge** hotel – high-Victorian gingerbread architecture at its best – and the unexciting ruins of the **Titchfield Hotel**, Port Antonio's first, once owned by Errol Flynn. The peninsula is largely somnolent and peaceful, characterized by large and rather dilapidated wooden houses, while the town's only proper strip of sand, **Folly Beach**, has been tidied up, planted with palms and removed from the public domain.

Back in the centre of town, compact **Musgrave Market** is the liveliest spot; friendly, easy-going and crammed with stalls selling appetizing fruits and vegetables, there's also a busy trade in fish, meat and clothes, with a handful of crafts and souvenirs. Walking up West Street, past numerous shops and the grassy lawn where the **ferry** used to leave for Navy Island, **Boundbrook Wharf** is the loading point for the few bananas still shipped off the island (see box, p.112). This is the place that inspired the banana boat song *Day O* – "Work all night for a drink of rum, daylight come and me wanna go home." Today the backbreaking work is much simplified, with bananas packaged centrally and mechanically loaded.

On the East Harbour side of town, the red-brick Anglican **Christ Church** on Bridge Street, Romanesque in design, is the most prominent of Port Antonio's houses of worship. Built on the site of an earlier church in 1840, its memorials date back to the late seventeenth century. The eagle lectern was donated in 1900 by the Boston Fruit Company (owned by Dow Baker – see box, p.112), which built its significant wealth from the banana trade.

Across the road from the church, a stiff half-mile walk uphill takes you to the rather run-down **Bonnie View Hotel**. The views are magnificent from here; you can look over the twin harbours, and from the lovely back garden see into the heart of the Blue and John Crow mountains. Hiking trails start from here, and with a bit of advance notice, the hotel can organize half-day horseback tours of the area (from US$30/person).

Errol Flynn Marina and Navy Island

Port Antonio has long been recognized as having one of the loveliest natural harbours in the world, and the entire waterfront of the West Harbour has undergone a massive multimillion-dollar redevelopment, the **Errol Flynn Marina** (℡715 6044, Ⓦwww .errolflynnmarina.com). Opened to great acclaim in 2002 by former Prime Minister P.J. Patterson, it's designed to appeal to mega-yachts and (as yet nonexistent) small cruise ships, with state-of-the-art docking **facilities**, elegant landscaped gardens, a pool, and gift shops in pastel-coloured wooden buildings. You'll also find a *Devon House* ice-cream parlour here, along with a good restaurant and tour company offices. Perhaps controversially, the entire development is secured behind enormous gates, with security guards vetting all comers; the atmosphere is no doubt refreshing after Port Antonio's street bustle, but ghettoizing the yachties just seems to reinforce age-old divisions.

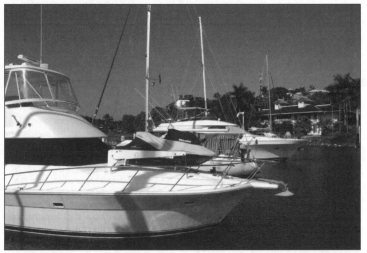

▲ Errol Flynn Marina, Port Antonio

The largest of the small islands that dot the Portland coast, **NAVY ISLAND** lies just off the mainland, and is closed to the public. The British Navy used it in the eighteenth century – hence the name – and Captain Bligh landed here in 1793, bringing yet more breadfruit from Tahiti (see p.110). A later adventurer, Errol Flynn, immediately bought it as a private retreat for entertaining Hollywood starlets – one of the myriad Flynn myths says that he lost it in a poker game less than a decade later. The 64-acre island, covered in lush vegetation, good beaches and trails, now belongs to the Port Authority; it's rumoured that an upmarket resort will be built on the site, but until then Dickie's son (see "Eating", below) can take you on a cruise around it.

The Folly

At the end of Allan Avenue (known locally as Folly Road), which runs east along the coast, is the second of the town's peninsulas, **Folly Point**. Covered with low-lying scrub, it's home to a cricket ground, and at its end, a **lighthouse**. You'll need to attract the attention of the keeper to let you into the pretty flowered garden that surrounds the lighthouse and they'll expect a donation; you can't climb the lighthouse but you're free to walk over the rocks in front of it, a favourite fishing spot.

Before you reach the lighthouse, a right fork brings you to the **Folly**, the sorry ruin of what was, briefly, one of the grandest houses in Jamaica. Built in 1902 for American banker Alfred Mitchell and widely applauded as a model of mock-Grecian architecture, the concrete house was a model of ostentation – until the roof collapsed in 1935, a victim of shoddy construction and the short-sighted use of salt water in the cement. Only the pillars and half a staircase remain standing, though restoration has made some improvements. Quirky and evocative, the shell's dramatic presence has not been lost on film-makers – it's been featured in movies and pop music videos by the likes of Shabba Ranks and Lauryn Hill. Just across the water, tiny **Woods Island** was once joined by a stone causeway, and Mitchell had a small zoo built on it for his pet monkeys. Swimmers can cover the short distance to create their own private retreat, though take care as undercurrents can be strong.

Eating

Port Antonio offers a number of inexpensive Jamaican eating **choices**, with two great vegetarian options. *Norma's* is the town's one sophisticated spot; for more fine dining you'll need to head eastwards (see p.122). Look out for barbeques around town at sunset; some do scrumptious foil parcels of spicy curried conch with okra.

A & K Deluxe Restaurant 23 Boundbrook Crescent. Very popular with locals, this is the cheapest eating place in town, serving soups and (small) meals for J$250, such as rundown, liver or callaloo for breakfast, and stew beef, cow foot and baked chicken for lunch.

Anna Bananas Allan Ave. Slightly upmarket seaside restaurant on a raised wooden boardwalk overlooking the bay. It's one of the better inexpensive places to eat with good salads, seafood and curry goat. Breakfast, lunch and dinner daily; there's also a pool table.

Dickie's Best Kept Secret Main road just west of town ☎809 6276. Easily missed as it's nestled on a knoll as you round the far bend of Port Antonio's West Harbour, this simple wooden shack is a surprising and fabulous choice. Served in owner Dickie's kooky lounge, the beautifully presented and moderate five-course dinners include dishes like ackee on toast, garlic lobster, steamed fish and veg options; order the morning before you want to eat. Breakfast also available.

Dixon's Food Shop Bridge St. Take-out joint with tables upstairs serving delicious home-made vegetarian food – tofu stew, stir-fried veg and salads – at rock-bottom prices. Wholemeal bread daily, plus garlic and raisin loaves each Friday. Weekdays, lunch only.

Golden Happiness Corner of Harbour and West streets. Large diner with a huge menu of reliable Chinese food with a Jamaican twist. Very cheap to boot.

Miss Shine-Eye Boundbrook Wharf. Some say hers is the best jerk chicken in Jamaica – it's certainly the best in Port Antonio. Fri evening and Sat only.

Norma's on the Marina Port Antonio Marina. *Norma's* name speaks for itself in Jamaica; with tables by the waterfront and a large open kitchen, you can watch the chefs prepare your food, upscale yet mid-priced. Menu includes steaks and sophisticated seafood.

Oliver's Survival Beach Allan Ave, next to *Anna Bananas*. Really excellent and inexpensive Ital food and fresh seafood is served at this easy-going and basic little restaurant with outdoor tables by the water.

Pier View Jerk Centre 21a West Palm Ave. Pleasant garden joint with a proper jerk pit; serves moderately priced pork, chicken or fish, cooked over charcoal.

Shadows 40 West St. Excellent omelettes for breakfast and good Jamaican and Chinese meals, served at a pleasant bar with gazebo or in an indoor, a/c room.

Yosch Cafe Royal Mall. Surprisingly sophisticated café/bar serving club sandwiches, burgers, seafood and pizza, alongside espressos, and drinks in the evenings. Mon–Sat till 10pm.

Drinking, nightlife and entertainment

Port Antonio isn't exactly bursting with good places to **drink**, but there are a few quiet spots and a couple of lively **nightclubs** which fill up from midnight. If you want to join the locals, the rum bars on Allan Avenue (known as Folly Road) are a great spot for a drink on the water's edge. Other good bars include *Shadows*, at the restaurant/guesthouse of the same name (see above), and *KFC Bar*, a great spot with a view over the harbour, hidden away down the road behind *KFC* (and related only by name).

In late September/early October, the prestigious **Port Antonio Blue Marlin Tournament** attracts serious anglers from all over the world, with numerous events in the evenings (contact TPDCO on ☎715 5324).

The Hub 2 West Palm Ave. A good, if rather testosterone-charged choice, with late-night drinking on Friday and Saturday. Popular with local officers of the law.

K-S Kozy Knook Allan Ave. The archetypal Jamaican drinking hole, with a circular bar and lots of white-rum drinkers fuelling the chitchat and dominoes action.

La Best Nite Club West St, above the main square. Currently the town's trendiest spot with big nights Fri and Sat drawing all the parish's winers and grinders for the latest dancehall.

Pier Lounge 21 West Palm Ave. Friendly upstairs bar known as Beenie Bob's Place with balcony and late hours (open daily until 3am), occasional live music and an oldies hits night every Saturday.

Roof Club 11 West St. Long-standing fluorescent-streamer-bedecked nightclub with a countrywide reputation as a relaxed place for a serious night out. Busiest for Thursday's "Ladies' Night" and weekends when La Best is closed. DJs pump out an eclectic mix of reggae/dancehall, soca, hip-hop and R&B, with occasional oldies nights.

Listings

Banks and money Most banks lie on Harbour and West streets, though better exchange rates are available at FX Trader in the City Centre Plaza on Harbour St, and Kamal's supermarket, 12 West St (open 9am–7pm, including Sundays).

Car and bike rental Eastern Car Rentals, at 16 Well St (☎ 993 4364), will deliver to your hotel, as will Derron's, east of town at Drapers (☎ 423 2449). High-season prices start at US$90/day.

Doctors Dr Daniella Speed in Boundbrook (☎ 993 3564) is recommended; Dr M. Valenti at 38 West St is a holistic practitioner.

Hospital The public hospital is on Nuttall Rd (☎ 993 2646).

Internet access The Portland Parish Library, in the marina park, has the best connection in town; J$200/hr, while Don J's is an Internet café at Royal Mall.

Police The main station is on Harbour St (☎ 993 2546). Call ☎ 119 in an emergency.

Post office The main branch is on Harbour St opposite the clock tower (Mon–Fri 9am–5pm).

Scuba diving Lady G'Diver (☎ 995 0246, ⓦ www.ladygdiver.com) based at the Errol Flynn Marina is the only scuba operator in the area, offering dives (from US$84 two dives/same day), certification courses 3–5-day PADI (US$400) and equipment rental (snorkels and fins US$10, kayaks US$12/hr).

Taxis The main rank is in the central square, or call the Port Antonio taxi cooperative/JUTA on ☎ 993 2684.

Telephone Eastern Communication at 28 Harbour St (Mon–Sat 8am–10pm, Sun 10am–10pm) offer inexpensive international calls.

East to Boston Bay

Made all the more alluring for its delicious sense of faded glamour and relative lack of visitors, the rugged stretch of coast east of Port Antonio is one of the most attractive parts of Jamaica. It's a fairy-tale landscape of lush, jungle-smothered hills rolling down to a coastline studded with fantastic beaches, such as **Frenchman's Cove**, **San San** and **Winnifred**, and swimming inlets like the **Blue Lagoon**, a fabulous aquamarine pool of salt and fresh water made famous by the eponymous 1980 movie. A series of smart hotels vie for business with a handful of less expensive guesthouses, and you can plump for dinner-jacketed feasts at their salubrious restaurants or for more authentic jerk cooking at **Boston Bay**.

Accommodation

The coastline east of Port Antonio is crammed with great places to **stay**, though none is as cheap as you'll find in town. Bear in mind, too, that transport links are poor, and if you don't have a car you'll be reliant on taxis. Expect to pay J$500–700 for a charter to Port Antonio, and J$200–300 for shared taxis. All the hotels listed here are marked on the map on p.120. If you're looking to rent a **villa**, attractive *Moon San*, 300ft above the Blue Lagoon, (☎ 993 7600, ⓦ www.moonsanvilla .com; ⓞ) has four bedrooms with kitchen and living room, and passes to French-man's Cove are included; a cheaper, yet clean and organized three-bedroom house is available to rent from Mrs Viola Blake (☎ 750 0360 or 856 0427, ⓔ georges reynolds@gmail.com), opposite the Trident Hotel two miles from town.

119

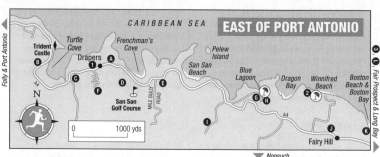

ACCOMMODATION				RESTAURANTS	
Bayview Villas	B	Mikuzi	J	Bush Bar	D
Drapers San	A	Mocking Bird Hill	F	Cynthia and Painter's	2
Gee Gam	D	Moon San Villa	G	Jamaica Palace	C
Goblin Hill	I	San San Tropez	E	Mille Fleurs	F
Great Huts	K	Sweet Harmony	L	San San Tropez	E
Jamaica Palace	C			Sir Pluggy's Jerk Centre	3
Kanopi House	H			Woody's	1

Bayview Villas Just east of Port Antonio ☎993 3118, ⓦwww.bayviewvillas-ja.com. Owned by Caribic Vacations, this small, renovated hillside hotel has attractive wood-panelled rooms with fans and a/c. There's also a pool with great views and a lovely flower garden. Breakfast included. ⑤

Drapers San Drapers ☎993 7118 or 362 4771, ⓦwww.go-jam.com. Funky, friendly, Italian-run guesthouse with an eclectic collection of rooms, some with kitchen, some with shared bathroom. Breakfast is included in the rates, and tasty Italian or Jamaican evening meals are also available. ②–③

Gee Jam San San ☎993 7000, ⓦwww .geejamhotel.com. Hip recording studio with shaded forest walkways between seriously classy villas and eco-huts, plus there's an astonishing view of almost the entire Portland coastline. Each unit offers sleek linen and batik fabrics, digital accessories, sea-facing verandahs; some have a steam room or jacuzzi. Hilltop villa *Panorama* could be the island's classiest house with its 360-degree view of both sea and mountain. Restaurant, gym, pool and access to a seafront spa. ⑨

Goblin Hill San San ☎993 7443, ⓦwww .goblinhill.com. A genteel complex of villas with a classy whiff of old Jamaica. With lovely contemporary decor, each villa is staffed with its own cookhouse keeper, and there's a pool, bar and tennis courts on site, as well as extensive grounds that offer grand views of San San. Passes to Frenchman's Cove are included. ⑥

Great Huts Boston Bay ☎353 3388, ⓦwww .greathuts.com. Unusual option in a superb location

atop low cliffs with a small private cove. Run by enigmatic American doctor Paul Rhodes, the resort offers a slightly eccentric take on Jamaica's African origins with a collection of tents and huts – from rustic to luxurious – connected by winding paths; all have fans and mosquito nets, some have tub/ jacuzzi. Breakfast included. Twenty percent of rate goes to a local charity, and long-stay volunteering opportunities available. ③–⑤

Jamaica Palace Just east of Port Antonio ☎993 7720, ⓦwww.jamaicapalace.com. Quirky fantasy hotel, designed to resemble a European chateau with a huge black-and-white tiled patio and a swimming pool in the shape of Jamaica. Rooms are comfortable, with large beds, a/c and marble bathrooms. ⑥

Kanopi House ☎1-242/368 6281, ⓦwww.kanopihouse.com. Indulge your Blue Lagoon fantasies at these astonishing eco-sensitive and secluded luxury jungle treehouses set amidst towering banyan, with paths snaking around the lagoon to a tiny private cove. Excellent attention to detail, friendly staff, fine local food and great rums provide a homely feel. Also backpacker rates (③) for more basic cabins. ⑨

Mikuzi Winnifred Beach, Fairy Hill ☎978 4859 or 813 0098, ⓦwww.mikuzijamaica.com. Rustic yet gorgeous two-bedroom cottage with funky decor, kitchen and verandah, and a range of smaller, one-bed studios of varying quality, all at the top of the rutted track down to Winnifred Beach. ①–④

Mocking Bird Hill San San ☎993 7267, ⓦwww .hotelmockingbirdhill.com. Eco-friendly hotel, set in a peaceful location in the hills above San San and filled with sculptures and paintings by artist and co-owner Barbara Walker. The airy rooms feature bamboo furniture and balconies, and there's a pool and a superb restaurant. ⑥ San San Tropez San San ☎ 993 7213, ⓦ www .sansantropez.com. This genial Italian-run property, best known for its restaurant, also offers spacious rooms that sleep four (for the same price per room as for two people). The rooms have king-size beds, a/c, cable TV, and private bathrooms with hot and cold water. ⑥

Trident Castle, Frenchman's Cove and San San

A few miles east of Port Antonio, pretty **Turtle Cove** beach is followed by the fantasy **Trident Castle** – a huge, white Disney-like edifice which looms up suddenly. It began life in the 1970s as a relatively modest home for European baroness Zigi Fami, who also owns the *Jamaica Palace*. She was forced to sell after financial troubles, and the new owners got increasingly carried away with elaborate additions. Robust enough to have survived Hurricane Gilbert with barely a lost slate, the castle is occasionally rented out, but is otherwise not open to the public.

Continuing three miles east from Port Antonio you arrive at **Frenchman's Cove**, whose eponymous hotel (☎ 993 7270, ⓦ www.frenchmanscove.com; ⑤) – with lavish tropical gardens and stunning beach – was once one of the area's most sumptuous hotels, frequented by royalty and A-list celebrities in the 1950s and 1960s. Though the hotel villas have deteriorated, the grounds are still beautifully maintained. The **beach** (daily 9am–5pm; US$6), though small, is one of the most splendid in Jamaica, with a curve of fine sand enclosed by verdant hills, and a freshwater river, its bottom alluringly lined by white beach-sand, running straight into the sea. Sun loungers and food and drink are available, as are **boat tours** to nearby beaches or the Blue Lagoon (US$20), guided **horseback riding** (US$25/hr), and **bike rental** (US$20/day). The easily missed entrance is opposite the eighteen-hole San San Golf Course (☎ 993 7645).

Two miles east, **San San** (US$6 entry) is a narrow but gorgeous strip of white sand beside a wide crescent bay, with rich reefs a few yards from the shore that provide excellent snorkelling. Like many north coast beaches, however, San San has fallen to the more unsavoury demands of the tourist industry. Once a lively locals spot, it's now fenced-off, presumably to stop "undesirables" (in other words, regular Jamaicans) from getting anywhere near foreign guests. Opposite the beach is the tiny but beautiful **Pelew Island**, also known as Monkey Island despite a lack of primates. It's great for snorkelling or lazing if you're up to the swim out there.

The Blue Lagoon

The **Blue Lagoon** is where 14-year-old nymphet Brooke Shields (and now-obscure cherub Christopher Atkins), playing child castaways on a deserted island, frolicked naked in the movie of the same name. Enclosed by high cliffs and forest, which give a deep green tint to the noticeably turquoise depths, the lagoon is a result of several underwater streams running down from the mountains. The whole effect is very picture-postcard, and swimming here is serene, with a layer of chilly fresh water covering waves of warm sea below. The lagoon drops to 198ft at its deepest spot – just enough for World Freediving Champion David Lee to set the new world record here: in 2002 he dived without assistance to 167ft in three minutes 45 seconds. Lee's parents run scuba/watersports operator Lady G'Diver (see p.119), which offer dive packages and courses in specialist freediving at the lagoon.

Facilities at the Blue Lagoon are nonexistent – a 2005 land dispute led to the close of the attractive wooden restaurant over the water – and though you can swim for free, inevitably a few touts have sprung up to cash in on parking fees. If you agree to pay, going over J$300 would be exorbitant. Alternatively, consider

THE BLUE MOUNTAINS AND THE EAST | East to Boston Bay

staying at the stunning new *Kanopi House* resort on the lagoon's opposite side (see p.120), hidden amongst the trees and boasting its own small beach.

Winnifred Beach

Two miles or so on, **Winnifred Beach** is one of the most appealing beaches in all Jamaica; to get there, turn down the road just east of the *Jamaica Crest Hotel* at the start of **Fairy Hill** village, and follow it for half a mile or so through a neat housing scheme. If you're driving, park where the tarmac ends and continue on foot; if it hasn't rained heavily you can drive right down onto the beach.

Used as the setting for the Robin Williams movie *Club Paradise*, the wide, golden crescent of sand is supremely laid-back and justly popular with Jamaicans. The small reef just offshore is perfect for snorkelling (you'll need to bring your own gear) and protects the bay from the waves, ensuring clear, calm, bright-blue water that shelves gently from the sand. At weekends, local operator Scotty offers children's horseback rides along the sands (J$350), and fishermen will provide boat trips to nearby Monkey Island (1hr; US$10/person). At the western end, a small mineral spring offers a freshwater rinse (the changing facilities are best avoided).

Winnifred beach has good, unobtrusive food and drinks stalls at the centre of the beach, but tucked into the beach's western corner, ⚑ *Cynthia and Painter's* (☎562 4860) is by far the best, offering delicious, delicately seasoned platefuls of ackee and saltfish, chicken, fish and excellent grilled lobster – food is cooked to order, so you're best off phoning in advance or putting in a lunch request as soon as you arrive at the beach. Cynthia has also spearheaded the campaign to keep Winnifred beach public; like so many others on Jamaica's north coast, the government has been moving to develop it exclusively for tourism, and local businesses have quite rightly fought to keep it open. In the meantime, local people are to be seen cleaning the beach, and you may be asked to pay a small unofficial "fee". You're under no obligation to pay (most Jamaicans refuse), but there's no harm in giving a small tip to anyone you see genuinely tidying up the place.

Boston Bay

The once-pretty public beach at **BOSTON BAY**, further east along the A4, is now largely eroded as a result of damage caused by hurricanes Gilbert and Ivan. The little sand that's left is nonetheless the base for taking in some of the best **surf** in Jamaica – you can hire boogie and surf boards (US$10–15/day) from various local characters (ask for Alton).

In any case, Boston has long been better known for its collections of **jerk stands**. Jerking of meat originated in this part of the country – the Maroons hunted wild pigs and smoked the meat to preserve it – and the pork and chicken on sale here is reckoned by many to be the best in Jamaica (if, by some reports, not always as good as it once was). The stalls are all quite similar and the on-commission touts can be aggressive, but if in doubt head to *Mickey's* restaurant, farthest down the small lane at the village's western end. The food is still excellent and authentic, though, cooked for hours over large charcoal pits. You'll pay around J$400 for half a pound of chicken, and J$600 for half a pound of pork; both are best eaten with roast yam, breadfruit or a hunk of fresh hard-dough bread. If you've room in your bags, buy a jar of the fiery home-made jerk sauce – you won't find better anywhere.

Minibuses and shared taxis run to Boston Bay from Port Antonio.

Eating, drinking and nightlife

This coast east of Port Antonio is not exactly bursting with **eating and drinking options**, and many visitors dine in their hotel restaurants – a couple of these are nonetheless excellent and are open to non-guests (phone to reserve a table). The renowned **jerk stands** at Boston Bay (see opposite) of course offer excellent, inexpensive fare, as does *Cynthia and Painter's* at Winnifred Beach (see opposite), alongside the usual assortment of local cookshops. You can have sophisticated drinks in the attractive bars of *Mocking Bird Hill Hotel* or *Jamaica Palace*, or otherwise at basic rum joints in friendly Drapers or Long Bay. *Great Huts* resort at Boston Bay has a Saturday night Jamaican cultural show with costume-clad children from Manchioneal performing a range of old-time dances to hypnotic drum rhythms. If you're after serious **nightlife**, you'll need to head into Port Antonio, or else look for lively sound-system parties at **Boston Bay** or nearby **Blackrock** at weekends or on Wednesdays.

Bush Bar *Geejam Hotel*, San San ☎ 993 7000. The wonderful contemporary-designed terrace is the highlight of this high-end Jamaican restaurant, serving a three-course evening meal with wine for US$70, great cocktails, plus a top-notch breakfast.

Jamaica Palace Just east of Port Antonio ☎ 993 2020. Elegant, expensive European-style restaurant. The menu is big on steaks, with some German dishes.

Mille Fleurs *Mocking Bird Hill Hotel* ☎ 993 7267. A soothing terrace setting and imaginative – and often delicious – concoctions based on Jamaican staples. There's a daily vegetarian option, and the puddings are sublime.

San San Tropez San San ☎ 993 7213. Flavoursome and authentic, if slightly overpriced, Italian cooking: home-made spaghetti and *fettuccini* with tomato, seafood or pesto sauce; fantastic thin-crust pizzas; and Italian-style grilled fish with tomatoes. The crème caramel, made on site, is delightful.

Sir Pluggy's Jerk Centre Fair Prospect. Simple little bar in the village just before Long Bay; some say it makes the best jerk meat in the area.

Woody's Drapers. Inexpensive and friendly café east of *Jamaica Palace*, with great burgers (including veggie), sandwiches and Jamaican staples such as fish with pumpkin rice or pepperpot soup.

Long Bay to Manchioneal

Below Boston Bay, the main road cleaves to the coastline and passes through **Errol Flynn country**, with great views of both pounding surf and rolling pasturelands. The erstwhile screen idol bought a 2000-acre estate here in the 1950s, and his widow, Patrice Wymore, still manages the groves of coconuts and guavas and its grazing beef cattle – though the prime seafront property has been on sale for some years.

Errol Flynn

By the time he arrived in Jamaica in 1947, **Errol Flynn**'s movie career was already in decline. The era of the swashbuckler was drawing to a close, and the Australian actor – star of classic movies like *The Sea Hawk* and *Captain Blood* – had begun to fall from favour with the studios. Nonetheless, sailing ashore in his yacht *Zaca* (now owned by *Superclubs* hotels), Flynn quickly worked his way into local legend. Well known for his powers of seduction, formidable drinking and addiction to gambling, the star reputedly lost Navy Island off Port Antonio in an unfortunate poker bet.

Flynn loved Jamaica, buying the *Titchfield Hotel* in Port Antonio, plus Navy Island, and later, with his third wife **Patrice Wymore**, setting up a ranch near Boston Bay. A string of celebrities attended the wild parties at his hotels – but unsuccessful efforts to resurrect his movie career and continuing bouts of heavy drinking and ill health were already taking their toll. During his final years, Flynn spent much of his time at Titchfield with the teenage actress Beverley Aadland. On his death in 1959, Aadland asked that Flynn be buried in Jamaica, but Wymore insisted that his body go to Hollywood. Today, despite the tarnishing of his reputation through tales of his exploitation of local girls, many people in the area remember the one-time heartthrob with affection.

Four miles of bumpy tarmac later, **Long Bay**, with its gorgeous swath of surf-pounded honey sand and laid-back counter-culture atmosphere, is a marvellous place to get away from it all, and it lies conveniently close to the fabulous **Reach Falls**, where Tom Cruise got amorous in the movie *Cocktail*. Past the falls, the fishing village of **Manchioneal** offers unaffected charm, with one simple but attractive accommodation option.

Long Bay

Unusually for Jamaica's sparsely developed eastern tip, a mini-tourist industry has existed in **LONG BAY** for more than twenty years; its wide crescent of sand, laid-back atmosphere and great surf attracts numerous backpackers, and some have chosen to settle and open guesthouses. It's a far cry from north coast resorts – simple, friendly beach bars draw equal numbers of locals as tourists, and the wholes place feels a bit like Negril must have in the 1960s, good-natured and vaguely alternative, with a lot of ganja smoking and general hanging out.

There isn't much to the village, which has grown up piecemeal on either side of the main road. The north end of the beach is where you'll find a small **surf** scene (though Boston Bay is rated better by professionals). The beach bars can help you find a board, and they'll also know of anyone who'll take you out **fishing**. **Swimming** is excellent here, too, particularly if you're feeling a little jaded towards the usual placid Jamaican shores, but watch out for a dangerous undertow and riptides; it's best not to swim out further than you can stand. Try, also, to get up early for the staggering **sunrise** over the ocean. At the south end of the bay a steep rutted track winds uphill to the quiet community of Rose Garden, which has great views and a couple of guesthouses.

Buses and **shared taxis** run daily to Long Bay from Port Antonio and cost about J$200. If you're driving, be aware that there's no petrol on sale between Port Antonio and Long Bay – the first station you'll reach is just as you enter the village. A small supermarket at the southern end of the community sells basics (plus ice cream and alcohol), while the **library**, opened by residents in 2003, lies behind the **post office**, with local information and **Internet** access. Beach bars *Chill Out* and *Blaze on the Bay* can guard your bags while you look around for **accommodation** (there are numerous basic options in addition to those listed below). At night, be sure to lock the door to your room or villa; despite exuding care-free relaxation, Long Bay is not free from theft.

Accommodation

Blue Heaven Resort Long Bay ☏715 4336 or 448 9605, ⊛www.blueheavenjamaica.com. One small cottage and two rooms (one sleeps three) in a funky concrete house on low cliffs at the bay's northern end, with a creek running down to a small pebble beach. Breakfast included. ❷

Glass House Long Bay ☏913 7475 or 891 0516. Smart and good-value five-bedroom house with large verandah right on the beach, boasting eclectic, homely decor and use of a kitchen. Services of a cook/cleaner are optional. ❸
Jamaican Colors Ross Craig, 3 miles south of Long Bay ☏893 5185 or 457 7786, ⊛www .hoteljamaicancolors.com. Set in a beautiful spot on the cliffs with a walkway down to a private cove, the seven smart and colourful two- to four-person bungalows have hot-water bathrooms, a/c and

TV/DVD. There's a swimming pool and jacuzzi, and the French owners serve great pizza and classic French dishes at the on-site bar. Continental breakfast included. ❸–❹

Likkle Paradise Long Bay ☏913 7702 or 528 8007. Two rooms (with TVs) in the home of ever-gracious and knowledgeable local Herlette Kennedy (guests share the kitchen); attractive decor, a peaceful flowered garden and a good view of the centre of the beach from the small upstairs verandah make this an appealing option. ❷
Monica's Hide-Out Long Bay ☏843 3328. Very basic though reasonable option with two bedrooms (one twin) in a small wooden house, each with tiled floor, fan and tiny private bathroom. Friendly atmosphere and central-beach location. ❶

Rose Garden Pool Villas Rose Garden ☎913 7431, in UK ☎0207 338 3869; ⓦwww.jamaican-grill.com /rose garden. Gorgeous one-bed studio with own pool and a standard three-bedroom house, located high above the bay. Good discount for renting whole property. ❸–❻

Rose Hill Cottage Rose Garden ☎913 7452, ⓦppz.irieweb.net. Just off the main road, this simple but attractive two-bedroom cottage has a kitchen and sea-facing verandah, owned by genial German author Peter-Paul Zahl. Dinner included. ❸

Seascape Long Bay ☎576 0082, ⓔsaintsteven1 @gmail.com. Recently renovated three-bedroom villa on the beach, with large living/dining room and wonderful verandah. Housekeeper and cook on request. Advance booking preferred. ❷–❸

Eating, drinking and entertainment

The two main beach bars/restaurants are currently *Chill Out* and *Blaze on the Bay* (hurricane damage tend to mean locations and ownerships vary); the latter serves the best-value food and drink (try the excellent steamfish) and has a great sound system. *Sweet Daddy* at the bay's northern end is a stalwart local cookshop also serving tasty food, while the *Mid-Way* bar does a roaring trade in rum and dominoes. The classiest place to eat locally is *Jamaican Colors* (see opposite) three miles south; French owner Bob cooks reasonably priced lobster, calamari and steaks, and serves great cocktails. Ask around for the location of weekly **dances** (Fri–Sun); they tend to rotate around East Portland to draw the biggest crowd.

Manchioneal and Reach Falls

South of Long Bay, the road passes by some marvellously rugged coastline and, four miles on before crossing the Christmas River, you'll pass **Kensington**, the birthplace of Father Hugh Sherlock who composed Jamaica's national anthem in 1962. Enclosed by a tunnel-like covering of trees and utterly pitch-black at night, the hairpin-bend stretch of road nearby is locally known as "see me no more". A couple of miles further, the road inches into the pretty fishing village of **MANCHIONEAL**. Here brightly painted stalls selling roast fish and conch soup border the road, and canoes line up on the sand; there's also a petrol station, and you can sup a Red Stripe at the diminutive *Titus Bar* or eat fresh fish on the breezy terrace of the *B & L* restaurant. Ask around for sightings of **manatees** (locally known as sea cows) here; they can occasionally be seen gambolling in the water.

▲ Exploring Reach Falls

Across the bay at **LONG ROAD**, and offering gorgeous views of the harbour, a great **accommodation** option is *Zion Country Cottages* (☎993 0435 or 451 1737, Ⓦwww.zioncountry.com; ❷–❸, including breakfast) signposted from the main road. Run by enthusiastic Dutchman Free-I, the Rasta-oriented, eco-friendly complex spreads down the cliffs to a small shingle beach with hammocks, while flowers and plants wreathe the pathways. Totally rebuilt after Hurricane Gustav in 2007, the four bright cabins share showers, and dinner is also available. Free-I does excellent informal **tours** of the surrounding area, including hikes along the volcanic rocks of the local coastline to impressive blowholes and natural swimming pools, and offers excursions into the mountains and to Morant Point (plus airport pick-ups).

Reach Falls

Between Manchioneal and Long Road, a road swings three miles off the main road through some dazzling countryside to **Reach Falls** (Wed–Sun 8.30am–4.30pm; US$10; ☎993 6606/83). This is one of the loveliest spots on the island, with the Drivers River running through some sumptuous rainforest before cascading over the falls into a wide, green pool. The thirty-foot waterfall allows for an invigorating water massage, and (if you can muster the courage) there's an exhilarating jump from the top. You can also go on a thirty-minute (guided) climb upriver – picking your way across slippery rocks and swimming through deep pools. You can ask to be taken to the base of **Mandingo Cave beyond**, though it's quite a tricky climb. Movie fans might recognize Reach Falls as the place where Tom Cruise cavorts with his lady love in the film *Cocktail*.

Recently redeveloped by the government's Urban Development Corporation (Ⓦwww.udcja.com) with a new visitor centre, craft shops and restaurant, the site has been the subject of a long and drawn-out land dispute, with many locals far from pleased with the result, leaving youngsters no longer able to act as informal guides. A round-trip **taxi** from Port Antonio to the falls costs around US$50; if you're short of funds you could take a route taxi for J$220 (around J$150 from Long Bay) to the signposted turn-off from the A4 and hitch the rest of the way.

The Rio Grande valley

Portland's interior – the **Rio Grande valley** – is a fantastically lush and partially impenetrable hinterland of tropical rainforest and waterfalls. The **Rio Grande**, one of Jamaica's major rivers, pours down from the John Crow Mountains through a deep and unspoilt valley of virgin forest. Despite its beauty, the area is little explored; many people visit **Nonsuch Caves** or do **rafting trips**, but there is also superb river and mountain **hiking**.

Many of the rivers and springs here are named after local Maroon leaders – Nanny, Quao, Quashie and Quako – and the major remaining Maroon settlement is **Moore Town**. If you're craving rustic isolation, some of the other **villages** beyond have lovely settings and fascinating names – Alligator Church, Comfort Castle – indeed, the only thing holding up booming eco-tourism here is the abominable road, which in its higher reaches is barely navigable by car.

Nonsuch Caves and Athenry Gardens

Four miles south of Port Antonio, on the outer fringes of the Rio Grande valley, **Nonsuch Caves** and **Athenry Gardens** (open on cruise-ship days 9am–5pm; US$8.80 with complimentary rum or fruit punch; ☎779 7144) are a mildly

Hiking in the Rio Grande valley

Hiking in the lower limestone valleys of the John Crow Mountains is entirely different to the Blue Mountains – hotter and wetter, you may want to use a waterproof jacket, though staying wet and cooling off at mineral springs could well be a wiser alternative. A guide is essential for most hikes: ask at *Ambassabeth Cabins* in Bowden Pen (see p.129) or *Sister Ivy's* in Cornwall Barracks for local help; otherwise book a **tour** in Port Antonio with **Valley Hikes** (Unit 41, Royal Mall, ☎993 3881), **Grand Valley Tours** (12 West St ☎993 4116, ⓦwww.portantoniojamaica.com/gvt.html) or Kingston-based **Sun Venture Tours** (☎960 6685, ⓦwww.sunventuretours.com). Rates range from US$35 per person for a half-day to US$150 for the two-day trek to Nanny Town – all can arrange home-stays with local families.

A couple of trails (e.g. Road End or Scatter Water Falls, from Berridale) can be done without a guide, but most hikes follow old pig-hunters' routes or even former council "roads" – now heavily overgrown – and require the help of an expert. Among the best trails are: the **Cunha Cunha Pass** (6 miles; 4hr) following the old Maroon **"Freedom Trail"** finishing close to Bath in St Thomas; the **Guava River Trail** (7 miles; 7hr) from Bellevue, with plentiful waterfalls; **Coopers Hill to Nanny Town** (10–15 miles; 2 days), through untouched forest to the site of the eighteenth-century hideaway, a scattering of overgrown ruins that remains an important symbol of Maroon history, allegedly haunted by the ghosts of vanquished British soldiers; and **White River Falls** (4 miles; 7hr), starting from Millbank, a tough and slippery climb through virgin forest to a series of seven cascades.

entertaining first stop. The fourteen ancient subterranean chambers were used by Taino Indians in pre-Columbian times and now house large stalactites and plenty of bats. Guides deliver a well-oiled patter throughout, pointing out fossils of fish and coral from one and a half million years ago when Jamaica was still underwater. Back in the sunshine, stroll around the expansive **gardens** which command a magnificent coastal view and are packed with ginger lilies, bougainvillea and royal poinciana trees.

Rafting the Rio Grande

Once a means of transporting bananas, **rafting** down the majestic Rio Grande is now Portland's most popular attraction, ever since Errol Flynn raced with his friends in the 1950s. It's a delightfully lazy way to spend half a day, although the sun can get fierce.

From the put-in point at **Berridale** six miles southwest of Port Antonio, the thirty-foot bamboo rafts (each with a raised seat) meander down the river for two hours through outstanding scenery, poled downstream by a captain and stopping periodically for swimming or to buy snacks. Tickets are sold at Rio Grande Experience in Berridale (daily 9am–4pm; US$65/raft; ☎993 5778) and by hotels and tour offices in Port Antonio. The trip is one-way terminating at Rafters' Rest in St Margaret's Bay (see p.129), so if you're **driving**, leave your car at Berridale and have an insured driver take it down for US$15, or else use a **taxi** – to Berridale and back to Port Antonio costs around US$20. If you're desperate to save cash, the Berridale route taxi from Port Antonio (J$120) runs close by the put-in point, and route taxis to Port Antonio from Kingston and Buff Bay pass the entrance to Rafters' Rest regularly.

You'll also find people touting **unofficial rafting trips** in Port Antonio for a lower price. Don't hand over the cash until you've finished the journey at Rafters' Rest, and don't go with anyone who makes you feel uncomfortable.

Moore Town, Millbank and Bowden Pen

Eleven miles inland, **MOORE TOWN** is Jamaica's principal Maroon settlement, founded, so the legend goes, by **Nanny** (chieftainess of the Windward Maroons and now a National Hero) in the mid-eighteenth century. Today, it's a small place at the end of a winding rocky road, with few signs and little apparent sense of its historical importance, though it does have a precarious **cricket** pitch by the river where fielders need to stand up to their ankles in water. You should, as a matter of protocol, check in with the Maroons' **colonel** – the present chief, Colonel Stirling, who assumed leadership in 1995, lives some way up the village, though you'll learn more from his elderly predecessor, Colonel Colin Harris, whose house is the first on the right after the post office. There's no charge for looking around but donations are expected. **Bump Grave**, a monument to the "indomitable and skilled chieftainess" Nanny – and supposedly the place where she's buried – is in the town's small central square.

Alternatively, you can find a local guide and hike the forty minutes up to the fabulous pools at **Nanny Falls**, or organize a longer trek with the **operators** noted on p.129. Moore Town is also renowned as the home of Mother Roberts, a spiritual healer practised in the art of Pukkumina (see p.290) with legendary powers. People come from all over to visit her AME (African Methodist Episcopal) Zion Deliverance Centre, a small flower-decked church as you enter the village. Healing sessions are held regularly 9am to 6pm by donation. Moore Town is served by frequent **route taxis** from Port Antonio, though few run on Sundays. Take a **picnic** as cookshops are hard to find. If you want to **stay**, you'll be limited to lodging with a local family, or continuing to picturesque **CORNWALL BARRACKS**, where the formidable Ivelyn Harris, rents out a one-room cabin (☎806 0161; ❸) in her lushly planted garden. Known locally as Sister Ivy, she is an expert herbalist and alternative-medicine practitioner.

The Windward Maroons

When the Spanish left Jamaica in 1660, they armed their newly freed slaves and encouraged them to fight a guerrilla war against the British. Calling the guerrillas *cimarrones* (meaning wild or untamed), the word was corrupted by the British to **Maroons**. With their numbers boosted by runaway slaves from the sugar plantations, the Maroons set up small communities in inaccessible locations, with the **Windward Maroons** establishing themselves in the Blue and John Crow mountains and the Trelawny Maroons making a base in Cockpit Country. The groups raided British settlements for weapons and supplies, and by the 1720s they had become a serious threat to colonial order.

The Windward Maroons had their headquarters 2000ft up at **Nanny Town**, virtually inaccessible to British soldiers, who were unfamiliar with the terrain. They only discovered it after a black slave led them there in 1728, and were periodically slaughtered on their forays into the rainforest to destroy it. Eventually, in 1734, army captain Stoddard dragged swivel guns up the south side of the John Crow Mountains and bombarded Nanny Town, destroying most of the 140 homes and forcing the Maroons to move south. Still, the British couldn't flush them out completely – five years later a peace treaty was signed, giving the undefeated Maroons a semi-independent status that they retain today, as well as 500 acres of land in the Rio Grande valley.

Today, the Windward Maroons have been virtually assimilated into the wider Jamaican population. Though some of the elders remain fiercely proud of their heritage – and a handful still speak the traditional Coromantee language – most young Maroons see little opportunity in their mountain villages and move to the cities. Within a generation there are likely to be few pure-blood Maroons left.

Little-visited **MILLBANK** – the last sizeable village in the Rio Grande valley – nestles deep in the John Crow Mountains, five miles south of Moore Town (take the right fork at Seaman's Valley via **Alligator Church**, where a perilous bridge crosses the river), and contains one of the three National Park **ranger stations** (see box, p.98). This is prime Maroon country, and many of the village's elders – a healthy diet and clean mountain air mean many are pushing 100 – will happily tell you historical tales, while younger locals can escort you to derelict Maroon settlements. The setting is spectacular: rainforest surrounds you and the perfume of wild ginger lilies hangs heavy; it's also the starting point for several **hikes** (see p.127), among them to the seven high cascades of **White River Falls**.

The only **place to stay** in the area is the wonderful 🍴 *Ambassabeth Cabins and Campsite* (☎ 395 5351 or call JCDT ☎ 960 2848; ❶) at **BOWDEN PEN**, a half-hour walk southeast of Millbank. Driving is possible in dry weather; otherwise you might be able to get a lift in a 4WD from the ranger station. Run by knowledgeable local Linnette Wilks, the basic wooden cabins have no electricity but fresh mineral-water-fed taps – and bags of atmosphere. Traditional Maroon meals are prepared on an open fire, and local guides are available. Arrange your stay in advance; the owners can organize transportation from Kingston or Port Antonio. Past *Ambassabeth*, the old Maroon **Cunha Cunha Pass** (see p.127) leads to Bath in St Thomas.

West of Port Antonio

The A4 winds west from Port Antonio, crisscrossing the old railway track torn up by Hurricane Allen in 1980, and threading through tiny villages peppered with stalls selling fruit and vegetables. You can stop for a freshwater splash at **Somerset Falls**, head inland to the maroon community of **Charles Town**, and stay at the **River Edge** retreat near **Annotto Bay**. **Buses** run between Port Antonio, Annotto Bay and on to Kingston every hour.

St Margaret's Bay, Hope Bay and Somerset Falls

Five miles west of Port Antonio, tiny **ST MARGARET'S BAY** is where the Rio Grande empties into the sea underneath an iron bridge dating from 1891. Just by the bridge, a side road leads towards **Rafters' Rest**, a pretty colonial building serving as journey's end for Rio Grande rafting trips (see p.127). You can also usually book an excursion here from a posse of touting operators. Past Rafters' Rest, St Margaret's Bay proper is an appealingly neat settlement spreading back from the roadside, and once served as the last-stop-but-one of the Jamaica Railway. The old railway station itself serves as a simple restaurant and bar. For **accommodation**, 🍴 *Rio Vista* (☎ 993 5444, ⓦ www.riovistajamaica.com; ❹–❺) is a beautifully situated hotel on a bluff with stupendous views of the Rio Grande. Offering attractive rooms in the main house or a self-contained one-bed villa with kitchen, there's also a pool and delicious meals on request. Otherwise, the quiet *Pleasant View Guesthouse* (☎ 913 3058; ❷) in the hills above town has spacious hot-water rooms with two double beds, fan, TV and a pool facing verdant mountain slopes.

Between St Margaret's Bay and Hope Bay, lush landscaping marks the entrance to **Somerset Falls** (daily 9am–5pm; US$9; ☎ 383 6970, ⓦ www.somersetfalls jamaica.com), part of the cascading Daniels River. Guides lead you up a stairway to have a dip in the "cool pool", and your entrance fee also buys a boat ride through the gorge-like rocks to the spectacular "hidden falls" beyond, cascading into a

20ft-deep pool perfect for a natural power shower. There's a smart **restaurant** serving Jamaican and fast food, well-appointed rooms to rent (❹), and sporadic reggae concerts and "Soca Sundays".

HOPE BAY is home to a string of shops and rum bars, with Linton's **Crafts Shop** selling woodcarvings, jewellery and drums at cheaper prices than in Port Antonio. Take a journey inland for marvellous **river swimming** in the upper reaches of the Swift River, a half-hour drive through cocoa groves and mountain valleys (turn left at the small suspension bridge). If you wish to **stay**, a budget option just upstream from the main road has two basic but clean wooden cabins (☎860 7483; ❶) rented by local Rasta Chuckie, while two miles west of town at **Black Hill** is a tranquil and funky Italian-run roots resort, *Ital Village* (☎898 5323, ☯www.italvillage.com; ❷), surrounded by fruit trees and hidden away down a side track from the hilltop.

Buff Bay, Charles Town and Annotto Bay

Heading west, more awesome views of the Blue Mountains are accompanied by relentless fields of coconut palms and banana groves which line the road. At one time they formed part of the United Fruit Company's Kildaire Estate, and today the former great house serves as an efficient rest stop with restaurant, gift store and sparkling bathrooms. Farmers come to sell their wares in the dingy covered market at easy-going **BUFF BAY**, a largely unremarkable town, though you may wish to poke around **St George's** Anglican church, dating from 1814 when it replaced the original structure built in 1681.

Aside from Kildaire, the best place to **eat** in Buff Bay – if you're a jerk pork fan – is the ⽊ *Blueberry Hill* jerk centre, just east of town on the knoll of a hill, which offers meat some say is better than Boston Bay's. If you're looking for somewhere to **stay**, the *Blueberry Guesthouse* (☎913 6814; ❶–❷) has clean rooms with TV and hot water. The town's annual highlight is the **A Fi We Sinting** festival, held on a Sunday each February (look out for posters), with fashion shows, crafts, music, storytelling and dub poetry packing in crowds from miles around.

Though Buff Bay has little to keep you, two-miles inland brings you to **CHARLES TOWN**, a settlement of Maroon origin home to an interesting museum, the **Asafu Yard** (call in advance on ☎445 2861; by donation). Local Maroon Colonel Frank Lumsden is glad to guide people around the drums, crafts and displays on spiritual traditions and medicinal plants, while the area also provides good hiking to an old coffee plantation and reconstruction of a traditional Maroon village two miles upriver. Further inland, the road climbs into the Blue Mountains past Fishdone Waterfall (see p.101), but bear in mind the route to **Section** collapsed in 2004 – check in Buff Bay or Charles Town if repairs have been carried out.

Ten miles west of Buff Bay, **ANNOTTO BAY** is a busy, tatty little market town named after the red annotto dye once produced here. The red and yellow **Baptist church**, built in 1892, has an entrance guarded by old cannons, the meagre remains of British Fort George. For **food**, head to the *Human Service Station* just east of town, which serves delicious fish, fried chicken and natural juices right by the sea.

The countryside **inland of Annotto Bay**, sheltering under the eaves of the Blue Mountains, makes a welcome change from coastal vistas; turn in at the Annotto Bay All Age School and follow signs to **River Edge** (☎944 2673, ✉riveredge99 @hotmail.com), twenty minutes' drive through banana groves and a flower farm. Built around the cool, clear waters of the Pencar River is a friendly, family-run combination of restaurant, swimming spot and retreat, with relaxing pools and massages even on offer. You can **stay** here in a choice of airy dorm beds or private studio apartments with cooking facilities (❶–❸); camping also available with showers and bathrooms nearby.

3

Ocho Rios and the north coast

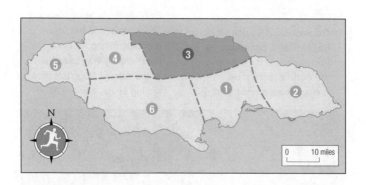

CHAPTER 3 # Highlights

✳ **Faith's Pen** This string of roadside stalls dishes out all the Jamaican favourites – jerk chicken, conch soup, curried goat, roast fish – each delicious and very cheap. A matchless Jamaican eating experience. See p.142

✳ **Firefly and Blue Harbour** Noel Coward's hilltop home oozes history and has one of the best views on the island, over Port Maria bay. His former beach house below is an intriguing and great-value accommodation option. See p.151

✳ **Robins Bay** This peaceful, largely Rasta community is ideally placed for exploring the north coast's most unspoilt countryside, and has two great places to stay. See p.154

✳ **Cranbrook Flower Forest** One of the loveliest gardens in Jamaica, with its own large river pool, grassy lawns to picnic on and a canopy zip line tour. See p.157

✳ **High Hope Estate** Set amid botanical gardens high over St Ann's Bay, this small, intimate hotel is one of the best on the island – and more affordable than most in its class. See p.158

✳ **Bob Marley's Mausoleum** The drive inland through dramatic rolling hills is a breathtaking way to arrive at the King of Reggae's final resting place. See p.160

▲ Canopy tour at Cranbrook Flower Forest

Ocho Rios and

the north coast

T he **north coast** is the most developed area of Jamaica outside the capital, boasting numerous things to do and an energetic atmosphere. A new highway between Montego Bay and Ocho Rios has halved journey times between the two cities, opening up the last stretches of undeveloped coastline to an onslaught of resort expansion.

The attraction of the north coast is obvious: barrelling through the diverse parishes of St Mary, St Ann and Trelawny, the highway passes stunning scenery – sweeping cane and coconut plantations, mangrove swamps, luscious farmland and miles of white-sand **beaches** with reefs less than a hundred feet out to sea. Yet this "touristy" coast can sometimes seem like Jamaica at its most forlorn – sights are often contrived and expensive, resorts are mostly fenced-in all-inclusives and ingrained hustling can make interactions feel like a sales pitch.

Much development is centred on the "garden parish" of **St Ann**, so called because of the area's immensely fertile soil. St Ann has also spawned luminaries such as **Marcus Garvey**, **Bob Marley** and **Winston "Burning Spear" Rodney**, and is considered the spiritual centre of the island. The nucleus of the parish and the home of the famous **Dunn's River Falls**, **Ocho Rios** is Jamaica's most popular holiday destination, with high-rise blocks, buzzing jet skis and thumping nightlife. But just a few miles to the east, the quiet coastal communities of **Oracabessa** and **Port Maria** are disturbed by little other than birdsong, with deserted coastline ideal for hiking and waterfall hunting. West of Ocho Rios, **St Ann's Bay** makes a refreshing change to

---

Public transport around Ocho Rios

Jamaica's haphazard **minibus system** offers both inter-city routes and stopping services along stretches of old road through the villages between 6am and 7pm, with a reduced service on Sundays, and little or nothing in the later evening. If you're going to Kingston or Montego Bay, the most reliable option is the more expensive **Knutsford Express Bus** (see p.22), with two daily services. In the interior, most areas have just one daily service, usually departing at the crack of dawn and returning to base in the early evening, though you may be able to pick up a route taxi. Internal Air Link (℡975 3773) flights go to Boscobel Aerodrome, a twenty-minute drive from Ocho Rios; a cab to town should cost about US$25.

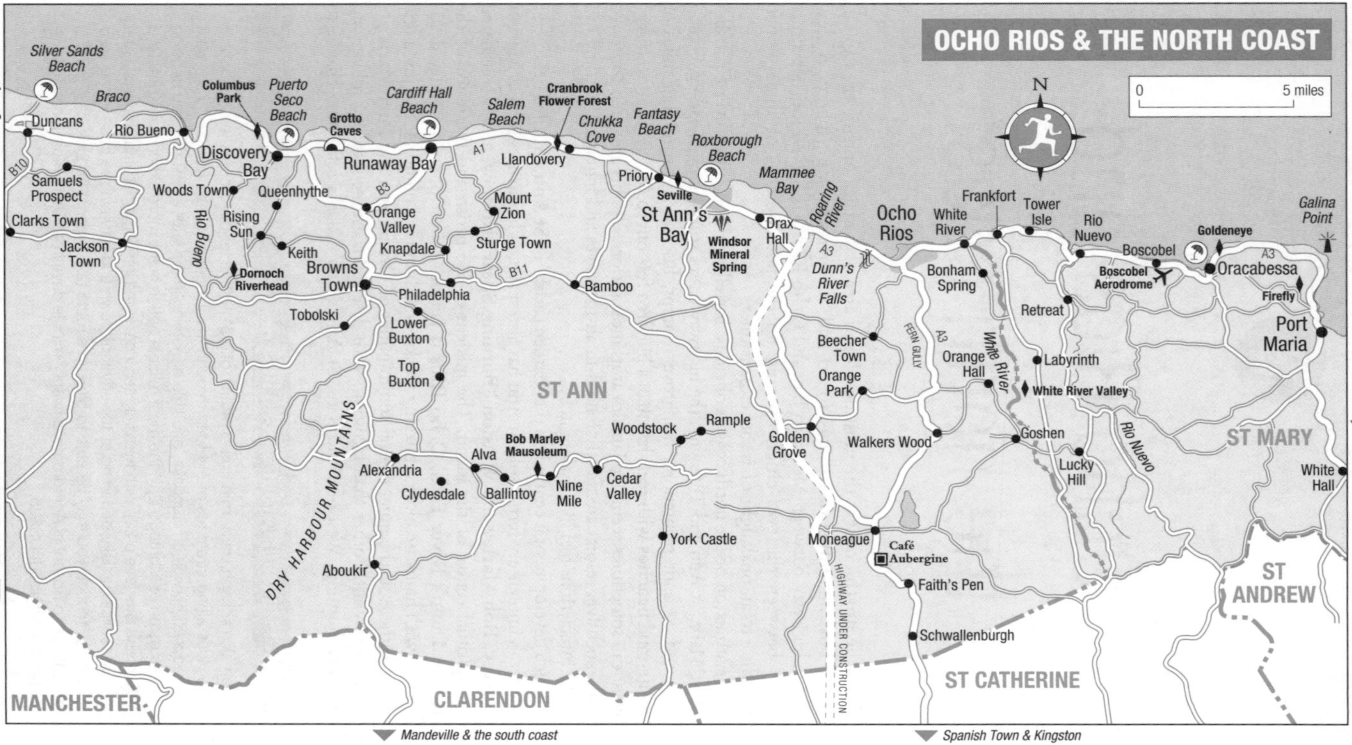

OCHO RIOS & THE NORTH COAST
0 5 miles
N
Montego Bay
Watson Town
Black River & the south coast
Mandeville & the south coast
Spanish Town & Kingston
Robins Bay & Port Antonio
Silver Sands Beach
Braco
Duncans
B10
Samuels Prospect
Clarks Town
Jackson Town
Rio Bueno
Columbus Park
Puerto Seco Beach
Discovery Bay
Woods Town
Rio Bueno
Queenhythe
Rising Sun
Keith
Dornoch Riverhead
Grotto Caves
Cardiff Hall Beach
Runaway Bay
B3
Orange Valley
Knapdale
Browns Town
Tobolski
Philadelphia
Lower Buxton
Top Buxton
A1
Salem Beach
Llandovery
Mount Zion
Sturge Town
B11
Cranbrook Flower Forest
Chukka Cove
Fantasy Beach
Priory
Seville
Bamboo
St Ann's Bay
Roxborough Beach
Windsor Mineral Spring
Mammee Bay
Drax Hall
Roaring River
A3
Dunn's River Falls
Ocho Rios
Beecher Town
Orange Park
FERN GULLY
White River
Bonham Spring
Frankfort
Tower Isle
Rio Nuevo
Boscobel
Boscobel Aerodrome
Goldeneye
Oracabessa
A3
Firefly
Galina Point
Port Maria
Retreat
Labyrinth
Orange Hall
White River
White River Valley
Goshen
Lucky Hill
Rio Nuevo
ST MARY
White Hall
ST ANN
DRY HARBOUR MOUNTAINS
Alexandria
Clydesdale
Alva
Ballintoy
Bob Marley Mausoleum
Nine Mile
Cedar Valley
Woodstock
Rample
Golden Grove
Walkers Wood
York Castle
Moneague
Café Aubergine
Faith's Pen
Schwallenburgh
HIGHWAY UNDER CONSTRUCTION
Aboukir
MANCHESTER
CLARENDON
ST CATHERINE
ST ANDREW

the glitz of its neighbour. Further west, sporadic tourism development is interspersed with peaceful villages like **Rio Bueno** and **Duncans** – and fantastic beaches. **Inland**, winding, leafy lanes pass through marvellous scenery; smack in the middle of St Ann is Bob Marley's birthplace and the site of his mausoleum, where a cache of Rasta guides welcomes hordes of reggae disciples.

Ocho Rios and around

Light years away from the sleepy fishing village of a few decades ago, **OCHO RIOS** (usually just called "Ochi") has long been overtaken by the tourist industry. Developed specifically as a resort, planners often overlooked aesthetics in the chase for foreign dollars. Each week thousands of cruise-ship passengers disembark here (especially from December to March), and Ochi is fully geared up to easy-access tourism with numerous neon-fronted in-bond stores, visitor-oriented restaurants and several slickly packaged attractions. Ochi isn't the best choice for the classic Caribbean beach holiday – the meagre strips of hotel-lined sand just can't compete with Negril and Montego Bay. Yet in spite of its scenic deficiencies and the fact that local culture takes a bit of a back seat, Ochi's town and tourist area are one and the same, with less of the "sitting duck" atmosphere of the Montego Bay strip, and it does boast a certain infectious energy. Harassment here too, has become only a minor irritation.

"Ocho Rios" is a corruption of the Spanish name *chorreros*, referring to the "gushing water" of the many local waterfalls – there are not "eight rivers" here. In contrast to its poetic name, the town has a somewhat violent history as the site of several bloody battles that took place when Spanish governor **Don Christobel Arnaldo de Yssasi** refused to give in to the British after their capture of the island in 1655. Major skirmishes took place at Dunn's River in 1657, Rio Nuevo in 1658 and Shaw Park in 1659, when Yssasi's men were attacked by a group led by his erstwhile ally, **Juan de Bolas**, a former slave who had defected to the British. In 1660, Yssasi fled the island, but local Spanish legacy remains in a smattering of place names and through the fragrant **pimento** tree, first discovered by the Spanish in St Ann and commercially planted here ever since.

The **British** left a more pervasive mark, with their huge sugar cane, lumber and cattle farms, though most planters were absentees. Ocho Rios remained little more than a fishing harbour until the twentieth century, when **tourism** and **bauxite** began to physically sculpt the land. In 1923, a great house at Shaw Park became Jamaica's first exclusive **hotel**, and by 1948 it had been joined by the *Sans Souci Lido*, *Silver Seas* and *Dunn's River* (now *Sandals*). Perpetual crop failures led local planter **Alfred DaCosta** to chemically analyse the St Ann earth, finding that the soil contained high levels of **bauxite**, the chief raw material used to produce aluminium. Foreign companies Reynolds and Kaiser bought up huge tracts of land, and in 1968 forty acres were reclaimed from behind what is now Ochi's Main Street. The harbour was dredged, and Reynolds built a deep-water pier, while Jamaica's Urban Development Corporation imported sand and built another jetty for cruise ships. More than three decades later, their efforts have brought about the firmly established resort town of today.

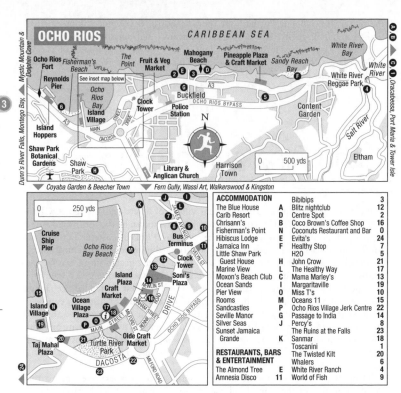

Arrival, getting around and information

All **buses** pull in at the transport terminus in the middle of town adjacent to the police station, which backs onto the bypass road. You're within walking distance of most hotels, but taxi drivers are on hand. If you're **driving** in from Montego Bay or the west, the coast road forks as you enter town; left takes you onto the one-way section of Main Street, where the majority of hotels are located, while right takes you along DaCosta Drive, bypassing downtown, and with Milford Road, which leads to Fern Gully and, eventually Kingston. If you drive in from the east, you enter town via the bypass and there are three signposted exits onto Main Street. **Cruise ships** dock at the pier off Main Street; taxi drivers line up to meet those who haven't already arranged tours – it's around US$5 into town.

The clock tower and the car park next to Ocean Village Plaza are all unofficial **taxi ranks**; plentiful tourists can also mean inflated fares – if in doubt haggle, as there is always another taxi waiting. As a rule of thumb, expect to pay about US$10–12 to charter a taxi from downtown to the Tower Isle area east of town or to Dunn's River Falls. To call a taxi, JUTA (☎974 2292) and Maxi Taxi (☎974 2971) are both reliable, as are the drivers noted under "Tours" below. **Shared taxis** running along Main Street can be flagged down anywhere at the roadside. For most drives around town, you'll pay around J$100; trips to Boscobel or Oracabessa will cost about J$180. For **car rental**, see p.147 – but if you're spending most of your time in town, walking is an easier option. **Information** desks are located at the

Cruise Ship Pier and at **TPDCO** (The Tourist Product Development Company; Mon–Fri 9am–5pm; ☎974 7705), upstairs in Ocean Village Plaza on Main Street – both can advise on activities and hotels, and dispense useful local maps. Weekly newspaper *The North Coast Times* is a valuable entertainment resource.

Numerous **tours** are on offer near Ochi, among them a variety with Chukka Cove (see p.157), horseback-riding with Hooves (see p.157), downhill cycling through the Blue Mountains (see p.96), ATVs and zip lines at H'Evans Scent (☎427 4866, ⓦ www.hevansscent.com) and Helicopter Tours (see p.139). You could also hire an independent driver – reliable ones for local sightseeing are Clifton Riley (☎375 8174), Dawn Clarke (☎774 1202) or "Cool Marco" Kura (☎784 3099) – the latter offering off-the-beaten-track days out. Drivers charge US$100–200 per day – a bargain for three or four people – but make sure you negotiate in advance which stops will be made and what entrance fees are payable.

Accommodation

The fashion for **all-inclusive resorts** is plain to see both east and west of town, with several *Sandals* resorts (one right by Dunn's River Falls) accompanied by two *Superclubs* properties, and in the centre of Ochi, the skyline-dominating *Sunset Jamaica Grande*. Condo resorts are also popular – blocks of family-friendly, self-catering apartments grouped around a pool. Budget travellers are not so well catered for, though there are a few rooms for less than US$50; triple and quad rooms also cost little more than a double.

There are hordes of **villas** around Ocho Rios, renting from US$2000 up to US$15,000 per week and beyond – some represent good value when sleeping up to twelve. For bookings contact: the Jamaica Association of Villas and Apartments (☎974 2508, ⓦ www.villasinjamaica.com); *Prospect Plantation*, which rents out five luxurious seafront villas (☎994 1373, ⓦ www.prospect-villas.com); *The Cottage at Te Moana* (☎974 2870, ⓦ www.harmonyhall.com) – a funkily designed ocean property; or, if money is no object, *Rio Chico* (☎1-305/284-1300 ext. 4238 in US, ⓦ www.riochico.com), which sits below Dunn's River Falls.

The Blue House White River, Ocho Rios ☎994 1367, ⓦ www.thebluehousejamaica .com. Superb deluxe B&B with immaculate, tasteful rooms. The highlight is possibly the best Jamaican-fusion cooking on the island, encompassing traditional, Chinese and Indian styles. Breakfast and dinner are served family-style, while the genial hosts are a mine of information and offer islandwide tours. A pool and nearby spot for river bathing are great for relaxation. ❻

Carib Resort Main St, Ocho Rios ☎974 0305. Quiet and quaintly furnished apartments in a two-storey building overlooking lively Mahogany Beach, with manicured gardens and access to the sea. All units have small balconies and ocean views; some have a/c and TV. ❹

Chrisann's Tower Isle, St Mary ☎975 4467, ⓦ www.chrisannsresort.com. Good-value, attractive condo resort east of town. Clean, well-maintained studios and one- to three-bedroom apartments with a/c, cable TV, fully

equipped kitchen and access to the pool and mini private beach. ❹–❻

Fisherman's Point Cruise Ship Pier Rd, Ocho Rios ☎974 2837, ⓦ www.fishermanspoint.net. Located in a low-rise building close to the beach, these clean, comfortable apartments all have private balconies, a/c, cable TV and kitchenettes. Friendly staff, small pool and on-site *Coconuts* restaurant are great extras. ❻

Hibiscus Lodge 83–87 Main St ☎974 2676, ⓦ www.hibiscusjamaica.com. Set back from the road in beautiful gardens, this is one of Ochi's most attractive hotels. The clean, pleasant, cliffside rooms all have balconies. Other highlights: a pool, jacuzzi, tennis court, sun deck, sea access, excellent restaurant and a bar with swinging seats. Rates include breakfast. ❺

Jamaica Inn Main St, Ocho Rios ☎974 2514, ⓦ www.jamaicainn.com. The most attractive (and expensive) hotel in Ochi, tasteful and elegant, with a gorgeous private beach, pool and sophisticated oceanfront spa. Rooms have a/c, beautiful blue and white decor and ocean-facing balconies. No children under 14; jacket and tie required for dinner. All-inclusive deals available. ❾

Little Shaw Park Guest House 21 Shaw Park Rd ☎974 2177, ⓦwww.littleshawparkguesthouse .com. Easy-going, family-owned place set in gardens above town, with space for camping (US$25). Homely rooms with cable TV, fan and private hot water bathrooms; most have kitchen facilities. The friendly owners offer local tours. ❸

Marine View 9 James Ave ☎974 5753. One of few budget options downtown, rooms here are basic but reliable, some with ceiling fan, others with a/c and TV; all have private bathrooms with hot water. Bear in mind James Ave is noisy and slightly seedy at night. ❷

Moxon's Beach Club Boscobel, St Mary ☎975 7023, ⓦwww.moxons-beach-club.com. East of town with a reef offshore, this hip hotel offers good-value luxury, with restaurant/bar and deep colours in various rooms, some with gorgeous verandahs. The original owner was Timothy Moxon who played Strangeways in *Dr No*; and the hotel had a long list of celebrity patrons in the 1960s. ❺–❼

Ocean Sands 14 James Ave ☎974 2605, ⓔOceanSands@worldlinks.com. Good-value, comfortable rooms with sea-view terraces and private bathrooms. Other pluses include a small private beach, pool, and a charming restaurant on a wooden jetty. ❸–❹

Pier View 19 Main St ☎974 2607. Busy, friendly, laid-back apartments next to the beach and popular with young people. Self-catering units available; all rooms have fridge, cable, fan or a/c, and access to the pool. Discounted rates for longer stays. ❸

Rooms Main St ☎974 6632, ⓦwww.roomsresorts .com. All-inclusive *Superclubs* beach resort downtown offering a great pool, gym, restaurant and bar. Comfortable rooms vary in size (ask for sea or pool view); all have a/c, cable and Internet. Rates include Continental breakfast. ❸

Sandcastles Main St ☎974 2310, ⓦsandcastles ochorios.net. In front of the beach (free access) and close to shops, these airy apartments have a/c, cable TV and kitchenettes. Good for families – the pool has a slide and a children's area – and there's an attractive restaurant and bar. ❹

Seville Manor 84 Main St ☎795 2900, ⓕ795 2901. Friendly small hotel popular with holidaying Jamaicans. All rooms have a/c and cable TV and are spacious and immaculate. ❷–❹

Silver Seas 66 James Ave ☎974 2755, ⓦwww.silverseashotel.com. Slightly faded and wonderfully atmospheric hotel with a peaceful ambience, despite its downtown location. Rooms are simple and comfortable; all have sea views and private verandahs. Large garden, pool and bar on site. ❸–❹

Sunset Jamaica Grande Main St, Ocho Rios ☎974 2200, ⓦwww.sunsetjamaicagrande.com. One of Jamaica's largest hotels, this grandly refurbished all-inclusive features 730 amenity-packed rooms, an open-air lobby complete with waterfalls, five restaurants, eight bars, private beach with watersports, fitness centre, five pools, tennis courts, disco, spa, a children's activity programme and the atmosphere of a ritzy shopping mall. ❼–❾

The Town

Although compact enough to explore on foot, the busy streets of Ocho Rios hold little interest for sightseers – though if trawling shopping malls or hanging out in a bar is your thing, you're well catered for. The attractions instead lie just outside of town, and days in Ochi itself are best spent lazing on the beach. Running parallel to the sea, **Main Street** houses the majority of hotels, bars, shopping plazas and restaurants, as well as craft markets and the post office. Opposite the clock tower and forking off towards the sea from Main Street, **James Avenue** has a somewhat seedy feel and is home to plenty of low-key, Jamaican style eateries, the odd ganja hustler and several no-frills clubs.

Most of the town's tourist activity centres around the main **beach** – variously known as Mallards, Turtle and Ocho Rios Bay (daily 8.30am–6pm, with last entry to the beach at 4.30pm; J$250). Tucked under the hotels and accessible from the western end of Main Street near the *Pier View* and *Sandcastles* hotels, the white-sand beach is wide and well maintained, with showers, changing rooms, bars and plenty of activity. However, the water is prone to patches of sea grass, and occasional reports of pollution mean that this isn't one of the north coast's most appealing beaches, particularly when it's overshadowed by the bulk of docked cruise ships.

At the far western end of both the beach and Main Street, the **Island Village** complex is a popular place to spend an hour or two. A combination of shopping mall and entertainment centre, it's been carefully designed to imitate the prettiest aspects of Caribbean architecture, with wooden shacks in washed-out ice-cream colours selling classy holiday souvenirs, clothes and jewellery. The large central square has a striking bronze statue of Bob Marley, guitar in hand, and a covered stage hosts musical events and free cultural entertainment – dance, drumming, and, inevitably, Marley tributes – at sporadic points throughout the day.

Ocho Rios Fort and Mystic Mountain

If you head west of town beyond Main Street, past the small shacks of the Fisherman's Beach and the bauxite factory gates, you'll reach the town's only historical feature, **Ocho Rios Fort**, now in the shadow of giant docked cruise ships. The fort was built by the British in the seventeenth century and restored in 1780 to defend against a feared French attack, but there's little to see other than two cannons, taken from the now derelict Mammee Bay Fort and placed here in the 1960s. Just past the fort and the Island Hopper helicopter pad from where you can take helicopter tours of the island (☏974 1285, ⓦwww.jamaicahelicopterservices.com) is the beginning of the **"One Love Trail"**, a pretty three-mile seaside path. The trail gives easy access to Ochi's three busiest tourist attractions, Mystic Mountain, Dolphin Cove and Dunn's River Falls, and you'll find toilets en route close to Clarke's Art Studio, a flower-wreathed, green-painted wooden house on the cliffside with gorgeous views of a small waterfall cascading down to the beach below.

Watersports, boat cruises and river adventures

Although there isn't that much underwater at Ocho Rios main beach – you'll find richer pickings east of the harbour or at the reef at the bottom of Dunn's River – the sand is lined with watersports concessions. Prices are set and displayed at boards by the entrances, and offerings range from jet skiing and banana boats to water-skiing and parasailing. Kayaks and windsurfers are also on hand. Half- or full-day deep-sea **fishing** for blue marlin or sailfish is available (from US$450), as are glass-bottom boat rides along the coast to Dunn's River Falls. For **scuba diving**, try Garfield (☏395 7023) or Resort Divers (☏974 5338, ⓦwww.resortdivers.com) – the best spots are Devil's Reef at the eastern end of town and a couple of shipwrecks further out to sea.

The coast reverberates to sound systems aboard **pleasure cruises**. Day-trips go to Dunn's River for snorkelling and climbing the falls (3–4hr; US$75, including open bar and/or lunch); romantic or soca sunset cruises (2hr; US$60, including drinks; dinner cruises also available). Contact Heave-Ho (180 Main St ☏974 5367, ⓦwww.heaveho charters.com) and Red Stripe (121 Main St ☏974 2446, ⓦwww.fivestarwatersports .com). Heave-Ho also has a weekend cruise to Santiago de Cuba (negotiable).

Some of the most fun activities are tubing, kayaking and rafting on the White River just to the east of Ochi. **Calypso Rafting** (☏974 2527, ⓦwww.calypsorafting.com) offers calm, risk-free trips, while **White River Valley** (daily 8am–6pm; US$8; ☏917 3373, ⓦwww.wrvja.com) and **Chukka Cove Adventure Tours** (☏972 2506, ⓦwww .chukkacaribbean.com) fight it out for the cruise and all-inclusive market, with free pick-up from most hotels to their purpose-built landscaped "villages", high up the White River valley, with **tubing** and kayaking along different sections (3hr; US$70). Bear in mind that the rapids are only mildly challenging even after heavy rain, and these days fear of litigation from potential accidents has led to overcautiousness.

▲ Ocho Rios Bay

A mile or so from the fort is the latest pocket-emptying addition to Ochi's tourism roster. **Mystic Mountain** (☎974 3990, ⓦwww.rainforestbobsledjamaica.com) boasts a kilometre-long chairlift through the forest canopy to the mountain's peak, where a visitor centre greets you complete with restaurant, pool with tube and a small yet fascinating exhibition on Jamaica's myriad sporting achievements. From here, capitalizing on Jamaica's *Cool Runnings* fame, a two-person "bobsled" takes you on a whirlwind rollercoaster through the trees, while nearby a series of zip lines is possibly the island's best canopy tour. If you want to take in all three rides (and you're likely to feel you're missing out if you don't) it'll set you back US$125; even so, this is better value than buying each separately, at around US$50 per ride.

Dolphin Cove and Dunn's River Falls

Just beyond the end of the One Love Trail is **Dolphin Cove** (daily 8.30am–5.30pm; ☎974 5335, ⓦwww.dolphincovejamaica.com; US$19 entrance fee for day-long access). The main draw at the theme-park style complex is the chance to swim with the bottlenose dolphins kept in a fenced-off section of the bay (changing facilities and lockers on-site). There are a variety of programmes ranging from US$46 to US$200 (children under 6 discounted or free), allowing anything from a stroke to a swim with dorsal pull and photos included. Programmes start daily at 9.30am, 11.30am, 1.30pm and 3.30pm; book a few days ahead. While swimming with dolphins is undeniably a great experience, operations like this generally encourage the capture and trade of wild (very often female) dolphins, with little study of local stocks. For further information visit the Jamaica Environmental Trust website at ⓦwww.jamentrust.org. Elsewhere in the complex, there's a pool containing sharks and rays, a "Jungle Trail" with stops for petting macaws and touching starfish and snakes, a small beach where you can rent snorkel equipment and canoes, and a restaurant and gift shop.

From Dolphin Cove, a ten-minute stroll along the boardwalk brings you to **Dunn's River Falls** (daily 8.30am–4pm, beach closes 6pm; US$20, plus a tip for the guide; ☎974 2857, ⓦwww.dunnsriverja.com). Jamaica's best-loved waterfall and a staple of tour brochures, the falls are overdeveloped but still breathtaking, and remain the island's major tourist honeypot. Masked from the road by restaurants, craft shops and car parks, the wide and magnificent 600ft waterfall cascades over rocks down to a pretty tree-fringed white-sand beach that's far cleaner than the one in town. There's a lively reef within swimming distance, and snorkel gear is available to rent from several touts.

Impressively proportioned, with water running so fast you can hear it from the road below, the falls are surrounded by dripping foliage and more than live up to their reputation, despite the concrete and commerciality. The main activity is climbing up the cascade, a wet but easily navigable hour-long clamber. The step-like rocks are regularly scraped to remove slippery algae, and the thing to prevent a stumble is to form a hand-holding chain led by one of the very experienced guides. It's thoroughly exhilarating, as you're showered with cool, clear water all the way up – wear a bathing suit. There's a restaurant and bar and full changing facilities at the beach and at the top of the falls. Frequently hundred-strong queues form along the beach; to avoid the crowds arrive late in the afternoon (last climb at 4pm), when cruise passengers are aboard their ships.

An alternative to the crowds and the admission price of Dunn's River Falls are the **unmaintained waterfalls** above the enclosure. To get there, take the main route to Dunn's River but carry on up past the car park to where the tarmac ends. Follow the dirt path into the bush to your right for five minutes, and there are several more waterfalls higher up the road, though you may need a local companion to find them. Kingston-based Sun Venture Tours (☎960 6685, Ⓦwww.sunventuretours.com) offers a six-hour tour of the area (US$65/person, minimum group of four) with local guide and ranger "Brother Mike".

Shaw Park and Coyaba River Garden

A twenty-minute drive starting along Milford Road takes you to two of Ochi's better-known pastoral attractions. Both are on the un-signposted Shaw Park Road (turn right from Milford Road 150 yards from the main roundabout on DaCosta Drive in the direction of Kingston). About a hundred yards from Milford Road, a left turn and a steep twenty-minute drive brings you to the 1922-foot peak of **Murphy Hill** (sometimes called Governor's Hill), which provides handsome views over Ocho Rios. A right turn from the fork takes you past some swanky private homes to the **Shaw Park Botanical Gardens** (daily 8am–5pm; US$10, plus a tip for your guide; ☎974 2723, Ⓦwww.shawparkgardens.com), a mere 550ft above sea level but boasting stunning aerial views nonetheless. The former grounds of a long-gone hotel, Shaw Park is a little-visited attraction these days, which means you might get the place almost to yourself. The creatively planted 25-acre gardens are resplendent with unusual flowers, plants and trees – including a huge banyan – set amidst grassy lawns, and there's also a near-perpendicular (but non-swimmable) waterfall.

About five minutes further up Shaw Park Road, the more intimate **Coyaba River Garden and Mahoe Falls** (daily 8am–5pm; US$5 for the garden, US$10 including falls; ☎974 6235, Ⓦwww.coyabagardens.com) is a much more packaged attraction than Shaw Park (with café and gift shop), and is well worth an hour of your time. Wooden walkways allow easy viewing of the heliconias, anthuriums, hot-pink ginger lilies and rampant vines, and flowerbeds are bisected by streams teeming with mullet, koi, crayfish and turtles, with occasional glass panels providing a view of the underwater goings-on. Housed in an elegant cut-stone building, the **museum** has a limited but thoughtful collection of exhibits, from Taino *zemis* (talismans used to ward off evil spirits) to a nineteenth-century man-trap, photographs depicting post-emancipation life, and displays on St Ann's own Marcus Garvey and Bob Marley. The falls are in a beautiful spot overhung by mahoe trees.

Fern Gully, Walkers Wood and beyond

Carrying on along Milford Road past the Shaw Park Road turn-off brings you into **Fern Gully**, a densely vegetated and steeply inclining three-mile stretch of the A3/A1 road to Kingston, made famous by the arboreal splendour of the five hundred or so varieties of fern that smother the roadside banks. First planted in the 1880s, the ferns are overhung by tall trumpet and mahoe trees, which filter the sunlight to create a cool, green-tinged tunnel. Moist and sheltered, the gully environment is ideal for ferns, but exhaust fumes from heavy traffic have damaged and even wiped out some of the species. Recent heavy rains have also severely disrupted the water table over the whole area, reducing the gully to a vehicle-crunching series of water-filled potholes, which often cause traffic jams. You can walk up from Ochi in about twenty minutes, but traffic combined with lack of walkways and persistent roadside vendors make this distinctly uncomfortable.

While you're in the area, the **Wassi Art pottery works** at Great Pond (Mon–Sat 9am–5pm; free) make an interesting distraction; turn off Milford Road at the colourful signposts just before Fern Gully, then left at the fork in the road 250 yards further. The small, family-owned commercial factory produces some of the island's better ceramic pieces. Tours take you through each stage of production, from clay processing to pot throwing, painting and firing, and you can buy the works at cheaper prices than at local gift shops.

Once beyond the leafy canopy of the Fern Gully hill, the landscape opens up, with eye-popping views across the pastures and hillocks of the interior, with misted Blue Mountain peaks just visible. The first community that you'll come to is **WALKERS WOOD**, home of **Walkerswood Caribbean Foods**, whose products – including its famous fiery jerk seasoning – are exported all over the world. A **guided tour** of its factory (US$15, including tastings and complimentary drink; ☎917 2318; cooking demonstrations and classes by special arrangement) combines a trip to the herb and spice garden with an excellent history of Jamaican culinary culture, followed by a buffet lunch at the on-site jerk pit. Day tours, including to Walkerswood, are available from **Maxi Tours** (☎974 2971, ⊛www.maxitoursjamaica.com). The gift shop has some wonderfully quirky bags, earrings and mobiles by local artist Nancy Burke (aka Inansi), as well as recipe books and Walkerswood products.

Continuing along the A3, through emerald fields dotted with dilapidated gingerbread houses and restored plantation homes, you eventually reach **MONEAGUE**, a quiet roadside town that's worth a stop for its sole **restaurant**, the elegant, intimate ꙮ *Café Aubergine* (Wed–Sun noon–late, last orders 9pm; ☎973 0527), set in a beautiful colonial-era building with verandah seating. The linen tablecloths and tastefully rustic decor come as a bit of a surprise after roadside cookshops, and the food – European with a Caribbean twist – is well worth the forty-minute drive from Ochi. Starters include conch in lemon vinaigrette, and mains like roast goose and lobster in a garlic sauce (mains US$20–40). A good wine list and soothing atmosphere complement the cooking. Easily missed, the restaurant is marked by a nondescript sign at the southern end of town, just past a near-hairpin bend.

If *Café Aubergine* is beyond your budget, a ten-minute drive along the A3 south of Moneague brings you to one of Jamaica's best-loved street-food institutions, ꙮ **Faith's Pen**, a string of smoking food stalls. Blackened by years of barbecue cooking, the stalls do a cracking trade with the steady stream of traffic passing between Kingston and Ochi – though the new super-fast toll road has undoubtedly impacted. Each stall sells a variation on the same theme (go for the cook with the longest queue): roast yam and saltfish, jerk chicken or pork, ackee and saltfish, roast corn, curry goat, mannish water or fish/conch soup, alongside beers and natural juices. You eat at benches, with whizzing cars and the strains of Irie FM blaring from ghetto blasters serving as background music.

Though not the most picturesque place for a meal, Faith's Pen is the consummate on-the-road eating experience.

East of town

The clamour of Ocho Rios's Main Street recedes as you head east of town, but one place you shouldn't pass by is **Mahogany Beach**, a quiet-ish beach (free admission) set in landscaped gardens just past the *Hibiscus Lodge* hotel. Occupying a pretty strip of sand with good snorkelling and swimming, and boasting a good beach bar and grill, natural spring pool and even a massage hut (US$60/hr), Mahogany is Ochi's most attractive chill-out spot, worth a visit by day or night. At weekends, jerk meat and fish is grilled outside and there's an uptown party atmosphere, aided by sound systems.

Beyond Mahogany, in amongst the glamorous frontages of all-inclusive hotels, the studios of **Irie FM** are marked by a colourful billboard opposite the Coconut Grove shopping centre. Irie was Jamaica's first reggae-only station and remains the island's most popular – airwaves were previously dominated by American soul, gospel and country. Since its first transmission in 1990, Irie has championed the cultural legitimacy of a musical genre branded subversive until the early 1970s. Today, the station provides the soundtrack for the nation. Wherever you go, you'll hear the music, the popular talk shows and the patois jingles: "Irie FM – a fi wi station" or "My radio dial stuck pon Irie FM, and guess what – me nah bother fix it". Steel Pulse, Burning Spear, Aswad and Third World, among many others, have recorded at Irie's Grove Studios, and the station has brought a bit of Kingston-style culture to Ochi.

Past Irie FM, Main Street merges into the A3 coast road and crosses the bridge over the sluggish **White River**, which marks the parish boundary of St Ann and St Mary. Several tour operators offer tubing, kayaking and rafting here (see box, p.139), accessed from various points on Bonham Spring Road (turn inland just west of the bridge), which also leads to Upton, home to the sumptuous Sandals Golf and Country Club, rated as one of Jamaica's finest **golf courses** (see p.35). Back on the main road and half a mile into St Mary, the former haunt of planter Harold Mitchell has been reincarnated as **Prospect Plantation** (daily; ℡994 1058, ⓦwww .prospectplantationtours.com; 3–5 hours; US$44–90), now owned by Dolphin Cove. The traditional tour is designed to introduce the more sedentary visitor to the delights of tropical farming with an hour-long jitney ride through sugar cane and groves of coconut, pimento, lime, ackee, breadfruit and soursop trees, stopping to spot butterflies, feed ostriches and sample fruits. You'll feel less like a member of a cattle herd if you indulge in the **camel safari**, **mountain bike** or **horseback** rides through the plantation or down into White River gorge, the site of Jamaica's first hydroelectric plant – though they're significantly more expensive.

A few minutes' drive east of Prospect is **Reggae Beach** (Mon–Fri 9am–5pm, Sat & Sun 9am–6pm; US$9.50). One of Jamaica's prettiest beaches, it's been earmarked for hotel development for years, but in the meantime new management have sadly hiked up the entrance fee to render it out of reach of locals. It's nonetheless a very picturesque curve of yellow sand with shady palm groves, with no hustlers and just one laid-back restaurant serving up fresh grilled fish. Formerly an immensely popular venue for stageshows, look out for new events which may be held here.

Beyond the beach, the coast road is intermittently lined with hotels and condos in the area known as **Tower Isle**, broken only by the wonderful **art gallery Harmony Hall** (℡974 2870, ⓦwww.harmonyhall.com), exhibiting a variety of local and national artists' work. Just east of here, a new housing development has almost obscured the **Rio Nuevo Battle Site** (pronounced "No-vo"; Mon–Fri 10am–5pm, Sat–Sun 10am–2pm; US$5), centred around a rather nondescript monument 150 yards from the road on the ocean side. Commemorating the final skirmish that made Jamaica a British rather than a Spanish territory in 1658, the area was donated to the Jamaica National Heritage Trust who have created a small yet mildly interesting exhibition on the area's Taino, Spanish, Maroon and British heritage. Despite this, few tourists visit and you're more likely to find courting couples enjoying the sea breeze under the shade of bamboo.

Eating

Ochi's **restaurants** aim to please the foreign palate, with Italian, Indian, Chinese and American cuisines vying for your custom alongside Jamaican staples. Most places stay open until at least midnight. For fine dining, also consider driving to *Café Aubergine* (p.142), while closer to St Ann's Bay, *Scotchies* (see p.158) is another superb jerk centre. If you've a sweet tooth, *excellent* ice cream chain Devon House I-Scream has a branch at Island Village. For lunch snacks, try the callaloo loaves and patties at The Golden Crust Baking Co (72 Main St), or even at chain Juici Patties (61 Main St). Jamaican fast food in the form of patties, burgers and chicken is available at the ubiquitous 24-hour Mother's (17 Main St), and there's also a branch of Island Grill (12 Main St), good for jerk delights. Street food, of course, is the most inexpensive bet, with jerk chicken vendors around Mother's wheeling out their oil-drum barbecues once the sun sets, the air filling with the heady smell of charcoal smoke and spicy grilled meat.

Inexpensive

Centre Spot 75 Main St. Close to the *Hibiscus Lodge* hotel, this small lunchtime joint is the best value in town. It serves strictly Jamaican food, very tasty and dirt-cheap. Closed after 5pm.

Healthy Stop 28 James Ave. Pleasant upstairs restaurant with a range of natural juices, excellent soup and an emphasis on vegetarian food.

The Healthy Way Ocean Village Place. Energetic and efficient vegetarian take-away with a couple of tables, offering veggie/ tofu burgers and patties, porridges, soups, Ital juices, fruit salad, cakes and a different main dish each day. Breakfast and lunch only.

Ocho Rios Village Jerk Centre DaCosta Drive. Reputedly the best jerk in town, this joint is popular with locals and passing motorists and gets pretty lively on weekend evenings.

Percy's 6 James Ave. Excellent homely local restaurant specializing in seafood and fish. Food is cooked to order and is very good value.

Sanmar Ocean Village Plaza. Chinese and Jamaican fusion, popular for lunchtime eating among Ochi's office workers (take-away with one seated table). Try Jamaican curry shrimp with Chinese fried rice. Daytime only.

Whalers Fishing beach (just west of Island Village). Overlooking the water, this two-storey timber building is the best of the collection of places here, selling inexpensive fresh grilled or steamed seafood, as

well as a gorgeous conch soup (breakfast and lunch only).

White River Ranch White River, just off the main road east of town. Busy, late-opening joint with tables outside, known as much for its sizzling jerk chicken and pork as it is for escovitched fish, though the conch soup is pretty good, too.

World of Fish 3 James Ave. Popular place for a late supper (lunch is served, too). Fish is prepared any which way, with bammy, festival or rice and peas. Open Mon–Sat until 2am.

Moderate

Bibibips 93 Main St. Set back from the road, this restaurant/bar has tables overlooking the sea, and is one of the better, if a little overpriced, choices in town. Menu includes devilled jerk chicken or lobster, coconut curry chicken, Ital wrap and all the usual Jamaican favourites. There's a great cocktail list too.

Coco Brown's Coffee Shop Island ("Burger King") Plaza. If you're fed up with chicken and rice 'n' peas then this is your place – foods on offer include a variety of sandwiches and cakes, plus there's tea and Blue Mountain espresso coffee.

Coconuts Restaurant and Bar Behind Fisherman's Point, on road to the cruise-ship pier. Attractive spot with a large terrace overlooking the bay and a wide-ranging menu of steaks, fajitas, potato skins, wraps, salads and traditional Jamaican fare. A good place to while away an evening; the friendly staff make a mean cocktail.

Mama Marley's Main St, opposite the entrance to *Jamaica Grande*. Bob-themed bar, restaurant and gift shop owned by the Marley family. The food and atmosphere is far from the Ital lifestyle Bob espoused; nevertheless the lobster curry and ackee and saltfish are nice enough and prices are reasonable.

Miss T's 65 Main St (just off the road by the clock tower). A fantastic addition to Ochi's eateries, the helpful staff serve up all the Jamaican favourites (oxtail, curry goat, seafood, roast yam and saltfish) in an attractive and peaceful garden. Plus there's a good range of natural juices.

The Ruins at the Falls 17 DaCosta Drive. Popular upper/mid-range restaurant on a terrace at the foot of a largish waterfall. It offers an extensive buffet menu of Chinese and international dishes, but the unusual setting alone makes it worth a visit.

Expensive

The Almond Tree *Hibiscus Lodge* ℡ 974 2813. Romantic clifftop setting, friendly service and a great gourmet menu, featuring superb seafood.

Evita's Eden Bower Rd ℡ 974 2333. The best-advertised (if a little overpriced) pasta and pizza on the north coast, served on a gingerbread verandah overlooking the bay. Large choice of starters, salads, soups and desserts; main courses include fettuccine bolognaise, linguine with pesto, seafood and "Lasagne Rastafari" with ackee, callaloo and tomatoes.

Passage to India Soni's Plaza, 50 Main St ℡ 795 3182. Attractively decorated rooftop restaurant serving excellent Indian cuisine. The menu is comprehensive: tandoori meats, chicken jalfrezi or masala, rogan josh, lots of seafood curries and vegetarian dishes. The starters are particularly good, as are the lassi yogurt drinks and desserts.

Toscanini Harmony Hall ℡ 975 4785. Under the eaves of pretty Harmony Hall, a ten-minute drive east of the centre, this is Ochi's best restaurant. The menu features all the Italian classics, from carpaccio to home-made pasta and meat dishes such as veal escalope with prosciutto and parmesan, and there are also daily specials and vegetarian options. Service is great, and the puddings are sublime. Closed Mon.

Nightlife and entertainment

Though it's not Kingston or Negril, Ocho Rios does have **bars** and **clubs** open every night of the week. James Avenue hosts several (seedier) joints – usually pretty harmless and good fun, though it is the town's red-light district and you might not want to walk it late at night. A number of restaurants (see opposite) also function as bars: *Evita's* holds occasional Latin theme nights with dancing; *Toscanini* offers a sophisticated bar ambience; *Bibibips* is great for a drinking session, with occasional live reggae; *Coconuts* features a large, circular bar with "until whenever" hours; the busy, open-air *White River Ranch* is a good bet for drinking white rum with enthusiastic locals and loud music; and finally *Ocho Rios Village Jerk Centre* also offers lots of rum bar-style banter. Occasional sound-system dances and concerts are held at **Reggae Beach**, a couple of miles east of town, **Crane Ridge Resort** (17 DaCosta Drive) and at *White River Ranch* (see p.144), while **Mahogany Beach** ranges from sound systems to lower-key music by candlelight – look out for flyers and ask around. Another possibility is an evening pass to one of the all-inclusive hotels (US$50–100), such as "Jamaika-Me-Krazy" at the *Jamaica Grande* (see p.138), including food, drinks and entertainment. Alongside regular nightspots, go-go clubs are a big part of the local nightlife scene, attracting crowds of Jamaican men and women alike. There are several go-go joints around Ocho Rios, the most enduringly popular being *Shades*, east of town in Content Garden, with a different music policy every night and not-for-the-fainthearted "Freaky" events featuring live sex shows.

Finally, the stellar **Ocho Rios Jazz Festival** brings Ochi to life every June, with concerts at venues around town. For more information call the tourist board or the Jazz Hotline (℡ 927 3544). The Jazz Festival website (Ⓦ www.jamaicaculture.org /jazz) posts line-ups and information.

Bars

Glenn's Restaurant and Cocktail Lounge Tower Isle. Out-of-town steak restaurant with cheesy 1970s decor, tinkly jazz as background music and occasional live performances.

H20 Coconut Grove Shopping Centre, Main St. New bar owned by internationally famous reggae songstress Tanya Stephens, featuring a games night (Wed), and a house band with open mic (Fri/Sat) – where you just might catch the owner and her friends on stage. Closed Mon.

John Crow 10 Main St. Smart and decent bar with sports screens and a friendly vibe. Also has fast food and Jamaican staples with tables out in the open air to watch the world go by.

Oceans 11 Fisherman's Point Rd. Overlooking Island Village beach near the cruise-ship pier, this slick spot is a great place for a bite or a cocktail; daytimes are taken over by cruise hordes, but serves as a club warm-up 8pm–1am, with karaoke Tues, happy hour Fri and live music Sun.

The Twisted Kilt Harbour Shops, Main St. New Irish pub/sports bar with great burgers, fish and chips, large drinks menu and a Latin night Sat with dancing on the attractive roof terrace.

Clubs

Amnesia Disco 70 Main St, above the Mutual Security building ⓦ www.theamnesia.com. Proper nightclub with indoor, a/c dancefloor and outdoor bar area, open Wed–Sun only. Wednesday is quieter, with free entry; Thursday is the busy Ladies' Night when women get in free; Friday offers pure dancehall at the After Work Jam; Saturday is Party Night; and on Sunday there's oldies music.

Blitz Main St, next to the Village Hotel. New club on the block whose most popular nights are Tuesday with an *Oceans 11* after-party (one price for both venues), and Wednesday International Night with hotel shuttles and drinks promotions.

Jimmy Buffet's Margaritaville Island Village, ⓦ www.margaritavillecaribbean.com. Part daytime family-fun venue with pool and water slide, part all-hours bar, this Jamaican institution is best known for its wet 'n' wild club nights, which attract hordes of locals and tourists alike. Specializing in potent cocktails and other drinks promotions, each night is themed with Wednesday Pool Party the busiest night; entrance is US$25 or US$15 if you arrive in swimwear, and covers all drinks and access to the torchlit beach. Weekends see bigger-name DJs; check flyers around town for a full programme. Food served until 10pm.

Reggae Inferno 7 James Ave. No-frills local disco. Formerly the *Roof Club*, here the music policy is dancehall and more dancehall, with some R&B thrown in. Women get in free and it's a lively place to let your hair down and meet young locals. Best at weekends/holidays. Cover J$250.

Shopping

The town's three **craft markets** (daily 7am–7pm) have enticed many a hapless soul to leave Jamaica laden with "Yeh mon it irie" T-shirts or fake dreadlocks, yet among the dross you'll find really nice T-shirts, paintings and sculptures, and vendors have a wicked line in sales banter. The main market is to the right of Ocean Village Plaza, while the excellent Olde Craft Market is nearby on the other side of the road; talented artist Gayle James, who paints on canvas, ceramics and even skin, is based here. Pineapple/Coconut Grove market is less cluttered, east past *Hibiscus Lodge*.

Ochi's Main Street houses eleven open-air **shopping plazas**, lined with identical, soulless, **in-bond shops** selling imported jewellery, watches and china, as well as the occasional upmarket craft shop – the scourge of market vendors, who claim that cruise-ship companies ferry prospective buyers straight into the air-conditioned calm rather than onto the street, with a cut of the profit. There's a lot more scope to barter in the markets. Alternatively, check out the sources of market **sculptures** and **ceramics** at Clarke's Art Studio (see p.139), a tiny, green-painted wooden shack just west of town, or the Wassi factory at Great Pond (see p.142; it's cheaper than the Wassi Art Shop at Soni's Plaza).

Don't miss the gorgeous **art gallery** and shop at Harmony Hall east of town near Tower Isle (see p.143), which features works by renowned contemporary artists as well as Caribbean books, set in a beautifully restored great house. Reggae Yard in Island Village has a reasonable selection of **reggae**, while Music World at Taj

Mahal Plaza has soca, reggae and calypso favourites. The best place to get the latest mix CDs is at the craft markets (they're around J$500 each).

Listings

Airlines Air Jamaica has a local office (☎ 974 2566) for flight confirmations and information; for other airlines see Montego Bay listings, p.190. Domestic services are available to and from Boscobel Aerodrome (☎ 975 3101).

Banks and money Most of the banks are easily located on Main St near to the craft market, with several ATMs. Cambio King, 12 Ocean Village Plaza (Mon–Sat 9am–5pm), and Cambio Express, 19 Main St (Mon–Fri 9am–6pm, Sat 9am–5pm) are reliable for currency exchange; Cool Card (☎ www.coolcorp.com) has an a/c cambio at 11 Main St (Mon–Sat 9am–4pm) and ATMs. Western Union at *Pier View* hotel (3 Main St) or Triple Supersave Supermarket, 70 Main St, offer wire transfers (☎ www.westernunion.com).

Car rental Many international firms have branches in Ochi. Otherwise local companies may give you a better deal: Caribbean Cars, 99A Main St (☎ 974 2513, ☎ www.caribbeancarrentals.com); Island, 4 Carib Arcade, Main St (☎ 974 2666, ☎ www.islandcarrentals.com); Sunshine, 154 Main St (☎ 974 2980) and Villa (☎ 974 2474).

Doctors Dr Prakash Kulkani, 16 Rennie Rd (☎ 974 2012), offers a 24hr service. The Williams

Medical Center is at 74 Main St (☎ 795 2482). The Holistic Medical Centre, 40 Ocean Village Plaza (☎ 974 6401), offers homeopathy alongside regular medical care and operates an air ambulance.

Hospitals The nearest is at St Ann's Bay (☎ 972 2272), a fifteen-minute drive from Ocho Rios. In an emergency call ☎ 119; or 974 6401/6404 or 818 5944 for a private ambulance.

Internet Best in town is Computer Whizz at Island Plaza by Burger King (J$300/hr), while EZ Access at the Little Pub Plaza is also a/c (J$200/30min).

Police The police station (☎ 974 2533 or 4588) is on Evelyn St behind the Texaco garage that faces the clock tower; in emergencies call ☎ 119.

Post office The permanently busy post office is on Main St opposite the main craft market (Mon–Fri 8am–5pm, Sat 8am–noon).

Telephones Phonecards are available from *Mother's* on Main St, the post office and pharmacies. Digicel, 70 Main St, sells local network SIM cards for as little as US$10. Inexpensive overseas calls can be made from the Xerox Centre in Ocean Village Plaza, which also has payphones nearby.

Around Ocho Rios

East of town, as the in-your-face glitz of Ocho Rios recedes, the coast road glides through some of the most beautiful scenery on the north coast. The main settlements, **Oracabessa** and **Port Maria**, are slow, close-knit communities where tourism has taken hold in a more sensitive manner, and the small guest-houses and restaurants that pepper the roadsides are generally overlooked by those who prefer sports bars and jet skis to quiet exclusivity. Low-key glamour has a lengthy history here, however, having long been a haunt of the rich and famous. Noel Coward and James Bond creator Ian Fleming both lived here, and their old homes, **Firefly** and **Goldeneye**, are still standing. Firefly has been transformed into a prime tourist site, with Coward's former guesthouse *Blue Harbour* an ideal spot from which to explore the area, while *Goldeneye* is the centrepiece of the most exclusive villa complex in Jamaica. Beyond Port Maria, the road swings inland and the coastline extends in an unbroken series of forested outcrops interspersed by deserted, volcanic-sand beaches and beautiful waterfalls reachable only on foot or by boat. Hiking uncovers breathtaking vistas

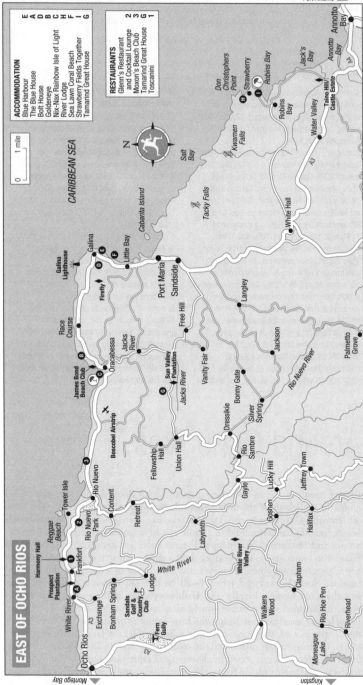

EAST OF OCHO RIOS

Port Antonio ▲

Montego Bay ▲

Kingston ▼

CARIBBEAN SEA

N

0   1 mile

ACCOMMODATION
Blue Harbour   E
The Blue House   A
Bolt House   D
Goldeneye   B
Nix-Nax Rainbow Isle of Light   C
River Lodge   H
Sea Lawn Coral Beach   I
Strawberry Fields Together   F
Tamarind Great House   G

RESTAURANTS
Glenn's Restaurant
  and Cocktail Lounge   2
Moxon's Beach Club   3
Tamarind Great House   G
Toscanini   1

– best undertaken from **Robins Bay**, where eco-minded accommodations offer reasonably priced guides and tours.

West of Ochi, the coast road sees plenty of tourist traffic, though the invasiveness of large-scale development is generally restricted to the beachside – such as at the established resort neighbours of **Runaway Bay** and **Discovery Bay**. Elsewhere, low-key guesthouses and boutique hotels can be sought out. With its thriving market and Georgian architecture interspersed with weather-beaten clapboard houses, **St Ann's Bay** is the small, unpretentious capital of St Ann, while the ruined Spanish capital of **Seville** is just a few minutes away. Further west, the boundary of St Ann and Trelawny parishes marks a distinct change in the landscape, from languid hills to rugged hillocks, while undeveloped yet energetic interior communities like **Brown's Town** perch on the fringes of Cockpit Country (see Chapter 4), with **Bob Marley's Mausoleum** the major attraction.

East to Oracabessa

Lit in the afternoons by an apricot light that must have prompted its Spanish name, *Orocabeza* ("Golden Head"), **ORACABESSA** is a delightfully sleepy little town, with friendly citizens and a mere handful of tourists visiting at any one time. Some sixteen miles east of Ocho Rios, it is centred around a covered fruit and vegetable market (main days Thursday and Friday), a police station and a few shops and bars. A centre for the export of **bananas** until the early 1900s, the wharves around the small natural harbour closed in 1969, taking with them the rum bars, gambling houses and most of the workers. It took until the mid-1990s for Oracabessa to begin to develop as a low-key resort, when the **Island Outpost** corporation (whose owner, Chris Blackwell, has family connections with the area) bought up seventy acres of prime land – from Jack's River to the west of town to the *Goldeneye* estate at the eastern outskirts.

Island Outpost's grand plans resulted in the creation of the **James Bond Beach Club** (Tues–Sun 9am–6pm; US$5; ☎ 975 3399), off Main Street at the end of the Old Wharf Road (signposted just west of Oracabessa). The area comprises a stylish strip of sand with a collection of brightly painted changing rooms, a bar and a restaurant, yet it receives a mere handful of visitors during the week. Locals do venture down at weekends, however, and the expansive oceanfront lawns, often used to stage large-scale concerts like **Fully Loaded** at the end of August and Boxing Day's **Teen-Splash**, make a wonderfully breezy outdoor venue. For most people though, snorkelling to see the stingrays that live in the waters surrounding the beach, and guided jet-ski safaris along the coast are the order of the day. If you prefer to stay away from the glitterati, the small adjacent **fisherman's beach** is an equally appealing place to swim, and the Rasta carvers who've built a shack on the sand sell seafood meals and drinks.

East of the town's petrol station, Oracabessa merges into the residential community of **Race Course** (named after a long-gone track), where gates, walls and trees mask **Goldeneye** (see p.151), the unassuming white-walled bungalow designed and purpose-built by Ian Fleming, sometime military man and creator of James Bond, who wrote almost all of the 007 novels within its walls.

Away from the coast, at the far western end of Oracabessa, a junction crowded with fruit vendors and **taxis** marks the start of the notoriously potholed B13 inland road. Wreathing through foliage-lined village **Jacks River**, the road leads onwards to the well-signposted **Sun Valley Plantation** (daily, 1hr 30min tours at 9am and 1pm; US$15), one of the north coast's most attractive plantations, concentrating on bananas and coconuts. The charming low-key tour explains the growth processes of the two

From Errol Flynn to Ralph Lauren, Jamaica has always attracted the rich and famous, but the island also served as inspiration for the ultimate (albeit fictional) symbol of glamour – **James Bond**. As a commander in the Naval Intelligence Division of the British army, Bond's creator, Ian Fleming, first visited Jamaica in 1943. Staying in the Blue Mountains, he was immediately taken with the island's sensual pleasures and declared that he'd be back to put down permanent roots after the war. By 1947, he'd paid £2000 for a plot of land on Jamaica's north coast that had once served as Oracabessa's racecourse, and engaged local workers to build the elegant beach house that he'd designed himself. Naming it after a bungled NID anti-German operation he'd been involved in, **Goldeneye** became his winter retreat and a source of competition with neighbour **Noel Coward**, who insisted that his Blue Harbour (see p.153) was far superior to Fleming's spartan bachelor pad. A series of magazine articles penned by Fleming on the joys of his island paradise soon lured a fashionable set to Jamaica, and Goldeneye played host to such luminaries as Sir Anthony and Lady Eden, Truman Capote, Lucian Freud, Graham Greene, Evelyn Waugh and Cecil Beaton. Cocktails by the pool and snorkelling with his "Jamaican wife" Blanche Blackwell (mother of Island Records' Chris Blackwell) soon began to take up most of Fleming's time. It wasn't until his other lover and soon-to-be wife, Lady Anne Rothermere (ex-wife of the British newspaper baron), became pregnant in 1952 that he got down to any serious writing. He cranked out *Casino Royale* on a rickety old Remington typewriter with the jalousies shut to block out the distracting sea view.

Clearly besotted with the island, Fleming exploited the Jamaica connection by taking his hero's name from the author of the classic book *Birds of the West Indies* – and many of his characters were inspired by Jamaican friends. Pussy Galore, in the *Goldfinger* novel, was said to be a tongue-in-cheek representation of Blanche Blackwell. Two novels, *Doctor No* and *The Man with the Golden Gun,* were set here (scenes for the movie versions were filmed in Kingston and Westmoreland respectively), and the island served as the fictional San Monique in *Live and Let Die.* And of course 007 wouldn't have dreamed of drinking any other coffee than his favourite Blue Mountain brew. Fleming later wrote "Would these books have been born if I had not been living in the gorgeous vacuum of a Jamaican holiday? I doubt it."

Fleming returned to Goldeneye each January to spend two months writing, but the years of hard drinking and partying began to take their toll and by the late 1950s his health had seriously deteriorated. Fleming survived long enough to supervise Cubby Broccoli's movie version of *Dr No*, filmed in Jamaica with Chris Blackwell as location manager. In the first few months of 1964, Fleming returned to Goldeneye and wrote his last 007 novel, *The Man with the Golden Gun*, infusing the pages with a strong sense of nostalgia for Jamaica. Though his Bond novels had by then sold some forty million copies, Ian Fleming died on August 12, 1964, without ever really knowing what a sensation he had created. Four months after his death, the release of the movie version of *Goldfinger* signified the beginning of worldwide Bond mania.

fruits, taking in trees and flowers, and including drinks, a light meal and fruit tasting. Close by is *Tamarind Great House*, a sumptuous guesthouse serving gourmet food (see opposite). Further inland and you are firmly off the tourist track in the gorgeous scenery of the **St Mary interior**. Market communities like **Dressikie** and **Gayle** have numerous local swimming spots if you ask around.

Practicalities

In addition to a large **all-inclusive**, the family-oriented *Beaches Boscobel Resort and Golf Club* (ⓦ www.beaches.com), there are some really lovely **guesthouses** and **rental villas** around Oracabessa, from simple to extremely plush.

⚑ *Goldeneye* (Oracabessa ☎ 975 3354, ⓦ www.islandoutpost.com; ❾) is one of Jamaica's most exclusive hotels and a regular haunt of the rich and famous, centred on Ian Fleming's beautifully restored Jamaican home. The one- to three-bedroom villas are secluded and indescribably inviting, with matchless attention to detail, outdoor bathrooms and access to the private beach where Fleming cooled his toes. *Tamarind Great House* (Crescent Estate, near Jacks River, Oracabessa ☎ 995 3252; ❹–❺), the palatial home of a welcoming English family, boasts ten spacious and good-value guest rooms with four-poster beds. There's a pool, as well as beautiful views of the surrounding orchards and valley below. Sailing and snorkelling trips are available, as are gourmet meals, including a full English breakfast. *Nix-Nax Rainbow Isle of Light* (off Main St, Oracabessa ☎ 975 3364; ❶) is a local institution – a friendly guesthouse run by American/Jamaicans Dominica and Dickie, with a range of basic but clean rooms. There's a definite collective feel here – communal kitchen, walls adorned with consciousness-raising adages, and alternative therapies and massage available. The Rainbow Basic School is located at the base of the building.

Decent **places to eat** around Oracabessa are few and far between: easily the best option is ⚑ *Tamarind Great House* at nearby Jacks River (see above), where host Gillian Chambers cooks up delicious three-course meals (approx US$30), served on the hotel's elegant verandah. You'll need to book in advance (☎ 995 3252) and take a charter taxi from Oracabessa if you don't have your own transport. *Nix Nax* coffee bar on the town's Main St (opposite the guesthouse of the same name) is a new addition, with vegetarian sandwiches and snacks, while there are a number of local cookshops, like friendly *Oracos* adjacent to the market, or jovial *Dor's Sea Cliff Fish Pot* the other side of town at Race Course, which serves superlative fresh fish, lobster, conch soups and has a nice circular bar for lounging, perched atop a cliff. Nearby, *Club Tan Jan* is a spacious and attractive backroom bar with pool table, and a simple lunch menu including a veggie (tofu) choice. **Drinking** choices are limited to numerous hole-in-the-wall rum shops such as *Tropical Hut*, a fairy-light-strewn bar in Race Course with occasional oldies parties, or several lively bars at Jacks River, with sound systems Friday and Saturday nights.

Firefly and Port Maria

Heading eastwards three miles from Oracabessa, you pass Jamaica's most northerly tip at the Galina Lighthouse and then the community of **Castle Garden**, home to Noel Coward's beach house **Blue Harbour** (now a superb guesthouse; see p.153), from where he stumbled upon the historical site that was to become ⚑ **Firefly**, perched high on the hilltop above (turn off the main road by the *Casa Maria* hotel, about two miles west of Port Maria). Coward bought the land from local politician Roy Lindo for £150, and from its construction in 1956 to the playwright's death in 1973, *Firefly* became the Jamaican home of both Coward and his partner Graham Payn. Now it remains the area's only organized attraction (daily except Fri and Sun and public holidays 9am–5pm; US$10 for guided tours).

The house was built on the site of a former **Taino settlement** – with artefacts found both here and across the hillside – before later becoming the stamping ground of pirate extraordinaire Sir Henry Morgan (see p.85), who used it as a vantage point during his reign as governor; gun slits in the bar recall the buccaneer days. Acquired by Island Outpost in 1992, the house remains much as Coward left it: his studio with a painting on the easel; the drawing room – where illustrious guests from Sophia Loren to Audrey Hepburn and Joan Sutherland were entertained – complete with two polished pianos; kitchen cupboards full of yellowing bottles; and the table freshly laid as it was on the day the Queen Mother came to lunch in 1965. Coward died here and is buried on the property. A statue of him by UK-based artist Angela Conner overlooks his favourite view. Even if you're not a Coward fan, it's worth coming up to Firefly for the panorama alone; one of the best on the island, it takes in Port Maria bay and Cabarita Island, with the peaks of the Blue Mountains poking through the clouds and to the west the lighthouse at **Galina Point**. You can even see Cuba on a clear day.

A series of twisting outcrops protecting a natural harbour mark your arrival in the diminutive capital of St Mary, **PORT MARIA**. As you round the last bend, a stunning view of tiny and forested **Cabarita Island** is revealed, right in the middle of the bay and well known for its variety of bird species. Once one of Jamaica's most picturesque towns – nestled around a crescent bay with lots of cut-stone and faded gingerbread fretwork alluding to more auspicious times – it's rather a scruffy place with little to keep you. West of the centre and marked by two sizeable royal palms at its gates is the quaint cut-stone **St Mary Parish Church**, dating back to 1861, with the weathered gravestones of its cemetery extending down to the sea. Nearby, in the middle of the playing field, is a monument to black freedom fighter **Tacky** (see box opposite), while the covered fruit **market** (main day Friday) is a maze of dingy paths winding through piles of yams, bananas and assorted local produce – called "ben-dung" (literally, "bend down") with items spread out on the ground. A bridge crossing the murky Ochom River brings you into the centre, where the streets of yellow stone and timber are laid out in a rough grid. Bear in mind that the centre effectively shuts down on Wednesday afternoons – not a good time to appreciate the usual hustle and bustle. At the eastern end of town is Pagee Beach, where you can arrange a combined fishing trip and visit to Cabarita Island (approx US$25)

▲ View from Firefly

The Tacky Rebellion

In the late eighteenth century, Port Maria saw one of Jamaica's bloodiest rebellions against slavery, an uprising that sowed the seeds for emancipation eighty years later. Led by a runaway slave known as **Tacky** (a European spelling of the Ghanaian name Tekyi, meaning "the great"), who was said to have been a chief of Coromantee descent, the rebellion sparked violent protests throughout the island. It aimed at a complete cull of whites and the creation of an all-black colony. The revolt began on Easter Sunday 1760, when Tacky and a small group of slaves from local estates murdered their overseers and marched to Port Maria, killing the storekeeper at Fort Haldane and seizing arms and ammunition. Five months of fighting ensued, with £100,000 worth of damage to nearby plantations. However, the thousand-strong slave army could not compete with British military force, which utilized loyal slaves and **Maroons** (following the 1739 treaty) in guerrilla warfare. The rebellion was savagely quashed and severe punishments meted out: Tacky was captured by Maroon marksmen and killed, his head cut off and displayed on a pole in Spanish Town; others were chained to stakes and burned alive, gibbeted or hung by irons, as an example to others contemplating sedition. It's said, however, that in one last defiant gesture, Tacky's sympathizers removed his body under cover of night and gave him a proper burial. After Tacky's death, many of his followers committed suicide rather than live enslaved. Three hundred Africans died fighting, with fifty more captured and executed and three hundred transported abroad. Only sixty whites lost their lives.

with local fisherman "Wiggle". He moors his boat at one end of the greyish sand, which, although strewn with sea grass and debris, extends in a long picturesque sweep backed by palms.

Practicalities

A number of **hotels** lie just west of Port Maria – but look no further than ⚓ *Blue Harbour* (PO Box 50, Castle Garden ☎725 0289 or ☎505-5861244 in the US, Ⓦwww.blueharb.com; ❹, including all meals; room-only option also available). Built in the 1950s by Noel Coward to house his guests, a main house with verandah on two sides as well as three seaside villas (4–12 beds), all have an astonishing view and may be rented whole or room-by-room. The current owners have done an excellent job in preserving the original atmosphere, and yet the property has a wholeheartedly Jamaican feel, with friendly, laid-back and helpful staff. There's a saltwater pool, a tiny beach and plenty of seclusion. Nearby, the gorgeous villa *Bolt House* (Galina, ☎994 0303, Ⓦwww.islandoutpost.com /io_villas; ❾) was built by Blanche Blackwell (mother of Island Records impresario Chris) on a bluff below *Firefly*, and affords the same stunning views of Port Maria bay. Beautifully furnished and boasting walls hung with contemporary art, the villa epitomizes classy, secluded luxury, with two bedrooms, dining and living rooms and a lovely pool, all set in landscaped gardens. Lower down the road, *Sea Lawn Coral Beach* (Castle Garden ☎419 6758; ❶–❷) offers camping and budget rooms Rasta-style. There's a grassy garden down to the sea and owner/fisherman Michael Higgins also offers local tours.

Port Maria has plenty of small **restaurants** serving tasty Jamaican fare. *Essie's Faith*, in the town square next to Courts, and the *Almond Tree*, both serve up reliable meals, while *Solos*, a long-standing no-frills bar is situated by Pagee Beach at the east end of town, with the freshest cooked-to-order fish around; it also hosts dancehall nights most Saturdays or Sundays. The only late-opening bar/club is the open-air *Roof Club* above *Essie's*, which gets going late at weekends. The annual **Fisherman's Regatta**, on the first Wednesday after Independence Day (August 6) showcases a competition to catch the largest marlin, as well as seeing all the local sound systems lined up on the town's streets.

East to Robins Bay

The road east of Port Maria swings inland, allowing the coastline to remain undeveloped, with disused plantations, ruined villages, and a plethora of fruit trees growing wild. A hiker's paradise, there are scores of attractive black-sand beaches and deserted **waterfalls** to explore – notably **Kwamen Falls**, a twenty-foot drop into a deep blue lagoon, and **Tacky Falls**, better accessed by boat but equally impressive.

The best place to explore the area is from **ROBINS BAY**, about twelve miles from Port Maria. Signposts for *Robins Bay Village Resort* and *Strawberry Fields* indicate the turning, and the road meanders along a craggy section of coastline. A right turn at the signed crossroads leads you past the incongruous concrete of *Robins Bay Village Resort*, and you finally arrive in the tranquil calm of **Strawberry**, named after the *Strawberry Fields* campsite popular with American hippies in the 1970s, whose free-love shenanigans drew sighs of consternation from local people. These days, the site is occupied by a campsite-come-hotel, ⚘ *Strawberry Fields Together* (☎999 7169 or 610 8658, ⓦwww.strawberryfieldstogether.com; ➍–➐; one week all-inclusive eco-adventure package US$2700; volunteer groups welcome), a collection of cabins and villas offering varying levels of luxury, centred around the pretty white-sand cove from which Spanish governor, Don Christobel Arnaldo de Yssasi, fled the island in 1657. Some units offer a kitchenette, and a gorgeous one-bed seafront apartment comes with a raised jacuzzi, breakfast bar over the sea, and an attractive natural wood interior. Good food (vegetarians catered for) is served – try the sweet plantain porridge for breakfast. Day passes to the property cost US$15, covering use of showers, as well as volleyball, table tennis, and use of a barbeque and wood-burning pizza oven. With miles of pristine land nearby, eco-oriented **tours** of the area (US$25–100) are available, including mountain biking and possibly the best **ATV/quad bike** tour on the island. More leisurely pursuits including boat/fishing trips, and an invigorating River Water Therapy Experience, with river gorge hiking, natural whirlpool massage and rock climbing.

A few minutes' walk farther takes you to ⚘ *River Lodge* (☎995 3003, ⓦwww.river-lodge.com; ➋, breakfast included), run by German Brigitta Fuchslocher, a restful, alluring complex built around the restored ruins of a Spanish fort. Rooms make full use of remaining stone walls, and offer attractively minimal decor with shared or private bathrooms. A river running through the grounds offers swimming in the wet season, and the beach is a short walk away. The delightful thatched restaurant/bar serves plentiful fresh fish, while there's a yoga deck surrounded by lush forest. A short hike upstream passes a series of rock pools and cliffs, eventually opening out into a clearing with bamboo towering overhead; guides are available for all local hikes.

Elsewhere in the village, a couple of quiet, friendly bars offer good Jamaican food, and local fine artist/sculptor Busha has some of the most detailed wood carvings to be found anywhere on the island (ask for directions; ⓦwww.crazy-inspirations.de). Closer to the main road, the 1650-acre **Taino Hill Estate** (formerly Green Castle; ☎322 7188, ⓦwww.greencastletropicalstudycenter.org) is well worth a visit, aiming to preserve local ecology and cultural heritage. Local guides lead you on an excellent "Orchids and Organic Tour" (US$30), with an historical overview of the 300-year old plantation and a demonstration of the production of organic coconut oil.

St Ann's Bay and around

If you're a James Bond fan, you'll be interested to know that four miles west of Ochi, behind the Roaring River generating station, is the private beach where Ursula Andress emerged from the sea as Honey Ryder in *Dr No*. Otherwise, the area is now dominated by the 846-room *Club Hotel Riu Ocho Rios* at **MAMMEE BAY**. Formerly an attractive spit of white sand named after the Mammee apple trees that grew here, the towering all-inclusive offers an exterior more Benidorm than Jamaica; a slightly more tasteful interior and "Rastafari bar" as concession to local culture doesn't quite compensate.

Beyond, the coast highway merges with the inland road through **Steer Town**, now effectively an Ocho Rios bypass for traffic heading to Kingston. Westwards, the coast road avoids the centre of **ST ANN'S BAY** entirely, with the town stretching up the hillside inland. Characterized by its porticoed shop-fronts, sloping streets and old-fashioned atmosphere, it's small enough to cover on foot in an hour, with two central thoroughfares, Bravo and Main streets, meeting in a crossroads. The Main Street shops and **market** (Fridays and Saturdays) hog the action, and dominating from the top of the street is the town's distinctive 1860 **courthouse** (observation gallery open to the public). In the middle of a nearby roundabout, Christopher Columbus strikes a noble pose above sunken ships, and just before the road forks, the pretty Catholic church of **Our Lady of Perpetual Help** is constructed of stone reclaimed from an earlier structure – Peter the Martyr Church, the first stone church in Jamaica, built in 1524 by the Spanish in Sevilla Nueva. The quieter left fork of Main Street holds the **library** (Mon–Sat 9.30am–5.30pm; Internet access), with its **Marcus Garvey memorial statue** out front proclaiming the words "We Declare to the World – Africa Must Be Free".

Christopher Columbus and the Tainos at Seville

The north coast is sometimes referred to as **"Columbus Country"**, as the conquistador got his first sight of Jamaica at St Ann's Bay. Sailing in during his second voyage in 1494 to claim new territories for King Ferdinand and Queen Isabella of Spain, Christopher Columbus was so impressed by its beauty that he named it **Santa Gloria**. He was rather less enamoured during his fourth and final voyage in 1503, when his unseaworthy caravels forced his crew to spend an unhappy year marooned here, awaiting rescue from compatriots in Hispaniola. Plagued by illness and worried by a partial mutiny, Columbus used bribery and superstition (his prediction of a solar eclipse led them to believe he was a god) to coerce indigenous Tainos into providing food for them.

Columbus died in Spain in 1506, but his son **Diego** was appointed Governor of the Indies. He directed **Juan de Esquivel** to establish the first Spanish colony on the island, **Sevilla Nueva**, in 1510. Situated on the site of the Taino village of **Maima**, Sevilla Nueva eradicated Jamaica's Amerindian population in fifty years. The *encomienda* system of serf labour – the antithesis of the unfettered Taino lifestyle – was brutally enforced, and *caciques* (Taino chiefs) selectively murdered. With their society in tatters and forms of authority destroyed, the Tainos were easily branded and enslaved. Alongside Africans, transported to the island by the Spanish for the purpose, they were conscripted to build the new city. Less robust than the Africans, the Amerindians were unable to bear a life of slavery; ill treatment and European diseases soon eradicated those who didn't commit suicide. But while the Tainos expired, New Seville rapidly developed into a sizeable town, with churches, irrigation and a wharf. Its occupation lasted only until 1534, however, when the marshy, disease-inducing environment was abandoned in favour of Villa de la Vega, or Spanish Town.

Born at 32 Market St in St Ann's Bay in August 1887, the **Right Excellent Marcus Mosiah Garvey** was one of the most powerful black rights activists of the twentieth century. His outspoken denunciations of colonialism and racism and his concrete efforts to unite and empower the African diaspora influenced politicians, musicians and academics alike. Rastafarians call him a **black prophet**, and his philosophies form the basis of their faith (see "Religion" in Contexts, p.292).

Reputedly of Maroon descent, Garvey was the son of a master stonemason with an uncompromising attitude, who pursued multiple lawsuits against those who had slighted him on racial grounds. Though lack of funds ended the young Garvey's formal schooling at fourteen, he continued to study privately and spent long hours in his father's library. Prodigious from an early age, Garvey was made foreman of his uncle's printery at eighteen. But small-town living offered scant opportunities, and in 1906 he moved to Kingston and found work as a printery foreman – a significant coup when supervisors were usually white. As an activist in the fledgling trade union movement, Garvey was disturbed at the injustice meted out to black workers, and he left in search of better prospects in Costa Rica. There, he worked on a banana plantation and set up workers' newspapers to publicize the deplorable conditions for West Indian migrants. During a stint in England in 1912, he read up on black nationalists at Birkbeck College – Booker T. Washington's seminal text *Up From Slavery* informed Garvey's increasing militancy. In 1914, he returned to Jamaica and formed the **Universal Negro Improvement Association** (UNIA) "to champion Negro nationhood by redemption of Africa; to make the Negro race conscious, to advocate self-determination, to inspire and instill racial love and self-respect". But Jamaica's middle classes weren't ready for such radicalism, and Garvey immigrated to the USA in 1916 to seek a more sympathetic audience. Black Americans identified so strongly with him that by 1920 the UNIA had become the largest black pressure group ever to exist in the US, with a membership of millions. Though outlawed in most of the colonies, Garvey's self-published *Negro World* achieved the largest circulation of any black newspaper in the world. With the financial backing of thousands who bought shares, Garvey formed the Black Star Line Shipping Company to foster trade links between black nations and enable repatriation to the African homeland.

Though known principally as a "Back-To-Africa" advocate, Garvey was equally concerned with improving the situation of blacks wherever they found themselves. His assault on post-colonial nihilism was his greatest achievement, countering feelings of inferiority and powerlessness fostered during enslavement, and advocating black pride by emphasizing the historical achievements of Africans: "Up you mighty race, you can accomplish what you will". Garvey was regarded as a subversive by white America, and his supporters saw his 1922 two-year imprisonment on a trumped-up mail-fraud charge as an attempt to muzzle the message. Pressure from UNIA members secured his release, but in 1927 he was deported back to Jamaica on a wave of publicity. A loss of momentum ensured that the **Black Star Line** foundered, and Garvey never recaptured his early success. Tiring of constant battles with authority, he moved the struggle to the UK, where he died in obscurity in 1940. His importance was only recognized posthumously – in 1964 his remains were returned to Jamaica and interred in Kingston's National Heroes Park. In the 1970s, reggae music inspired a resurgence of Garveyism in Jamaica, with Rastafarian musicians like Burning Spear immortalizing his life and work. Today Marcus Garvey's ideas remain central to the Jamaican national consciousness.

The house where he was born is a private residence, but a parade in his honour takes place every August 17, and the library itself is a good source of information on Garvey's life. For more on the great man, see the box above.

At the far eastern end of town, by a rough track beyond the Windsor Girls' Home, is the small yet remarkable **Windsor mineral spring** (known as "Fire Hole"; free, though donation of J$500 expected). Strangely understated and looked after by a couple of local guys, a muddy hole bubbles with sulphur gas and can be lit to impressive effect with flames dancing across the water. Reggae artists have used the site in music videos, but visitors are few and far between save from an occasional tour group from Ⓦ www.tourwise.org.

To the west of St Ann's Bay, ⚑ **Seville Great House and Heritage Park** (daily 9am–5pm; ☎ 972 2191 in advance for a 45min tour; US$5) is one of few true heritage sites on the island, focusing on the birth of the nation from its three separate origins; Tainos, Africans and Europeans. The **museum** displays numerous artefacts such as Taino *zemis* (talismans to ward off evil spirits), as well as describing the customs and cultures of each group. Outside, replica Taino and African huts provide an idea of what the early settlements looked like. The wide lawns at the front of the property also serve as the venue for the Easter Monday **kite festival**, attracting flyers from all over the world and thousands of spectators, and a lively **Emancipation Jubilee** festival (31 July–1 Aug), with music, food and presentations.

Hidden in cattle pastures and woods on the beach side of the highway (marked by a commemoration plaque), the **ruins** of the old village of **Sevilla Nueva** – Jamaica's first Spanish settlement – are now an overgrown wasteland dotted with crumbling remains: a water wheel, parts of Peter the Martyr Church, a sugar mill, the 1509 castle-home of the first Spanish governor, a Taino village and slave settlement. The only way to see Seville is on a **horseback trail ride** courtesy of Hooves (2hr 30min; US$70; ☎ 972 0905, Ⓦ www.hoovesjamaica.com), which meanders from the great house to Seville, finishing up at the sea, where you can ride your mount in the water. West of Seville is the village of **PRIORY**, a favoured selling spot of jerk vendors and home to an appealingly deserted, clear water public beach.

Chukka Cove and Cranbrook Flower Forest

Half a mile or so west of Priory, the mountains recede and the road cuts through cattle pastures and sugar-cane flats, once home to a huge sugar plantation, the Llandovery-Richmond estate, established in 1674 – you can just make out the factory chimneys from the road. Signposted on the coastal side is **Chukka Cove** (☎ 972 2506, Ⓦ www.chukkacove.com), the most prestigious equestrian facility and polo ground in Jamaica (weekend matches open to observers). The stables are the home base of **Chukka Cove Adventure Tours**, which offer a variety of expensive excursions (US$70–100 with transportation and drinks) including a fabulous three-hour beach horseback ride (swimming your snorting mount below barren volcanic cliffs, used as a backdrop for scenes from the cinematic epic *Papillon*), an ATV tour and a new dogsled safari). Chukka Cove also serves as the main north coast venue for **Carnival** each April, with all the soca music and dancing you can handle – for more details, contact TPDCO in Ocho Rios (see p.137).

A mile or so past Chukka Cove, a tiny signposted road cuts inland towards ⚑ **Cranbrook Flower Forest** (☎ 770 8071; daily 9am–5pm; US$10), an exquisitely landscaped, 130-acre nature park with grassy lawns, tilapia fishing pond, resident peacocks and a swift-running river with marvellous swimming pools for adults or splashing children alike. No ghetto-blasters or vendors are allowed, and it's the perfect place for a picnic or barbecue in the purpose-built gazebos. Beyond the pond and lawns, pathways overhung with tropical flowers, tree ferns, philodendrons and sheaves of giant bamboo run parallel to the riverbank. Strategically placed steps lead down to the deeper pools, but for the best swimming you'll need to walk half a mile to the **riverhead**, a gorgeous 20ft-wide pool where the river gushes up from the rocks. Surrounded by lush greenery, the turquoise water is cool and refreshing. Cranbrook also boasts a few sun **orchids**, with plans to create a dedicated orchid house. In conjunction with Chukka Cove (see p.157), the park's latest attraction is an adrenaline-fuelled **canopy tour** (2hr 30min; US$88) with nine zip-line traverses of varying lengths and degrees of fear factor, whizzing you through the treetops. It's best to bring your own food and drink to Cranbrook, though you can buy snacks from the tuck shop and bar.

Practicalities

Staying in St Ann's Bay has its advantages, especially if you have your own vehicle; you escape the dust and bustle of Ochi while being close enough to enjoy its good points, and can relax in less restricted surroundings. Intimate and luxurious, **High Hope Estate** (PO Box 11, St Ann's Bay ☏972 2277, Ⓦwww.highhope estate.com; ⑤–⑦, including breakfast) located just above the town, is an eclectically furnished seven-room hotel, featuring great views, a pool, botanical gardens, excellent food and free access to a stunning private beach at *Colombus Cove*. Illustrious past guests include Charlie Chaplin, Kurt Vonnegut, and more recently, Annie Lennox, who wrote much of her album *Bare* in the Pineapple Room. The only property on the left past High Hope, **TeresinaJamaica** (Top Road, Sussex Estate, St Ann's Bay ☏972 5936 or 857 9557, Ⓦwww.teresinajamaica .com; ③) is a well-presented three-bedroom chalet set in the hills, boasting wooden floors, private bathrooms, ceiling fans and small verandahs; great Jamaican food is served. For budget dormitory/guesthouse accommodation, turn inland at Priory to Circle B Farm (☏913 4511; ①–②), a friendly option on a working plantation with communal kitchen. Camping available.

The usual selection of patty shops and Jamaican **eateries** line Main Street in St Ann's Bay, while *Seafood Specialist* by the town's turn-off on the main road is a breezy, enduringly popular eatery with fish tea and "crack conch" – marinated, deep-fried pieces of tender meat so-named because, like the drug, they keep you going back. A mile or so east of St Ann's Bay at Drax Hall (unsignposted, neighbouring the gas station), *Scotchies* jerk restaurant have extended their winning Montego Bay formula of good quality jerk in attractive gardens and a lively atmosphere, while right next door is the unlikely location for the *Irish Rover* pub, run by Jamaican former Belfast resident Winston Samuels. Lunch specials include pies, steaks and baked potatoes, plus there are imported beers, football screens and live jazz at weekends. Back in St Ann's Bay by the main road is *Jus' Cheers*, a popular venue for sound-system dances and crowded Wednesday **karaoke**. Other dances and **stageshows** are held on Sundays at Priory beach – its circular bar is a nice place for a drink, too.

Runaway Bay and Discovery Bay

Halfway between Ocho Rios and Falmouth, the neighbouring mini-resorts of **Runaway Bay** and **Discovery Bay** bask in isolated indolence, with little in the way of either natural beauty or manufactured attractions. **Buses** and **shared taxis** from Montego Bay and Ocho Rios arrive and depart from points all along the main road through Runaway Bay, and from the A1/B3 intersection in Discovery Bay. Theories abound as to the **naming** of the bays; while it's assumed that "runaways" were Spanish troops fleeing the British in the seventeenth century, it more likely refers to Africans who made the risky ninety-mile canoe trip to Cuba and freedom. Baptized into Catholicism, calls for their return were denied on the grounds that Catholics couldn't live among sectarians. Also contrary to popular belief, Discovery Bay does not hold the dubious honour of being the place where Columbus first stepped onto Jamaican shores; that accolade goes to Rio Bueno a few miles down the road. The bays are both well blessed with luxuriantly lively **snorkelling** and **dive sites**, including sunken ganja planes. Reliable operators include Jamaqua dive shop at resort *Club Ambiance* (℡ 973 4845, Ⓦ www.jamaqua .com), and Resort Divers (℡ 881 5760, Ⓦ www.resortdivers.com).

RUNAWAY BAY is the more developed of the two towns, a lackadaisical melee of no-frills rum joints and commercial centres running along a three-mile strip from the satellite community of **SALEM** to the east, where you'll find the majority of shops and restaurants, to the main "square", marked by a post office and the road to Browns Town inland. The **all-inclusive hotels**, which have fenced in the best stretches of beach, are spread throughout, but as all holiday business takes place inside, the town itself appears pretty somnolent. For swimming, sugary-sanded **Cardiff Hall public beach**, opposite the Shell petrol station, is popular with locals, and the **fisherman's beach** at Salem is less pristine but full of atmosphere. Even better is to jump in a shared taxi to lovely Puerto Seco beach in Discovery Bay (see below). If you're a golfer, check out the *Superclubs* **golf course** opposite *Breezes* (℡ 973 2436; US$45 greens fee for eighteen holes), which is open to non-guests.

Midway between the two bays, the *Bahia Principe* resort at **Pear Tree Bottom** is notable islandwide for the storm of protest it created upon construction. Formerly a pristine forested hillside and mangrove wetland with reef just offshore, a 2006 legal ruling declared that the government had breached the law in awarding a permit. Shortly after, workers on the site rioted over unfair conditions, including working twelve-hour shifts for between J$800 and J$1000 (at the time US$15), and over the company's decision to bring in cheaper workers from the Dominican Republic; police responded with tear gas and gunfire. Nearby, the **Green Grotto and Runaway Caves** (US$20 for a 45min guided tour; daily 9am–4pm); is the area's sole managed attraction. The site has a nature park with fishing (you catch, they cook), while the limestone caves themselves are expansive and well lit, with an underwater lake 120 feet below sea level. The grotto may have been used as a hideout by fleeing Spanish troops and as a Taino place of worship, but much more recently it gained notoriety as a nightclub – a surfeit of gyrating dancers badly damaged the delicate formations, which are fortunately now growing back. Guides are properly trained and informative, and they work hard at injecting plenty of humour into their tours.

More pacific than its neighbour, the crescent harbour of **DISCOVERY BAY** is dominated by the red-stained sphere of the Kaiser **bauxite** plant, from where much of Jamaica's two million tons of "red gold" is exported annually to US refineries. The plant also acted as "Crab Cay", the fictional base of Dr Julius No in the first of the James Bond movies. A Texaco petrol station and clutch of shops is the main focus, though **Puerto Seco beach** (daily 9am–5pm; J$300, including use of full facilities) offers gleaming sand, crystal-clear water and a gently shelving shoreline that's good for children. The name means "dry harbour" in reference to Columbus's reluctance to land in a bay with no source of fresh water. The eastern curve of Discovery Bay's horseshoe is dominated by luxurious villas, and on the opposite outcrop, the University of the West Indies Marine Research Laboratory (℡ 973 2241) houses the island's only **decompression chamber**. Rounding the bay, the basic stone structure and rusting ironware of **Quadrant Wharf** are visible, built in 1777 by the British, fearful of possible French attack. Nearby, **Columbus Park** (daily 9am–5pm; free) is a well-signposted yet rather dull museum with colonial-era artefacts including a water wheel and cannon.

Practicalities

For accommodation, **all-inclusives** dominate: *Superclubs'* (Ⓦwww.superclubs.com) *Breezes,* with every facility possible including an eighteen-hole golf course, and *Hedonism III,* the second branch of the infamously "adult" resort, with nude beach and risqué ambience. The *Franklyn D Resort* (Ⓦwww.fdrholidays.com) is specifically family-oriented, with round-the-clock childcare. There are many luxury **villas**, which can be cost-effective for large groups – contact JAVA (Ⓣ974 2508, Ⓦwww .villasinjamaica.com). For **guesthouse** accommodation, Runaway Bay is the better bet. *House Erabo* (Ⓣ973 4813, Ⓦwww.house-erabo.com; ❷) is an attractive and spotless three-bedroom (with en-suite) guesthouse on the western edge of town, with steps leading down to a small private beach. *Piper's Cove* (Ⓣ973 7156, Ⓦwww .piperscoveresort.com; ❹), a newly built complex of one-bedroom apartments in a pretty landscaped garden with pool and private beach. *Runaway Bay HEART Hotel* (Cardiff Hall Ⓣ973 6671, Ⓦwww.runawayheart.com.jm; ❹) offers outstanding service due to its designation as a hotel training school, set amidst immaculate gardens overlooking a golf course, with pool and beach shuttle.

The bays' fancy **restaurants** are all within hotels, and you have to buy an expensive day or evening pass to eat there. For semi-fine-dining, however, try the *Cardiff Hall Restaurant* at *Runaway Bay HEART Hotel,* with Jamaican and international cuisines accompanied by wonderful service. A number of Jamaican eateries are signed off the main road; best bets include *Ultimate Jerk Centre,* between the bays opposite Green Grotto, a lively place serving up delicious helpings of spicy pork and chicken, and plenty of white-rum (open until at least 1am), and *Sharkies Bar and Grill* at Salem beach, with succulent lobster and roast fish dinners served alfresco. Patties, coconut bread and pastries are available from *Bayside Pastries* near the post office in Runaway Bay, and from *Spicy Nice,* beside the petrol station in Discovery Bay. As most people head into Ocho Rios for their **nightlife**, the twin bays are not exactly jumping, though occasional sound systems are advertised. Non-guests can buy an evening pass to all-inclusives (US$50–80), covering dinner, drinks, a floorshow and disco – *Breezes* and *Club Ambiance* are particularly lively. Numerous **bars** line the main road, some of which serve as go-go clubs with plenty of rude, semi-naked gyrating late into the night. In Discovery Bay, *Nancy's* is a breezy and less raunchy open-air local joint. In Runaway Bay, the suitably named rooftop bar *Tek it Eazy* has music most nights and **karaoke** every Tuesday, and *Flavours* at Cardiff Hall beach has a stage for larger dances and busy Sunday bashments (parties).

Car rental is available from Caribbean Car Rentals in Runaway Bay (Ⓣ973 3539) or from Salem Car Rental (Ⓣ973 4167, Ⓦwww.salemcarrentals.com.jm).

Marley's mausoleum and the St Ann interior

Both the B3 from Runaway Bay and the inland road from Discovery Bay lead high in the hills to bustling **BROWN'S TOWN**, a sizeable inland community with fantastic views and booming central **market** (main days Wed, Fri and Sat). Pillars of sugar cane, yams and dasheens caked in red alluvial earth are ferried in by farmers and sold by formidable female higglers, while bootleg name-brand clothing and tawdry knick-knacks sell by the bucketload. Even the shops are worthy of a root – Charley & Son on Main Street is a treasure-trove of ancient books with yellowing covers, tacky postcards and intriguing miscellany, while

The legacy of the ambassador of reggae is impossible to overemphasize, with his lyrics today continuing to strike a chord across every social stratum. Born February 6, 1945, **Robert Nesta Marley** was the progeny of an affair between 17-year-old Cedella Malcolm and 51-year-old Anglo-Jamaican soldier Captain Norval Marley, stationed in the Dry Harbour mountains as overseer of crown lands. Marley's early years, surrounded by a doting family and the rituals of rural life, had a profound effect on his development. He clung to his African heritage and revelled in the cultural life of Kingston, where he spent most of his later life. Marley was known as a spiritual individual, emanating energy and charisma, but he was also a lover, fathering eleven children by various women including those by his wife, **Rita Anderson**, his 1966 marriage which lasted until he died. Appropriately enough, his 1970s' membership of Rastafarian sect the Twelve Tribes Of Israel gained him the name Joseph, "a fruitful bough" according to the Bible.

Fusing African drumming traditions with Jamaican rhythms and American rock guitar, Marley's music became a symbol of unity and social change worldwide. Between 1961 and 1981, his output was prolific. Following their first recording, *Judge Not,* on Leslie Kong's Beverley's label, his band, The Wailers (Marley, Bunny Livingstone and Peter Tosh), went on to record for some of the best producers in the business; most agree that their finest material was recorded in collaboration with volatile genius Lee "Scratch" Perry. In 1963, the huge hit *Simmer Down* meshed perfectly with the post-independence frustration felt by young Jamaicans, and the group's momentum of success began in earnest. International recognition came when the Wailers signed to the Island label – owned by Anglo-Jamaican entrepreneur Chris Blackwell, who Marley saw as his "interpreter" rather than producer. The first Island release was *Catch a Fire* in early 1973, and the eleven albums that followed all became instant classics. With the help of Blackwell's marketing skills, reggae became an international genre. Differences with Blackwell led to the departure of Livingstone and Tosh in 1974, but Marley continued to tour the world with a new band called *Bob Marley and the Wailers*.

In the run-up to a performance at the 1976 Smile Jamaica concert – staged by the government to quell rising tensions in a factionalized election campaign – gunmen burst into Marley's home and tried to **assassinate** him. The attempt was bungled, and most of the shots hit manager Don Taylor (who made a full recovery), though Bob and Rita incurred minor injuries. Undeterred, a bandaged Marley went on stage, choosing to leave after the concert to recover and record in Britain and the US, a period which produced the album *Exodus*. Two years later, he returned to perform at the historic **One Love Peace Concert**, the result of a short-lived truce between the political garrisons of the PNP and JLP. He was the headline act of a line-up that also included Peter Tosh spitting vitriol at the politicians, and Marley ended his performance by enticing archenemies Michael Manley and Edward Seaga on stage to join hands in a show of unity. But Marley's call for unity and freedom was not restricted to Jamaica; one of his greatest triumphs was performing the protest anthem *Zimbabwe* at the independence celebrations of the former Rhodesia.

In the midst of a rigorous 1980 tour, Marley was diagnosed as suffering from cancer; he died a year later in Miami, honoured by his country with the Order of Merit. Marley died without making a will, and years of legal wrangles resulted in his widow being granted the lion's share. Rita Marley's Bob Marley Foundation (🌐www.bobmarley foundation.org) continues to sponsor the development of new artists and to manage Bob's legacy, and many of the Marley children have also forged their own musical careers. Ziggy, Cedella and Sharon found success as the Melody Makers, while Damian **"Junior Gong"**, his son by 1976 Miss World Cindy Breakespeare, is a new star with three albums and an equal number of Grammys. **Steven Marley** has found success as both producer and recording artist, and US-based Kymani has a number of reggae/hip-hop hits to his name. In the hearts of both Jamaican and global fans, though, the master's voice can never be equalled.

nearby **restaurants** are good for Jamaican food; try *Colbys* for natural juices. Few visitors choose to **stay** here, but if you want to soak up more of the atmosphere try *Meditation Heights* (☎917 9495; ❶–❸) at the top edge of town (take a left fork beside the Cool Oasis petrol station). Buses from Runaway Bay arrive two or three times a day; taxis are much more convenient.

Further inland, **Alexandria** is a hamlet on the stunning cross-country B3 route to Mandeville (see p.259), but a left turn onto a (signposted) narrow road winds through communities **Alva** and **Ballintoy** to the only tourist attraction in the St Ann interior: the **Bob Marley Centre and Mausoleum** (daily 8am–8pm; US$20; ☎843 0498 or 467 2400, ⓦwww.bobmarleymovement.com) at his former home of **Nine Mile**. The red-earthed pastures, distant Cockpits and sweeping hills and gullies of the Dry Harbour Mountains are a photographer's dream, though the viciously potholed road will demand most of your attention. You can make your own way here with a rental car or taxi charter (a round-trip from Runaway/ Discovery bays or Ochi should cost US$80–100), or alternatively, you can sign up

▲ Guides at The Bob Marley Centre and Mausoleum

for a tour: Chukka Cove's Zion Bus Line (☎972 2506, ⓦwww.chukkacove.com; US$100; 6hr with pick-up, drinks and lunch included) operates a vehicle designed to look like a 1970s country bus with a pumping Bob Marley soundtrack, though cynics may find the ambience too "gift-wrapped Jamaica". A straightforward bus tour is operated by Tourwise (☎974 2323, ⓦwww.tourwise.org).

You know you're in Nine Mile when you see the red-gold-and-green flags flying high above a fenced compound – if you're driving, park directly in the compound car park rather than on the road. Once you've paid the entrance fee, one of a throng of Rasta guides takes you into the centre proper. There's a prayer space at the first plateau, sometimes occupied by orthodox Rastafarians, and to the right is the wooden shack that Marley lived in between the ages of six and thirteen, complete with the "original" single bed he sang of in *Is This Love*. Opposite is a barbecue where he cooked up Ital feasts during rural retreats, and the "meditation stone" where he rested his head for contemplation, immortalized in the song *Talkin' Blues*. You leave cameras and shoes outside before entering the **mausoleum**, painted with Rasta colours and depictions of black angels that encases the marble slab that holds Marley's remains. A stained-glass window filters red, gold and green sunlight over the stone, while candles, incense, fresh flowers and scribbled tributes make the mausoleum one of the more uplifting aspects of a place that in celebrating Marley's death seems to succeed in highlighting the yawning gap left by his passing. Some Rastas – who eschew the concept of physical death – argue that Nine Mile is not his resting place and that, like Haile Selassie, Bob's bones will never be found. The latter may yet prove more apt than it might seem; conspiracy-minded Jamaicans have begun to suggest that Rita Marley's stated aim of moving his remains to Ghana (causing great consternation) has secretly already taken place.

In some ways, the centre is a bit of a disappointment, the abundance of concrete and high prices giving the impression of a theme-park cut off from the community; there's also an undercurrent of hustle – you'll doubtless be offered overpriced ganja. There's a sizeable gift shop and vegetarian restaurant on-site. Despite all of this, nothing can detract from the beauty of the locale, the home of the original "Natural Mystic". If you want to linger, you can stay in the on-site luxury rooms with stone floors, balconies and jacuzzis (US$220 all-inclusive); in a basic **hotel** opposite the complex (US$50; shared kitchen); or pitch you, own **tent** for a small fee. The place comes alive each **February 6** on Marley's birthday, sometimes featuring one of the Marley children (see the website or contact the Bob Marley Foundation (☎927 9152).

Rio Bueno to Duncans

West of Discovery Bay the new highway traverses the Rio Bueno (which doubles as the St Ann–Trelawny parish border) before cutting inland. A right turn just beforehand leads to **RIO BUENO**, a quiet village of crumbling eighteenth-century buildings cowering in the shadow of a towering animal-feed factory and lumber export dock – fortuitously absent when the place was used as a set for *A High Wind in Jamaica*. It's popularly agreed that the "crescent harbour" here was where **Christopher Columbus** – having spent a night anchored off St Ann's Bay during his "discovery" of the island in 1494 – decided to land, recording the bay's rapidly running river and horseshoe dimensions in his diary. Columbus made a lucky choice as Rio Bueno also boasts one of Jamaica's deepest harbours. History is also present in the form of a ruined British **fort**, named after secretary of war

Henry Dundas, and dating back to 1778, and in the blue- and white-painted **St Mark's Anglican church**, built at the sea's edge in 1833. The original **Baptist church** was burnt to the ground by hostile Anglicans – the present incarnation above town was erected in 1901. The only other reason to linger here is to peruse the excellent Gallery Joe James, an inviting **art gallery** set in a seventeenth-century warehouse, itself part of the *Hotel Rio Bueno* (T 954 0048; ④). Enigmatic James is a well-known Jamaican artist, and the gallery includes paintings, masks and a stunning cedar Medusa, a carved sculpture with flowing locks of snakes. You can also **eat** seafood lunches (US$12–20) or take a drink at the breezy hotel restaurant, *The Lobster Bowl,* right over the water. To the west, a vast all-inclusive has seen fit to open up – *Breezes Rio Bueno* (T 954 0000, W www.superclubs.com; ⑦) strives to re-create a "real" Jamaican town with its own town square (minus traffic, goats and dirt) and extensive facilities.

If you're after more pastoral delights, head for a swim inland at the (hard to find) Bueno's source, **Dornoch Riverhead**, a deep, cliff-edged swimming hole surrounded by silk cotton trees and throngs of mosquitoes (take the road to Woods Town and continue towards Seaford Town; it's hidden from the leafy lane and you may need local help – a rough track crosses the road where you can park up and walk the final 300 yards westwards). Baptist missionary and anti-slavery activist William Knibb baptized converts here, and a spiritual, spooky ambience lingers. Elsewhere inland, history is everywhere in a landscape strewn with the crumbling chimneys of unidentifiable sugar factories and stone churches built by Baptist missionaries.

With the highway speeding off towards Montego Bay, it's easy to miss the turning for **DUNCANS**, a peaceful village huddled under the hills of Cockpit Country, with a clock tower timepiece that hasn't worked for over twenty years. Most visitors passing through come to stay at the restful and secluded **villas** of *Silver Sands* (PO Box 1, Duncans T 954 7606, W www.mysilversands.com; ③–⑦), a wide and windswept beach with powdery white sand and superlative swimming – accessed from just west of town. Around 100 privately owned holiday homes are decorated in varying styles and degrees of luxury, many rented out for a minimum of three nights – some sleep up to twelve for around US$5000/week. The **coastline** here is sublime, though the *Silver Sands* beach has a hefty US$25 a day fee for non-guests.

Montego Bay and Cockpit Country

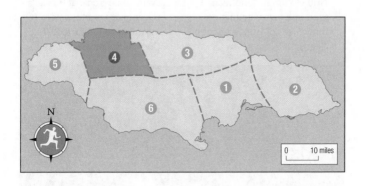

CHAPTER 4

Highlights

* **Doctor's Cave Beach** Powdery white sand and gin-clear waters make this the ultimate place to take a dip in the warm Caribbean. See p.178

* **Horseback riding** Swim your mount through the sea at the *Half Moon* hotel stables, or take a leisurely ride through the gorgeous plantation of Good Hope on the fringe of Cockpit Country. See p.185 & p.196

* **Meal at the Houseboat Grill** Gourmet Caribbean food in a lovely setting on the waters of Bogue Lagoon. See p.188

* **Falmouth** As well as boasting some of the most impressive Georgian architecture in Jamaica, this small market town has a lively but unhurried atmosphere. See p.193

* **Cultural Tours** Experience Jamaica's enthralling history through the vivid theatrical performance at Outameni, or the story of the Maroons at Flagstaff. See p.195 & p.200

* **Albert Town adventures** Make the hair-raising descent onto Quashie River Sink, have a swim and a picnic at Bunker's Hill or take a gentle walk in the unique egg-box foothills of Cockpit Country. See p.199

▲ Doctor's Cave Beach

Montego Bay and Cockpit Country

J amaica's second-largest city, the seaside settlement of **Montego Bay** is one of Jamaica's premier tourist honeypots. Framed by a cradle of hills and sitting pretty in a sweeping natural harbour, with fabulous **beaches** hemmed in by a labyrinth of offshore **reefs**, it's furnished with enough natural attributes to fill any brochure, and its slick tourism suits the commercial, easy-access tastes of cruise shippers. Montego Bay remains the reigning old madam of Jamaican resorts: gossipy, belligerent and overdressed, but also absorbing, spirited and lively, particularly during its world-renowned summer reggae festival, **Sumfest**. The coastline to the east of town has been snapped up by upmarket all-inclusives, strung out alongside souvenir malls and golf courses. Most famous of these is **Rose Hall Great House** and its massively embellished legend of Voodoo and sexual intrigue, though the sun-bleached Georgian-era town of **Falmouth**, marooned from coast-road action following construction of the new North Coast Highway, offers a welcome respite from the resort ethic as well as the unusual prospect of a night-time swim in the nearby phosphorous lagoon. Inland, the landscape rises sharply as you enter rural St James, where districts such as **Montpelier** and **Kensington** were once absorbed by huge **sugar estates**, worth the trip alone for their magnificent settings covered with acres of citrus. The verdant **Great River valley** here offers good freshwater **swimming** at lovely oases such as Nature Village Farm, as well as **tubing** or **rafting** in the silky green waters, or hand-feeding a hummingbird at the beautiful **Rocklands Bird Sanctuary** high above the bay.

Less than two hours' drive from the centre of Montego Bay lies an area so untouched by any kind of holiday development that it's something of a parallel universe to the coastal resort ethic. The mainly uninhabited limestone hillocks of **Cockpit Country** are the antithesis of palm trees and concrete, and the few settlements that cling to the edges of this almost lunar landscape are some of the most beguiling on the island. Some are still home to descendants of the once-mighty **Maroons**, escaped slaves who waged guerrilla war against the British. Though **Accompong**, on the southern side of the Cockpits, is still a semi-autonomous state governed by a Maroon council, these Trelawny Maroons of western Jamaica welcome visitors, and as a result, the west is one of the better places to learn a little Maroon history firsthand.

Montego Bay

MoBay, as it's locally known, nestles between the gently sloping Bogue, Kempshot and Salem hills, and extends some ten miles west to the haunts of the suburban rich at Reading, and to the plush villas and resorts of Ironshore and Rose Hall to the east. Planeloads of foreigners flood in every day, seduced by a heavily marketed Caribbean dream of swaying palm trees, lilting reggae and cocktails at sunset, and although the flow has slowed a little in recent years (with many heading straight for the more expansive charms of Negril), the city in many ways still delivers. It's made up of two distinct parts: touristy **Gloucester Avenue**, vigorously marketed as the "Hip Strip", and the city proper, universally referred to as **"downtown"**. The split between the two is so sharp that the majority of tourists never venture further than the Strip on foot, dividing their time between the unbroken string of beaches, shops and restaurants, though the air of enforced tourist-friendliness can be a bit disquieting. Downtown offers a more accurate and vibrant picture of Montegonian life, and though it's short on specific sights, the malls and markets here provide MoBay's best shopping possibilities. MoBay's holiday mask slips along its **western** stretch, an ugly sprawl of factories and gas containers, whose main concession to the tourist trade is the **Freeport cruise-ship pier**.

When Columbus anchored briefly in Montego Bay in 1494, he was charmed enough to name it *El Golfo de Buen Tempo* (The Bay of Good Weather). The Spanish were less romantic, dubbing it *Manterias*, a derivation of *manteca* (pig fat), after the lard they produced and shipped from here in large quantities. Eventually, the English corruption, "Montego", stuck. By the time the Spaniards hastily fled the island in 1655, the city was little more than a village. Its subsequent development was heavily influenced by two factors. First was the presence of the **Maroons** in neighbouring Cockpit Country (see p.271), an African-Jamaican band of militarily skilled former slaves whose frequent attacks on British settlements kept the town from prospering until the peace treaty of 1739. By this time, plantation **sugar production** was booming, the harbour thronging with ships, and lavish cut-stone town houses and inns spreading back from the waterfront. The 1831 **Christmas Rebellion** (see p.181) nonetheless nearly destroyed it. The most important of the violent slave revolts that prefaced emancipation began in the foothills behind the town, and saw almost every estate in the area burnt to the ground.

After the collapse of the sugar trade, Montego Bay spent a hundred-odd years in limbo, and it was not until the early twentieth century that it entered another period of growth, beginning when Sir Herbert Baker advocated the redemptive powers of the Doctor's Cave waters. MoBay metamorphosed into the ultimate **tourist town**; rich North Americans and Europeans built holiday homes around Doctor's Cave, or arrived on banana boats to stay in the town's first hotel, the *Casa Blanca*. The town's population increased fourfold between 1940 and 1970, with Jamaicans from all over the island moving in to work at the hotels. In the 1960s, the Freeport peninsula was constructed on reclaimed land, assuring its position as a premier port of call for Caribbean cruises. More recently, MoBay has achieved fame as the base for Jamaica's summer **reggae festival**, Sumfest (see p.182), while the Air Jamaica Jazz and Blues festival and debauched college antics of Spring Break inject shots of adrenaline at other times of the year. The beaches have been attractively overhauled, and determinedly tourist-friendly, MoBay feels on the upswing.

Arrival, information and getting around

Over eighty percent of visitors to Jamaica arrive at **Donald Sangster International Airport** (ⓦwww.mbjairport.com; ticket, flight and baggage information line ☎952 3124), right by the sea a mile from the Gloucester Avenue Hip Strip. It's fully geared up for the newly arrived tourist, with a 24-hour **cambio**, ATM machines and numerous hotel transport and car-rental booths. **Luggage trolleys** aren't permitted past immigration, but red-capped porters will carry your bags for a small charge. Larger hotels provide free airport transfers; alternatively you can charter a **taxi** from the omnipresent JUTA drivers. A ride to Gloucester Avenue, Queen's Drive or downtown should cost no more than US$10; if you're on a very tight budget and travelling light, you could consider one of the local **shared taxis** (see p.171) that leave from the petrol station past the airport's car park, and run down the Strip into downtown MoBay. Note that there's no public bus service.

If you're heading straight for Negril or Ocho Rios, check at JUTA and at hotel booths in the arrivals area, which run **bus transfers** for guests in Negril and Ocho Rios hotels; space allowing, you may be able to jump in one for US$25–35 per person. Otherwise, make for the busy downtown **bus terminus**, behind the

---

Organized tours

Hundreds of **tour companies** operate out of Montego Bay; most have booths at the airport and offices along Gloucester Avenue and offer similarly priced trips to plantations (such as Croydon, John's Hall and Hilton High) and great houses like Rose Hall (see p.185) or Greenwood (see p.192). For more on the activities available, visit ⓦwww.attractions-jamaica.com and ⓦwww.montego-bay-jamaica.com.

In addition to standard **tours**, Barrett Adventures (☎382 6384, ⓦwww.barrett adventures.com) offers interesting options, from customized packages to waterfalls, plantations, beaches and Cockpit Country, to horseback rides at Good Hope; prices start at US$60 per person per day. Otherwise, a raft of operators do standard trips to Dunn's River Falls, the Appleton Estate and to Negril; try Caribic Vacations, 69 Gloucester Ave (☎979 3421, ⓦwww.caribicvacations.com) or Tourwise, 14 Sunset Blvd (☎952 4916, ⓦwww.tourwisejamaica.com). Standard tours usually mean sitting with twenty others on an air-conditioned bus, and paying through the nose for the privilege; you'll often get a better (and cheaper) sense of Jamaica by hiring a **local driver** and doing some independent sightseeing. Dale Porter, aka Rasta Shaka (☎316 2184), is recommended, as is Danny of Danny's Taxi and Tours (☎707 4767 or 979 4318); both charge around US$120 per day for two people, or US$25 per person per day for groups of four or more. Your itinerary could include stops for excellent cultural tours at Outameni, the Rastafarian Village, or the new Flagstaff Maroon Heritage Tour. For details of hiking and caving in Cockpit Country, see p.199.

Soft adventure options include **Caliche Rafting** (☎940 1745, ⓦwww.whitewater raftingmontegobay.com), based in the St James hills in beautiful Montpelier, which offers excellent trips (1hr 30min–2hr; US$80–90) along the Great River, water levels permitting, or a gentler Grade II Rainforest Tour, with rafting, rope-swinging and a swim in a mineral pool; Canyon White-water is a more demanding, adrenaline-fuelled Grade 4 trip. **Chukka Caribbean** (☎684 9934, ⓦwww.chukkacaribbean.com) is the biggest operator on the island, offering river-tubing or kayaking along the Great River (4hr); jeep "safaris" into the St James interior (4hr), with swimming and a waterfall climb; and other unusual options like the "Flight of the Witch" (2hr), in which you buckle on a harness and swing through the treetops of the Rose Hall estate, an ATV/ quad bike safari (2hr) at Rose Hall, or horseback riding through hills and sea (3hr); all include transfers and cost between US$70 and US$100.

169

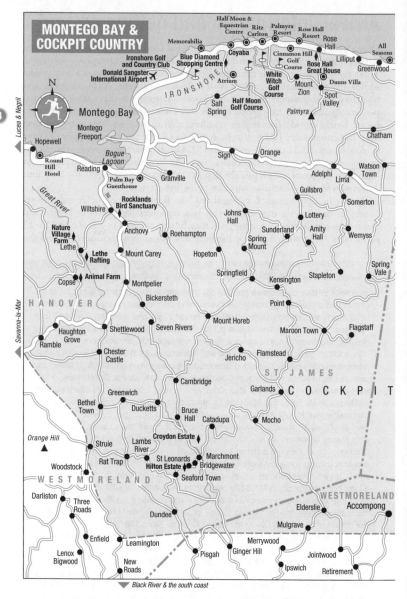

MONTEGO BAY & COCKPIT COUNTRY

N

Lucea & Negril

Savanna-la-Mar

Montego Bay

Hopewell

Round Hill Hotel

Montego Freepoort

Bogue Lagoon

Reading

Palm Bay Guesthouse

Rocklands Bird Sanctuary

Wiltshire

Nature Village Farm

Lethe

Lethe Rafting

Animal Farm

Copse

HANOVER

Haughton Grove

Ramble

Shettlewood

Chester Castle

Bethel Town

Greenwich

Ducketts

Orange Hill

Struie

Woodstock

Rat Trap

Lambs River

Croydon Estate

St Leonards

Hilton Estate

Marchmont

Bridgewater

Seaford Town

WESTMORELAND

Darliston

Three Roads

Enfield

Leamington

Lenox Bigwood

New Roads

Pisgah

Ginger Hill

Merrywood

Ipswich

Jointwood

Retirement

Elderslie

Mulgrave

Accompong

WESTMORELAND

Dundee

Anchovy

Mount Carey

Montpelier

Bickersteth

Seven Rivers

Cambridge

Bruce Hall

Catadupa

Mocho

Garlands

C O C K P I T

ST JAMES

Maroon Town

Flagstaff

Flamstead

Jericho

Mount Horeb

Point

Kensington

Stapleton

Springfield

Hopeton

Roehampton

Johns Hall

Spring Mount

Sunderland

Amity Hall

Wemyss

Lottery

Guilsbro

Somerton

Adelphi

Lima

Watson Town

Chatham

Sign

Orange

Salt Spring

Half Moon Golf Course

Palmyra

Spot Valley

Mount Zion

White Witch Golf Course

Dunns Villa

Rose Hall Great House

Cinnamon Hill Golf Course

Coyaba

Memorabilia

Blue Diamond Shopping Centre

Ironshore Golf and Country Club

Donald Sangster International Airport

Atrium

IRONSHORE

Half Moon & Equestrian Centre

Ritz Carlton

Palmyra Resort

Rose Hall Resort

Rose Hall

Lilliput

Greenwood

All Seasons

Granville

Great River

Spring Vale

Black River & the south coast

fire station at the corner of Howard Cook Boulevard and Barnett Street, from where minibuses run to all destinations (for Negril, you may have to change at Lucea or Savannah-la-Mar). If you're arriving at the bus terminus, charter a taxi to Gloucester Avenue or Queen's for around US$10. You can also take a cheap **shared taxi** from here to points all over the city; ask somebody to show you the relevant departure point.

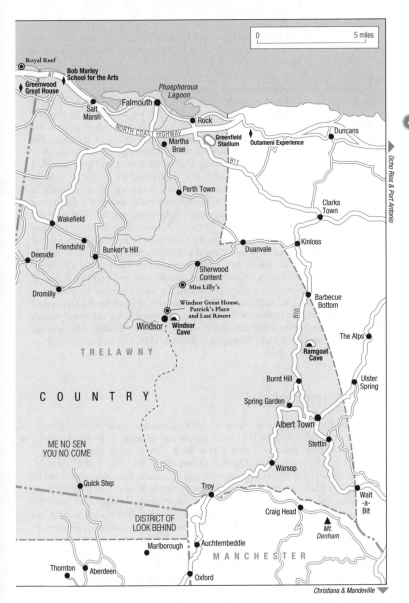

Public transport all around town is provided by the **shared taxis** that run set routes, convenient for short hops along the Strip or to get to the beaches if you're not staying right on Gloucester Avenue. They charge around J$100 per person, and J$150 for trips out of town (bear in mind that rates change constantly with inflation and fluctuating petrol prices). Most start at the bus station or Fort Street near Gully Market (see p.179), but you can flag them down anywhere en route. If you want to charter a **private taxi**, there are legions of drivers along Gloucester Avenue – be prepared to haggle and always settle the price before you get in; most rides from Gloucester Avenue around town cost US$10. Downtown taxi parks are located at the intersection of Market and Strand streets, and by the bus station off Howard Cooke Boulevard (prices are always less downtown than on the Strip).

The **Jamaica Tourist Board** office (Mon–Fri 8.30am–4pm, Sat 9am–1pm; ☎952 4425) is at 18 Queen's Drive opposite the airport, offering maps, flyers and limited advice on hotels, restaurants and attractions. The *Jamaica Tourist* free newspaper, available from all over town, is also a useful resource. Musical events – concerts and special club nights – are usually announced by banners, as well as on the radio. For comprehensive online information, check out ⓦwww.montego-bay-jamaica.com.

If you're staying on the Strip, **walking** is the best option and you shouldn't experience any problems even at night, but downtown it's better to walk in company until you get your bearings (see p.178 for more on staying safe). Tailbacks during rush hours (7.30–10am and 4.30–6.30pm) make **driving** a frustrating experience, and though good for independent sightseeing, you'll find that all the Strip attractions are reachable on foot. Between 7am and 2am there are **parking fees** between *Margaritaville* and the far end of the plaza in front of Fantasy Craft Market; pay at stores east of Doctor's Cave Beach. If you park illegally, your vehicle will be towed away to the pound on Creek Street and you'll be charged a hefty fee and suffer bureaucratic hassles. Outlets selling permits close at 8 or 10pm – though restrictions are rarely enforced after 5pm. Avoid the whole scenario by parking in the lots adjacent to Coral Cliff (see p.178) or close to Cornwall Beach. **Car rental** companies have airport booths, with local operators based along the lower section of Queen's Drive/Sunset Boulevard. Rates are high (US$60–80/day), but there are reductions for weekly rentals. Motorbikes (from US$35/day) and scooters (from US$25/day) are also available.

Accommodation

Most **accommodations** here are up to international standards, with air conditioning, TV, phone and safety deposit box. Most people stay adjacent to the beaches along buzzing **Gloucester Avenue** – aka the **Hip Strip** – but if you're after something a little quieter, opt for a hotel on **Queen's Drive**, above and to the east of the strip, which has fabulous sea views and is connected to Gloucester Avenue by shared taxi (if you make like you're a guest, you may be able to use the lift down to the Strip from the *El Greco* and *Montego Bay Club*). There are a few worthy **budget** places near the beaches, and places **downtown** are all considerably cheaper. Many hotels include free airport transfers and beach shuttle. It's rarely difficult to find a vacancy, unless you hit town during Sumfest (July–Aug) or the Jazz Festival in January.

Montego Bay is prime **all-inclusive** territory, with the swankiest enclaves out at suburban Ironshore – more monoliths are completing construction. Some of Montego Bay's wealthiest visitors head for *Round Hill* resort, eight miles out of Montego Bay near Hopewell (see p.196), one of the island's classiest hotels and a regular haunt of the rich and famous.

Gloucester Avenue, Queen's Drive and around

Altamont West 33 Gloucester Ave ☎952 9087, ⓦwww.altamontwesthotel .com. This is an excellent option close to all the action and Walter Fletcher Beach. Modern, businesslike rooms have all mod cons and useful amenities like hairdryers and CD players. There's a pool, sun deck, wireless Internet throughout and great restaurant/wine bar. Breakfast included. ❶

Bayshore Inn 27 Gloucester Ave ☎ 952 1046, ⓔ theporkpit@hotmail.com. Cheerful gingham-swathed rooms with cable and a/c, above a great jerk restaurant. Reduced weekly rate available. ❸

Beach View Apartments Gloucester Ave ☎ 971 3859, ⓦ www.marzouca.com. Appealing and inexpensive self-contained apartments in a great location. All have tiled floors, big bathrooms and living area with kitchenette; one can sleep six, the others four. Tours available, including to Cuba. ❸

Caribic House 69 Gloucester Ave ☎ 979 6073, ⓦ www.caribicvacations.com. Small hotel by Doctor's Cave Beach, popular with backpackers. The three categories of room are all neat, with a/c and fridge; some have a communal balcony over the street. Beware of noise from the basement bar. ❸

Casa Blanca Gloucester Ave ☎ 952 0720 or 1215, ⓦ www.casablancajamaica.com. MoBay's very first resort hotel shows signs of wear and tear but offers plenty of 1950s period charm – mahogany fittings and walls lined with shots of famous former guests. Fantastic location on low cliff between Doctor's Cave and Walter Fletcher beaches, plus a gorgeous pool. Check ahead, as the hotel had been scheduled to open after a long closure. ❺

Doctor's Cave Beach Hotel Gloucester Ave ☎ 952 4355 or 4359, ⓦ www.doctorscave.com. One of the better Strip hotels, opposite Doctor's Cave Beach. Communal areas have funky decor and tropical landscaping, plus pool, jacuzzi, restaurant, bar and gym. Rooms are pretty uniform, but the real draw is the very friendly atmosphere. Rates include breakfast. ❻

El Greco Queen's Drive ☎ 940 6116, ⓦ www.elgrecojamaica.com. Complex of self-contained apartments perched high above the Strip (access via a lift from opposite Doctor's Cave Beach), an excellent choice if you want some independence. Modern suites have balconies and kitchens; there's a pool and tennis courts; rates include breakfast and beach pass. ❺

Gloriana 1–2 Sunset Blvd ☎ 979 0669–71, ⓦ www.hotelgloriana.com. Cheap and cheerful hotel popular with Jamaicans as well as budget travellers. Rooms are bright, basic but adequate, there's free wi-fi, a restaurant, plus a reggae soundtrack at the poolside bar. Student discounts. ❷–❸

Jamaica Grandiosa Queen's Drive, entrance on Leaders Ave ☎ 979 3205, ⓔ jamaicagrandiosa @hotmail.com. A large complex with something of a ghost-town atmosphere, but staff are friendly and the good-value rooms (tiled floors, queen-size, some with fridge) surprisingly bright; go for one on the top floor with a wooden ceiling. Pool and restaurant. ❹

Knightwick Corniche Rd ☎ 952 2988, ⓔ knightwick@hotmail.com. Several large, comfortable rooms in an elegant hacienda-style family guesthouse, conveniently situated above *Coral Cliff*. A good breakfast (included) is served on the verandah. One of the best options on the Strip, with great rates, especially for triple rooms. ❸–❹

Relax Resort 26 Hobbs Ave, above Queen's Drive ☎ 952 7218, ⓦ www.relax-resort.com. Efficiently run by a dynamic Jamaican family, this is a reliable option with pretty landscaping and well-maintained rooms and apartments with kitchen, plus a deep, large pool, gym, restaurant/bar and free beach, airport and shopping shuttles. ❹

Ridgeway Guesthouse 34 Queen's Drive ☎ 952 2709, ⓦ www.ridgewayguesthouse .com. Conveniently located behind tourist informa-tion and near the airport, a homely and friendly option with eight lovely rooms with tiled floors (fan or a/c), wooden furniture and marble bathrooms; some have fridge, kettle and sea views. Free beach shuttle. ❸

Toby Resort Corner Gloucester Ave & Sunset Blvd ☎ 952 4370, ⓦ www.tobyresorts.com. Long-established place with an appealing location in pretty gardens, within easy walking distance of the beaches. Rooms are ageing a little, but comfortable nonetheless with rattan furnishings, and there are two pools, a restaurant and two bars. ❹

The Wexford 39 Gloucester Ave ☎ 952 2854, ⓦ www.thewexfordhotel.com. Overlooking the only green space on the Strip, with lovely sea views, this reliable MoBay old-timer has clean, bright rooms, with tiled floors, tropical-style decor and king-size beds. Apartments with kitchenette are available, plus there is a pool, bar and busy restaurant. ❺

Downtown and out west

Brandon Hill Guest House 28 Peter Pan Ave, Brandon Hill ☎ 952 7054, ⓦ www.brandonhill guesthouse.com. Quiet option with a lovely lobby mural (though the eye is more drawn to the "No schoolgirls in uniform" sign). It's a thoroughly respectable place, though, with neat, spacious (twin bedded) rooms with a/c, plus bar and pool. Turn right off Union St at the garish orange/purple building. ❷–❸

Comfort Guest House 55 Jarrett Terrace, Barnett View Gardens ☎ 952 1238, ⓕ 979 1997. Family-run place with a Christian slant – ideal for those seeking a reserved but friendly atmosphere. The comfortable rooms have a/c and TV, and there's a communal lounge and a sun deck. ❷

Ora Vista Guest House Richmond Hill, off Union St ☎ 940 7075. Friendly guesthouse overlooking downtown, popular with Jamaicans and offering

▲ ❷, ❸, Ⓐ, Ⓑ, Ⓒ, Ⓓ, Ironshore & Ocho Rios

Depart

DOWNTOWN
MONTEGO BAY

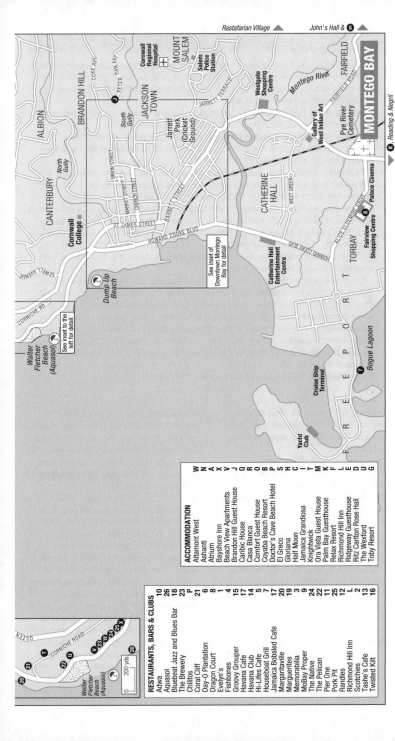

Rastafarian Village ▲   John's Hall & **6** ▲

MOUNT SALEM

Cornwall Regional Hospital

Salem Police Station

Westgate Shopping Centre

Montego River

FAIRFIELD

J

JACKSON TOWN

BRANDON HILL

ALBION

COKE AVE

PETER PAN AVE

JARRETT TERRACE

FAIRFIELD ROAD

Jarrett Park Cricket Ground

South Gully

Gallery of West Indian Art

Pye River Cemetery

MONTEGO BAY

North Gully

CANTERBURY

UNION STREET

MARKET STREET

CHURCH STREET

CATHERINE HALL

WEST GREEN

K Reading & Negril

4

MONTEGO BAY AND COCKPIT COUNTRY

Cornwall College

ST JAMES STREET

BARNETT STREET

HOWARD COOKE BLVD

See inset of Downtown Montego Bay for detail

Palace Cinema

Fairview Shopping Centre

8

TORBAY

SEWELL AVENUE

CORNICHE RD

Dump Up Beach

See inset to the left for detail

Catherine Hall Entertainment Centre

ALICE ELDEMIRE DRIVE

HOWARD COOKE BLVD

Walter Fletcher Beach (Aquasol)

Cruise Ship Terminal

Bogue Lagoon

7

F R E E P O R T

Yacht Club

ACCOMMODATION
Altamont West	W
Ashanti	N
Atrium	A
Bayshore Inn	X
Beach View Apartments	V
Brandon Hill Guest House	J
Caribic House	Q
Casa Blanca	R
Comfort Guest House	O
Coyaba Beach Resort	B
Doctor's Cave Beach Hotel	P
El Greco	S
Gloriana	H
Half Moon	C
Jamaica Grandiosa	T
Knightwick	M
Ora Vista Guest House	K
Palm Bay Guesthouse	F
Relax Resort	L
Richmond Hill Inn	E
Ridgeway Guesthouse	D
Ritz Carlton Rose Hall	U
The Wexford	G

RESTAURANTS, BARS & CLUBS
Adwa	10
Aquasol	26
Bluebeat Jazz and Blues Bar	18
The Brewery	23
Chilltos	P
Coral Cliff	21
Day-O Plantation	6
Dragon Court	8
Evelyn's	1
Fishbones	4
Groovy Grouper	15
Havana Cafe	17
Havana Club	14
Hi-Lifes Cafe	5
Houseboat Grill	7
Jamaica Bobsled Cafe	17
Margaritaville	20
Marguerites	19
Memorabilia	3
MoBay Proper	9
The Native	24
The Pelican	22
Pier One	11
Pork Pit	25
Randles	12
Richmond Hill Inn	L
Scotchies	2
Tashe's Cafe	13
Twisted Kilt	16

QUEEN

CORNICHE ROAD

Walter Fletcher Beach (Aquasol)

0 — 200 yds

175

Watersports

Montego Bay is justifiably famed for its turquoise waters and reefs, some swimmable from the beach. Deeper reefs are alive with fish, rays, urchins and occasional turtles and nurse shark. Pamphlets and information are available from the Montego Bay Marine Park office (see box opposite).

Guided dives (around US$65), certification courses (around US$400) and dive/snorkelling equipment rental (from US$20) as well as snorkelling tours are offered by **Captain's Watersports and Dive Centre** at *Round Hill*, Hopewell ☎956 7050, ext 378; **Resort Divers** at *Holiday Inn*, Ironshore ☎953 9699; and **North Coast Marine Sports** at *Half Moon*, Ironshore ☎953 2211 or 406 9252.

Boat trips, with an open bar and lunch depart from *Pier One* downtown and sail around the bay, with a stop for reef snorkelling. MoBay Undersea Tours (☎940 4465 or 952 5860) run trips aboard *Calico*, the only wooden sailing ship in town (3hr daytime cruise US$45; 2hr evening cruise US$35). Sailing from Doctor's Cave Beach and *Sandals Montego Bay*, two beautifully maintained catamarans, *Tropical Dreamer* and *Day Dreamer*, cruise along the coast to *Margaritaville*'s water slides, there's a snorkelling stop, and ladies get a foot massage. Trips (☎979 0102; 3hr cruises US$70 including transfer from local hotels) operate daily; families in the morning, with afternoons a racier, adults-only affair.

Comprehensive watersports are available at Aquasol on Walter Fletcher Beach (see opposite), while *Breezes* watersports centre at Doctor's Cave has jet skis and parasailing (both US$55 for 30min). From *Pier One*, MoBay Undersea runs trips on a **semi-submersible** vessel (Mon–Sat 11am & 1.30pm; US$45 including transfer from local hotels); go in the morning for the best light or at night for nocturnal marine life. **Glass-bottom boats** operate from all the main beaches (30min; US$15–20). Jet skis are available all over the place for US$80 for half an hour. A fully equipped **sport fishing boat** costs around US$750/day; try Captain's Watersports at *Round Hill*, Marlin Madness (☎896 7279) or Salty Angler (☎863 1599).

lovely bay views. Rooms are simple but clean, with or without a/c. There's a pool, guest kitchen, sun deck, lounge and Jamaican and Cuban food available. ②–③

Palm Bay Guesthouse Bogue Crossing ☎952 1795, ☏940 0411. A great and busy budget guesthouse just off the shared-taxi route into town. Neat, tile-floor rooms have fan or a/c, phone and cable TV. Jamaican restaurant plus shaded bar/jerk centre. ②

Richmond Hill Inn Richmond Hill, off Union St ☎952 3859, ☉www.richmond-hill-inn.com. Former planters' house whose lofty setting offers easily the best views in town. Communal areas with pool, lots of greenery and delicious 1970s touches. Bright rooms have tiled floors, microwave, fridge and patio – some with a view. Excellent value. ③

Ironshore and around

Atrium 1084 Morgan Rd ☎953 2605, ☉atrium @cwjamaica.com. Just off the main road by Blue Diamond Shopping Centre, these spotless, modern apartments have full kitchens and living areas, and there's a pool on site. ⑥

Coyaba Beach Resort Ironshore ☎953 9150, ☉www.coyabaresortjamaica.com. Classy, tranquil resort with elegant, modern rooms with balconies and thoughtful extras. Gorgeous gardens with pool, tennis courts, fitness centre, spa, restaurants and bars, plus private beach. Sports, afternoon tea and entertainment included. ⑥

Half Moon Golf, Tennis and Beach Club Ironshore ☎953 2211, ☉www.halfmoon-resort.com. Queen Elizabeth stayed in this exclusive resort, as do the perma-tanned über-rich. It's heavy with glitzy colonial-style atmosphere. Shopping village, equestrian centre, golf course, lagoon where you can swim with dolphins, 54 private pools, tennis courts, disco, six restaurants and numerous bars. 220 luxury rooms plus private villas. ⑨

Ritz Carlton Rose Hall ☎953 2800, ☉www.ritzcarlton.com. This huge, super-luxurious property feels like a country unto itself, with 427 rooms and every imaginable amenity: golf course, spa, pools, legions of restaurants and bars. Even the sun loungers come equipped with flags to raise to get a drink without moving more than your hand. Manufactured beach and very manufactured atmosphere. ⑨

The Hip Strip: Gloucester Avenue and the beaches

Though it stretches for less than two miles, Montego Bay's glittering **Hip Strip** is the focal point of many a Jamaican vacation. Dazzling **beaches** with protected offshore coral reef are located here, leading to development of the whole of **Gloucester Avenue** and stretching north into **Kent Avenue**. The Strip goes all out to cater to tourists' every need, but its shiny commercialism does make it feel a bit unreal, as though visitors and Jamaican workers here are all playing out designated roles in a sort of open-air tropical theme park.

The southern end of the Strip – where it shoots off from the wide junction with Howard Cooke Boulevard – is split in two, with its easily missed upper section (Fort Street), running parallel. Tucked away here around steep steps up to Queen's Drive is the **Fort Street Craft Market**, a bartering stop that's best bypassed in favour of the craft market downtown (see p.181). The uninspiring hulk of stone next door, **Fort Montego**, dates back to the eighteenth century, built by the British to guard against foreign attack, but its cannons were fired only twice, both times with disastrous results. In a salute to celebrate the capture of Havana in 1760, one cannon misfired and killed its operator, while in 1795 it mistakenly opened fire on one of its own vessels, the *Mercury*, carrying a cargo of dogs to hunt down Maroons; inevitably, the shots missed.

Opposite the fort and Craft Market, the **Aquasol Theme Park** at **Walter Fletcher Beach** (daily 10am–10pm; J$400; ℡979 9447) offers comprehensive watersports facilities, from jet skiing to glass-bottom boat rides, tennis and basketball courts and a go-kart track (J$300 per ride). An attractive decked bar (open until late every night), a locals restaurant and a wide expanse of curving sand with clean changing rooms and showers have made the beach popular, though there are inevitable attendant hangers-on. Beware of the water after heavy rain, when the town's gullies discharge into the sea.

Montego Bay Marine Park

Until 1991, MoBay's offshore reefs remained open to attack from plunderers, spear fishers, divers, boat anchors and industrial pollution. In an attempt to stem the destruction, **Montego Bay Marine Park** (℡952 5619, ⒲www.mbmp.org) was created, Jamaica's first national park with environmental regulations enforced by rangers. Running west from Sangster Airport to Great River, just past Reading, the park comprises nine square miles of coral reef, sea-grass and mangrove, divided into watersports, fishing and fish nursery zones. Within the park, it's illegal to mine sand, damage or move coral, shells and seaweed, fish without a permit, spear-fish or drop litter, while successful past initiatives include the introduction of buoys along the major reefs, so that pleasure-cruise snorkelling stops don't result in damaged coral, and the replacement of large mesh used for fish and lobster traps with smaller mesh to allow young specimens a chance to reach maturity. Though funding and staff shortages and the lack of policing of regulations make it difficult to run the permit system effectively, 2010 has seen renewed investment through the Marine Mania project, aimed at educating fishermen on alternative means of income, alongside increased patrols and restriction signs. Tours are also available for educational trips by the rangers; phone the number above. Donations in cash or kind (particularly depth gauges) are gratefully accepted. If you're interested in learning more, visit the Resource Centre on the top floor of the row of shops and offices adjacent to the *Pier One* club (see p.189).

Though Gloucester Avenue runs parallel to the sea, the water is mainly obscured by buildings. The only place to fully appreciate the sweep of the bay is from the Strip's only **green space**, opposite the restaurants and bars at Miranda Ridge; it's a favourite spot for football, and there are a few benches to take in the view. The bucolic illusion is rudely shattered just past the park by the neon facade of **Margaritaville** (daily 10am–3am; ⓦwww.margaritavillecaribbean.com), a mini-watersports park-cum-restaurant-cum-bar, with a smoking volcano belching vomit-like lava down the walls. A temple to crazy tropical fun, the bar and outdoor eating deck jut out over the sea, while there is a jacuzzi, sun deck and a 110ft water slide. Water trampolines and floating sun decks add to the attraction for MoBay's Spring Break; in February, it's wet T-shirts and beer-drinking competitions all round. Directly opposite, with a thatched roof constructed by African artisans complete with faux-tropical ephemera (including a life-sized plastic elephant), is the **Coral Cliff** complex, where the slot machines and air-conditioned bar never close – always a lively place to stop for a drink.

Beyond, past the seamless parade of bars, cafés and in-bond shops, the magnificent **Doctor's Cave Beach** (daily 8.30am–sunset; J$500; ⓦwww.doctorscavebathing club.com) is Montego Bay's premium portion of gleaming white sand. The beach was put on the map in the late nineteenth century when Doctor Alexander McCatty founded the *Sanatorium Caribbee*, a private bathing club that's still in existence. In the 1920s English chiropractor Sir Herbert Baker was so impressed by the curative potential of the waters that he published an article extolling their efficacy. The beau monde flocked and MoBay's tourist industry was born. The

Staying safe and dealing with hustlers

Though Kingston is home to the country's most impoverished ghettos, Montego Bay, too, has some pretty hairy areas, most of them fringed around the city centre. Given that the vast majority of visitors never choose to set foot downtown, foreigners do stick out away from the Strip, though you're not likely to be robbed the moment you step out. Pickpocketing is a risk, however, so it pays to take **common-sense precautions** like not taking out wads of cash when paying for items, using ATMs in daylight only and keeping cameras in a closed bag. Equally, looking purposeful as you explore and saving the map and guidebook reading for later will help you to blend in.

At one time, a defining characteristic of MoBay was constant interaction with **hustlers**, who earn a living selling crafts, hair braiding or services as a guide or driver. A concerted effort to "clean up" the Strip has seen a reduction in levels of harassment, and these days, you'll find approaches increasingly rare. But unless you're encased in an all-inclusive you will at some point be accosted by someone trying to sell you something. It's tiring and irritating, but it's also easy to lose perspective, visitors bristling with tension and regarding every encounter as adversarial. People need to make a living, and whether or not harassment becomes a problem depends largely upon your attitude. Hustlers play on guilt and use psychological trickery. Lines like "Don't you remember me from the hotel/car rental shop/airport/beach?" are designed to suck you into a dialogue. Of course you've never met them, but once you've stopped, the sales pitch begins. If you ignore the outstretched hand or catcall, you may be upbraided for thinking yourself too good to talk to a regular Jamaican. The best approach is to acknowledge the seller, and say you're not interested in a friendly but straightforward manner – and you don't need to stop walking. Don't try to avoid the issue by giggling or hinting that you may be interested another time; and if you're white, don't fall into the liberal trap of buying things you don't want just to avoid looking racist. Keep your sense of humour, treat sellers as people and you'll minimize problems.

rapidly deepening, crystal-clear waters really are the best in town and facilities are excellent, though it gets very crowded at weekends and the prattle of entertainment at *Breezes* next door can grate. Beach umbrellas, sun loungers or snorkelling equipment available (at high cost), and there are beautiful corals offshore. The membership-only **clubhouse** offers a games room, gym and steam room, but regular changing rooms are also well equipped. There are several snack counters, as well as the *Groovy Grouper* restaurant and bar (see p.187).

A short walk further, **Cornwall Beach** (9am–6pm; J\$350) is a compact but gorgeous swathe of white sand, with gently shelving waters and good snorkelling. Recently reopened, it's seen as the hippest new bathing spot, given greater impetus by its status as venue for the Reggae Sumfest after-party in August. Right opposite, the diminutive **Fantasy Craft Market** is tucked behind a row of duty-free stores and take-outs, massively oversold by its vendors, but you may pick up a bargain. The hotels peter out as Gloucester becomes **Kent Avenue** at the junction with Sunset Boulevard, and continues to hug the coast before ending abruptly at the airport runway wall. The thin but attractive parallel strip of public sand, **Dead End Beach** (also known as Buccaneer or Sunset Beach) is shallow, with good snorkelling, and is popular with Jamaicans. Viewing the sunset from here is fabulous, though the atmosphere is plagued by noisy and occasionally startling landings and takeoffs.

Shooting away from the sea, **Sunset Boulevard** is home to a few forlorn shops and bars, countless car-rental outlets and the rather grand **Summit Police Station**, which boasts its own pool. At the airport roundabout, the boulevard meets **Queen's Drive**, a fast traffic route looping across the hill above (locally known as "top road"). Pavements are sporadic here and walking risky, though the views over the bay are fantastic.

Downtown

After the flamboyance of the Strip, **downtown** MoBay announces itself with a curve of grass-fringed white sand at the southern end of Gloucester Avenue. **Dump-Up Beach**, as it's known, looks pretty enough from a distance, but is in fact one of the dirtiest parts of the bay, as untreated waste from downtown squatter settlements drain directly into the sea via rainwater gullies. It's not a place to swim or chill out, though local soccer matches take place here, alongside packed gospel meetings with Jamaicans in their finery overflowing marquees erected for such occasions. At the wide crossroads with Queen's Drive at the end of the Strip, Howard Cooke Boulevard shoots off to the south, passing the *Pier One* nightclub, a couple of playing fields and the **Catherine Hall Entertainment Centre**, stage show venue and home of Reggae Sumfest (see box, p.183).

Carrying straight on from the Strip at the traffic lights takes you onto **Fort Street**, the main route into the centre of town and a clamorous affair, with dancehall flooding out from store-fronts and all manner of pushcarts and vehicles jostling for space with the thick human traffic. A short way along and to the right, a small sunken garden area houses the **parish library** (Mon–Fri 9.30am–5.30pm, Sat 9am–4pm), which carries a fair stock of Caribbean books. Crossing the bridge and turning left takes you to the **post office**, and at nearby, lively **Gully Market** (the correct name, William Street Market, is seldom used), hard-dough bread and callaloo are sold from supermarket trolleys, and fruit and veg spill over.

Running parallel to Fort Street to the east, **Orange Street** is lined by shabby shops and dingy bars that back onto the Canterbury squatters' community. The zinc-roofed clapboard dwellings cover the entire valley behind, petering out at the red-earthed playing fields of MoBay's main high school, Cornwall College. To the west, squeezed into the space between Fort Street and Howard Cooke Boulevard (south of *Pizza Hut* and *KFC*) is the Bay West shopping mall; pop in to sample ice cream sold at the Devon House outlet, or the veg delights of *Adwa* (see p.187).

Sam Sharpe Square and the craft market

Fort Street comes to an end at **Sam Sharpe Square**, the heart of downtown, characterized by its central fountain, permanent stream of honking traffic, and jumble of old and new architecture. **The Cage**, now a craft shop, was originally built in 1806 as a lock-up for disorderly seamen and runaway slaves; their shenanigans so damaged the original wooden walls that they were replaced by the red-brick and stone that stands today. In 1811, the belfry was installed, used to ring out a 2pm curfew; after a second ring at 3pm any slaves still on the streets were locked up. Just outside, National Hero Sam Sharpe (see box opposite) is commemorated in a rough **bronze statue** by Jamaican sculptor Kay Sullivan, which depicts him in full evangelical flow before a crowd of converts.

▲ Sam Sharpe statue

Sam Sharpe and the Christmas Rebellion

During the course of just over a week, slavery in Jamaica received the blow that would kill it forever. The **Christmas**, or **Baptist**, **Rebellion** began on December 27, 1831; by its end on January 5, 1832, twenty thousand slaves had razed nearly 160 sugar estates, causing damage to the value of £1 million – then a massive drain on the British exchequer. It was the largest slave uprising in Jamaican history, and it set in motion the process that led to the abolition of slavery in 1834 and full emancipation in 1838.

The rebellion was led by **Sam Sharpe**, a house slave working for a MoBay solicitor. Though Sharpe took on the surname of his master in accordance with tradition, his sideline as deacon of the town's Burchell Baptist Church made him anything but servile. Baptists were slavery's most outspoken critics, rightly seen as a threat by the British establishment. The church taught Sharpe to read, and through international newspapers he learned of English anti-slavery sentiments and became convinced that emancipation in Jamaica was imminent, a reality that planters were trying to suppress. A powerful orator, Sharpe formed a **secret society** and planned a nonviolent withdrawal of labour over the Christmas period. Talk of the insurrection spread fast through St James estates, and even the planters became uneasy as December 1831 drew to a close. By the night of the 27th, passions were running high. Peaceful protest soon degenerated into anarchy; tipped off by estate owners, the militia were out in force, and more militant slaves responded by lighting bonfires at the highest point of the Kensington estate to signify the start of a full-scale **rebellion**. Others followed suit and within days western Jamaica was burning as the cane fields and great houses were destroyed one by one. The response of the British militia was brutal. Though damage was predominantly restricted to property and only fourteen whites died, soldiers gunned down one thousand slaves, and magistrates handed down a further three hundred execution orders during the emotional six-week trial that ensued. Sharpe himself was hanged in the MoBay square that today bears his name. He was buried in the harbour sand, though his remains were later exhumed and interred in the vault of Burchell Memorial Church.

To the left of The Cage is MoBay's town hall, **Montego Bay Civic Centre**. Opened in 2001, the handsome Georgian-style structure contains an unmemorable museum on Jamaican history (Tues–Fri 9am–5pm, Sat 10am–3pm; J$200) and a theatre space. To the east next to the centre, Market Street holds the hulking **Burchell Memorial Church** where Sam Sharpe lies buried, while the western section towards the sea has been pedestrianized. Towards the street's end, the main **craft market** is a surprisingly hassle-free place to shop if you don't treat the inventive sales pitches as bamboozling. The 200-odd stalls sell every type of Jamaican craft, and there are a couple of good, cheap, local eateries.

Branching off east from Sam Sharpe Square's southern corner, **Church Street** is the most architecturally interesting of downtown's busy thoroughfares. Dominating it is **St James Parish Church** (if locked, ask at the rector's office opposite or call ⊤ 952 2775), built from creamy cut stone in the shape of a Greek cross. It was considered the showpiece of the parish when completed in 1782, and it underwent major repairs after a 1957 earthquake. Inside, the virtues of Rosa, first wife of John Palmer of Rose Hall (see p.185), are commemorated in a John Bacon verse and sculpture set to the left of the altar, while stained-glass windows depict the crucifixion. Outside, the neglected graveyard contains the weathered graves of planters, many standing at erratic angles since the earthquake. Facing the church is the weathered yet elegant facade of the **Town House**, constructed in 1765 by merchant David Morgan, serving as a private home, church manse, Masonic lodge, synagogue, hotel (Queen Victoria stayed here) and restaurant.

St James and Barnett streets to Jarrett Park

Striking south from Sam Sharpe Square, **St James Street** is a lively strip of shops, with tatty hole-in-the-wall emporia vying for space with neon signs and sidewalk vendors, fighting to be noticed against a background symphony of reggae and shouts of "sky juice" and "peanuts and Wrigley's". Beyond, **Barnett Street** is the least tourist-friendly part of downtown, a raucous belt of mini-malls and traffic fumes, which after St James Street is also good for shopping, though not of the duty-free and T-shirt variety. Barnett Street holds a notorious **police station** and lock-up, a run-down colonial structure where inmates sleep ten to a cell on concrete floors and officers make appeals for donations. Turn down Railway Lane for **Charles William Gordon Market** (known as Fustic Market; main days Wed and Sat). Straddling the disused railway tracks and impoverished homes that make up MoBay's most notorious ghetto, it's a visceral whirl of tarpaulin-covered mounds of earthy yams alongside deep-orange pumpkins, scallion and thyme, and a kaleidoscope of fruits, while numerous higglers make up temporary beds beside their pitches in the pungent indoor meat section.

Back on St James St heading east, a turn onto Creek Street leads a few hundred yards to the **Dome**, an incongruous circular structure with a wooden roof built in 1837 to protect a bubbling water source. The upper floor was originally occupied by the "Keeper of the Creek", who supervised MoBay's only source of fresh water until 1894. Past the Dome, Creek Street rises uphill, changing names and eventually reaching **Jarrett Park** (☎940 3710), MoBay's cricket ground and the original site of Reggae Sunsplash (Bob Marley performed here in 1979). Even if you're not a cricket fan, attending a match is highly entertaining, as much for the dancehall that booms out during breaks in play as for aficionados' impassioned commentaries. Tickets (US$5–10) are sold at the gate, but you should get to high-profile matches early.

The downtown fringes and Freeport

Just south of Jarrett Park, Barnett Street opens up and passes over the Montego River, from where the roadside takes on an incongruously lush aspect; giant bulrushes and emerald reeds flourish in the greyish water, and egrets roost in remaining poinciana and palm. Beyond the river is large landmark **Westgate Shopping Centre**, and past here the road heads through MoBay's last remaining cane fields before connecting up with the coast road towards Negril; just past the left-hand turn-off for Fairfield, a side road to the right leads to the **Gallery of West Indian Art** (see p.190), a marvellous repository of works from Jamaica and the wider Caribbean and a great place to learn about the local arts scene.

Back at the Westgate plaza, fairly good – and attractive – **Fairfield Road** strikes inland towards Adelphi and, ultimately, Cockpit Country. Two miles or so eastwards is the entrance to the **Indigenous Rastafarian Village** (☎410 1770, ⓦwww.rastavillage.com; US$25 2hr tour, US$100 full day including lunch and river swimming), the brainchild of enigmatic local Izza and a surprisingly good tour, offering a modern interpretation that shatters myths about the world's most stereotyped religious movement. Once across the river, you're led through medicinal gardens, a drumming circle and a wooden "village", all the while listening to an enlightening talk on the movement's history, conception of nature, and its place in today's world. The road beyond here is overhung with dripping foliage, and passes over swift streams to the Cockpit foothills, the tarmac barely gripping the edges of steep valleys lined by tiny hamlets such as **Kensington**, the key flashpoint of the Christmas Rebellion – there are no specific sights, but the countryside is gorgeous if you have your own transport.

Every year, Jamaica's best-loved art form overwhelms Montego Bay as **Reggae Sumfest** takes to the stage. The build-up is frenetic: flights are overbooked, beaches throng with fans and the line-up – which reads like a reggae hall of fame – is worried over on radio talk shows. By the time sound and light equipment arrives, the city's hotel rooms are booked-out and every scrap of cardboard is appropriated by entrepreneurs to be sold as "reggae beds" – an essential piece of equipment for tired legs.

Sumfest usually takes place in mid-August, kicking off with a beach party on the Sunday featuring top sound systems, fashion shows and food stalls. "**Mad Monday**" follows with a street party – a take on outdoor jams like Kingston's Passa Passa. Wednesday's **Top Ranking**, is staged at the *Pier One club* and aimed at serious reggae aficionados – you can get close to the performers and it's a night to remember.

Sumfest proper takes place just along the road from *Pier One* at the Catherine Hall Entertainment Centre. Thursday's show is a showcase for the current biggest names in dancehall and has a more raw feel than Friday and Saturday nights – the mostly local crowd is packed to the edges of the arena. Jamaican audiences know their music and are notoriously hard to please; people waste no time demonstrating their appreciation with firecrackers or setting a lighter to a stream of hairspray or anything else combustible – or not, with some blistering heckling and, occasionally, bottle-throwing. By the time, Vybez Kartel or Mavado take to the stage in the early hours, the atmosphere is truly electric. The show is almost always good-natured despite on-stage rivalries, and aside from lyrics and posturing you'll also be treated to some truly rude dancing courtesy of "dancehall queens". Friday and Saturday nights have a more international feel. The new generation of roots artists add a cultural flavour, and grizzled old dreads wave enormous sticks of ganja in the air. A fabulous PA bounces all your favourite tunes around the hills surrounding the town.

Specialist travel agents (see p.20) offer festival packages that include accommodation and entrance fees, and **ticket** outlets (including JTB offices) are found in all the resorts. Entry to the Sumfest beach party costs around US$15, Top Ranking US$25 and Ignition and the Summit around US$50; the Monday street party is free. A season ticket (around US$150) covers entry to all the main nights, and a VIP version (around US$200), gives access to the backstage and front of stage areas – though the latter isn't really worth bothering with unless you're an autograph-hunter or photographer. Combined Fri–Sat passes cost around US$90, or VIP US$120. For **information**, check out ⓦ www.reggae sumfest.com, call ℡ 953 2933, or contact JTB worldwide (see p.46).

The festival tradition began in 1978 when revellers enjoyed five nights of roots reggae at Jarrett Park – with a heady combination of ganja and rum. This "**Reggae Sunsplash**" set a positive tone; international attention was captured, and a year later a capacity crowd rocked to a killer line-up with Bob Marley at the helm. The quintessential 1980s shows drew huge crowds and "good musical vibes" – a contrast from the cool reserve and sometimes farcical posturing of today's stageshows. In the 1990s, legal wrangles and venue changes left Sunsplash struggling for success. In 1993, **Reggae Sumfest** muscled in, snapping up the Montego Bay location and outshining its rival. Nonetheless, Sunsplash rose from the ashes in 2006 (ⓦ www .reggaesunsplashja.com) with its first show in seven years, staged at the 200-acre Richmond Estate. Sadly, its return lasted just one year, and Sumfest still remains Jamaica's most popular festival, despite being somewhat marred in 2005 when obscenities and homophobic lyrics led to a (temporary) ban on Beenie Man and other artists who remain supremely popular locally. In the eyes of some, the event has become sanitized in its quest to appeal to foreigners, but it continues to attract some simply brilliant line-ups – recent years have seen sets from Beres Hammond, Buju Banton and Sizzla, as well as Ini Kamoze, Toots and the Maytals and the late Alton Ellis, plus huge international stars from Ne-Yo and Kanye West to Alicia Keys and Nas. And with 60,000 tickets sold, it remains unmissable.

At the south-western edge of town, Howard Cooke Boulevard merges at a cross-roads with Alice Eldemire Drive; left heads past the Fairview Shopping Centre and meets the main road west to Reading and, ultimately, Negril, while right leads to **Freeport Peninsula**, backed to the south by the mangroves of the Bogue Lagoon and to the north by commercial wharves and the **cruise-ship pier**, a collection of expensive shops and restaurants. Past here are a series of expensive apartment complexes and the high-rise *Sunset Beach* hotel. There's not much to see here, but it's worth coming for a sundowner on the roof of the *Houseboat Grill* (see p.187), or a game of pool and a tasty lunch at the posh **Yacht Club**, ostensibly for members only but covertly accessible to tourists; shared taxis ply the route.

Ironshore and Rose Hall

Heading east from the Sangster airport roundabout, Queen's Drive becomes a dual-lane highway, skirting the runway and the low-income community of Flankers. After a mile or so, there's a left-hand fork following the perimeter of the airport to the fishing community of **WHITEHOUSE**, a largely quiet residential zone – bar a *Sandals* all-inclusive and airport noise – seldom visited by tourists and refreshingly hassle-free, with a great local seafood restaurant (see p.187).

With endless reefs and postcard-perfect beaches, the coast east from here has long been the preserve of expensive hotels, and a number of brand new mammoth all-inclusives and condos together with glitzy shopping malls, ensure the upmarket feel lingers. The plush residential belt of **IRONSHORE** is home to palatial private residences and three of the island's best **golf courses**: the eighteen-hole Superclubs Ironshore Golf and Country Club (℡953 3681), the Half Moon

▲ White Witch golf course

The White Witch of Rose Hall

Jamaica's most famous horror story centres on **Annie Palmer**, the "White Witch of Rose Hall". A beautiful young woman, Annie Mary Patterson's early years are cloaked in mystery. Born in either England or Ireland, she was the only child of small-time property owners John and Juliana Patterson, who brought her to live in Haiti, where she learned the Voodoo art. The date of her arrival in Jamaica is unknown, but it's said that she came to Kingston as a fresh-faced seventeen-year-old in search of a husband. Being young and white, she was granted access to high society and her brooding good looks soon captured the attention of John Palmer, incumbent of Rose Hall and grand-nephew of its architect, also John Palmer. They married in March 1820, but the union was not a happy one; seven years on and bored with her insipid husband, Annie took a young slave lover. Palmer found out and whipped her severely; Annie took her revenge by poisoning his wine and smothering the dying man with a pillow. She went on to murder two more husbands, and seduce and murder a succession of white book-keepers and black slaves. She was a cruel and sadistic mistress even to those slaves she wasn't sleeping with, meting out excessive punishments for misdemeanours.

However, Annie's cruelty proved to be her undoing, and she was **murdered** in her bed in 1831. No one knows for sure whose hands encircled her neck, but some accounts point to an old and powerful balmist whose pretty granddaughter had been in competition with Annie for the attentions of a young English book-keeper until the older woman set an "ol' hige" vampire upon her rival, killing her within a week.

Gripping as it is, there's barely a shred of truth in the story (though it's retold in bodice-ripping style in Herbert DeLisser's novel; see Contexts). Annie Palmer did exist (she's buried in a concrete grave, where the tour concludes), but by all accounts she had no discernible tendencies to sadism or lechery. She may have become confused over the years with Rosa Palmer, the original mistress of Rose Hall, who did have four husbands, but she was said to be unwaveringly virtuous. Nonetheless, most Jamaicans believe in something more sinister, and visiting mediums swear to strange visions and buried effigies in the grounds, while the house retains a vestige of creepiness.

Golf Club (☎953 3105) and the *Ritz Carlton* hotel's White Witch course (☎953 2800). Amongst the large developments you can still find the occasional appealing bar or **restaurant**, however, such as *Scotchies* jerk centre or living-museum-cum-bar *Memorabilia* (see p.188).

Some of the island's best **horseback riding** is found at the Half Moon Equestrian Centre (☎953 2286, ⊛www.horsebackridingjamaica.com; closed Sun), an immaculate facility that's home to many ex-racehorses. Beginners are welcome on the Jungle Jaunt, a forty-minute trek with a short lesson (US$60), but the best option is the Sand Shuttle (1hr 30min; US$80), a ride through the hotel gardens and onto the beach, where you ride out into the waves, swimming your horse back to shore. Dressage, showjumping and polo lessons are also on offer (around US$50), as are pony rides for kids (US$20) and guided **mountain-bike rides** (1hr 30min; US$45). Other on-site soft adventures such as zip line and ATV/quad bike tours are offered by Chukka Caribbean (see p.169).

Romanticized plantation history comes into its own at **ROSE HALL**, six miles east of MoBay and site of the infamous **Rose Hall Great House** (tours daily 9am–6pm; US$20), the inspiration for Jamaica's best-loved piece of folklore. Built between 1770 and 1780 by planter and parish custos (mayor) John Palmer, the dazzling white stone structure, set back from the A1 and surrounded by gardens and a swan-filled pond, is difficult to miss. The mechanical 45-minute tours make much of the embellished legend of Annie Palmer, the "White Witch of Rose Hall" (see box, p.185); starting in the gift shop, you gasp at blurred photos sent in by previous visitors that supposedly show the face of an unknown woman in the mirror or a bat in a chandelier, and gawp at Annie's bedroom, symbolically redecorated in shades of red, and the terrace from which she allegedly pushed a maid to her death. As the house was unoccupied and widely looted during the nineteenth century, almost all of its current contents have been transported from other great houses or from overseas. The silk wallpaper and magnificent mahogany staircase are attractive (if not from the right period), and the fake food laid out on the dining table adds a touch of kitsch.

The grounds are also lovely, though these too have a violent (and authentic) past. On Good Friday in 1963 the district was the site of the "**Coral Gardens Massacre**", a bloody altercation between police and Rastafarians – then commonly viewed as vicious, anti-white, drug-crazed maniacs – whose right of way through the Rose Hall grounds to their vegetable plots was being threatened by property speculators developing the house into the tourist attraction it is today. After months of contention, a policeman sent to arrest the dissidents was attacked, and a petrol station was set on fire. During the ensuing bloodbath eight Rastas died, and an unofficial "war on Rastas" was declared islandwide, with hundreds thrown into jail and their locks forcibly sheared off. Obviously, nothing marks the spot, though local Rastafarians commemorate the killings at Sam Sharpe Square in MoBay each Easter.

If you fancy a splurge on **lunch** after visiting the great house, the White Witch Clubhouse has a beautiful setting amid the greens of the *Ritz Carlton*'s golf course, with lovely views of the coast and an international menu. To get there, turn right (rather than left for the great house), and follow the signs.

Past the great house and a towering condominium development, the road swings past the *Hilton Rose Hall*, whose expansive **golf course** contains a beautiful waterfall seen in the Jamaican James Bond classic *Live and Let Die*. The hotel is also home to the **Sugar Mills Falls**, a water-park complex with cascading waterfalls, a thrill slide, and a "lazy river" for tubing and swimming and several pools. It's great fun for kids and adults alike, and non-guests can buy a day pass that includes all food and drink for US$75 (10am–6pm; children US$40).

Eating

Resort status ensures a fair share of swanky **restaurants** alongside usual Jamaican eateries – though many restaurants within the hotels offer quite bland "international" fare or watered-down Jamaican dishes. Some tourist restaurants offer free pick-ups for dinner guests; look out for flyers. If you're in the mood for a serious splurge, head west of town to *Round Hill* in Hopewell for the Monday-night beachside dinner, a supremely romantic candlelit affair (see p.196); at the other end of the scale, there are a string of eateries to the west of Hopewell churning out seafood for an enthusiastic local crowd. For Sunday **brunch**, the *Wexford* hotel on Gloucester Avenue has an all-inclusive Jamaican feast (8am–1pm; J$1500) served on its terrace.

The best Chinese take-away is the very inexpensive *King Palace,* in the City Centre mall on Fort Street near the Strip. Also downtown, Centre Point Mall on Harbour Street has a branch of Jamaican supreme **fast-food** spot *Island Grill*. For patties, branches of renowned *Tastee's* are at each end of Barnett Street, while *Juici Beef* is on St James St. On the Strip, *L'Oven Best* on Doctor's Cave Beach is good for snacks, but you have to pay to come on to the beach even if you just want to eat. *Calypso Gelato*, opposite the *Casa Blanca* hotel, offers a huge range of gorgeous Italian ice cream, from soursop to pannacotta and hazelnut, plus coffees and sandwiches.

Phone numbers are given only where you might need to reserve a table.

Inexpensive

Adwa 1st Floor, Baywest Shopping Centre, Harbour St and Westgate Shopping Centre. Two branches of this fabulous vegetarian take-away – pick up lunch here before heading on excursions. Serves breakfast (porridge, wholewheat ackee, veg or soya patties), and lunch (salads, veg stew, curried tofu and pulse and vegetable combinations), plus smoothies, juices and power drinks.

Coral Cliff 165 Gloucester Ave. Upstairs at this contrived American-style gaming lounge is the *Rum Jungle bar*, decked out in theme-park style with life-sized pirates swinging from the rafters and a canopy of plastic fauna and flora. You nonetheless can't go wrong with the unlimited quality Jamaican lunch buffet here for US$10, which also has a passable pasta bar.

Evelyn's Kent Ave, Whitehouse. Basic locals' seafood joint right on the water (turn right after *Sandals*), serving all things piscatorial with rice, bammy or, unusually, roti, the last a great accompaniment to the curried conch or Indian dahl. Great cooking and inexpensive prices.

Fishbones Sunset Blvd. Rustic little Jamaican outdoor eatery near the strip, with a reliable and inexpensive range of seafood Jamaican style, plus chicken and curry goat.

MoBay Proper Fort St ⓦwww .mobayproper.com. Brilliant, inexpensive little place on the approach to the Strip, offering a welcome remedy to the all-encompassing Americana hereabouts. Jamaican lunches and dinners (red peas soup, stewed chicken, steamed or brown-stewed fish, curried conch), all served up on the verandah or indoors. Popular Friday night fish fry.

Pork Pit Gloucester Ave. The Strip's obligatory jerk spot, and very good it is too, with a shaded dining area and well-seasoned, inexpensive, chicken, pork, shrimp, ribs and fish grilled over a proper pimento-wood fire. There's yam, festival and hard-dough to help soak up the pepper, and a tasty, hearty pumpkin or chicken soup, too.

Scotchies Ironshore, near the *Holiday Inn Hotel*. A bit out of the way, but worth the effort if you're after some excellent jerk cooking; pork, chicken, fish and seafood are served with festival, breadfruit, yam or sweet potato. You eat at palm-thatch-shaded tables set back from the road.

Tashe's Café St James Place, Gloucester Ave. Popular kiosk café situated in the courtyard of a small plaza between Doctor's Cave and Cornwall beaches. No-nonsense local and American breakfasts, burgers and home-made cakes, alongside fresh juice and passable coffee.

Moderate and expensive

The Brewery Miranda Ridge, Gloucester Ave. Late-opening spot above the Strip, offering an extremely varied menu with daily specials, a big burger selection, lots of seafood, salads and some Mexican fare. Good value, and pretty views from the semi-open-air dining area.

Chilitos Shops 1&2, Doctor's Cave Beach Hotel. New spot with an informal vibe and a small but inviting menu of "Jamexican" food; the jerk chicken tacos are a clear winner, the beef less so. Small a/c lounge bar with happy hour 5–7pm.

Day-O Plantation Fairfield ⓣ952 1825. A great romantic spot, this elegant hillside restaurant in a plant-wreathed colonial building feels a world away from the flimsy glitz of the Strip. The Jamaican and international food is wonderful; smoked marlin, jerk snapper and conch creole, plus grilled fillet steak with Béarnaise sauce, pork with sherry and egg noodles and a spicy fruit and veg "Curry Caribe". Great service.

Dragon Court Fairview Shopping Centre, Alice Eldermire Drive ⓣ979 8822. Newish Chinese place whose plush a/c dining room has the dubious honour of overlooking the sewage ponds. The food is far better than the view, though, with a huge menu including nice veggie choices. Take-away and delivery available.

Groovy Grouper Doctor's Cave Beach, ⓦwww.groovygrouper.com. On a deck overlooking the sand, it's best at night, when bay lights twinkle in the greenery. Menu features conch fritters, salads and burgers as well as escovitched or steamed fish, jerk shrimp pasta and steaks. Best value is the all-you-can-eat Friday night seafood buffet (US$25).

Havana Café 47 Gloucester Ave. Tiny rooftop restaurant with good, mid-priced Latin and International cooking (though expect a wait), great *mojitos* (when there's fresh mint available) and bags of atmosphere – especially when there's a Salsa DJ or band in.

Houseboat Grill Freeport Rd ℡ 979 8845. Fantastic, unique setting in a converted houseboat moored on Bogue Lagoon. You board by way of a rope-pulled launch, and a window in the floor allows perusal of the marine life gliding underneath. The sophisticated menu offers imaginative takes on local seafood (including choose-your-own lobster) and meat and vegetarian choices. You might find sautéed mahi mahi with shrimp bisque and truffled chickpea puree, or seared duck breast with a merlot and mustard demi-glace, beetroot mash and roast veg. Desserts are satisfyingly indulgent, and service is great. Closed Mon.

Marguerites Gloucester Ave ℡ 952 4777. Right on the seafront next to *Margaritaville*, and with tables under the stars or in the open-sided dining room, this is perfect for a romantic dinner, with faultless formal service, upscale atmosphere and a delicious Continental menu specializing in seafood; the crème brûlée is excellent.

Memorabilia 27 Mahoe Bay, Rosehall Main Rd. An unexpected, highly original beach bar and restaurant worth the drive east of town for (just before Coyaba resort). Decked out with all manner of oddments and photos, the friendly bar is well stocked and the menu covers Jamaican and international foods – you'll get some of the best steam fish in MoBay here – while the music mix is as eclectic as the furniture.

The Native 29 Gloucester Ave ℡ 979 2769. The best place on the Strip for a sit-down Jamaican breakfast or full meal, taken on the shady, plant-filled verandah – but not cheap, so take advantage of reduced-rate buffets and lunch specials. The "Boonoonoonoo's Platter" of ackee, curry goat, jerk chicken and escovitched fish, rice and peas and plantain is a good introduction to local cooking.

The Pelican Gloucester Ave ℡ 952 3171. This long-established, mid-priced restaurant is a MoBay institution, and its leatherette booths are perfect for a reliable Jamaican meal. Highlights include cornmeal porridge or Ameri-Jamaican breakfasts, lunch specials (from fricassee chicken to cow foot) and desserts (rum pudding and coconut- or banana-cream pie).

Pier One Howard Cooke Blvd. With tables laid out along a breezy pier and great views down the coastline, this is a pleasant, mid-priced spot for lunch or dinner, with salads and fish or steak sandwiches alongside usual Jamaican dishes as well as scallops in Red Stripe or seafood pasta. At the Sunday Seafood Market you can choose your fish by the pound and have it cooked any-style.

Twisted Kilt Gloucester Ave ℡ 952 2660. Irish-American pub with a wonderful verandah over the beach next to the *Casa Blanca* hotel. The mid-priced food is very good – with quality chunky burgers and shepherds pie, though the highlight is the succulent jerk pork served on mash potato. Fresh juices are a welcome and surprising addition with the sports screens overhead.

Drinking, nightlife and entertainment

Montego Bay has many lively **nightspots**, but aside from the buzz around *Margaritaville* and *Coral Cliff*, you have to search them out. *Groovy Grouper* at Doctor's Cave is great for a drink by the sea after dark, and the *Houseboat Grill* (see above) is superb for cocktails and bar snacks; Friday nights here attract the expat crowd. Also on the more sedate side, *Coyaba* hotel in Ironshore has jazz and finger foods during its Friday half-price cocktail hour (from 6.30pm). Next door, *Memorabilia* (see above) has a wonderful bar by a private section of beach.

At the other end of the scale, the *Dead End Bar*, at the end of Kent Avenue beyond the Strip, is often busy. MoBay's **club** scene centres around *Margaritaville* and *Pier One*; both get going at 11pm (around US$15 unless an all-inclusive night). Also on the Strip, *Havana Café* (see p.187) offers free salsa classes Tues, Thurs and Fri, with karaoke Sat, and a DJ party later on. If you're well up on dancehall culture, you might want to take in **Exact Mondays**, a street dance in the flavour of Kingston's Passa Passa (see p.78), in downtown MoBay, on the balcony across from the Hype Stripe barber shop on Barnett Street, with music from Pure Playazz.

Live music is surprisingly thin on the ground in MoBay, with the *Groovy Grouper* putting on the odd show and the sands of Doctor's Cave throwing an occasional full-moon party, while *Coral Cliff* features occasional big-names reggae old-timers. The large music events of the year are August's Reggae Sumfest (see box, p.183) and the Air Jamaica Jazz and Blues in January (see Basics, p.32); smaller one-off events are advertised on Irie FM or on posters. Sound-system jams are a better prospect, sporadically at *Aquasol* or venues in Ironshore.

There are two **cinemas** in town: the Palace Multiplex off Alice Eldemire Drive (T971 5550) and Diamond Cinema in Ironshore (T953 9540). **Roots plays** are staged at the Montego Bay Civic Centre and occasionally at the Chatwick Gardens Centre, 10 Queen's Drive (T9522147). For more serious theatre, catch one of the excellent Montego Bay Little Theatre Movement productions at Fairfield Theatre (T952 0182).

Bars and clubs

Aquasol Walter Fletcher Beach. Right by the sea, the open-air bar is a lovely spot for a drink (try the excellent margaritas) or Jamaican food staples, and the beach itself is also a regular venue for stageshows and sound-system jams. The upstairs disco, *Dreamz*, is now a go-go dancing joint only.

Black Pearl Blue Diamond Shopping Centre, Ironshore. The latest club to join the MoBay nightlife roster promises the glitziest and trendiest nights out in town, with a multi-level dancefloor, fish tanks, VIP section, three bars and a young, upscale ambience.

Bluebeat Jazz and Blues Bar Gloucester Ave. Upmarket, icily a/c (and non-smoking) little bar with high-tech jazz-themed decor, offering expensive cocktails and great live jazz or blues nightly (9pm–1am).

The Brewery Miranda Ridge, Gloucester Ave. Friendly bar with a dancefloor, popular with an upmarket and young-ish crowd who spill out onto the attractive decked bar. Nights change regularly, but there's usually karaoke Thurs, and a DJ or live music Fri and Sat.

Coral Cliff 165 Gloucester Ave Wwww.coralcliff jamaica.com. Free (and often very good) live music from the in-house band most nights, including "Retro Wednesdays" courtesy of Merritone Music. Open 24hr, it's a good bet even in the wee hours.

Havana Club Gloucester Ave. New upscale cigar and jazz bar just north of Doctors Cave Beach Hotel, favoured by guests of the smartest hotels and local top brass.

Hi-Lites Café 19 Queen's Drive. Very sleepy bar, but a great escape from the Strip and worth visiting for the wonderful view across the bay.

Jamaican Bobsled Café 69 Gloucester Ave. At the heart of the strip, this bar is bedecked with memorabilia from Jamaica's Olympic bobsled team of *Cool Runnings* fame. You can have your picture taken in the team's sled,

while there are great drinks, pizza, and a busy, friendly atmosphere.

Margaritaville Gloucester Ave, Wwww .margaritavillecaribbean.com. Hugely popular bar-cum-restaurant-cum-club – if you're looking for guaranteed action, this is it, and if you don't mind gigolos galore and sunburnt tourists, it's great fun. Big sports screen TVs, 52 different flavours of margarita and 32-ounce "bongs of beer" keep the atmosphere buzzing, and nights run to various themes, always with a packed dancefloor. Thurs is usually Latin night with dance classes, and things heat up at the weekends; Sat is busiest with big-name DJs. Cover is US$12 Wed–Sat, US$6 rest of the week. Good food if you fancy something un-Jamaican.

MoBay Proper Fort St Wwww.mobay proper.com. The best place on the strip to get a flavour of downtime Jamaican style, drawing a loyal crowd for verandah drinks or a round of pool; board games are kept behind the bar. Pool and skittles tournament Tues, jam on Wed, karaoke Thurs, old hits Fri and jazz Sun.

Pier One Howard Cooke Blvd Wwww .pieronejamaica.com. Popular MoBay old-timer, with a roster of club nights and sports events shown on big-screen TVs. The waterside setting is great for a drink anytime, but best is the packed Friday night Pier Pressure, with dancehall, hip-hop, R&B and soca on the decks and a mostly local crowd demonstrating all the latest dances.

Randles Hart St. Brilliant oldies club (ska, R&B, soul) in a large open-air building downtown. Popular with an eclectic mix of Jamaicans, and though you won't feel unwelcome, this is strictly non-tourist territory so go with someone local. Thurs & Sun only. Small cover charge.

Richmond Hill Inn Union St. A lovely spot for a sunset drink by the pool. The setting – on its very own hill at the top of Union St – is spectacular and intensely romantic; the view covers the whole bay.

Shopping

Countless malls are given over to **in-bond shopping for the cruise ship crowd**, with identical jewellery, perfume and leather goods; City Centre Mall on Fort Street is the least ostentatious, and the Half Moon Shopping Village in Ironshore, easily the most. At the latter check out Caribbean designer store Staysies (ⓦ www.staysies.com) for attractive and colourful clothing and jewellery from across the region. The Montego Bay Shopping Centre – usually referred to as the LOJ (Life of Jamaica) Mall – on Howard Cooke Boulevard is better for general purchases, with clothes shops and a branch of Fontana Pharmacy, great for gimmicky souvenirs. For miscellaneous odds and ends, including red, gold and green string vests and car-mirror tassels, browse the untouristy stores downtown, on St James and Barnett streets. The former also holds a branch of Sangster's **bookstore** and Dominion Stationery, with an excellent selection of 1970s postcards.

The biggest and best craft market is the Harbour Street complex (daily 7am–7pm) packed with straw- and wicker-work, belts, clothes, jewellery, T-shirts and woodcarvings, and with vendors who expect a bit of bartering. The Fort and Fantasy craft markets along the Strip (daily 8am–7pm) are worth a look but tend to be a little more expensive, with more insistent sales pitches. The higher-end Gallery of West Indian Art at 11 Fairfield Rd, Catherine Hall (ⓣ 952 4547, ⓦ www.gallery ofwestindianart.com), has a huge range of **artworks** from the wider Caribbean and is renowned for hand-carved and painted wooden animals. On the Strip, seek out shops Heaven 67 by Doctor's Cave, which has a superior selection of jewellery, books, artworks and clothing, and Stoosh, at Miranda Ridge, with cool shirts (look for the 2000lbs range), swimwear and Starfish candles and oils.

Downtown **record stores** offer the Jamaican speciality of custom-made reggae CDs (around US$4), as well as albums on CD and vinyl. Worth a visit, for the enthusiasm of owner Ainsworth Palmer coupled with his large collection, is Federal Records, 14 Strand St, while El Paso at 3 South Lane by Sam Sharpe Square is also good. For quality sound-system session CDs and bootleg recordings of stageshows (US$5) check Clapper's Mobile Music Box in the Church Lane car park; ask for a test play before you buy.

Listings

Airlines Air Jamaica ⓣ 1-888/359 2475 or 952 4300; Airlink ⓣ 1-888/247 5465 or 940 6660; American Airlines ⓣ 1-800/744 0006; Continental ⓣ 1-800/231 0856 or 952 5530. All are based at the airport.

Banks and exchange FX Trader (Mon–Sat 9am–5pm) is best for exchange, above the *Pelican* restaurant on the Strip – it also handles Western Union transfers. Cambio King, at the Casa Montego mini-mall opposite Doctor's Cave is also good. Banks with ATMs congregate at Sam Sharpe Square; there are also ATMs on Gloucester Ave near Cornwall and Doctors Cave beaches (the latter doles out US dollars) and at the airport.

Car and bike rental Car rental companies have offices at the airport or on Queen's Drive/Sunset Boulevard. International companies: Bargain ⓣ 952 0762; Budget ⓣ 952 3838; and Hertz ⓣ 979 0438. Local operators are usually cheaper; most reliable are: Alex's ⓣ 940 6260, ⓦ www .alexrental.com; Danjor, 34 Queen's Drive ⓣ 940 2679, ⓦ www.danjorcars.com; Island, Sangster Airport ⓣ 952 5771, ⓦ www.islandcar rentals.com; Prospective, 28 Union St ⓣ 952 011, ⓦ www.prospectivecarrentals.com.

Consulates Only the Canadian Consulate (ⓣ 952 6198) and US Consulate (ⓣ 952 0160) have offices in Montego Bay; both are on Gloucester Ave. UK citizens should call the British Honorary Consul (ⓣ 953 3301 or mobile 999 9693). Embassies and other consulates are all based in Kingston (see p.81).

Doctors Most hotels have a doctor or nurse on duty or on call. A recommended practitioner is Dr Anthony Vendryes, whose surgery is at the *Royal Court* hotel on Sewell Ave (☎979 3333).
Hospitals Cornwall Regional Hospital, Mount Salem (☎952 5100 or 6683), is the best public hospital outside Kingston. The best private institutions are Doctor's Hospital in Fairfield (☎952 1616) and the MoBay Hope Medical Clinic at Half Moon Shopping Village, Rose Hall (☎953 3649 or 9310). In an emergency dial ☎119 for an ambulance.
Immigration Immigration Office, Floor 3, Overton Plaza, Union St ☎952 5381; Mon–Thurs 8.30am–4pm, Fri 8.30am–4pm. For visa extensions, go early to avoid the queues.
Internet On the Strip, the Cyber Café at Doctor's Cave Beach offers expensive access at US$2 for 15min). Access is far cheaper away from Gloucester Ave; try Computers for Less on the 1st floor of Baywest Mall (Mon–Sat 9am–6pm); or Cellular King at 9B Westgate Plaza (Mon–Sat 9am–6pm).
Laundry Most hotels have a laundry service, but there are some fairly good coin-operated laundries. Try Fabricare at 4 Corner Lane (☎952 6987) and Westgate Plaza (☎940 0492).

Pharmacies There are plenty of pharmacies downtown. Try Best Care, 10 St James St (Mon–Sat 9am–10pm, Sun 9am–9pm); Clinicare on Sam Sharpe Square (Mon–Sat 9am–8pm, Sun 10am–6pm); Fontana, Montego Bay (LOJ) Shopping Centre (Mon–Sat 8am–7pm). There are no pharmacies on the Strip; the Sunset Supermarket sells basic toiletries.
Police Montego Bay has four police stations. Visitors are usually told to take crime reports directly to the Tourism Liaison Unit at Summit station on Sunset Blvd (☎952 1540). Other stations are located in Catherine Hall (☎952 4997) and downtown at 14 Barnett St (☎952 1557). If your car is impounded you should go to the pound on Creek St; otherwise, contact the police station at 27 Church St (☎952 5310). In an emergency, dial ☎119; the Woman Inc rape crisis line is ☎952 9533.
Post offices The two main post offices are on the corner of Fort St opposite the library, and at 120 Barnett St. There is a postal agency (Whitesands PO) on Gloucester Ave next to Doctor's Cave Beach; you can pick up post-restante mail at all three, but Whitesands is the least frenetic.

Around Montego Bay

Away from the shops and the beaches, there's plenty to see around Montego Bay. Some, such as the **Greenwood Great House**, have a quiet charm and seductive natural beauty, and the wealth of Georgian architecture at sleepy **Falmouth** is deliciously un-touristy; worth a few hours if not an overnight stay. As well as the determinedly tourist-friendly managed attractions like water parks, zip lines and **raft trips** down the Great River from Lethe, the MoBay surrounds offer many less contrived sights, from the sweeping lawns and river swimming at Nature Village Farm to the **St James interior**, where the rolling hinterland pastures are spectacular in places. St James was prime plantation territory under the British and a few of the old estates have kept their land and opened it up to the public. Polished boiling pots and repointed stone mills illustrate the mechanics of the sugar industry, and lavishly restored great house interiors froth over the planters' lifestyles. However, there's little to commemorate one of the most significant phases in Jamaican history: the Christmas Rebellion of 1831, which began in St James and set the wheels in motion for the abolition of slavery.

Inland, **Cockpit Country** is without doubt the most bizarre landscape in Jamaica, an uncanny series of improbable lumps and bumps covering roughly five hundred square miles of Trelawny and St James parishes, south of Montego Bay. One of the most intriguing parts of the island, a visit here is worthwhile not only for its fantastic scenery but also its intriguing history.

East along the coast

East of Rose Hall (see p.184), coastal development becomes more sporadic, and bar the enormous new *Iberostar* complex, resorts are thinner on the ground. Beyond here, the fast coast road passes scrubby mangrove swamps and opens up with a magnificent sea view at diminutive **GREENWOOD**. Perched on a hill overlooking the sea, the classy stonework of ⚑ **Greenwood Great House** (☎ 953 1077; daily 9am–6pm; US$15) is deservedly declared a National Heritage site by the JNHT. Surrounded by luscious gardens, it has none of the flashy allure of Rose Hall, but is of far more interest, retaining most of its original contents as well as a wonderfully listless, frozen-in-time eighteenth-century ambience. Built in 1790 by relatives of the Barrett family of Wimpole Street fame (see p.104), the house contains the owners' original library and an eclectic collection of ancient musical instruments, a court jester's chair and custom-made Wedgwood china. The Barretts seventy-foot verandah commands a panorama of the sea unbroken by land, and you really can see the curvature of the earth. The tour, ending at a bar in the original kitchen, is more enjoyable than the breakneck run around Rose Hall. Though the Barretts owned 84,000 acres hereabouts, worked by some 2000 Africans, there's little information on the less savoury realities of the plantation era other than a cursory reference to a man trap used to catch runaways and a leg iron displayed like an ornament.

▲ Greenwood Great House

For **eating and drinking**, head for the *Far Out Fish Hut* on the main road at the eastern edge of Greenwood, a locals' fish spot with a laid-back seaside setting and a thatch-roofed bar. Pick your fish from the catch of the day and have it roasted in foil or escovitched, and eat it with bammy and a cold beer. There's more Jamaican food on offer at *Turtles Inn*, half a mile further down the road and worth a visit for the home-made conch soup alone. Just past here, some enterprising locals have landscaped a pretty little slip of white sand and clear water known as **Citizen's Beach**. It's a lovely, breezy spot for a drink or a snack, particularly on Sundays when local families come down, and it occasionally serves as a venue for sound-system jams, too.

If you want **to stay** in the area, *Dunn's Villa Resort* is well-signposted two miles inland from Rose Hall and Greenwood (☎953 7459, ⓦwww.dunnsvillaresort .com; ❸). A small family-run resort with pool, jacuzzi, restaurant and mountain bikes, rooms are pleasantly decorated; haggle on the price; rates include breakfast. Right on the coast at Greenwood, the *All Seasons Resort* (☎953 1707; ❹) is an intimate grouping of apartments around a driftwood-decorated bar, with smallish air-conditioned rooms and fully equipped kitchenette.

Falmouth and around

Just past Greenwood, the road passes through the parish border of St James and Trelawny. Though it's best known today for both its magnificent yams (sixty percent of Jamaica's yam crop is grown here) and as the home parish of world record sprinter Usain Bolt (see p.71), Trelawny's history is dominated by the plantation era; at the height of the plantocracy there were 88 **sugar estates** here worked by tens of thousands of slaves, and the parish capital, **FALMOUTH** – 23 miles east of MoBay and named for the English birthplace of parish Governor Sir William Trelawny – became the main port of call for sugar ships. Slaves were traded and goods unloaded, while planters built elegant Georgian town houses. In the late eighteenth century, Falmouth boasted 150 houses and a cage where the market now stands (akin to the one still standing in Montego Bay's Sam Sharpe Square – see p.180), used for locking up drunken sailors found on the streets later than the 6pm curfew. Though slavery ended within fifty years of the town being declared parish capital in 1790, Falmouth's natural harbour ensured Trelawny's prosperity, and it thrived where others declined, even after emancipation. However, the advent of the steamship – the first docked at Jamaican shores in 1837 – spelled the first step in the town's declivity. The harbour wasn't deep enough for larger vessels, and by 1890 Falmouth had become something of a ghost town – traders left for Montego Bay or Kingston, and their houses began to slowly rot. In 1896, however, the Albert George Market was built, and Falmouth's status as **market town** still ensures a bustling centre each Wednesday, with fruit and veg, bootleg clothing and brightly coloured fripperies set out along the pavements, in traditional "bend down" style.

At the time of writing, a new **cruise-ship dock** with obligatory shopping mall was under construction at the town's eastern seaboard, with divers contracted to physically move over 150,000 "valuable" corals from a section of reef making way for the shopper-happy hoards. The development has divided locals between those looking to conserve the town's sleepy aspect and those predicting economic upliftment, and it remains to be seen exactly what the impact will be. For now, at least, Falmouth is an easy-going place, boasting a high concentration of **Georgian architecture** – though many buildings are in a terrible state of disrepair. Two-hundred-year-old timbers crumble onto the tarmac, and once majestic properties serve as dilapidated shelters for chickens and stray dogs. Periodic calls for it to be granted "heritage" status are left largely ignored, but a wander through the streets provides an unadorned – and sometimes chilling – glimpse into Jamaica's past.

The Town

Now entirely bypassed by the main highway (turn coast-wards at one of three signposted junctions), Falmouth's centre retains its original grid formation, with main streets fanning out from **Water Square**, named in allusion to the town's status as the first in Jamaica to have piped water. The non-functioning central fountain marks the spot of a stone reservoir that once held fresh water pumped by water wheel from the Martha Brae River. The square has numerous remaining antiquated wooden shop-fronts, combined with cane and coconut vendors and crowds of shoppers. To the side, the **Albert George Market building** holds a largely unmemorable collection (Mon–Sat 9am–5pm; free) of bits and bobs from Falmouth's illustrious past. Buses to Montego Bay and Ocho Rios arrive and depart outside Courts department store.

Some of Falmouth's most impressive constructions – the sagging **Tharp House** a block east, the porticoed **post office** in the middle of Market Street and the old **courthouse**, built overlooking the sea in 1895 – are still in commercial or municipal use, though badly in need of structural attention. Immediately striking as you enter or leave town to the east is the conical roof of the 1810 **Phoenix Foundry** behind the locked gates of **Central Wharf** (close to the new cruise-ship terminal) – where sugar, rum and slaves were traded during Falmouth's heyday – along with several dilapidated warehouses and disintegrating plasterboard set dressings from the filming of *The Wide Sargasso Sea*.

A block west of Water Square, the stately and carefully restored **Baptist Manse** on Market Street is thought to have been inhabited by nonconformist Baptist preacher and anti-slavery campaigner **William Knibb**, whose efforts did much to facilitate emancipation. Two blocks south on the corner of King and George streets is the chunky **William Knibb Memorial Baptist Church**, where, on the momentous date of August 1, 1838 when Africans were given full freedom, Knibb declared "The Monster is Dead" to the large crowd gathered to celebrate and thank the man who had been so instrumental in the process. Slave irons, collars and whips were ceremonially buried under a raised memorial in the grassy churchyard; Knibb is also buried here. Inside the church, a marble plaque "erected by the sons of Africa" depicts their interment of the implements alongside the biblical quote "Ethiopia shall soon stretch out her hands to God". Another plaque marks the demise of Knibb's 12-year-old son, whose "death was occasioned by fever from excess of joy" at the voluntary manumission of slaves by the members of the congregation, who, a year before formal emancipation managed to conclude that "slavery is incompatible with Christianity". The church and grounds are often locked; if you want to get inside you'll need to ask Mr Mac, who runs the Leaf Of Life hardware store on nearby King Street (make a donation to church funds).

Falmouth was built on land originally owned by plantation magnate Edward Barrett, and it was even once known as Barrett Town. The Regency-style **Barrett House**, at 1 Market Street, was built in 1799, with a brick base and weatherboard upper storey supported by wooden columns; the upper half has now completely disintegrated and there are sadly no immediate plans to restore it. The house also has a tenuous literary connection. Having survived his three sons, Barrett left his estate to his daughter on the condition that the man she married took the Barrett name – the house was built by her husband, Charles Moulton Barrett. The couple moved to England and had two sons, one of whom fathered the poet **Elizabeth**

Barrett Browning. The last historical site in town is the 1791 **St Peter's Anglican Church** on Duke Street, surrounded by a sun-bleached cemetery brimming with faded gravestones and grazing goats.

If you're interested in learning more about Georgian Falmouth, contact local resident and US expat Jim Parent, who runs **Falmouth Heritage Renewal Inc**, 9 Market St (☎617 1060) and sometimes organizes walking tours. The organization has restored various buildings and also runs an NGO focusing on training unemployed youth in carpentry and restoration. The Georgian Society of Jamaica has also produced an informative booklet, **Falmouth 1791-1970**; it's available from the society's headquarters (18 Hillcrest Ave, Kingston 6 ☎927 9570). If you want to **stay** right in the town (rather than the beach to the east, see below), the only option is *Falmouth Resort* (29 Newton St ☎954 3391; ❷), a quiet hotel with a bar and basic rooms with air conditioning and TV. There are loads of **restaurants** and **snack shops** around town – try the *A&A Exquisite Restaurant* on Thorpe Street, which is clean and homely and serves tasty Jamaican and vegetarian food.

Out of town

On the eastern side of Falmouth the new cruise-ship port takes up a good chunk of the coastline, while beyond mangrove and white sand lie close to the mouth of the Martha Brae River. The community of **ROCK** (which also has its own exit from the highway), is home to the **Oyster Bay phosphorous lagoon**, enclosed by a casuarina-covered promontory, and which owes its name to the incandescent illuminations of microorganisms. After dark, the water shines bright green when agitated, and you can see the trails of fish. *Glistening Waters*, a marina, good-value seafood restaurant and bar right on the lagoon (☎954 3229), offers night-time boat trips costing US$25 for a thirty-minute jaunt; bring your swimsuit and plunge into the eerie depths. Local man Michael Currie (☎348 1028) operates a similar trip to the lagoon in his glass-bottom boat, with a more relaxed attitude and reggae soundtrack. Ask for Currie a mile or so east at 🍴 *Time 'n' Place* (☎954 4371, 🌐www.mytimenplace.com; ❹; follow signs for *FDR Pebbles* resort from the highway and it's located next door), a lovely laid-back guesthouse/bar/restaurant right on the white-sand beach. The property features Thai-style stilted wooden cabins – some with air conditioning and TV, and others with pull-out futons for families – while jerk chicken, fish, steaks, burgers and delicious smoothies are also served to non-guests.

On the inland side of the highway close to Rock is the 25,000-seat Trelawny All-purpose stadium, constructed to hold the opening match of the Cricket World Cup in 2007 and given a new lease of life as the venue for the high-profile **Jamaica Jazz and Blues Festival** (see p.32) from 2010. Nearby, highway signposts for the **Outameni Experience** alert you to one of Jamaica's newer and more absorbing attractions (Coopers Pen, Trelawny ☎954 4035 or 617 0948, 🌐www.outameni.com; shows daily at 3pm, phone to confirm; US$30); a theatrical journey through the different periods of Jamaican history from Taino Amerindians through slavery, independence, and right up to present-day dancehall culture. A series of reconstructed shops and dwellings within a purpose-built warehouse provide the location for enthusiastic and talented actors to portray cultures and intrigues from each tumultuous era, and with just a touch of poetic licence, you gain a convincing insight.

Heading inland from Falmouth, a lone road threads from Water Square, under the new highway and onward for about three miles to the **Martha Brae River**, Trelawny's longest waterway, notable chiefly for **rafting**. If you want to have a go, follow the battered signs to the put-in point at Rafter's Village (daily 9am–4pm;

1hr 30min; US$50 per two-person raft; ☎ 952 0889, Ⓦ www.jamaicarafting.com), which has a small swimming pool and decent gift shop. The leisurely trip begins with complimentary rum punch and takes you past banks overhung with silk cotton, mango, and towering banyan trees festooned with vines. There are a few craft stalls, floating bars and a constant mosquito offensive – bring repellent.

The Martha Brae road is also the route to 𝕏 **Good Hope Great House** (PO Box 50, Falmouth ☎ 610 5798 or 469 3444, Ⓦ www.goodhopejamaica.com), ten miles or so along a well-signposted yet muddy and rutted road. Built in creamy English stone, the Tharp family home is a Georgian dream house overlooking a 2000-acre working plantation, ringed by the conical hillocks of Cockpit Country which are best seen when the mists roll away at dawn across the surrounding valleys. The house is rented out as an exclusive villa with space to sleep seventeen (contact for rates), a serene nod to colonial excess with antique furnishings and gardens full of flowers and hummingbirds. The estate also rents out an equally gorgeous three-bedroom cottage, right by a river pool fringed by bamboo (US$2900 per week in low season, US$4500 in high, including staff and all meals). If you can't stay here, however, you can explore the grounds on **horseback** on one of many well-kept mounts. You go at your own pace, and it's a very different kettle of fish to the staid resort trail rides – it may well be just you and your guide. A hack (1hr 30min; US$50; book on ☎ 469 3443 or 3444) takes you past original cut-stone buildings, the old sugar-processing room (now used for Good Hope citrus) and on through coconut plantations to a small waterfall where you can take a dip. You'll also pass the workshop of master potter David Pinto, whose beautifully crafted plates and sculptures are reasonably priced (classes and workshops in clay pottery are held here in conjunction with Ⓦ www.andersonranch.org). Mountain biking and river tubing are also on offer.

Beyond Good Hope, the road weaves onwards to Bunkers Hill, a lovely rural community in Cockpit Country (see p.199).

Southwest of MoBay

West of Montego Bay, the smooth coastal highway to Negril hugs the shoreline, offering beautiful views of the turquoise, reef-studded water. Shooting off from the main road just past Reading, the well-signposted B8 inland road plunges straight into the verdant **St James interior**, paralleling the Great River valley with occasional glimpses of lush palms and ferns in the chasm below. Most visitors venture here to tube the river or sail through the treetops with slick Chukka Caribbean (see p.169), or to raft down the river from **Lethe**, although there are more worthy attractions further on, including the eco-oriented **Animal Farm**, the **Rocklands Bird Sanctuary** and the unique German settlement of **Seaford Town**. The B8 is the route from MoBay to Savannah-la-Mar and the south coast, so traffic is pretty heavy.

If you don't have a car and are heading somewhere near the B8, you can take a Sav-la-Mar bus and get off as near to your destination as possible, completing the journey on foot. **Transport** can be a problem in the rural areas beyond, so your best bet is to join an organized tour or hire a private driver (see p.169).

Hopewell

The first sizeable town west of Montego Bay, the straggling residential community of **HOPEWELL** is famous mainly for its one **hotel**, *Round Hill* (PO Box 64, ☎ 956 7050, Ⓦ www.roundhilljamaica.com; ❾), draped across an entire hillside just east of town and one of the classiest in Jamaica. Designed in part by Ralph Lauren, with an elegant 36-room hotel building and 29 eclectically furnished villas, the 98-acre property exudes taste and opulence. JFK and Jackie, Audrey Hepburn, Clark Gable and Queen Elizabeth II gave the hotel a reputation for glamour that today attracts an autograph book of famous names. *Round Hill* has unfortunately fazed out external use of its facilities without paying for annual beach membership – but for those on the island for some time, the pool, tennis courts, gym, restaurant, spa and watersports are an attractive option. On Mondays the hotel hosts a wonderful candlelit beach party open to non-residents, with tables and chairs shifted onto the sand, barbecued food and live music (US$70/head).

Aside from Round Hill the **coastline** is not ideal for swimming, but there are occasional sandy spots such as **Steamer Beach**, past the murky fishermen's beach, marked by the rusting iron shell of a wrecked boat, which gets packed in the early evening and on weekends when kids descend, dominoes slap down on verandah tables, and sound systems string up. A good stop for a **seafood meal** is directly in front of the fishing beach west of town, where a couple of simple places offer conch soup and steamed or fried fish. Local's **eatery** *Love Bird* on Bamboo Hill is also a good option for ackee and saltfish, chicken and curry goat. Before moving on, visit the small **gallery** of local potter Sylvester Stephens past the Shell petrol station on your left as you drive west. His garden has an interesting if bizarre collection of giant pots and clay figures nailed to wooden posts.

Inland to Seaford Town and beyond

A few miles before Hopewell, by the traffic lights at **Reading**, the B8 veers away from the coast into the St James interior with a tortuous ascent up **Long Hill**. Toward the top, there's a well-signposted left-hand turn toward **LETHE**, a pretty village set amid cool and vividly green hills, with a graceful stone bridge straddling the Great River, built by slaves in 1820. **Lethe Estate** (☎ 956 4920) offers **rafting** here; the 45-minute trip (US$50 for two people, US$80 including transfers from MoBay) takes you past banks dripping with vines. Due to heavy rainfall the water often takes on a muddy aspect, but it's still safe for swimming. There are a few turbulent shallow spots where the bamboo rafts scrape the bottom, but the raftmen are highly experienced.

On the road up to Lethe you'll notice signs for the turn-off to 𐅮**Nature Village Farm** (Mon–Fri 10am–6pm, Sat & Sun 11am–7pm; free; ☎ 912 0172, ⓦ www .naturevillagefarms.com), several miles along a potholed road at the appropriately named Eden. A marvellous place to get away from it all, this scenic spot on the Great River has sweeping manicured lawns, bamboo groves and a restaurant on a deck overlooking the water; there's also a go-kart track, net/basketball and volleyball courts and soccer pitches, and a sauna and gym. Cooked-to-order Jamaican food (curried shrimp, sandwiches, salads, omelettes) is excellent and inexpensive. Swim in the river or kick back with a game of pool.

Just two miles beyond Lethe at Copse, the road curves; look out for a signposted dirt road to the left which leads down to **Animal Farm** (Mon–Fri tours by arrangement, Sat & Sun 10am–5pm; J$1000; ☎ 815 4104, ⓦ www.animalfarm jamaica.com), with some gorgeous vistas over Cockpit Country along the way. A delightful, environmentally conscious smallholding run on solar energy and biogas from pig dung, it makes a worthwhile stop, especially if you're travelling with children. There's an array of exotic birds, cages containing mongooses and snakes, plus a petting zoo and herb garden, all of which explained by knowledgeable guides. Children's donkey rides are available, and a path leads down for swimming in the Great River.

After the Lethe turn-off, residential **ANCHOVY** is notable for the fabulous **Rocklands Bird Sanctuary and Feeding Station** (daily 2–5pm; US$10; ℡ 952 2009) indicated by a battered sign along a potholed turn-off just before the town. The flowered home of the late Lisa Salmon, a celebrated ornithologist, hummingbirds here are confident enough to drink sugar water while perched on your outstretched finger. More than a hundred varieties of bird have been sighted, including orange quits, vervain and the streamer-tailed doctor – Jamaica's national bird – but it's the iridescent colouring and thrumming wings of the hummingbirds that make the prettiest visitors; feeding peaks at around 4pm. A nature walk is included in the entry fee, but serious ornithologists should call ahead for specific hikes with knowledgeable Fritz, who can take you on trails beyond the property (US$20). If you want to **stay** at Rocklands, you can rent a three-bedroom cottage (➒).

The B8 rises to 2000ft and passes through the citrus groves of **MONTPELIER**, before the road forks; a right turn takes you over the interior mountains on an incredibly pretty route to Shettlewood and Sav-la-Mar, while a left fork passes through marvellous countryside to **SEAFORD TOWN**. At first glance, this is just another rural community, but you'll soon notice that a lot of the older residents are white. In 1834, the British administration, fearing that emancipation would result in widespread chaos and an exodus from the plantations, began a pre-emptive programme of European settlement. To establish a "civilizing" white presence throughout Jamaica, and, more importantly, snap up the best land before the slaves could (thus keeping Africans at work on the lowland plantations), it drafted in more than a thousand Germans, promising them prosperity after a set period of indentured toil. Between 1834 and 1836, 251 Germans settled in Seaford Town, a 500-acre plot of land donated by Lord Seaford of Montpelier. Other immigrants scattered throughout the interior and blended in; Seaford Town remains the only Jamaican community to be deliberately established.

The new arrivals, many unused to farm labour, found life in rural Jamaica difficult, and when first year rations ran out, became as impoverished as their black neighbours. Hardship and tropical diseases depleted their numbers, and many survivors emigrated to the US. Enough remained, however, for their legacy to be obvious. Despite intermixing, a tradition of intermarriage has ensured that quite a few of the town's residents still have blonde hair, blue eyes and (almost) white skin. The diminutive **Seaford Town Historical Museum** (daily 9am–5pm; US$2), on a grassy knoll below the Catholic Church, tells the story of Seaford's German heritage, with photographs of the original settlers and a list of their names and occupations (one man was a comedian). It's usually locked; head up to the HEART/NTA school and ask for Mrs Shakes. Beyond the museum, little German culture has been retained; traces are seen in older houses' pointy roofs and gingerbread fretwork – fast being eclipsed by incredibly garish new-builds – but German speakers are restricted to the very old, and residents eat rice and peas rather than sauerkraut.

If you want to **stay** here, the HEART/NTA training school above the museum operates a guesthouse (℡ 995 2067; ➋) in a lovely old wooden building, staffed by students; breakfast is included. Otherwise, pillar of the community Jeanette Lynch offers B&B in her modern home at nearby Bridgewater (℡ 640 6134; ➋, including breakfast), above a verdant valley.

East of Seaford Town, pretty villages like **ST LEONARDS** and tiny **MARCHMONT** – look out for the local bush doctor's home, painted red, gold and green – are accompanied by citrus and pineapple plantations, occupying the last stretches of accessible land before the Cockpit hillocks make large-scale farming commercially impossible. **CATADUPA** was once the main tourist stop of the train line from Montego Bay to Kingston; today, goats pick at the sleepers near the peeling paint of the gingerbread station house. Beyond, **MOCHO** has the disparaging honour of informing the colloquial insult of Mocho residents being the ultimate country bumpkins; the *Dictionary of Jamaican English* calls Mocho "a place of symbolic remoteness – a rough, uncivilized place".

Cockpit Country

Thousands of years of rainwater flowing over porous limestone created **COCKPIT COUNTRY** (Ⓦ www.cockpitcounty.com), a rugged **karst topography** of impenetrable conical hillocks dissolved on each side by a drainage system of sinkholes and caves. The area is peppered with bizarre place names throughout: Me No Sen You No Come, Wait-a-Bit (where the police station sign is subject to many a photographer's lens), Quick Step and Rest and Be Thankful District. It's also known as the **"District of Look Behind"**, in

Hiking and caving in the Cockpits

Despite popular disbelief, **hiking trails** do exist in Cockpit Country. Windsor, Albert Town and Flagstaff are the most accessible starting points, where you should hire a local guide – essential not only to stop you getting lost but also in case of accident. The main ten-mile trail starts at **Windsor** and runs straight through the middle to **Troy** on the southern outskirts, though it gets very overgrown towards the middle. The first few miles are relatively easy, but in the heat of the day it's an arduous eight-to-ten hour trek; you're in the midst of foliage most of the time with few open vistas, and you'll certainly feel a sense of achievement at the end. Alternatively, the first couple of hours from Windsor give you a pretty good idea, and if you set out from Troy, the trail is mostly downhill and a lot easier – the best plan is to base yourself at Windsor, hire a guide and get yourselves to Troy early enough to make the hike back before nightfall.

Well-organized **guided tours** point out rare plants and birds, such as Sun Venture in Kingston (☎960 6685, Ⓦ www.sunventuretours.com), though more community-based trips are offered by brilliant **Cockpit Country Adventure Tours** (☎610 0818 or 869 3429, Ⓦ www.stea.net), a part of South Trelawny Environmental Agency (STEA) in Albert Town. Its trips are led by local guides whose commitment to sustainable community tourism is admirable, organizing nature walks, trips to wet caves such as Rock Spring, campfire picnics, and walks along Barbecue Bottom Road in search of medicinal plants. A great option is a trip to gorgeous village **Bunker's Hill**, from where you take a walk to Dromilly Cave, and then to a picnic spot by the Clear River, with a deep pool and lunch of anything from pepperpot or *janga* (freshwater crayfish) soup, to rundown, roast yam and sweet potato. Most walks are fairly easy-going, but for longer treks you'll need a stout pair of shoes or boots, a waterproof, something warm for the evening, a torch and water bottle. Don't forget mosquito repellent. Allow double your usual walking time for chopping foliage.

Cavers find Cockpit Country irresistible, despite a lack of infrastructure. Around 250 caves network the area, but only Windsor is easily accessible. Cockpit Country Adventure Tours run trips into cathedral-sized Quashie River Sink; it's a tough scramble down steep slopes – not for the unfit. Other explorations are led by **Jamaican Caves Organisation** (Ⓦ www.jamaicancaves.org). Caving in Jamaica (Ⓦ users.skynet.be/sky 33676/index1.html) is another good source of information. Alan Fincham's essential book *Jamaica Underground* lists all the island's caves; you can visit his website at Ⓦ www.fincham.co.uk.

reference to the justifiable paranoia of English soldiers who made hot, comfort-less and usually ill-fated missions here tracking **Maroons**, whose superior local knowledge and guerrilla strategy brought most sorties to a bloody end. To this day, the Cockpits are thought by superstitious Jamaicans to be the stamping ground for spirits and duppies. In fact, the Maroons here have been established on the tourist trail for much longer than the more secretive Windward Maroons of the east (see p.128).

Cockpit Country is largely uninhabited. Feral pig hunters make regular forays into the interior, but otherwise locals congregate at villages like **Windsor**, **Albert Town** and **Accompong**, where the economy is based on small-scale farming, coffee, and – cloaked by thick foliage – ganja. The legendary Coptic, one of Jamaica's wealthiest ganja exporters, allegedly grew his stock here in the 1970s and 1980s. Only a fraction of the area is accessible, and you can't get far independently, but the scarcity of tourists and pristine environment make the area unforgettable. It's a sanctuary of untouched beauty, particularly in the early mornings when low-lying mists and a silence broken only by bird calls give it an almost primeval feel.

If you're **driving** from Montego Bay, you can take either of the narrow, potholed roads that lead off the A1 near Westgate Plaza, though a quicker route is to head inland from Falmouth along the B11, which strikes off the new highway at Rock. Most makes of regular car will suffice, but a 4WD is preferable. Cockpit Country is poorly served by **buses**, with limited services from Falmouth to Clarks Town, Sherwood Content – the best place to catch a lift to Windsor – and Albert Town. If all that sounds like hassle, you might want to join an **organized tour** from MoBay (see p.169). Maroon Attraction Tours (☎952 8753; from US$50/person) are the only carriers authorized to visit Accompong, but most tour companies offer trips to Windsor or Flagstaff. Once you're there, local people are extremely amenable with **lifts**, for free or sometimes a small charge.

Maroon Town and Flagstaff

Accessed either from Seaford Town (see p.198) or from Montego Bay via **KENSINGTON** – which boasts huge historical significance as the place where the first fires of the Christmas Rebellion were lit (see p.181) – **Maroon Town** has no contemporary Maroon connections. The road here, however, holds marvel-lous views over gaping valleys; John Crow vultures whirl high on the thermals and though you're only fifteen-odd miles from Montego Bay, the contrast couldn't be more striking. Just south, nearby **FLAGSTAFF** is the location of the new Maroon Village Heritage Tour and Trail (☎326 1868 or 421 3473, Ⓔ michael.grizzle@yahoo.com; US$20/person), which draws on the fasci-nating yet bloody history of the Trelawney Town Maroons (see Accompong, below). Local culture is exhibited at a visitor centre through traditional foods, crafts and dramatic sketches, while there's a choice of three guided trails (1hr 30min) through Cockpit Country's fascinating flora and fauna to the historical remnants of the British occupation of Trelawney Town, with explanations of maroon lifestyles. A bed-and-breakfast programme also operates within host homes across the community (❷–❸), offering an excellent insight into life in the Jamaican interior.

Accompong

Sitting on one of the steep hillocks that make up outer Cockpit Country, **ACCOMPONG**, the last remaining Maroon settlement in western Jamaica, boasts breathtaking views. Named after the brother of Maroon hero Cudjoe, Accompong came into being in 1739, when, as part of the peace treaty that ended the first **Maroon War**, the British granted the Maroon people 15,000 acres of land to create a semi-sovereign community; a missing zero in fact meant that only 1500 acres were made available, a matter of continuing contention. Several such communities, including Trelawney Town in St James (see Flagstaff, above), were also given land, and the Maroons set about a peaceful farming life. In 1795, however, a Trelawney Town Maroon caught stealing a pig in downtown Montego Bay was publicly flogged, ironically by one of the runaway slaves the Maroons had captured and returned to the plantations in accordance with the peace treaty. His kinsmen rebelled once again and the second Maroon War flared up. Though the Trelawney Town Maroons could muster only 300 fighters, the British took no risks and sent in 1500 soldiers and hunting dogs to track them down and wreck their villages. Accompong, the only Maroon village that chose to remain neutral, was allowed to stand.

Accompong is still ruled by a **colonel**, elected every five years – the current incarnate is police inspector Ferron Williams (it's considered proper protocol to call on him when you arrive). Accompong colonels still hold real power; they ensure citizens abide by the town's constitution, and mete out justice for petty crimes. Though most Maroons value their level of autonomy (they pay no taxes or rates), independence has ensured years of state neglect. However, things are looking up: the village boasts a new access road and coverage by mobile phone networks.

Though Accompong is making a determined effort to retain its heritage, there's a sense that it's a losing battle. Though older residents claim direct descendancy from Maroon leaders Nanny and Cudjoe, there are relatively few "real" Maroons left. During the last thirty years two-thirds of the population have left for jobs elsewhere, the secret "Coromantee" language has vanished, resurfacing only in traditional songs and ceremonies, and Maroon culture has become less important to a younger generation more interested in dancehall than goombay drums or Akan chants. The most interesting time to visit is the annual **Accompong Maroon Festival**, held on January 6, with day and night celebrations.

Accompong Maroon Festival

Every January 6, Maroons from all over the island celebrate the anniversary of the 1739 peace treaty. Like everything else in Jamaica, Accompong festivities start late. Under a towering mango tree (known as the **Kindah Tree**), a male pig (according to Maroon tradition) is roasted or boiled and eaten communally – bringing luck to all that partake. The highlight of the day (at around 10am) is when Maroon leaders, adorned by the vines used as camouflage by their ancestors, make their way up from the **Peace Cave**, where they have drummed, danced and chanted since dawn. Goombay drums beat complicated rhythms in anticipation, and a hornblower sends the haunting tones of an **abeng** horn (a cow horn once used as a means of communication) echoing across the hills, signalling the approach of the elders. The drumming reaches a climax and the assembled mass joins in with call-and-response Akan war songs. At around 2pm, the procession moves through the village, paying respects at the homes of former colonels and those too old to participate, finishing at the **Bickle Village** parade ground for speeches and whirling dancing, sprinkled with a traditional dash of white rum. Eventually, drums make way for towers of speakers, and the party continues all night, sometimes with live reggae. Note that there's an entry fee to the village festival, and that timings vary – get there in the morning, and go with the flow.

The village

Accompong is ranged along a precipitous main street; as you drive in you'll most likely be met by one of many **tour guides** (US$20/person), who relate the town's history and introduce you to local characters. The **community centre** contains a small museum with exhibits on the wider history of black Jamaicans as well as Maroons, with items such as calabash gourds, an Ashanti stool and Taino axe, as well as goat-skin goombay drums. Next door is a skills training centre with computers and small library (book donations appreciated). From the museum, you'll be led up the hill to **Bickle Village**, with traditional Maroon thatch-roofed huts, and to the sacred **Kindah Tree**, a giant specimen of the common mango, adjacent to which there's a battered sculpture of a Maroon in battle by Leonard Perkins. Local women give an overview of medicinal uses at the **Herbal Garden**, before you're (on request) led to the **Peace Cave**, where the treaty with the British was signed, in the valley below. It's so small and insignificant that it's hard to imagine history was made here; it's a couple of miles' walk through undulating hinterland that's more of an attraction, however. The village **church** sits atop a hillock overlooking the town, and, on the lower half of the main road, there's a **memorial to Cudjoe**, co-signatory of the 1739 treaty.

There are several ways to get to Accompong, the easiest by **driving** north from Maggoty in St Elizabeth (see p.256) to Vauxhall, and following the signs. It's a fabulous drive with spectacular vistas, though the sheer drops can be a bit disquieting, especially when you meet another vehicle. You can also drive up from Albert Town, skirting the southern edge of Cockpit Country along the B10/B6, or travel via Elderslie and Jointwood from the west. There are a couple of places to **stay**, the best choice being *Mystic Pass Villas* (☎770 3680 or 792 6166; ③), two thatch-roof buildings affording wonderful views over the Cockpits; waking up here is unforgettable. The wood-floored villas are surprisingly modern, with mozzie-netted double beds, immaculate bathrooms, an outdoor hot-water shower with a view, and a fridge; some have kitchens, though ask if meals can be provided.

Windsor

Smack in the middle of Cockpit Country's accessible northern edge, **WINDSOR** is a gorgeous spot, cradled by high cockpits and with impossibly lush foliage permanently threatening to overtake the dirt tracks that serve as roads. It's reached via the tiny village of **Sherwood Content**, remarkable for the unlikely fame granted it by its most celebrated son, Usain Bolt, the 100m and 200m world record holder and Olympic sprint champion – a couple of signs decorate the village in the name of "Lightening Bolt". Unless you're lucky enough to catch Usain at home, Windsor is still the main attraction, with tour buses occasionally pulling in to **Windsor Cave**, at the end of the signposted track. Documented to stretch as far as three miles underground, it's an eerie maze of dripping water and huge, twisting columns of fused stalagmites and stalactites. Its innocuously small mouth exhales a clammy wind, except at dusk, when hundreds of bats – the cave is home to eleven species – sweep majestically out to feed. Experienced cavers can explore on their own, following the slippery path for two and a half hours before emerging deep in the mountains and walking back to Windsor, but others will need a guide. Franklyn Taylor, aka Dango, owner of the red-gold-and-green bar, leads tours for US$20–40.

Franklyn's also your man for **hiking**, as Windsor is the starting point for the only trail that crosses Cockpit Country. If you're of a botanical bent, resident Windsor biologist Susan Koenig leads informative walks for US$30; for the best experience, go at night. Franklyn or Susan can also introduce you to local guides

Flora and fauna of the Cockpit Country

Soil forms only a thin cover over the Cockpit limestone, and as the rock soaks away most of the rainfall, the area's **plant life** has had to adapt in order to survive. As a result, visitors see a proliferation of species that make the most of their rather limited means. Bromeliads collect dew and rainwater in the tanks between their leaves, while the thick, waxy leaves of other plants, such as the tiny orchids that colonize dead wood, take advantage of high humidity. There's a huge range of **bird life** here, including 27 of Jamaica's 28 endemic species; this is one of the few places you'll see – and hear – profusions of shrieking green parrots. The feral **pigs** that root through the undergrowth are descended from those reared by the Maroons, and with hundreds of caves, **bats** are common – 21 varieties are found in the region. The limestone also provides a perfect cover for the **Jamaican boa**, or **yellow snake**. For more on the area's unusual environment, visit ⓦ www .cockpitcountry.com.

who charge around J$2500 per day. There's not much else to Windsor save for a few fields of coffee and swimming spots along the Martha Brae River, which rises by the cave. If you want to **stay**, the stately 🏛 **Windsor Great House** (☏ 997 3832 or 361 4659, ⓦ www.cockpitcountry.com; ❷) opposite Franklyn's shop as you enter Windsor, is the best-equipped option, with nine simple rooms in the main house and an annexe; some have cold-water showers, others share communal facilities (or you can bathe in the cool Martha Brae). Meals are taken on the huge verandah. Bear in mind that Windsor is primarily a research station – rooms are often booked up by visiting biologists and aren't really geared towards the needs of vacationers. Nonetheless, if you've even a passing interest in Cockpit Country, or fancy a little solitude, this is a magical place to spend a night or two. Every Wednesday, the owner, Mike Schwartz and partner Susan Koenig host a "meet the researchers" dinner (four courses US$30 per head plus alcohol), part of an ongoing project to develop and fund research; an excellent way to experience the allure of the Cockpits with bats leaving their roosts under the great house's roof, insects ceasing their attentions and the whistling sounds of the forest taking over.

There are also a couple of other options: administered by Franklyn (contact the Great House for bookings), a modest house owned by Texan Patrick Childres (❶) is basic but with water piped in from a spring and battery-operated electric lights – you cook over a fire or on a stove, and can bathe in a nearby spring; or the *Last Resort* (☏ 931 6070 or 700 7128, ⓦ www.jamaicancaves.org /last-resort-jamaica.htm; ❷), a pretty two-storey house with verandah, flush toilets, gas stove, piped river water and solar electricity – it's also the HQ of the Jamaican Caves Organisation (see p.199). Finally, you can also stay just outside Windsor at *Miss Lilly's* **bar** and **shop** (☏ 788 1022, or contact Windsor Great House; ❷), herself an aunt of sprinter Usain Bolt, in Coxheath, just past Sherwood Content on the road towards the great house. It's also good for a drink or game of dominoes; foodstuffs and provisions are on sale. Rooms are clean, with fan, shared cold-water bathroom, and meals are available; Bolt himself puts his success down to the strength of the Trelawny yams he grew up eating – so the cooking must be good.

Albert Town

If you fancy a slightly more lively base for exploring the Cockpits than Windsor, head to **ALBERT TOWN**, a friendly hillside community (though expect plenty of staring from kids). Though a veritable metropolis compared to Windsor, it has only thirty-odd buildings with a few more residences extending down into the valley. As the base of the excellent **South Trelawny Environmental Agency** (STEA) and its tour company, Cockpit Country Adventure Tours (see p.199), it's also the starting point for several tours, and the office in the main square offers a wealth of useful information.

Some 65,000 farmers produce yams in Trelawny, a fact celebrated in Albert Town's annual **Trelawny Yam Festival**, a hugely popular celebration of the enormous tubers that are the backbone of the parish's economy, held on and around Easter Monday. Thousands of people, locals and tourists, jam the streets to witness culinary displays, best-dressed goat and donkey competitions, yam head-balancing races and ultimately the crowning of the Festival King and Queen. Associated events include a 10km road race, DJ and singing competitions and gospel concerts.

The easiest route into Albert Town is via the B11 from the north coast at Rock, joining the B10 at Clarks Town, a poor excuse for a road but with fantastic views and some of Jamaica's best white-knuckle driving; the **Barbecue Bottom** district is notable for its scarily steep roadside cliffs. STEA also do pick-ups from Falmouth or the airport, and shared taxis run up from Falmouth for around J$250. There's no formal **accommodation** in Albert Town, but a number of local families offer bed-and-breakfast with meals at extra cost (contact STEA for reservations; ❶–❷). Good **eating** and **drinking** spots surround the square.

5

Negril and the west

NEGRIL AND THE WEST

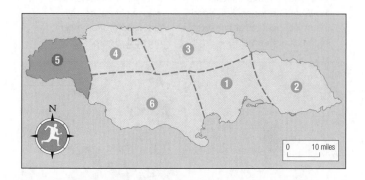

CHAPTER 5 # Highlights

✳ **Snorkelling and scuba diving** Negril's coral reefs are the finest in Jamaica, with a wealth of marine life, year-round warm water and excellent visibility. See p.216

✳ **Royal Palm Reserve** A tranquil and lovely nature reserve with wooden walkways snaking through the groves of majestic royal palm trees and abundant bird life. See p.217

✳ **Sunset-watching** An institution in Negril, where everyone heads to the cliffs of the West End for cocktails and the most spectacular sunsets in Jamaica. See p.219

✳ **Half Moon Bay Beach** No jet skis, no hustlers and no hotels – just a peaceful and pristine stretch of sand. See p.227

✳ **Fishing-village life** Eat some of the finest food in the west at the *Lost Beach* resort on the fishing beach of Broughton, or take in the lively coastal village feel at Bluefields Bay, with low-key accommodation and engaging residents. See p.231 & p.235

✳ **Mayfield Falls** A series of waterfalls and river pools in the hills of Westmoreland whose natural beauty remains, for the present, unspoilt. See p.233

▲ Royal Palm Reserve

Negril and the west

S plit in two by the parishes of Hanover and Westmoreland, sybaritic **Negril** has a front-row sunset seat, the longest continuous stretch of white sand in Jamaica and a geographical remoteness that provides this ultimate chill-out town with a uniquely insouciant ambience. "Discovered" by wealthy hippies in the 1970s, Negril is immensely popular with those who favour fast living and corporeal indulgence – but even though the main menu items are still sun, sea, smoke and sex, there are plenty of natural attractions too, including the Great Morass, the **Royal Palm Reserve** and some marvellous reefs.

Away from this traveller's mecca, **Hanover** is the island's smallest parish, and despite the deceptively steep-looking rise to the **Dolphin Head Mountains**, it's also the flattest, ensuring the island's lowest rainfall and invariably sultry weather. The decaying grandeur of sleepy **Lucea** has been slated for heritage development for years, but aside from a new all-inclusive, there's little tourism development along its stretch of coast, though deserted coves beg for exploration. To the south, the flat coastal plains of **Westmoreland** were once Jamaica's foremost **sugar-growing** area, and cane plantations still surround the main commercial town, parish capital **Savanna-la-Mar**. Inland, the water-bound attractions of **Mayfield Falls** and **Roaring River Park** offer picturesque diversions, while beyond, quiescent coastal villages backed by rugged hills project an air of pastoral neglect, with undeveloped beaches dedicated to fishing rather than aloe massages and sun loungers. Villages like **Bluefields**, neighbour **Belmont** – birthplace of reggae revolutionary **Peter Tosh** – and **Whitehouse**, are lively once you scratch beneath the surface, and they offer a good variety of low-key accommodation, ideal if you want peace, quiet and few other foreign faces.

Negril

Jamaica's shrine to permissive indulgence, **NEGRIL** metamorphosed from deserted fishing beach to full-blown resort town in three decades. By the 1970s, this virgin paradise with seven miles of palms and pristine sand, offering beach camping, ganja smoking and chemically enhanced sunsets, had set the tone for today's free-spirited attitude. Thanks to deliberately risqué resorts like **Hedonism II**,

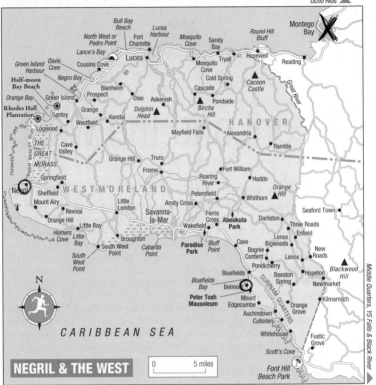

Negril is widely perceived as a place where inhibitions are lost and pleasures of the flesh rule. The traditional menu of ganja and reggae (Negril has a deserved reputation for **nightlife** and **live music**) draws a young crowd, but the north coast resort ethic has muscled in, too. All-inclusives pepper the coast, and even though undeveloped beachfront land is now limited, are still being built. One consolation is that resorts can be no taller than the highest palm tree, which has so far prevented really high-rise development taking hold, while encouraging smaller independent properties.

Concurrent with Negril's dramatic expansion and reputation as "sin city" is an over-quota of **hustlers** – though its occasional edginess fluctuates between tame and irritating depending on current policing and the time of year. Nonetheless Negril shrugs off minor annoyances and it remains supremely chilled-out – conversations start and end with "Irie" or "no problem" – and addicts come back year after year for the best sunsets in Jamaica. Pristine miles of sand with comprehensive watersports, open-air dancing to rated Jamaican musicians, a wide range of eating and drinking joints and gregarious company are all on offer. Many visitors have stayed on permanently, and the consequent blurring of the distinction between tourists and locals makes for a relaxed, natural interaction that's a refreshing change from other resort areas. For an entertaining introduction, read Mark Conklin's novel, *Banana Shout* (see p.307), based on the outlandish real-life events that shaped the beginnings of Negril as a tourist resort.

Jamaican nightlife

Unsurprisingly for the country where reggae was born, music is Jamaica's strongest cultural suit. From the lilting tones of ska and rocksteady to sweetly soulful lovers' rock or the militant posturing of roots reggae and bass-heavy dancehall, music is omnipresent here, and you're never far from a booming speaker. The best way to take in some tunes is to immerse yourself in the nightlife scene, whether a sound-system jam or a state-of-the-art nightclub. And if you prefer your reggae live, regular stageshows feature the cream of the island's artists.

Clubs

The party spirit is deeply imbedded in most Jamaicans, who like to dress up and let loose at weekends (head out in a floppy T-shirt and shorts and you're guaranteed to feel underdressed). There's a lively club scene in all of the larger towns, at its most authentic in Kingston, home to some of the island's best-known and busiest venues, all of which are packed with patrons from Wednesday to Sunday. The nightlife scene is also reasonably good along the north coast: Negril in particular is very buzzy once the sun goes down, with a good club, *Jungle*, and a string of beach bars that host dancing on the sand to DJs and live bands every night (see p.223); while Montego Bay's aptly named *Pier One* (see p.188) boasts one of the best locations on the island, laid out along a pier by the sea. Most indoor clubs are sweaty and smoky in the extreme, though: the music is super-loud and dancers vie with each other as to who can dress the best and move the most. With the notable exception of low-key spots like the marvellous *Roof Club* in Port Antonio (see p.119), Jamaican clubs more than hold their own with US or British venues, with contemporary decor, fancy lighting and crisp sound-systems, and while music policy is equally international, running the gamut from R&B to hip-hop, reggae (in all its forms) is the mainstay. The best nights are usually Fridays and Saturdays, but most clubs also hold less frenetic oldies parties, usually on Sundays or Wednesdays, with DJs spinning vintage reggae, rocksteady and even the odd ska tune. And happily, a night out in Jamaica won't break the bank; cover charges are low, and there are frequent "ladies' nights" and drinks promotions.

DJ at *Jungle* nightclub, Negril ▲

Clubbers in Kingston ▼

Sound-system parties

Altogether less formal than the clubs, sound-system parties (known as dances) have long been the stalwarts of the Jamaican nightlife scene, staged all over the island at weekends by big-name sounds such as Stone Love. Loyal followers travel for miles to hear their favourite sound system spinning exclusive tracks and, on a good night, to see an established DJ take to the mic to improvise lyrics over the latest rhythms. Part club and part stageshow, sound-system sessions are held at fenced-in open air "lawns", with the beer, rum and ganja consumption intensifying as the night rolls on. However, the new Noise Abatement Act means urban parties are usually closed down after 2am, and the best dances are often those held in remote country areas, where the music is left to play till dawn and the atmosphere is invariably friendly. In recent years, free street jams such as Kingston's infamous Passa Passa have come to dominate the sound-system scene, staged on almost every night of the week in all of the island's larger towns (though most frequently in Kingston) and hugely popular both with visitors and Jamaicans from all walks of society. Places for the dancehall royalty to see and be seen, resplendent in the latest bling-bling fashions, street dances are also an arena for dance crews to "bring out" their new moves in the lights of the video cameras that transmit the best parties on local cable TV. And though many of the best parties are held in decidedly dodgy areas, the fact that they bring in much-needed income means that the locals make sure they're trouble-free, so there's no need to worry overly about safety – but you may want to tag along with someone local until you get a feel for the scene.

▲ Street dance, Kingston

▼ *Passa Passa* street jam, Kingston

▼ Kingston DJ

Stageshows

Held throughout the year at open-air venues, Jamaica's **stageshows** offer the chance to see stellar line-ups of the island's best artists for a fraction of the price of a ticket back home. Attending a concert is an essential part of any reggae-lover's Jamaican vacation, and the tips below should help you have a night to remember.

▶▶ Big shows such as Air Jamaica Jazz or **Sumfest** adhere to published timetables, but at smaller concerts, it's not uncommon for the first act to take to the stage at 1am. Events vary, so ask around before you decide what time to leave your hotel room; arriving at midnight will ensure an adequate view and enough stamina to last until the end (the same goes for Jamaica's clubs, too).

▶▶ If it rains on the evening of a show, it's likely to be a washout – Jamaicans wouldn't dream of leaving home if there's a possibility of getting wet.

▶▶ At events such as **Rebel Salute** with a huge line-up of artists, the music can continue till daybreak, so wear clothing suitable for the night-time chill and early morning sun – and don't forget your dark glasses. There are few pleasures more satisfying than watching the sun come up as the cream of the performers take to the stage.

▶▶ Jamaican entertainers can be unreliable, and it's well worth checking that the artists you've come to see have turned up before buying a ticket.

▶▶ Don't worry about eating before a show. Vast quantities of goat curry, mannish water (goat soup) and fried fish are available at almost every stageshow. Mobile vendors sell confectionery as well.

▶▶ Patrons often demonstrate appreciation of an act by throwing **firecrackers** or employing home-made flame-throwers (achieved by way of an aerosol can and a lighter); it's not aimed at hapless tourists, so move away if you don't like it.

Damian Marley ▲

Jamaica Jazz and Blues Festival, Trelawny ▼

Crowds at Sumfest, Montego Bay ▼

Negril's isolation – before the coast road was laid in 1959, it was completely cut off from the mainland by the Great Morass – has been central to its history. Even its Spanish name, *Punto de Negrilla* or "dark point", referred to its remoteness as much as to the black eels that once thrived in its rivers. During British rule, Negril's seclusion was used both to protect British ships and to attack Spanish vessels en route to and from Cuba. It also provided an ideal hideout for **pirates** in the eighteenth century (see p.217), and for the export of **ganja** in more recent years. In 1996, overzealous coast guards opened fire on a plane owned by Island Outpost boss Chris Blackwell, assuming that the cargo was drugs rather than, as was the case, members of the band U2 and country singer Jimmy Buffet; fortunately the volleys missed and a tragedy was spared. The town also played a part in war: in 1814, fifty English warships and 6000 men, including 1000 Jamaicans from the West Indian Regiment, sailed from Negril to Louisiana to fight the Battle of New Orleans.

Though it's hard to imagine once you've seen today's overdeveloped strip, in the late 1960s Negril's population was under a hundred; it was only in the 1970s that Negril's charms were brought to wider attention by hippies from overseas. Developers were quick to step in and by the early 1980s the once-empty curve of beach was smothered with all the trappings of a full-blown resort. International attention was captured by tales of debauchery at the notorious *Hedonism II* resort, and Negril's reputation as Jamaica's devil-may-care hot spot was assured. Though summer hurricanes slow the pace of development by altering the shape of the beach, 1990s infrastructural projects and a brand new highway to Montego Bay have ensured that the resort continues to grow, often at the expense of the local environment. Even Bloody Bay, until 2000 entirely unspoilt, now has three all-inclusives on its sands. Nevertheless, it is still possible to find the laid-back charm and gorgeous scenery that first brought tourists to Negril.

"Rent-a-dread"

Jamaica is a carnal kind of country, and while there's no sex tourism industry as such, monetary-based holiday liaisons are a well-established convention. Fuelled by tropical abandon and the island's pervasive sexuality, the lure of the "big bamboo" prompts some unusual partnerships. Middle-aged women strolling hand in hand with handsome young studs have become such a frequent sight that pejorative epithets – **"Rent-a-dread"** or **"Rastitute"** – for the young men who make a career out of these cynical liaisons have entered the lexicon.

The butt of many jokes, the stereotypical Rastitute is a muscle-bound model of the latest mini-trunks and sneakers, with a head topped off with dreadlocks – or extensions if he can't manage the real thing. However, not all gigolos come in the same package; a Rastitute can also appear as an Ital-style Rasta, wooing with talk of natural living and preaching sex with white tourists in the name of racial unity.

In a country of scant possibilities, becoming a gigolo is a very practical career move. Negril is a centre for this kind of trade-off, and many women regularly return for an injection of "Jamaican steel", some forming relationships that span several year's holiday time. As a result, single women are universally assumed to be out for one thing only - prepare yourself for a barrage of propositions.

Male tourists are less involved in the holiday romance scenario, but **female prostitutes** are common and men should expect to be frequently propositioned. If you do choose to indulge, practise safe sex; one in five prostitutes are HIV-positive and STDs – including syphilis – are rife.

Negril's drug culture

As any aficionado can tell you, Jamaica's best **ganja** (marijuana) – well-flavoured and incredibly potent – grows in the fertile local Westmoreland earth. The trade to eager tourists plays a significant, if covert, part in the local economy. Many devotees make annual pilgrimages to find a place to chill out and partake of the local weed. Herb is a part of daily life in Negril, so don't be surprised if your first potential supplier is your hotel porter, and you lose count of the men who hiss "sensi" as you pass them in the street. Don't feel that you can light up wherever you choose, though – marijuana is as illegal here as it is anywhere else on the island, and there are plenty of undercover police around who can and do arrest tourists and locals alike for possession.

Though Negril has been an unofficial ganja centre since its hippie heyday, there's also a great deal of **cocaine** and **crack** use around town. It's not especially noticeable, but a certain furtiveness around the late-night beach bars lets you know that it's there for the taking. Negril is also one of the few places on the island where you're likely to be offered locally abundant **magic mushrooms**, considerably larger and stronger than those in cooler countries. Some restaurants include them in cakes or omelettes and serve foul-tasting mushroom tea, such as *Jenny's Favorite Cakes* (also serving up potent ganja cake) on the West End Road, while *Tedd's* on Sheffield Road mixes up mushroom-flavoured daiquiries.

Arrival, information and getting around

Buses from Montego Bay and Lucea drop passengers just before the central round-about – if you're staying on Norman Manley Boulevard, drivers will drop you off outside your hotel. Buses from Savanna-la-Mar and Kingston terminate at the bus park on Sheffield Road, from where you can **charter a taxi** to the West End or beach for US$7–10, or take a **route taxi** for J$150-250. Private taxis charge anything from US$50 to US$75 for the MoBay to Negril ride; alternatively, try hitching a lift with a hotel transfer bus (approx US$25/person). Domestic **flights** land at Negril Aerodrome at Bloody Bay (T957 3016). Taxis are waiting but fares can be ridiculous; a reasonable price is US$10–15. Reliable **taxis** and minibuses for longer **tours** and airport pick-ups include John's On-Time Taxi (T880 1520 or 481 0157), Floyd Wilson (T771 0962), Tony Vassell at Tykes Bikes (T957 0388) and Verne Francis (T957 3112). **Taxi** companies include Candycabs (T957 9224) and Negril Transportation Services (T815 6782). The Negril branch of JUTA (T957 9197) can also line you up with a driver.

Negril doesn't really have a "town centre", just a roundabout right on the coast that feeds its three streets: Norman Manley Boulevard, which runs parallel to the Long Bay and Bloody Bay beaches and the Great Morass wetlands; the quieter West End/Lighthouse Road – recently renamed One Love Drive, to the confusion of most locals – winding along the cliffs; and **Sheffield Road**, the route to Savanna-la-Mar.

You don't need a **car** if you're staying in town. **Walking** is fine and shared **route taxis** run the length of the beach and West End Road all day every day, charging around J$200 from the roundabout to the lighthouse or Bloody Bay – flag them down anywhere. You can also rent **bicycles**, costing around US$15 per day and an excellent way to explore the surrounding area; **rental** and **bicycle tours** are available from Rusty's X-cellent Adventures, situated past the lighthouse (T957 0155, Wrusty.nyws.com/services.htm). Rusty promotes a series of mountain bike trails through ex-ganja landing strips and deserted beaches, and there are championship mountain-bike races in February each year. **Mopeds** or **dirt bikes** rent for US$30–45 per day from Tykes Bikes (T957 0388). Alternatively, if you're staying on the cliffs, you could flag down a glass-bottom boat on its way to the beach – *Famous Vincent Elvira* is a good choice, though at US$12 one way, not the cheapest way to travel.

As Negril tends to attract those who want to stay put and relax, tours are not such a big business. Most operators offer the same list as in the Montego Bay chapter (p.169), along with a few south coast tours; the best standard trip includes a crocodile search along the Black River (approx US$75/person), together with a visit to the YS Falls and perhaps the Appleton Rum Estate; the nature tour to Mayfield Falls (US$65/person) is also a good bet. Local operator Divine Tours International (℡957 3838, ⓦwww.divinetoursinternational.com) is an experienced outfit with foreign-language guides, while Conch Tours (℡869 0900, Ⓔleeanne_47@hotmail.com), run by friendly American LeeAnne Criscenti, is a smaller operation with individualized service. Alternatively, you could rent a vehicle or a driver (see opposite) and go under your own steam: aside from the destinations listed above, great day-trips include **Roaring River Park** and the **Blue Hole** garden, and **Paradise Park** on the south coast, which has its own private beach, river pool and horseriding; you could also combine a trip here with the Peter Tosh Mausoleum at Belmont).

The helpful **Tourist Product Development Company** (TPDCO) is on hand for **information**, located at Time Square Plaza on Norman Manley Boulevard (Mon–Fri 9am–5pm; ℡957 9314); it stocks freesheets with local maps, listings and news. Worth checking out also is ⓦwww.negril.com for information on the latest goings-on and accommodation deals.

Accommodation

There are thousands of **beds** here – from five-star all-inclusives to backpacker hangouts and boutique hotels to undistinguished apartment blocks. More popular, the **beach** (Norman Manley Boulevard) reeks of commercialism and is the place to stay if you want to be right at the centre of Negril's party culture. Many hotels have commandeered areas of beach with sun loungers and security, while smaller hotels and those on the inland side of the road use whatever piece of sand is closest. Inland properties are cheaper, but as they back straight onto the Great Morass, bugs can be a problem. The quieter **West End** has a degree of privacy that the

---

Spring Break

Every year, between the end of February and Easter, upwards of twenty thousand American college students arrive in Jamaica for **Spring Break** – and well over half go straight to Negril. Heavily promoted by the Jamaica Tourist Board, it's a non-stop carnival of fun if you're 19, and a rude shattering of the (relative) peace if you're not. This is the one time of the year when hotels can guarantee one-hundred-percent occupancy. If wet T-shirt competitions, drinking challenges and dancing in piña-colada flavoured foam are your thing, then this is the time to head for Negril – otherwise be warned. *Margaritaville* is the self-appointed headquarters for Spring Break in both MoBay and Negril; all the beach bars put on **special events**, and the season is sponsored by Red Stripe and Appleton.This is also a good time to see **live music**, with some of Jamaica's best DJs and bands making the most of a large, enthusiastic audience. Travel agents specializing in Spring Break packages include *Student Travel Services* (℡1-800/648 4849 in US, ⓦwww.ststravel.com) and *Sunsplash Tours* (℡1-800/426 7710 in US, ⓦwww.sunsplashtours.com). For further information check ⓦwww.negril.com/SpringBreak.

beach lacks and boasts several of the loveliest hotels in Jamaica as well as some attractive budget options, though its steep open-access cliffs make it a bad choice if travelling with children.

As planning regulations prevent building anything higher than a palm tree, much accommodation in Negril is in traditional palm-thatched or tile-roofed **cottages**; though cooler than concrete, many are ludicrously easy to break into. Wherever you stay, make sure that doors and windows are secure and check ID before you let anyone in.

All-inclusives congregate around **Bloody Bay**, away from the polluted South Negril River, on some of the prettiest stretches of Negril's beach; a couple of less obtrusive ones are listed, while notable among the rest are *Hedonism II* (Ⓦ www .hedonismresorts.com), the original "risqué resort", with nude beach, swingers' month and night-time fun in the hot tub; and the especially luxurious *Breezes Grand* (Ⓦ www.superclubs.com).

The beach

Charela Inn ☎ 957 4277, Ⓦ www.charela.com. French-Jamaican-owned place with gardens, pool, four-poster beds and an air of cultured elegance. Folklore and jazz/reggae shows twice-weekly. Three-night minimum stay; includes continental breakfast. ❺–❻

Country Country ☎ 957 4273, Ⓦ www.country jamaica.com. Brightly painted cottages set in a pretty garden with a small strip of beach. The rooms are spacious and each has a fridge, a/c, ceiling fan and cable TV. Rates include breakfast, served at the attractive beachside bar/restaurant. ❻

Couples Swept Away ☎ 957 4061, Ⓦ www .couples.com. Extensive landscaped gardens, great facilities and a sound environmental policy make this a better all-inclusive. Numerous racket sports, gym, regular and Olympic-size pools, jacuzzis, saunas, steam rooms, aerobics, spa and water-sports, plus elegantly furnished rooms, beach grill and veggie bar, and highly rated main and separate Thai restaurants. From $350. ❽

Golden Sunset ☎ 957 4241, Ⓦ www.thegolden sunset.com. Long-established and reliable, though across the road from the beach, it offers clean good-value rooms or cabins with fans, kitchenettes and private or shared bath. ❷–❹

Idle Awhile ☎ 957 3302, Ⓦ www.idleawhile.com. Sophisticated small hotel with beautifully designed rooms, all with a/c, TV and wi-fi. Includes free pass to *Swept Away*'s sports facilities. Beachside *Chill-a-while* restaurant (see p.224). ❺–❻

Kuyaba ☎ 957 4318, Ⓦ www.kuyaba.com. A classy hotel. The king and honeymoon suites have stylish Mexican tiling, calico fabrics, plasma TVs and large bathrooms with jacuzzi. More basic wooden cottages are also available. Good restaurant on site. ❹–❺

Mom's Place ☎ 957 3349. Run by a friendly Jamaican couple, a simple and homely set of

rooms by the beach. All have bright decor, fans and private bathrooms, some have a/c. Café/bar on the premises. ❷

Moondance Villas ☎ 1-800/621 1120 in US, Ⓦ www.moondancevillas.com. Most luxurious choice beachside; a collection of beautifully designed pastel-coloured villas with huge wood-panelled rooms and raised jacuzzis, plus gorgeous grounds with pools, a full staff and all mod cons. Five-bed villas are best value. ❾

Negril Tree House ☎ 957 4287, Ⓦ www.negril -treehouse.com. A clean, comfortable and appealing complex of rooms and villas. The bar is built around a tree, and there's a restaurant, pool, jacuzzi, plus watersports and massage room. Buffet breakfast included. ❺

Negril Yoga Centre ☎ 957 4397, Ⓦ www .negrilyoga.com. Yoga centre and guesthouse overlooking the Great Morass. Attractive cottages of varying degrees of comfort, surrounded by heaps of greenery. Whole food cooking, guest kitchen, and yoga and pilates classes available. ❷–❸

Nirvana on the Beach ☎ 957 4314, Ⓦ www .nirvananegril.com. Attractive a/c three-bed wooden cottages with kitchens in a spacious, shaded, sandy garden, dotted with sculptures and hammocks. Friendly atmosphere and kooky decorative touches. Very reasonable for groups of four or more. ❹–❻

Roots Bamboo ☎ 957 4479, Ⓦ www.roots bamboo.com. Friendly, efficient and one of the most popular budget options. Cottages are small and faded but cosy; some have private showers. Camping with 24-hr security available. Jamaican restaurant on site. Often noisy due to twice-weekly gigs. ❶–❷

Sunset at the Palms Bloody Bay ☎ 957 5350, Ⓦ www.sunsetatthepalms.com. Elegant wooden cabins in lush gardens, plus friendly service and great facilities make this the most attractive and private all-inclusive in Negril. On the morass side, the resort has access to a section of beach opposite. Price includes all sports and morning yoga class. From $400, non all-inclusive available. **7**

Valentine Villas Trombone's Place ℡ 957 5279, ⓦ www.valentinevillas.com. Amidst all the beach action, this small property has four clean if slightly pricey cabins; but also a bright and luxurious "bamboo suite" right over the water – one of the nicest rooms in Negril. **3**–**5**

Westport Cottages ℡ 957 4736. Budget travellers' haven at the roundabout end of the beach overlooking the Morass. The basic cabins are starkly furnished but comfortable, with fan, mosquito nets, outdoor bathroom and communal lounge and fully equipped kitchen. **1**

Whistling Bird ℡ 957 4403, ⓦ www.negriljamaica .com/whistlingbird. Beach cottages set in a lovely overgrown garden with cook-to-order restaurant and wireless Internet throughout. Private but also family-friendly. Wheelchair access. **4**

West End

Banana Shout ℡ 957 0384, ⓦ www.bananashout .com. Italian-owned, clean and attractive cottages in gardens or right on the cliffs. Each unit has kitchenette, fan, hammocks on the verandah and Haitian artwork. There's a diving platform, sun deck, private cave and exceptional sunset views. **4**–**5**

Catcha Falling Star ℡ 957 0390, ⓦ www .catchajamaica.com. Newly refurbished hotel in ideal clifftop location, featuring a range of private and attractive rooms, from wood-panelled cottages to apartments within a main villa; each has verandah and full amenities. Relax in the exquisite pool or enjoy superb food and cocktails at *Ivan's Bar*. **5**–**8**

The Caves ℡ 957 0270, ⓦ www.islandoutpost .com. Gorgeous, romantic small hotel set behind Fort Knox-inspired gates. Eleven cottage-style rooms are funkily designed and equipped with batik bathrobes and CD players, while the Aveda spa, sauna and jacuzzi with sunset view are faultless; guests can also have a massage in one of the caves below, with the sea lapping nearby. **9**

Citronella ℡ 957 0379 or 0550. This private, tranquil and good-value property next to the *LTU Pub* offers luxury away from the oft-irritating resort schmaltz of today's Negril. Five luxuriously furnished self-catering cottages sleep up to seven and are set in sprawling cliffside gardens with sea access. **5**

Jackie's on the Reef ℡ 957 4997, ⓦ www.jackiesonthereef.com. Wonderful relaxing health spa/retreat three miles east. Remarkably well designed for a thorough recovery

from urban stress, with expansive airy rooms (including a mystical geodesic dome), large verandah, saltwater pool and open-air massage hut on the shore. A full range of holistic therapies are on offer, and tasty wholesome meals are served. Vibrant owner Jackie is the perfect advertisement for her treatments. Three-night minimum; rates include breakfast, dinner and daily yoga or meditation. **5**–**6**

The Judy House Westland Mountain Rd ℡ 424 5481, ⓦ www.judyhousenegril.com. Two homely and great-value cabins set amidst gorgeous and secluded flowered gardens a short walk from the sea. Each has a fan, hot-water bathroom, well-equipped kitchenette, mosquito net and deck; one also has a/c. **3**

Lighthouse Inn II ℡ 957 4052, ⓦ www .lighthouseinn2.com. Good-value option at the far end of the cliffs. Simple attractive cabins are scattered within a beautiful garden, all have verandah and small kitchenette, though there's a breakfast and dinner package at the good on-site restaurant. Student discounts. **2**–**3**

LTU Villas ℡ 957 0382, ⓦ www.theltu.com. Spacious, great-value apartments in quiet gardens opposite one of Negril's best bars, the *LTU Pub*. Each room has two double beds, lounge and fridge, some have balcony and a/c. **3**

Moonlight Villa ℡ 957 4838, ⓦ www.moonlight villa.com. Spacious rooms in an attractive ocean-front villa, all with large beds and fridge. Private sun deck and outside grill for barbecues. **2**–**3**

Negril Escape ℡ 957 0392, ⓦ www.negrilescape .com. Extensive boutique-esque resort with a friendly, funky vibe and range of rooms, themed from India to Morocco. Each has a/c, TV, wi-fi and balcony with hammock; some have king-size bed or kitchenette. Great facilities like dive centre, pool, restaurant and spa. The resort also hosts superb monthly reggae shows. Breakfast included. **3**–**6**

Negril Moves ⓦ www.movesnegril.com. In the village a few minutes' walk from the cliffs. A comfortable and spacious house with a/c, kitchen-lounge, giant verandah and attractive garden; good family option with double and bunk rooms, sleeps two to six. **3**

New Moon Cottage ℡ 957 4305 or 417 6848, ⓔ newmooncottage@gmail.com. Clean and quiet rooms in a Jamaican family home, with communal kitchen. Camping available. **1**

Primrose Inn c/o Gus Hylton ℡ 771 0069 or 640 2029, ⓦ www.negril.com. Comfortable "home from home" option set back from the road with a huge ackee tree outside. Rooms are off an open corridor laced with hammocks; each has fan and most a (cold-water) bathroom. **1**–**2**

Rockhouse ☎957 4373, ⓦwww.rock househotel.com. Enviable location on a rock peninsula with ladders down into an azure cove; this is a unique, stylish and comfortable hotel. Thatched studios or villas, each with glass-door patio overlooking the ocean, outdoor shower, fan and bamboo four-poster bed. Magnificent, innovative thatched bar/restaurant. The Rockhouse Foundation is Negril's leader in social responsibility. ⑤–⑧

Tensing Pen ☎957 0387, ⓦwww.tensingpen .com. Stylish and exclusive retreat in pretty clifftop gardens. Imaginatively decorated wood and stone cottages are graced with bamboo furniture and have an individual touch. There's a restaurant (breakfast included) and yoga room. Two cliffs are linked by a tiny suspension bridge. ⑥–⑧

Villas Sur Mer ☎957 0377, ⓦwww.villassurmer .com. Unfailingly stylish throughout, this renovated property features sumptuous thatched wooden cottages with sea access via a cave under the road, plus a six-bed luxury villa on the clifftop with marble bathrooms and breezy living room. Full staff, pool, jacuzzi, cable and wi-fi. ⑨

Wendy's B&B Beaver Ave ☎481 0157, ⓦwww.wendybbnegril.com. Four miles east of Negril, this country cottage has two comfortable rooms with bathrooms, a peaceful atmosphere and gorgeous sea view. The friendly hosts offer good tours and airport pick-ups. Includes full breakfast, changing each day. ②–③

Xtabi ☎957 4336, ⓦwww.xtabi-negril.com. Lovely West End veteran with flowering gardens and network of caves. Oceanside rooms are in wooden cabins with private sun deck and swimming platforms, or there's garden-side apartments with kitchen. Features a pool plus open-air restaurant/bar. ③–⑥

The beach

Negril beach is a near-perfect Caribbean seashore with inviting whiter-than-white sand and swaying palms and sea grapes. Bathing here is Negril's trademark feature; the water is translucent and still, and the busy reefs ornately encrusted. It's also packed with tourists, locals and holidaying Kingstonians, and while it's great for lively socializing – the banter runs as freely as the rum cocktails – the high concentration of human traffic inevitably draws vendors and high-octane hustlers. As well as the usual crafts, hair braiding and aloe massage (the last must have been invented in Negril), you'll be offered sex and drugs with alarming frequency.

▲ Glass-bottom boats, Negril River

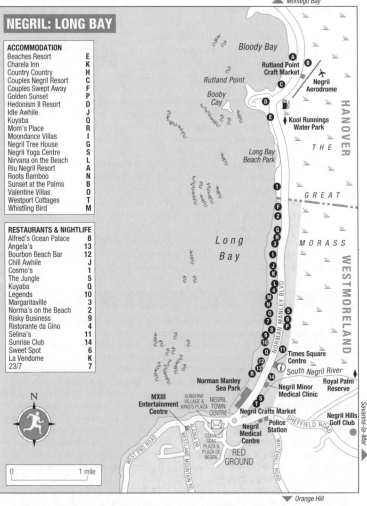

NEGRIL: LONG BAY

ACCOMMODATION

Beaches Resort	E
Charela Inn	K
Country Country	H
Couples Negril Resort	C
Couples Swept Away	F
Golden Sunset	P
Hedonism II Resort	D
Idle Awhile	J
Kuyaba	Q
Mom's Place	R
Moondance Villas	I
Negril Tree House	G
Negril Yoga Centre	S
Nirvana on the Beach	L
Riu Negril Resort	A
Roots Bamboo	N
Sunset at the Palms	B
Valentine Villas	O
Westport Cottages	T
Whistling Bird	M

RESTAURANTS & NIGHTLIFE

Alfred's Ocean Palace	8
Angela's	13
Bourbon Beach Bar	12
Chill Awhile	J
Cosmo's	1
The Jungle	5
Kuyaba	Q
Legends	10
Margaritaville	3
Norma's on the Beach	2
Risky Business	9
Ristorante da Gino	4
Selina's	11
Sunrise Club	14
Sweet Spot	6
La Vendome	K
23/7	7

Though many hotels guard "their" portion of beach with security and floating buoys, the law keeps beaches public up to the shoreline and you can walk the first couple of miles in an hour or so, though it's a hot and thirsty business in the sun. The beach is roughly divided by the bank of all-inclusives at the outcrop splitting Long Bay and Bloody Bay. Stretching north from the roundabout, **Long Bay** by day is a rash of bronzing bodies and flashing jet skis, and by night a chain of bars dedicated to reggae, rum punch and skinny dipping. At the northern end, hotels give way to the grassy stretch of **Long Bay Beach Park**, with picnic tables, changing rooms and considerably fewer people; it's also the venue for the hilarious annual **Donkey Derby**, usually held early in February. **Cosmo's**, a long-established restaurant close by in the Bloody Bay direction, is one of the best places to hang out if you're not staying at a beach hotel, with hammocks strung between the trees (J$100 entrance). Beyond, on Norman Manley Boulevard,

Kool Runnings Water Park (Wed–Sun 11am–7pm; ☎957 5400, ⓦwww.kool runnings.com) has tubes, water slides, a slower river and trampolines designed for kids looking for more adrenalin-fuelled action.

The final stretch of Negril's seven miles of beach is crescent-shaped **Bloody Bay**. Named for the crimson innards of whales once butchered here, it's now home to two particularly unattractive *Riu* all-inclusive resorts. Just beyond, the remaining piece of construction-free beach is where guests of the more attractive *Sunset* resort on the morass side come to bathe. Nearby you'll find the *Office of Nature,* an open-air barbecue run by friendly, if business-conscious Rastafarians; there's lots of local activity here on public holidays and Sundays, and the beach is backed by dense mangrove and woodland; on weekdays it's almost deserted, so keep a eye on your belongings.

The small forested islet in the centre of Bloody Bay, **Booby Cay**, appears in the epic movie *20,000 Leagues Under the Sea,* based on the Jules Verne novel. It's named after the **booby bird**, or sooty tern, an ocean dweller that takes a brief respite to lay eggs, though centuries of egg collection and hunting mean you're unlikely to spot one. Hotels hold barbecues here, and you can usually get a fisherman to take you across (US$20) – ask near the main craft market.

Beyond Bloody Bay, the coast is fringed by mangroves until it reaches horse-riding and bathing spot **Rhodes Hall Plantation**, and a few miles further, **Half Moon Bay**, one of the prettiest coves in all Jamaica (see p.227).

Watersports

Two large reefs parallel to the West End and four along the beach make **snorkelling** and **scuba diving** major Negril highlights. Despite environmental damage, the reefs are sumptuous, crowded with soft and hard coral, brilliantly coloured sponges and fish, octopuses, sea stars and even the odd turtle or nurse shark. There are several **sunken wrecks** that have become artificial reefs, including a ganja-smuggling plane that misjudged its landing at Negril airstrip. Snorkel equipment is available at hotels and watersports operators (US$20/day). All operators are based along the first mile of beach: Marine Life Divers (☎957 9783 or 957 3245), Sun Divers (☎957 4503 or 957 5340), and Negril Scuba Centre (☎957 4425) are all reputable – the latter also teaches in French and German. **Water-skiing, parasailing,** and **jet-ski** rentals are available along the same stretch; go with a legal operator and sign papers in their office rather than renting informally – accidents have been known to happen; try Aqua Nova Sports at *Coral Seas Beach Resort* (☎957 9226).

Glass-bottom boats are well represented (US$25 for a 90min trip); touts also sail along the cliffs, as do **canoe owners**, offering impromptu pleasure or fishing trips. Rates vary (about US$50 per half day); also ask at the fishermen's beach behind the craft market. If you're really serious you can hire a **sport fishing boat** from most cruise operators listed below – or from Spread Eagle Fishing Co (☎957 5170) or Stanley's (☎957 6341 or 957 0667); bait, tackle and beverages usually included. **Cruises** are an excellent way to see the local coastline, whether daytime cruises to Rhodes Hall Plantation or Half Moon Beach, or at sunset (US$45–70/person), most include snorkelling and snacks and have an open bar. Try Cool Runnings (☎957 4323), Red Stripe (☎640 0873) or Wild Thing (☎957 5392).

For a more tranquil experience good **sea kayaking** tours are available east of town at Little Bay, through Seaspray (☎433 8823, ⓦwww.seasprayadventures.com; US$50/ half day). If your tastes are more adrenaline-oriented, grade two **white-water rafting** is available inland on the Cabarita river, through Jamaica Whitewater (☎810 9922; 3hr 30min; US$80/person including pick-up, instruction and lunch).

Negril's women pirates

One of Negril's proudest moments came when the reign of **Calico Jack Rackham**, the most notorious buccaneer to terrorize Jamaican waters, was brought to an end here in November 1720. Rackham – called "Calico" in reference to his preferred underwear – and his crew had moored their captured sloop in Bloody Bay to celebrate recent plunders, unaware that their every move was being shadowed by one Captain Barnet of the British Navy. Made inattentive by rum punch, the pirates were quickly overwhelmed. Some surrendered instantly, but two, in particular, put up a mighty struggle – even turning their weapons on their more malleable crew members. Eventually, they were subdued – at which point naval officers were astonished to find that they were **women** in disguise. Famously bloodthirsty in battle, **Anne Bonney**, Rackham's former mistress, and **Mary Read** formed a ruthless double act and were instrumental in earning Rackham his infamy as a freebooter. At their trial, victim Dorothy Thomas noted that "they wore men's jackets and long trousers… each of them had a machete and a pistol in their hands, and cursed and swore".

Rackham was executed, his body displayed in an iron frame at the Kingston cay that now bears his name. Bonney and Read were also sentenced to death, but were spared when they declared themselves pregnant and were eventually reprieved. Anne Bonney disappeared from recorded history, while Mary Read died of yellow fever and is buried in St Catherine.

Sheffield Road and the Royal Palm Reserve

Negril's centre is focused on the roundabout feeding the three main roads – and most people leave the beach or cliffs only to change money, buy petrol or find a ride out of the area. However, **Sheffield Road** is the least tourist-oriented part of town and the closest approximation of a real heart, with the police station, market stalls, petrol station, restaurants and constant crowds dodging beeping mopeds. To the right of the roundabout are two rather tatty **shopping plazas** – Coral Seas Plaza and Plaza de Negril, the latter used by locals more than tourists; the car park in front is known as **Negril Square**, a base for taxi drivers, low-key hustlers and would-be guides. Nestled behind is **Red Ground**, a residential area that visitors seldom see, but which houses most of Negril's permanent population.

East out of town on Sheffield Road, the Negril Hills Golf Club (☎957 4638) is an extremely hilly and attractive 18-hole, 6600-yard, par-72 course. The topography makes for a challenging game, and there's a clubhouse and restaurant on site. Accessed by means of a signed left turn beyond the course, the 289-acre **Royal Palm Reserve** (daily 9am–6pm; US$10; ☎957 3736, ⓦwww.jpat-jm.net) was created in the 1980s at the southern side of the **Great Morass** as a means of protecting this crucial wetland. The royal palm cluster here is one of the largest single collections of the tree in the world; tall and magnificent but devoid of coconuts, the palms have a stately presence that lends the reserve a patently tropical air. Wreathed in creepers and vines springing up from the nutrient-rich bog below, the trees are thick enough in places to block out views of the hills behind. Peat channels are now fishponds, and there's a rickety birdwatching tower.

A system of boardwalks here allow you to go deep into the morass without getting wet; the best point at which to view this rare habitat. Jamaica's second-largest **wetland**, it comprises six thousand acres of rivers, peat bogs and grasses running parallel to the beach. Fed by rivers from the Orange and Fish River hills, the area

Rapid growth and unplanned development have had a devastating effect upon Negril's delicate ecosystems. Norman Manley Boulevard cuts straight through what was originally swampland, jet skis and anchors have played havoc with the reefs, and mangrove-felling has allowed the sea and hurricanes to slim down the precious beach and smother portions of reef with earth and sand that the trees once filtered. The population explosion meant that houses built on captured land lacked water supplies, garbage removal and sanitation facilities until relatively recently. Now thankfully Negril has a US$15-million water treatment plant and reservoir, which has minimized the amount of untreated sewage flowing into the sea, although link-up is still proving beyond some people's means. With healthy support from Negril citizens, the **Negril Coral Reef Preservation Society** (NCRPS) has placed 45 mooring buoys at key points on the reefs and successfully lobbied for marine park status like that afforded the Montego Bay waters (see p.177); it was granted in March 1998. The **Negril Environmental Protection Trust** (NEPT) has a wider brief, declaring eighty square miles from Green Island to Salmon Point as the **Negril Watershed Environmental Protection Area**, with action required on all fronts: from reforestation projects to combating the burning of hardwoods for saleable charcoal, to rescuing sea turtles deprived of their beach nesting grounds, and education programmes in local schools. Recently, NEPT has engaged larger hotels in the **Blue Flag Campaign**, which provides beach marine certification to those active on beach erosion and effective coastal management – not an easy task. To find out more about both groups, visit their offices at Marine Park, next to the main craft market (@negril.com/ncrps, ☏957 4626).

is crucial to the supply of fresh water, acting as a giant natural filter, protecting reefs from being smothered by silt, and acting as a sanctuary for insects, shrimp, rare plants and birds – commonly seen include Jamaican euphonias, parakeets and woodpeckers. Land crabs enjoy one of the few remaining perfect habitats in Jamaica and are a common sight during the summer breeding months. The morass has long been threatened by pesticide and sewage pollution and proposals to remove peat fuel, but thankfully public outrage has put a stop to the cut-and-drain activities of the government-owned Petroleum Company of Jamaica (PCJ).

The reserve land is still owned by the PCJ, which, after years of mismanagement, finally leased it to the Negril Environmental Protection Trust (NEPT; see box) in 2001. There's now an on-site **café** and small **museum** with rather desultory exhibits and explanations of wetland ecosystems and bird varieties. However, the **guides** who take visitors on a 45-minute tour are informative and enthusiastic, and there are useful labels posted on trees and other plants. Dawn or dusk bird watching is available with advance booking, and you can also fish (US$10) for tarpons and tilapia.

The West End

Beyond the overpriced cocktails and hallucinogenic sunset-watching at the infamous *Rick's Café*, the **West End** cliffs are the last vestige of truly laid-back Negril. The ostensible serenity, however, follows an extended period of economic decline in the late 1990s, when the more obvious appeal of the beach eclipsed its popularity. Nevertheless, immaculate reefs and the thrill of diving from a cliff straight into fifteen feet of the crystal-clear Caribbean remain unbeatable, and with some top accommodation options and several popular evening joints, life has truly been brought back to the area.

The West End Road, now also re-branded as **One Love Drive** (see Ⓦ www .onelovedrive.com), begins at the roundabout in the centre of town and twists and turns along the cliffs for some three miles, becoming Lighthouse Road at Negril lighthouse and meandering for another two coastal miles before winding inland to Orange Hill and ultimately Sheffield Road. The first stretch is the liveliest, with jerk shacks, bars, juice stalls and craft shops – including the official A FiWi or Vendor's Plaza **craft market** – lining each side, as well as one tiny **beach** where fishermen moor their canoes – check the cleanliness of the water. The fancy King's Plaza and Sunshine Village shopping malls are just beyond, but the true West End begins over the next blind bend; the road narrows and the hotels that carve up the rest of the cliffs begin in earnest. Nonetheless, the relative quietude here can mean that you've got some of the best places entirely to yourself.

As this is Jamaica's extreme westerly point, the **sunset view** from the West End is the best you'll see. Most evenings the sky blazes with absurdly rich oranges, pinks and blues that intensify as the sun dips behind the horizon, eventually merging into the deepest of blues, with a moon reflected way out to sea. Sunset-watching is an institution; most bars and restaurants offer sunset happy hours and the half-hour or so before dusk is the closest the West End gets to hectic. Coach parties descend in droves upon Negril's biggest (and rather tired) cliché: **Rick's Café**, the venue of sunset cliff-diving demonstrations by local boys, who enjoy

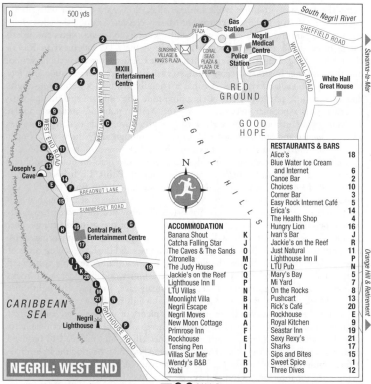

ACCOMMODATION

Banana Shout	K
Catcha Falling Star	J
The Caves & The Sands	O
Citronella	M
The Judy House	C
Jackie's on the Reef	Q
Lighthouse Inn II	P
LTU Villas	N
Moonlight Villa	B
Negril Escape	H
Negril Moves	G
New Moon Cottage	A
Primrose Inn	F
Rockhouse	E
Tensing Pen	I
Villas Sur Mer	L
Wendy's B&B	R
Xtabi	D

RESTAURANTS & BARS

Alice's	18
Blue Water Ice Cream and Internet	6
Canoe Bar	2
Choices	10
Corner Bar	3
Easy Rock Internet Café	5
Erica's	14
The Health Shop	4
Hungry Lion	16
Ivan's Bar	J
Jackie's on the Reef	R
Just Natural	11
Lighthouse Inn II	P
LTU Pub	N
Mary's Bay	5
Mi Yard	7
On the Rocks	8
Pushcart	13
Rick's Café	20
Rockhouse	E
Royal Kitchen	9
Seastar Inn	19
Sexy Rexy's	21
Sharks	17
Sips and Bites	15
Sweet Spice	1
Three Dives	12

NEGRIL: WEST END

▲ View of the cliffs from *LTU Pub*

being the centre of attention while cameras click, drinks are paid for with plastic tokens, and (often poor) bands churn out Marley classics. Though the cliffs are at their highest around *Rick's*, many other clifftop hotels and **restaurants** are superb for a sunset drink and swim; best is probably at the *LTU Pub* (next to *Rick's*), though the *Sands* bar at the *Caves* hotel is an exclusive sunset-watching venue, and the *Rockhouse* boasts sea access from a stylish bar and restaurant, and complete seclusion. *Drumville Cove* hotel also has a friendly attitude towards non-guests and a spectacular portion of cliff. Being limestone, the cliffs are also riddled with caverns, with a popular network below the *Xtabi* restaurant, and the popular *Pushcart* restaurant located above the large Joseph's Cave, made famous in movies *Dr No*, *Papillon* and *20,000 Leagues Under the Sea*, though sadly there is no longer access from above (you can view it by boat, however).

Rick's marks the last of the major development; from here on hotels are interspersed with near-wild coastline, and the **Negril Point Lighthouse** stands proud 100 feet above sea level at Jamaica's westernmost tip. Built in 1894, the 66-foot tower flashes a solar-powered beam ten miles out to sea, though it still contains the acetylene gas canisters that originally provided the power, the hand-wound pendulum that once regulated the beam, and plenty of brass fittings. Port authority workers are usually willing to take you up all 103 leg-quivering steps. Look out for the quaint (listed) crumbling outhouses and the far-reaching roots of a huge silk cotton tree. Below the lighthouse is a beautiful cove, now connected to the chic Caves hotel and reached via a precarious wooden ladder, with rocks smooth enough to lie on and an accessible small cave. Just past the lighthouse the road forks as the cliffs peter out and coastal winds whip the sea into a frenzy. Swimming becomes risky here, though there's plenty of undeveloped land perfect for **mountain biking** (see p.210). Beyond, there's a markedly rural atmosphere, though a 6000-room highly questionable resort village and marina had received planning permission at the time of writing. Some two miles beyond the lighthouse is the wonderful *Jackie's on the Reef* spa and retreat (see p.213), before the tarmac swings into the interior to Orange Bay.

Negril Hills and Little Bay

Inland from Negril's West End, the terrain rises into the dry limestone peaks of the **Negril Hills**, habitat of non-venomous **yellow boa snakes** occasionally seen slithering across the road. The area is best approached from Sheffield Road in Negril – turn off by the Texaco petrol station and continue over the hill. At its summit is **Whitehall Great House**, a crumbling piece of colonial architecture that enjoyed a brief stint as a disco in the early 1980s, but has lain uninhabited since being gutted by fire in 1985; recent reports of robberies make it an unsafe area to stop at. As an aside, the 187-acre estate is also home to the grave of Robert Parkinson, a plantation owner who had the dubious honour of giving his name to Parkinson's disease.

Past Whitehall the route descends into the valley, giving wonderful views of the cane fields in the basin below. A right turn a few miles on leads you back to Negril's West End, and continuing straight ahead is quiet **ORANGE HILL**, with flowered duck ponds and a host of quietly convivial **bars** – though the village's greater island-wide fame is undoubtedly for the strength of its ganja, grown in the surrounding fertile hills. Orange Hill merges into residential **RETIREMENT**, home to the distinctive **Jurassic Park Art Garden and Restaurant**, marked by a giant cast-iron pterodactyl on its gate. This is the creative outlet of local ironworker Daniel Woolcock, whose enormous sculptures of flamingos, hibiscus flowers and a five-foot-long centipede overlook a basketball court, restaurant/bar and shady gazebo.

Past Retirement the road forks: one branch connects with the Negril to Sav-la-Mar road, while the other weaves its way back down to the coast at the pleasant but dishevelled inlet of **Homer's Cove** (also known as **Brighton Beach** to locals). The once-pristine beach here has been mostly eroded by sand mining, but it's still a nice place for a swim, and there are a few vendors selling drinks and snacks. You can also arrive here along a dirt track directly from Negril along the shoreline on foot or by bike.

Under a mile after Homer's Cove, **LITTLE BAY** is an extremely attractive, tranquil piece of coastline with a couple of low-key eateries and **accommodation** options: the smartest is *Seaspray Villas* (☎433 8823 or 3065, ⓦwww.seasprayvillas .com), a gorgeous oceanfront house with verandah and saltwater pool sleeping two to six people and renting for as little as US$1200 per week off season, including the services of a cook and free use of kayaks. Non-guests can also rent kayaks here (US$20 for 2hr), or arrange a guided kayaking tour (ⓦwww.seasprayadventures .com). More basic lodgings with communal kitchen are to be found at *Romie's Ocean View* (☎442 3721; ❶), as well as bikes for rent. Although locked up behind high gates as a result of ownership disputes, you may be able to find someone to take you round **Bob Marley's Place**, an attractive wooden seafront house built by Marley in 1972 for himself and girlfriend Esther Anderson, which became the setting for *Talking Blues*. The garden has a small mineral spring pool, large enough to swim just a couple of strokes.

From Little Bay you can continue east along the beautiful, rugged coastline by bike or on foot, to **Broughton** and the *Lost Beach Resort* (see p.231).

Eating

Negril's cosmopolitan eateries offer some of the finest cuisine in Jamaica. There is a high proportion of **vegetarian** options alongside chicken and fish, and you'll also find a lot of **pasta** and **pizza**, with many restaurants run by expat Italians – popular with the large number of Italians who visit in the early summer. Jamaican fare tends to be lower-priced, with numerous vendors in shacks along the first stretch of West End Road selling roast or fried fish, jerk chicken and soup; names change frequently, but the *Sea View Bar and Grill* (aka the *Corner Bar*) currently does excellent jerk and fish. There are dozens of **jerk vendors** in Negril, all wheeling out their oil-drum barbecues as dusk falls, but particularly recommended for jerk chicken are *The Best in the West* on Norman Manley Boulevard and *Three Dives* on West End Road. Some of the smarter restaurants offer free pick-up; call in advance. Beach bars *Risky Business*, *Legends* and *Margaritaville* all serve various forms of hamburgers and chips, alongside Jamaican fare.

For snacks and patties, try Tan-Tan at the back of the Plaza de Negril – its callaloo and cheese loaf and vegetable and beef patties are the cheapest in town. Ice-cream and fruit vendors make regular rounds of the beach if you can't be bothered to move; otherwise look out for Calypso Gelato, delicious Italian-style ice cream made by Italians in Montego Bay and sold at various outlets, including at the Blue Water Ice-cream Parlour on West End Road.

Sheffield Road

The Health Shop Tait's Plaza. This tiny, friendly little vegetarian place in the plaza just past the roundabout sells some of the tastiest patties in Jamaica (go early, as they run out fast), with fillings like spicy veg, lentil and soya. Daily cooked lunch, and in-season natural juices – try the soursop and tangerine.

Sweet Spice Known among locals as one of the best Jamaican restaurants in Negril, it serves all the standard dishes, to take away or eat in, plus a few unusual ones – at moderate prices.

The beach

Angela's *Bar-B-Barn Hotel*, Norman Manley Blvd ☎ 957 9793. Good, mid-priced Italian restaurant on breezy and attractive upstairs terrace. Delicious thin-crust pizza, pasta dishes and other Italian specialities.

Chill Awhile *Idle Awhile*, Norman Manley Blvd. Tasty, cheap to moderately priced Jamaican breakfasts, plus fresh juices, vegetarian pastas, salads, and lots of seafood and burgers – all served up in attractive gardens on the beach.

Cosmo's Norman Manley Blvd ☎ 957 4330. One of the best, busiest spots right on the beach, equally popular with Jamaicans and tourists. Excellent and inexpensive seafood – the conch soup is a speciality – and the usual selection of chicken and fish variations. A bargain.

Kuyaba *Kuyaba* hotel ☎ 957 4318. Thatch-roofed, open-sided and upscale restaurant with innovative decor and consistently good food. The frequently changing menu might include lobster in white wine and garlic, steaks, snapper with coconut callaloo and vegetarian dishes. Great burgers and pepper shrimp lunch.

Norma's *Sea Splash* hotel, Norman Manley Blvd ☎ 957 4041. One of three award-winning island restaurants owned by chef Norma Shirley.

The moderately priced menu features nouvelle Jamaican cuisine, with creative salads, pastas, soups like pumpkin bisque with sherry, and fantastic seafood – try the marlin sushi. Breakfast and lunch menus are especially good value.

Ristorante da Gino *Mariposa* resort, Norman Manley Blvd ☎ 957 4918. Expensive Italian restaurant set on a pretty outdoor terrace, serving pastas, seafood (try the *scallopine al burro*), and a decent meat menu, such as pork fillet with gorgonzola.

Selina's Norman Manley Blvd. Excellent all-day breakfast joint with friendly service and extensive menu – eggs, bagels, banana pancakes, all freshly made. The Blue Mountain coffee is roasted on site, and Selina mixes a killer Bloody Mary. Book exchange, and great for local information.

Sweet Spot Norman Manley Blvd. Great little local's lunchtime spot with large portions of chicken, fish and shrimp cooked all ways, plus ackee and saltfish for breakfast, curry goat and fresh juices.

Sunrise Club Norman Manley Blvd. Smart, friendly, Italian-run restaurant-cum-bar on the morass side, specializing in fine yet mid-priced Italian food. The wood-fired brick oven turns out probably the best pizza in all Jamaica, and honours are also due for the coffee – Blue Mountain, Italian style, unbeatable. In addition the menu includes tasty pink gnocchi and a range of lobster dishes.

La Vendome *Charela Inn* ☎ 957 4648. Celebrated, sophisticated, expensive French/Jamaican cuisine – duck à l'orange, veal with veloutée sauce, snapper in coconut. Vegetarian options, plus home-made ice cream, excellent bread and good wine list.

West End

Alice's West End Rd. Large portions of great Jamaican food at this new, popular spot with a large landscaped yard and loud sound system. Escovitched fish a great option here.

Canoe Bar West End Rd. One of few Jamaican places on the West End to serve great international food, too – with great-value seafood pastas, potato wedges, sandwiches and cakes. Great chilled vibe, wi-fi, and set on its own tiny beach.

Chicken Lavish West End Rd ☎957 4410. Choice spot for domino players. It serves chicken and fish, Jamaican- and Chinese-style, steaks and pork chops, all inexpensive.

Choices West End Rd. Brightly painted outdoor café with low prices and all the Jamaican staples. Popular with both locals and tourists, particularly at breakfast.

Easy Rock Internet Café West End Rd. Not just the best place to check your emails, this is a good breakfast and lunch option, serving bagels (try the jerk pork with mango salsa), home-made cakes and pastas too. There's also a book swap.

Erica's Opposite the *Rockcliff Hotel*, West End Rd. Small shack featuring home cooking by Erica herself. Seafood is a speciality, with excellent, and reasonably priced, lobster.

Hungry Lion West End Rd ☎957 4486. Some good vegetarian food, with seafood as well. A walled courtyard affords privacy, though the food has dropped in quality due to long-running popularity. Try the green lentil shepherd's pie, lobster in lemon butter and black-bean chilli. Desserts are a highlight, especially the coconut cream pie.

Jackie's on the Reef Lighthouse Rd ☎957 4997. Meals must be ordered in advance, but the menu is innovative and health food oriented, and the setting romantic and unusual, a couple of miles from town. Moderately priced dishes include grilled tuna with sesame noodles, sun-dried tomato pasta, and marvellous chicken tacos for lunch.

Just Natural West End Rd. Inexpensive, fresh Jamaican food, callaloo omelettes, pasta, burritos and vegetarian options, in a beautiful shady garden.

Lighthouse Inn II West End Rd. Imaginative, intimate restaurant set in an overgrown garden out of town. An original mix of Caribbean and European cuisines and a homely feel make this one of the best mid-priced options.

Pushcart West End Rd. A new upscale restaurant and bar in prime spot over Joseph's Cave, serving straightforward but high-quality Jamaican food (the jerk pork and oxtail are highlights) at moderate prices. Service is friendly and professional, and it's also a great spot for an evening drink.

Rockhouse West End Rd ☎957 4373. One of Negril's finest restaurants, romantically set on a boardwalk right over the sea. Good value for money and an imaginative menu that includes seafood bouillon in a coconut shell, conch fritters and a range of favourite Jamaican fish and meat dishes.

Royal Kitchen West End Rd. The best pure Ital and vegetarian option in town, there's a different stew each day, home-made ginger beer, and natural juices with what's in season. Inexpensive.

Sharks West End Rd. Popular with locals and tourists alike, for the big portions of good-quality Jamaican food and the very friendly service from Shark and family. Inexpensive.

Sips and Bites West End Rd. Large open yard, very friendly, popular with taxi drivers for breakfast. Serves unadulterated Jamaican cuisine at very reasonable prices.

Three Dives West End Rd. Popular, inexpensive jerk centre in a cliffside garden, with particularly good lobster and a nightly bonfire.

Drinking and entertainment

Most **bars** want you to spend the sunset with them and provide drinks promotions or happy hours as an incentive. As the cliffs give the best view, bars along the West End tend to be livelier at dusk, with the action most nights moving to the beach later on. If you want some local flavour, try the darkened interiors of the **rum bars** and **beer shacks** along Sheffield Road or West End Road near the roundabout.

There is only one proper **club** in town, *The Jungle*, so most of the weeknight dancing is offered by **beach bars** using their portion of sand as a dancefloor – though there are a couple of West End options, too. A nightly rotation system shares the business around, and DJs play mostly reggae dancehall or dance music, with **live music** usually consisting of a no-name reggae band singing Bob Marley covers. Ask around to see what's happening – you can usually walk from one beach venue to another. Negril's risqué reputation also means it boasts a number of go-go clubs; scantily clad women gyrate for drinkers and post-Jungle clubbers; perhaps surprisingly, they draw a mainly local clientele of both sexes.

Large **stageshows** featuring well-known reggae artists are advertised on roadside billboards and through a car-with-megaphone system, rarely starting before 11pm and going on until between 2am and 5am. Main **venues** for large shows are *MXIII*, *Central Park* and *Negril Escape* on the West End, and *Roots Bamboo, Bourbon Beach*, *Alfred's*, or *Risky Business* on the beach; cover charges start at US$10. There's usually huge reggae extravaganzas around Spring Break, **Negril Carnival** – held in late April, with costume parades and all-night dancing – and at the **Bob Marley Birthday Bash on February 6**. To a lesser extent, the birthday of Westmoreland's own Peter Tosh, in October, sometimes draws big-name acts. At New Year, Easter and Independence Day in August, it's always worth the 40-minute drive to Savanna-la-Mar for big-name, all-night shows. **Sound-system jams** take place pretty much anywhere each weekend; Red Ground, Orange Hill and West End Road are usual locations; ask around. **Jazz** fans will find occasional gigs at *Roots Bamboo* and the *Charela Inn*.

The beach

Alfred's Ocean Palace Norman Manley Blvd. Busiest bar on the sand, with thrice-weekly live reggae and crowds of vacationers dancing within their fenced-off section. Can be great fun but watch out for the hustlers on gig nights. Bob cover songs earlier in the night, raw dancehall later.

Bourbon Beach Bar Norman Manley Blvd. Known for years as *De Bus*, though the trademark London bus used in *Live and Let Die* has mysteriously disappeared. There's piped-in or live music every night in a large covered beach area. The jerk chicken is famously good.

The Jungle Norman Manley Blvd. Negril's only purpose-built nightclub, across from the beach, with gaming lounge, sports bar and jerk food. Thursday's "Ladies' Night" is one of the best and most popular club nights in the country, with seemingly half of western Jamaica's youth sweating and gyrating to a surprisingly original music selection (free for women until midnight). Open Wed–Sun until 5am. Cover US$9 for men, US$6 for women.

Margaritaville Norman Manley Blvd. Large beach bar/restaurant with nightly bonfire, beach volleyball, two-for-one drink offers and TV screens for sports fans. Themed nights include Karaoke Monday and Beach Party with bonfire Tuesday or Wednesday. Hugely popular at weekends with American students and locals alike.

Risky Business Norman Manley Blvd. A top beach spot for live music and sound systems – much like *Alfred's*, drawing a varied crowd of tourists, locals and hustlers. Up- and downstairs bars and good jerk for snacking on later.

Roots Bamboo Norman Manley Blvd. Still one of the best and liveliest places to take a drink on the beach. The music's usually good-quality reggae and dancehall, with guest sound systems and live acts Wednesdays and Sundays.

West End

Ivan's Bar *Catcha Falling Star*, West End Rd. One of the best hotel bars (open to non-guests), rebuilt after damage from Hurricane Ivan. Great for excellent cocktails and finger foods like crab cakes, jerk shrimp and strips of tenderloin, enjoyed in a supremely romantic setting on the clifftop.

LTU Pub West End Rd. Laid-back venue offering cliffside drinking, diving, snorkelling and a moderately priced, mixed menu: seafood, stuffed jalapeno chillis and jerk favourites. Ask the barman to make you a Bob Marley – the five-shot red, gold and green special can take a while to get down.

Mary's Bay West End Rd, next to *Easy Rock Café*. A welcome addition to the West End with great vibes, music and whisky assured by genial Scots hosts. Right over the water, you can arrive on foot or moor your boat. Food menu includes bargain breakfasts, lobster and burgers.

Mi Yard West End Rd. High-rise bar that's tourist-friendly but positively Jamaican. Open 24hr for music, dominoes, drinking and jerk; always busy once the beach bars start to slow down after 2am.

On the Rocks West End Rd. Attractive cliffside circular bar currently in vogue for its Wednesday dancehall sessions on the large lawn, with an up-for-it local crowd arriving not before 11pm.

Rick's Café West End Rd. Newly rebuilt yet still overpriced touristy place with reggae covers band alongside the traditional (and impressive) spectacle of local boys diving from the high cliffs.

The Sands at *The Caves*, West End Rd. Negril's most exclusive hotel now has an attractive public bar to match, but it's strictly for sunset, 4–7.30pm only. Nonetheless, it's markedly atmospheric and unpretentious.

Seastar Off West End Rd (turn inland just before *Rick's*). This hotel's "Saturday Night LIVE Twisting by the Pool Party" has fast become a high point of the entertainment scene, with live drumming and band plus buffet meal included for US$15 (7pm–midnight).

Sexy Rexy's West End Rd. Just beyond *LTU*, this small shack has as good a clifftop view as anywhere in the West End. Rexy is an entertaining local character and will cook up tasty fried fish if you're hungry.

Shopping

The best place to buy **crafts** is at the main craft market at the roundabout end of Norman Manley Boulevard, with around a hundred stalls and a full spread of merchandise, though be prepared for sales banter and a good haggle. Dedicated craft shops also pepper the West End and along the beach; especially good is A FiWi Plaza (otherwise known as Vendors' Plaza or Hi-Lo Plaza), and the ramshackle collection of huts opposite the *Rockhouse Hotel,* both on West End Road.

For unusual items try the shop at *Kuyaba* on the beach, which prides itself on stock that you can't find anywhere else in town, like painted tin "country buses" and brightly enamelled tropical fish. Well-known Negril-based artist Geraldine Robins sells excellent **batik** and hand-painted T-shirts and fabrics from her shop at *Margaritaville*, and Gallery Hoffstead in A FiWi Plaza (see p.219) has original prints and sculpture. The *Rockhouse* gift shop offers a pretty array of **beach wraps** and other attractive items; Sarongs to Go on the West End Road also has a good selection. Ja-Ja Originals (Ⓦwww.jajaoriginals.com) at the *Coco La Palm* hotel sells **paintings** by local Jamaican artists as well as elegant gold and silver **jewellery** and will custom-make items – vastly better than the **in-bond shops** dotted around.

Sunshine Plaza, on the West End, stocks interesting knick-knacks, kitsch holiday souvenirs as well as swimwear; one of the better shops is Countrywide, which also has a reasonable selection of **books and maps**. For **music**, try The Office/22's Music Café, close to *Mary's Bay* bar on the West End Road, or if you're looking for **recording facilities** or to arrange dub plates with top Jamaican artists, go to Jah Freedom Recording studio (Ⓣ957 0037, Ⓦwww.jahfreedom.com) also on the West End.

Roots Man Corner, at the roundabout, is the place to get natural remedies. The best **supermarket** is Hi-Lo on the West End, while the stalls at the top end of Sheffield Road have cheaper and fresher fruit and veg. Wise Choice, opposite *Tensing Pen*, is a reasonable grocery. Daley's liquor store, near the start of West End Road offers discounts on bulk buys of **beer** or **spirits**.

Listings

Airlines Air Jamaica Ⓣ952 4300 or 4100; American Airlines Ⓣ952 5950; British Airways Ⓣ952 3771; Continental Ⓣ952 4495; Timair (Ⓣ957 5374) and Intl Air Link (Ⓣ940 6660) have offices in Negril (for aerodrome, see p.210).
Banks & money 24hr ATMs can be found at Scotiabank by the roundabout and at the Bloody Bay gas station by the Negril Aerodrome; NCB in Sunshine Village has an ATM, counters and wire transfer facilities (Mon–Thurs 9am–2pm, Friday 9am–4pm); both banks offer exchange and credit cash advances – as do cambios Gold Nugget

(Mon–Sat 9am–5pm) and Time Trend Financial Co, both on Norman Manley Blvd (Mon–Fri 9am–5pm, Sat 10am–3pm; Ⓣ957 3242). Black market touts hang around Negril Square; if you use them, try and get a Jamaican to accompany you. Western Union (Mon–Thurs 9am–5.30pm, Fri & Sat 9am–6pm) has an outlet at Hi-Lo in Sunshine Village.
Car and bike rental Choices Ⓣ957 3490; Dollar Ⓣ957 4110; Jus Jeep, West End Rd Ⓣ957 0094/5; Vernon's, Plaza de Negril and Norman Manley Blvd Ⓣ957 4522 or 4354. Manufactured in Jamaica, Patrick Mazuka's Island Cruisers can

be rented from the office on Norman Manley Blvd (℡ 957 9187). Bikes can be rented from Jah B's on Norman Manley Blvd (℡ 957 4235) or Banmark (℡ 957 0197); Kool Bike Rental (℡ 957 9224) and Tykes Bikes (℡ 957 0388), all on West End Rd.

Internet Best service is from: Surf n Talk, between Merrils 1&2 on Norman Manley Blvd; Easy Rock Internet Café or Bluewater Internet Café on the West End. Mi Yard is open 24hr (slow service).

Laundry West End Cleaners, off Hylton Ave at the top of Lighthouse Rd (℡ 957 0160), is rather inaccessible but will pick up and deliver between 8am and 10pm daily. Washing costs J$100 per pound, including soap.

Massage Massage is a Negril institution. Try *Jackie's on the Reef* (℡ 957 4997); Catherine McLean (c/o *Tensing Pen* ℡ 957 0387). Dr Peggy Daugherty (℡ 818 0682) is a naturopathic doctor specializing in deep tissue and cranio-sacral massage.

Medical services Negril Minor Emergency Clinic, Norman Manley Blvd (℡ 957 4888; open 24hr),

or Dr Dale Foster (℡ 957 9307). There is an optician at Kings Plaza, West End Rd. Nearest hospitals are at Savanna-la-Mar (℡ 955 2533 or 2133) or Lucea (℡ 956 2233). In an emergency, dial ℡ 119 for an ambulance.

Petrol Negril has two petrol stations: on Sheffield Rd at the junction with Whitehall (24hr), and Petcom by Negril Aerodrome (daily 6.30am–11pm).

Pharmacies Key West Pharmacy, 11 Sunshine Village (Mon–Sat 9am–8pm, Sun 10am–6pm); Negril Pharmacy, 14 Coral Seas Plaza (Mon–Sat 9am–7pm, Sun 10am–2pm).

Post office West End Rd next to A FiWi Plaza; Mon–Fri 9am to 5pm.

Telephones and communications Phone boxes opposite the main craft market and at Plaza de Negril; phonecards available from pharmacies or the post office. Phone booths available at Sunshine Village, by *Catcha Falling Star* hotel, and by the *House of Dread* bar. The Negril Calling Centre (9am–11pm) in Plaza de Negril offers relatively cheap calls, as does Bluewater Internet Centre.

North and east of Negril

After Negril's glittering hedonism, the rest of western Jamaica can come as quite a surprise. Restaurants remain wholeheartedly traditional, with mannish water and eye-rollingly insouciant service replacing waffles and exhortations to "have a nice day". Locals tend to be more genuinely friendly, if a little surprised that you've torn yourself away from a resort, and unfettered by high-rises, the countryside is magnificent.

Towards Montego Bay, the highway through the parish of Hanover soon passes the bounteously situated **Rhodes Hall Plantation**, an ideal spot for riding and diving, and there's swimming at the marvellously secluded **Half Moon Bay Beach** which is a far cry from the resort onslaught. There's a good concentration of roadside bars and rest stops around **Green Island** and **Orange Bay**, and market town **Lucea** breathes more life into the area as you head northeast. The mini-museum at Alexander Bustamante's **Blenheim** birthplace is the only "official" site on the northern side of the central **Dolphin Head** range of hills, and as most people choose to remain within sight of the Caribbean Sea, much of the land remains uncompromisingly indifferent to tourism.

The southwest coastline offers a contrast in landscapes, albeit on less serviceable roads than to the north. Alluvial plains occupy the western half of Westmoreland parish, with the multi-tributaried **Cabarita** river meandering down from the Dolphin Head Mountains through vast cane fields, to arrive at the parish's concrete capital, **Savanna-la-Mar**, where brisk trade and honking horns fight against the soupy humidity. Since Indian workers first entered the scene in the mid-nineteenth century, the wetlands here have also been employed for the cultivation of **rice**, particularly in the coastal areas near to linear community **Little London**. A few miles inland from Sav-la-Mar, **Roaring River** marks its entrance above ground with a spectacular blue swimming hole, having carved out an inky cave on its way, and more fabulous swimming is available at **Mayfield Falls**.

Hills rise up once more to the east of the parish, hiding lush stretches of coastline and beach below at **Bluefields Bay**; a series of **low-key hotels** and guesthouses are perfect to appreciate the area's unhurried charm.

North along the coast

North of Negril, long tracts of mangrove break occasionally for a villa or sea view, with the first point of real interest **Rhodes Hall Plantation** (℗957 6883, Ⓦwww.rhodesresort.com); a 550-acre coconut, banana, plantain, pear and coconut farm with two private **beaches** with reef and a freshwater mineral spring bubbling under the brine. Volleyball and football pitches and a restaurant/bar back onto the beaches, as do two semi-luxurious two-bedroom **cottages** (❹–❻). **Horseback riding** is also an option; the well-kept mounts trot into the hills and along the beach (US$60–70). The pristine **mangrove swamp** here is home to a few wild Jamaican **crocodiles** – if you can't see any in the open section, you'll usually find some sunning themselves in a fenced-off enclosure.

A couple of miles beyond nearby **ORANGE BAY**, unspoilt **Half Moon Bay Beach** (℗957 6467 or 531 4508; daily 8am till late), is full of the paradisiacal charm that originally brought tourists to Negril. The wide curve of white sand has no braiding booths or jet skis (though all-inclusives do visit on Sundays), just a little sea grass and some small islets; nude bathing is acceptable, snorkelling equipment cheap and the **restaurant** (daily 8am–10pm) serves excellent sandwiches, chicken and fish, as well as freshly caught lobster at US$18/lb. The overgrown flat track behind the restaurant was once an illegal airstrip used for ganja smuggling. Set back within the trees are three basic wooden cabins with fan and verandah (❷) for overnight stays, while **camping** is also possible (US$10/tent); security is provided.

Three or four miles up the coast is **GREEN ISLAND**, a scruffy harbour town which is also home to the only secondary school for miles around – consequently much of Negril's burgeoning youth population commutes here daily. If there are few good reasons to stop here, just up the coast **Cousin's Cove** has a lot more rootsy appeal. Visitors could be forgiven for thinking this is just another sleepy community, but a read of Guy Kennaway's two hilarious novels about Jamaican village life, *One People* (see p.307), quickly dispels the sentiment. Accessed by means of two turns of the main highway, the first (more scenic) turn-off is somewhat hard to find, and the second at the far end of the village is confusingly marked "Davis Cove"; readers of the novels may not be surprised by the sign mix-up. Cousin's Cove has a lovely enclosed bay and a couple of places to **stay**. *Cove House* (❸) is an attractive four-bedroom villa owned by Kennaway (for bookings Ⓦwww.cousinscovehouse.co.uk, or in Jamaica phone Nerissa ℗427 1965). Next door is *Byron's Bar*, where someone can be found for fishing or boat rides. Just after the second turn-off on the main road, *Sunset Village* (℗899 7400; ❶) is a simple local bar offering lodging in a couple of wooden huts in its well-maintained garden. Nearby on the inland side of the main road at **Lance's Bay**, the main attraction is **Ron's Arawak Cave** (daily 9am–5pm; 2hr tour US$10; ℗426 6315), signposted from the road. The impressive cave is a mile long, with intricate stalactite formations and faint markings on the wall made by bat guano miners, themselves long since gone. You can also stay not far from the cave at *Sweet Breezes* (℗370 4733; ❷, with breakfast), an attractive collection of simple rooms set in a grassy clearing with space for **camping**.

Lucea and around

Another three miles, past stunning coves like **Bull Bay Beach**, where Henry Morgan (see p.85) moored ships during his respectable period as governor of Jamaica, **LUCEA** (pronounced Lucy) was a flourishing port town during the plantation era, its wharves thronged with ships exporting locally produced sugar. These days, only the occasional shipment of molasses leaves the docks, while agriculture here is focused on production of **Lucea yams**, a tasty tuber with excellent storing properties, exported in vast quantities to the Jamaicans who migrated in the nineteenth century to work on sugar plantations and the Panama canal in Central America.

Despite being the capital of Hanover, Lucea is no showpiece; peeling paint pervades and even the best buildings display broken windows or sagging walls. Despite this, it's a nonetheless beguiling jumble of austere stone architecture and salt-and-sun-bleached clapboard houses, gaudy store-fronts, and snack and rum bars, all clustered around a seething central bus park. Just beyond, the **Cleveland Stanhope Market** spills out onto the streets on Saturdays, and nearby is the imposing exterior of the once-majestic Georgian **town hall** and old **courthouse**, restored after decades of neglect. The roof of the courthouse is topped by an incongruously large **clock tower**. Still keeping perfect time after more than 170 years, the size of the clock betrays its misplacement – it was originally destined for St Lucia (Lucea's Spanish name was Santa Lucea) but arriving here by mistake, locals became so attached to it that they refused to exchange it for the modest timepiece originally ordered, raising the difference through public collections. The tower was built with funds from a local German planter, hence the distinctive nippled rooftop dome of a German army helmet. The town hall overlooks the official (traffic-clogged) town square, formally dedicated as **Alexander Bustamante Square** by England's Queen Elizabeth in 1966, and used as a period set for parts of the movie *Cool Runnings*.

Lucea's western portion contains many older buildings; noticeable is the cut-stone steeple of **Hanover Parish Church**, dating back to 1725 with some fine monuments, while the cemetery's walled area is a **Jewish burial ground**, presented in 1833 to the large Jewish community who settled here during Lucea's commercial heyday. Toward the sea behind the church, **Rusea's School** (Mon–Sat 8am–4pm; free) was established in 1777 by a benefaction from French religious refugee Martin Rusea, so grateful for the help he received when washed ashore at Lucea that he bequeathed his estate to the parish; disgruntled relatives contested the will for ten years after his death in 1764, without success. The school moved to the present site, an old army barracks, in 1900. Just past the school, through a small truck-repair yard, is near-derelict **Fort Charlotte**, restored in 1761, though no one is sure when the foundations were first laid. Three original cannons remain, and it has a sweeping view across the harbour. Also on the Negril side, scrubby playing fields mark the way to **Watson Taylor Beach**; it's not one of Jamaica's best beaches but the swimming is reasonable and water clean. Overlooking the beach and accessed most directly from the main road by the Catholic Church is the interesting though run-down **Hanover Museum** (Mon–Fri 8.30am–4.30pm; J$150; ☏956 2584). A former barracks, the red-brick building has served as a prison, police station and firing range, while blackened timbers attest to the fire that almost destroyed it in 1985. In honour of the settlements discovered at nearby Mosquito Cove (see p.230), there's a small collection of Taino artefacts flanked by a traditional silk cotton tree canoe, and the main museum offers a surprisingly comprehensive glimpse into local history, with several aerial photos of Hanover, old English weights and measures displayed alongside records of the West African ancestors of various Lucea citizens, and a copy of a harbour map hand-drawn by Captain William Bligh, who lived in Lucea for four years.

Chief Busta

Wild-haired and brutishly handsome, **Sir William Alexander Bustamante**'s physical stature, charismatic appeal and legendary appetite for women earned him a fond notoriety in the ribald world of Jamaican politics. Born Alexander Clarke on February 24, 1884, into an impoverished family working on the Blenheim estate, Bustamante rose to political prominence through a mixture of insight, cunning and cynical manipulation of the illiterate populace who worshipped him as **"Busta"** or simply "Chief".

He left Jamaica at nineteen in search of better prospects, and his years away are veiled in mystery, though he's said to have laboured and cut cane alongside other migrants. He returned nearly thirty years later with an assumed surname and enough wealth to become a small-time money lender, a shrewd move that gave him clandestine influence before he entered the political arena. The Jamaica that Bustamante returned to was still firmly languishing under Britain's imperial grip. Working conditions for those lucky enough to have a job were abysmal, and the polarities between the ruling browns and whites and black majority were as sharp as ever. Settling in Kingston, Bustamante began to win worker's support through outspoken condemnation of inequality. By 1938 his "fire and brimstone" warnings of racial violence and black revolution (designed to scare the colonial authorities into action) were almost realized; fanned by Bustamante's inflammatory rhetoric, a violent confrontation between police and workers broke out at the West Indies Sugar Company in Frome, Westmoreland, sparking a wave of strikes that brought the island to a near standstill. Eclipsing the tentative support for black nationalist labour leader St William Grant, Bustamante formed the **Bustamante Industrial Trade Union** – still the main union today – and became the leader of the labour movement among the rank and file.

In 1940, distressed at the volatility of his speeches, the government seized on Bustamante's union involvement and imprisoned him as the ringleader of the 1938 unrest. On his release in 1942, he formed the **Jamaica Labour Party** and swept to victory in the island's first election in 1944, trouncing his first cousin Norman Manley's People's National Party so decisively that Manley lost even in his own constituency. Though the PNP enjoyed a few years of power between 1955 and 1961, it was the JLP that ruled through independence in 1962, and Sir Bustamante (he was knighted by Queen Elizabeth II in 1954) who danced with Princess Margaret during the ensuing celebrations. He remained active in politics until 1967 and died a National Hero on August 6, 1977, at age 93.

The Lucea Infirmary is adjacent to the museum (☏ 956 2911). A visit here in 1995 inspired American gerontologist Paul Scott Rhodes to set up JAFIS, a charity that brings financial and practical aid, such as wheelchairs and sheets, to thirteen hospitals around Jamaica as well as homeless shelters, and also encourages visits to the residents. If you wish to donate or take part in JAFIS' working vacations, phone ☏ 350 0077 or email ✉ DrPaulShalom@yahoo.com.

You're unlikely to want to **stay** in Lucea, but if you favour rural communities, a good choice is *Global Villa* (☏ 956 2916, 0121 554 1410 in the UK, ⊛ www.global villajamaica.com; ❷–❸), a friendly, clean air-conditioned guesthouse west of town at Esher. For **eating**, numerous Jamaican restaurants and cookshops are found around town and the market. All **minibuses** connecting MoBay and Negril stop at Lucea's central bus park; fares are around J\$250 to either destination.

Blenheim and the Dolphin Head Mountains

From Lucea town centre, a twenty-minute drive inland along the B9 will take you to **BLENHEIM**, birthplace of National Hero Alexander Bustamante (see box above). The shack in which Jamaica's first prime minister grew up has been converted into a small but interesting **museum** (daily 9am–5pm; J$250; call JCDT ☎956 3898 for more details) celebrating Bustamante's life and achievements. Though the building was gutted by fire late in 2005, refurbishments have largely been completed, and the grounds make a great picnic spot, with plenty of shade and staggering views.

The surrounds form a part of the **Dolphin Head Mountains**, a languid series of low-lying hills said to resemble a dolphin – though no one seems to know *where* you get this perspective. The range rises to 1789ft and is known for its abundant bird life, plus 23 endemic plants, including species of orchid and bromeliad. Most of the hillocks are partially cultivated by small-scale farmers, and there's none of the cool air or remoteness of full-scale ranges like the Blue Mountains (see Chapter 2). There are no **organized tours** in the area, though you may be able to arrange an ad hoc guide at the tiny village of **Askenish** on the Lucea East River, the nearest settlement to the highest peak, or at Mayfield Falls in Westmoreland (see p.233).

Mosquito Cove to Tryall

Just east of Lucea, the sprawling monstrosity that is the *Grand Palladium Lady Hamilton Resort* looms into view, while a couple of miles further east, a turn-off from the highway at *Eddie's Highway Pub* leads to pretty **Mosquito Cove**, named for the perfect breeding ground of the Maggoty River shallows; several tributaries meet here, spanned by a tiny stone bridge. The pesky mites didn't deter the Amerindians – **Taino settlements** were based here, though not a hint of them remains today. Instead there's a small **beach** of pebble-strewn yellow sand lined by wind-bent palms – assorted flotsam and jetsam hint at the strong undertow, so stick to paddling. There are a couple of bar-cum-jerk spots and craft stalls nearby.

Inland of Mosquito Cove, horses graze in clipped pastures dotted with the odd run-down windmill, relics of the plantation days when the land was part of the Kenilworth estate. A superb example of old industrial architecture, Kenilworth's **great house** now serves as the HEART (Human Employment and Resource Training) Academy, a further education college, signposted just past the cove (daily 9am–5pm; free; ☎953 5315). There are no guided tours, but you can go in and have a look around the surrounding mills, boiling houses and distillery, all now under the protection of the Jamaica National Heritage Trust.

A mile or so further on the coast road is the Blue Hole Estate, base of **Chukka Caribbean Adventure Tours** (☎953 5619, ⓦwww.chukkacaribbean.com). The well-organized company offers several kinds of trip into Jamaica's western interior, popular with large parties from the Montego Bay cruise ships and all-inclusive hotels (see Montego Bay listings, p.169). Its classic "Horseback Ride 'n' Swim" tour (2hr 30min; US$75/person) takes riders through lush mountain scenery and through the shallow waters of the Blue Hole Bay itself.

Some ten miles west of Montego Bay, a towering **water wheel** at the roadside marks the old **Tryall Estate**, a once huge sugar plantation destroyed in the Christmas Rebellion (see p.181) that's now Jamaica's most prestigious **golfing hotel**. Until 1996, *The Tryall Club* (☎956 5660, ⓦwww.tryallclub.com; ❾) hosted the annual Johnnie Walker golf tournament, due to its well-kept, smoothly undulating eighteen-hole course. Reputedly it's the most challenging on the island, though you'll need deep pockets to examine it; non-*Tryall Club* guests pay US$170 per round plus mandatory caddie service. The hotel, in the plantation's refurbished great house, is unstintingly luxurious; rooms come with every conceivable trapping and most of the self-contained villas have private pools. The spacious beach is fully equipped for watersports, and there are tennis courts and a waterfall pool on site.

Negril to Savanna-La-Mar

Leaving Negril behind, Sheffield Road sweeps past cane fields neatly bordered by the Fish River hills en route to Savanna-la-Mar. After nine miles, a cluster of buildings around a petrol station signifies the start of **LITTLE LONDON**. Though the years have blurred racial origins, the town's population was once dominated by Indians who came to work as indentured labourers in the cane fields. There's little of obvious interest here; as you enter the town, a signposted right turn takes you to **Jamwest Raceway**, a drag-racing strip with bimonthly events (call ☎957 9360 for details) and, if you're hungry, a stop at *Winnies Kingfish Bar & Kitchen* reveals really good Jamaican cooking, including Ital specials. A turn right at the central crossroads, however, leads you down a paved road to the coast at **Broughton** and the idyllic **accommodation** option, ⚲ *Lost Beach Resort* (☎640 1111, 1-800/626 5678 in US, ⓦwww.lostbeachresort.com; ❸–❹); miles away from the frenzy of Negril but close enough by car to enjoy its amenities. Located right on a beautiful beach, each cabin or suite is spacious and comes with kitchenette, plus there's a swimming pool, bar and superb **restaurant** on site. Lobster and conch can be bought directly from local fishermen and then cooked by you or in the hotel's kitchen – which also serves possibly the finest roast breadfruit and ackee and saltfish breakfast anywhere in Jamaica (open to non-residents). Horseback riding, watersports and kayaking are also available.

Capital of Westmoreland it may be, but there's little to keep you in commercial **SAVANNA-LA-MAR** (known to most people simply as **Sav**). It's the area's main shopping centre, but as the profusion of low-lying concrete keeps the air still, it's a hot and uncomfortable place and most people depart as quickly as possible. Lying almost at sea level, successive hurricanes have flattened Sav through the centuries; in 1748 the wind drove the sea far enough up needle-straight thoroughfare **Great George Street** that boats were left dry-docked in the middle of the road. Today, most of the main street is taken up with pharmacies and general stores selling the usual assortment of imported designer bootlegs, though this is the place to go if you want some true Yardstyle string vests, bandannas, barely-there dancehall attire or **reggae music** from street vendors, all at half the price of Negril. Great George Street ends abruptly at the seashore, where you'll find the rough-around-the-edges main fruit and vegetable **market**.

All **buses** connecting Negril, Montego Bay, the south coast and Kingston stop at the bus park east from the top of Great George Street. With so many pleasant options nearby, there's no reason to **stay** in Sav-la-Mar, but you could join regulars and stay at *Orchard Great House* (☎955 2737; rooms have a/c and TV, plus there's a bar and pool; ❷) on Amity Road; or the smarter, businesslike *Hotel Comingle* on Hudson Street (☎918 1465; ❸). For the best vegetable patties for miles around, *Lucky Tree Pastry* is on the road leading out of town eastwards to Bluefields, and there are a couple of good eateries just west of town on the Negril road, serving jerk and Indian curry and roti. Nearby, the *Llandillo Centre* is Westmoreland's largest outdoor music venue, with major **reggae** shows throughout the year; look out for posters.

Inland from Sav

The flat savannah lands north and west of Savanna-la-Mar have proved ideal for the cultivation of cane, long meaning strong local ties to the **sugar industry**. A huge cane-processing factory lies at **FROME**, about five miles north of Sav, which handles most of the cane from neighbouring plantations (see box, p.232). Though the factory is not officially open to the public, you can arrange a tour by calling ahead (☎955 6080).

Of probably more interest to visitors, a few miles east near the small community of **Petersfield**, is **ROARING RIVER PARK** (daily 9am–5pm; US$15), approached on a badly rutted road that you'll probably need directions to find, though there are signposts from Sav. Still surrounded by cane fields, extensive **caves** by the river have been developed with tourists in mind, though it's still distinctly low-key. Unfortunately, the area suffers from unpleasant hustling from unofficial "tour guides"; make sure you get an official park guide from the TPDCO ticket office, who will take you on a trip round the caves and surrounding gardens. Bear in mind that on Saturdays the caves are accessible, but the landscaped park and gardens are closed – shake any persistent hustlers off firmly. Aside from this, the site is really very pretty – watercress grows wild along banks planted with palms and crotons, and the forested hillside rises up unbroken. Concrete walkways and lighting let you appreciate the full magnitude of the caverns, which range from broom cupboard to auditorium in size. Bats flit about, and there are two mineral pools for a disquieting swim in pitch-blackness – the water is said to rejuvenate. The caves are marred only by graffiti carved into the rock and jagged edges where the quartz has been levered off and sold.

The gorgeous **Blue Hole Garden** (daily 8am–6pm; US$8; ☏ 955 8823, ⓦ www.jamaicaescapes.com) is located a five-minute drive or ten-minute walk further; take a left turn and continue through the village – no guide is necessary. Overhung with trees and flowers, the thirty-foot-wide natural spring of refreshing chilly azure water is said to be bottomless – the true depth has never been charted. The surrounding gardens are well kept and packed with unusual trees, anthuriums, narcotic white trumpet flowers, and every variety of heliconia; the helpful staff will answer any questions you have. There is also a sculptured pool to immerse yourself amid gushing mini-waterfalls. The tranquil atmosphere of the place is well worth experiencing overnight – if you want to **stay** there are two simple thatched cabins (❷) right in the garden (with mosquito screen and outdoor shower

Sugar wars

The centre of some of Jamaica's most violent labour disputes, **Frome sugar factory** was built in 1938 by British company Tate and Lyle's subsidiary West Indies Sugar Company as the most modern facility in the West Indies. It is now government-run under the Sugar Company of Jamaica.

The factory has long been beset by industrial disputes. Constructed during a period of high unemployment, it drew job seekers in their thousands. Most were unlucky, and even those who were given jobs received a pittance far lower than the salary they'd been promised. Under the fiery leadership of **Alexander Bustamante**, the workers banded together in protest. The dispute swiftly turned ugly; cane fields were set on fire and a full-scale riot broke out on May 3, 1938. The unrest left four dead from police bullets and one hundred demonstrators, including Bustamante, in jail.

Frome's volatile reputation endures, and it has been the centre of more recent difficulties, triggered by the **decline** of the Jamaican sugar industry. Inadequate technological advancement, combined with the crippling effect of having to compete in a free market following the WTO ruling that led to the removal of preferential tariffs to EU countries, has had a devastating effect. Re-mechanization is often argued to be the only solution, but the inevitable loss of hundreds of manual jobs has understandably generated animosity. Though local producers are making attempts to diversify, Frome remains the largest single employer in Westmoreland, and the only solution may be to follow Brazil's lead and look to the production of ethanol. Two hundred years after sugar made Jamaica the richest of Britain's colonies, the future of the crop in Jamaica has never looked less secure.

▲ Mayfield Falls

and toilet), and **camping** is allowed (US$20); another, smarter, wooden cottage is located on the hill above, with a kitchen, living room and large verandah with marvellous view (❹). **Food** and **drink** is available from the *Lover's Café*; for a relatively remote spot, the Jamaican menu is excellent, including vegetable patties, garlic bread, spicy dumplings, fish and Ital options.

Another five miles inland, on the Westmoreland side of the Dolphin Head Mountains (see p.230) are the 22 mini-cascades and numerous swimming spots at **Mayfield Falls**. Two (non-amicable) tour operators, Original Mayfield Falls (☎953 3034 or 3046, ⓦwww.mayfieldfalls.com) and Riverwalk at Mayfield Falls (☎957 3444, ⓦwww.riverwalkatmayfield.com), have sites a hundred yards apart on opposite sides of the river and charge the same entry fee (US$18). Both offer the identical experience of a tranquil guided walk (leave a tip) through bamboo-shaded cool water with swimming holes every twenty yards – a fabulous, sensuous treat compared to the contrivances of the more famous Dunn's River Falls (see p.230). It's not the easiest of places to find, however, if you're going independently: signs dot the route from Frome and Roaring River (and from Tryall via Pondside in Hanover), but you may have to ask for directions multiple times. To avoid getting lost, go with a local or join the Original Mayfield Falls' round-trip tour from Negril or MoBay (US$85 including lunch). Wear a swimming costume and bring flip-flops as the stones are tough on bare, wet feet – mosquitoes can also be a problem. Hiking guides are available for walks in the surrounding hills.

Bluefields and Whitehouse

The contiguous coastal communities east of Savanna-la-Mar are laid-back places, with picturesque fishing beaches and reef-fringed shallows backed by hillsides dense with forest and farmers' smallholdings. Inordinately relaxed, a few communities have become favoured destinations for eco-tourism, with some returning year after year.

233

The coast road becomes the A2 along this stretch, and, around three miles from Sav, passes **Paradise Park** (Mon–Sat 8.30am–4.30pm; US$7; ☎848 9826, ©paradise1 @cwjamaica.com), marked by a drive of royal palms. A 2000-acre cattle ranch and dairy, the estate also offers swimming in the Sweet River, hiking in beautifully varied terrain (guides are available), and hour-long **horse rides** (9am–3pm; US$40; moonlit midnight rides possible), which pass along a private white-sand beach and around the eighteenth-century great house.

After the Ferris Cross junction (to Montego Bay), the A2 sticks close to the sea and passes through long, linear community **Cave**, before arriving at **Bluefields Beach**, marked by signs to *Bluefields Beach Park*, a collection of units selling drinks, jerk chicken and full Jamaican meals, which gets very busy at weekends. The *Fresh Touch* restaurant is thought of as the best, with tasty fried and steamed fish served up by Miss P. The narrow white-sand public beach here, together with the

Peter Tosh

Consciously controversial, **Peter Tosh** (born McIntosh) was Jamaica's best-known lyrical agitator. Born an only child in Belmont on October 19, 1944, he was raised by an aunt in the west Kingston tenement yards dominated, at the time, by the explosion of harmony groups that transformed post-independence Kingston into a hotbed of aspirations. Every newly arrived country "bhuttu" (or bumpkin) wanted to be a singer and Tosh followed suit, embarking on a mission to reveal home truths from a ghetto perspective. He saved to buy his first guitar and in 1964 formed vocal trio The Wailers with teenage allies Bunny Livingstone and Bob Marley. In 1972 they signed to Chris Blackwell's Island label, and recorded *Catch a Fire* and *Burnin'* together while Tosh put out tracks on his own Intel Diplo HIM label (Intelligent Diplomat for His Imperial Majesty), all the time becoming increasingly bitter over pay and personal disputes with the man he referred to as "Whiteworst". By 1974, he and Bunny Livingstone had gone their separate ways.

Having already earned a reputation as the Wailers' social conscience and an uncompromising egotist, Tosh took on the mantle of chief critic of what he called Jamaica's "**Babylon shitstem**" (system), publicly berating politicians for double standards and hypocrisy and lighting spliffs on stage with a cool disregard for the law. His bellicose militancy did him no favours with the island's police; in 1975 he was busted on a trumped-up ganja charge and beaten to within an inch of his life. As soon as his wounds had healed, he answered back with *Whatcha Gonna Do*, a cocky release chiding the futility of police brutality, smokers' anthem *Legalize It* and the defensive *Can't Blame the Youth* – inevitable airplay bans ensured record sales and Tosh cemented his position as the roots reggae revolutionary.

Tosh stayed in Jamaica, but his status and fortune – collaboration with the Rolling Stones in 1978 and a deal with EMI attracted global recognition – drew awkward parallels with the sufferers' lot he expostulated. In a country where money and fame draw a barrage of demands from old friends, causes and shady characters, the intensely spiritual and suspicious Tosh began to display signs of paranoia, believing himself both a victim of an establishment assassination conspiracy and haunted by duppies. His prophecies of destruction were fulfilled on September 11, 1987, when **gunmen** opened fire in his living room, killing him and two friends, and wounding five others. Rumours of the motive spread, some arguing that renowned "bad man" assassin Dennis "Leppo" Lubban was demanding financial retribution for a prison stint he saw as Tosh's rap, others muttering of a government-backed gagging.

Remembered by Jamaicans as a formidable ladies' man with a razor-sharp wit, Tosh himself provided his best biography; the "Red X" tapes, shot on scratchy film in a darkened room, show him philosophizing on his mantra, reggae and Rastafari and form part of the essential Tosh documentary *Stepping Razor Red X*.

deserted fishing beach at **BELMONT** beyond, are the main attractions of the area, and with a range of basic to exclusive **accommodations**, they're a good place for to relax and meet local people.

BLUEFIELDS is where pirate Henry Morgan sailed from to attack Panama in 1670, and the calm seas and sheltered bay have attracted every generation of Jamaican settler. The most interesting building is the privately owned but now virtually derelict **Bluefields House**, uphill from the police station. It was once a temporary home to Philip Gosse, "father of Jamaican ornithology" and inventor of the modern aquarium, who researched *Illustrations of the Birds of Jamaica* and *A Naturalist's Sojourn in Jamaica* during an eighteen-month residence in 1844–45. In the gardens stands a **breadfruit tree** said to be one of the first in Jamaica, planted by Captain Bligh when he brought seedlings from Tahiti (see p.110). Bluefields merges imperceptibly into **Belmont**, birthplace of the late **Peter Tosh** (see box opposite). His body lies a mile east through the village – in a small red-gold-and-green **mausoleum** (daily 9am–5pm; US$15) just off the main road, decorated with stained glass, photos and press cuttings. It's much less of an affair than the Marley mausoleum in St Ann (see p.160) and is often deserted. Upgrades by Tosh's family – his mother lives in a modest house at the back of the property – means there's now a small car park, along with CDs and T-shirts on sale and hand-painted signs that exhort you to light up a spliff on your way in.

Without your own transport you'll have to rely on **buses** and **route taxis** between Savanna-la-Mar and Whitehouse, which although running frequently on weekdays, can be virtually nonexistent on evenings and Sundays. For local **information**, as well as **Internet** access, visit the Bluefields People's Community Association (T373 6435) at Belmont "Square" – the main crossroads. For **food**, *Belmont Sands Ocean Edge* ("Miss Dorrit's") serves great fresh fish and chicken by the beach – though best-value food cooked alfresco is found at *Robert's* a short way beyond.

Accommodation

Bluefields Villas Bluefields T 202/232 4010 in US, W www.bluefieldsvillas.com. Scattered along the bay are five beautifully furnished villas in old-world colonial style; all fully staffed, with beach, jetty, pool, jacuzzi and fabulous ocean views. Villas sleep two to twelve people. All-inclusive: US$5000 to US$8000 per week, for four in low season.

Horizon Belmont T 955 8823, 602/942 7633 in US, W www.jamaicaescapes.com. Friendly guesthouse at the eastern end of Belmont, with two smart cabins, each with kitchenette (though a cook is available) and wonderful outdoor shower. Small private beach and jetty, tours available. ❹

Natania's Guesthouse Colloden, Whitehouse T 963 5349 or 883 3009. An attractive house set in gardens with sea view and swimming pool. All have private bathroom, TV and a/c. Meals and drinks available, served on the spacious verandah overlooking the sea. ❸

Nature Roots c/o Brian, Belmont T 955 8162 or 384 6610. Great budget option, near the sea at the heart of the village. Basic cabins rent whole or by the room, each with kitchenette and bathroom.

Rasta owner Brian is a fountain of knowledge on the area and can provide boat and hiking tours; meals available. ❶

Shades Cottage Belmont T 441 1830, W www.shadescottage.com. Next to *Nature Roots*, Bigga and family rent seven rooms, each with double or twin beds. There's a bar squeezed in between the cabins, and meals are provided on request. Negotiable for longer stays. ❶

Shafston Great House c/o Frank Lohmann, Bluefields (call ahead for pick-up) T 869 9212 or 997 5076, W www.shafston.com. Inexpensive option above the bay, with one of the best views this side of the island. Large rooms with en-suite or shared bathroom, plus pool, bar/ restaurant, pool table, hammocks and extensive grounds, in which there's an adrenaline-pumping canopy zip line. All-inclusive, ❺

Sunset Cottage Belmont Dist, Bluefields PO T 955 8007. Right on the rocky shoreline in the centre of Belmont, a collection of somewhat kitsch rooms, each with bathroom, kitchenette and verandah. Laundry, and a gazebo over the water for chilling out. ❷

Whitehouse and Font Hill Beach Park

As you continue along the A2 – through land known as **Surinam Quarters** in honour of the English who resettled here when the formerly British colony was captured by the Dutch in 1667 – the scenery becomes drier, with swathes of pasture and plenty of cattle. The road swings away from the coast, but there are still some nice places to swim; ask locals to direct you to the best spots. Formerly the best of the bunch, a beautiful beach-fringed isthmus just before **Culloden** village, is now the site of the first all-inclusive on the south coast, the problem-plagued *Sandals Whitehouse European Village*. Why people would visit Jamaica to stay in a European village is anybody's guess, and the resort certainly split the community. While offering seasonal employment, the desecration of such a pristine natural environment outraged many. The crocodiles formerly resident of the mangrove swamp here proved very hard to eradicate; the resort then suffered a series of infrastructural and political disasters, with the resignation of a senior government official in 2006 amidst allegations of corruption.

One of the main fishing ports on the south coast, **WHITEHOUSE**, just beyond Culloden, offers little beach life but plenty of commercial bustle with a fruit and vegetable **market** (Wed & Sat) and **fishing beach**, where on afternoons you can see huge hessian bags of flapping specimens weighed and bartered over, while women scale furiously. Boats return here from trips that can last as long as a week, with the fish transported islandwide.

Past Whitehouse, a popular spot amongst Jamaicans for a day or two by the sea is the signposted **Font Hill Beach Park** (Mon–Sun 9am–5pm; J\$250, J\$120 for kids), part of the wider Font Hill Wildlife Sanctuary. There's a small beach bar and ice cream shop, though visitors usually bring picnics to eat on the lovely, if compact, stretch of clean white sand, with good snorkelling at the offshore reef. Across the road is the entrance to the three-thousand-acre sanctuary – originally established for swimming and leisure, though also serves as a refuge for the endangered **American crocodile**. About two hundred of the crocodiles live in the swamps at the eastern edge, and many bird species – doves, pelicans, egrets and herons – are to be found. If you want to **stay** here, the smart *Font Hill Villas* each have air conditioning and cable TV (☎462 9011; ❸), while guided walks are organized for guests and non-guests alike. Buses between Black River and Sav-la-Mar or Whitehouse can drop you outside the entrance.

The coast road marks the Westmoreland/St Elizabeth border with a cache of purpose-built fish and bammy stalls at **SCOTT'S COVE** (also know simply as **Border**), manned by enthusiastic vendors who crowd around anything that stops.

6

The south

CHAPTER 6

Highlights

❋ **Black River safari** Jamaica's longest river, complete with water hyacinths, mangroves full of roosting egrets and surprisingly tame crocodiles. See p.243

❋ **Pelican Bar boat trip** Thwack through the waves in a fishing pirogue and enjoy an ice-cold beer at the bar, built on a sandbar a mile offshore. See p.249

❋ **Jack Sprat, Treasure Beach** Funky and laid-back, this is the quintessential south-coast beach bar. See p.251

❋ **Milk River Spa** This wonderfully ramshackle colonial-era spa hotel offers the chance to soak away aches and pains in the second-most radioactive water in the world. See p.254

❋ **Pepper shrimp, Middle Quarters** Spicy and delicious, the peppered river shrimp sold at the roadside here are legendary. See p.255

❋ **YS Falls** Surrounded by spectacular rainforest-edged farmland, the falls here come equipped with a Tarzan-style rope swing over the water. See p.255

❋ **Appleton Estate rum distillery tour** Hemmed in by the egg-box cockpits in the gorgeous Nassau Valley, the scenery here is as spectacular as the effect of tasting seventeen luscious varieties of rum and liqueurs. See p.257

▲ *Jack Sprat*, Treasure Beach

6

The south

Mass tourism has yet to reach Jamaica's **southern** parishes – the beaches aren't packed with sun-ripened bodies and there still remain some great off-the-beaten-track places to visit. If you're after watersports and heavy-duty nightlife, stick to the coastal resorts, but if you want to catch a glimpse of Jamaica as it was before the boom, head south. It takes a bit of extra effort to get here, and you'll need a car or a tour to see some of the more remote highlights, but it's definitely worth it.

The parishes that make up south-central Jamaica are immensely varied, with the landscape ranging from mountain to scrubby cactus-strewn desert, and from typically lush vegetation to rolling fields more redolent of the English countryside. To the west, in the beautiful parish of St Elizabeth, **Black River** is the main town, an important nineteenth-century port that today offers popular **river safaris** and a handful of attractive colonial-era buildings. If you're after somewhere to stay and swim, **Treasure Beach** is a better target; it's an extremely laid-back place with lovely black-sand beaches and some unique accommodation options fast making it a major destination in the south. As for touring around, you can make for the **Appleton Estate rum distillery** on the cockpit fringes, the fabulous **YS waterfalls** or drive around the tiny villages of the attractive and untouristed **Santa Cruz Mountains**.

Further east, the parishes of Manchester and Clarendon are less diverse and a little less appealing. Manchester, with its cool evenings and misty mornings, has the major town of **Mandeville**, a very English inland touring base that makes a pleasant, if unspectacular, change from the coast, and the much smaller market town of **Christiana**, an unspoilt retreat with a single, delightful old hotel. Along the coast, there's marvellous river and sea swimming, and some great fish restaurants at Alligator Pond, while the combination of mineral spring and black-sand beach at **Guts River** provides one of the most picturesque spots on the entire island. The parish of Clarendon is total farming country, with large citrus groves in the north and sugar-cane fields everywhere else, but it offers a handful of unusual places to visit including the mineral spa at **Milk River**.

Although remnants of the once lucrative **bauxite** industry are still around (in the form of massive empty factories and dried-up red mud lakes) it is **agriculture** that has and continues to be, despite St Elizabeth's dry climate, the main stay of the local economy, producing most of the country's agricultural surplus – and which is why it's known as Jamaica's "breadbasket". Recently, **tourism** has begun to make an impact, though it is unlikely ever to approach north coast levels. The emphasis is on small-scale, community-based, environmentally friendly tourism, avoiding the disruption to traditional lifestyles that the industry has caused elsewhere on the island.

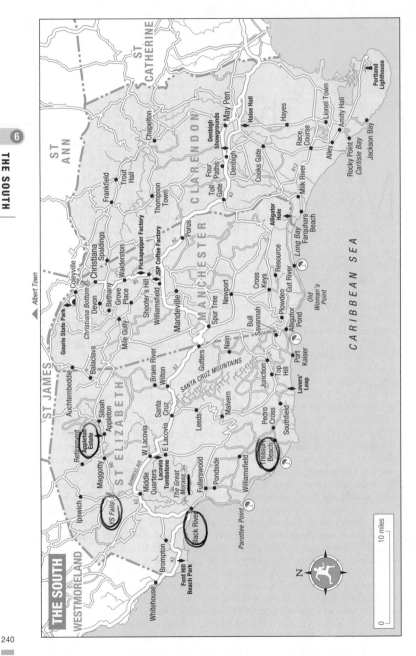

THE SOUTH

WESTMORELAND

ST JAMES

ST ELIZABETH

MANCHESTER

CLARENDON

ST ANN

ST CATHERINE

CARIBBEAN SEA

Albert Town

N

0   10 miles

Ipswich
Whitehouse
Brompton
Font Hill Beach Park
Black River
Parottee Point
Maggotty
Retirement
Appleton Estate
YS Falls
Auchtembeddie
Siloah
Appleton
Balaclava
Middle Quarters
Lacovia
W Lacovia
E Lacovia
Tombstone
The Great Morass
Fullerswood
Pondside
Williamsfield
Santa Cruz
Leeds
SANTA CRUZ MOUNTAINS
Malvern
Nain
Braes River
Wilton
Gutters
Treasure Beach
Pedro Cross
Southfield
Top Hill
Junction
Lovers' Leap
Port Kaiser
Alligator Pond
Old Woman's Point
Plowden
Gut River
Resource
Farquhars Beach
Long Bay
Alligator Hole
Milk River
Race Course
Alley
Rocky Point
Carlisle Bay
Jackson Bay
Lionel Town
Amity Hall
Portland Lighthouse
Hayes
Halse Hall
May Pen
Denbigh Showgrounds
Denbigh
Cooks Gate
Four Paths
Toll Gate
Chapelton
Thompson Town
Frankfield
Trout Hall
Coleyville
Christiana
Spaldings
Devon
Christiana Bottom
Bethany
Grove Place
Mile Gully
Shooter's Hill
Williamsfield
Pickapepper Factory
JSP Coffee Factory
Walderston
Mandeville
Spur Tree
Newport
Porus
Bull Savannah
Cross Keys
Gourie State Park
A1
B6
BAMBOO AVE
N2
A2
A2
B12

Getting around

Regular **buses** and **minibuses** ply the main routes between Kingston and Negril, giving easy access to the main towns of May Pen, Mandeville, Santa Cruz and Black River. From these centres, a network of buses and route (shared) taxis fan out to smaller towns like Christiana, Treasure Beach and Malvern. **Driving** is the best way to see the hidden parts of the south although car-less travellers can also opt for taking a relay of route taxis that link with each other trekking to smaller towns where most public transportation doesn't go. Many of the main attractions in the interior, however, like YS Falls and Appleton, are somewhat off the beaten track and can be hard to reach without your own set of wheels. That said, Jamaican roads are not for the faint-hearted and in the south they are notoriously bad. Potholes packed with marl or gullies on the smaller, coastal roads (a result of poor drainage and a series of bad hurricanes in the last few years), will, if you approach them aggressively, take the bottom out of your car or at least damage your tyres.

The south coast

Though without the turquoise seas and white-sand beaches of the north, Jamaica's southern coastline is among the most spectacular on the island. The scenery is wild and unspoilt, with giant cacti standing sentry at the roadside and thickets of makka thorn bushes, wetland morass and twisted mangroves giving way to glimpses of undeveloped coves, the volcanic sand twinkling in the sunlight. You'll need a car to see most of it at your own pace as buses and minibuses tend to stick to the main, inland roads, leaving route taxis to make side-trips down to coastal villages as required.

Of the area's towns, **Black River**, the largest in St Elizabeth, merits a visit for its crumbling architectural gems and **river safari** into the Great Morass. Further round the coast, close-knit, laid-back **Treasure Beach** is probably the best place on the island to just stop, chill out and de-stress for a couple of days. It offers a brand of community tourism that's entirely different from anywhere else in Jamaica, a fact that the island's visitors are fast catching on to. Further east still, there are the seafood restaurant and quiet beaches of **Alligator Pond** and the mineral spa at dry and dusty **Milk River Bath** is the perfect place to soothe away any aches and pains.

If you spend any time in this part of Jamaica, you'll appreciate the importance of the local **fishing industry**. Tiny fishing villages are scattered along the coast, with boats pulled up on stretches of the beach; even in tourist areas like Treasure Beach, fishing remains vital to the local economy. Many of the fishermen head for the **Pedro Banks**, a series of sandy cays in rich, but treacherous, fishing waters some eighty miles south. Over the years, full-scale communities have become established on these tiny blips in the ocean, and the abandoned behaviour of the fishermen and the few women who live on them semi-permanently are the stuff of local legend. However, things on the cays are more organized these days, with a police post ensuring some semblance of order, and two-way radio transmitters, provided at cost price by the Treasure Beach community organization BREDS (see p.250), giving fishermen a vital link with the mainland. The cays are the preserve of Jamaica's hardiest fishermen, so not a destination for a day-trip, but if you want to try your hand at fishing JA-style, ask around at any of the fishing villages.

Black River and around

Although it's St Elizabeth's largest town, **BLACK RIVER** is a quiet spot, and most travellers only nip in briefly to take a boat trip on the river in search of crocodiles, or stay a couple of nights whilst exploring the delights of western St Elizabeth. It wasn't always this way, though: in the mid-nineteenth century the town derived substantial wealth from the trade in logwood, used to produce black and dark-blue dyes for the textiles industry and exported in great quantities from Black River's port. For a brief period the trade helped to make the town one of the most influential in Jamaica, with electricity, the telephone and the car all first introduced to the island here, and a big racecourse west of town. However, with the introduction of synthetic dyes, the trade in logwood began to dry up, and today, the only signs of those illustrious days are some wonderful but decrepit old gingerbread houses. Just beyond Black River going east is secluded **Parottee**, which has also begun to promote its fledgling tourism product. Visitors are slowly coming to this quiet fishing village to explore nearby swamplands and go birdwatching, take boat tours to **Pelican Bar** – a ramshackle bird's-nest of a bar built on a sand bar half a mile off Parottee Point; see p.249 – or simply enjoy miles of the pristine, all-to-yourself, golden-sand beaches just beyond the main road. If you have time to spare, Black River and Parottee are worth a couple days of gentle exploration.

The nicest thing to do in Black River itself is to take a stroll along the **waterfront**, particularly attractive around sunset, and check out the old wooden buildings, many with gorgeous colonnaded verandahs and gingerbread trim and most in a perilous state of near-collapse. The **Waterloo Guesthouse**, built in 1819, is reputed to have been the first place in Jamaica to get electricity – installed to provide air conditioning for racehorses kept in the old stables – and to have boasted the island's first telephone. Nearby, the **Invercauld Hotel** (no longer a hotel and at time of writing closed to the public) was built in 1889. With its lavish fretwork and spacious floor plans, it reflects the confidence of the town during its heyday. As you head back towards the town centre, you'll see goats roaming the grounds of **St John's**, the tidy parish church; it dates from 1837 and has marble monuments to Robert Munro and Caleb Dickenson, benefactors of two of the schools at nearby Malvern.

Practicalities

Buses and **minibuses** stop in the typically chaotic bus-park behind the market, just off the High Street. Given that few tourists stop over in Black River, much less Parottee, there's a surprisingly decent selection of places to stay. Most of the cheaper options are just east of town on Crane Road, across the iron bridge and running parallel to the coastline towards Parottee. *Ashton Great House* (☎965 2036, ✉theashton@cwjamaica.com; ③–④) enjoys a completely stunning hilltop setting, with eye-popping views over the St Elizabeth/Westmoreland plains and the Santa Cruz Mountains. The 200-year-old great house bursts with period charm, all creaking, waxed wood floors and antique furniture. Rooms in the main house are the most characterful, but there are also appealing newer ones; all have air conditioning or fan, cable TV and phone. *Anke's Place* (62 Parottee Rd ☎ 965 2578; ❸), located across the bridge in Parottee, is an eclectic beachfront hideaway tucked away at the end of a long grass lawn, and has two small self-contained wooden beach cottages with one large room each, kitchenette, queen-size bed, mosquito nets and bathrooms with outdoor shower. Fresh seafood is the order of the day in this seaside town and *Cloggy's on the Beach* (Crane Rd) has a lovely setting by the sea, with tables under thatched gazebos, on the sand or inside by the bar. This is the best place in town for a cup of conch soup, curry conch or lobster, or a plate of fish (steamed with okra and pimento is lovely), served with rice, bammy and festival. *Tasty Food Restaurant* (Brigade St), inside an old, stone warehouse near the river, serves good home-cooked meals, such as brown stews of chicken and fish and curry goat. For snacks, try *Sunrise Bakery* (High St), which is well known for its traditional baked goods.

The Great Morass and the Black River Safari

The main reason most people come to the town is for a **boat safari** on the **Black River** itself, which, at 44 miles, is Jamaica's longest. The river – so named because the peat moss lining the river bottom makes the crystal-clear water appear an inky black – is fed by various tributaries as it makes its way down from Balaclava, on the Manchester/St Elizabeth border. It's the main source for the **GREAT MORASS** – a 125-square-mile area of wetland that spreads north and west of Black River and provides a swampy home for most of Jamaica's surviving crocodiles as well as some diverse and spectacular bird life. It's the best place to spot the crocodiles, a rapidly dwindling bunch now protected by law, who once lived in great numbers around the coast of Jamaica until hunting and the deterioration of the swamplands began to take their toll.

The boat tour is a very pretty trip into the Great Morass, although the term "safari" promises rather more excitement than it delivers. You do have a virtually guaranteed sighting of crocodiles (albeit fairly tame ones, most of which answer to their names), and there are some marvellous **mangrove swamps** where you can normally spot flocks of roosting egrets as well as whistling ducks, herons and jacanas, and you may run into the occasional shrimp- or crab-fisherman in his dugout canoe. To go on the sixty-minute tour (approx. US$16–17/person), turn up at the dock or contact **St Elizabeth River Safari** (☎ 965 2374) or **Black River Safari Boat Tours** (☎ 965 2513). Theoretically, you should be able to go straight away; there aren't any definite departure times but there is a minimum passenger load of three unless you are willing to pay an additional charge. Ask your tour operator about stopping at *Miss Lou's*, for some scrumptious crabs and a cold beer. For a more one-of-a-kind, adventurous and academic exploration of the river, contact **Irie Safaris** (☎ 965 2211, ⓦ www.lostriverkayak.com). It's run by wetland ecologist Lloyd Linton, who not only puts a more scientific spin on the standard safari tour but also runs **specialized ecology trips** (by prior arrangement only; rates negotiable). His latest venture – kayak tours (US$40/person) – couples a trip up the Black River with a one- to two-hour kayak of the virgin morass that is the upper reaches of the Broad River, one of the tributaries that feeds the Black River. Inaccessible by motorized boats, kayakers can enjoy the calm of the crystal waters while being guided by knowledgeable staff. You can also include a Black River safari on a boat trip from Treasure Beach (see p.249) or Parottee, which tends to be a less touristic way to see the river and its inhabitants.

Treasure Beach and around

South of the main A2 road between Black River and Mandeville, snoozy **TREASURE BEACH** is the bright spark of south-coast tourism. A string of laid-back fishing villages tucked under the Santa Cruz Mountains amidst some of Jamaica's most beautiful countryside, the area is the ultimate antidote to the island's more commercialized resorts. Tourism is very much a community concern here: many of the accommodation and eating places are owned by local families, and as there are no fenced-off all-inclusives to create a barrier between the locals and the visitors, everyone mixes easily together. One of the safest areas in Jamaica, this tight-knit, proud community has both a solid tourist infrastructure and a strong sense of its own traditional values. It's a tiny spot, with no neon beach-bars or jet skis and sun loungers on the beaches, and attracts a mix of hip, bohemian jet-setters and young backpackers who simply want to unwind and absorb Jamaica's gentler, more pastoral side. There's a good and ever-expanding range of **accommodation** options, including a delightfully eclectic collection of villas and beach cottages to rent, some great places to **eat** and a couple of diverting attractions, while the bays that make up the area feature some spectacular undeveloped golden-sand **beaches**.

The **Santa Cruz Mountains** rise up from the sea just east of Treasure Beach and run northwest, providing a scenic backdrop for the village and protecting the area from rain clouds coming from the north. As a result, Treasure Beach has one of the driest climates in the country, and the scrubby, desert-like landscape – red-earth savannahs strewn with cactuses and acacia trees – is often reminiscent of the African plains. Despite the dry weather, though, this is very much farming country, and you'll see rolling plantations of carrots, scallions, thyme, onions and watermelons scattered around the area. You may also notice that many of the residents have a very distinctive appearance – red or blonde hair; blue, green or yellow eyes; light skin and freckles – that is said to be the result of intermarriage between locals and a crew of Scottish sailors who were shipwrecked here in the nineteenth century. Whatever the reason, Treasure Beach's "red" men and women, as they're known, are famed islandwide for their unusual beauty.

Treasure Beach itself is made up of a string of loosely connected fishing settlements; the community is the closest point in Jamaica to the **Pedro Banks**. Many locals make month-long trips to the cays, braving dangerous seas and the elements in order to bring home what are often very rich pickings. Chances are, you'll stay on the long sandy sweep of **Frenchman's Bay**, where tourism has largely displaced fishing as the main industry, or smaller **Calabash Bay**, where you can still see brightly coloured fishing boats pulled up on the beach below the newly constructed villas and guesthouses. To the east, **Great Bay** remains a basic fishing village with a sprinkling of guesthouses and some spectacular scenery, while west of Frenchman's Bay the road runs out of town past Billy's Bay, home to some of the more upscale villas in Treasure Beach, some pretty deserted beaches and a lot of goats.

Arrival, information and getting around

Public-transport links with Treasure Beach are not great, although several **minibuses** and **route (shared) taxis** run daily from Black River and from Mandeville via Junction or Santa Cruz (you'll have to change bus/route taxi). A regular taxi costs around US$20 each way from Black River, more from Mandeville. If you're **driving**, there are several approaches to Treasure Beach. From the main A2 road between Santa Cruz and Mandeville, turn right at

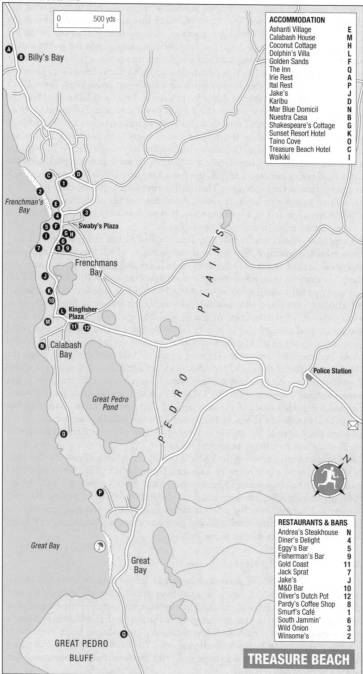

Fort Charles & Black River

0   500 yds

A   **B** Billy's Bay

Frenchman's Bay

C   **D**

2   **1**

E

4   **3**

5 **F**   Swaby's Plaza

I   **G** **H**

7   **8** **9**

Frenchmans Bay

J

K

10

L Kingfisher Plaza

M

11   **12**

N Calabash Bay

Great Pedro Pond

O

P

Great Bay

Great Bay

Q

GREAT PEDRO BLUFF

Police Station

Pedro Cross, Lovers' Leap, Junction & A2

Back Seaside

ACCOMMODATION	
Ashanti Village	E
Calabash House	M
Coconut Cottage	H
Dolphin's Villa	L
Golden Sands	F
The Inn	Q
Irie Rest	A
Ital Rest	P
Jake's	J
Karibu	D
Mar Blue Domicil	N
Nuestra Casa	B
Shakespeare's Cottage	G
Sunset Resort Hotel	K
Taino Cove	O
Treasure Beach Hotel	C
Waikiki	I

RESTAURANTS & BARS	
Andrea's Steakhouse	N
Diner's Delight	4
Eggy's Bar	5
Fisherman's Bar	9
Gold Coast	11
Jack Sprat	7
Jake's	J
M&D Bar	10
Oliver's Dutch Pot	12
Pardy's Coffee Shop	8
Smurf's Café	1
South Jammin'	6
Wild Onion	3
Winsome's	2

TREASURE BEACH

Gutters (opposite a large gas station) and follow the road south towards Nain and then Junction, where you veer right and head through Southfield and roughly 25 minutes later Pedro Cross, just north of the coastline. A turn-off to the left at Pedro Cross leads towards the coast – continue straight, past the police station and down a narrow winding road and you'll see a sign to the left for Great Bay or straight to Treasure Beach. You can also get to Pedro Cross from Santa Cruz via Malvern, a spectacular but bumpy drive on a badly pot holed road. From Black River, you can either take the A2 to Santa Cruz and turn south there, or take the small signposted right turn from the A2 just past Parottee at Fullerswood, from where a tiny, winding road runs though a series of quiet hamlets and then follows the coastline into Treasure Beach, past some bizarre ironshore rock formations and a string of small bays. Otherwise, the easiest way to get here is to organize a **private transfer**: Treasure Tours (T 965 0126, W www.treasuretours.info) and most local hotels can organize pick-ups from Kingston or MoBay airports as well as transportation for excursions. Though Treasure Beach is developing fast, there are still no cambios or banks in town; the nearest are in Southfield, Santa Cruz, Black River or Junction, a bustling town at the crossroads of Alligator Pond and coastal communities including Treasure Beach.

There's no official tourist office in Treasure Beach, but the town does have a comprehensive **website**, W www.treasurebeach.net, which lists accommodation and local sites of interest. Otherwise, most hotel and guesthouse operators are happy to share their local knowledge and arrange excursions; BREDS (see p.250) has also opened a small office in the King Fisher Plaza that acts as an informal information centre and **Internet café**. Several hotels including *Jake's* and *Sunset Villa* provide wireless service to guests and non-guests hanging out at their restaurants; otherwise bring your own laptop and surf with a sea view and a cold beer at *Jack Sprat* (see p.251), the first public "hotspot" in the area. As signs dotted along the roadsides announce, Treasure Beach is "bike country", and given the inconsistent state of the roads, periodically reduced to gullies following the severe flooding that has hit the area in recent years, a bicycle is an excellent way to **get around**. Andy Nembhard (T 438 1311) rents his mountain bikes for individual use and for guided tours of the area, and he also operates hiking and kayaking trips. Tours include a three- to four-hour kayak trip to Pelican Bar and a hike through Back Seaside (see p.250) of the Pedro Bluff in Great Bay. Rates depend on distance and how many people on the tour.

If you're interested in seeing the YS Falls, Gut River, Alligator Pond or other parts of the island from a base here, try **Treasure Tours** (T 965 0126, W www.treasure tours.info), a locally operated tour company that offers a personable experience. Run by the friendly, efficient and knowledgeable American émigré Rebecca Wiersma, Treasure Tours also offers transfers from MoBay and Kingston airports (as well as other resorts), hotel, villa and guesthouse booking and a taxi service for Treasure Tours guests staying in the area.

Accommodation

There is a wide variety of **accommodation** in Treasure Beach, from full-blown resorts and chic boutique hotels to numerous guesthouses and villas, the latter charging lower rates (US$50 per double is average) than in more developed parts of the island. More places are springing up all the time and, in addition, seemingly every other house is a rentable **villa**; these vary from simple beach cottages to luxurious and elegant homes with all mod cons. For a full listing of all accommodation options including villa properties, visit W www.islandoutpost.com/jakes and www.treasurebeach.net.

Ashanti Village Billy's Bay ☎ 433 1593 or 387 4887. Two, two-storey houses with one- and two-bedroom units, private bathrooms, kitchens, fans and small verandahs sit amidst a garden. The property's friendly owners live on-site, gladly share their local knowledge and will prepare meals for an additional cost. ❷–❹

Calabash House Calabash Bay ☎ 965 0126. Right on the sea, this is a cute, clean little place with four simply decorated rooms, a/c, private bathrooms, communal kitchen and large dining and living room. You can have the whole place (sleeps eight) or rent a room only. ❹

Coconut Cottage Frenchman's Bay ☎ 320 8867, 807/473 7595 in Canada. Three-storey house opposite Frenchman's Bay in downtown Treasure Beach. It includes five en-suite bedrooms with fans and screened windows, a small outdoor verandah on the second floor, fully equipped (shared) kitchen and a roof terrace. ❷

Dolphin's Villa Calabash Bay ☎ 823 3184. A five-minute walk from Calabash Bay beach, *Dolphin Villa* has five modestly decorated, clean bedrooms, some with a/c, others with fans and mesh, all en-suite. There is a communal kitchen and living area with a TV. Centrally located, the house can be rented by the room or as a whole. ❸–❹

Golden Sands Frenchman's Bay ☎ 965 0167, ✉ goldensandguesthouse@yahoo.com. A long- standing budget option in a prime position right on Frenchman's Beach. The basic, tile-floor rooms are either on the beach or a stone's throw from the beach, with fan or a/c, screened windows and en-suite bathrooms. All share a communal kitchen. There's also an apartment option with kitchen and dining room but no a/c. ❷–❸

The Inn Great Bay ☎ 965 0228 or 239 564 8976. The first small "hotel" in the fishing community of Great Bay, *The Inn* has six rooms, all en-suite with a/c; the rooms upstairs have tiny verandahs. Two minutes' walk from the beach and a small mini-mart. Guests can use the communal kitchen and dining area for their meals. ❷–❹

Irie Rest Billy's Bay ☎ 965 0034. Extremely friendly place set back from, but within walking distance of, the beach. Rooms are simple and inviting, with a/c, screened windows and en-suite bathrooms; some have huge screened verandahs. There's a cool communal area with a stereo and satellite TV. Great value. ❷

Ital Rest Great Bay ☎ 473 6145, 284 6186, ⓦ www.italrest.com. Two cottages only at this gentle, friendly and beautifully landscaped place within walking distance of a lovely swimming cove; each has separate rooms upstairs and down (ask for upstairs for the views and the breeze – there is no electricity) and a kitchen. A small bar with ping-pong table, meals are available on request and for an additional cost. There are also bicycle rentals. Turn right just before the *Sea Crab* restaurant and then take the first right. ❷–❸

🏃 Jake's Calabash Bay ☎ 965 3000, ⓦ www.islandoutpost.com/jakes. Run by the dynamic Jason Henzell, perhaps the main player in the local tourism scene, *Jake's* is a unique spot, bursting with imagination and personality. Each of the gorgeous, quirky rooms has its own hand-done decor, with earthy colours and intricate attention to detail; common touches include outdoor showers with mosaics of shells and coloured glass. Most of

Relaxation therapies

Treasure Beach's relaxed vibe lends itself well to a bit of pampering and luckily for visitors there are two independent masseurs and a new full-service spa offering just the cure for all your aches and pains.

Based in a small enclave at the entrance of Treasure Beach, herbalist and self-professed healer **Shirley Genus** (☎ 965 3820 or 366 1726) offers a great herbal steam bath prepared with organic herbs – a fantastically soothing experience. A fifteen-minute steam with a one-hour massage is US$90. Rates include round-trip transport from local hotels.

Treasure Beach's first full-service spa is the **Driftwood Spa** (☎ 564 2406) at *Jake's* (see above), where a small team of trained therapists offer an array of treatments including traditional Swedish, hot stone and aromatherapy massages, facials, mani-pedis, coffee and brown sugar scrubs and cooling mint wraps. Yoga and Pilates are also offered on most weekends (in season) and sometimes during the week. Also at the spa is Joshua Lee Stein (☎ 389 3698; 1hr US$75), who practises from a beautiful seafront therapy room and offers unique Intuitive Bodywork Massage that blends various traditional techniques with movement and healing energy.

the rooms have a/c, all feature mosquito nets and are screened, plus they have CD players and coffee makers. There's a fabulous saltwater pool, a good restaurant, a TV/library/games room and a bar that draws a genial local crowd. Standard garden-view rooms start at ④; suites, cottages and villas, ⑨.

Karibu Frenchman's Bay ☎965 0149 or 387 7231, 617/354 1719 from the US, ⓦwww.karibu cottage.com. Set behind the beach on a hillside, *Karibu* consists of two two-storey houses with verandahs overlooking the sea and access to the roof for sunning and night time chilling out. Cottage one sleeps up to six people, while cottage two has two, two-bedroom apartments, each with their own kitchen/living/dining rooms. ②–⑤

🏃 **Mar Blue Domicil** Old Wharf, Calabash Bay ☎965 3408, ⓦwww.marblue.com. A stylish boutique hotel on a secluded stretch of beach, with fabulous attention to detail. Spotless and fresh, rooms have a/c, balconies overlooking the sea, minibars and CD and DVD players, too. The new verandah villa suites have king-sized beds, small living areas and one has a private plunge pool. There are two small pools on the property, a bar and an excellent restaurant – breakfast is included in the rates. ⑦

Nuestra Casa Billy's Bay ☎876/965 0152, ⓦwww.billysbay.com. *Nuestra Casa* is a traditional English B&B run by Lillian Brooks and her son Roger Chamberlain, both expats who've made their home in Treasure Beach and rent out three simple and clean rooms in their villa at great budget rates. There's a shared living room and kitchen, sun deck and great English breakfast included. Good value

for money, across the road from the sea, and run by a very pleasant staff. ②–③

Shakespeare Cottage Frenchman's Bay ☎965 0120. Excellent budget option, with four basic but clean rooms in the main house, all with fans and shared bathrooms, and a kitchen for guests to use. In the new house, there are three simply decorated, clean, fan-only en-suite rooms; top rooms have small balconies with sea views – there's also a one-bedroom cottage for rent. ①–③

Sunset Resort Hotel Calabash Bay ☎965 0143, ⓦwww.sunsetresort.com. Incongruously and fabulously kitsch resort in a lovely seaside setting with Astroturf around the central pool and wonderfully gaudy Hawaiian-esque decor in the rooms. All are spacious, with a/c, wireless Internet access, fans, satellite TV and coffeemaker; self-catering cottages are also available. There's a restaurant on site. ④–⑤

Taino Cove Old Wharf ☎965 0126. Quiet and secluded this two-storey hotel features twelve en-suite rooms with a/c and high, artisan-designed wooden ceilings. There's also a pool and small, private beach cove. ⑤

Treasure Beach Hotel Frenchman's Bay ☎965 0110. A timepiece in the middle of Treasure Beach, this hotel remains the area's only full-blown resort with two pools, extensive gardens and a restaurant and bar. The newer suites with oceanfront views all have a/c, ceiling fan and satellite TV. ④

Waikiki Calabash Bay ☎965 0448. Rangy place set back from the road and overlooking the beach, with basic, clean rooms with fans and shared or private bathrooms. Brilliant if you're on a budget. ③

The town and the beaches

Spread on either side of the main coast road, Treasure Beach has no town centre as such, though things are busiest between *Jake's* in **Calabash Bay** and the *Treasure Beach Hotel* at the western corner of Frenchman's Bay, where restaurants and hotels line the road. Most people, though, divide their time between their hotel and the beautiful undeveloped **beaches**, most of which have fine black sand, body-surfable waves and crystal-clear water once you get out past the breakers; however, you'll need to watch the **undertow**, which can get strong at times; ask locally about present conditions. The best swimming is along the wide sweep of **Frenchman's Bay**, where there are few underwater rocks and several beach bars for snacks and drinks. The sweep of sand here is wide enough for late-afternoon football games amongst local lads, and it's a great spot to watch the sun go down. If you're not staying along Frenchman's and thus don't have direct access to the sand, you can get onto the beach via numerous footpaths. Frenchman's is also the departure point for **boat trips** along the coast, a brilliant way to see the area. You'll probably be approached by various operators on the beach (some of whom have questionable safety standards); best plan is to ask at your hotel who will recommend someone to you, or get in touch with Dennis "Shabba" Abrahams (☎965 3084, mobile 435 3779, ✉dennisabrahams@yahoo.com), an excellent and experienced boatman whose fishing pirogue is the fastest (and one of the most comfortable) in Treasure Beach.

An excellent and unusual excursion is to **Pelican Bar**, a sandspit offshore of Parottee Point, where enterprising local man Floyd has constructed a bar on stilts in the middle of the sea (2hr; $75). Other boating excursions offered by Dennis include a trip to Landacre beach for sunbathing and snorkelling (1–4 hr; $120). He'll also take you to *Little Ochi* (see p.252; 3hr 30min; $120); a ride up the coast and along Black River to see the crocodiles (4hr; $120); and line fishing ($60/hr). All prices are for two people, and there are good reductions for larger groups.

Another option is a sunset cruise on **Shabba's Shallow Bar** (a home-made catamaran partially shaded with a thatch roof that covers the bar; $20/person) that cruises from the famous twisted Buttonwood tree at the end of Jack Sprat beach to Great Bay and the Pedro Bluff when the weather is nice and the sea is calm. Joseph "Blacka" Brown (☎376 9944) is another reliable tour operator who offers a popular Kingfish Cook-Out tour – a day-long trip (weather permitting) that takes you to a private beach where he will cook up king fish or lobster and serve drinks. Call for prices and more information.

Great Bay and out to Lovers' Leap

On the outskirts of Treasure Beach, just beyond Pedro Cross police station, a turn-off to the right leads to **Great Bay**, the least geared for tourism of Treasure Beach's mini-communities, but perhaps the most physically beautiful, with a fabulous beach and a sprinkling of low-key guesthouses. This is primarily a fishing community, as demonstrated by the large Fishermen's Co-op building on the beach where the paved road ends, and many of the locals are regulars at the Pedro Banks. Aside from exploring the beach (there are several paths over rocky outcrops that lead to secluded coves), the only other thing to do in Great Bay is

▲ Fishing boats, Treasure Beach

BREDS

This nonprofit association was established in 1998 by Jason Henzell of *Jake's* and Peace Corps volunteer Aaron Laufer to promote awareness of Jamaican cultural heritage, sports development, entrepreneurship and healthcare for the residents of Treasure Beach. **BREDS** (☎965 0748, ⓦww.breds.org), short for "bredrin", Jamaican slang for friend, has had a tangible positive impact on quality of life in Treasure Beach. BREDS embodies the strength of this close-knit community, very much a place where people look out for one another. By way of grants and donations, as well as the profits from annual events such as the triathlon and fishing tournament and sale of T-shirts and postcards, BREDS raises money that has gone to hurricane relief funds (building homes and donating fishing boats), paying for remedial teachers, constructing a playground and most recently creating a partnership with **Jamaica National Foundation** that aims to nurture (amongst other initiatives) local entrepreneurship. The organization is always on the lookout for visitors who can contribute to the cause (*Jake's* even offers Voluntourism opportunities – see their reception for details), whether in cash or kind. BREDS merchandise is also on sale at *Jake's*. For more on upcoming projects, visit the website or drop in at their main office, The Source by BREDS and Jamaica National (otherwise known as The BREDS Store), located at Kingfisher Plaza. It's also the area's only Internet café and business centre (you can send faxes, print and copy).

to head for **Back Seaside**. Described by Sally Henzell – of *Jake's* fame – as "God's own golf course", Back Seaside is a magnificent portion of undeveloped coastline in the shadow of Lovers' Leap that's home to numerous types of cacti, tall golden grass and age-old thatch palms, all of which support several species of sea birds. On the other side of the Great Pedro Bluff, and reachable via a fifteen-minute walk through strangely English-looking pastureland (only the palm trees give the game away), it's a great spot for a coastal walk or a spot of shell collecting.

Out to Lovers' Leap

At some point, most Treasure Beach visitors take a trip out of town up to the sheer cliffs of **LOVERS' LEAP** (daily 9am–7pm; free; call in advance about dining, ☎965 6577), where the Santa Cruz Mountains drop nearly two thousand feet to the sea. According to legend, two young lovers – slaves at a nearby plantation – came here while running away from their owners. They were followed to the edge of the cliffs and, preferring to die rather than be separated again, threw themselves into the sea. It's hardly gripping stuff, but there's a restaurant and bar on site and a balcony that takes in the breathtaking sea-to-sky view, making it a good spot for a breezy lunch or an evening drink while watching the sun go down. Lovers' Leap is signposted off the main road at Southfield seven miles east of Treasure Beach. On the way back to the coast, you can stop at *Tender Chick Restaurant* in the little town of Southfield, which serves great Jamaican "cookshop" staples (lunch and early dinner) and ice cream in a pleasant setting.

Eating and drinking

Evenings are pretty low-key in Treasure Beach, but there are plenty of excellent options for **food**, most offering, unsurprisingly, excellent locally caught seafood. Most of the places are small-scale affairs, but a few – *Jake's*, *Sunset Villa's Restaurant*, *Andrea's Steak and Seafood* – accept credit cards.

If you're cooking for yourself, you'll find several small **groceries** in Treasure Beach with a limited selection of goods – but for a big shop, you'll need to go to

Black River, Southfield or Junction. Vans selling fruit and vegetables pass through Treasure Beach a couple of times a week; ask locally.

Andrea's Steakhouse and Seafood Restaurant Mar Blue Domicil, Old Wharf ☎ 965 3408. Priding themselves in serving only the finest quality filet of beef and other choice cuts, proprietors (and husband-and-wife-team) Axel and Andrea provide hands-on service and delicious four-course meals in a romantic setting. Pricey but worth it, especially for special occasions. Meals must be ordered in advance of arrival.

Gold Coast Kingfisher Plaza, Calabash Bay. Mom-and-Pop restaurant that's best for take-out as it lacks atmosphere. Delicious Jamaican fare, curry goat, stew chicken and rice and peas to name a few. Serves lunch only.

Jack Sprat Calabash Bay. With tables under sea-grape trees and a sandy path down to the beach, this is the perfect place for a relaxed meal. Shellfish (conch, shrimp and lobster in season) as well as fish cooked any style are served with bammy, rice and peas, and salad. There is also a hearty conch soup available alongside excellent pizzas (bases are handmade on the spot, and toppings include fresh pineapple and proper pepperoni). Pastries, cakes and Devon House ice cream satisfy the sweet tooth, and prices are very reasonable.

Jake's Calabash Bay. Open-air restaurant within the hotel, this is usually one of the busiest places in town, serving moderately priced Jamaican fare with a sophisticated twist. The breakfast, lunch and dinner blackboard menus change daily; highlights include banana porridge, pumpkin soup and home-made coconut ice cream. Tables are under shade trees, and there's a good, if small, wine list.

M&D Bar Calabash Bay. Run by the formidable Maureen Powell and her partner Delvin, *M&D's* is a bar and well-stocked grocery on a corner of the Treasure Beach main road. On the weekends, Delvin cooks up jerk conch, chicken and pork and a massive pot of deliciously spicy conch soup. A great place to people-watch and get to know the local happenings, find a seat on the curb with a foil "plate" of food or a cup of conch soup and watch Treasure Beach go by.

Oliver's Dutch Pot Maylen Plaza (also known as Lazza's Plaza), Treasure Beach Main Rd. Occupying one of the few open shops in the plaza, *Oliver's* serves up good Jamaican fusion food in a dimly lit, homely setting. Lunch and dinner.

Pardy's Coffee Shop Treasure Beach Main Rd across from *Waikiki*. Centrally located on the main road, offers a good breakfast at a reasonable price and also serves lunch.

Smurf's Cafe Frenchman's Bay. Formerly home to the *Trans-Love Café*, this spot serves up some of the most delicious and well-priced breakfasts (starting at J$300) in the area. Tasty breads and pastries are available to order as well as freshly ground coffee beans. Open daily from 6am.

South Jammin' Frenchman's Bay. Unpretentious and popular open-sided bar offering a comprehensive mix of burgers, pizza and seafood; local and international breakfast fare is served, too. Other highlights include two pool tables and sports events on satellite TV.

Winsome's Place Frenchman's Bay. Beach shack with limited seating serves up flavourful home-cooked meals by Winsome. Nice local vibe; serves lunch only.

Nightlife and entertainment

Treasure Beach isn't a nightlife hot spot, and during the week, evenings out will generally consist of after-dinner **drinks** at any of the restaurants listed above or at the area's few bars, which often keep quite late hours if the punters are drinking. In addition to the places listed below, there are numerous rum shops in and around town for a spot of white-rum drinking and ol' talk. Things get busier on the weekends, with the occasional special event happening at local bars or in the hotels; for a dancehall fix ask locals about street dances in the area (a party that usually spreads from a local rum bar to the middle of a road) or listen out for "town-criers" (cars that drive around with loudspeakers strapped to their roofs) who announce everything from plays to parties. Not to be missed are the hugely entertaining in-car sound-system clashes occasionally put on hereabouts; several local men have installed ridiculously powerful sets in their cars, and the clash usually consists of two rivals attempting to outdo each other in terms of sound quality and selection, as decided by crowd response.

Dougie's Bar *Jake's*. Relaxed in-hotel bar that's usually filled with a friendly crowd of sophisticates and locals. A great spot for a sunset cocktail or a glass of wine.

Eggy's Bar Frenchman's Beach. The first beach bar shack you'll see as you make a right out of *Waikiki*, *Eggy's* is a Treasure Beach institution – no-frills, simple drinking; occasional grilling of fresh catch; and always lots of locals (particularly fishermen) catching up on gossip. Great at sunset.

Fishermen's Bar FIrst lane on the right after *Jake's* and before *South Jammin'*, Frenchman's Bay. *Fishermen's* has a small indoor disco and pool table out back, and a thatched bar and restaurant. This easy-going local hangout is a reliable if slightly shady spot open long after everywhere else has closed. Very popular on the weekends with both locals and tourists.

Jack Sprat Calabash Bay. A good place for a drink or a lesson in the art of dominoes, with a great selection of music – from rock-steady to roots reggae.

South Jammin' Calabash Bay. A reliable late-night hot spot with a consistent crowd of followers, this sports bar opposite *Waikiki* on the main road is a Treasure Beach stalwart. It'll be open for breakfast before you get up and closed well after you leave.

Wild Onion Frenchman's Bay. A vibesy, down-to-earth Jamaican one-stop bar/lounge/disco with a cool alfresco dancefloor, pool tables and restaurant serving light meals. On weekends there's a great mix of locals dancing and visitors checking out the scene.

Alligator Pond to Alligator Hole

At first glance, the ramshackle fishing village of **ALLIGATOR POND** – ten miles east of Treasure Beach, and reachable from the A2 via a direct road from Gutters – is not one of the most attractive spots on the south coast. But if you're passing, it's worth stopping to get the feel of a part of Jamaica pretty much unsullied by tourism, and to eat some superb **seafood**. Where the main road into Alligator Pond opens up into an unofficial town square, a dirt road to the right leads to several small shacks selling lobster and fish fresh from the boats. By far the most popular of these is *Little Ochi* with a lovely setting right on the beach and a collection of tables housed in brightly painted fishing boats on stilts. There's always a steady trade here, but it's particularly busy on weekends, with hungry folk pouring in from Mandeville and even as far as Kingston, and reggae blaring from columns of speaker boxes. The fresh fish, shrimp, lobster and conch – hand-selected by you and cooked in every way possible alongside bammy and festival

Manatees

The **manatee** – an aquatic mammal that looks rather like a large, fat seal with a bigger snout and a smile – is found in the warm waters of the Atlantic Ocean and in the Caribbean Sea. Known locally as the sea cow, it's a very secretive creature; little is known about its reproductive habits, for example, and scientists have found it tricky to monitor its numbers. The nature park at Alligator Hole is the only place in Jamaica, and one of few places in the world, where you've an excellent chance of seeing them in the wild.

Fully grown, manatees can reach up to fourteen feet in length, although the great size is no cause for concern as they are strictly vegetarian – eating as much as four hundred kilos of sea grass per day – and known for doting on each other and their young. Columbus probably spotted them when he first came to Jamaica in 1494 (although he claimed that he had seen mermaids), and there were certainly plenty around back then.

Sadly, their slow and gentle lifestyle meant that they were (and are) easy prey for fishermen; accordingly, even though they are now protected, fewer than three thousand are believed to survive in the Caribbean and only a hundred in Jamaica.

– certainly taste great eaten in the sea air, but the wait can be sizeable: an hour or more at busy times. If you're not bothered by having a sea view, head back down the main road and take the left turn just before the Cayman church. In an orange-painted thatch-roof shack, with tables in the garden out back, *Bunch of Grapes* is a family-run affair with a similar flair. Fish, conch and lobster are sold by the pound (you select what you want from the fridge) and either brown-stewed, steamed, fried or curried and served with rice or bammy.

There's little reason to **stay** in Alligator Pond itself, though if you do, you can try the small, friendly guesthouse *Venue Sunset Lounge* (℡ 804 0330) in Wards Bay, a five-minute drive east of *Little Ochi*. Rooms are basic and rather dingy, but cheap, and it's a lovely spot for a drink in the sea breeze or a plate of fish. In the other direction from *Little Ochi* (take either of the Kasier turn-offs, and follow the road past the Sports Ground), the *Sea-Riv Hotel* (℡ 450 1356 or 360 7609) is a far better option, right on a nice stretch of black-sand beach, with a swimmable river running into the waves. Rooms are surprisingly appealing, with ceiling or standing fans, tile floors and plain white linens. Ask in town or at *Little Ochi* for directions.

There's no tourism scene here as such, but there's a bar at the water's edge, and local families arrive at the weekends for a day on the beach. It's also a great spot for watching the sun set – or the moon rise over the hills, which slip down to the sea in the unmistakeable shape of an alligator's head. Incidentally, the usual peace of this very secluded area is interrupted once a year on the second week of January when Tony Rebel's **Rebel Salute** stage show is held at the Kaiser Sports Ground; if you're attending the show, try to get a room at the *Sea-Riv Hotel* (℡ 450 1356 or 360 7609), as traffic jams on the minor roads leading to the A2 are horrendous.

Alligator Hole

From the square in Alligator Pond, a road leads east for eighteen miles to Alligator Hole and Milk River. What Jamaicans call a "lonely road" (with a shiver of misgiving), it's a lovely drive through an isolated area known as **Canoe Valley**, or the Long Bay Morass, much of it along the coast, with goats and sea birds usually your only company. The area is barely touched by development and remains a naturalist's paradise, with the dry, cactus-strewn slopes in the west giving way to mangrove swamps as you head further east – brilliant for birdwatching. In several places, you can access the beautiful, completely deserted stretch of brown-sand **beach** along Long Bay. It's not really a place to swim – the water is usually rough and currents strong – but it's a marvellous spot for a walk, with plenty of driftwood and shells to collect. Halfway along this stretch, the road passes **Gut River**, one of the most picturesque places on the south coast. The river runs under the road towards the sea, emerging in a clear blue stream edged by coconut palms and huge aloe plants, where you can swim, and watch frigate birds and egrets flap lazily around.

Continuing east towards Milk River, you'll pass the tiny nature park of **Alligator Hole** (daily 9am–4pm; free), the part-time home of a small number of **manatees**. It's a peaceful place to stop, with a small visitor centre housing displays on manatees and Caribbean ecosystems. If you're lucky, you'll see the manatees come in for their daily feed, usually in the late afternoon, supplied by the caretaker-managers who hang out by the park, drinking, playing dominoes and selling cold beer and soft drinks. It's a truly paradisiacal spot. **Crocodiles** (known locally as alligators) also inhabit the area, although they are seen less often, and lots of people swim in the cool, clear waters here.

About 200m up the road towards Milk River, and reachable via a path on the left (inland) side of the road, **God's Well** is a deep sinkhole, surrounded by greenery and with a deep-blue pool just visible at the bottom. Said to be inhabited by the ghosts of a Taino maiden and a scuba diver who drowned here whilst trying to establish the sinkhole's depth, it's a rather eerie spot. Throw a stone over the edge and it seems to take an age to reach the water, the sinkhole's sheer sides providing a satisfyingly loud and deep thump as it hits. The guys at Alligator Hole will usually be able to take you here if you ask.

Milk River Spa

The **hot mineral springs** near **MILK RIVER**, only a couple of miles inland from Alligator Hole, were first discovered in the early eighteenth century. Mineral spas were subsequently built in the area – first opened to the public in 1794 – and are today housed in the basement of the *Milk River Hotel* (☏ 610 7745-6; rates include breakfast and dinner; ❹–❺). The hotel is a lovely old wooden building, with comfortable, if rather sparse, mostly en-suite rooms and inexpensive meals on offer, and, though there's nothing spectacular about the area, the dry climate and the laid-back atmosphere make it a very pleasant place to spend a night.

Renovations on the main baths, including new tiles and mosaic designs, have added to its appeal as well as the opening of three additional, larger baths at the far end of the hotel – currently only open on busy days, although there are future plans to make them private and more akin to the typical spa experience (complete with comfy robes and herbal teas) for in-house guests only. Many of the guests at the hotel and spa are return visitors who swear by the curative powers of the water for a range of ailments from rheumatism to gout, nerve diseases and sciatica. Other visitors find their curiosity tinged with concern about the high radioactivity levels of the baths – more than fifty times that of the waters at Vichy in France – although the staff will assure you that this is quite harmless so long as you don't stay in for more than an hour. You get free use of the spas if you're staying at the hotel; if you're visiting, they cost J$400 for fifteen minutes; water massages are also available for an additional cost. Besides the spa, there's little to the village of Milk River other than the usual crowd of schoolchildren and smattering of churches, although there are rumoured plans to build a large all-inclusive hotel close to the spa. The river itself is named for its colour in the early morning, when it is shrouded in mist; swimming is not a great idea, given that the river is the home of a number of crocodiles. Two miles beyond the spa, past rows of giant cacti, is the tiny fishing village of **FARQUHARS** which has, at its western end, a passable black-sand beach where you can swim in the ocean. Expect lots of good-natured attention from the locals, as tourists very rarely venture this far.

Inland to Mandeville

The A2 highway speeds inland from Black River, passing through some attractive countryside before making the long climb up Spur Tree Hill to **Mandeville**. The main road passes through **Bamboo Avenue**, with its walls of tall bamboo, and there are several interesting detours worth taking, particularly in the interior of St Elizabeth. There are gorgeous **waterfalls** at YS, **hiking** possibilities in the **Black River Gorge**, and the quiet and completely untouristed villages of the **Santa Cruz Mountains**. You can also visit a **rum factory**, beautifully placed among fields of sugar cane at Appleton, on the southern edge of Cockpit Country (see Chapter 4).

Accommodation options in the area are limited, though there are a couple of decent places at Santa Cruz and Maggotty, and you may want to consider visiting on day-trips from a base on the south coast or in Mandeville. **Getting around** is a breeze if you've got a car; public-transport links into the interior are not brilliant, though minibuses and route taxis do run to most parts – for a couple of places, including YS, you'll need to charter a taxi for a short part of the trip.

Middle Quarters and YS Falls

As you drive northeast from Black River, you'll reach an intersection directing you north for Montego Bay or east towards Santa Cruz and Mandeville. Head east towards Middle Quarters and you will soon see the bright multicoloured perimeter walls of the Bubbling Spring Mineral bath on your left-hand side. Under the direction of the enterprising Mr Fagan, **Bubbling Spring** features a large refreshing open-air pool of (scientifically tested) "healing" mineral waters (Mon–Sun 8am–6pm; US$15; ☏850 1606). There's also a bar with food and drinks and a gift shop. After taking a dip continue east and you'll reach **Middle Quarters**, a small crossroads where groups of women sell spicy, salty **pepper shrimp** fished from the Black River. Feel free to sample from the proffered bags before you buy; reckon on around J$200 for a small bag. Buy some to add to your picnic if you're heading to the YS Falls or take a few minutes out to crunch them on the roadside and have a chat with the women. Incidentally, don't be intimidated by the fiercely competitive approach of the sellers – they are often all members of the same family and if one is lagging in sales for the day, she will usually be thrust forward to clinch the deal. Try Billy (☏366 4182), whose shop is the last one in the first set of shops on your left after the big corner in Middle Quarters. Friendly and knowledgeable about the area, Billy sells peppered shrimp as well as fried chicken and Jamaican boiled corn. Otherwise, to enjoy some shrimp in a more relaxed setting, head past the ladies to *Grassy's*, a wooden shack to the left of the road, with a shady grove/deck for eating. Trade is busy here, and the shrimp always fresh and delicious (they also tend to be bigger than those sold on the road); fabulous *janga* (shrimp) soup is also available.

Shortly after Middle Quarters, a left turn takes you two and a half miles north to **YS** (pronounced "why-ess"), an area dominated by the **YS farm**, home of the magnificent YS Falls. The name is thought to derive from the farm's original owners in 1684, John Yates and Richard Scott, whose initials were stamped on their cattle and the hogsheads of sugar that they exported. Today the farm covers around 2300 acres and raises pedigree red poll cattle – a Jamaican breed that you'll see all over the country. The **YS Falls**, a series of ten greater and lesser waterfalls, are great fun (Tues–Sun 9.30am–3.30pm; closed on public holidays, ⊛www .ysfalls.com; US$15). A jitney pulls you through the farm's land and alongside the YS River to a grassy area at the base of the falls, where there are changing rooms and toilets. You can climb up the lower falls or take the wooden stairway, which leads to a platform beside the uppermost and most spectacular waterfall. There are lianas and ropes for aspiring Tarzans, and pools for gentle bathing at the foot of each fall as well as a spring water swimming pool on the flat for lounging. Depending on river conditions, tubing is also available on the lower

Rum and raison d'être

Rum – once known as rumbullion or kill-devil – is Jamaica's national drink, and you couldn't choose a better place to acquire a taste for the stuff. Jamaica was one of the first countries to make rum commercially and it still produces some of the world's finest. Overproof is the drink of choice for the less well-off – it's cheap, lethally strong (64 percent alcohol) and, supposedly, cures all ills. If you can't handle the overproof, the standard **white rums** are the basis for most cocktails, while more refined palates go for the **darker rums**. During the ageing process these rums acquire colour from the oak barrels in which they are stored and, as they get older, they slip down increasingly smoothly with no need for a mixer.

Distilling of sugar-cane juice started in Jamaica during the years of Spanish occupation, stepping up a few gears when the British took over in 1655 and rum became famous as the drink of the island's semi-legitimate **pirates** and **buccaneers**. The production process hasn't changed much over the centuries, although it has become fully mechanized, putting a number of donkeys out of work in the process. The sugar cane is squeezed to extract every drop of its juice, which is then boiled and put through a centrifuge, producing molasses. In turn, the molasses is diluted with water, and yeast is added to get the stuff fermenting away. After fermentation, the liquid "dead wash" is sent to the distillery, where it's heated, and the evaporating alcohol caught in tanks. It sounds simple enough – and it is. But when you discover that it takes ten to twelve tonnes of sugar cane to produce half a bottle of alcohol, which is then blended with water and a mixture of secret ingredients (molasses is almost certainly among them) to make the finished product, you begin to appreciate all those fields of swaying cane a little more.

part of the river – a gentle to moderately speedy 25-minute trip that includes five mini-rapids – for US$6. Or for the more adventurous, there's a canopy tour where once strapped to a harness you can zip through the treetops starting at the top of the waterfall and finishing just before the spring water swimming pool (US$30). Early morning is a good time to go, before the afternoon clouds (and the bus tours) draw in; take a picnic and a book and you can comfortably spend a few hours loafing around the gardens. Cold beers, soft drinks, coffee and simple snacks are offered in their well-stocked gift shop; there are also bathrooms and changing rooms on-site.

A car is extremely handy if you're heading for the falls, as they're a little off the beaten track, but if you're relying on public transport, buses run along the main A2 highway south of YS between Black River and Santa Cruz. Ask the driver to drop you at the junction, and you can usually find taxis waiting to run passengers up to the YS farm. There's nowhere to **stay** at YS – possible bases include Christiana (see p.263) or Black River (see p.242). If you're hungry for a roadside snack, check *Howie's*, a cookshop at the bottom of the YS driveway/road that serves great local dishes and undisputedly the best peanut porridge in the island.

Maggotty

East of YS and seven miles from the main A2 highway, **MAGGOTTY** resembles a small Wild West frontier town. It's a dry, dusty place, most of whose inhabitants work at the **Appleton Estate** rum distillery nearby (see opposite). Though there's little to see in town, there is some beautiful scenery in the area particularly YS Falls, where the river tubing, swimming and canopy tour make for a great day out. Infrequent **minibuses** run to Maggotty from Black River and Santa Cruz. If you're **driving**, the road north from the A2 highway is in far better condition than the road running east–west between Maggotty and YS.

The Appleton Estate Rum Tour

Three miles east of Maggotty, the **Wray and Nephew rum distillery** at **APPLETON** (Mon–Sat 9am–3.30pm; US$18; ☎963 9215, ⓦwww.apple tonrum.com) has a great setting in the Nassau Valley among thousands of acres of sugar-cane fields. At 250-years-old, this is one of the oldest rum producers in the English-speaking Caribbean and the best known of Jamaica's several brands. All of the rum produced here is sent for blending, barrelling and bottling in Kingston – though some barrels are sent back here to age in a warehouse viewed during the tour.

You'll need a car to get here, or you can take a taxi from Maggotty. Though you're free to drop in, it's a good idea to call ahead to arrange a guided visit, if only to avoid your visit coinciding with a big tour party. The hour-long **tour** starts with a complimentary drink and video session, followed by a visit to the factory (heavy with the sweet scent of molasses) and cobwebby, ageing house, and then outside to an old sugar press, where donkeys used to walk in circles to turn a grinder that crushed juice out of the sugar cane. Today it's all mechanized, though a donkey has been put back into service to demonstrate old techniques. The tour concludes in a "tavern", where you get to sample all seventeen kinds of rum and various rum-based liquors.

▲ Appleton rum distillery

Bamboo Avenue and Lacovia

Back on the main A2 highway, **Bamboo Avenue**, halfway between Middle Quarters and Lacovia, enlivens the drive to Mandeville. For several miles, *Bambusa vulgaris*, Jamaica's largest species of bamboo, has grown up on either side to create a pretty arch over the road. The place was once almost completely shaded by the bamboo, but the sun now streams in through gaps created by Hurricane Gilbert and, some say, by official neglect. There are several rest stops along the road where you can get a jelly coconut or a cold beer.

Just east of Bamboo Avenue, the village of **LACOVIA**, one-time capital of St Elizabeth, was once an important inland port for shipping sugar and logwood down to Black River for export. Today it is most notable for its **twin tombs**, just outside the Texaco petrol station, believed to contain the bodies of two young men killed in a local duel in 1723. One of the deceased is identified as Thomas Jordan Spencer and the coat of arms on his tombstone suggests a connection with the family of Britain's Winston Churchill and Lady Diana Spencer. Nearby, in the village of **Mountainside** (off the main road heading back towards the coast) is the small **Butterfly Dreams Farm** (Mon–Fri 10am–4pm; ℡ 881 8855, ⓔ butterflydreamsja@yahoo) which raises fourteen types of butterfly (mostly swallowtails) for release at local weddings. Well worth the detour, the half-acre property has a lab, greenhouse, small vivarium and, oddly, a few ostriches. Described as a living science class, knowledgeable employees take visitors on an (informal) guided tour that allows you to see butterflies in the various stages of their lifecycle. The farm can be tied into your road trip to or from Treasure Beach heading toward Lacovia and Santa Cruz, or as a day-trip (it's forty minutes away) from the coast.

Santa Cruz, Malvern and Spur Tree Hill

If you're in this part of the country, sooner or later you're likely to pass through **SANTA CRUZ**, the main settlement along the A2 and reckoned to be the hottest place in Jamaica. This rapidly expanding market town, once famous as a livestock trading centre, is noisy and frenetic at the best of times, and there's no particular reason to stop off here, although you can fill up on fresh patties and delicious juices at *Paradise Patties* on Main Street.

The road south from Santa Cruz to Treasure Beach and the coast is a beautiful (if slow) drive over the Santa Cruz Mountains. The drive takes you through a series of tiny villages and the quiet town of **MALVERN**. Like Christiana further north (see p.263), this is one of Jamaica's coolest towns, at around 2500ft above sea level. In the early twentieth century, it was an important summer retreat for foreigners and wealthy Jamaicans, though it's now almost bereft of tourists. Today, apart from a handful of top-notch schools and colleges established here in the 1850s, there's not much to the town, although the presence of returning residents who've made their money abroad is injecting an air of affluence – with grand houses springing up on the hilltops – and it's a pretty place to cruise around for a little while.

Heading east from Santa Cruz, the A2 continues to **Gutters**, on the Manchester/ St Elizabeth border and a turn-off for Treasure Beach, where it begins the long and rather tortuous climb up **Spur Tree Hill** to Mandeville. Once known as "man bump", the switchbacking hill provides dramatic views over the southern plains, the Santa Cruz Mountains, and down to the sea, and there are a couple of good

bars and **restaurants** to stop off at and enjoy the view: *All Seasons* on your right coming up serves a great jerk pork and chicken and an excellent jerk pork sausage on the weekends, while 400 yards further up, a handful of small bars specialize in curry goat and mannish water – *Neville's Curry Goat* (the first bar on the left after *All Seasons*) is a sweet and friendly, one-table "one-stop" cookshop and bar, frequented by truckers and locals alike.

Mandeville and around

You can almost feel the wealth in **MANDEVILLE**, Jamaica's fifth-largest town. Big money started to arrive here in the 1950s as a result of a now-defunct but once highly profitable **bauxite industry** that grew up around the town. More recently, returning expatriate Jamaicans, attracted by the cooler climate and the relatively low crime rate, have begun to invest their accumulated savings in large homes and small businesses around town, and Mandeville has grown at an unprecedented rate. Tourism has dipped in the last few years, although from the early days of the *Mandeville Hotel* in the 1890s, the town was popular with British soldiers who came to escape the heat of the coastal areas and to recuperate from their fevers and diseases.

Mandeville was founded in 1814 and still retains something of its early colonial air – most noticeably at the very English **Manchester Golf Club**, just west of the town centre. The first buildings were set out around **Mandeville Square**, a rather unkempt grassy space now also known as Cecil Charlton Park after a former mayor, and this is the best starting point for a brief walking tour of the centre. Built in 1819, **St Mark's Church** is on the south side of the park, behind the massed ranks of taxis, buses and vendors. The interior is pretty ordinary, but, as usual, there are plenty of goats nosing around in the churchyard, and you could happily spend a few minutes wandering among them and checking out the nineteenth-century tombstones. On the other

Community tourism

The creation of big tourist "ghettos" on Jamaica's north coast has completely disrupted traditional lifestyles there and means that, often, the only contact overseas visitors have with Jamaicans is when they're serving drinks or driving tour buses. In the face of its own gradually developing tourist scene, Jamaica's south coast, where the absence of large-scale beach resorts offers visitors more of a feel of the "real" Jamaica, is keen to escape such insensitive development. Planners and hoteliers are showing increasing interest in the concept of "**community tourism**", which aims to contain and control tourism by fostering closer connections between the tourist and the community. In Mandeville, Diana McIntyre-Pyke at the *Astra Inn* (☎ 962 7758 or 488 7207, ⊛ www.countrystyletourism.com), can organize a variety of local tours (Jamaican Taste, Nature, Roots, Health and Wellness) to the area. The cost is US$60 per person including food but not transportation or the fee for the community/host guide which is an additional US$50 for the day. She can also arrange homestays (US$40–$60).

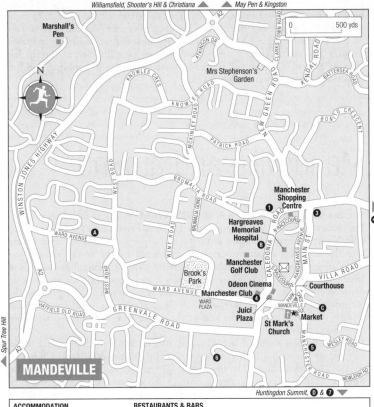

Huntingdon Summit, **D** & **7** ▼

ACCOMMODATION		RESTAURANTS & BARS			
Astra Country Inn	A	Beavers	4	The Link	2
Golf View Hotel	B	Bird of Paradise	1	Little Ochie	3
Hilltop Hotel	D	Bloomfield Great House	6	The Vineyard	5
Mandeville Hotel	C	International Chinese Restaurant	7		

side of the park, the limestone **courthouse** is one of Mandeville's original buildings, completed in 1820 and still normally crowded, while the **rectory** (now a private home) alongside the courthouse dates from the same year. The nearby **police station** – once the town jail and workhouse – is the last of Mandeville's original structures. North of here, at 25 New Green Rd, there is a **private garden** that will be of interest if you've a passion for anthuriums. Carmen Stephenson has the most impressive collection of plants in town, and she is a regular winner at the Mandeville Flower Show every May. Visitors can tour the garden (daily during daylight hours; US$5; call ☎962 2909 or 962 2328 to make an appointment); its well-ordered collection includes the rare white anthurium, orchids and **ortaniques** – a cross between the orange and the tangerine and Mandeville's contribution to the world of fruit.

Mandeville's hilly setting means a pleasantly cool climate; winter evenings can get quite cold, and you'll need a sweater. If you're here for a longer time, check out the old great house at **Marshall's Pen** (see opposite) or while away an hour with a visit to a local **factory** (see opposite).

Marshall's Pen and Factory Tours

Mandeville's more interesting sights are both a bit of a drive out of town. **Marshall's Pen** (by appointment only; ☎ 904 5454, ✉ asutton@cwjamaica.com) is a lovely old great house, built around 1795 and originally used in the preparation of coffee beans for export. The driveway you enter through was the "barbecue" where the beans were laid out to dry in the sun, and the ground floor of the house, with its massive cedar floorboards, was where they were polished prior to their shipment to the US and UK for roasting and grinding. Nowadays this area has been converted to living quarters and also serves, together with a couple of rooms upstairs, as an informal museum with fabulous collections of shells and stamps, from both Jamaica and abroad; Japanese and Chinese artefacts; and a tiny array of Taino relics. Under the direction of owner Ann Sutton, a conservation ecologist, Marshall Pen has become a good place for birdwatching (guided tours also by appointment only) and serious ornithologists can arrange to stay at the house for around US$40 per person per night.

If you have some time to kill while you're in Mandeville, you might want to visit a nearby factory. The **coffee factory** of Jamaica Standard Products (Mon–Thurs by appointment; J$200; ☎ 963 4211) is a couple of miles north of the town centre in Williamsfield. The factory roasts, grinds and packages beans for the superior Blue Mountain coffee as well as JSP's own – High Mountain – and Baronhall brands, grown at lower elevations. Since seventy percent of coffee drunk in Jamaica is instant, most of the coffee packaged here is exported – largely to Japan. The tour of the coffee plant, conducted by staff members and with an entirely uncommercial air, is brief but informative, taking you through all stages of processing from grading the beans to roasting – and the entire place smells wonderful. Afterwards you have a chance to buy the products at excellent prices.

Just beyond Williamsfield at the bottom of Shooter's Hill, the **Pickapeppa factory** (Mon–Thurs 9am–3pm; 45min tour J$200; ☎ 603 3441, ⊛ www .pickapeppa.com) makes a great detour, especially if you've developed a taste for its extremely addictive main product. In operation since 1921 and equipped with masses of ancient-looking, Heath Robinson-esque machinery, the factory is best known for its delicious Pickapeppa seasoning sauce, a piquant blend of tomatoes, onions, mangoes, raisins, tamarinds, hot peppers and a secret concoction of fourteen spices; once made, the sauce is aged for at least a year in oak barrels. The end product, sold mostly overseas but nonetheless a firm favourite on Jamaican restaurant tables, is utterly delicious and not as fiery as the Scotch bonnet sauce that's also made here.

Arrival and getting around

Buses into Mandeville arrive at the south end of Mandeville Square, a small village green in the town centre surrounded by banks, supermarkets and, usually, a crowd of people. Buses and minibuses for Kingston, Christiana, Santa Cruz and Black River (less often for the west and north coasts) leave from the same place at regular intervals, and the town's main **taxi rank** is alongside. If you're **driving** there are three separate entrances to town signposted from the highway – it's simplest to take the middle one, at the major roundabout, and follow New Green Road all the way into town. For sightseeing, a car is definitely a major asset; although you can see everything in the town centre on foot, getting out to Marshall's Pen will require wheels.

Accommodation

Although most accommodation in Mandeville is catered to business travellers, there are several places that offer budget – deals perfect if you're just passing through.

Astra Country Inn 62 Ward Ave ☎ 962 7758. A little out of the town centre, and a bit short on character. The rooms range in size, price and facilities (the budget ones are a great deal), and all have cable TV. **④**

Golf View Hotel 51/2 Caledonia Rd ☎ 962 4477, ⓦ www.thegolfviewhotel.com. Modern, well-equipped hotel designed around a central courtyard with a pool. The en-suite rooms, either a/c or fan, have attractive wood furnishings, phone, cable TV and balcony, and there's a restaurant and bar on-site. **④–⑤**

Hilltop Hotel Northern Caribbean University, Manchester Rd ☎ 523 2439, ⓔ hilltophotel @ncu.edu.jm. Clean, spacious and comfortable en-suite rooms with phone and cable TV, and a communal kitchen for preparing snacks and hot drinks. Most guests are visitors to the university, so there's not much of a holiday feel, but the staff are friendly and helpful. Rates include breakfast. **③–④**

Mandeview Flats 7 Hillview Drive, Balvanie Heights ☎ 961 8439. Built on a hillside, affording great views over town, this small guesthouse enjoys a quiet setting along pretty residential roads. Spacious and comfortable rooms, some with kitchenettes and small living spaces; all have cable TV, phone and fans. Breakfast is included; dinner prepared on request. **④–⑤**

Mandeville Hotel 4 Hotel St ☎ 962 2460. One of the oldest hotels in Jamaica and fully refurbished. A pleasant and easy-going place to stay right in the heart of town, but a little on the expensive side. Facilities include a restaurant, bar and large pool, and the rooms and studios have phone and cable TV. **④–⑦**

Eating, drinking and nightlife

As you'd expect from such a peaceful town, Mandeville **nightlife** is pretty tame, though there is a cinema, the Odeon, on Caledonia Avenue (☎ 962 1354 or 7646). But there are some good **restaurants** and a lot of fast-food options and snack outlets at the ubiquitous malls (particularly at the Manchester Shopping Centre). The central bus park at twilight is your best bet for jerk chicken and delicious roast yam.

Restaurants and snack bars

Bird of Paradise Cobblestone Plaza, 1 Brumalia Rd ☎ 962 7251. This brightly painted, modern restaurant/café serves tasty international fare (pastas, Tex-Mex) and local fusion food at a moderate price. There is also a bar upstairs that serves frozen drinks and wine. They also serve brunch on Sundays.

Bloomfield Great House Bloomfield ☎ 962 7130. Wonderfully restored house, with grand steps leading up to a verandah dining area that affords lovely views over Mandeville. The menu is varied, fairly sophisticated and expensive, with mains ranging from fillet mignon, chicken parmigiana and lamb chops to coconut curry shrimp and lobster and chickpea vegetable stew. If you're not dining, come anyway for an early evening drink.

International Chinese Restaurant 117 Manchester Rd. Great, reasonably priced Chinese food that can be selected from an extensive menu; a short drive from town.

Little Ochie Leaders Plaza ☎ 625 3279. The first franchise of the original in Alligator Pond, this lively spot is a replica of its big sister, serving delicious seafood in a variety of styles amidst a casual, local vibe.

Bars and clubs

Beavers Ward Ave Located in the former home of Fayors Entertainment Center, Beavers is a low-key open-air bar with a great flashback party on Wednesdays and Latin night on Saturdays.

The Link 80 Caledonia Ave ☎ 962 3771. Cosy, friendly little bar, usually busy with a mixed crowd – young and old, local and foreign.

Manchester Club corner of Caledonia Rd and Ward Ave. Definitely a colonial feel at this golf club, but a decent place for an early-evening drink if you're cruising around.

The Vineyard Manchester Rd. A small upscale (wine) bar and restaurant offering tasty snacks and classy drinks. Popular with expats and locals, food is served from 2pm onward.

Christiana and May Pen

The south's two other main towns sit in splendid isolation, with the emptiness of the interior between them. North of Mandeville, the hills around the small market town of **Christiana** offer a view of a very different, more rural, Jamaica, while unattractive **May Pen**, to the east, is only worth a visit for its annual agricultural show.

Christiana and around

The steep Shooter's Hill heads north from Mandeville, climbing up above the ugly, former Alcan bauxite plant, with its lake of red mud. Just over halfway up the hill, you'll come to **WALDERSTON**, a small village at the crossroads. Continue ten miles north for **CHRISTIANA**, a small market town for the surrounding agricultural community, where potatoes, yams, ginger, coffee and cocoa are grown. Lofty and cool, three thousand feet up in the hills, the town was a popular resort for "old-style" tourism in the 1940s and 1950s, when beaches and tanning were less fashionable than they are today. If you have a car, Christiana also makes a decent base for visiting Appleton and Maggotty to the west (see p.256) or Bob Marley's mausoleum to the northeast in Alexandria (see p.160).

A hike to the lush gorge at **Christiana Bottom** is the big thing to do here. Take a right turn by the post office in town and then follow the left fork at the crossroads to a standpipe where you can park if you're driving, though it's perfectly walkable from the centre of Christiana. Continue down an often muddy track through prolific ferns and bamboo to a **waterfall** and a cold but refreshing pool. (It's not easy to find the way, so if you get lost ask for the "blue hole".) North of town, beyond the village of **Coleyville**, the **Gourie State Park** (daily during daylight hours; free) has a number of lovely hiking trails through its pine woods; the cool air up here makes for especially pleasant hiking. To get to the park from Christiana, turn left off the main road towards Albert Town at the signposted potato-processing factory; follow the road, bearing left, and keep going until you reach a thatched gazebo in a clearing. (The road is pretty rough, but is usually driveable.) To the right of the gazebo, trails lead into the forest (look out for wild strawberries at the side of the path), while to the left are **Gourie Caves** and **Oxford Caves**, which offer some challenging caving. With a good flashlight you can explore on your own, but the underground routes are tricky and a guide (ask at *Villa Bella*) is strongly recommended.

Practicalities

The lone **hotel** in Christiana, *Hotel Villa Bella* (☎964 2243, Ⓦ www.villabella .com; ❸–❹), three miles from the town centre, is one of the most delightful small hotels in Jamaica. There is no pool or unnecessary fripperies, but the place retains a colonial-era feel and is dotted with interesting curiosities – plenty of Art-Deco furniture, nineteenth-century china, old prints and the hotel's original guest book from 1941. *Villa Bella* can also organize a variety of **tours** of the local area, including mountain biking, caving and hiking. The **restaurant** at *Villa Bella* has standard international and Jamaican fare at moderate to expensive prices and a nice indoor dining area (you'll find it's too cold to eat outside in the winter). Otherwise, the main road has a smattering of inexpensive snack bars and patty shops and a particularly popular jerk stand/restaurant (*Bull's Jerk Center*) right before the cross-roads heading to Walderston.

Regular **minibuses** run up Shooter's Hill from Mandeville and head straight into town – ask them to drop you off if you're heading for *Hotel Villa Bella*. If you're driving, the hotel is signposted on your right just before you enter town; bear left and keep straight on for the town itself.

May Pen and around

Heading east from Mandeville, the A2 road runs out of the parish of Manchester through **Porus**, a lengthy village easily identified by its displays of citrus fruit strung up by the roadside. While there are no real points of interest along the route, the drive is beautiful and easily punctuated with stops for fruits sold by vendors that line the main road, snacks at *Paradise Patties* in the little town of Porus and the hard-to-miss two-storey, neon-lit *Juici Patties*, which serves staples like chicken, beef, vegetable and lobster patties and everything in between, including fried chicken, ackee and saltfish, soup, banana bread and ice cream. The end of the winding road out of Porus leads you into **Clarendon**, one of Jamaica's least enthralling parishes. A right turn at Toll Gate takes you down to Milk River Spa on the south coast (see p.254), while continuing straight ahead brings you to the parish capital of **MAY PEN**, a light industrial centre and an important market town with a population of over forty thousand. The highway actually bypasses the town, which is handy as there is no reason at all to stop there unless your bus is breaking its journey. However, if you're here during the **Denbigh Agricultural Show**, a three-day fair held in the Denbigh showgrounds just west of town – normally over the last weekend in July or the first weekend in August – then it's certainly worth stopping off. The event features displays of agricultural produce from each of the country's parishes, exhibits of prize livestock and a show-jumping event. There's also plenty of live entertainment, including singers, dancers and reggae bands, and the usual array of food vendors and craft stalls.

Contexts

Contexts

History

The first inhabitants of Jamaica were the **Tainos**, Amerindians who spoke the Arawak language and arrived in Jamaica around 900 AD, making their way from present-day Venezuela and Guyana aboard dugout canoes. A peaceful people whose subsistence depended on farming and fishing, they lived in scattered settlements all over the island. Estimates of Taino numbers at the time of Columbus's arrival in Jamaica are hugely varied, but it's possible that there were as many as a million. Although Tainos living in the small islands of the eastern Caribbean were raided by the more warlike **Carib Indians**, there's no evidence of Carib attacks on Jamaica.

The arrival of the Spanish

Christopher Columbus first set foot on Jamaica on May 6, 1494, when he landed at Rio Bueno on the north coast during his second "voyage of discovery" in search of a western sea route to Asia. He had little interest in Jamaica (which he named Santiago), but claimed it for Spain nonetheless. During his fourth and final voyage in 1503, he made an unfortunate return, his ships running aground on the coral reefs at St Ann's Bay (for more on which, see p.155), but Spanish settlement of Jamaica didn't begin in earnest until 1510, when a group of settlers from Hispaniola headed by Governor Juan de Esquivel set up a base at Sevilla Nueva, near modern-day Ocho Rios on the north coast, and set about searching for gold. They didn't find any, and nor was Sevilla a good site; surrounded by swampy land, the tiny Spanish population soon found its numbers threatened by fever. In 1534, King Charles I permitted a transfer of the capital, and the Spanish decamped south to Villa de la Vega, known today as **Spanish Town**, which remained Jamaica's capital until 1874.

Though farms were established throughout the island, Spanish Jamaica remained largely undeveloped, serving mostly as a stopping-off point between the mother country and the richer colonies of the Spanish Main. Nonetheless, the Spanish still managed to obliterate any traces of the native population, who fell victim to European diseases in their thousands and suffered severely from the legendary cruelty of the Spanish; by the time of the British conquest in 1655, the entire Taino population had been wiped out.

Because the Tainos didn't provide the labour force that the Spanish required, they began importing **slaves** from Africa within a decade of arriving in Jamaica, and there is evidence from this period of the first runaway slaves, the *cimmarones* or **Maroons** (see p.271), who gradually developed settlements of their own and who were to prove a constant thorn in the side of the British after 1655.

The British conquest

Spanish Jamaica was not a well-protected colony; in 1596, for example, English adventurer Sir Anthony Shirley landed with five hundred men at Passage Fort near present-day Kingston and completely **sacked** Spanish Town. Spain provided little or no assistance in defending the place, and gave scant impression of caring for its colonists.

In 1654, Britain's "Lord Protector" Oliver Cromwell, distrustful of sections of his armed forces whom he suspected of plotting the restoration of the monarchy, decided to send them against Spain's American possessions, far away from home. The British were well aware of the immense Spanish wealth in the area; for over a century, British pirates and buccaneers like Francis Drake had been making a good living from looting Spanish ships and cities. Cromwell sent fifteen vessels under the command of General Robert **Venables** and Admiral William **Penn**.

After a disastrous first assault on Hispaniola, they set sail for neighbouring Jamaica, which they knew to be a modestly prosperous and poorly defended place, and landed at **Passage Fort** in May 1655. After the previous sackings, there were few Spanish left to fight for Jamaica; the capital was quickly overrun. The Spanish did hold off the British on the north coast, however, and in 1657, forces sent over from Cuba engaged the British at Los Chorreros, present-day Ocho Rios. In 1660, troops led by British governor Edward D'Oyley finally defeated the Spanish at the battle of **Rio Nuevo**, near Ocho Rios. As they fled for Cuba, the Spaniards freed and armed their slaves to continue the fight; these freed slaves proved an important boost for the growing band of **Maroons**. Penn and Venables, meanwhile, returned to Britain with little booty to show for their efforts and, despite the conquest, were promptly imprisoned in the Tower of London.

Port Royal and the buccaneers

Immediately after the British conquest of Jamaica, defence of this newly won prize became the first priority. **Fortifications** were built on either side of Kingston harbour, with five separate forts created on the uninhabited island of **Port Royal**. In 1661, Edward D'Oyley became Jamaica's first non-military governor and, in 1664, the first **local assembly** was summoned. Sir Thomas Modyford became governor and encouraged local **buccaneers** to make Port Royal their base for attacks on Spanish dominions. These buccaneers had started out as a ragged collection of outlaws living on the island of Tortuga; by the mid-seventeenth century, they had evolved into a disparate but skilled collection of pirates, attacking ships around the region. The British saw a way of using buccaneers to their advantage. By giving them official sanction as **privateers** and letting them use Port Royal as a base, they would provide some defence for the young colony; equally important, they would harass the Spanish enemy, attacking their cargo ships, and would be obliged to deliver ten percent of their haul to the British authorities in Jamaica.

Port Royal became a boom town. The security provided by the forts and the wealth of the privateers encouraged traders to set up, exporting sugar and spices and importing slaves and supplies for the growing population. Although Spanish Town remained the capital city, government figures set up home on the island alongside the merchants, and Port Royal became one of the wealthiest places in the world. However, its ascendancy was short-lived; a devastating **earthquake** in 1692 plunged most of Port Royal into the sea, and sent its residents fleeing for a new home across the harbour in modern-day Kingston.

By the 1670 **Treaty of Madrid**, the Spanish recognized British rule in Jamaica, and the brief era of the privateers was over, though there was to be one last fling. Henry Morgan, most famous of the privateers, launched an attack on the Spanish colony of Panama, sailing from Bluefields Bay on Jamaica's southwest coast. Though he claimed that he was unaware of the peace treaty, Morgan and Governor Modyford were recalled to Britain. Modyford was sacked to appease the Spanish, while Morgan, having insinuated his way into royal favour, was made lieutenant-governor in

Modyford's stead, returning to Jamaica with a new brief – to stamp out piracy by persuading his former colleagues to turn to a life of peace.

Naturally enough, many of the privateers, now officially termed "**pirates**" to mark their loss of favour, refused to give up their thrilling and financially rewarding lifestyles and continued to torment shipping in the Caribbean throughout the eighteenth century. But their heyday was past, and a succession of high-profile successes by the authorities – particularly the capture in 1720 of Calico Jack Rackham (see p.85) – inexorably turned the screw on the remaining bandits.

Sugar and development of the Jamaican economy

Though initially unimpressed with his new charge, Oliver Cromwell soon came to appreciate Jamaica's strategic importance, and issued a proclamation encouraging emigrants from Britain and other parts of the Empire with offers of land grants and other financial incentives. Jamaica began to mutate from an insignificant colony into a much-prized possession, and the key factor in this change was **sugar**. Though first planted in Jamaica by the Spanish, cultivation of sugar cane became a major phenomenon only under British rule, and as Europe developed an ever sweeter tooth, the number of sugar estates here grew by leaps and bounds, expanding eightfold between 1673 and 1740. During the eighteenth century, the island became the biggest producer of sugar in the world.

Many of the **planters** were absentee landowners who spent most of their time in Britain and delegated control of their estates to overseers. These planters amassed extraordinary fortunes from their Jamaican possessions, and this wealth brought with it significant political power and influence in London. This, in turn, was used to nourish and protect the sugar trade, with huge duties levied on sugar imported from elsewhere and the price of Jamaican sugar kept artificially high. Given the lavish lifestyle led by the planters in Britain, practically none of the profits of sugar were ploughed back into developing Jamaica, although every plantation had its **great house**, the elegant hilltop mansions that still survive to this day.

Slavery

The success of the sugar industry and the wealth of the planters was, of course, predicated upon the appalling inhumanity of **slavery**. The development of the sugar estates called for a mammoth workforce, and with no indigenous labour available, the planters embarked upon the importation of slaves from Africa in earnest.

The **slave trade** was dominated by British merchants, whose ships sailed first to the west coast of Africa carrying trinkets and other goods to barter for the human cargo. From Africa, ships loaded with slaves sailed direct to Kingston, the region's key transhipment point, where those strong enough to have survived the **Middle Passage** leg of this transatlantic trade triangle were unloaded into warehouses and sold at auction. From there, the ships would return to Britain, now laden with the Jamaican sugar, rum and spices. It's estimated that between **twelve and fifteen million** people were transported from Africa as slaves, and they brought great wealth to the traders, reflected – among other things – in the development of the major port cities of Bristol and Liverpool.

Little attention, meanwhile, was paid to the plight of the West Africans, drawn principally from the tribes of the Coromantee, the Fula, the Ashante, the Ibo and the Mandingo. As the needs of the colonies expanded, **raiding parties** were sent into the African interior to hunt for more victims, who were marched across the continent to stockades on the coast. From there, the journey to Jamaica could take between six and twelve weeks, with the slaves enduring the most deplorable conditions imaginable – kept in chains in the hold of the ship, packed into galleries one above the other and jammed into spaces so small that they couldn't stand or lie at full length. With no sanitation facilities and barely any food, huge numbers died of disease or malnutrition; many others committed suicide if the chance arose, leaping from the ship rather than continue in captivity.

Despite the high rate of loss, it continued to be profitable for the slavers to ply their trade, and every year, several thousand slaves survived the Middle Passage to become labourers on the estates or, on a smaller scale, domestic workers in the homes of white settlers. Unsurprisingly, many of the transported slaves – uprooted from home and family and prohibited from using their own language – found the prospect of life on the plantations impossible, and there was continual **conflict** between slaves and slave owners. **Living conditions** for the slaves were invariably squalid, and discipline was brutal, with severe punishments meted out to any wrongdoer – in his 1740 treatise *A New and Exact Account of Jamaica*, Charles Leslie noted of Jamaica's planters that "no Country exceeds them in a barbarous treatment of slaves, or in the cruel Methods that they put them to death". Torture, designed as much to humiliate as to punish, was commonly imposed, and followed by a slow, painful death.

Slaves were at the whim of cruel overseers, few of whom would ever be taken to task, however badly they treated those in their charge. **Religion** went some way to improve living conditions – converted slaves were usually given Sundays off to attend church, while church leaders encouraged planters to treat slaves as human beings rather than "chattel" – and when food supplies to the island were disrupted in the 1770s during the American War of Independence, slaves were often allowed to cultivate and market their own foodstuffs. Yet this was hardly an altruistic gesture – malnourished slaves did less work, so it was in every planter's interest to keep his lifeblood alive at the least possible cost to himself. For every slave owner who made some small effort to ensure the physical well being of his slaves, there were ten more who cared little or nothing for their well being – it was easier and cheaper to simply buy some more should slaves die or be put to death. Life on the plantations remained unimaginably horrible for all but the slave owner and his family.

Rebellion

Given the conditions on the estates, it's hardly surprising that **slave revolts** were a feature of Jamaican life from the time of the British conquest right up until emancipation in 1838, always dreaded by the authorities and invariably crushed with appalling brutality. Dissenters were severely flogged and their wounds rubbed with salt, lime and pepper before being slung up from the waist in the sun for several days; they were then taken down to have the soles of the feet and the armpits seared, the heart and entrails removed and burned in front of the still-living victim; the heads of hung or burned slaves were routinely cut off and displayed on poles as a warning to others considering revolt. Despite such grisly punishments, slave rebellions in Jamaica – occurring, on average, every five years during the eighteenth century – were both more numerous and on a larger scale than in the United States or elsewhere in the British West Indies.

Comprised of slaves armed and freed by retreating Spanish troops in 1660, alongside runaways from British plantations, the **Maroons** (a corruption of the Spanish *cimarrones*, meaning "wild" or "untamed") lived in inaccessible parts of the Blue and John Crow mountains in the east and Cockpit Country in the west. Initially, most Maroons were of **Coromantee** descent, from the region of modern-day Ghana, and despite the upheaval of slavery, their shared language and traditions helped to organize strong communities in their new environment. As numbers grew, they periodically plundered British settlements for arms, animals and supplies, and they proved an effective deterrent to colonists who were considering settling in inhospitable areas like Portland.

Although British soldiers made regular forays against them, the Maroons had become such a serious threat by the 1720s that forts and barracks were built at the edges of their territories, and the British military might was turned towards wiping out this troublesome fifth column. Special troops were brought in, including a large party of Mosquito Indian trackers from Nicaragua but, in extremely difficult and confusing terrain, they were often outmanoeuvred by the skilled **guerrilla tactics** of the Maroons. In places that now carry evocative names like "The District of Look Behind", whole parties of British soldiers were slaughtered, though one was normally left alive to carry the message of comprehensive defeat back to the authorities.

By 1739, the superior firepower of the British had gained the upper hand, although it was apparent that winning a war against this "invisible enemy" would be costly and drawn-out. Accordingly, the First Maroon War was ended by a **peace treaty**, signed in the Maroon stronghold of Accompong by British commanding officer Colonel Guthrie and **Cudjoe**, the Maroon chief. The terms were that the Trelawny Maroons should stop attacking British settlements, return all future runaway slaves and provide assistance in the event of internal rebellion or foreign invasion. In return, they were granted freedom, fifteen hundred acres of land in Cockpit Country (around present-day Accompong) and a degree of autonomy, including the administration of justice in all cases except for those involving the death penalty. One year later, the Windward Maroons – those encamped in the Blue Mountains – signed a similar deal.

For two generations the peace held, and the Maroons lived as a semi-sovereign state within Jamaica. Both sides kept to the agreement, most notably in 1760, when Maroons helped to suppress the **Tacky rebellion**. However, in 1795, the public flogging of two Maroons in Montego Bay outraged the Trelawny Maroons community, and hostilities quickly flared again. Plantations were burned and planters killed, and the British army rushed to quell this internal conflict. For a while, the **Second Maroon War** followed the path of the First, with soldiers ambushed as they ventured into unfamiliar territory, and the Maroons inflicting heavy losses. However, the British were better organized this time and had at their disposal both enormous hunting dogs imported from Cuba, and warriors and trackers from Jamaica's other Maroon settlements. A peace offer was made by British General Walpole and the Maroons surrendered, although not until several days after the terms of the peace offer had lapsed. Using this pretext, the British revoked the promise that Maroons should be allowed to stay on their land, and five hundred of the Trelawny Maroons were **deported** to the freezing climate of Nova Scotia (although not before General Walpole had resigned in disgust at the authorities' duplicity). The deported Maroons stayed in Nova Scotia for just a year before setting sail for Sierra Leone – from where, generations earlier, many of their ancestors had been brought to Jamaica as slaves.

Most of the Maroon communities in Portland and at Accompong in Cockpit Country remained relatively undisturbed by the ructions of the Second Maroon War and, protected by the 1739 peace treaty, continued to maintain a semi-independent status within the island that persists to this day.

There were a number of reasons for this. The island's mountainous **geography** encouraged rebels by providing places to escape and hide, while the high level of absentee slave-owners also encouraged revolts either through the cruelty of the overseers or, conversely, because of a lack of attention to the risks of rebellion. In addition, **social and religious ideas** fermented disorder, with abolitionists arguing the case against slavery at the turn of the nineteenth century. Meanwhile, the creation of the first independent black-led republic in the world following Toussaint L'Ouverture's 1799 revolution in **Haiti** provided slaves with a concrete example of a successful revolt.

Though brutally crushed, Tacky's rebellion in 1760 (see p.153) was the major slave revolt of the eighteenth century, while the 1831 **Christmas rebellion**, led by Sam Sharpe (see p.181), was the most serious slave uprising in the island's history. The scale of the rebellion and the brutality with which it was crushed intensified the abolition debate, both in Jamaica and in Britain, and accelerated the emancipation that Sharpe had been seeking.

Jamaica 1670–1834

The eighteenth century saw the Jamaican authorities plagued as much by the threat of **foreign invasion** as they were by domestic insurrection. Skirmishes with French troops from nearby San Domingo led to a frenzy of **fort building** around the coast (and in parts of the interior, to contain the threat of the Maroons), and all of Britain's great naval commanders served time here, many of them based at Port Royal. The presence of such force undoubtedly contributed to the fact that there was not to be another foreign invasion. Though the French took advantage of Britain's preoccupation with the 1775 **American War of Independence** and launched a series of invasions that left Britain's West Indian possessions limited to just Jamaica, Barbados and Antigua, Jamaica itself was saved from invasion by Britain's conclusive victory at the Battle of **Les Saintes** off the Windward Islands in 1782, which saw the destruction of the French Navy by British forces under Admiral Rodney, and removed the threat of attack from the island for several generations.

Without the threat of invasion to contend with, the early nineteenth century saw Jamaica consumed with problems more close to home, as conflicts arose between the interests of the early settlers and those of the mother country. As Creole society developed, and a new generation of whites who had actually been born in Jamaica grew up, there were increasing demands for political power to be kept entirely on the island. Accordingly, in 1729 the British Crown recognized the **local assembly** as the source of all legislation on Jamaican matters, replacing the Crown's governor as the chief authority on the island.

Throughout the eighteenth century, power remained in the hands of the white planter class, with the right to vote given only to property owners. Gradually, given the sexual proclivities of the planters, who routinely enforced sex on their female slaves (planter diarist Thomas Thistlewood chronicled some 4000 sex acts with 138 women during his time in Jamaica), a "mulatto" or **mixed-race class** emerged who looked to their white fathers for an education and opportunities that were denied to people of pure African origin. Although this mulatto class were not officially granted equal rights until 1832, many of its members exercised considerable political influence and were to prove far more sympathetic to the black cause than white planters had been.

Nineteenth-century Jamaica

In the early nineteenth century, forces inside and outside Jamaica brought about a sea change in the fortunes of the different racial groups. In 1807 the British parliament prohibited its colonies from trading in slaves, but the **abolition of slavery** itself – heavily opposed by the West Indian lobby, who feared the collapse of the local economy – was not finally passed until 1834. Despite the islandwide jubilation, the slaves were not yet given unconditional freedom; they were expected to continue working for their former masters, unpaid, for a six-year "apprenticeship". In 1838 the apprenticeship system was abandoned and the former slaves were, at last, free to demand wages or work elsewhere. Many left the hated estates at the first opportunity, establishing small farms on squatted or rented land, or settling in the "**free villages**" set up by missionaries throughout the island. Lots were either sold or donated to former slaves, who in turn helped to build the church and school that the villages were based around.

The drain of workers from the estates, and the reluctance of many estate owners to pay proper wages, forced them to turn to alternative sources of cheap labour. Already, during the 1830s, when the white ruling class were keen to avoid seeing Jamaica's fertile interior settled by black ex-slaves, 1200 Germans had been brought to the island and granted land at present-day Seaford Town once they had worked on the estates for five years. Other workers were brought from China, the Middle East and other parts of Europe, but India was to provide the great majority of the new **indentured labour**. Under a scheme approved by the Jamaican assembly in 1845, 35,000 **Indians** were brought to the island before the Indian government banned further traffic in 1917. The estate owners promised that, once the workers had paid off the cost of their passage from India, they would be able to earn decent money to send home, before returning themselves at the end of their contracts. In practice, the Indians became the new slaves – working for scant pay under terrible conditions – and the majority never had the chance to return home.

The sugar industry took another major blow in 1846, when the Sugar Duties Act forced Jamaica's sugar producers to compete on equal terms with others worldwide; simultaneously, the development of **beet sugar** contributed to a drop in price and reduced demand for cane sugar. Although the industry was far from dead, this series of setbacks forced the island to end its reliance on a single crop. **Banana** cultivation was introduced in the 1860s and, for a while, became the boom crop as demand for the new fruit soared in Europe and America. By the end of the nineteenth century, the older economic pattern of the Jamaican community had faded completely and a new organization was emerging.

Post-emancipation problems

Jamaica's estate-owners were given a total of £20 million compensation for the loss of their slaves (most of which went to repay debts owed to merchants in Britain). There was no such compensation for the newly freed slaves, for whom life remained far from easy. Their first problem was **land**. Without somewhere to grow crops, black Jamaicans had little choice but to return to the plantations as poorly paid wage-labourers; getting their own land guaranteed a degree of independence and provided a bargaining tool for higher wages. The planters were equally aware of this issue, however, and made it as hard as possible for the ex-slaves to get land, imposing high rents and taking action against squatters who tried to occupy unused land. The second issue was the one-sided **administration of justice**; the planter class dominated the magistrates' courts and imposed heavy-handed penalties for squatting and other minor wrongs.

The downturn in the country's economy that followed the abolition of slavery and the introduction of free trade in sugar also took its toll on the freed slaves. Wages were kept pitifully low, taxes were imposed and unemployment rose as plantations were downsized or abandoned altogether. As food shortages intensified, unrest among Jamaica's black population grew, eventually coming to a head in 1865 when the **Morant Bay rebellion** (for more on which, see p.109) broke out in St Thomas. Fearing that the uprising would spread throughout the island, Governor Eyre ordered a show of strength from the armed forces. Little mercy was shown, as 437 people (including the rebellion's leader, **Paul Bogle**) were killed and executed, and thousands more flogged and terrorized.

This brutal suppression caused horror throughout Jamaica and Britain, and provoked considerable change in the colony. Governor Eyre was ordered back to Britain and dismissed for his part in the atrocities, while his assembly abolished itself and, in 1866, Jamaica became a **Crown Colony**, with direct rule from Britain via a legislative council. Although this set back the cause of responsible government on the island for almost a century, it enabled certain reforms to be passed that would never have got past the planters and their representatives in the assembly. New courts were established, a police force created and the Church of England was disestablished on the island. Roads and irrigation systems were improved, more money was spent on education, and in 1872, the capital city was transferred from Spanish Town to **Kingston**. This move was long overdue; most of Jamaica's trade – from slaves to rum – had been processed through Kingston's harbour for two centuries, bringing colossal wealth in its wake, and by any criteria the city was the right place for the seat of government.

There were downsides to the changes, of course. Taxes were raised to finance the reforms, and the unrepresentative political system frustrated the island's fledgling democratic movement for nearly eighty years. On the whole, the new system kept the peace while preserving the status quo; the whites retained all political and social authority, while the blacks were sufficiently mollified that there was little threat of upheaval for the rest of the century. Nonetheless, landowners bemoaned the government's financial extravagance and inefficiency, while black leaders pointed to the lack of any radical change.

Away from politics, meanwhile, the 1890s saw the arrival of the island's first **tourists**, many sailing from North America on the banana boats that plied between the east coast and Port Antonio in Portland.

Jamaica in the twentieth century

The early twentieth century saw considerable **economic prosperity**, with particular booms in the banana and tourism industries. And the new wealth was no longer confined to the whites – **George Stiebel**, Jamaica's first black millionaire, used his fortune to design some fine buildings, particularly Devon House in Kingston, and his example proved an inspiration to others. Inevitably, though, most of the new wealth bypassed the black masses, and serious **poverty** remained throughout the island. People were increasingly drawn to the new capital city to look for work, but many were left stranded in Kingston slums with little prospect of income or employment. **Natural disasters** also took their toll. In 1907, the capital was partially flattened by a devastating earthquake, and there were major hurricanes throughout the 1910s.

By the 1930s, as the **Great Depression** took hold worldwide, the positive effects of the economic boom had pretty much evaporated. The banana crop had been decimated by disease, and never regained its former export heights, while sugar revenues fell precipitately as demand dried up. Unemployment spiralled, and riots in Kingston and around the island became commonplace, as did **strikes**; in 1938, a major clash between police and workers of the West Indies Sugar Company factory at Frome left several dead. Protests and looting followed islandwide, and in the wake of the dispute, strike leader **Alexander Bustamante** founded the Caribbean's first **trade union** – the Bustamante Industrial Trade Union (BITU). An associated political party was born, too, with the foundation of the **People's National Party (PNP)** by the lawyer **Norman Manley**. Both events gave a boost to Jamaican nationalism, already stirred by the campaigning of black-consciousness leader **Marcus Garvey** during the 1920s and early 1930s, and increased the pressure for political reform and improvement in the condition of the workers.

World War II and the road to independence

Jamaica served as an important Allied base during **World War II** (and thousands of islanders contributed to the war effort more directly by volunteering to fight for Britain), while the need to provide increased supplies of food to the mother country led to the expansion of sugar and other food industries. Economic development continued by way of both increased tourist arrivals and of the emerging bauxite industry, which began commercial export in 1952.

On the political front, a **new constitution** in 1944 introduced universal adult suffrage, and the same year saw the first elections for a locally based government to work in conjunction with the British-appointed governor. The vote was taken by the **Jamaica Labour Party (JLP)**, formed by Bustamante in 1943 after he split from Manley's PNP. The two parties gradually drifted in the ideological directions that they (loosely) retain to this day, with the JLP adopting a basic liberal capitalist philosophy, and Manley's PNP leaning more towards democratic socialism.

When the PNP finally took over the reins at the 1955 election, one of Norman Manley's first priorities was the issue of independence. As it was impractical for Caribbean colonies to "go it alone", the idea of a West Indian confederacy was floated; by 1958, the ill-fated **West Indies Federation** was launched, with its capital in Port of Spain, Trinidad. However, it never really stood a chance. Jamaica refused to accept the principle of federalism, arguing that it must be allowed to protect its own economic interests, even where these clashed with the other islands, while traditional inter-island rivalries left many Jamaicans suspicious that they would have to subsidize their smaller, less successful neighbours. In a **referendum** called by Manley in September 1961, Jamaica voted categorically to leave, prompting the Federation's rapid disintegration. Disheartened though they were, the British had little choice but to accept the decision of the electorate. Within a year they had granted Jamaica its **independence**.

Independence and the Manley era

On August 6, 1962, Jamaica became an independent state within the British Commonwealth, with Bustamante as its first prime minister. The early years of independence were marked by rising prosperity, as foreign investment increased, particularly in the bauxite industry. The JLP continued in power until the key **elections of 1972**, when Jamaicans rejected the JLP's US-friendly liberal economic programme and voted in droves for the PNP, now led by Norman Manley's charismatic son Michael. The next eight years of PNP rule represented a crucial period for Jamaica. Until 1972, economic and political power had rested predominantly with white and mixed-race Jamaicans. **Michael Manley**'s rousing slogans, such as "Power for the people" and "Better must come", the latter borrowed from Delroy Wilson's hit reggae tune, exemplified his desire to improve the conditions of the black majority and to challenge the status quo.

His **major reforms** included a minimum wage, a literacy campaign, the distribution of land to small farmers, more public housing and an improvement in funding for the island's education and healthcare sectors – all of which were financed by businesses that had been largely protected from taxation, in particular the internationally owned bauxite industry. The strategy backfired, however, when the bauxite companies promptly scaled down their Jamaican operations, reducing the country's foreign-exchange earnings, and this blow was compounded when the 1973–74 oil crisis further increased pressure on government spending. In the light of this, Manley sought to promote a greater degree of **self-sufficiency**, encouraging the use of Jamaican, rather than imported, products. In **foreign affairs**, meanwhile, Manley rejected close ties with the US in favour of friendship with Fidel Castro's Cuba. Needless to say, the American reaction was furious; economic sanctions were applied and foreign investment nosedived. Fearing higher taxation and even the introduction of communism, wealthy white Jamaicans left in droves, withdrawing their capital and skills at the time that they were most needed.

Jamaican politics became increasingly polarized and antagonistic, with the JLP (by now led by **Edward Seaga**) launching blistering attacks on the "communist" administration. The 1976 election – won by the PNP again – saw a disturbing increase in **political violence**, particularly in the ghetto constituencies of Kingston, which the political parties had turned into **"garrisons"** by distributing guns to their supporters and encouraging them to drive away opponents through intimidation. Manley's response to the violence was to impose a **state of emergency**, establishing a non-jury "Gun Court" and passing severe anti-crime legislation that allowed it to impose life sentences for anyone convicted of unlawful possession of a firearm.

The PNP's **second term** sounded the death knell for Manley's brand of democratic socialism. Foreign investment had fallen precipitately, local capital had been withdrawn from the island, and despite the empty shelves in the supermarkets, the cost of imports continued to outstrip exports. The government turned to the International Monetary Fund for assistance, and the resulting curtailment of public spending and the drastic cuts in social programmes alienated many erstwhile supporters. Violence flared again during the 1980 election campaign, with hundreds of people killed in shoot-outs and open gang-warfare. Amid the carnage, the Jamaican people turned to the JLP for a new vision for their country.

The JLP in power

The first foreign leader to visit the newly elected President Ronald Reagan in Washington, Edward Seaga's **realignment** of the two neighbouring countries was perhaps his most important change in policy. The US took steps to open its markets to foreign imports and to encourage outward investment, most notably with the enactment of the Caribbean Basin Initiative (economic aid in return for free elections and cooperative governments), and foreign capital began to find its way back to Jamaica. However, Seaga was obliged to continue the cutback of government services, and his honeymoon with the Jamaican people proved short-lived. A snap election in 1983 was boycotted by the PNP, but re-elected prime minister Seaga was unable to give the island's economy the boost it required, and rising poverty and unemployment combined with his lack of charisma led to a fall in support. In 1989, Michael Manley were returned to office, and the PNP were to remain in government for the next eighteen years.

The PNP years

Despite widespread fears of a return to the politics of the 1970s, the new-look Manley administration proved very different. The emphasis now was on continuity of policy, and although foreign relations with Cuba were restored, there was no more anti-American rhetoric. The demands of the World Bank and the IMF continued to be met and a generally liberal economic policy followed. In 1992 Manley resigned the premiership on the grounds of ill health, leaving his successor, **P.J. Patterson**, to continue the policy of continuity. The first black man to become Jamaica's prime minister, Patterson went on to defeat Seaga and the JLP in the 1993 general election, a loss from which Seaga never fully recovered; having lost successive elections in 1997 and 2002, Seaga resigned from politics in 2004. Despite having limped to victory for a further two terms, the PNP received a much-needed shot of adrenaline in 2006, when Patterson resigned as the PNP's leader and **Portia Simpson Miller** became Jamaica's first female prime minister. Far removed from the white (or nearly white), male, upper-class hegemony that has dominated Jamaican politics since independence, and employing plenty of Christian rhetoric along with the spin, "Mama P" proved hugely popular with the masses. Nonetheless, she proved no less able to deal with the key issues of crime, poverty and unemployment than her predecessors, and in 2007, a tightly contested election was eventually taken by the JLP under their new leader, **Bruce Golding**.

Jamaica today

Twenty-first century Jamaica is an intriguing mix of extreme juxtapositions. This tiny developing country with its brutal history of slavery and social injustice has nonetheless managed to produce a succession of truly remarkable writers, musicians and athletes, not to mention dictating many of the defining features of youth culture the world over, from dreadlocks to pseudo-patois. But for all its successes and its sense of inherent hipness, contemporary Jamaica is tarnished by many negatives. The backbone of the island's economy now rests on tourism, bauxite and the **remittances** that overseas Jamaicans send to family back home, the latter accounting for a colossal twenty percent of GDP – roughly equivalent to tourism revenues. A huge amount of money is spent on promoting Jamaica as a **tourist** destination, and so far the island is holding its own despite the global recession, with just under 64,000 more visitor arrivals in 2009 than in 2008, and an annual count of more than a million and a half stayover guests – an affirmation, perhaps, of the immense appeal of Jamaica's cultural and physical attributes. **Bauxite** production has long recovered from the blow the industry took in the 1970s, although sharp falls in prices worldwide following the recession have meant lower earnings overall – and as the island's processing plants are all foreign-owned, relatively little of the industry's profits remain in Jamaica in any case.

The potential of **agriculture** remains vast, with great products and superb farming conditions. Nontraditional exports such as ackee and seafood have made significant increases in recent years, while premium Blue Mountain coffee is seen as one of the few traditional crops that has the potential for growth, but the sector is floundering. The WTO's 1997 removal of preferential tariffs to European markets for Caribbean producers has left Jamaica's small-scale producers unable to compete with huge US-backed operations in Latin America and all but decimated the banana industry. The **sugar** industry is in crisis, too, though overseas aid, government bailouts and efforts to diversify via production of ethanol (as a gasoline additive and as a cleaner-burning fuel) from sugar cane may yet prevent it from collapsing completely. Despite its potential to turn the economy around, farming remains an unattractive prospect as a career choice, especially because Jamaican produce has to compete with goods imported from the US; go to any market in Jamaica, and you'll see American potatoes, cabbages and carrots on sale for significantly less than their locally grown equivalents – hardly an incentive for the hard-pushed consumer to buy Jamaican, nor for farmers to continue to produce crops. Jamaica's imbalance between earnings and spending has been further exacerbated in the last couple of decades by a staggering increase in other **imports**, too. The streets and shopping malls are chock-full with flash cars and other foreign accessories, from foods to phones or brand-name clothing, though there's no sign of any corresponding increase in export production to pay for it all. Remittances, meanwhile, have declined significantly as the economic downturn bites overseas.

Jamaica's foreign **debt burden** – some US$10.2 billion at the time of writing, the fourth highest per capita in the world – is another tale of woe. Debt serving accounts for nearly half of the government's expenditure, leaving little to allocate to urgently needed domestic programmes such as education and health. Retrenchment, built on interest rates that average around eighteen percent, has hit hard: unemployment stands at around eleven percent, and the glamour of the tourist resorts belies a lot of poverty in Kingston and rural areas.

The other major issue for most Jamaicans – and the one that makes the most headlines overseas – is **crime**: the island has the unwelcome distinction of having one of the highest per-capita murder rates in the world – around 1500 per year, or five per day, and a terrible reputation for violent crime in its inner cities. The "garrison communities" established during the 1970s are now run by gangsters known as "area leaders" or dons, and they – with the help of their contacts in every walk of Jamaican life, from the police to the government to the army and coast-guard – have turned the island into one of the key transhipment points for cocaine being smuggled from South America to the US, bringing criminality to ever more sophisticated and brutal levels. Initiatives such as **Operation Kingfish** have had some success in tackling organized crime, while the installation of several British police officers in prominent positions within the Jamaica Constabulary Force is part of a wider programme of cooperation between the Jamaican force and international police agencies to find more effective ways of policing the nation. Cynics, however, point to fact that the police fatally shoot at least 200 Jamaicans each year as evidence that so-called **vigilante justice** has been unofficially adopted as the principal way for the police to deal with violent crime. Capital punishment is often mooted as the ultimate deterrent to criminals, but until Jamaica joins Barbados and Guyana in adopting the pro-hanging **Caribbean Court of Justice** to replace Britain's Privy Council as the island's final court of appeal, it's unlikely that any of the nine people currently on the island's Death Row will go to the gallows.

Amid all of these crushing problems, however, Jamaica does have plenty to celebrate. The island's **athletes** provided some positive headlines at the 2008 Olympics in Beijing, notching up six gold, three silver and two bronze medals to the delight of Jamaicans everywhere. Team Jamaica then went on to wow the world at the World Championships in Berlin in August 2009, where their medal tally included three golds and three world records for sprinter **Usain Bolt**, still the fastest man in the world at the time of writing. Jamaica's sporting success is a truly awesome feat for such a tiny nation, especially one with so much less in the way of resources and facilities for its sportsmen and women. And culturally, too, Jamaica remains a world leader, with the county's musicians – from the pre-eminent Bob Marley and his son Damian "Junior Gong" to Sean Paul and the countless dancehall DJs imitated worldwide – topping the charts in every corner of the globe. Jamaica today remains a country of dichotomies: home to the worst of the worst, perhaps, but also the best of the best.

The environment

From parched savannah plains and dry limestone forest to low-lying rainforest and wetland swamps, with richly vegetated, undulating hills and lush pastures in between, Jamaica's landscape and topography vary immensely, and harbour a rich array of plant, bird and animal life.

With a total area of a thousand-plus square miles, Jamaica is the third largest island in the Caribbean archipelago, after Cuba and Hispaniola. Unlike many of its neighbours, however, more than half of it stands over 1500ft above sea level, providing mist-shrouded peaks as well as brilliant white-sand beaches. Other than the metamorphic, sedimentary and igneous volcanic rocks of the Blue Mountains – Jamaica's oldest geological feature – most of the island's surface area is covered with soft, sedimentary **limestone**, at its thickest in central and western areas such as Cockpit Country, where rivers have carved out a labyrinthine network of conical hillocks surrounded by deep sinkholes and caves.

Trees and shrubs

Though Jamaica's deforestation rate is high, some thirty percent of the island is still shrouded in a thick cloak of trees, and even in urban areas, there's plenty of green to be seen. Trees are often planted for their shade-giving properties; the **guango**, with its bromeliad-smothered spreading branches, is common, but the most arresting and majestic is the towering **silk cotton**, which often reaches more than 130ft in height, its huge buttressed roots spreading elegantly to meet the ground. Naturally buoyant and easily carved, silk cottons were hollowed out into dugout canoes by Tainos, and their fruits contain the cotton-like kapok. **Logwood** is extremely common and was once grown commercially for the dark-blue dye extracted from the trunk and roots. In 1893 it surpassed cane and coffee as the island's main export, but synthetic alternatives subsequently ended the trade. Bees flock to the perfumed yellow blossoms, and logwood honey is said to be the best available. The **annotto** was also exploited for the intense orange-red dye extracted from seed pods growing in clusters around its attractive pink flowers. Tainos used it as their principal body paint and it was a prime commodity during Spanish occupation, though it's extremely rare today.

You'll encounter the marbled, blue-tinted wood of the **mahoe**, the national tree, in countless craft items. Fast-growing and indigenous, the mahoe has a short straight trunk that grows up to 65ft, broad leaves and distinctive hibiscus-like flowers that change from yellow to orange and deep crimson as they mature. The rich red wood of Jamaican **mahogany** is regarded as some of the best in the world, but has been so heavily exported that few trees are left – the custom of stripping the bark from young trees to extract a dye helped to decimate populations. Those remaining grow in remote areas such as Cockpit Country and the Blue and John Crow mountains, and can attain a height of 130ft.

The archetypal Caribbean tree, the **palm** comes in numerous shapes and sizes. Ornamental varieties include the **royal palm**, a 100-foot-high specimen that's often planted along driveways to impressive effect; close relative the **cabbage palm** manages a whopping 130ft and has thicker, messier-looking fronds. There are several pseudo-palms in Jamaica, of which the most attractive pretender is the magnificent **travellers' palm**, a member of the banana family – the name refers to mini-ponds at the base of the leaves that provide a convenient water source. Fronds fan out from the base in an enormous peacock's-tail shape that can measure 30ft.

Jamaica's geographical location and geological origins make the island highly susceptible to the elements, particularly during the rainy seasons (roughly May–June and Sept to mid-Oct), when tropical waves, as storms are called, cause islandwide flooding, landslides and road closures. These are mere trifles, though, in comparison to the devastation wrought by the **hurricanes** which blow through the region between June and November each year. Though many bypass the island entirely, Jamaica has suffered extensive hurricane damage over the years, most notably from **Allen** in 1980, **Gilbert** in 1988, **Ivan** in 2004 and **Dean** in 2007, the latter sweeping through the south and east coats and causing such devastation that then Prime Minister Portia Simpson-Miller postponed the general election and declared a month-long state of emergency while the island licked its wounds and repaired the worst of the damage. Ivan, meanwhile, was even more devastating, resulting in seventeen deaths, thousands of destroyed homes, power lost for days, and severe damage to banana, coffee and sugar production, fisheries and roads.

Flowering trees and shrubs

If you fly over Jamaica's interior or look closely at any rural panorama, you'll notice occasional patches of deep red courtesy of the **African tulip** or "flame of the forest"; flowering sporadically throughout the year, its clusters of blooms often cover entire outer branches. Known for the gorgeous crown of deep-scarlet blossoms that adorn many a hotel garden, the **poinciana** or "flamboyant tree" also produces long brown seed pods, often polished and used as shaker instruments. More familiar as a Christmas pot plant in temperate climes, the **poinsettia** grows into a lovely tree here, with a huge spread of bright green leaves that turn deep red in the cooler winter months. Twenty-nine varieties of **cassia**, meanwhile, provide showy cascades of blossoms, most commonly in pink or yellow; equally common is the **bauhinia** or "poor man's orchid", a prolific purple-flowered shrub with cloven-hoof-shaped leaves. The tree of life, **Lignum vitae** – so called because of its many medicinal uses – blooms with Jamaica's **national flower**, a subtle, light-blue shower. Highly resinous, its wood is heavy enough to sink in water and was extensively used in shipbuilding and as a suitably painful material for truncheons.

Fruit trees

Bearing Jamaica's national fruit, the ubiquitous **ackee** is identifiable by its crimson seed pods, which burst open when ripe to reveal the edible yellow arils. Almost as prevalent are the spreading branches of the **breadfruit**, decorated by serrated, hand-like leaves and pockmarked, matte-green fruits. **Cashew** trees are common and produce both fruits and nuts. Similar in appearance to red ackee pods, cashew "apples" produce the nut but can also be cooked and eaten. The oily liquid in the shell is poisonous, while the sap produces an indelible ink. The source of many a souvenir, the large globular fruits of the **calabash** are hollowed and dried for use as dishes and containers, or filled with pebbles to make maracas. **Cocoa** trees are easily identifiable, with shiny dark-green or red leaves and ten-inch oval pods that grow in clusters from branches or sometimes the trunk, turning from light green to brown when ripe; the sweet pulp around the beans inside can be eaten when raw.

Versatile **coconut palms** are everywhere, with every part of their fruit used – be it for food or floor mats. The Jamaica Tall coconut palm has been largely eradicated by lethal yellowing disease (you'll see the frond-less trunks dotted around) and has been widely replaced by the hardier hybrid **mayapan**, a squat ten-footer with straggly yellowed leaves and orange-tinted nuts. Diminutive **guava** trees grow wild throughout the island and are also cultivated commercially for their green-skinned, pink-fleshed fruits, but the king of the fruit trees are the many varieties of **mango**, with their dense covering of finger-like leaves and branches heavy with fruits during the summer season.

Coastal trees

Jamaica's surviving **mangrove swamps** are central to the health of coastal ecosystems, affording protection from hurricane surges, filtering earth sediments and nutrients and providing a protected nursery for fish and crustaceans. Nonetheless, they often fall victim to short-sighted development, bulldozed to make way for hotel developments and to facilitate sand mining, or used as fuel for charcoal kilns. Though not naturally a coast-dweller, the **Indian almond** flourishes along the length of Jamaica's shores. Branches grow symmetrically, and though they don't taste much like conventional almonds, the nuts can be eaten once the outer pods turn brown. A staple of all Jamaican beaches, the **sea grape** varies considerably in shape according to its environment; on exposed shores it lies low and twisted, but with less buffeting it can attain a height of 50ft. The flat, round leaves are distinctively veined and turn a deep red as they mature. Once they've turned purple, the grapes are edible, if a little sour. Fortunately very rare and definitely one to avoid is the **manchineel**, which grows to about 40ft, with a wide-spreading canopy dotted with indistinct green fruits and flowers, all of which are extremely poisonous – even standing below a manchineel during rain incurs blistering. Luckily, you're only likely to chance upon a manchineel in the most remote areas, and cases of run-ins are unheard of.

Ganja cultivation

Though there are two annual growing seasons, Jamaica's most infamous crop is mainly reaped between August and October, when the buds have received the full benefit of the summer sun. Plants can reach a height of 7ft, and are usually grown amongst other tall crops at very remote and usually small plantations. After the plants are harvested, the outer leaves are discarded and the potent buds hung up and cured. Marijuana, or **ganja**, is not particularly easy to raise – many cultivators liken the task to bringing up a sickly child. Seeds must first be carefully germinated, then planted in open ground and stringently guarded against pests and birds. As buds attain maturity, the farmer must spend increasing amounts of time at the plot, feeding, watering and tending his crop as well as defending the valuable stems against thieves. Many farmers use pesticides and expensive conventional fertilizers, though this is frowned upon and seen to produce a tainted version of the real thing; local organic fertilizers such as bat guano are preferred to ensure top potency. Growers also face losing it all to the hands of the Jamaica Defence Force, who conduct regular **eradication programmes** as the fields reach maturity. Helicopters scour the hills for likely plantations, while a ground crew sweeps through the countryside burning or spraying the plants with powerful insecticide. Unscrupulous soldiers are frequently known to accept a bribe in return for burning only a portion of the fields or not arresting the farmer, though as many policemen sell or smoke cannabis themselves, undocumented and highly profitable confiscations are reputedly common.

Plants

Of Jamaica's abundance of plants, some of the most striking are the **cacti** that flourish in the dry scrub of the Hellshire hills and south-coast plains. Some, such as the two **dildo** varieties, grow as tall as 20ft, stretching skywards between clumps of viciously thorned **makko** bushes. The inner stems of **torchwood** cacti are dried and lit as home-made torches in rural areas and bear a yellow fruit, while the **dildo pear** has a red fruit; both are edible. **Prickly pear** and the "smooth pear" or **cochineal cactus** are also common, the latter known as "roast pork" for its taste when cooked. Of climbing varieties, most spectacular is the **queen of the night**, which boasts a huge and powerfully scented flower that only blooms after dark. The endemic **god okra**, with its edible stems and crimson fruits, is often vested with supernatural powers as its aerial roots spread so far over rocks and trees from their triangular main stem that they appear to have no earth to support them. The epiphytic **spaghetti cactus**, meanwhile, has 6ft skinny green stems that hang down from dead or living trees, and bears miniature white flowers and berries. The flat-lobed prickly **tuna** cactus is widely used in bush medicine, said to cure dandruff, reduce swelling and relieve chronic pain.

Jamaica's **vines** are equally unusual. The rampant forest **cacoon** has a huge circular bean pod the colour of a burnished conker, while strings of shiny red and black seeds from the **John Crow bead vine** turn up on craft stalls island-wide. The rare, triffid-type **duppy fly trap** bears the largest flower in Jamaica – an eight-inch, purple heart-shaped centre from which 23-inch fly-catching spurs extend. A rotting-meat odour attracts flies to the inside of the flowers, where they are covered in pollen and released to pollinate other plants. Growing prolifically throughout the island, the mimosa family's fascinating **shame'o'lady**, resembling a miniature bracken, closes its leaves to expose thorns on its stem at the slightest touch as protection against foraging animals. Equally intriguing is the epiphytic **wild pine bromeliad**, its 3ft pineapple-like leaves flourishing wherever there's a tree to host it. The rainwater collected between the leaves supports a variety of insects and even frogs, and the most protected specimens boast a pale crimson flower.

Aloe vera

Jamaicans are so convinced of the curative power of fast-growing **aloe vera** or "sinkle bible" (a corruption of the botanical name *sempervivum*) that many dispense with titles altogether and simply call it the "healing plant". Noticeable for its thick, spiny-edged clusters of leaves growing close to the ground, aloe is the workhorse of Jamaican healing. It's used to treat sunburn (for which it's particularly effective), heat rashes, cuts, bruises, burns and all insect bites; mixed with water to make an eye wash that soothes conjunctivitis; used to condition sun-damaged hair; prepared as a treatment for skin conditions like eczema and psoriasis; and drunk with garlic to cleanse the blood – a daring feat, as it's very bitter.

Rastafarians use aloe in place of the Biblical hyssop, but you're most likely to encounter it in the hands of hustlers who peddle bottles of "aloe massage" (aloe gel mixed with water) on north-coast beaches. As aloe plants flourish throughout the island, you can usually find it for free, and it's much more effective (and hygienic) to use aloe straight from the plant than in a preparation. To extract the gel, slice the stem in two, cut off the serrated edges, lightly scrape the mauve jelly and wipe it on. Be careful not to get it on clothing – it can leave a stubborn stain.

Many Jamaicans, particularly in rural areas, still make frequent use of **"bush medicine"** or **"balm"**. A system of African herbal medicine introduced to Jamaica by slaves, it was fundamental to Maroon civilization for three hundred-odd years and is used to treat anything from the common cold to impotence. Herbs are taken as an infusion or decoction (usually as a tea), as a poultice, or in a hot "bush bath". Many households have a pot of cure-all **bush tea** permanently on the hob, made up of diverse ingredients like lemon, fevergrass, soursop, breadfruit leaves and pepper elder. Perhaps the most widely used single herb is **cerassee**, a climbing vine made into a very bitter tea – you can buy ready-made teabags if you develop a taste. It's said to cure practically everything, but is particularly good as a blood purifier and allegedly discourages mosquitoes. Inevitably, there are loads of plants geared around **male virility** – chainy root, jack-in-the-bush, medina, janta (or cow-hoof leaf), quassia – the list of "front end lifters" goes on and on, and many concoctions are now commercially bottled (see Basics, p.30). Ganja is boiled into a tea for asthma and eye problems; **leaf of life** is said to conquer colds, hypertension and bronchial problems; **tuna cactus** is used to treat dandruff, nerves and chronic pain such as arthritis. Many of the medicinal herbs have wonderfully fanciful names; among the best are **search mi heart** and **shame o' lady**, both used for colds and stomach problems, but the prize goes to **ram goat dash along**, good for arthritis and debility. Healing properties are also attributed to simple **fruits and vegetables**. Soursop is said to calm the nerves, and its leaves are used to help testy babies go off to sleep. Papaya (paw-paw) is reputed to relieve indigestion; guava leaves are good for diarrhoea; tamarind soothes itchy skin and chicken pox; and coconut water cleanses the bladder.

Flowers

Jamaica's rich soil supports 3003 varieties of flowering plant (28 percent of which are endemic), from the lavish exotics of the lowlands, exported worldwide, to the delicate iris, begonia and azaleas of cool mountain climates and the hibiscus, ixoras and bouganvillea that feature in almost every garden. A favourite of hotel landscapers, the brush-like deep-pink bracts of the **red ginger** hide the small, white true flower that grows from each tip once fully open. A close relative is the **torch ginger**, which boasts one of the showiest heads in the world, a deep-crimson cluster of thick waxy petals nestled among leaf blades that grow to 15ft. Also ubiquitous are the forty vividly coloured varieties of **heliconia**. Most popular are the various red shades of aptly named **lobster claw** and the red, gold and green cascade of the **hanging** heliconia, which looks like a series of fish hanging from a rod. Equally prevalent is the **anthurium**, a heart-shaped and shiny red, pink or white bract with a long penile stem protruding from the centre, and the spectacular **bird of paradise**, a mauve, bent stem which resembles a bird's head graced by a deep-orange crest.

Jamaica boasts 237 species of **orchid**, approximately 25 percent of which are endemic; many are so small that you'll need a magnifying glass to appreciate them, such as the pea-sized **Lady Nugent's purse**, commonly seen in the Blue Mountains and Cockpit Country.

Hedges and fences are beautified by several varieties of flowering shrub; the ubiquitous bougainvillea ranges from red to deep magenta, white, orange and pink. Hibiscus take on an abundance of hues and shapes but are distinguishable through the generic pollen-tipped stamen that grows from the centre. The lacy coral hibiscus has a cluster of tiny curling red petals and an unusually long stamen topped by another red frill, and there are hundreds of hybrid varieties.

Fauna

Aside from its creepy crawlies and bats, Jamaica's animal life is pretty poor in comparison to its flora, and there are few large mammals. **Camels** made a brief and inopportune appearance in the eighteenth century, transported by planters to carry sugar and rum on the estates, but their preference for smooth ground and sand dunes made them unsuited to Jamaica's uneven and precipitous terrain. They spooked other livestock and had more or less died out by the late nineteenth century, when historian Edward Long described them as "the most useless animals on the island". Planters also introduced the **mongoose** in 1872, which quickly wiped out the Jamaican cane and rice rat population, as well as decimating the island's snakes. Together with rats and mice first introduced via the galleys of Spanish ships, burgeoning populations of mongoose pose a significant threat to other Jamaican creatures, including the hutia or **coney**, a nocturnal rabbit-sized rodent that lives in hollowed trees or rock crevices. The only other indigenous mammal is the **bat**, of which there are 21 varieties; Jamaicans call them all "rat-bats" (the country's huge moths are called rat-bats, too). Some bats are solitary tree-dwellers, but huge colonies inhabit Jamaica's caves, from which their droppings, or guano, have been harvested as a fertilizer, particularly prized for its effect on ganja plants.

Birds

Approximately 250 species of bird frequent Jamaica's skies, though many are migratory or come to the island only to breed. There are 25 indigenous species and 21 varieties found nowhere else in the world, which represents a greater level of endemism than in any other Caribbean island. Quick-moving, brightly coloured **hummingbirds** epitomize Jamaican bird life at its most spectacular; the red- or black-billed streamertail, or **doctor bird**, is the national bird, though only males have the characteristic trailing double tail-feathers (reminiscent of an old-fashioned doctor's coat) and iridescent green breast. At under two inches, the **vervain** or bee hummingbird is the second-smallest bird in the world. Its darting aerial techniques, surprisingly loud squeaky call and insect-like buzzing are far more notable than its grey-brown plumage. Another common nectar addict (and a frequent visitor to hotel breakfast terraces), the black-and-yellow **banana quit** punctures flowers with its curved bill and often hangs upside down from a twig to ensure a favourable feeding position, while glossy black, sharp-beaked **greater Antillean grackles** are to Jamaica what pigeons are to England. Noisy and social, they live in groups and their harsh clacking call, broken by a gentler whistle, forms a constant background music. Commonly seen around cattle, the **white egret** often roosts on a ruminating rump in a mutually rewarding relationship that provides the egret with a constant supply of insects and the cow some relief from bloodsuckers.

Few sights are more evocatively Jamaican than the sight of a distant **John Crow vulture** swooping high over the hills. Though ugly and awkward on the ground, this scavenging carrion bird comes into its own in the air as it scans the land for the scent or sight of dead meat. Typically scrawny, its messy black plumage and bald red neck and head make it a convenient euphemism for people considered dirty, lazy or ugly. Easily recognizable by its harsh rasping cry is the 2ft **red-tailed chicken hawk**, dark brown and black with a white breast and russet tail feathers, which feeds on rats, mice and occasionally chickens. Jamaica has two types of night-hunting **owl**, both surrounded by superstition. The eerie cry of the "**screech owl**", or white owl, is said to bring bad luck, despite its useful function as a vermin exterminator, while the **Jamaican brown owl** or "patoo" feeds on moths and lizards, and has a deep, hoarse cry that's said to be a harbinger of death and destruction – it's certainly disquieting on a dark night.

Reptiles and amphibians

There are 24 species of **lizard** in Jamaica including the **iguana**; the endemic Jamaican version, *Cyclura collei*, grows up to 5ft in length and has been recently rediscovered in the Hellshire hills, having thought to have become extinct. However, most of the lizards you'll see are one of the seven varieties of *Anolis* – *lineatopus* has a mixed pattern of brown markings, while *Anolis grahami* and *garmani* are bright green and can darken their skin if threatened. A variety of gecko, **croaking lizards** provide a throaty night-time call and are extremely common. There are six varieties of **snake** in Jamaica, none of which are poisonous. The largest is the Jamaican **yellow boa**, which grows to around 7ft and is bright yellow/orange when young, maturing into a beautiful yellow and black; during the day it rests in trees and sinkholes and is rarely seen. Popularly called the trophy dophy, the 1.6ft **thundersnake**, cream-coloured with rows of brown squares along a russet stripe, is said to be able to soothe sprains; chunks of its body are marinated in white rum, which is rubbed into the skin – its willingness to be handled makes it easy to catch. Jamaica's two species of **grass snake** (*Arrhyton funereum* and *dromicus*) are also known as black snakes, both attain a size of about a foot and are uniformly brown with a white underside; they're found under logs or leaf litter.

A south-coast swamp inhabitant, the American **crocodile** has been so extensively hunted that it's now classed as endangered, and has been protected by law since 1971. The Black River Morass is one of the last places it lives wild, growing up to 12ft. Generally nonaggressive unless threatened, Jamaican crocodiles live mostly on small fish. There are 22 varieties of **frog** in Jamaica. Since their introduction in 1890 by the then-governor's wife Lady Blake, who apparently found their sound soothing, whistling frogs provide a regular night-time chorus throughout the island. There is one variety of **toad**, commonly called "bull frog", introduced from Barbados in 1844 as an insect killer, but most often seen squashed flat on country roads.

Insects

By far the most noticeable Jamaican insects are the 120 varieties of **butterfly** and **moth** ("rat bats" to Jamaicans), which appear in all shapes, sizes and colours. Most striking but extremely rare is the six-inch **giant swallowtail** butterfly, seen only in the lower slopes of the eastern John Crow Mountains, matched in size by the multiple species of giant moth. **Spider** species are comparatively few, and though there are none of the huge and hairy tarantula types, there are some pretty big ones; the orange, red and black **silk spider** measures around six inches. Its many-layered webs are an arachnaphobe's nightmare; at 3ft wide with attachment lines extending as far as 6ft, they have been known to trap small birds. Encountered only by the foolishly inquisitive, **brown** and **black widows** live under rocks and leaves and, though dangerous, do not carry a fatal bite. Often referred to as "white ants", Jamaica's seventeen species of **termite** construct the lumpen nests you'll see on tree trunks.

Marine life

Much diverse marine life is found around Jamaica's reefs. The sixty or so coral varieties include rotund **brain** coral, patterned with furrowed trenches; branching umber **elkhorn** and **staghorn**; stalagmite-like **pillar** coral; and cool-green **star** coral. Extremely striking are the **gorgonian** group of intricate soft coral **sea plumes**, **sea whips** and purple **sea fans**. Around the reefs, brilliant yellow **anemones** and red, brown, purple and green **sponges** provide a splash of colour, some growing up to three feet in diameter. **Crabs, Caribbean spiny lobsters** and spotted **moray eels** inhabit the crevices between corals. Harmless unless provoked, when they can inflict serious bites, morays open and close their mouths in a constant snarl as they draw oxygenated water over the gills. The patches of sandy sea-bed and sea-grass fields between harbour spiny black sea **urchins**, and the less spiky round white urchins. **Sea cucumbers** are long, thin and off-white, sifting through the sea floor to feed on deposited nutrients, while five-armed orange and green **starfish** and queen **conch snails** move slowly along, encircling grass blades with their stomachs to ingest encrusted organisms. One of the most stunning inhabitants of the sea floor is the flat manta or **stingray**, often partially buried in sand. Though nonaggressive, it has a serrated tail-spine that is venomous but can only be used if the ray is partially immobilized by a bite or a badly placed foot.

Despite the effects of overfishing, there are still over seven hundred varieties of fish in Jamaican waters. The commonest include multicoloured **parrot** fish, electric-blue creole **wrass**, red and yellow **snappers**, ornate **damselfish**, striped **grunts**, glassy **sweepers**, spiny **puffers**, and rarer **tarpon** and **trigger fish**. The slender yellow and blue **trumpetfish** suspends itself vertically in the water awaiting smaller victims to drift by and into its mouth. Larger specimens include **grouper, jackfish, kingfish, tuna, marlin, bonita** and **wahoo**. The scourge of spear fishermen, silvery-sleek predatory **barracudas** impart a nasty bite if provoked, though the common **nurse shark** is benign unless attacked or cornered. In deeper water, **dolphins** are a common companion to boats.

Though increasingly rare, hawksbill and loggerhead **turtles** still lay their eggs on Jamaican shores, despite the continuing threat of capture. The Caribbean **monk seals** that once inhabited offshore cays are now believed to be extinct, and Jamaica's cutest sea mammal, the **manatee**, or sea cow, is extremely endangered; there are only about a hundred left in Jamaican waters, mostly along the less-developed inlets of the south coast.

Threats to the environment

The Jamaican environment has long suffered the effects of unplanned development and a lack of environmental awareness. While many of its **reefs** are still the beautiful underwater gardens of hotel brochures, they are under serious threat. Studies have reported that the island has damaged 95 percent of its reefs in the last fifteen years as a result of overfishing (and destructive fishing practice), as well as sand mining, coral collection, industrial pollution and mass tourism. Dynamiting and chemical bleaching, which stun fish up to the surface for an easy catch, have had disastrous effects upon reefs, which depend upon clean, clear water for their survival. A symptom of unusually high sea temperatures worldwide, coral bleaching has been reported on eighty percent of reefs around Jamaica's shores – killing the algae within the polyps and leaving the still-living coral to starve.

On land, **deforestation** and its associated problems are a major concern. Slopes stripped both by human hand and as a result of hurricane damage are overly susceptible to soil erosion and landslides, threatening hundreds of already rare animal and insect species and wreaking havoc with the island's ecosystems. Deforestation has been particularly severe in the Blue Mountains, which represent the watershed for the entirety of eastern Jamaica, causing annual droughts and floods. For an island with such a high rainfall, Jamaica is in the perverse situation of facing a permanent

Environmental and conservation associations

Environmental matters in Jamaica are the responsibility of the **National Environmental Planning Agency** (Ⓦ www.nepa.gov.jm), which ensures (with sometimes negligible success) sustainable development and devises and enforces environmental legislation. The **Jamaica Conservation and Development Trust** (Ⓦ www.greenjamaica.org.jm), has responsibility for Jamaica's national parks, among other things, while the website of the Environmental Foundation of Jamaica (Ⓦ www.efj.org.jm) has links to some of Jamaica's many environmental NGOs, which are useful for obtaining information on specific environmental concerns throughout the island; the Jamaica Environment Trust (Ⓦ www.jamentrust.org) is another source of up-to-date information on environmental issues.

drought entirely of human making. In the Yallahs Valley, a century of misuse – slopes cleared for coffee cultivation or slash-and-burn farming techniques – has left the area vulnerable to the torrential rainy season deluges, which have flooded the valley and dumped huge amounts of earth onto former farmlands, leaving the slopes above bald and impossible to cultivate. The situation became so desperate that the government intervened as early as 1961, creating the Yallahs Valley Land Authority to rehabilitate the area through planting Caribbean pine, mahoe and eucalyptus to restabilize the slopes, although a lack of funding has resulted in poor maintenance and the flooding is ongoing. Bauxite mining, meanwhile, has come at a heavy price: caustic red mud deposits are often inadequately disposed of and seep into the watersheds to poison rivers and lakes. Elsewhere, though eighty percent of household waste is collected by the government, the remaining twenty percent is simply dumped in open areas and gullies, resulting in poor hygiene, increasing levels of vermin and polluted water.

However, all is not lost. Thanks to the efforts of **nongovernmental conservation organizations**, there has been a marked increase in public awareness of environmental issues over the last few years. Jamaica has established three **national parks** (Montego Bay Marine Park, Negril Marine Park, and the Blue and John Crow Mountains National Park), and the area offshore of Negril has also been designated a marine park. A further six sites are proposed for protected status, including Cockpit Country, the Dolphin Head Mountains in Hanover, Black River, the Hellshire Hills and the coastline around Port Antonio.

Religion

With over 250 denominations and the world's highest number of churches per capita, **religion** is a Jamaican vocation, and in this fundamentally non-secular society, faith features in every aspect of daily life. Popular ideology is governed by biblical dogma, and most Jamaicans are devoutly religious and have an astonishing ability (and propensity) for quoting lengthy passages of scripture. Sunday piousness is fervently observed, reggae stars devote entire performances to unadorned preaching and the most popular newspaper agony columnist is addressed "Dear Pastor". Churches are at the heart of all Jamaican communities, providing subsidized housing, education, healthcare and a strong social focus – and this centrality is fundamental to Jamaican religion, in all its myriad forms.

The development of Jamaican religion

The antecedent of most contemporary Jamaican cults and Christian sects is a wider **African religious tradition** that arrived with the first wave of slaves. As the white ruling class didn't deign to give their "chattel" Christian religious instruction until the late eighteenth century, African religions flourished under the British plantocracy, with the constant influx of new slaves keeping belief systems and practice alive – something the planters attempted to quash by banning drumming and persistently breaking up ceremonies.

Moravian, Baptist and Methodist **missionaries** began arriving in the late eighteenth century, however, and slowly set about proselytizing increasing numbers of slaves, while also attempting to convince the planters that slavery in itself was inherently un-Christian. Owners were faced with a choice between having their slaves attend church on a Sunday or flaunt their heathen proclivities on a daily basis; they grudgingly bowed to the former, and a mass church culture was born. Sunday mass became the only sanctioned gathering for slaves and, ironically, contributed to emancipation, as firebrand black-activist preachers used their sermons to whip congregations into political action.

After emancipation, the British took a belated interest in the spiritual lives of black Jamaicans and tried to "civilize" them into orthodox Christianity, but the majority of former slaves preferred to practise aspects of their folk culture or combine their traditions with western Christianity. The time was ripe for a uniquely African–Jamaican phenomenon. Some twenty years after the abolition of slavery, a new **religious fervour** swept Jamaica, initially carried along by the momentum of the newly popular Native Baptists and other Christian denominations but essentially resting upon the Revival, Pukkumina, Zion and Myal Afro-Jamaican cults that have remained active in Jamaica ever since. The **Great Revival** of 1860–61 was one of several religious revivals (others took place in 1831, 1840, 1865 and 1883) that signified a resurgence both of religious practices banned under slavery and of a desire among blacks to rediscover and celebrate their African origins. It marked the beginning of a Jamaican religious tradition that threatened carefully constructed colonial hierarchies, and white Jamaicans were horrified at this "grossly perverted religious fervour" and "scenes of debauchery and hideous caterwauling".

By the end of the nineteenth century, the white Jamaican elite was panic-stricken by the phenomenal popularity of the church led by self-declared messiah **Alexander Bedward**. His August Town branch of the Native Baptist Church adapted conventional theology, proffering a combination of black power and faith healing – Bedward blessed the waters of Hope River and thousands flocked to Kingston for baptism or a miracle cure. He also prophesied that he would sprout wings and fly to Zion on December 31, 1921, and Bedwardites from all over Jamaica and the Caribbean descended upon Kingston to witness his departure; Bedward stayed put, but used the mass gathering as an opportunity to spread the message. Inevitably, Bedward's black-nationalist tendencies led to several clashes with the state; in 1895 he was tried for sedition but acquitted on the grounds of insanity, and eventually he was arrested as a vagrant and committed to Kingston's Bellevue asylum, where he died in 1930.

Christianity

Christianity arrived in Jamaica with the Spanish, who built the island's first **Roman Catholic** church at Sevilla Nueva in St Ann (see p.155) in 1524. The British promptly outlawed Catholicism in 1655, and it was not freely practised again until 1792; of the eighty percent of Jamaicans who describe themselves as Christian today, only around six percent are Catholic.

The British divided the island into the ecclesiastical **parishes** and established what later became known as the **Anglican Church of Jamaica**, still the island's dominant denomination. The second largest is the Baptist church, first brought to Jamaica by African-American ex-slaves George Lysle and Moses Baker in 1783. The **Native Baptist movement**, as it was then known, incorporated numerous African rituals into more orthodox forms of worship and was widely supported at its peak, with impressively large and still-functioning churches springing up all over the Jamaican interior throughout the nineteenth century. Following emancipation, the Baptists were the first to set up **free villages** for liberated slaves and became a main instigator and provider of free education for black Jamaicans.

Approximately ten percent of Jamaicans are **Methodists**, which in Jamaica is a faith strongly influenced by the African religious tradition and often connected to Revivalism (see below). Methodism arrived on the island in 1789, when missionaries from the Wesleyan Missionary Society set up the Coke Church in Kingston, and assured potential converts that their own religious traditions would survive within the blanket of the Methodist Church.

In recent years, the fundamentalist tenets of US Bible-Belt churches have also proven immensely popular, with many Jamaicans becoming **Seventh-Day Adventists** and **Jehovah's Witnesses**, while the Pentecostal Church and the Church of God also have significant followings.

Revivalism and Kumina

Essentially spiritualistic, the **Revival** movement combines African and European religious traditions into a uniquely Jamaican form. It centres on the African acceptance of a synthesis between the spiritual and temporal worlds, an animist philosophy of a supernatural power that organizes and animates the material universe. Spirits are seen to have a distinct influence upon the living and, accordingly, must be respected, pacified, praised and worshipped through ritual dances, offerings and prayer. There are two branches within Revivalism: **Zionism** and **Pukkumina**. More overtly Christian, Zionism deals only with the heavenly spirits and angels of the Bible, while the more African Pukkumina worships earthbound "ground spirits" such as deceased ancestors. Known as bands (the collective plural is always used), Revivalist congregations have a female (**mother**) or male (**shepherd** or **captain**) leader who acts as general adviser and governs meetings. Ceremonies are held in consecrated **mission/seal grounds** or **poco yards**, which are specifically designated by spirits and marked by a tall central pole flying coloured flags to attract passing spirits and identify the site. The **tabernacle** – decorated with symbolic candles, fruits, herbs, flowers and holy pictures, and containing an earthenware jug of water used in the rituals – is either in the open air, a temporary bamboo structure or, increasingly, a concrete building. Liturgies include the singing of "**Sankeys**" (hymns penned by the American evangelist Ira David Sankey), dancing, drumming, clapping, and multiple-spirit possession (sometimes called **trumping**). Once inside a physical host, the spirit becomes an adviser to the whole flock and is controlled by the shepherd, who interprets messages received in tongues or through the movements of the possessed. The drumming, chanting and dances are all of African origin, as are the traditional goatskin burru or kette drums (see "Music", p.297). Today, revivalism is concentrated in the eastern end of the island, and its increasingly ageing followers wear flowing white or coloured robes and cover their heads in a turban-style wrap.

Usually described as the most African of Jamaican cults, **Kumina** (also concentrated in the east) is less formally organized than Revival, and though still centred on connections between spiritual and temporal worlds and the evocation and worship of ancestors, it focuses on music to a far greater extent – call-and-response chants backed by complicated, hypnotic drumming rhythms provide the music for the worshippers, who dance around the drummers in a ring and often "catch the spirit", as possesions are called. Though a relatively obscure practice today, Kumina has made an indelible mark on Jamaican culture; the intricate and precise patterns of its **drumming** have had far-reaching influence upon latter-day forms such as reggae, and Jamaica's national dance company, NDTC, incorporates numerous Kumina movements into performances.

African death rituals

Believed to be a prime time for the release of wicked duppies, **death** in Jamaica is traditionally surrounded by rituals designed to smooth the passage from one world to another. If a death occurred at home, mirrors were turned against walls to prevent reflections that could portend further deaths, and the house was ritually swept out with new palm brooms. The deceased would be washed by two family members who began at the head and feet and met in the middle, and the body was then placed with their head at the foot of the bed to confuse any lurking duppies. These practices are fast dying out, however, but one tradition that's still often observed is the **Nine Night** or "death watch", originally staged over the nine days and nights following a death. Friends and relatives meet to remember and celebrate the deceased and ensure that their duppy doesn't return to haunt the living; food is cooked and consumed, stories told and rum imbibed. Today, observance is usually restricted to the ninth night only, and sound-system speakers often take the place of drums and anecdotes.

Obeah

Obeah (from the Ashante term *obayi*, meaning a malicious spirit) is the belief in a form of spiritual power that can influence events – from curing disease to providing good fortune or wreaking revenge. Though dismissed by many as primitive nonsense – and theoretically outlawed, though prosecutions are rare – obeah, or "duppy business", is taken seriously, and it's not uncommon for Jamaicans, particularly in rural areas, to call upon the services of an obeah practitioner, who (for a fee, of course), will invoke or dispel a curse. They often give their supplicants bags of special powders – comprised of roots, herbs, ashes, earth (perhaps grave dirt), blood, feathers – to sprinkle on the subject and bring on the desired effect, which is reversible only by a more powerful obeah-man.

The jiggery-pokery of obeah also manifests itself in ghosts or **duppies**, as they're called in Jamaica. The idea of the duppy originates from the African belief that each person has two souls; after death, one goes up to heaven while the other may linger in the temporal world and can be easily persuaded by an obeah-man to do good or evil to the living. Believers consult obeah-men if they feel they've been "fixed" or cursed, and there are countless rituals, charms and substances used to ward off or invoke the spirits. A traditional superstition warns that when walking on lonely roads at night, you should carry handfuls of stones or matches and drop them as you go to ensnare any inquisitive ghoul – unable to count beyond three, the duppy is forced to remain on the spot in a perpetual inventory.

Alongside the ghosts of regular people, there are also specific fiends that haunt children's bedtime stories and have become intermeshed with Jamaica's folklore and culture. The **Ol' Hige** is a bloodsucking hag who leaves her skin at night to seek out succulent babies and feast on their blood. A crossed knife and fork and Bible kept near a child's crib are said to ward off her attentions, but she can only be stopped by finding her skin and dousing it with salt and pepper. The **Rolling Calf** is a night phantom that appears as an enormous red-eyed bull draped with clanking chains and walking with a sickly rolling gait; to see it is dangerous and to be attacked means certain death. The only duppy to appear during the day, the **River Mumma** combines the African belief in a river spirit with the Western mermaid legend. Appearing as a ravishing young woman, she sits near deep pools on river banks and exposed rocks, bewitching passing males with her beauty; once beguiled, the love-struck victims are pulled down to the river bed and drowned.

Rastafari

From the reds, golds and greens that colour everything from shop hoardings to belts and buses, and the beaming dreads that adorn commercials and tourist brochures, the outer trappings of Jamaica's newest and most visible religious movement are inescapable. **Rastafari** has influenced all aspects of society from art and craft to politics, academia, language and particularly music, but the movement was not always looked upon so favourably. The last thirty years have seen a complete societal volte-face from widespread revulsion and persecution (a favourite police pastime in the 1960s was to arrest Rastas on ganja charges and shear off their locks – as sacrilegious as the cutting of hair is to Sikhs) to the tentative acceptance of today. Nevertheless older Jamaicans still retain a deep-seated prejudice against the "Blackheart Man", and despite a few notable exceptions, dreadlock-wearing Rastafarians are poorly represented within the professions. Some more well-to-do supporters prefer to defend the faith without

Inherently patriarchal, the traditional Rastafarian attitude towards **women** takes direction from Biblical concepts of woman as an impure and a potentially corrupting influence upon man, a position upheld particularly zealously by Bobo dreads (see p.295). Initially, women ("daughters" or "sistren") could only be recognized within the movement and be shown their own innate sin through the guidance of a "king-man", the physical and spiritual ruler of the Rasta **queen** who takes responsibility for balancing her thoughts and for her spiritual development – without a man, women cannot know the faith. Women are expected to be receptive to spiritual instruction at all times, and – unlike men – are required to cover their hair when praying. They must never be seen in public without a hat or headscarf and must dress modestly, avoiding revealing clothes (particularly trousers) and make-up. Women are considered unclean during **menstruation**, when they're not permitted to prepare food for others or attend communal prayer sessions, and in orthodox Rasta communities are often completely isolated and excused from chores. Traditionally, women are also greatly excluded from worship, prohibited from leading rituals and sharing the chalice and sometimes excluded from the most significant nyabinghis. However, since the 1970s and the rise of the more egalitarian Twelve Tribes group, women have begun to assert themselves within the Rastafarian movement, taking respected positions in the hierarchy and participating in all celebrations, often with the active support of their progressive male contemporaries.

displaying the frowned-upon outer trappings – wearing locks is not deemed essential to "knowing" Rastafari, as followers assert that they do not merely "believe" in Rastafari, but know and feel their faith.

Beliefs

The Rastafari faith has its roots in the teachings of black activist and National Hero **Marcus Garvey** (see p.156). He advocated an anti-imperialistic, pro-black philosophy and prophetically urged Jamaican followers to "Look to Africa, where a Black King shall be crowned." When **Ras Tafari Makonnen** was crowned Negus of Ethiopia in 1930, taking the title **Emperor Haile Selassie**, King of Kings, Lord of Lords, Conquering Lion of the Tribe of Judah, Jamaicans looked to their Bibles and interpreted his title as proof of divinity. Garvey was christened the Black Moses and Selassie became a messiah sent to redeem black people from their suffering at the hands of white oppressors.

Rastafari places Africans as the direct descendants of the original Hebrew Israelites, and Africa as the promised land, offering a restructuring of black identity and an emphasis on black culture lost and maligned by centuries of "slave mentality". As a colonized country, Jamaica is part of the white, Western system of corruption and "downpression" – **Babylon** – which will ultimately destroy itself through its own innate wickedness in an appropriately apocalyptic manner.

The first tenet of Rastafari is the acceptance of Haile Selassie as the second coming of God, or **Jah**. The **Kebre Negast**, the Ethiopian version of the Christian Bible, places him in a legendary line of Ethiopian kings stretching directly back to King Solomon and Queen Sheba; it states that the Ark of the Covenant (and therefore the God of Israel) rests in Ethiopia rather than Jerusalem, and that Selassie was the 225th incarnation of the divinity – a latter-day Christ. Though the Rastafarian elders granted a private audience with Selassie during his 1966 visit to Jamaica reported that he said "Holy priests, warriors and traitors, be still and know that I am He," Selassie never publicly acknowledged himself as a god and was said to be frightened rather than gratified by the adulation he received. Selassie died in 1975, but to Rastafarians, he became even more powerful – it is believed that only the evil truly die, and as the Rastaman lives his life in the appropriate spiritual manner, his soul is immortal.

A second central doctrine of Rastafari is African **repatriation**. This became a real possibility through Haile Selassie's gift of land at Shashamene in Ethiopia for black people to return "home" to. Though the few who made the journey found life in Shashamene just as harsh as it was in Jamaica, the belief in Africa – particularly Ethiopia or **Zion** – as a spiritual home persists amongst older Rastas. Younger followers, though, point to Selassie's 1966 public comments, in which he advised Rastafarians to "liberate themselves in Jamaica" before removing to Africa. In the 1970s, the new cry of "liberation before repatriation" emerged, alongside a blossoming politicization. Traditionally, Rastas do not vote and refuse to enter the corrupt world of "politricks", but following Selassie's words, the movement became intensely political, with popular adherents such as Peter Tosh publicly decrying the manifestations of the bloodsucking Babylon "shitstem" (system). This politicization has been taken further in the new millennium, with several Rastas standing for office in local and national elections. Meanwhile, Rasta groups have applied to the British Queen Elizabeth for reparations in compensation for slavery; the request was denied on the grounds that the UK "can't be held responsible for something that happened 150 years ago".

Rituals

Most Rastafarians abide by basic principles based on interpretations of the Bible. Proverbs 15:17 – "Better is a dinner of herbs where love is, than a stalled ox and hatred therewith" – is the source of the strict **Ital** (natural and unprocessed) **diet**: no salt in cooking, no meat (pork, lobster and shellfish are particularly avoided, though many Rastas eat small fish – anything larger than twelve inches is probably predatory and representative of cannibalistic Babylon), and few dairy products. Animal byproducts such as lard are also prohibited, as are alcohol, cigarettes and chemical stimulants. However, **ganja** – or "herb", as Rastas prefer to call it – is seen as a religious sacrament, as referred to in Psalms 104:14 "He causeth the grass to grow for the cattle, and the herb for the service of man." Though many followers smoke pretty much continually to aid their meditations, or "reasonings", ganja is primarily used at prayer meetings, when the communal pipe (chalice, cutchie or chillum) is stoked with the finest herb available, blessed with a prayer and passed round the group to the left. Alleged to have first grown around King Solomon's grave, the "holy herb" is said to enable deep penetration of thought as well as permitting a higher level of spirituality that transcends the petty distractions of the Babylonian world. **Reasoning** is central to the Rastafari faith, designed to reveal truth and elucidate the wickedness of the world and the Rasta position within it. Alongside these ad hoc sessions, Rastafarians hold more organized gatherings, centred on drumming and reasoning and known as **grounations** or **nyabinghis**.

Dreadlocks are also believed to be a biblical directive; Leviticus 21:5 commands that "They shall not make baldness upon their head, neither shall they shave off the corner of their beard, nor make cuttings in the flesh." Orthodox Rastafarians cover their hair in a wrap or a knitted hat called a **tam**, believing it indiscreet and immodest to show it off. The reference to cutting the flesh informs Rasta opposition to surgery; most prefer to trust in herbal **bush medicine** and supplement their diet with a variety of stamina-building fruit drinks and herbal tonics such as the "roots wine" concoction consumed by Rastas and nonbelievers islandwide.

Finally, the Rastafarian **colours** of red, black, gold and green have a deep significance. Red symbolizes the blood spilled in Jamaican history, black is the African skin of 97 percent of the population, gold is the hope for the victory over oppression and green represents the fertile land of Jamaica – and Ethiopia.

The development of the faith

After being kickstarted in the 1930s by Marcus Garvey, the **Rastafarian** movement quickly attracted some vociferous advocates, so provoking widespread antagonism in the broader society. One of the most provocative early sympathizers was **Claudius Henry**, head of the self-made Kingston-based African Reform Church and something of a charlatan. Aligning himself with Rastas through public speeches on white corruption and the necessity of repatriation, in 1959 he enraged the poorest sections of Jamaican society through the sale of thousands of cards purporting to be tickets back to Africa. Hundreds of eager exiles sold up and descended upon Kingston on October 5, only to be disappointed as Henry reneged on his promises. The movement was further maligned when Henry's church was raided and a quantity of detonators, guns, swords and conch shells packed with ganja were seized. Henry was imprisoned, but reports that his son was training a crack team of armed Rastas in preparation for an overthrow of the government led to a national manhunt and an islandwide state of emergency – a public-relations disaster for a movement that prides itself on pacifism and tolerance.

Among early Rasta elders of a more sincere nature, **Leonard Howell** stands out as one of the most influential father-figures. He established a Rasta commune at **Pinnacle**, an abandoned great house near Sligoville in St Catherine, where converts lived a self-sufficient lifestyle praising Jah, growing food crops and cultivating ganja. Despite countless police raids, the community flourished for more than thirteen years until Howell's 1953 arrest and permanent committal to the Bellevue asylum. Those Pinnacle members who were not incarcerated drifted back to the slums of west Kingston, establishing the Back'o'Wall and the Dungle strongholds described in Orlando Patterson's seminal novel *The Children of Sisyphus* (see "Books", p.308) and setting up Jamaica's oldest Rastafarian camp at Bull Bay, east of Kingston. (Howell's descendents still occupy the land to this day, however, and the Jamaica National Heritage Trust declared the site a national monument in 2009.)

By the late 1950s, Rastafari was a serious faction in the volatile sphere of Jamaican religion, with at least fifteen different sects practising in Kingston alone. Yet the wider view, fuelled by hysterical press reports, was of a drug-crazed, violent underclass plotting the mass murder of white Jamaicans. Police harassment ensued throughout the 1960s, with Rastafarian communities bulldozed without notice and countless followers beaten, thrown into jail and relieved of their locks. However, come the 1970s, things began to look more favourable for Rastafarians. Poor Jamaicans in their thousands began to identify with the movement's militant analysis of a wicked state and its apparent disdain for the lot of the black sufferer. Michael Manley was the first politician to use the Rasta faith to his advantage. During a visit to Ethiopia in 1970, Manley was presented with an ornamental staff by Haile Selassie, a sacred relic that he dubbed the "**Rod of Correction**" and transported to every election meeting in every small village during the 1972 election campaign. Always up for a little showmanship, Jamaicans greeted the appearance of the sacred rod with evangelical fervour, and Manley reinvented himself as the Rastas' ally, employing their lexicon in speeches and calling himself the "people's Joshua", able to lead Jamaicans into deliverance. He swept to victory on election day with the tacit support of the Rastafarian community and its many sympathizers. Governmental recognition of Rastafari was lent untold weight by the worldwide influence of **Bob Marley and the Wailers**, who brought international attention to Jamaica and forced an acknowledgement of the movement's legitimacy at home, and suddenly – almost overnight – the tide of public antipathy turned. Dreadlocks became chic, and reggae Jamaica's number-one export, but these halcyon days were short-lived. With popularity came a certain commercialization of the faith, with many Rastas turning to the financial gains of the international ganja trade rather than to Jah. Conspiracy theories about infiltration by the CIA were supported to a degree even by Manley, who believed that his programme of "economic socialism" was deliberately destabilized by the US government. Twinned with the death of chief ambassador Marley in 1981, this general degeneration meant a loss of international prominence and local momentum, but Rastafari continues to develop its political and ideological strategies on home ground, remaining one of the most unique, challenging and fascinating of contemporary religions.

Though true figures are probably far greater, it's estimated that there are around 100,000 Rastafarians in Jamaica today, many of whom have a more egalitarian view of the faith than older adherents. Many embrace the faith superficially, wearing locks as a hairstyle rather than an expression of faith, becoming "Rent-a-dreads" (see p.209), smoking the sacred herb and pontificating about Jah, Ethiopia and their personal friendship with brother Bob but lacing their ganja with cocaine and washing down their jerk pork with white rum.

Sects

Though there have been many attempts to coordinate the Rastafarian movement, there are hundreds of divergent belief strands, sects and methods of worship. Some prominent Rastas (including several of the Marley family) have moved towards the more Christian-oriented **Ethiopian Orthodox Church**, while others have joined the **Twelve Tribes of Israel** sect (as Marley himself did). Well-organized and well-connected, Twelve Tribes is now one of the more prosperous branches of Rastafari, with chapters in the UK and America, as well as one of the more progressive, with women taking a far more equal role. Members must read a chapter of the Bible every day and are assigned a name and a colour based on twelve "houses" related to birth months and corresponding to the twelve tribes.

At the other end of the spectrum, members of the reclusive and strictly orthodox **Bobo** sect are the high priests of Rasta, following the teaching of the late Prince Emmanuel Charles Edwards in choosing to reject wider society and live self-sufficiently in semi-rural communes called **camps** (the largest being at Bull Bay, just east of Kingston), wearing their locks wrapped tightly in a cloth turban rather than the conventional knitted tam, and sometimes dressing in long, flowing robes. Prayer meetings are continuous, and members leave only to sell the palm brooms and leather sandals made on site or to purchase foodstuffs that the commune is unable to produce.

Music

Close your eyes practically anywhere in Jamaica and you'll hear **music**. Radios blare on the street, buses pump out nonstop dancehall and, come Friday or Saturday night, the vibrations of a thousand sound systems waft through the evening air. Music is a serious business here, generating an average of a hundred record releases per week (the highest anywhere in the world) and influencing every aspect of Jamaican culture from dress to speech to attitude. **Reggae**, and specifically DJ-based **dancehall**, dominates, but Jamaicans are catholic in their musical tastes: soul, hip-hop, jazz, rock'n'roll, gospel and the ubiquitous country and western are all popular.

The evolution of Jamaican music

Jamaica has long been a musical island. The simple rhythms of the Amerindian Tainos were adopted by the Maroons; and the drumming, Coromantee chants and songs of their Myalist religious ceremonies and related **Kumina** dance movement became the island's first established musical form. Principal instruments included the bamboo and Coromantee nose flutes, abengs (cow horns), conch shells and strum-strums – home-made banjos fashioned from a hollowed calabash strung with horsehair. These provided the melody, but by far the most important instruments were the gumbe and ebo **drums**, supplemented by **percussion** from shakers, scrapers and graters. But while the Maroons were sounding their drums and abeng horns through the hills, plantation slaves were expressing themselves in a considerably more restricted environment. Recognizing the drum as a principal instrument of African warfare, the British tried to smother the provocative music of their minions, going so far as to prohibit "the beating of drums, barrels, gourds, boards or other such-like instruments of noise".

Yet African musical traditions survived, most notably in the annual **Jonkonnu** masquerade parade, contemptuously dubbed "Pickaninny Christmas" by the whites. Jonkonnu was originally a religious ceremony using music and dance to

---

Traditional Jamaican dance

The syncretism of African and European culture in the plantations and beyond is particularly visible in Jamaican traditional **dance**. Much of it emanates from the moves performed at Myal or Revival religious ceremonies, and most dances are purely African, often revolving around "dip and kotch", up-and-down movements or shuffling, hip-swinging styles that parallel the counterclockwise movements of ritual dance. One of the most interesting dances is **etu**, traditionally danced at Nine Night ceremonies (see p.290). It revolves around a process called "shawling", where the Revival Queen throws a scarf around the neck of a fellow dancer who is ceremoniously dipped back, giving each individual a chance to demonstrate some solo footwork from the standard pose of a slight but flat-footed bent-kneed crouch. Still actively practised in Portland, **brukins** is danced to celebrate the emancipation of Africans from slavery; groups of red and blue sets perform in a mock contest before the king and queen of each colour.

Many of Jamaica's most well-known dance forms are incorporated into performances by the island's professional dance companies, and you can see practically every style ever danced at the annual Heritage Festival held each October in Kingston.

evoke spirits – and named for its principal rhythmic component, the jawbone of a cow or horse played by scraping a stick across the teeth – and appropriated on the plantations to become a secular travelling pantomime. It incorporated British fife and drum marching rhythms and featured the fixed characters of a cow- or horse-headed leader followed by a king, queen and policeman, with companies of **Set Girls**, grouped by coloured sashes and skin tone. Jonkonnu has pretty much died out today, although it is resurrected as a tourist attraction around Christmas time. Other celebrations, such as those marking the end of the plantation year, were more European in flavour, with English maypole and morris dancing, and French quadrilles.

Another significant development was the rise of the **folk song**, created by workers in the cane and banana fields as a way to alleviate the arduous hard labour – an oral tradition that survives today. In the enormous canon of Jamaican folk music, there are traces of African, British, Irish and Spanish musical and vocal traditions, and heavy doses of Nonconformist hymns, arrangements and singing styles. Each of these influences is blended with characteristic Jamaican wit, irreverence and creativity. There are songs for courting, marrying, digging, drinking, playing ring games, burying – and just for singing, too. One of the all-time classics is *Hill and Gully Rider*, a timeless ode to transport on an island strong on hills and weak on roads.

The roots of reggae: burru to mento

After emancipation, the arrival of free African workers rekindled support for the less European aspects of Jamaican music and society. The Great Revival of 1860–61 (see p.288) saw a massive resurrection of support for Myal, Kumina and Afro-Pentecostal religious forms, all of which used drumming, chanting and singing as an integral part of worship. The new prominence of the master **burru** drummer and his topical, wickedly humorous social commentary signified the return of the **drum** to the heart of Jamaican music. A version of the African griot (a travelling one-man information agency who brought gossip and news to rural communities), the burru man originally accompanied fertility rites and played in plantation canefields to keep machetes swinging to a steady pace, but later became a sort of smutty strolling minstrel. Characterized by their innuendo and wicked wordplay, burru songs dealt with situations seen as taboo in everyday speech. Musically influenced by Pukkumina and Revivalist drumming, the burru man would accompany himself on a three-part set of drums known today as **akete**, beating out complicated rhythms that would eventually work their way into Rastafarian music and develop into ska, rocksteady and finally reggae.

Over time, burro men added a booming rhumba box (a wooden box with a hole on one side covered by metal strips that are plucked for an elementary bass sound) and home-made bamboo fifes, piccolos and fiddles to their repertoire. By the turn of the twentieth century, groups of burro men were banding together to perform at jump-ups and parties, singing souped-up and sophisticated versions of traditional folk songs – burru had become **mento** and Jamaican popular music was born. With a syncopated rhythm that got hips gyrating and bodies dipping forward or back in Kumina-esque abandon (a style of movement revived in the "bogle" dance of the early 1990s), pelvis-centred mento was closely related to calypso – the music of Trinidad and Tobago – through both a predilection for rhythmic and lyrical bawdiness and its humorous social commentary. Mento dominated the Jamaican music scene for the first decades of this century. You'll still see mento trios – often referred to as calypso bands – performing welcome songs at north-coast hotels or forming the "authentic Jamaican culture" portion of an all-inclusive floor show.

Big bands to ballads

By the early 1940s, mento was waning in popularity as thousands of young Jamaicans left the island to fight for Britain in World War II or find work in Cuba, Latin America and the US. They returned with a taste for new rhythms and musical styles – *rumba*, *salsa* and *merengue* – as well as new musical technology – phonograph records and cheap radio sets, widely available and affordable for the first time. Taking their influence from black Americans Count Basie and Duke Ellington, meanwhile, **big bands** such as the Eric Deans Orchestra found moderate success playing international standards and cleaned-up versions of mento hits at hotel floor shows. The best of these were put on vinyl by West Indies Recording Limited (WIRL), a record label owned by then-entrepreneur and later prime minister Edward Seaga. However, despite the quality of these tightly orchestrated performances, the big bands were bypassed by the majority of Jamaicans in favour of the radio stations beaming black-American R&B from transmitters in Florida.

By the early 1950s, Jamaica's music scene was concentrated in a few pockets of southwest Kingston that were later to spawn the island's best-known musical luminaries. The desperately poor communities of Trench Town, Jones Town, Denham Town and Greenwich Farm offered plenty of dancehalls and street corners where quick-thinking impresarios like **Duke Reid**, **Prince Buster** and **Clement "Coxsone" Dodd** played for the people on huge mobile disco sets, taking the latest R&B or blues to areas where few could afford to see a big band play live. Reid and Dodd were the first to exploit the full commercial potential of the **sound system** (see p.302), vying with each other to see who could spin the best selections (often acquired on record-buying sorties to the US), and employing the braggadocio that characterizes today's dancehall posturing. An ex-policeman who always carried a firearm, Reid was prone to arrive at a dance dressed to the nines in sequins and leather, his guns cocked and ready to discipline any contenders to his throne.

By the mid-1950s, R&B's star had faded and the fickle Jamaican consumer was tiring of American imports. Quick to catch on to a new opportunity, men like Reid, Dodd and Leslie Kong began recording music themselves – primarily soft and soulful ballads – using established vocalists and players who had cut their teeth on the big-band circuit. The Gaylads, Jackie Edwards, Owen Grey, Jackie Opal, Laurel Aitken, and Bunny and Skully were backed by some of the best musicians Jamaica has ever produced – Roland Alphonso, Tommy McCook and "Deadly" Headley Bennett on saxophone, Don Drummond and Rico Rodriguez on trombone, Jerome "Jah Jerry" Haines and Ernest Ranglin on guitar, Lester Sterling on trumpet and keyboard virtuoso Jackie Mittoo. Initially, the producers used the WIRL and Federal studios to record, but as soon as finances allowed, Reid and Dodd (among others) built their own rudimentary studios, naming them after their most popular labels, **Treasure Isle** and **Studio One** respectively. Around this time, too, Chris Blackwell founded Island Records, which would go on to become arguably the most famous label in Jamaican music. It was a halcyon age for Jamaican music, a time of cooperation and innovation.

Ska licks

By the late 1950s, musicians and singers began flirting with the philosophies of **Rastafari**. Some went down to the Dungle in Kingston or Adastra Road in the Rasta-dominated Wareika foothills and jammed with master drummers like **Count Ossie** and his **Mystic Revelation of Rastafari** band. Reworked in 1993 to massive commercial success by Jamaican DJ Shaggy, their *Oh Carolina* was one of the most influential tracks they recorded, a perfect example of the fusion of Kumina drumming, harmonic singing and unique rhythm that was later to develop into ska, rocksteady and finally reggae. The Rasta drummers became well known on the Kingston entertainment scene via their regular performances at the popular "Vere Johns Opportunity Knocks" variety show (held every week at the Ambassador Theatre in Jones Town), and went on to perform regularly at other Kingston venues.

For Jamaican musicians, the late 1950s and early 1960s were a time of intense creativity, a period of exploring new rhythms and pushing the boundaries of jazz, R&B and Rasta drumming – an explosive combination that sometimes saw drummers and instrumentalists pitched against sound-system wattage. Meanwhile, session musicians were conducting their own experiments, using the exaggerated shuffle rhythm of R&B and syncopated mento sounds. Somewhere along the way, the staccato, guitar-and-trumpet-led sound of **ska** emerged and captured the Jamaican musical imagination with effortless ease.

Following independence from British colonial rule in 1962, the future seemed full of possibilities. You can hear the euphoria in the music of the time – joyous, up-tempo ska tunes that seem now not to express a care in the world – and the small independent record labels in west Kingston were at the cutting edge. Ska lyrics provide a window into the evolution of Jamaica and its music. With its home-grown roots and dancefloor beat, ska expressed the mood of the ghetto dweller. Tommy McCook grouped together the cream of the session musicians to form the now-legendary **Skatalites**, who released a host of massively popular instrumental tracks, like *Guns of Navarone*, and backed most of the era's popular singers – including Millie Small, who shot to international fame with *My Boy Lollipop*, and gave Chris Blackwell's Island label its first smash hit. Other prominent ska tracks included Justin Hinds and the Dominoes' *Carry Go Bring Come*, the Ethiopians' *Train to Skaville* and a host of others on Beverley's, Federal, Treasure Isle and Coxsone Dodd's Studio One and Coxsone labels.

Rude boys to rocksteady

As the post-independence glow began to fade, Jamaica's ghetto youth became increasingly dissatisfied with their meagre slice of the pie, and the **rude boy** era of police brutality and ghetto dissent began. Rude boys were cinematically celebrated by Jimmy Cliff's portrayal of urban rebel Ivan in *The Harder They Come*, and musically documented in early Wailers cuts like *Rule Them Rudie* and *Let Him Go (Rudie Get Bail)*. Their fractious stance also generated the Wailers' 1964 *Simmer Down*, an appeal for calm among the youth.

While the musical critique of free Jamaica continued in releases like the Skatalites' 1966 *Independent Anniversary Ska*, subtle changes occurred in the music itself as Jamaicans began to demand something more leisurely. Producers accorded and began to slow down the tempo, guiding their artists toward a more benign lyrical

The art of the rhythm track

Through what's known in Jamaica as the **rhythm track**, the bass lines and chord sequences laid down during the rocksteady and reggae eras have become the foundation for practically all Jamaican music recorded thereafter. Realizing that there are only so many chords to play, or pressed for time when studios charge by the hour, the island's musicians and producers have capitalized on the best chord and bass-line combinations, manipulating and reinterpreting them so often that most of the classic rhythm tracks have established names, usually gleaned from the song title with which they first appeared. Working as full-time studio session musicians throughout the rocksteady and early reggae eras, the likes of singer, bassist and arranger Leroy Sibbles and the "rhythm twins", **Sly Dunbar** and **Robbie Shakespeare**, created many of the rhythms that backed hundreds of 1970s' reggae cuts and are still reworked into today's dancehall; producer Bunny Lee, meanwhile, was one of the first to release multiple versions of a song backed by the same rhythm track; today, this has become normal practice, with all the prominent Jamaican artists recording a vocal version over whatever rhythm track is currently in vogue. Within contemporary dancehall, certain rhythms – from "punany" and "pepper-seed" in the 80s and 90s to "dutty wine" and "willy bounce" in the new millennium – become hugely popular, with specialized dances to go with them (as Usain Bolt demonstrated to the world at the 2008 Beijing Olympics with his performance of the "nuh linga" dance).

The upshot is that listening to Jamaican music can feel like an exercise in déjà vu; you may or may not have heard a particular song before, but once you've listened to a fair portion of rocksteady and early reggae, you'll certainly be familiar with most of the classic rhythm tracks. And once you've listened to the radio for a couple of hours, you'll get to know the currently popular dancehall rhythms.

output. The rude-boy lament continued in cuts like *007 (Shanty Town)* from Desmond Dekker and the Aces; but by 1966 Hopeton Lewis had produced *Take It Easy*, and Stranger and Patsy were singing emollient **rocksteady** tracks about love and relationships in *When I Call Your Name*. *Happy Go Lucky Girl* and *Only A Smile* by John Holt and the Paragons, *Queen Majesty* by the Techniques and *I Caught You* by Brent Dowe's Melodians also did something to temper the pressure in West Kingston. Characterized by the addition of the "one drop" drumming style and a more melodic tone, rocksteady carried the swing and swiftly eclipsed the ska sound. The king of the era was **Alton Ellis**, who put a name to the movement with his *Get Ready Rock Steady* track. It was a prolific time for Jamaican music, with labels like Studio One and, primarily, Treasure Isle pumping out the tunes, many set to rhythm tracks that still continue to be heard to this day (see above). However, rocksteady was a short-lived movement, and by 1968 it had been superseded by the tighter guitars, heavier bass and sinuous rhythm of reggae.

Reggae to roots rock

So many artists contributed to the development of **reggae** that it's impossible to say who originated the genre – it's most likely that this ubiquitous Jamaican sound developed organically as a natural progression from rocksteady, but Toots and The Maytals' 1968 single *Do The Reggay* (sic) certainly cemented a name that Rastafarians may tell you derives from *rex*, meaning king. Hence reggae is the "king's music" – an apt allegory, as the appearance of reggae coincided with an explosion in the popularity of the Rastafarian movement.

From 1970 onwards, Jamaican music took an increasingly religious stance, with its main lyrical themes drawing reference from the tenets of Rastafari: repatriation, black history, black pride and self-determination. **"Roots and culture"** were the lick, and reggae became a fully fledged protest music. It was anathema to the establishment, who saw a menacing, subversive message from a dirty and violent source and banned it wherever possible – though the rum-bar jukeboxes played whatever the radio stations wouldn't. It wasn't until after Bob Marley and the Wailers signed with Island Records in 1972, to international acclaim (see p.161), that reggae was given islandwide approval for the first time.

A time of intense musical productivity, the 1970s stand out as the classic period of Jamaica's best roots reggae. But while **Burning Spear** was singing *Marcus Garvey* and *Slavery Days* and Joseph Hill's **Culture** provided apocalyptic warnings of the time when *Two Sevens Clash*, the era also offered a sweeter side; the angelic crooning of more mainstream artists like **Dennis Brown** and **Gregory Isaacs** found an eager audience, their style becoming known as **lovers' rock**. Though their lyrics rested mostly on love and affection, lovers' artists also had some bite; tracks like Junior Byles' *Curly Locks* (a song about the controversial move of falling in love with a Rastaman) highlight the uneasy relationship that Rasta and reggae still had with wider Jamaican society.

Dub to DJ business

As the 1970s wore on, studio technology became increasingly sophisticated. Producers began manipulating their equipment, using reverb or echo machines, overdubbing techniques and snatches of dog barks or gunshots to produce some of the most arresting and penetrating music ever to emerge from Jamaica – **dub**. Employing a remarkable level of inventiveness with often limited means, Jamaican engineers such as dub pioneers **King Tubby**, **Prince Jammy** and **Scientist** predated the advent of the digital sampler by ten years and brought reggae back to basics, stripping down songs so that only bass, drums and inflections of tone remained. Snippets of the original vocals were then mixed in alongside sound effects and two-line DJ sound bites. Like ska, dub remained a primarily instrumental music for a short time. Before long, scores of DJs clamoured to produce a dub voice-over, and producers plundered their archives and released dub versions of old cuts, while DJs provided the voice-over and even vocal tracks had a dub flip-side.

The cult of the **DJ** had begun in the sound systems, with resident DJs improvising a couple of lines of introductory patter at the beginning of a record. The ecstatic crowd responses encouraged them to spin it out, and soon they were delivering full-length monologues over the music, discussing topical events as well as the state of play on the dancefloor. The craft was mastered by **U-Roy** – inspired by the earlier efforts of Count Machouki and Sir Lord Comic – who released talk-based singles to great success throughout the 1970s with roots sound systems like the venerable King Tubby's Hi-Fi, Stur-Gav, Tippertone, Sir George and Killamanjaro providing the backing for their live appearances. Meanwhile, the DJs' trade was expanded when Big Youth started talking over records in his cultural style, followed by the likes of King Stitt, Dennis Alcapone, I-Roy, Jah Stitch, Tappa Zukie, Prince Jazzbo and Dillinger, whose *Cocaine Running Around My Brain* scored a hit in the UK. As the violent elections of 1976 and 1980 saw the pressure in Kingston building up, the sound systems multiplied and the DJs "chatted" on the mike about the times, analysing the position of the ghetto

The cult of the sound system

Since the mid-1950s, when Duke Reid and Coxsone Dodd discharged the first shots in a battle of heavy wattage, mobile discos known as **sound systems** have been intrinsic to the Jamaican music scene. Laying the foundations of each stage in reggae's development, sound systems provide an opportunity to test crowd response to new lyrics or rhythms and inspire Jamaicans to follow their sound of choice with vehement loyalty. A simple arrangement of high-powered amplifiers and momentous columns of speakers customized to give a heavy, belly-rolling bass, the sound system began as a way of bringing the music to those who couldn't afford nightclub or stageshow cover charges. And so it remains; the sound system jam is now the major form of entertainment for young Jamaicans, with outdoor events such as the legendary Passa Passa and the many subsequent street dances breaking new artists and tunes and – of course – allowing the opportunity to display prowess at the dances that go with each new rhythm. Some sound system devotees go to hear their favourite **selector**, the man who employs an almost clairvoyant intuition to play just what the crowd wants, while others come for the prospect of hearing DJs chatting live lyrics. Overall, though, it's the unique "dancehall vibe" that most people come to savour, with patrons dressed to the nines in the very latest fashions, dancing in the light of the inevitable video camera or posing for the photographers from local dancehall websites.

Since the early days when Dodd would set up on an opposite Kingston corner to Reid and try to poach his crowd with a mightier bass and a craftier playlist, **rivalry** has been central to sound-system culture. The battle to be known as the best is fought out at "**clashes**", where two sounds play on one night, and crowd appreciation is the mark of the winner. Buying a larger amp or a new set of speakers is one way of achieving dominance, but the most popular method is still to spin an exclusive track voiced over by the latest DJ or singer (though CDs have replaced the "dub-plate" acetates of the vinyl era).

Today, the main players in the Jamaican sound-system scene are the inimitable **Stone Love**, whose raw reputation and killer selectors still prompt followers to travel for miles to hear them play. And the sound system phenomena isn't restricted to Jamaica, either, with Mighty Crown from Japan and King Addies from New York being two of the more popular sets from overseas, both of which regularly play at parties in Jamaica. For more on sound system parties, see the *Jamaican nightlife* colour section.

youth in Jamaica from a dread perspective and offering cultural distractions by setting the psalms to song. Newcomers U-Brown, Ranking Joe, Josey Wales, Charlie Chaplin and Trinity continued in the same vein, touring Jamaica and the Caribbean with sound systems, and paving the way for the dancehall explosion of the 1980s.

In 1981, the Jamaican reggae industry was left in shock as Bob Marley succumbed to cancer and the music fraternity realized the enormity of their loss. Jamaica came to a standstill for two days as mourners viewed his coffin and lined the roads to watch the entourage on the final procession to Nine Mile. Though not the greatest singer to emerge from Jamaica, Marley's influence and songwriting talent were immeasurable, and following his demise, reggae struggled to regain its direction and purpose. Groups like **Black Uhuru** recorded a succession of roots albums for Island, but the musical tide had already turned towards the DJ, and Marley's legacy of cultural consciousness began to seem less appropriate to the world of cocaine-running and political warfare in the ghettos. The roots reggae scene also took a further blow in 1999 with the death of the "Crown Prince of Reggae", Dennis Brown, one of Jamaica's most prolific – and sweetest – singers.

Slackness in the dancehall

These days, you're far more likely to be assailed by a clamourous barrage of raw drum and bass and shouty patois lyrics than hear Bob Marley or Burning Spear booming out from Jamaican speaker-boxes. Known as **dancehall** (because that's where it originated and where it is best enjoyed), this is the most popular musical form in contemporary Jamaica. The genre first surfaced around 1979 and was cemented in 1981 when flamboyant albino DJ **Yellowman** exploded onto the scene with his massive hits *Married in the Morning*, *Mr Chin* and *Nobody Move*. Yellowman's lyrical bawdiness and huge popularity signified the departure from roots reggae and cultural toasting (the original term used to describe the Jamaican talking-over-music that inspired US rappers) to the sexually explicit and often violent DJ-ism that took hold in the 1980s. Though none were rawer than Yellow, who added energetic stage performances and self-deprecating humour to the expletives, other DJs – fuelled by a positive response from their Jamaican audience – emulated his lewd approach, and sexually explicit lyrics – or "**slackness**" – began to proliferate.

In 1985, Wayne Smith's hit *Under Me Sleng Teng* – voiced for a King Jammy's rhythm of the same name – heralded the start of the computer age in the dancehall. Studios switched from analogue to digital recording formats, and producers seized upon computerized rhythms as a quicker and cheaper way of putting out a record. The mixing board had become an instrument unto itself, with a new breed of producers like Bobby Digital, Donovan Germaine, Mikey Bennett, Dave Kelly, Jeremy Harding and Patrick Roberts becoming the Reids and Dodds of the 1990s and DJs becoming the island's biggest stars. Vocalists also clamoured to ride the digital rhythms – singers like Frankie Paul, Michael Palmer, Little John, Beres Hammond, Barrington Levy, Pinchers, Wayne Wonder and Sanchez got the sweetness out of the rhythms.

Dancehall is massive in contemporary Jamaica, though it's not to everyone's liking. Many charge the genre with wider moral decline as the DJs become the gangsta rappers of reggae, with flash cars, designer clothes and, in some cases, a seemingly limitless enthusiasm for automatic firearms and rough sex. Homophobia, too, is

Dancehall queens

Weekends in Jamaica mean sound-system dances islandwide, and here, **fashion** goes hand-in-hand with the music. In a society where single-parent families dominate, making women the sole breadwinners, parties are a time to let loose and forget the domestic drudgery in favour of some of the rudest dancing and most glittery glamour on the planet – as demonstrated in the 1997 Jamaican movie *Dancehall Queen*, named for the women who have long ruled the roost at Jamaican sound-system parties.

Whether it's a latticework leatherette G-string and bra ensemble or a concoction of carefully arranged silver plastic straps, topped off with a neon wig, thigh-high boots or killer heels, dancehall wear is loud, proud and deliberately ostentatious. The outfits are for one purpose: the sheer hype and self-promotion of making an impression at a party and performing the suggestive gymnastics of the latest dances to mesmerizing effect. **Dancehall queens** are the icons of sound-system culture, a league of ghetto princesses ruled for years by a light-skinned uptown Kingstonian named Carlene, whose killer dress-sense, athletic dancing style and pneumatic body earned her the local status of a Hollywood film star. New faces are constantly arriving on the scene – in 2002, Japanese dancer Junko "Bashment" Kudo stunned locals by becoming the first of several non-Jamaicans to win the annual Dancehall Queen competition staged in Montego Bay, itself an excellent opportunity to get a flavour of this quintes-sentially Jamaican phenomenon.

The producers

From the late 1950s to the late 1960s, **Duke Reid** and **Coxsone Dodd** dominated Jamaica's music scene, commanding heavyweight respect among the music fraternity and churning out the majority of the island's hits. This pair of musical titans are widely credited with controlling Jamaican recording as the industry shifted focus from ska to rocksteady. Their "big fish in a small pond" infamy has shaped the way that the industry works at a basic level: a producer raises enough funds to buy a studio; he then hires a team of musicians or a master keyboard programmer to lay down the rhythm tracks, and scouts for a talented arranger to look after the daily running of recording sessions and audition hopeful vocalists. The producer then selects the right combination from his pool of vocalists, songs and rhythm tracks, puts it all together, presses vinyl copies and releases the record, inevitably taking no chances on its success by handing out favours – payola – to ensure the tunes are played on the radio and at dances.

Though the reign of Dodd and Reid remained watertight until the late 1960s, the prevailing mood had changed by the early 1970s. Artists got sick of being paid a single fee while the producers reaped the royalties, and in-house arrangers balked at doing all the work while the producers sat back and enjoyed the rewards. As starting a label was merely a matter of raising the funds for studio time and record pressing, a new breed of **independent producer** emerged. Many lasted no longer than a couple of releases, but the likes of Jack Ruby, Harry "J" Johnson, Bunny "Striker" Lee, Henry "Junjo" Lawes, Sonia Pottinger and Clancy Eccles were more long-standing, and produced some of the finest reggae of the era. The most infamous and instrumental independent producer, though, was the eminent "Upsetter", **Lee "Scratch" Perry**, who started out as a bouncer for Prince Buster and graduated to running Coxsone's Studio One, where he worked with Marley and the Wailers on the definitive singles (*Small Axe*, *Sun Is Shining*, *Duppy Conqueror*, *Satisfy My Soul*) that were later reworked on albums for Island Records. In the late 1960s, Perry built his **Black Ark** studio and established the famous Upsetter label, releasing classic tracks such as Junior Murvin's *Police and Thieves*, Max Romeo's *Sipple Out Deh* (*War Inna Babylon*) and the Congos' definitive roots reggae LP *Heart of the Congos*. Perry remained at reggae's cutting edge until the late 1970s, becoming one of the chief innovators of dub as a patron of the late King Tubby. But his legendary – and often consciously cultivated – mental instability (planting records in his garden, burning down his studio in a fit of pique) and refusal to compromise his increasingly eccentric musical vision led to a decline in sales.

The digital age of the 1980s heralded a new era for reggae, as producers were able to release material with even fewer resources behind them. Big names such as Prince Jammy churned out electronic dancehall rhythms alongside fellow luminaries Bobby Digital, Gussie Clarke, Mikey Bennett and Donovan Germain, Philip "Fatis" Burell and Steely and Cleevie, while Dave Kelly and Jeremy Harding carried the swing throughout the 1990s and are still producing today.

a regular theme; although high-profile DJs such as **Buju Banton** (whose 1990s song *Boom Bye Bye* has become synonymous with anti-gay sentiments in Jamaica music) have bowed to pressure from campaigners and no longer perform their more inflammatory hits overseas, many still publicize their views whilst back in Jamaica. However, though some dancehall does seem intent on a glorification of violence and bigotry, much of it simply reflects the lives of thousands of ghetto dwellers for whom brutality and prejudice are a daily reality. Essentially, dancehall is a raw, rude, hard-core music designed to titillate and tease its Jamaican audience on home ground and beyond. Whether you like the lyrics or hate them, it's unlikely you'll be able to resist dancehall's compelling rhythm and infectious hype, and while you're in Jamaica, it's futile to try.

For the definitive history of Jamaican music, consult Steve Barrow's and Peter Dalton's *Rough Guide to Reggae*, and for a musical trip through the years, try Island's unbeatable *Tougher Than Tough* four-CD collection.

Reggae in the twenty-first century

Undoubtedly, dancehall dominates contemporary Jamaican music. Yet those worried about moral depravity can take heart: dancehall culture is going through another transitional phase, as the battle between cultural and dancehall artists intensifies. In 1993, the conscious lyrics and staunch Rastafarian stance of singer **Garnet Silk** managed to conquer the dancehalls at the time when "gun and gyal" lyrics were the sole signifiers, and his immense popularity started the momentum for today's resurgence of cultural reggae. In 1994, Silk was killed in an explosion, but the likes of the massively popular Morgan Heritage, Luciano, Richie Spice, Etana, Jah Cure and Tarrus Riley have carried on where he left off, using musicians rather than keyboards and writing their own material. Singers Sanchez, Beres Hammond and Wayne Wonder provide sweet love songs for the romantically inclined, while Queen Ifrica, Lady Saw, Tanya Stephens, Macka Diamond and Spice provide the woman's touch. Reggae has even made moves into the pop arena: Grammy Award-winner Shaggy scored worldwide hits with *Boombastic* and *It Wasn't Me*, platinum-selling uptown boy **Sean Paul** has scored several No.1s on the US *Billboard* chart, and Grammy-winner **Damian "Junior Gong" Marley** has shot to global fame on the back of his brilliant second album, *Welcome to Jamrock*, a sizzling record with guest performances from brothers Stephen and Ziggy as well as a slew of international names.

Nonetheless, dancehall continues in its classic abrasive form, with the likes of Busy Signal, Elephant Man and Mr Vegas continuing to release hit after hit. The ongoing feud between **Beenie Man** and **Bounty Killer** continues to rumble on, but these stalwart DJs (some might say old-timers) are being eclipsed by the new dancehall kings, **Vybez Kartel** and **Mavado**, who have taken rivalry to ever higher levels: most young Jamaicans having chosen their side and give passionate support to either "Gully" (Mavado) or "Gaza" (Kartel).

Books

The selection below represents the best available books written about Jamaica, alongside some of the authors' personal favourites. All are available from ⒲www.amazon.co.uk and www.amazon.com, or from specialist Caribbean publishers such as Sangsters (⒲www.sangsterbooks.com), UWI Press (⒲www.uwipress.com), Peepal Tree (⒲www.peepaltreepress.com) and LMH (⒲www.lmhpublishingjamaica.com). Titles marked with 🏃 are particularly recommended.

Travel and diaries

Patrick Leigh Fermor *The Traveller's Tree*. The classic Caribbean travelogue describing Leigh Fermor's visit in the late 1940s, before tourism had really started in the region, though only the last chapter covers his time in Jamaica, with specific reference to the developing Rastafari movement in west Kingston.

🏃 **Linda Gambrill** (ed) *A Tapestry of Jamaica*. A collection of the best articles from thirty years of Air Jamaica's brilliant in-flight magazine. Covering sport, music, travel, fashion, people, art, history and folk tales, as well as a whole section on the inimitable Miss Lou, this is an essential collection, made all the more poignant by the sheer love of the island that comes through in the final "memories" section.

🏃 **David Howard** *Kingston*. Comprehensive treatment of Jamaica's irrepressible capital, with a solid historical perspective alongside plenty of informed social commentary and a trot around all the sights and sounds of Kingston.

Brian J. Hudson *The Waterfalls of Jamaica*. A wide-ranging ode to Jamaica's gorgeous cascades (though not a guidebook in the practical sense), it looks at the main waterfalls and their exploitation as tourist attractions, with illustrations ranging from eighteenth-century prints to contemporary photographs. Food for thought as you idle away an afternoon at YS or Reach.

Matthew Lewis *Journal of a West Indian Planter*. Fascinating diaries of Lewis, an early nineteenth-century English novelist, describing his brief visits to his Jamaican estates and cataloguing the lifestyle and living conditions of the island's slaves.

Lady Maria Nugent *Journal of Residence in Jamaica 1801–5*. Lady Nugent was the wife of one of Jamaica's governors, and her diary, though often naive and patronizing, paints an interesting picture of how the "ruling class" lived.

🏃 **Chris Salewicz** *Rude Boy – Once Upon a Time in Jamaica*. Part history of Jamaica, part travelogue written by a true Jamaica-phile, it evokes some of the innate paradoxes of Jamaica with humour and delicacy.

🏃 **Frank Fonda Taylor** *To Hell with Paradise*. Exhaustive history of the beginnings of the Jamaican tourist industry, with great black-and-white photos and early adverts. Offers some marvellous insight into the prejudices and condescensions of the first visitors.

Anthony Winkler *Going Home to Teach*. Engaging story of novelist Winkler's own experiences as a white Jamaican returning to live on his native island during the "anti-white" climate of the late 1970s. Very good on the politics of the period.

Fiction

Russell Banks *The Book of Jamaica*.
Narrated by an academic who bases
himself in Jamaica whilst writing a
novel about the Maroons, this is a
slow starter that eventually manages
some compelling commentary on the
island's society in the 1970s, from the
prejudices of his landlords or the magic
worked by a Maroon colonel to the
lifestyles and attitudes of the Jamaicans
that live and work around him.

Louise Bennett *Anancy and Miss
Lou*. Jamaica's oral tradition of
storytelling may be fading, but these
are the classic folk tales told in patois
by the late Louise Bennett, the greatest
of modern Jamaican storytellers.

Margaret Cezair-Thomson
The True History of Paradise and
Pirate's Daughter. Poignant and
beautifully written, the former is a
history of Jamaica as told by various
generations of a Jamaican family,
from the Scottish wife of a planter to
an African ex-slave to a modern-day
uptown girl in Kingston. The latter
is a brilliantly imaginative tale of a
Portland family whose lives become
intertwined with Errol Flynn, with
evocative descriptions of their life
with him on Navy Island.

Colin Channer (ed) *Iron Balloons*.
Written by participants of the
Calabash Writers Workshop, an
offshoot of Jamaica's marvellous
literary festival (see p.32), this pacy
collection of short stories, set in
Jamaica and the US, gives voice to
some wonderful new writers alongside
more established names such as Kwame
Dawes and Channer himself.

Colin Channer *Waiting In Vain*.
This tale of a modern-day romance
between a Jamaican man and an
American woman perfectly evokes the
Jamaican communities of England,
New York and Jamaica itself. Great
holiday reading.

Mark Conklin *Banana Shout*.
Engaging and occasionally hilarious
account of an American draft dodger's
adventures as he sets up home in
Negril during the 1970s.

Herbert de Lisser *The White Witch of
Rose Hall*. A blend of Gothic horror and
purple prose, this richly embellished
account of the island's best-known
ghost story tells the tale of Annie
Palmer, mistress of Rose Hall Great
House, whose three husbands all died
in suspicious circumstances.

Perry Henzell *Power Game*. Long,
entertaining story of power seekers
at different levels in Jamaican society
– politics, the army, the banks, the
drug trade. Henzell catches local
language and atmosphere with the
same skill he used in his movie *The
Harder They Come*.

Marlon James *John Crow's Devil*.
Centred on the battle for the
souls of the village of Gibbeah, this
is a powerful, perfectly paced novel
from one of the most exciting new
writers to emerge from Jamaica in
years, with crackling dialogue and a
plot which keeps you riveted to the
last. Brilliant stuff.

Evan Jones *Stone Haven*. Long-winded
but readable historical novel that
picks its way through modern issues,
from 1920s attitudes to colour to the
problems of post-independence.

Guy Kennaway *One People*.
Entertaining and brilliantly
funny take on life in a tiny coastal
town in Westmoreland. It perfectly
evokes rural Jamaican life, from the
patois chat to the clandestine shenanigans of the locals. Essential.

Roger Mais *The Hills Were Joyful
Together*, *Brother Man* and *Black
Lightning*. *Hills* is a bleak, compelling
picture of life in a Kingston ghetto in
the 1950s, with a harsh look at law

and order Jamaica-style, by one of the country's earliest novelists. *Brother Man* details the emergence of Rastafari in Kingston via the gentle "Brother Man" himself, while *Black Lightning* is an intense and atmospheric account of the life of a brooding sculptor living in the Jamaican bush.

Alicia McKenzie *Stories from Yard*. With settings ranging from a Brazilian beach to the streets of Kingston, this wide-ranging collection of short stories are sweet, funny and sometimes very sad.

Terry McMillan *How Stella Got Her Groove Back*. In McMillan's lightweight but enjoyable tone, this semi-autobiographical tale tells the story of a holiday romance that turns serious, written as a result of the author's experiences during holidays in Negril.

Brian Meeks *Paint the Town Red*. Moving portrayal of an uptown Kingstonian's first day of freedom after serving a prison term for his involvement in a politically motivated shooting in the run-up to the 1980 election. The descriptions of life in the ghetto are particularly gripping – and brutal.

Orlando Patterson *The Children of Sisyphus*. Famous, uncompromising picture of the poorest of Kingston's poor, fighting for survival on the margins of society, and of Dinah, a prostitute who tries to leave them behind and move up in the world. One of the first novels to try to present a fair picture of the Rasta community.

Geoffrey Philp *Benjamin, My Son*. A Jamaican living in Miami returns to the island for the funeral of his father, a politician loosely modelled on several recognizable Jamaican leaders, and becomes embroiled in the shady world of Jamaica's political scene: gunmen, obeah-men and all.

V.S. Reid *The Jamaicans*. Juan de Bolas was a slave liberated by the Spanish when the English captured the island in 1655. Reid's fictionalized account tells of his life in hiding and struggle against the English.

Jean Rhys *Wide Sargasso Sea*. Poignant, beautifully written view of post-emancipation Jamaica, with Antoinette, a young Creole girl, and Rochester, her English boyfriend, trapped by declining financial circumstances and his inability to understand the realities of local life. Written as a prequel to Bronte's *Jane Eyre*.

Kim Robinson & Leeta Hearn (eds) *Twenty-two Jamaican Short Stories*. Excellent short-story collection that covers some of the more chilling psychological aspects of Jamaican life. Venerable authors include Olive Senior, Dennis Scott, Hazel Campbell and Trevor Fearon.

Tony Sewell *Jamaica Inc.* Gripping and intelligent fictional history of a strangely familiar political family dynasty.

Sistren Collective *Lionheart Gal*. Recently reissued, this brilliant collection penned by members of the Sistren Theatre Collective sheds light into the hopes, dreams and realities of women's lives in Jamaica, and though the island has gone through many changes since the initial publication, all the voices strike a contemporary chord and, as most are written in patois, provide a lovely window into the local lingo.

Vanessa Spence *The Roads Are Down*. Excellent and amusing first novel of a cross-cultural love affair, set in modern-day Kingston and the Blue Mountains.

Michael Thewell *The Harder They Come*. Novel inspired by Perry Henzell's brilliant movie, telling the story of Rhygin – country boy turned rude boy – who comes to Kingston and gets caught up in gangs and ganja.

Anthony Winkler *The Great Yacht Race*, *The Painted Canoe* and *The Lunatic*. Set just before independence, *The Great Yacht Race* is a hilarious look at the lifestyle of Montego Bay's erstwhile "ruling class" as the lawyers, journalists and hotel owners go through scandal after scandal in preparation for their annual boat race. *The Painted Canoe* is a powerful, evocative tale of a Jamaican fisherman and his relationship with the sea, while *The Lunatic* is a poignant but amusing tale of a Jamaican madman, who wanders the island talking with the trees and bushes, and his encounter with Inge, a sexually voracious German tourist (see also p.83).

History and politics

Warren Alleyne *Caribbean Pirates*. Alleyne debunks the myths about the region's leading pirates – from Blackbeard to Henry Morgan – in a series of brief portraits.

Clinton Black *Port Royal* and *Tales of Old Jamaica*. *Port Royal* is a solid history of the city once known as the "wickedest place on earth"; *Tales* has brief accounts of some of the key events in the island's past, recalling the capture of Jamaica by the British, the story of "Three Fingered" Jack Mansong, and the women pirates Anne Bonney and Mary Read.

Trevor Burnard *Mastery, Tyranny and Desire*. Based around the diaries of Thomas Thistlewood, who kept a regular journal during his forty years as a plantation owner in Jamaica, this compelling and accessible book provides a chilling insight into life in the colonial era, from Thistlewood's obsessive detailing of his sexual exploits to the appalling punishments and routine humiliations he meted out to his slaves.

James Ferguson *A Traveller's History of the Caribbean*. Concise and well-written overview that provides a good introduction to the region's history.

John Gilmore *Faces of the Caribbean*. Excellent and essential sociohistory of the Caribbean, covering everything from slavery to reggae, cricket and the environment.

Michelle Harrison *King Sugar – Jamaica, the Caribbean and the World Sugar Economy*. Solid history of the Jamaican sugar industry – and the fortunes it made for British planters.

Rupert Lewis & Patrick Bryan (eds) *Garvey: His Work and Impact*. Twenty-one articles on the historical background to Garveyism, his influence on Jamaica and his worldwide legacy.

Michael Manley *The Politics of Change – A Jamaican Testament*. Interesting overview of the proposed transformation of the island under Manley's PNP government, written as it got underway in the early 1970s.

Tony Sewell *Garvey's Children: The Legacy of Marcus Garvey*. Readable account of Garvey's black-power movement and the inspiration it has provided for black nationalists in Jamaica and abroad.

Religion, culture and society

Leonard Barrett *The Rastafarians* and *The Sun and the Drum*. The former is one of the most comprehensive accounts of the movement, explaining its origins and politics and looking at related religious movements like the Twelve Tribes of Israel sect. The latter is an in-depth look at the influence of

African traditions in Jamaican culture, including language, witchcraft and folk medicine.

Derek Bishton *Black Heart Man – A Journey into Rasta*. Succinct, well-researched foray into the origins and development of the Rastafarian movement in Jamaica, with discussion of Garvey and a host of less-well-known black theorists.

Adrian Boot & Michael Thomas *Babylon on a Thin Wire*. Evocative photographic portraits of 1970s Kingston from one of the most renowned photographers of Jamaican culture, backed up by cynical and informed text.

Lloyd Bradley *Bass Culture – When Reggae Was King*. Very readable history of reggae written, for once, by a man of Jamaican origin rather than a US academic. Entertaining and pretty comprehensive, though a bit short on contemporary detail.

Barry Chevannes *Rastafari Roots and Ideology*. Comprehensive, accessible study of Rastafari, tracing the history of the movement and detailing religious practice, and with a chapter dedicated to orthodox Bobo dreads to boot. Essential reading.

Laurie Gunst *Born Fe Dead*. Gripping account of the dark

side of political and drug-related violence in Jamaica, reissued with updates and a new postscript. Ably researched with the help of Jamaicans in Kingston and New York, this traces the development of Jamaican posses from political lackeys to drug-trafficking gangsters.

Polly Pattullo *Last Resorts – The Cost of Tourism in the Caribbean*. Important, well-researched critique of the tourist industry and its impact on the islands.

M.G. Smith, Roy Augier & Rex Nettleford *Report on the Rastafari Movement*. Published in 1960, the first academic study of Jamaica's home-grown religion. Dated but accurate description of the contempo-rary make-up, history, beliefs and rituals of Rastafari.

Ian Thompson *The Dead Yard*. An absorbing exploration of contemporary Jamaica that paints a depressingly accurate portrait of the realities of life for Jamaicans at home and in the diaspora. Though the rather melodramatic title is an indication of the author's tendency to go for the headline-friendly jugular, this is nonetheless an exemplary commentary on the island's history and current affairs, and makes essential reading for any Jamaica-phile.

Music and art

Steve Barrow & Peter Dalton *The Rough Guide to Reggae*. Comprehensive, definitive handbook on reggae music, with sections on the UK, US and African scenes as well as a comprehensive rundown on things in Jamaica.

Cedella Booker *Bob Marley*. Very personal account of Marley's life and death written by his mother, light on the music but heavy on family anecdotes, plus the occasional (and most entertaining) catty swipe.

Adrian Boot & Chris Salewicz *Bob Marley – Songs of Freedom*. Boot's fabulous photos and Salewicz's spot-on text make this one of the better Marley bios, with lots of input from the family and first-hand interviews.

David Boxer & Veerle Poupeye *Modern Jamaican Art*. Lavish tome with text from Jamaica's premier art historians, and high-quality plates of the best and most familiar works.

Jeremy Collingwood *Bob Marley – His Musical Legacy*. Coffee-table heavyweight, lavishly illustrated with little-seen photographs as well as shots of contemporary magazine covers, record labels, concert flyers and newspaper clippings, all of which set the tone for the informed and sensitive text on Marley's career as it developed from his early days in Kingston to international stardom. A detailed discography, too.

Lee Jaffe *One Love – Life with Bob Marley and the Wailers*. An American photographer who hung out with Bob et al in the 1970s, Jaffe tells his story via interviews with Roger Steffens. The text is interspersed with Jaffe's wonderful photographs (some previously unpublished), which perfectly document the era.

David Katz *Solid Foundation* and *People Funny Boy*. *Solid Foundation* is a history of the first thirty years of Jamaican music, from mento to the dawn of dancehall, as told by the musicians themselves. The 200-plus interviews include producers (Coxsone Dodd, Prince Buster, Junjo Lawes), musicians (Sly and Robbie) and all the essential artists, from members of the Skatalites and Toots and the Maytals to Burning Spear, U-Roy and Frankie Paul. Katz's *People Funny Boy* is the definitive biography of the eccentric genius Lee "Scratch" Perry.

Beth Lesser *King Jammy's* and *Dancehall*. The former is a brilliant bio of the Waterhouse dancehall maestro, which provides the definitive lowdown on the man himself as well as a host of artists

from Wayne Smith to Bounty Killer; while *Dancehall* gives a wider overview of the scene in Jamaica from the 1980s onwards.

Chris Morrow *Stir It Up*. LP-sized tribute to Jamaican record-cover artwork, with all the best efforts in full colour.

Norman C. Stolzoff *Wake The Town and Tell The People*. Though rather academic in tone, and written firmly from the somewhat anthropological perspective of a non-Jamaican, this nonetheless provides some solid background to the sound-system scene, from the genre's early days to a blow-by-blow account of a Killamanjaro dance.

Petrine Archer Straw & Kim Robinson *Jamaican Art*. Comprehensive account of the development of modern Jamaican art, well illustrated with the work of all of the major painters and sculptors, from Edna Marley to Kapo.

Don Taylor *Marley and Me*. Taylor was Bob Marley's one-time manager, and his chatty if rather badly written account – focusing on girlfriends, politics and controversy – is more sensationalist than White's (below).

Timothy White *Catch a Fire*. Exhaustive and loving biography of Bob Marley (including a detailed discography), with an in-depth look at the early Jamaican music scene; plenty of obeah and superstition mixed in with plenty of supposition on the thoughts and feelings of the great man and those who surrounded him.

Flora and fauna

C. Dennis Adams *Flowering Plants of Jamaica*. Useful introductory guide to Jamaican flora.

James Bond *Field Guide to Birds of the West Indies*. The classic bird book,

from which Ian Fleming took the name of his fictional hero, though generally considered to have been supplanted by the Downer/Sutton book.

Audrey Downer & Robert Sutton *Birds of Jamaica: A Photographic Field Guide*. The definitive field guide on the island's birds, with handy sections on the island's principal habitats and birding "hot spots".

Alan Fincham *Jamaica Underground*. The ultimate guide to caving in Jamaica, with reams of background info and some 300 plans of the islands's caverns, sinkholes and underground rivers.

Eugene Kaplan *A Field Guide to the Coral Reefs of the Caribbean and Florida*. Attractive guide to the region's reefs.

G.W. Lennox & S.A. Seddon *Flowers of the Caribbean*; *Trees of the Caribbean*; *Fruits and Vegetables of the Caribbean*. Handy pocket-size books, with glossy, sharp, colour pictures, and a good general introduction to the region's flora.

Food and drink

Norma Benghiat *Traditional Jamaican Cooking*. Handy and engagingly written guide to the island's traditional dishes, from ackee and saltfish to curry goat and rice and peas, with all of the classic recipes and a lot more. *The Food of Jamaica*, by Benghiat and John Demers, is another reliable option.

Mike Henry *Caribbean Cocktails and Mixed Drinks*. All of the classic recipes based mostly on rums and fresh juices.

Caroline Sullivan *Classic Jamaican Cooking*. The Jamaican version of Mrs Beeton, little changed since its first publication in 1896. Excellent recipes, anecdotes and the essential "Herbal Remedies and Household Hints".

Helen Willinsky *Jerk – Barbecue from Jamaica*. Do-it-yourself jerk manual.

Language

Language

Language

Tune into the talk-show-dominated radio and you'll soon see that Jamaicans enjoy nothing better than a good debate, taking great delight in outwitting each other in verbal battles. Although the official language is English, **patois** is the working mode of expression, and its validity as either legitimate language or corrupted slang continues to provoke much debate on the island.

Patois is an incredibly creative and constantly evolving idiom; new words are constantly coined to suit every development and fall into common use with astonishing speed, while older phrases – yesterday's "buzzwords" – disappear without a trace.

Understanding Jamaican Patois by L. Emile Adams is a user-friendly description of patois grammar and language usage, and includes a small dictionary; the list of some of the most obvious idiosyncrasies below should help you to understand what you're hearing.

- Women are commonly referred to as "him": "Wha! Shelley pregnant! Him never tell me!"
- "H" is often not voiced, but makes up for the discrepancy by adding itself to plenty of other words. Hence "So yu is 'Enry from Hin-glan, don't?" ("don't" is used to mean "aren't you", or "isn't it?").
- There are plenty more random additions and absences: "shrimp" is often "swimp", "spliff" is "scliff", "vex" is "bex", "little" is "likkle", "ask" is "aks".
- Plurals are either ignored or conveyed by adding "dem"; hence "two feet" becomes "two foot", and "the girls are cooking for me" is "de gyal dem a cook fe de I".
- If somebody calls you "fatty", "whitey" or "big batty gyal", they are (usually) simply being direct rather than attempting to insult. Follow Jamaicans in their directness and convey your meaning as simply as possible. Don't waste time with endless unnecessary pleasantries – "please" and "thank you" will suffice (though don't pass someone on a country road without wishing them good morning/afternoon/evening).

Rasta linguistics

The Rasta challenge to all things Babylonian includes an assault upon all that "downpresses" the black man via language. As a means of resistance, Rastas have reclassified words as a way of correcting perceived racial bias and turning negatives to positives; hence greeting someone with "hello" might illicit the cool response "We're not in hell and I'm not low". Rasta linguistics is one of the most creative elements of Jamaican patois, breaking down words, analysing syllabic connotations and reading significance into every nuance; hence understand becomes **overstand** (because if you comprehend something, you're above it rather than beneath it), oppress (up-press) becomes **downpress.** The most recognizable aspect of Rasta linguistics is the use of "I" to emphasize unity (Inity) and positivity as well as to protest against the coercive control of language. Hence create becomes **I-rate**, continually becomes **I-tinually**, creation is **I-ration**.

Selassie I is interpreted as proof of Haile Selassie's omnipresence: **Selasee eye**. It isn't difficult to see why there are so many cryptic messages embedded in 1970s roots-reggae lyrics.

For a full description of the Rasta lexicon, read Velma Pollard's *Dread Talk*.

Patois glossary

The common words and phrases below have been written semi-phonetically, a sometimes clumsy medium but the only way in which to convey their sound in the available space.

Ago Verb meaning will or going to do something: "Me ago check yuh tomorrow".

Almshouse Militant or negative behaviour, a favourite attitude during sound-system clashes.

Babylon Government or the established and oppressive social system; also an insulting title for police.

Baby mother/father A person with children.

Badmind Jealous, covetous, bad intentions.

Bakra White man, traditionally a slave owner, probably derived from the Ibo "mbaraka".

Bandulu Trickery or a swindle.

Bashment A big party or dance.

Batty Backside/bottom.

Battyman/boy Homosexual male.

Batty riders Tight lycra hot-pants worn by dancehall queens for maximum buttock exposure.

Bhuttu Unsophisticated, simple country bumpkin; used as an insult. Also used these days for any uncouth, rude person.

Big up Boost yourself up (verb): "Big up yu chest" or "Big up yu status/yuself".

Blood Principally a swear word used with claat and hole. Can also be used as a respectful greeting signifying unity, as in "Wh'appen, blood?"

Blouse and skirt An exclamation of surprise.

Bly An opportunity, chance or escape from an unwanted chore: "De rain gimme a bly – me nah haffe go a wuk".

Boderation Annoyance, irritation.

Bombo Offensive expletive meaning backside, usually used in conjunction with claat or hole: "Move yu bombo-claat face from me".

Bow Verb meaning to indulge in oral sex; "**bow cat**" is a participant.

Brawta A little extra to make a better bargain, usually employed when bartering in a market: "Gimme me brawta, nuh?"

Breddah Friend, usually male: "Yes mi breddah!" **Bredren** is the plural form, used both as a noun and as an adjective; **breds** is the shortened version.

Breed To get pregnant, or be pregnant: "Mi wan' breed dat gal before year-end".

Broughtupsy Good manners as a result of a careful upbringing; often used to reprimand someone: "Dat child have no broughtupsy!"

Browning Light-skinned person, usually used for women.

Bruk Broken.

Brukout To let loose, usually at a party.

Buck To meet somebody: "Me will buck up wid yu later".

Bumper Backside/bottom.

Bun or **burn** Literally, burn. Used in terms of smoking: "Me bun de ganja long time"; as a condemnation: "Bun out de politician dem"; and to connote infidelity: "She give him bun with a nex man".

Cat Vagina.

Cha Exclamation, usually of surprise or distaste: "Cha! Me nah wan no man inna me life".

Chalice Pipe for smoking ganja, usually communally.

Charged Intoxicated, stoned: "Me get charged las' night".

Check Pay a visit: "Me ago check yu tomorrow". Also a term of platonic or sexual appreciation, as in "Me check fe di man's argument", and as a term for sexual advances: "De young bway try check big woman".

Chi-chi man Pejorative term for a homosexual man.

Claat/clot Literally, cloth, used with Raas, pussy, bumba as an expletive: "Tek yuh blood-claat hands off me!"

Cook an' curry Everything's been taken care of, as in "Me clean de whole house; everyting cook an' curry now".

Copasetic Cool, good: "Everyting copasetic".

Cork Full, as in "the dance cork tonight".

Cotch Rest up, chill out: "Sit dung and cotch with me". Also a verb to mean where a person sleeps: "Me a cotch by Evelyn's". Also used to denote bracing something: "Cotch de wheel wid' a rock".

Craven Greedy, desperate.

Criss Attractive, beautiful: "Maxine a criss, criss gyal".

Criss-biscuit Anything of excellence.

Cuss-cuss Argument.

Cut-eye A malevolent look: "Pure cut-eye me get from him".

Daggering Aggressive, athletic dancing, usually of a sexual nature.

Dally To go: "Me mus dally now".

Dawta Young woman, interchangeable with **sistah**.

Dead-stock Quiet, a non-event: "Dem promote pure dead-stock dance".

Dealing Dating, being in a relationship.

Dege-dege Small, measly: "She gimme one dege-dege piece of yam".

Deh-deh Be somewhere: "Me deh-deh" ("I am here").

Deh-pan Doing it, in control of matters: "Me deh-pan the repairs, man". **Deh-bout** is to be somewhere: "Him deh-bout somewhere inside".

Diss Disrespect: "Him a diss de programme" ("He's rudely disrupting our plans").

Don Literally a ghetto "area leader", but also used to describe any respected male: "Him a de don".

Draw card To trick or deceive; pull something sneaky.

Dread A person with locks (not necessarily of Rastafarian faith), or an adjective used to describe a bad situation: "De times dread".

Dun know Used to express total agreement.

Duns/Dunsa Money.

Dutch pot Heavy cooking pot.

Dutty Dirty, nasty or sleazy.

Dweet Do it: "Me dweet sweet, sis".

Ends A place, usually somewhere to chill out: "Mi deh pon a ends, still" ("I'm here relaxing").

Facety Impertinent, rude: "De touris' facety to rass".

Fassy Literally vagina, combined with **hole**, as in "Yow, fassyhole, who you talk to so?" Also, generally nasty, dirty and foolish.

Favour Resemble.

Feel no way Don't worry about it.

Fish Homosexual man.

Flex A person's way of behaving: "Ah so me flex, my yout" ("That's how I operate, young man").

Flop Losing face, usually in public and often associated with the performance of an artist or sound system.

Frenemy False friend.

Friend Apart from the usual meaning, can be used (rather confusingly) to refer to one's sexual partner.

Fuckery Irritating, bothersome, out of order: "Dis man is pure fuckery" ("This man is badly behaved").

Galang Expression meaning "Go away".

Gallis Man who has a way with the ladies.

Ganja Marijuana.

Gates Home: "Check me at me gates".

Ginnal Con man or trickster.

Gravalicious Greedy or avaricious.

Grind To have sex. A **grindsman** is a man particularly skilled between the sheets.

Guidance An inspirational goodbye meaning "Let God be with you".

Gwan Go on or carry on (verb). Also used to mean "go away" or "going to".

Gweh Go away.

Gyal Girl or woman.

Heartical Conscious, esteemed person: "He's my heartical bredren".

Herb Ganja, herbal marijuana.

Higgler Female market-trader, or a woman who brings goods to Jamaica from abroad to sell.

High grade Premium-quality ganja.

Hol' it down Be cool and restrained, to be on a low profile or stay quiet.

Hood Penis, also called a **wood**.

Hottie-hottie An attractive female.

I an' I Rasta-speak meaning me, I, we, mine, myself. **I-man** equally applies.

Idren Used by Rastas to mean friends or **bredren**.

Irie Adjective meaning fine or good: "You lookin' Irie tonight". Also used as a greeting.

Ishence Ganja.

Ital Anything natural (an Ital car wash is a river) or pure (a spliff without tobacco). Also describes Rastafarian meatless food cooked without salt.

Iyah Greeting to a friend: "What a gwan Iyah".

Jacket Child raised by a man who isn't his father (the father usually doesn't know).

Jagabat Nasty, unclean, sluttish woman.

Jamdown Jamaica. **JA** and **Jamrock** are also frequently used.

Joe Grind Term for a man sleeping with someone else's partner.

Jook Stab or pierce: "De rass fish hook jook me". Also penetrative sex.

Juggling Sound-system tactic of playing several tracks on the same rhythm, mixing them smoothly via two decks. Also just playing records in a dance.

Kiss me neck! An expression of surprise: "Kiss me neck! Price of rice gone down!"

Labrish Gossip, small talk. **Labba-labba** is to talk too much.

Let off Give something: "She nah let off she tings" ("She won't have sex with me").

Lick To strike a blow: "(H)im a lick down the pear tree". Also to smoke: "Me a lick de chalice Iyah". Also an adjective meaning hot: "Beenie Man a de lick!" ("Beenie Man is the best").

Lick shot Literally or figuratively firing a gun to demonstrate appreciation in the dancehall.

Licky-licky Subservient, sycophantic.

Likkle more See you later.

Live blanket Human body: "Darlin', you need a live blanket?" ("Would you like to have sex with me?")

Lock off Cease, desist; also hold a low profile.

Maaga Thin, scrawny.

Maama man Effeminate, probably gay man.

Mampy Fat woman, not necessarily derogatory.

Matey Girlfriend, often used to denote one of an attached man's multiple sexual partners.

More time Another way of saying "See you soon".

Mule Woman without children, usually incapable of conceiving. Also a person that smuggles drugs internally.

Murderation Violence: "De fight was pure murderation!"

Natty Used as an adjective or adverb to describe dreadlocks, also a greeting to a Rasta: "Wh'appen, Natty?"

Nature Libido: "Me nature rising".

Navel string Placenta; it's traditional for a new baby's navel string to be planted under a sapling.

Nuff Abundant or copious: "Me have nuff gyal". Often twinned with respect as a courteous greeting: "Nuff respect me breddah".

Nyam To eat, from the Hausa word "nyamnyam".

Obeah Jamaican witchcraft.

One love Greeting or farewell salutation. "**Love**" is used in the same way: "Love Iyah".

Ongle Only.

Oonoo You, them: "Oonoo wan' eat tonight?" ("Do you want any dinner?")

Pappy show Something utterly ridiculous and foolish.

Passa passa A disturbance, hullaballoo or scene, often caused by gossip. Adopted as the name of Jamaica's most popular street-jam.

Par Hang out with, shortened version of **spar**.

Pardner Savings club, where each member makes a weekly contribution, and in turn gets a whole week's collection.

Piece A gun, a girl, or sex: "Me get a nice piece las' night" ("I had sex with an attractive woman last night").

Pikney Child.

Pirogue Fishing canoe.

Pon On or upon.

Prentice Apprentice or protégé, usually young man; also shortened to prenta.

Pum pum Vagina.

Punany Vagina – again.

Pussy or punny printers Shorts even tighter than the **batty rider**.

Quail-up Fade, shrink, cower.

Queen Respectful title for a woman, usually a Rastaman's partner.

Raas Loosely translated as backside ("Mi fall dung pon me raas"), and an expletive when used with claat or hole: "That man is one nasty raashole". Can also express surprise or emphasize a point: "Wha de raas claat man a deal wid?"

Raggamuffin Respected and wily ghetto sufferer, often used in a musical context. Also used to refer to "street" style.

Rahtid Mild expletive or an expression of surprise.

Ramp Usually used in the phrase "ramp wid", meaning to interfere with or irritate.

Rastitute See **Rent-a-Dread**, below. Not to be confused with Ras, the abbreviation for Rasta, often used as a respectful greeting: "Wha'ppen, Ras?"

Reason Discuss and debate a subject.

Red Used to refer to a light-skinned person: "See de red man deh". Red also describes someone who has been smoking ganja.

Red-eye Greedy, envious.

Rent-a-Dread A man with locks who makes a living out of sexual relationships with tourists.

Respect Perhaps the most commonly used greeting or farewell in Jamaica.

Roughneck Ragamuffin rascal.

Rucktion Commotion, dispute.

Rude bway Bad boy.

Runnings Happenings, things that are going on: "Bway, runnings hard dis year" ("Things are tough this year").

Rush Assail: "Watch dem rush de gates" ("Look at them forcing their way in").

Salt Used as a verb to describe something unlucky or gone wrong; ie "Windies gwine lose the series – we salt fe true".

Science Obeah.

Screw Be annoyed, and look like you are. A **screw face** is a miserable character.

Seen Understand or comprehend what someone is saying. Usually used as a reply to a statement, as in "Uh-huh".

Sensimillia High-grade ganja; also shortened to **sensi**.

Session Sound-system jam: "Stone Love session gwine be wicked!"

Shock-out Looking good: "Me ago shock-out tonight ina mi criss new suit".

Shotta Rude boy, with all the appropriate notoriety that such status demands.

Sick Slang term meaning good: "Bounty new tune is sick!"

Siddung Sit down, often used by DJs to describe their lyrical flow: "Me siddung pon de riddim".

Sinting Something.

Sistren Woman/women generally, or close female friend.

Skank Rip off, con: "Me get skank at the mechanic today". Also an old-time dance.

Sketel Promiscuous, provocatively dressed woman.

Skin-teet Smile.

Skull Play truant from class or take a sickie from work.

Slackness Improper, lowdown, dirty, base behaviour; also used to describe rude dancehall lyrics.

Slam The sexual act.

Smalls Small change: "Beg you a smalls, boss?"

Spar Friend.

Spliff Marijuana joint.

Star Used as a salutation or qualifier in greetings: "Wh'appen, star".

Stoosh Snooty, condescending from a position of assumed superiority. Also means something of quality.

Sufferah Poor but righteous ghetto-dweller.

Sweetboy Attractive, well-dressed young man, perhaps financially supported by his lover.

Talawah Small but strong, applied to Jamaica itself in the motto: "She little but she talawah".

Tan Stay or stand: "Tan so back" ("Hold back").

Tek set To follow someone around or annoy them: "De youts tek set pon me all day, me never get no break".

Ting Object or woman: "A my ting dat" ("That's my girlfriend"). "Tings" can be male and female genitalia. Also the Jamaican pronunciation of "things": "Tings a gwan rough sah".

Trace To curse somebody or quarrel.

Version A cut of a popular rhythm-track.

Vex(ed) Irritated or annoyed.

What a gwan "What's going on?"

Wind/Wine Dance closely and suggestively, as per Tony Matterhorn's hit *Dutty Wine*.

Wuk Regular work or sex.

Wutless Combination of worthless and witless: "Pure wutless bway me meet at the show" ("I met some awful men at the show").

X-amount Huge, incalculable amount: "Me have x-amount of loving".

Yahso Here: "Park yuh car yahso".

Yard Home; also used as an alternative name for Jamaica: "No where no better dan Yard".

Yush An alternative for "hello".

Small print and

Index

A Rough Guide to Rough Guides

Published in 1982, the first Rough Guide – to Greece – was a student scheme that became a publishing phenomenon. Mark Ellingham, a recent graduate in English from Bristol University, had been travelling in Greece the previous summer and couldn't find the right guidebook. With a small group of friends he wrote his own guide, combining a highly contemporary, journalistic style with a thoroughly practical approach to travellers' needs.

The immediate success of the book spawned a series that rapidly covered dozens of destinations. And, in addition to impecunious backpackers, Rough Guides soon acquired a much broader and older readership that relished the guides' wit and inquisitiveness as much as their enthusiastic, critical approach and value-for-money ethos.

These days, Rough Guides include recommendations from shoestring to luxury and cover more than 200 destinations around the globe, including almost every country in the Americas and Europe, more than half of Africa and most of Asia and Australasia. Our ever-growing team of authors and photographers is spread all over the world, particularly in Europe, the US and Australia.

In the early 1990s, Rough Guides branched out of travel, with the publication of Rough Guides to World Music, Classical Music and the Internet. All three have become benchmark titles in their fields, spearheading the publication of a wide range of books under the Rough Guide name.

Including the travel series, Rough Guides now number more than 350 titles, covering: phrasebooks, waterproof maps, music guides from Opera to Heavy Metal, reference works as diverse as Conspiracy Theories and Shakespeare, and popular culture books from iPods to Poker. Rough Guides also produce a series of more than 120 World Music CDs in partnership with World Music Network.

Visit www.roughguides.com to see our latest publications.

Rough Guide credits

Text editor: AnneLise Sorensen
Layout: Nikhil Agarwal
Cartography: Ashutosh Bharti
Picture editor: Harriet Mills
Production: Rebecca Short
Proofreader: Amanda Jones
Cover design: Dan May
Photographer: Anthony Pidgeon
Editorial: **London** Andy Turner, Keith Drew,
Edward Aves, Alice Park, Lucy White, Jo Kirby,
James Smart, Natasha Foges, Róisín Cameron,
James Rice, Lara Kavanagh, Emma Traynor,
Emma Gibbs, Kathryn Lane, Monica Woods,
Mani Ramaswamy, Harry Wilson, Lucy Cowie,
Alison Roberts, Joe Staines, Matthew Milton,
Tracy Hopkins, Ruth Tidball; **Delhi** Madhavi
Singh, Lubna Shaheen, Jalpreen Kaur Chhatwal
Design & Pictures: **London** Scott Stickland, Dan
May, Diana Jarvis, Mark Thomas, Nicole Newman,
Sarah Cummins, Emily Taylor; **Delhi** Umesh
Aggarwal, Ajay Verma, Jessica Subramanian,
Ankur Guha, Pradeep Thapliyal, Sachin Tanwar,
Anita Singh, Sachin Gupta

Production: Liz Cherry
Cartography: **London** Ed Wright, Katie Lloyd-
Jones; **Delhi** Rajesh Chhibber, Rajesh Mishra,
Animesh Pathak, Jasbir Sandhu, Karobi Gogoi,
Alakananda Roy, Swati Handoo, Deshpal Dabas
Online: **London** Faye Hellon, Jeanette Angell,
Fergus Day, Justine Bright, Clare Bryson, Aine
Fearon, Adrian Low, Ezgi Celebi; **Delhi** Amit
Verma, Rahul Kumar, Narender Kumar, Ravi
Yadav, Debojit Borah, Rakesh Kumar, Ganesh
Sharma, Shisir Basumatari
Marketing & Publicity: **London** Liz Statham,
Jess Carter, Vivienne Watton, Anna Paynton,
Rachel Sprackett, Laura Vipond; **New York** Katy
Ball, Judi Powers; **Delhi** Ragini Govind
Digital Travel Publisher: Peter Buckley
Reference Director: Andrew Lockett
Operations Assistant: Becky Doyle
Operations Manager: Helen Atkinson
Publishing Director (Travel): Clare Currie
Commercial Manager: Gino Magnotta
Managing Director: John Duhigg

ROUGH GUIDES

SMALL PRINT

Publishing information

This fifth edition published August 2010 by
Rough Guides Ltd,
80 Strand, London WC2R 0RL
11 Local Shopping Centre, Panchsheel Park,
New Delhi 110017, India

Distributed by the Penguin Group
Penguin Books Ltd,
80 Strand, London WC2R 0RL
Penguin Group (USA)
375 Hudson Street, NY 10014, USA
Penguin Group (Australia)
250 Camberwell Road, Camberwell,
Victoria 3124, Australia
Penguin Group (Canada)
195 Harry Walker Parkway N, Newmarket, ON,
L3Y 7B3 Canada
Penguin Group (NZ)
67 Apollo Drive, Mairangi Bay, Auckland 1310,
New Zealand
Cover concept by Peter Dyer.

Typeset in Bembo and Helvetica to an original
design by Henry Iles.

Printed in Singapore

© Polly Thomas, Adam Vaitilingam and
Robert Coates 2010

Maps © Rough Guides

336pp includes index

A catalogue record for this book is available from
the British Library

ISBN: 978-1-84836-513-1

The publishers and authors have done their best
to ensure the accuracy and currency of all the
information in **The Rough Guide to Jamaica**,
however, they can accept no responsibility for
any loss, injury, or inconvenience sustained by
any traveller as a result of information or advice
contained in the guide.

1   3   5   7   9   8   6   4   2

Help us update

We've gone to a lot of effort to ensure that the
fifth edition of **The Rough Guide to Jamaica** is
accurate and up-to-date. However, things change
– places get "discovered", opening hours are
notoriously fickle, restaurants and rooms raise
prices or lower standards. If you feel we've got it
wrong or left something out, we'd like to know,
and if you can remember the address, the price,
the hours, the phone number, so much the better.

Please send your comments with the subject
line "**Rough Guide Jamaica Update**" to ©mail
@roughguides.com. We'll credit all contributions
and send a copy of the next edition (or any
other Rough Guide if you prefer) for the very
best emails.

Have your questions answered and tell others
about your trip at ®www.roughguides.com

Acknowledgements

Polly Thomas: Many thanks to Rob Coates for his dedication and good humour; Laura Henzell for another spot-on update; AnneLise Sorensen for smooth editing; and Harriet Mills for fabulous pictures. Thanks also to Dexter Lewis for his unstinting support.

Robert Coates: A big thank you to Adrian Harrison at JTB, Donahue Jarrett, Andre McGann, Michael Grizzle, Charlie, Suzie and Rodger at Lime Tree Farm, David Twyman, Jackie Kanopi, Jon and Rosemary at Gee Jam, Cynthia and Painter, Geraldine Scott, Leroy, Roy, and the late Michael Gleeson at Blue Harbour, Anna Williams, Elise Yapp, Dennis and Ludo High Hope, Susan and Jane at Catcha, Damian Salmon, Jackie Lewis, Easy Rock Sue and Alan Young. Elsewhere in Westmoreland, as ever Lippy Butler and Brian in Belmont, the Jeffrey family and the ever-hospitable Denise Johnson and family. As always it's great to work with Polly Thomas, and a big thank you also to AnneLise Sorensen for answering all my queries so thoroughly.

Readers' letters

Thanks to those readers of the fourth edition who took the trouble to write in with their amendments and additions. Apologies for any misspellings or omissions.

George Barnhill, Deanna Bergdorf, Scott Buschkuhl, Sasha Davidson, Dennis and Lucia Keim, Tony Kuhn, Steven and Claudia St Clair, Stephen Thorpe, Pepe Urquijo, Elise Yap.

Photo credits

All photos © Rough Guides except the following:

Introduction
Red hibiscus flower, Jamaica © James Benet/istockphoto.com

Things not to miss
01 Diving at Pirate's Cave © Paul Souders/Corbis
02 Blue Mountains rainbow © Robert Harding/eye ubiquitous
09 Sailboat and snorkellers, Negril © Interfoto/Alamy

Jamaican food and drink colour section
Ackee at Papine Market, Kingston © Mark Bassett/Alamy
Jerk stand, Mammee Bay © Cris Haigh/Alamy
Cocktail at Negril bar © Mark Bassett/Alamy

Jamaican nightlife colour section
Passa Passa street jam, Kingston © Debbie Bragg/www.everynight.co.uk
Damian Marley at Sumfest© Andre McGann
Jamaica Jazz and Blues Festival © Anthony Pidgeon/Redferns

Index

Map entries are in colour.

K

L

M

INDEX

I

INDEX

331

T

Map symbols

maps are listed in the full index using coloured text

—··—	County boundary	⊞	Hospital
———	Chapter division boundary	✈	Airport/airfield
═══	Road	★	Transport stop
-----	Path/track	⛽	Petrol station
▬▬	Railway	⊙	Memorial
———	River/canal	ⓘ	Tourist office
———	Wall	⊠	Post office
⋊	Bridge	⛳	Golf course
⧫	Site of interest	❗	Museum
∴	Ruin	◉	Accommodation
⌂	Cave	▣	Restaurant
	Reef	⬭	Stadium
⚒	Waterfall	▬	Building
♨	Spring	✚	Church
▲	Mountain peak	Cemetery	Cemetery
⌃	Mountain range		Park
⛯	Lighthouse	⩜	Marsh/wetland
⊥	Gardens	ⓐ	Beach

So now we've told you about the things not to miss, the best places to stay, the top restaurants, the liveliest bars and the most spectacular sights, it only seems fair to tell you about the best travel insurance around

 WorldNomads.com

keep travelling safely

Recommended by Rough Guides